Strategies for Work
with Involuntary Clients

Strategies for Work with Involuntary Clients

Second Edition

EDITED BY

Ronald H. Rooney

Columbia University Press

Columbia University Press
Publishers Since 1893
New York, Chichester, West Sussex
Copyright © 2009 Columbia University Press

Library of Congress Cataloging-in-Publication Data

Strategies for work with involuntary clients / edited by Ronald H. Rooney.
   p. cm.
Rev. ed. of: Strategies for work with involuntary clients / Ronald H. Rooney. c1992.
Includes bibliographical references and index.
ISBN 978-0-231-13318-0 (cloth : alk. paper)—ISBN 978-0-231-13319-7 (pbk. : alk. paper)
1. Social service—United States.   2. Involuntary treatment—United States.
I. Rooney, Ronald H., 1945–   II. Rooney, Ronald H., 1945– Strategies for work with
involuntary clients.   III. Title.

HV91.S735 2009
361.3'20973—dc22   2008035024

Casebound editions of Columbia University Press books are printed on
permanent and durable acid-free paper.

Printed in the United States of America

c 10 9 8 7 6 5 4 3 2

References to Internet Web Sites (URLs) were accurate at the time of writing.
Neither the author nor Columbia University Press is responsible for Web sites that
may have expired or changed since the book was prepared.

Contents

Illustrations

Preface

This book is about practice with involuntary clients, both those clients required to see a helping practitioner, such as juveniles on probation, and those pressured to "seek help," such as an alcoholic threatened with desertion by his or her spouse if he or she does not get help. The book is also about "involuntary practitioners" who may be as reluctant to work with involuntary clients as the clients are to work with them. When I entered graduate school, I intended to work with clients who wanted to work with me, who would be thankful for the insights I gave them, and who would pay my receptionist on the way out. The reality was that my clients then and later were often more interested in escaping the clutches of my agency and the law than in gaining an insight into their personalities.

Most of the intervention theory I was taught ignored these clients or considered them exceptions to the rules that apply to work with voluntary clients. When I became an instructor, I continued the tradition of teaching voluntary client methods to students who worked with involuntary clients. Independent-thinking students would ask, "But how does this apply to the people who don't want to see you?" and I would improvise answers adapting voluntary methods. This book is written in answer to those students and practitioners working with involuntary clients who find difficulty applying voluntary practice theories to involuntary practice. I suggest that involuntary clients are the rule in practice rather than the exception.

The book is written for students, instructors, and practitioners. While probably few students enter the helping professions hoping to work with people who don't want to work with them, many experience less than voluntary client contact through their field placement and internship experiences. Students should find the book useful in explaining and guiding involuntary practice on its own terms. Such practice often appears to be undertaken as a rite of passage to provide experience and toughness before graduating to work with voluntary clients. Students may also find parallels to their own situations as "involuntary" students: if they wish to graduate, they must take some required courses "for their own good" in addition to choices in elective courses.

The book is also intended for practice methods instructors who wish to add material about involuntary contact to balance sources that assume solely voluntary contact. Instructors teaching courses about social problems and practice settings that often include involuntary clients, such as child welfare, criminal justice, chemical abuse programs, will also find the book a useful practice supplement.

Finally, the book is written for practitioners who work with involuntary clients. While the book is based in the social work profession, the content is useful to other helping practitioners such as psychologists, psychiatrists, nurses, probation officers, and youth workers. The book addresses public-agency practitioners with legal mandates, large caseloads, feelings of being unappreciated, overworked, and underpaid, as well as private-agency practitioners who may not recognize that they are in fact working with involuntary clients.

The book is designed to help both involuntary practitioners and involuntary clients become at least semivoluntary. Guidelines are aimed at providing legal, ethical, and effective intervention. While involuntary clients differ from one another as much as they do from voluntary clients, involuntary clients share the fact that they did not *willingly* enter contact with the practitioner. Consequently, the book focuses most extensively on the socialization and contracting phase that involuntary clients have most in common. Guidelines for interventions after the contracting phase are more tentative, since there may be much variation according to the specific problem and setting. The book will help practitioners prepare for involuntary contacts by providing them with realistic role expectations so that they can make clearer decisions about when they must act and when they should not act. The guidelines should lead to less hostile and uncooperative encounters, to more successful contracts, and less "burnout" on both sides of the involuntary transaction.

Finally, the book reviews the philosophical debate about the conflict between social control and caring roles, and between rehabilitation and criminal justice goals. The issues are reviewed with an aim toward increasing awareness without proposing to resolve those issues herein. The book is designed to help practitioners now amid the ongoing debate.

Involuntary clients sometimes have fantasies that their practitioners will leave them alone, or forget about "helping" them. Practitioners also fantasize that they can make involuntary clients change if they can just find the right magic to make those clients think differently, or if they could exert enough force. This book supplies neither magic nor force. It will not provide the practitioner with a blueprint for making involuntary clients do what they do not want to do, continue to do it after intervention, and like it. The book does not provide a "laying on of hands" whereby the involuntary client is transformed into a "born again" voluntary client, thankful for insight and eager to modify his or her life patterns. It is not a manual for brainwashing or hypnotizing involuntary clients to bring them to their senses—or to the practitioner's point of view. Nor will the guidelines eliminate the need for professional judgment in making decisions.

Guidelines are based on available evidence about interventions that can be used legally, ethically, and effectively across involuntary settings and populations. Where that evidence is limited or inconclusive, alternatives are presented to help practitioners make informed choices. The book also draws on the practice literature from different involuntary populations and helping professions and on my case experiences and those of my students. Practice guidelines are frequently illustrated with selections from transcriptions derived from training videotapes, some of which were conducted with actual clients. In all cases, practitioners and clients provided informed consent and client identities are disguised. The book raises questions for further study and suggests ways that those questions can be tested.

The book is aimed at increasing understanding of the involuntary transaction and knowing how to act within it. As practitioners need to be able to explain to themselves and others why they carry out an intervention, Part 1 provides a foundation with a conceptual framework for understanding the involuntary transaction and influencing client behavior and attitudes in a legal, ethical, and effective fashion. It draws widely from sources in law, ethics, intervention effectiveness across helping professions and problem areas, and social psychology. Chapters are organized around brief summaries of relevant theory and research.

This second edition of the book revises, condenses, and updates the first edition. The original fourteen chapters of the book have been condensed into ten chapters, and a new Part 3 contains contributions from expert practitioners and theorists about practice with varied problems and settings. Each chapter closes with questions to guide discussion in classes and work groups. Chapter 1 introduces the involuntary client and system and contains updated materials from the chapters titled "Introduction to Involuntary

Practice" and "The Involuntary Transaction" of the first edition. Chapter 2 integrates new material on legal and ethical perspectives and integrates the chapters titled "The Legal Foundation for Work with Involuntary Clients" and "The Ethical Foundation for Work with Involuntary Clients" from the first edition. Chapter 3 updates information on effectiveness in work with involuntary clients; and chapter 4 on influencing behavior and attitudes contains a substantial revision on persuasion. Chapter 5 on assessing initial contacts contains new materials on reactance theory. Chapter 6 contains the former chapters titled "Socialization Strategies for Individual Involuntary Clients" and "Negotiation and Contracting with Involuntary Clients" into an integrated focus on the initial phase of work with individual involuntary clients, focusing on negotiation and contracting. Chapter 7 on task-centered intervention with involuntary clients contains the former chapter titled "Formalizing the Contract and Initial Task Development" and focuses on middle-phase intervention and termination. Chapter 8 contains new developments in work with involuntary families (the former chapter titled "Working with Involuntary Families"), and chapter 9 presents work with involuntary groups (the former chapter "Work with Involuntary Clients in Groups.").

Part 3 contains chapters by contributing authors on problem areas, populations, and fields of practice in which involuntary clients are encountered. Part 3 is divided into four sections. Section A features the contribution of motivational interviewing to work with involuntary clients. Chapter 10 by James Barber focuses on work with substance abusers. Melinda Hohman and Chris Kleinpeter "bring up what they don't want to talk about" in chapter 11 related to motivational interviewing with adolescents about health-related behaviors. Finally, Michael Chovanec contributes chapter 12 on group work practice with domestic violence perpetrators.

Section B explores the contribution of solution-focused treatment to work with involuntary clients. Cynthia Franklin and Laura Hopson present the use of solution-focused methods with involuntary clients in public schools in chapter 13; and Julie Altman and Debra Gohagan describe the use of solution-focused methods in child welfare in chapter 14.

Section C presents work with involuntary clients in varied settings and populations. Chapter 15 by Glenda Dewberry Rooney focuses on work with members of oppressed groups as involuntary clients. Chris Trotter explores work with involuntary clients in corrections in chapter 16. Tony Bibus applies the involuntary client framework to work with clients in employment settings in chapter 17.

Section D addresses mezzo and macro involuntary practice in the context of broader systems. Carol Jud and Tony Bibus explore applications of the involuntary perspective to supervision in chapter 18. I close the book with an exploration of nonvoluntary practitioners and the system in chapter 19 (formerly the chapter titled "The Involuntary Practitioner and the System").

This book would not have been completed without the support and encouragement of colleagues, students, practitioners, and clients from many settings. The support of chairs Jean Quam and Jim Reinardy from the University of Minnesota School of Social Work was essential. Most directly members of our writing group assisted Ron, Glenda, and Mike with their drafts: Nancy Rodenberg, Elena Izaksonas, Rachel Roiblatt, and Terry Lum. Nancy Zupfer did tireless, valuable work with references and indexing. I want to thank the contributing authors for their persistence and commitment in supporting the completion of this project. Finally, we want to thank reviewers from Columbia University Press for their helpful comments.

Ron Rooney

Part 1 _____

A Foundation for Work
with Involuntary Clients

_____

Helping professionals often assume that their clients want to work with them. Practice with clients who do not seek a helper but rather acquiesce to pressure to seek help requires different assumptions. Practitioners need to know when and why to act with involuntary clients as well as how to work with them. Part 1 lays a foundation for legal, ethical, and effective practice with involuntary clients by providing concepts and assessing empirical evidence about effectiveness. Chapter 1 introduces involuntary practice, and work with clients across a continuum of voluntarism is introduced. Chapter 2 builds a foundation of legal and ethical principles for involuntary practice. Intervention principles based on evidence of effectiveness are discussed in chapter 3; and principles of behavior and attitude change, in chapter 4. Chapter 5 then presents theoretical frameworks, such as reactance theory, to help assess initial interactions between practitioners and involuntary clients.

Chapter 1

Introduction to Involuntary Practice

Robert, sixteen, slouches in his chair, squinting at the young probation officer behind the desk. While Robert considers how he might escape the situation without too much hassle, his probation officer wonders about how to help Robert before he does further harm to himself and others.

Meanwhile, George, thirty-two, waits in the well-appointed lobby of a private family service agency to be screened for a domestic violence treatment group led by a clinical psychologist. Although George "chose" to seek voluntary treatment as an alternative to prosecution for battering his wife, he hardly considers his choice to have been free.

Alice, forty-five, is a developmentally disabled adult. She has lived alone in a poorly heated rural shack since her mother died a year ago. But Alice is not really alone, as she shares her home with the twenty cats she considers her friends. The cats also share her food, and Alice's neighbors have called Social Services asking that something be done for her safety. Perhaps an underlying issue in their request is the fact that Alice's shack is an eyesore that affects the neighbors' property values. An adult protective service worker is assigned to assess Alice's safety. Expecting an unpleasant meeting, she cautiously puts the assignment on the bottom of the pile in her in-basket.

Finally, Mr. Chou Vang stares impassively at the young social worker attempting to persuade him to accept services. They see one another through a mist of assumptions about what to expect from Asian elders, on the one hand, and from Caucasian social workers on the other. Though Mr. Vang has some concerns for his safety, he assumes that his family will handle anything that is needed and that accepting services from government strangers would bring shame upon him. In turn, the social worker muses about how "resistant" Asian elders are to services.

Robert, George, Alice, and Chou do not willingly seek the services of a helper or agency and hence are not at this point voluntary clients. This chapter introduces work with two types of involuntary clients. Many involuntary clients, such as Robert, are legally mandated to see a helper. Others, such as George, Alice, and Chou, are nonvoluntary clients who experience pressure that is no less real, though not legally mandated. As the practitioners who work with involuntary clients are often as reluctant as the clients, I also introduce the concept of the involuntary practitioner and describe the transactions between involuntary clients and practitioners. Since clients can be more or less voluntary at different times or depending on the issues, a continuum of involuntary contact is presented. The implications for involuntary status of membership in an oppressed group are also considered. The chapter concludes with questions for practitioners to ask about their work with involuntary clients.

Definition of Involuntary Client

According to Merriam-Webster Online (http://www.m-w.com/dictionary/client), a client is "a person who is under the protection of another, one who engages the professional advice or services of another, or a person served by or utilizing the services of a social agency." The definition best fits the circumstances of a voluntary client who recognizes a problem, is willing to tell someone about it, is willing to give that person permission to advise, and, finally, is willing to change in some way (Keith-Lucas 1972). A voluntary client does not experience external pressures to participate in services and is free to select helpers or "fire" them if services are not acceptable.

Does the dictionary definition of "client" readily include both voluntary clients and those who receive services, whether or not by choice? Are Robert, George, Alice, and Chou clients, by this definition? None of the four willingly engage professional advice, nor do they voluntarily utilize services, though Alice and Chou might eventually come under protection. Some authors suggest that the term *client* be reserved for those who choose a service without pressure to do so.

Involuntary clients have been defined as individuals who are forced by those around them, such as parents, spouses, neighbors, and police, to seek assistance from official helpers (Murdach 1980). They also include clients who must deal with a helping professional because they have behaved in ways considered annoying or troublesome to society (Cingolani 1984). Involuntary clients feel pressured to seek or accept contact with a helping professional. The aforementioned definitions contain the term *client* while recognizing constraints on free choice. To retain the use of the term *client*, there must be efforts to engage persons in involuntary circumstances as informed participants in constrained circumstances. Change is not targeted at the person as a whole, but rather at his or her illegal, harmful behavior. A sexual predator may find that there is a non-negotiable focus on his dangerous, illegal behavior toward others; but he can be engaged as a client around other goals, such as how to increase his freedom. If the person in involuntary circumstances has no opportunity to engage in actions to identify and increase self-defined goals, then he or she is an involuntary target rather than a client. The Social Work Code of Ethics provides guidance for service to clients, but no guidance is available for targets (National Association of Social Workers [NASW] 1999).*

Involuntary clients can be subdivided further into legally mandated clients and nonvoluntary clients, according to the source of pressure experienced. Legally mandated clients must work with a helping practitioner as a result of a current or impending legal mandate or court order (Hutchison 1987). Such mandated clients are often the majority of those seen in many public social service settings, human services departments, child welfare, probation and parole, and some psychiatric wards. The helping practitioners who work with them come from such professional fields as social work, psychology, psychiatry, counseling, marriage and family counseling, nursing, correctional counseling, and chemical dependency training. Many others are paraprofessionals with on-the-job training. Practitioners working in public settings with mandated clients are usually aware of the involuntary nature of their client contact since legal mandates describe practitioner responsibilities and often specify client rights. In common parlance, legally mandated clients are those understood to be involuntary clients. While legally mandated clients are an important group of involuntary clients, I suggest that they are not the only ones.

Nonvoluntary clients have contact with helping professionals through nonlegal pressure from formal or informal sources. For example, referral from a doctor, a school official, or an employer can represent a formal pressure to seek assistance. Referral from a spouse, partner, or family member represents informal pressure to seek help. Hence, while clients such as Robert are legally mandated to seek help, clients such as George and Alice are also involuntary clients but are considered nonvoluntary. Nonvoluntary clients

---

*I thank Charles Garvin for clarifying this discussion of the use of the term *client* when applied to persons in involuntary circumstances.

include those who accept services under pressure because valued services are unavailable elsewhere (Slonim-Nevo 1996). For example, though prospective adoptive parents generally might be considered voluntary, the adoptive children they seek are a scarce and valued resource. Hence, they may experience their contact with helpers, such as attending required training to qualify as potential parents, as "jumping through hoops." Similarly, women who seek refuge in a shelter for victims of domestic violence may voluntarily seek safety from possible abuse, yet chafe at the "package deal" of requirements implicit in the acceptance of the offer of service. For example, they may wish relief with no strings attached. They may object to restrictions against telephone contact with their partner or the requirement to attend groups. Nonvoluntary clients are more difficult to count because they are not defined by a legal status yet may be the majority of clients seen in public schools, hospitals, outpatient mental health settings, day treatment programs, group homes, shelters, drug and alcohol treatment programs, youth services, and family service agencies. Nonvoluntary clients include persons who are not required to participate in a service but are encouraged to do so, if such encouragement contains pressure (Altman 2003). Nonvoluntary clients may exert their freedom by refusing to accept a service when their perception of their own needs does not reflect that of the referral source (Barlow et al. 2005).

Informal pressures also come from the referrals of community members who attribute problems to persons whose behavior they consider inappropriate or deviant. For example, Ralph presented himself for counseling at a clinic because he was having some difficulties with his wife yet maintained that it was "nothing that we can't handle by ourselves." When the practitioner asked what he was seeking from counseling since he was capable of handling the problems, Ralph responded that he did not really want anything. Ralph continued that he and his wife were living with his mother, who had told them that they had to move out if they did not seek counseling for their arguing.

Responses such as Ralph's are usually interpreted as a reflection of his inability to accept responsibility for his problems. Voluntary clients are typically identified by the fact that they have acknowledged problems that concern them and lead them to seek help. Ralph acknowledges no problems other than perhaps needing to satisfy his mother. An attributed problem is one that others say that a client has (Reid 1985). Ralph's mother attributes marital problems to Ralph and his wife. Involuntary clients, both mandated and nonvoluntary, have problems attributed to them that they may or may not acknowledge: frequently they do not. For example, many of the clients in my child welfare practice had been found by a court to be abusive or neglectful yet did not acknowledge abuse or neglect as a problem. They did acknowledge, however, that the public child welfare agency was restricting access to their children and were willing to work to regain access. In later chapters, we will explore ways for working with both attributed and acknowledged problems.

Both legally mandated and nonvoluntary clients are involuntary because they feel forced to remain in a helping relationship through physical or legal coercion the unavailability of attractive alternatives, or both (Thibaut and Kelley 1959). Also, the individual may choose to remain in an involuntary relationship because the cost of leaving it is considered too high. For example, Robert might consider violating his court order yet decide that the costs of an increased sentence are too much. Finally, people are involuntary when they believe that they are disadvantaged in the current relationship because better alternatives are available. For example, George may feel disadvantaged if he expects to be a quiet, passive observer marking time in a domestic violence treatment group and finds instead that he is pressured to be active and that his own attitudes and behavior are scrutinized.

Factors influencing how pressured an involuntary client may feel include:

- How severe are the consequences should he or she refuse the service?
- How constrained are the client's choices regarding who might help him or her?
- How much input can he or she provide in the assistance offered by that helper (Slonim-Nevo 1996)?
- Who initiated the contact: the client or others?
- Does the potential client perceive a need for service?
- Does that potential client experience pressures to make life changes (Burstein 1988)?
- How receptive are helping professionals to the client's account of circumstances leading to contact?

The Involuntary Transaction

Both legally mandated and nonvoluntary clients are participants in an involuntary transaction. An involuntary transaction is a dynamic exchange of resources among clients, practitioners, and agencies occurring in a shifting legal and normative context and power imbalance such that the involuntary client would prefer to be elsewhere. In addition, involuntary clients are disproportionately more likely to be members of oppressed groups. The four parts of this definition are examined separately, and the concept of fate control is introduced.

1. The involuntary transaction is a dynamic exchange of resources (Hasenfeld 1987). It is commonly assumed that since clients want help and agencies wish to provide it, they share a common goal. In fact, however, the interests of the worker and those of the client are determined by their respective systems. Like all living systems, the agency and the client want to maximize their own resources while minimizing the costs of attaining them. Therefore a person becomes a client to obtain needed resources and tries to do so with minimal personal costs. The agency, via the worker, engages the client to obtain resources controlled by him or her while minimizing organizational costs. It is this exchange of resources that makes both systems interdependent.

The transaction is dynamic because the involuntary client and the practitioner can become either more or less voluntary over time. For example, a legally mandated client who enters a domestic violence treatment program may begin at a point of low voluntarism. If, however, he experiences assistance in dealing with anger and avoiding prosecution, he may become more voluntary. In contrast, a client who experiences increasing restrictions on behavior may become less voluntary. An example is an adolescent who had been removed for protection from a home where parents were law violators and cocaine users. She was cooperating with a plan for visitation with her parents when a violation of the plan occurred, causing the agency to suspend further visits. Her response was to run away from the foster home, becoming less voluntary, as her next placement was secure detention.

2. The involuntary transaction occurs in a shifting legal and normative context. Contacts between involuntary clients and practitioners are influenced by legal and professional mandates and by agency policies (Hasenfeld 1987). Legal mandates specify rights, responsibilities, and sanctions for law violations that govern practitioners and involuntary clients (Alexander 2003). Legal mandates are based in cultural norms for approved and unapproved behavior and are means for sanctioning unapproved behavior. Some norms are nearly universal, and others vary by culture and over time within a culture. Corporal punishment has been common in the United States and in other cultures and nations as an acceptable form of child discipline; only in recent decades has excessive parental discipline resulting in harm been identified as child abuse (Popple and Vecchiolla 2007).

3. The involuntary transaction occurs within a power imbalance such that the involuntary client would prefer to be elsewhere. While power differences are most obvious in legally mandated contacts, they take place in nonlegal transactions as well. Such imbalances of power between clients, practitioners, and agencies can occur in three circumstances: (a) the agency depends more on outside resources than on those provided by the involuntary client; (b) there is greater demand for agency services than there are supplies available;

or (c) the agency has a quasi-monopoly over access to services such that the client does not have ready access to alternatives; then (d) the client may have little choice but to accept services on the terms they are offered (Hasenfeld 1987). When George was given the "choice" of entering a program for batterers or of risking prosecution, he had to select from a limited supply of programs offering such services.

4. Members of oppressed groups are disproportionately represented among involuntary clients. Power imbalance falls disproportionately on them (Solomon 1983), as evidenced by the following: (a) alternatives to preferences enforced by the majority society are lacking; (b) prejudice against the group is depersonalized; (c) bias is not private or narrow but entrenched in the larger society; and (d) members of the group are visible and aware of the discrimination (McGuire 1980). By these characteristics, many social groups such as the poor, the aged, the disabled, refugees, women, children, gays, and lesbians are often oppressed. Of particular concern are persons whose racial status is different from that of the majority and who are readily identifiable by that majority society. As an immigrant member of an ethic minority group, Mr. Chou Vang is part of an oppressed group. Such persons are seen as disproportionately underutilizing services. His age and poverty also need to be taken into account.

Oppressed group status is compounded when an individual is a member of overlapping oppressed groups. The term *ethclass* describes the intersection of ethnic group and social class (Gordon 1994; Smith and Seitzer 2002). In 2003, between 8 and 10 percent of American households were headed by women with children (AmeriStat 2003; U.S. Census Bureau 2003). About 5 percent of non-Hispanic white and Asian households were headed by women with children. The figures were 22 percent for African American households headed by women and 14 percent for Hispanic households (AmeriStat 2003). The intersection of these statuses has highlighted the feminization of poverty and the growth of the so-called underclass (Abramovitz 1988).

It has been suggested that professions such as social work have always played a significant role in social control while service providers told themselves that they were providing disinterested help (Margolin 1997). Proponents of an anti-oppressive framework argue that a larger societal context must always be considered when factors such as racism and poverty play a role in the circumstances leading to social service contact (Delgado 2001; Pollack 2004). Use of an anti-oppressive perspective suggests that deviant or criminal behaviors are explained by more than bad individual choices (Kendall and Pollack 2003). Proponents of this approach suggest that marginalized groups receiving the most punitive forms of care is not accidental (Graham 2004).

Membership in an oppressed group often means disproportionate access to resources and substandard living conditions. Tax cuts in the George W. Bush administration disproportionately assisted the wealthiest 2 percent of the population (Francis 2001). Such actions, which disadvantaged certain groups, have been described as institutional racism (Longres 1990).

Members of oppressed groups often find their own behaviors, rather than limited access to resources or care, as the focus of change. Hence, the emphasis is on their "private troubles" as caused by problems and pathologies in their personal situations rather than "public issues" or access to resources (Mills 1971). Members of oppressed groups frequently come into contact with helpers as a result of a coercive referral from systems of authority such as the courts or schools (Devore and Schlesinger 1987). This contact is often conducted in transactions with "street-level bureaucrats" who must manage chronically limited and inadequate resources for dealing with their appointed tasks. The resource limitation in turn often leads these bureaucrats to become "people processors" who focus on rationing services and controlling and limiting clients (Weatherly and Lipsky 1977). The care members of oppressed groups receive is more likely to be institutional and custodial than private and individualized (Miller 1983). Low-income minority children are more likely to enter social-control institutions and foster care than are Caucasian middle-class children (Dewberry Rooney 2002; Understanding and addressing racial/ethnic disproportionality 2005; Sheppard and Benjamin-Coleman 2001). African Americans are overrepresented in U.S. prisons relative to their proportion of the population and their rates of drug-related offenses. (Racially disproportionate incarceration of drug offenders 2000). African American children comprise two-fifths of the foster care population but represent only one-fifth of the children in the United States. African American children are more likely to be removed from the home, less likely to be returned to the home, and more likely to receive inferior treatment while in care (Roberts 2002a).

The reasons why members of oppressed groups are disproportionately likely to become part of an involuntary transaction are not clear. Does it occur as a result of a lack of access to resources? Are members of oppressed groups subject to ethnocentric pressures to comply with norms of the majority group? For example, the children of immigrant parents may come under the scrutiny of child welfare services in part because child rearing customs in their country of origin may differ from those of their adopted home (Togo 2006). Oppressed groups as involuntary clients will be explored in greater depth in chapter 15.

Fate Control

The disproportionate power imbalance between clients and practitioners in involuntary transactions is influenced by the perceived or existing fate control. Fate control refers to the degree to which one member of a dyad can coerce or constrain the future goals or actions of a second member, if that second member decides to leave the dyad before the first member is ready. For example, many involuntary clients experience different levels of fate control in their dealings with helping professionals (Thibaut and Kelley 1959). Coercive power is the ability of the practitioner to restrain or compel a client to an act or decision by force or threat. Having fate control or the power to coerce does not mean that it must or will be used (Kipnis 1972; Hasenfeld 1987). The level of voluntarism is influenced by the degree to which clients experience *coerced or constrained choices*, that is: (1) some choices are rewarded, (2) others are punished, and (3) preferred alternatives are often not available.

1. *A coerced or constrained choice may be rewarded.* Clients may "agree" to perform many actions to obtain rewards. For example, under the 1996 welfare reform legislation, clients could be required to participate in work readiness programs to qualify for assistance (Hage 2004). While they were legally free to discontinue their job training, the consequence of losing financial assistance for food and rent is constraining.
2. *Coerced and constrained choices are sometimes made because preferred alternatives are punished.* George, the alleged domestic violence perpetrator, may have preferred to be released with a warning. If he chose to avoid treatment, however, that choice may have meant facing prosecution and a possible prison term.
3. *A coerced or constrained choice may be made as the least detrimental alternative* (Thibaut and Kelly 1959). Clients may also "volunteer" for a service because the desired alternatives are too costly or unavailable, or because they believe some service is better than no service at all. For example, parents referred to child welfare agencies in which risk is not considered imminent may "choose" to participate in Alternative Response programs that are ostensibly voluntary but may contain the implied threat that failure to "volunteer" will result in a child protection referral (Pecora et al. 2000; Rooney 2000).

Attempts by Involuntary Clients to Regain Power

In a circumstance of perceived fate control, involuntary clients have five options if they wish to attempt to regain power in an unbalanced power situation. They can: (1) offer resources that the practitioner or agency will accept in exchange; (2) look elsewhere for the resource; (3) coerce or pressure the practitioner to provide the resource; (4) become resigned to getting along without the resource; or (5) meet the agency or practitioner's requirements to get the resource (Emerson 1962).

Even when involuntary clients decide that they have no alternative to meeting the requirements of the resource, they still have control over the way they decide to comply. For example, involuntary clients can reframe the situation to some personal benefit by viewing their circumstances as an opportunity to learn how to deal with other unequal power situations, or by working on their own goals at the same time as meeting the conditions set by the sources of the pressure (Thibaut and Kelley 1959). How to help involuntary clients reframe their circumstances will be explored in chapter 6.

A Continuum of Voluntarism

Our discussion about perceived fate control and available alternatives suggests that clients can experience a range of voluntarism over time or at the same time, on different issues. A continuum of voluntarism is defined by different sources of pressure, coercive and constraining modes of exerting that pressure, and a range of freedoms lost or threatened (Epstein 1988; Ivanoff, Blythe, and Tripodi 1994; Trotter 2006). The degree to which personal freedoms are limited is influenced by participation in institutional settings with a range of restrictiveness (Hawkins et al. 1992). For example, limits on freedom of action and choices are extensive in many correctional and in-patient hospital settings, whereas participation in a shelter or group home often involves moderate restrictions with more freedom to make choices.

Hence, clients who experience legal mandates, high fate control, and high perceived loss of valued freedoms through placement in highly restricted settings might be expected to be *highly involuntary*. Conversely, should clients experience a legal mandate with high fate control yet low perceived loss of freedom, they might act as if they were the *inaccessible involuntary*. That is, if the client is willing to give up what the agency or practitioner has the power to take away, then the effect of coercive power is limited. For example, biological parents are sometimes challenged that if they do not have frequent, productive visits with their children in out-of-home care, they risk losing permanent custody of the children. If, however, the parents have lost the will or hope that their efforts can succeed or no longer feel committed to regaining custody, then such admonitions can be powerless to influence their behavior.

Between the highly involuntary and the inaccessible involuntary client groups are the *invisible involuntary clients* whose circumstances are often not recognized by practitioners. For example, the nonvoluntary clients described earlier who do not face legal mandates, yet experience high fate control and loss of valued freedoms, can be considered the *invisible involuntary*. George and Alice are examples of invisible involuntary clients who experience stronger negative reactions to services than do legally mandated clients experiencing less fate control. I describe them as invisible because their lack of voluntarism is often hidden from the practitioner and agency if the latter are only alert to legal mandates as a measure of voluntarism.

Involuntary status can change over time: clients can become more or less voluntary. For example, if an involuntary client attains some of his or her own goals or comes to value some of the changes influenced by others, then he or she can become more voluntary. Conversely, many clients experience a *widening net* whereby their voluntarism decreases. An example is a family serving as kinship providers for the children of a sibling who wishes to adopt those children. At this point, they were voluntary clients in the sense that they were willingly pursuing a resource controlled by the agency: the legal custody of the children in their kinship care. In the course of assessing the clients' readiness to become adoptive parents, the agency discovered that the man had become depressed and at one point had threatened to harm himself. Concerned about his readiness to become an adoptive parent, the agency now *strongly suggested* that he seek an assessment of his predilection for depression and psychological assistance for the concern. The prospective adoptive parents were now feeling less enthusiastic about the process, questioning all the "hoops" they were being made to jump, and considered withdrawing their application to become adoptive parents. Through sensitive work by the adoption worker, the parents came to see a psychological assessment as a fair part of a safety plan both for the children and the father, and their voluntarism was partially restored. Skills in how to pursue such semivoluntary contracts are presented in chapter 6.

A client may acknowledge some issues while denying others. For example, a young mother who was accustomed to leaving her children unsupervised in the evening for a couple of hours when she went to a bar may have, on returning home, struck a child who was whining and injured him. When she took him to the hospital, her account of the injury was not convincing to medical personnel, who contacted the child protection agency. Her memory of the prior evening was not clear, but she did tell the investigator about striking the child. She deeply regretted this and acknowledged that drinking may have played a role in her behavior; she continued, however, to believe that leaving the children alone did not endanger them (Littell and Girvin 2004). The point here is that she acknowledged the harm done, and the role of alcohol, to some extent, but did not acknowledge safety issues related to child supervision. Consequently, her voluntarism could be expected to vary according to the issue. The consequences of differing levels of acknowledgment of problems will explored in chapter 4; stages of change and the role of motivational interviewing will be explored in chapters 10 to 12.

Legal status does not necessarily predict willingness to cooperate with helping professionals. Practitioners often believe that involuntary clients are unmotivated to achieve goals for themselves (Ivanoff, Blythe, and Tripodi 1994). However, a revealing study of motivation for change at intake did not support this assumption. As might be expected, legally mandated clients were overrepresented among those who were not initially open to pursuing goals for personal change (O'Hare 1996). However, 25 percent of those who were legally mandated had already moved before first contact to considering decisions or taking action to change. Consequently, the assumption that legally mandated clients will not be motivated for change and that clients without legal mandates will be motivated for change is not well supported. In this book, readers can assume that motivation is rarely completely voluntary in any case and can be enhanced in most cases.

These combinations of objective and subjective factors of voluntarism make predicting which clients are really involuntary difficult. In fact, little hard data is available on voluntarism as a client characteristic (Clarkin and Levy 2004). Self-referral is, however, one clue in identifying voluntary clients. One meta-analysis of social work services in mental health found that 18 percent of the clients were self-referred. Only 2 percent of the studies explicitly identified clients as involuntary. The remaining 80 percent are more difficult to classify because they were referred by agency staff, by staff in other agencies, or self-referred in coordination with staff referral (Videka-Sherman 1988). This group probably contains both clients who are quite voluntary and others who are nonvoluntary and experiencing a range of perceived loss of freedoms.

Involuntary Practice Issues for Practitioners

Three major issues are raised by work with involuntary clients: (1) the practitioners who work with involuntary clients are often themselves at least in part nonvoluntary; (2) ignoring involuntarism creates frustration and confusion for involuntary clients and practitioners; (3) nonvoluntary practitioners often need to perform dual roles of helping and controlling.

Nonvoluntary Practitioners

Reluctance often occurs on both sides in the involuntary transaction. While involuntary clients are frequently plotting to escape, physically or psychologically, practitioners can also imagine more desirable working conditions than struggling with persons who are opposing their efforts to help. Helping professionals in these circumstances may therefore be termed nonvoluntary practitioners. Nonvoluntary practitioners often understandably prefer working with voluntary clients who ask "Who am I?" rather than with the involuntary client who wonders, "Who are you, why are you here, and when will you leave?"

Practitioners who work with involuntary clients come from all the helping professions. For example, psychologists and psychiatrists sometimes evaluate and provide treatment to nonvoluntary clients who do not wish to be evaluated or treated. Similarly, nurses often engage in discharge planning with patients who feel that their choices are limited. Family therapists frequently work with families in which at least some members are ambivalent about participating in treatment (Anderson and Stewart 1985). Since social workers often work in both public and private agencies, they frequently work with mandated as well as nonvoluntary clients. Counselors placed in hospitals, schools, clinics, and prisons are also likely to work with involuntary clients (Ritchie 1986). Finally, practitioners in private agencies and private practice also have frequent contact. For example, clients may be required to obtain an assessment or seek out treatment from a practitioner who does not have a mandated relationship with the client.

Ignoring Involuntarism

Assumptions based on voluntary clients can complicate involuntary practice (Cingolani 1984). The helping perspective can break down at the very beginning of treatment because of conflicting assumptions between clients and practitioners about who "owns" the problem. Frustration because involuntary clients frequently deny responsibility for problems attributed to them by others can contribute to practitioners blaming clients and labeling them as resistive or unresponsive. For example, maintaining silence or limited speech in initial contacts could be an expected response in an involuntary situation in which contact came under outside pressure. Such persons normally might be talkative under less pressured social circumstances. Similarly, expectations that clients will be honest and candidly share their experiences ignore the reality of consequences for such candor for involuntary clients (Ivanoff, Blythe, and Tripodi 1994).

Rein and White have suggested that ignoring the involuntary circumstances in which some client contact takes place has been pervasive in social work practice: "We mistakenly assume that clients always come voluntarily to the professional relationship in order to get help . . . [that] the help . . . is not coercive and does not get into questions of private faith, morals, or politics" (Rein and White 1981:624). They further describe practitioner beliefs that there is no conflict between individual and social needs, that power is not used, and that self-determination is always pursued as myths of the profession (Rein and White 1981). In fact, social workers control many important client resources and frequently act to represent the agency, the community, and others, rather than the client (Hasenfeld 1987).

Rein and White described three solutions practitioners use to deal with the dissonance created by the gap between the reality of power and professional myths of equality. One solution to the dilemma is to say "I am one with the client" while ignoring that other interests are also represented. A second is to maintain that "everyone really agrees" by focusing on compromise and ignoring the fact that differences of interest often remain. The third solution maintains that "I have a set of skills," which avoids consideration of differing interests between the client and the agency by focusing attention on those areas the practitioner alone can affect. Rein and White (1981) suggest, however, that these so-called solutions do not eliminate the dissonance, and a malaise results from the unsuccessful efforts to implement them. Cingolani (1984) suggests that a social conflict approach is more congruent with the circumstances of involuntary contact. In this view, therapy is a political process in which society sanctions use of power in a context of conflict of interest. Lacking such a social conflict approach or a view of involuntary transactions, practitioners are often left with blaming involuntary clients for noncompliance for sabotaging plans made for them by others, and with wishing that they might work with a more appreciative clientele.

We will go beyond these three solutions in this book. While at times performing the coach or advocate role, practitioners are rarely *one with the client* and in fact often perform dual roles. Negotiating and contracting strategies to clarify available choices is the focus of chapters 5 and 6. The focus is on practitioner skills, while attempting to avoid myopia about the client's broader environment and situation.

Performing Dual Roles

Practitioners who work with involuntary clients need to play *dual roles*. On the one hand, they have responsibilities to enforce the law and to protect society and other persons. On the other hand, they have responsibilities to coach and assist clients in problem solving. These responsibilities can overlap or conflict (Burman 2004; Trotter 2006). Settings influence how these dual roles are performed. For example, a practitioner in a private setting may be able to focus extensively or exclusively on the helping or coaching role. Practitioners in public settings, however, have protection responsibilities. As noted by Regehr and Antle, "social workers are often placed in the role of working for the greater good—for example, balancing the needs of a child with the individual rights of one or both parents, or balancing the risk to society of freeing someone charged with a criminal offense with the rights of the accused" (Regehr and Antle 1997:301). Hence, while social work practitioners may find themselves serving *vulnerable voluntary* clients who require resources and efforts to empower them to protect their rights and safety, they also often find themselves working with *involuntary clients* who are a threat to others. How to play multiple roles, including representing authority and acting as a coach, will be presented in chapters 5 and 6.

Involuntary clients are abundant, whether defined by legal status or response to coerced or pressured contact. Voluntarism varies on a continuum that shifts over time or at the same time according to the issue and source of pressure. In chapter 2, we explore legal and ethical bases for work with involuntary clients.

Discussion Questions

The following questions are addressed to readers of this book who are practitioners with involuntary clients, students, supervisors, or instructors.

1. How often do the clients in your setting arrive with problems attributed to them by others? What are the implications for making service plans based on attributed problems rather than concerns acknowledged by clients?
2. Where do the clients in your setting fit on the continuum of voluntarism? For those who would report that their clients are voluntary, do some of those clients make constrained choices to accept services?
3. Can you think of client experience examples that support the idea of a continuum of voluntarism? For example, have you noticed clients who vary in their level of voluntarism at one time depending on the issue?
4. Have you noticed clients whose level of voluntarism increases or decreases over time? For example, have you noticed the widening net phenomenon whereby an initially voluntary client becomes less so over time as a result of new pressures being brought to bear?
5. Have you experienced work with clients whose voluntarism begins at a low point and increases over time?
6. What are the implications for the fact that some issues regarding involuntary status relate to observable factors such as legal mandates and others relate to subjective responses?
7. How do you respond to the concept of the *invisible involuntary* client? What are the implications for practitioners of ignoring pressures experienced by nonvoluntary clients and failing to distinguish them from voluntary clients?

8. What are the implications of the fact that involuntary transactions frequently occur between members of oppressed groups and social service agencies in which the practitioners who serve clients often differ from them in terms of race, culture, and social class?

9. Have you experienced fate control in which some choices you would prefer are punished, some are rewarded, and some selected because they are the least detrimental alternative? For example, what is the experience of fate control with students in a degree program?

10. How are students like and unlike involuntary clients? How do their constrained choices differ from those of clients?

11. What are the implications for practitioners of performing dual roles of protecting society and supporting client self-determined goals?

12. How can helping professionals be like or unlike involuntary clients? Have you experienced feeling as if you were an *involuntary practitioner*? How does that experience affect job satisfaction? How have you experienced constrained choices in that process and attempted to increase your voluntarism by making the most of your choices?

Legal and Ethical Foundations for Work with Involuntary Clients

Practice with involuntary clients requires a legal and ethical foundation. The legal foundation determines the conditions under which practitioners can restrict behavior. Practice with involuntary clients often entails carrying out legal mandates and/or investigating harm to self or others. For example, child abuse and vulnerable adult investigations are designed to determine whether serious danger has or might eminently occur. This chapter presents guidelines concerning legally mandated investigations.

The ethical foundation guides practitioners in areas not covered by law. For example, the practitioner or employing agency may believe that harm is imminent but has not yet reached a legal threshold wherein involuntary intervention is appropriate. Practitioners need to know how to support maximum feasible self-determination. They also need to know when paternalistic or beneficent action can be in the client's best interests. This chapter provides guidelines for ethical intervention with involuntary clients, and offers practitioners assistance in answering questions about legal and ethical intervention with involuntary clients such as the following:

- How can I act to support due process and informed consent for involuntary clients?
- What are my responsibilities related to confidentiality?
- How do I avoid malpractice and reduce liability?

- How do I perform the dual roles of helping clients and protecting society?
- How can I support maximum feasible client self-determination and empowerment while acting to protect vulnerable persons and society?
- When am I justified in acting to limit self-determination or acting paternalistically in the client's best interest?

The Clash Between Legal and Helping Perspectives

Helping professionals have often been ambivalent about the expanding role of the legal system in protecting client rights (Alexander 2003). For example, practitioners often learn new legal procedures that can become obsolete by the time they appear in training texts (Sadoff 1982). In fact, the law plays such a large role in practice with legally mandated clients that practitioners have been urged to "think like lawyers" (Dickson 1998) and they have complained of being "belegaled" (Madden 1998:4). Attorneys and mental health professionals often approach the same situations from different perspectives, such that lawyers are more concerned with the sanctity of legal principles and advocacy of civil rights, while mental health professionals are more inclined to provide help regardless of issues of loss of liberty (Melton et al. 1987; Cull and Roche 2001). Some attorneys argue that this commitment to help often means that practitioners act as if client rights are forfeited on entry into a program (Martin 1981). Further, clients with mental illness or retardation and juvenile clients who are institutionalized are often members of oppressed groups with limited power to protect their own rights.

Practitioners working with involuntary clients are often caught in controversies over community and individual rights and frequently have to deal with fluctuating standards (Rhodes 1986; Regehr and Antle 1997). The pursuit of legal, ethical, and effective practice involves conscious use of practitioner influence to affect the behaviors, attitudes, and decisions of involuntary clients in some situations and conscious efforts to avoid influence in others. Public practitioners are often mandated to act to protect the community or defenseless persons from self-harm or harm from others (Fowler 2003). Similarly, practitioners in private settings often attempt to influence nonvoluntary clients to make wise decisions by bringing to bear agency, referral source, family, as well as their own pressures.

Helping professionals have rarely been trained in how to carry out their legal roles. Social workers, for instance, are advised in their professional code of ethics to "make every effort to foster self-determination on the part of clients," to consider their responsibilities to the client as primary, yet are also told to "adhere to commitments made to the employing agency (NASW 1999). As these directives often conflict, social workers are left with difficult choices (Reamer 1999). Confusion often ensues about the nature of the responsibilities to involuntary clients, family members, the agency, and the community (Regehr and Antle 1997).

One frequently cited solution to these dilemmas is for the agency-based practitioner to be guided primarily by law and agency requirements. In fact, many practitioners begin their professional work with legal in-service training or an informal, trial-and-error approach to learning the law, policies, and procedures, since these areas are often inadequately covered in their academic programs. This chapter next explores the growth of procedural safeguards for legally mandated clients designed to curb arbitrary discretion and guarantee fundamental fairness such that constitutional rights to life, liberty, and property are not endangered without due process. The perspective presented here is in line with Martin's observation that "rather than assuming there is an inherent conflict between rights and therapy, professionals must realize that appropriate therapeutic intervention includes client rights" (Martin 1981:9).

Principal Legal Issues in Work with Involuntary Clients

Our discussion of legal issues begins with a brief survey of due process, informed consent, confidentiality, and privileged communication, followed by liability and malpractice.

Due Process

Under the fifth, eighth, and fourteenth amendments to the U.S. Constitution, citizens are entitled to due process of law before they can be deprived of life, liberty, or property (Alexander 2003). The fifth amendment guarantees that individuals cannot be required to testify against themselves, while the eighth amendment guarantees freedom from cruel and unusual punishment and the fourteenth amendment states that a citizen cannot be deprived of his or her civil rights without fundamental fairness. Due process safeguards include some or all of the following: the right to adequate notice of charges, an open hearing before an impartial examiner, right to counsel, the rights to cross-examine and present witnesses, right to written decisions giving reasons based on facts, and the right to appeal decisions (Schroeder 1995). The specific forms of notice vary, and in some states there is a right to trial by jury (Saltzman and Proch 1990).

Informed Consent

Informed consent refers both to a process of continually informing clients about intervention plans and the use of forms so that those clients can provide consent to proposed treatment with adequate knowledge of costs, benefits, and alternative procedures (Reamer 1987). Informed consent is *not* satisfied by the mere completion of a written form (Rozovsky 1987). A valid consent form is not an open-ended, blanket agreement but rather an agreement to specific procedures based on adequate information.

Informed consent is relevant for conditions such as legally involuntary mental commitment, chemical dependency, use of restraints, aversive treatment, isolation, abortion, contraception, sexual disorders, and sterilization (Reamer 1987). Mental patients also have the right to be informed about treatment, to refuse treatment on religious grounds, and to participate in experimental treatment or research only after providing informed consent.

Valid informed consent must be obtained without coercion or undue influence such that a person is able to refuse or withdraw consent. However, according to Melton, "the available research raises substantial doubt as to whether most consent in health and mental health care is truly voluntary" (Melton et al. 1987:255). For example, Saltzman and Proch note, "Some hospitalizations which are called 'voluntary' are in fact only agreed to under the threat of commitment. Moreover, voluntary hospitalizations often turn into commitments when a voluntary patient seeks to be released" (Saltzman and Proch 1990:312). There have been court rulings that institutionalized mental patients are in inherently coercive situations. If release from the institution depends on patient cooperation, they may provide informed consent to intrusive procedures such as psychosurgery (ibid.).

Circumstances do exist, however, in which informed consent is not immediately required: (1) when actions must be taken in genuine emergencies to preserve life and (2) when a person has a mental illness or incapacitating chemical or alcohol dependency such that he or she is currently incapable of providing such consent (Reamer 1987). The ability to provide consent cannot be determined by membership in a general class of persons such as those with severe mental illness, but must be based on a mental status examination. If mental status fluctuates, it may be possible to give or withdraw consent during lucid phases. Standards used to determine competency include the ability to comprehend relevant facts, appreciate one's circumstances, understand and manipulate information, and test reality. Research on implementation of informed consent suggests, however, that the spirit of informed consent is often violated. Consent forms are often drafted in legal terms incomprehensible to clients, or are often presented as a mere formality, alternative forms of treatment are rarely presented, and full information about negative or harmful side effects is often omitted (Lidz et al. 1984). Rather than treating informed consent as pro forma, it should be an opportunity to engage in a collaborative relationship consistent with a therapeutic philosophy of basic respect for all people (Melton et al. 1987).

There are inherent difficulties in appropriately supporting the principle of informed consent. For example, the risks and benefits of an assessment cannot always be determined in advance. The power imbalance between practitioners and clients undermines free consent. Client ability to provide valid consent can also be reduced because of language or cultural barriers, diminished capacity, or the developmental capacity of juveniles (Regehr and Antle 1997). It is recommended that the practitioner clarify his or her role when serving two or more people, and not use interviewing skills to "trick" a client into disclosing information that might harm the client (ibid.). Another challenge for supporting informed consent is the fact that practitioners cannot precisely describe the outcome of contact, predicting all contingencies. Finally, while practitioners may offer choices within treatment, the treatment itself may occur because of coercive pressure (Ryder and Tepley 1993).

Confidentiality and Privileged Communication

Confidentiality refers to the obligation of helping professionals not to reveal without permission records or client information obtained in the course of practice (Saltzman and Proch 1990; Dickson 1998). Privileged communication refers to a client's right to prevent a helping practitioner from testifying against him or her in a court of law without his or her permission (Albert 2000). Some helping professions do not have privileged communication and others have it in some states but not in others (Schroeder 1995). Consequently, practitioners should be prepared for possible subpoena of records. Confidentiality of records such that the records or information contained therein could not be revealed without prior client consent is a goal of the helping professions. However, some professions have more legal rights in some areas than in others, such that at times helping professions can be court-ordered to turn over records. This often leads to keeping superficial records to avoid being legally required to turn over information that might be damaging.

Circumstances exist in which a practitioner is required to violate privilege. For example, if a client is currently suicidal or imminently violent toward a certain person, the practitioner is obliged to breach confidentiality for that person's protection or issue a warning to the intended victim (*Tarasoff v. Regents of the University of California* 1976). In addition, practitioners are legally required to report possible child abuse.

Practitioners need to make clear their relationship with clients from the beginning so that clients understand the circumstances under which their confidentiality may be violated (Melton et al. 1987). Clients often have legal access to their own records on notice, which should be provided, with the confidentiality of others referred to in the records protected.

Liability and Malpractice

Helping professionals have been increasingly faced with legal liability and malpractice concerns (Reamer 2003a, 2003b). Malpractice is negligent practice, inconsistent with the standards of a prudent professional in which: (1) a legal duty existed to a client; (2) the practitioner was negligent in performing that duty; and (3) the client was harmed by that negligence (Reamer 2003b).

Malpractice can be based on incorrect diagnosis or treatment, harmful effects of treatment, poor results, failure to consult or refer appropriately, injury resulting from violation of confidentiality, or a failure to warn (Saltzman and Proch 1990).

Malpractice has a longer legal history in the medical profession, in which the doctor's responsibility to the patient is clearer. For professionals such as social workers and family therapists, a definition of the duty owed to the client(s) is often less clear. In addition, a professional standard of care must be in place by which the action can be assessed as in accordance with a duty or dereliction of duty. The standard of care is sometimes hard to define, but practitioners are expected to act within established parameters (Madden 1998).

Additional concerns have been raised, however, about the liability of public agency employees, who are less frequently protected by immunity from litigation (Saltzman and Proch 1990). For example, child protection workers can be sued for failure to reopen or investigate possible child abuse, improper selection of or failure to monitor placement, wrongful removal or detention, and failure to locate permanent placements. The best protection against such suits is careful practice, following procedures that are compliant with the law, consulting with colleagues, reviewing ethical standards, obtaining necessary legal consultation, keeping good records, ensuring access to adequate supervision, and documenting decision-making steps (Reamer 2003a).

Legal Issues Applicable Across Populations and Settings

The first edition of this book contained extensive information about legal issues within a variety of settings and populations. As such information rapidly becomes dated and more specific information is needed to guide practice with a particular population, more extensive discussion is presented in the chapters in part 3 that deal with specific populations and settings. This chapter provides information about specific principles that apply across populations and settings, focusing on three issues: the least restrictive alternative principle, the right to treatment, and freedom from unnecessary treatment.

Least Restrictive Alternative

Some federal district and state courts have interpreted the fourteenth amendment to include rights to the least restrictive alternative such that when two methods are available that would achieve the same result, the individual is entitled to the form that would restrict least (Wodarski 1980). For example, courts can order involuntary commitment only when less restrictive alternatives are unavailable or inappropriate (Madden 1998).

Right to Treatment

Some courts and state statutes have moved to ensure that persons deprived of their liberty for purposes of treatment are entitled to adequate treatment that is not merely custodial (*Rouse v. Cameron* 1966). In defense of a right to treatment, Judge Johnson wrote: "To deprive a citizen of his or her liberty upon the altruistic theory that the interference is for humane and therapeutic reasons and then fail to provide adequate treatment violates the very fundamentals of due process. . . . If adequate treatment is not provided, it is equal to incarceration" (*Johnson v. Solomon* 1979:278). While the Supreme Court has not ruled that under the Constitution there is a right to treatment, the Court has strongly suggested that a person cannot be confined to ensure a better living standard and that fencing in the harmless to protect citizens from exposure is not justified (Alexander 2003). Involuntary commitment must contain proper treatment that is the least restrictive, patients must be informed of their rights, and care must be monitored to ensure that progress is reviewed (Reamer 2003a).

Since there is no constitutional right to medical care, those who are voluntarily admitted for treatment do not have the same access to a right for treatment as the involuntarily committed (Saltzman and Proch 1990). Informed consent is relied upon to protect the rights of voluntary clients. Clients must therefore be competent to provide voluntary, uncoerced consent while knowledgeable about consequences and alternatives. Voluntary hospitalization supposedly raises few legal questions since in theory there is no unwanted restriction of individual rights. Saltzman and Proch note, however, that "it may be difficult to determine the voluntariness of consent in certain situations which may be coercive by nature such as when someone is required to execute a consent for the release of full medical records to obtain welfare benefits" (ibid.:394). Under the schema suggested in chapter 1, this could be nonvoluntary contact based on formal pressures. Even those who are determined legally incompetent can be represented by guardians who act under the principle of substituted judgment as they believe the patient would have wanted (ibid.).

Freedom from Unnecessary Treatment

The courts seek to protect involuntarily hospitalized persons from unnecessary treatment. In the case of extreme procedures such as use of restraints, electroconvulsive shock, and lobotomies, the least restrictive principle requires adequate justification, including informed consent from the patient or a qualified conservator or guardian. Under the rights to privacy, use of some mind-altering drugs that have harmful side effects have been opposed as prohibiting freedom of thought (Melton et al. 1987).

Most nursing home residents are considered voluntary since they are treated in private facilities with the assumption that they are free to leave (Edwards and Sheldon-Wildgen 1981). Many nursing home residents, however, are placed without a hearing or adequate representation. Once again, these legally voluntary clients may be the "invisible" nonvoluntary with decisions often constrained by pressures from doctors, family members, physical inability to leave, and lack of alternatives (ibid.). However, nursing home residents who are Medicare or Medicaid recipients are protected by a bill of rights that includes, among others, the rights to be informed about their health and medical condition, to participate in planning total care and treatment, to refuse treatment, to be free from restraints except under specified conditions of care, to choose a physician, and to be free from physical or mental abuse (Omnibus Budget Reconciliation Act of 1987).

Legal guidance and protection of rights for clients considered legally voluntary are much more limited (Saltzman and Proch 1990). Hence, legally voluntary clients such as mental patients, health care recipients, nursing home residents, and children frequently make decisions that are coerced or constrained by other persons, situations, and a lack of alternatives. In the absence of legal guarantees, practitioners are urged to voluntarily extend similar protections to nonvoluntary clients as are accorded legally mandated clients. Nonvoluntary clients should have a right to privacy and to be left alone unless their overt behavior qualifies them for inclusion in a program (Martin 1981). Practitioners and clients can collaborate in obtaining the information needed for an nonvoluntary client to make an informed decision (Adams and Drake 2006). Clients should have the right to their own thoughts and opinions as a basic requirement to ensure freedom of speech and should be entitled to treatment that is the least restrictive with guaranteed quality of care.

Assessment of Legal Impact on Work with Involuntary Clients

The legal framework is one major element toward a goal of legal, ethical, effective practice. That framework is the basis for when to intervene involuntarily, when not to intervene, and how to protect the rights of clients in these circumstances. As a result of expansion of legal guidelines for legally mandated clients, practitioners, agencies, and institutions have become much more aware of client rights and protective statutes and are engaged in a continual updating of knowledge of changing standards (table 2.1).

These benefits have not been achieved without cost. For example, the expansion of due process procedures does not create more resources for direct service to clients and may reduce it because of more paperwork and court appearances (Dickson 1976). Emphasis on the law and procedures may lead practitioners to be unwilling to take risks or fail to advocate for fear of being sued (Barton and Barton 1984). Decisions to act are increasingly dichotomized between coercive action when legal grounds exist or inaction when legal grounds do not (Sadoff 1982). The focus on the rights of mandated clients has overshadowed the rights of nonvoluntary clients who often face unfair coerced choices. Nonvoluntary clients whose capacity to provide informed consent is often constrained by formal and informal pressures should have their rights protected, taking those pressures into account. Finally, many helping professionals have reservations about the least restrictive principle

Table 2.1   Questions regarding client legal rights in treatment programs

- Does the client meet program criteria?
- Are client rights explained in ways understandable to him or her?
- Are staff aware of client rights?
- Do goals reflect the least restrictive alternative?
- Has written informed consent been obtained from appropriate persons?
- Do clients have the opportunity to present complaints?
- Are treatment plans individualized?
- Are clients involved in goal development?
- Do plans identify and build on client strengths?
- Is adaptive behavior recorded as well as pathological?
- Are plans related to those goals?
- Are goals and progress reviewed periodically by an appropriate group that includes clients?
- Do records adequately protect confidentiality?
- Is abuse investigated?
- Are staff appropriately trained and supervised?

when they consider more restrictive means to be more effective and they often question a client's ability to judge this effectiveness (Barton and Barton 1984). Nevertheless, practitioners must work with procedural protections developed to protect the rights of legally involuntary and nonvoluntary clients (Martin 1981).

Ethical Guidelines for Work with Involuntary Clients

While law provides one foundation for legal, ethical, effective practice, it provides little guidance for practice with nonvoluntary clients whose consent is often provided under duress. In addition, laws and regulations do not cover all contingencies in work with mandated clients. An ethical foundation is needed to guide practitioners regarding client self-determination and appropriate paternalism contrary to a client's wishes about his or her own welfare. Finally, guidelines for practitioner behavior that integrate legal and ethical perspectives are provided.

Self-Determination and Autonomy

Most practitioners would agree that they are committed to client best interest. They disagree, however, about who their clients are and what constitutes their best interest (Reamer 1999). Guides for determining ethical responsibilities to clients must include a review of the concepts of self-determination and autonomy. *Self-determination* means action toward one's own goals, wishes, and desires. The concept can be further divided into *positive* self-determination, which means having the knowledge, skills, and resources necessary to pursue one's own goals, and *negative* self-determination, or autonomy, which refers to free acts, not coerced, or made under duress or undue influence (Reamer 1999; Strom-Gottfried 1998). For example, actions to assist a client in reaching her goal of alleviating her depression through a referral for counseling and a consultation for medication would support positive self-determination. Ensuring that her participation in the counseling program was not coerced would be in support of negative self-determination or autonomy.

Does self-determination take precedence in all situations? A critical problem occurs when the rights of one person conflict with the rights of another. Many believe that one person's self-determination stops where another person's begins (Reid 1984). In fact, avoiding harm to others is generally agreed on as legitimate grounds for limiting self-determination. According to Reamer, when a client acts to endanger others, the endangered person's right to the basic preconditions to action such as health, food, and livelihood take precedence over the client's right to freedom of action (Reamer 1999). Some have suggested that self-determination should be supported when the rights of others are protected; when client choices are realistic, rational, reasoned, and constructive rather than unexamined impulses; when those choices fit the law, agency, and society; and when those choices are within the client's capacity to self-determine (Biestek 1951). However, including all of these criteria would limit self-determination to socially acceptable, trivial goals (McDermott 1975). The NASW Code of Ethics adds "socially responsible" as a qualifier for client self-determination of goals (NASW 1999). Commitment to self-determination does not mean that the practitioner must support unwise client choices. Persuasive influence toward making better choices can be ethical in such circumstances (ibid.; Clark 1998). Clients can also be helped to distinguish between circumstances that are changeable and those that are not and they can be helped to review their full range of choices (Bernstein 1960).

Paternalism

There is less agreement on limitations to self-determination when such interference is justified solely by judgment of the client's best interest apart from immediate danger to others. Paternalism refers to limitations on client self-determination for a person's own good rather than the good of a third party (Reamer 1983). Paternalism may take three forms: (1) opposing client wishes, (2) withholding information from the client, or (3) providing deliberate misinformation, thereby manipulating the client to the practitioner's viewpoint. Paternalism is obvious when the client's explicit wishes for his or her own good are directly contradicted. Less obvious is paternalism in which information is withheld or the client is manipulated to concur with the practitioner's viewpoint. Paternalism is frequently practiced with clients not considered entirely rational, including children and those judged mentally incompetent (Abramson 1985). Practitioners who practice paternalistically usually assume that they are acting for the client's own good, that they are sufficiently qualified to judge that good, and that client welfare justifies their action.

Four client attributes are routinely used to justify paternalism: (1) that clients lack information that would lead them to consent to interference; (2) that clients are temporarily or permanently incapable of comprehending relevant information; (3) that clients have given prior consent to paternalism; and (4) that such consent is likely to be given later in any event (Reamer 1999). Reamer suggests that clients may give invalid prior consent to paternalism under duress of a threat of withdrawal of service (ibid.). Similarly, some chemical dependency programs have norms to prevent impulsive decisions to leave treatment (ibid.).

Three situational attributes are also used to justify paternalism: (1) that harmful consequences are likely to be irreversible without interference; (2) that a wider range of freedom can be preserved by restricting it; and (3) that there is an immediate need to rescue (ibid.).

This discretionary range in determining potential harm contributed to the legal movement to ensure due process. Paternalism is subject to abuse because paternalistic acts are often as motivated by organizational as they are by client interest (Abramson 1985). For example, confining patients to their rooms for a rest period may be also motivated by staff shortages during shift changes. Second, once a decision is made to limit self-determination through paternalism, the way is often paved for further limitation.

Frederic Reamer suggests that because of the potential for paternalistic abuse, practitioners and organizations are responsible for providing a compelling case for the need for paternalism rather than holding the client responsible for proving that paternalism is *not* needed (Reamer 1999). He suggests that ethics committees can be helpful for consulting on difficult cases and for educating practitioners and administrators and developing agency guidelines (ibid.).

Reamer further proposes guidelines for making paternalistic decisions. Temporary interference to determine whether the conditions of informed choice have been met is justified when clients threaten or actually engage in behavior, such as self-destructive actions or severely debilitating alcohol or drug use, that results in harm to themselves (Reamer 1999). This interference is justified long enough to determine whether: (1) the action would be incapacitating or fatal; (2) the choice is made voluntarily, knowledgeable of consequences, circumstances, and alternatives; and (3) the proposed interference would not cause physical or economic dependency on others or endangerment.

Beneficence refers to protective interventions made despite a patient's objections in order to enhance his or her quality of life (Abramson 1989). For example, *limited beneficence* refers to carefully circumscribed interventions designed to protect a patient and also not interfere with his or her civil liberties (Murdach 1996). For example, accompanying a patient who is hearing voices on a shopping trip could help the patient exercise his or her freedom to shop while assisting in dealing with the environment (ibid.). *Selective beneficence* refers to more extensive intervention in specific areas such as temporary hospitalization for those who threaten or attempt suicide (ibid.). *Extensive beneficence* refers to protective intervention in all principal aspects of a patient's life, which may be required for persons experiencing major psychoses, severe disabilities, or brain trauma (ibid.). Such decisions raise conflicts between autonomy and decisions in best interest. The principle of the least restrictive alternative would suggest that the level of beneficence proposed must be justified by meeting accepted standards and reduced when the need declines. There are no clear guidelines for such judgements. Reamer (1983) comments that, "If we err in the direction of too much intrusion, we risk alienating our client and the sins of commission. If we err in the direction of leaving too much alone, we risk nothing less than neglect and the sins of omission" (p. 268).

As a process to protect clients and ensure that practitioners and agencies act appropriately, Reamer suggests when policies are considered, the groups that are likely to be effected by the policy should be identified, the potential risks and benefits for different courses of action considered, colleagues and experts appropriately consulted, and then the decision made and documented (Reamer 1999). Congress suggests the acronym ETHIC to prescribe a process whereby one considers first the problematic situation:

Examines pertinent values (personal, societal, agency, client, professional);
Thinks about which ethical standard of a professional code of ethics applies;
Hypothesizes about consequences of decisions;
Identifies who will benefit and who will be harmed in light of commitment to most vulnerable; and
Consults with supervisor and colleagues about ethical choice (Congress 1999).
Reamer (1999) would add a final step of evaluation to incorporate a review of the actual outcomes of the decision.

Finally, Reamer proposes an ethics audit of practices that includes assessment of the clarity and comprehensiveness of summaries of client rights including confidentiality and privacy, release of information, informed consent, access to services, access to records, service plans and rights to participate in their development, options for alternative services, policies regarding termination of services, grievance procedures, and evaluation (Reamer 2000, 2001a, 2001b).

Legal and Ethical Guidelines for Work with Involuntary Clients

While the legal guidelines described in the preceding text are sometimes consistent with ethical guidelines, they often point the practitioner toward different decisions. Four general guidelines integrating the two perspectives for practitioner behavior with involuntary clients for which legal and ethical guidance is consistent are considered. These are followed by more specific guidance in a matrix of legal and ethical influences when these influences indicate different directions (table 2.2).

Table 2.2   General legal and ethical guidelines

- Facilitate informed consent and due process.
- Facilitate empowerment, co-planning, and contracting.
- Communicate honestly and avoid manipulation and deception.
- Advocate for social justice and fair treatment practices.

1. *Facilitate informed consent and due process.* As each citizen is constitutionally entitled to due process before rights can be endangered, all clients are entitled to be informed about their rights and programs for which they are eligible, as well as limitations to those rights and programs. But some therapists have argued that persons who have violated the rights of others forfeit the right of informed consent (Ryder and Tepley 1993). Practitioners do not have a societal mandate to determine whether a client has forfeited informed consent. Even if an involuntary client has perpetrated harm on others, that person is still entitled to be informed of alternatives, risks, benefits, and consequences. If the client is not competent to provide informed consent, such consent can be sought from proxies who can act to consider the issue as the person judged incompetent would have done, in line with their life goals and preferences. Practitioners should describe their own limits and obligations such that clients know about circumstances both in which they are legally entitled to confidentiality and in which practitioners might have to violate that confidentiality or act against client wishes.

2. *Facilitate empowerment, co-planning, and contracting.* One solution to the dilemma of determining who the client is entails facilitating the empowerment of involuntary clients within legal limits. Legal requirements do not preclude affirmation of the worth, dignity, and uniqueness of involuntary clients and their ability to resolve problems (Clark 1998; Adams and Drake 2006). Respect for individual worth and empowerment can be enhanced through the use of contracts. Contracting is a consensual agreement and acceptance of reciprocal obligations and responsibilities to perform certain tasks, and deliver goods within a time-limited period (Simons and Aigner 1985). Contracts are similar to involuntary service agreements used in mandated situations that specify target problems, goals, and client expectations. Service agreements, however, are often "corrupt contracts" imposed on captive clients without negotiation. Such service agreements are less contracts and more "notices of agency intent" or "notices of consequences" analogous to the citation a motorist receives when stopped by a police officer for speeding (Seabury 1979). Such a citation is not negotiated, though it may offer a coerced choice such as paying a fine or appearing in court.

Contracts with mandated clients are obviously not entirely consensual, as legal requirements are not negotiable. Other areas, however, are open to discretion and negotiation such that clients can participate in decisions affecting their rights, and their range of choices can be broadened (Raynor 1978). Contracting entails negotiation on such discretionary issues and exploring work on voluntary issues beyond mandated requirements. The practitioner can also help mandated clients be aware of areas that are not covered by their legal restrictions.

As nonvoluntary clients, by definition, do not face legal limitations, contracting is a particularly appropriate way to ensure that there is informed consent to proceed on agreed-upon problems without duress. Agency policies may specify that clients be aware of constraints involved in their decision to accept services. Specific guidelines for contracting with involuntary clients are explored in chapter 6.

3. *Communicate honestly and avoid manipulation and deception.* Professional codes of ethics proscribe exploitation of clients for the practitioner's own gain or satisfaction, and practitioners are urged not to use their expertise to dominate or manipulate clients. Manipulation, however, often occurs through keeping plans hidden, maintaining a mysterious distance, and not raising questions an unquestioning client should raise. As Keith-Lucas notes, "Some clients are still given the illusion of free choice when in fact they have been pressured or manipulated into a formal contract that has nothing to do with their real wishes" (Keith-Lucas 1972:334). In addition, there may be superficial agreement with client goals, masking a commitment to a hidden goal. The motto for such efforts might be: "Start where the client is in order to get him or her to where you want to go!"

Such withholding of information alleged to be for the client's good is paternalism, which should best be considered using the narrow ethical guidelines suggested earlier. Should voluntary clients choose to remain in a counseling relationship that utilizes deceptive methods, their continuation may be based on agreement concerning the overall goal of contact and satisfaction with progress in counseling. Mandated and nonvoluntary clients, however, suffer consequences in leaving such relationships, and should be protected from the use of deceptive methods when they have not agreed to or have been pressured to accept goals set by the practitioner (Harris and Watkins 1987). Hence, practitioners working with mandated and nonvoluntary clients should avoid use of deceptive methods. Such methods constitute an unethical paternalism and, because of manipulative practitioner behavior, do not lead to the development of a trusting working relationship.

4. *Advocate for social justice and fair treatment practices.* While the above guidelines refer to comportment with individual involuntary clients, practitioners also have ethical responsibilities to advocate for fair treatment for all

involuntary clients in their setting. The ethical practitioner should challenge demeaning, unfair, discriminatory practices and institutional restraints that limit client opportunities for change. For example, ethics committees can develop guidelines and training for the use of informed consent, which embodies the spirit of client protections, rather than pro forma use of written releases. Such practices may call for efforts to reform policies from within and form alliances with outside professional groups (Rhodes 1986; Clifford and Burke 2005). Unfortunately, many practitioners are better trained in methods for influencing personal rather than structural change and engaging in advocacy. If they do not engage in efforts to humanize services, they are susceptible to providing "social control with a smiling face."

Integrating Legal and Ethical Perspectives in a Matrix

The four guidelines described in the preceding section can be applied generally in involuntary transactions. To help the practitioner think about both legal and ethical issues simultaneously, an integrative perspective is needed that asks both legal and ethical questions and suggests possible actions based on those questions. The guiding issue in this perspective is to determine whether there are legal and ethical grounds for restricting client freedom. For such action to be legal and ethical, two sets of criteria need to be satisfied.

The legal questions are: (1) Do you have delegated legal authority to restrict freedom in this instance? (2) Does client behavior fall within the domain of that delegated authority (Keith-Lucas 1972)? (3) Is the decision to take action to limit client freedom based on clear, unbiased criteria? The principal ethical question is whether there is *imminent danger to self* or *others*. Ethical action to limit client freedom is justified when irreversible, clear, and present danger will occur if prompt and positive action is not taken. Also, when one person acts to endanger others, the endangered person's rights to health, food, and livelihood take precedence over the client's right to act freely.

When the answers to these four questions are affirmative, then action to at least temporarily limit freedom can be both legal and ethical (cell 1 in figure 2.1). Cells 2 and 3 refer to unbalanced situations in which legal criteria are met while ethical criteria are not (cell 2), or situations in which ethical criteria are met while legal criteria are not (cell 3). Finally, cell 4 refers to circumstances in which there are neither legal nor ethical grounds for interference. Specific guidelines for each cell are proposed below, with case studies to illustrate their use.

Figure 2.1   Legal–ethical matrix

	Ethical Criteria Met	Ethical Criteria Not Met
Legal Criteria Met	**Cell 1:** **Legal, Ethical Intrusion** 1. Clarify rights, responsibilities, roles 2. Distinguish non-negotiable requirements from free choices	**Cell 2:** **Intrusion Is Legal But Not Ethical** 1. Advocate for change in law or policy through internal advocacy or external organization 2. Overt or covert resistance of policy 3. Choose to leave agency or setting
Legal Criteria Not Met	**Cell 3:** **Intrusion Is Ethical, But Not Legally Based** 1. Practitioner must be guided by informed consent and self-determination if legal criteria or grounds for appropriate paternalism do not exist 2. Attempt ethical persuasion 3. Offer an incentive to influence choice 4. Advocate that the harm be made illegal	**Cell 4:** **Restrictions on Freedom Are Neither Legal Nor Ethical** 1. Act according to negative self-determination; avoid coercion of choices 2. Consider positive self-determination in assisting to reach goals

Cell 1: Limitations on Client Freedom to Act Are Both Ethical and Legal

To explore legal and ethical limitation of freedom, let us consider the following situation. Police have reported to a Minnesota public child welfare agency that two children, one and two years of age, were found home alone while the mother, Agnes Jones, nineteen, was found across the street in a bar.

1. *Does the practitioner have legal authority?* Following the sequence of legal and ethical questions suggested in figure 2.1, we ask first whether the child protection practitioner has authority and domain over the alleged action. Child protective service does have legal authority and domain over allegations of child abuse, neglect, and sexual abuse, and hence the child protection practitioner does have legal authority to investigate the allegation.

2. *Does client behavior fall within the domain of that authority?* Mr. Brown, the child protection worker, consulted agency criteria for assessing danger and found that leaving small children unattended is included within the behaviors justifying investigation.

3. *Is the decision to limit client freedom based on clear, unbiased criteria?* Agency criteria for assessing risk in such conditions include the following: (a) the child is exposed to dangerous surroundings and (b) infants or very young children are left alone or in the care of other children too young to protect them. Criteria are less specific in determining what constitutes dangerous surroundings. Less objective criteria require more discretionary interpretation and hence may be more subject to bias. For example, the agency's own criteria in this case guided Mr. Brown to rate the situation as low-risk if the "parent is remorseful; this is a first incident; the parent seeks help and there were extenuating circumstances" and to rate the situation as high-risk if the parent is "denying responsibility and blaming others."

Ms. Jones responded to the investigation by saying that she was out of the home for only a few minutes and was nearby, across the street. In addition, a neighbor was supposed to be checking in with the children. She raged that she should not have to spend all of her young life with babies and she had a right to go out occasionally and have a drink. Ms. Jones went on to say that she felt cooped up and wanted to get out to get her GED and a job.

By the agency's parental response criteria, Ms. Jones' children would have been considered at high risk. Such criteria emphasize parental motivation rather than considering normal situational responses to threatening situations. In chapter 4, we explore alternative explanations for responses to threatening situations. For now, it is sufficient to consider that a negative response to the possible threat of removal of children can be a normal situational response. On the other hand, superficial cooperation may indicate use of ingratiating strategies of self-presentation to neutralize a threat in a less than sincere fashion (see self-presentation strategies in chapter 4). As a consequence of the difficulties in attributing the "real" motivation for hostile and cooperative behaviors, practitioners should place higher emphasis on more objective criteria, such as the fact that the children were left alone, rather than on parental responses that may be aggravated by the involuntary nature of the transaction (Reamer 2005).

4. *Is there imminent danger to self or others?* Leaving small children unattended would also justify ethical action to limit Ms. Jones' freedom if such behavior endangered them. Norms vary in different cultures about child-rearing and child safety practices. For example, the age at which children are considered old enough to care for others varies, the length of time they can be left unattended varies, and the responsibility entrusted to an older child for getting adult help in times of possible danger also varies. It is sufficient

here to note that there may be a conflict between what Ms. Jones and her neighbors might consider unsafe practices and the definition of such by the investigating agency. When the practitioner is employed by a legally mandated agency and a legal threshold of danger to others is reached, the client's right to self-determine is temporarily superseded by the rights of others to act freely. In this case, the small children's rights to adequate supervision take precedence over Ms. Jones' right to free action.

Can such intervention to limit freedom be done in a way that maximizes self-determination within legal limits? General guidelines toward this goal follow; more specific guidance is provided in chapter 5.

The first task in ethical and legal intrusion is to clarify rights, responsibilities, and roles. First, the reason for contact should be explained clearly and nonjudgmentally, including the specific criteria that led to contact. Mr. Brown should then clarify what the authority invested in him requires that he and Ms. Jones do. Third, Mr. Brown should clarify Ms. Jones' legal rights. Fourth, any requirements for behavioral change should be interpreted narrowly and should not include implied conditions or threats. Finally, should those behavioral requirements entail work on goals that Ms. Jones does not share, she is entitled to an explanation of the rationale for them.

Next, the practitioner distinguishes non-negotiable requirements from choices the client can make. Mr. Brown can promote self-determination within legal limits toward the goal of achieving a semivoluntary contract by including non-negotiable requirements, negotiable items, and voluntary concerns of the client. Self-determination in mandated situations can be promoted in at least four ways: (1) reframing the client's own concerns to blend with mandated requirements; (2) emphasizing freedoms untouched by requirements; (3) clarifying areas for discretion and negotiation; and (4) addressing additional client concerns voluntarily or referring them to others. As some mandated clients may not wish to explore these voluntary concerns with a mandated practitioner, referral to other practitioners and the freedom *not* to work on any additional concerns should be emphasized. In sum, the mandated client can be helped to a measure of self-determination by clarifying choices to: (1) not comply with non-negotiable requirements and risk consequences; (2) comply with non-negotiable requirements; and (3) work on additional concerns with the practitioner or someone else.

In Agnes Jones' case, while maintaining the children safely was a nonnegotiable priority, establishing whether she could keep custody of them in her home with assistance was negotiable. Mr. Brown noted that he could see that she did care for her children and would not wish them harmed *and* that it was also true that the police report indicated that her small children were at home unsupervised and hence were by agency standards at acute risk. He asked how might the children have been able to take care of themselves if there had been a fire or other emergency. Since keeping the children safe from harm was a goal they both shared, he suggested that they could plan together for ways to improve her child care relief, including arrangements with friends and relatives, day care, and drop-in centers.

Mr. Brown also noted that indeed her drinking that evening and getting out of the house was her own business as long as it did not endanger the children. He also empathized with her feeling cooped up, taking care of babies all the time, *and* that it was also true that they were entitled to be in a safe place. He could refer her to others who might help with her goals of getting a GED and a job if she wished. She could also handle these concerns alone or choose to do nothing about these goals at this point. As the non-negotiable requirement was that the children be in a safe environment, court intervention that might involve removal of the children from the home could be avoided if they could agree on a plan for safety.

Cell 2: Limitations on Client Freedom Are Legal But Not Ethical

The preceding example assumes that the practitioner has the appropriate authority and that the behavior falls within the domain of that authority. A different circumstance of authority and domain would occur if during the course of a conversation between Ms. Jones and her counselor at a mental health clinic, she mentioned that she had left the children alone briefly while she took a "stress break." While the counselor would lack the authority or domain to directly intervene, the counselor is legally mandated to report allegations of possible child abuse and neglect to child protective services.

Although making such a report is legally mandated, is it always ethical to do so? Reamer suggests that if the mandated reporter considers the child to be at substantial risk, then the danger should be reported (Reamer 1999). However, Heymann suggests that reporting some allegations of abuse may be harmful if the loss of control happened once rather than as a pattern, if it happened several years ago rather than currently, and if it depends on an assessment of what will happen to the parties and the working relationship as a result of reporting (Heymann 1986). Both Reamer and Heymann describe situations in which reporting resulted in greater harm for clients than not reporting might have done and therefore suggest that there are instances in which following legal requirements to report alleged abuse or neglect would be unethical.

How does a practitioner determine when it is unethical to obey the law? Reamer suggests that while the obligation to obey laws to which one has freely consented ordinarily overrides one's rights to freely violate those laws, circumstances exist in which an individual's rights to well-being may override obedience to those laws (Reamer 1999, 2005).

The point at which the practitioner determines that those individual rights override laws is the problem. In the preceding abuse or neglect reporting example, Reamer and Heymann seem to be suggesting that the mandated reporter may be able to assess intuitively whether behavior or conditions meet objective standards for abuse and neglect as well as or better than trained child protection workers.

Bergeron and Gray (2003) report a complex situation of conflicting loyalties. In the first session of a support group of caregivers for the elderly, a caregiver reported that she was a single woman caring for her eighty-five-year-old mother as an only child with no relatives or friends to help her with caregiving. She was under high stress and said her doctor told her she needed to come a support group or she would have a nervous breakdown. She reported that she had recently raised her voice to her mother on several occasions and was afraid that her frustration and exhaustion would lead her to hit her mother. In the following weeks, Edith indicated some reduction in stress and thanked people for supporting her.

Should the facilitators have filed an elder abuse report after that first session? The authors developed an informed consent process including a confidentiality statement to manage such dilemmas. That statement noted that confidentiality would be honored except to seek supervision or in a case in which the facilitator suspects the caregiver has intentionally or unintentionally abused or neglected the care receiver. Such cases of suspected abuse would then be reported for investigation and intervention (Bergeron and Gray 2003).

Failure to make a mandated report of possible abuse or neglect is illegal. Practitioners should not make such determinations to violate the law unilaterally. Since clients should be appropriately informed at the beginning of contact about circumstances in which client confidentiality must be violated, they can be informed that a circumstance has occurred in which the practitioner is legally required to make a report. An appropriate ethical and legal response would be to make the mandated report and include, with client permission, any mitigating information, should it be the practitioner's opinion that current conditions do not indicate serious danger. While such reporting may well be harmful to the working relationship with the client, there is also danger when that relationship is valued more highly than risk to a vulnerable person.

Practitioners have at least three alternatives in situations in which intervention appears to be legal but unethical. First, they can advocate for changes in the law or policy either through internal advocacy or working with outside professional and client organizations. Similarly, those who consider current reporting laws too broad and require reporting in circumstances that are not considered harmful have alternatives to failure to report. They can advocate that reporting requirements be made more specific to include more serious evidence of harm.

Second, the practitioner may choose to overtly or covertly resist the law or policy. As suggested above, there may be instances in which obeying a law or policy appears to be unethical and some practitioners have chosen to violate the policy openly or covertly. For example, in a school program to assist students who were in danger of dropping out, practitioners discovered a policy that required students who missed more than six days in a semester for any reason to be expelled. Some practitioners chose to violate this policy by not reporting some absences that they considered justified.

There can be no firm guidelines about when the line between protection of client interest and obeying laws and policies is crossed. Practitioners are urged to attempt to deal with changing the law or policy openly. Should they choose to resist the law or policy covertly, they should do so with full knowledge of the potential consequences for themselves, their agencies, and their clients. They should consult with supervisors and other colleagues because a choice not to follow the law leaves the burden of proof to the practitioner that the decision was justified.

Finally, practitioners can choose to leave the agency or setting. There are some instances in which the law or policy that the practitioner considers detrimental to client interest appear to be unchangeable. Practitioners who consider practices to be unethical may choose to leave the setting and perhaps advocate more freely from the outside for changes.

Cell 3: Limitations on Client Freedom May Be Ethical But Are Not Legal

Intervention to influence client choices can be ethically appropriate in some situations in which a legal threshold to limit such choices has not been reached.

A neighbor contacted a county agency requesting that an investigation be made about the safety of Alice Donat (whom we met in chapter 1). Under the state law to protect vulnerable adults, a practitioner (Ms. Jones) was mandated to visit Ms. Donat and determine whether she might be in danger. Ms. Donat was forty-five and mentally retarded, and had lived alone in a poorly heated rural shack since her mother died the year before. Specifically, there was concern that she might not have adequate heating in the winter, and eating off the same plates as her cats might be contaminating her food.

As Ms. Donat had lived alone through two previous winters and was informed about heating resources available to her, Ms. Jones assessed that danger from this source was not imminent. Similarly, the cats had not contaminated her food and her health was good. Consequently, Ms. Jones decided there were insufficient grounds to support a petition to declare Alice incompetent. Following figure 2.1, while the practitioner did have the authority and the case fell within her domain, criteria for legal intervention were not met.

Is Ms. Jones' job complete with the determination that coercive action is not justifiable? When paternalism is not justified, Gadow suggests guidelines to assist clients in making informed choices: (1) helping clients clarify their own values and intentions; (2) asking clients what information they need in order to decide; (3) clarifying the practitioner's own position; and (4) stepping back and avoiding interference with client decisions once this process is complete (Gadow 1981). The client has a right to learn from experiences and even to fail when those actions are not incapacitating.

Four guidelines are suggested to influence practitioner decisions in situations such as the ones in the preceding text in which action seems ethically compelling but that cannot be required legally.

1. *If the behavior is not illegal, the practitioner cannot require the client to change and should be guided by informed consent and self-determination.* If harm to self or others has not met legal criteria, then the practitioner cannot coerce the client to change. However, coercion or ignoring the client are not the only alternatives. The practitioner does not have to support dangerous or unethical actions that are not illegal, and noncoercive influence may be attempted. A first step with Ms. Donat would be for Ms. Jones to assure her that she cannot be forced to leave her home or accept services if her situation does not meet legal criteria for acute or imminent danger.

2. *The practitioner can act ethically to attempt persuasion.* Persuasion means helping clients consider the possible consequences of their choices and exploring alternatives in terms of their own best interest. Persuasion is not the same as coercion when the influence attempt is open, does not resort to threats, and ultimately respects the client's power to decide (Clark 1998). In reviewing the alternatives and consequences, the practitioner may share his or her own opinions about the client's self-interest. The practitioner can explore voluntary concerns of the client and share the concerns of referring sources as a context for decision making. At the end of this exploration, the practitioner should accept the client's decisions about his or her own behavior rather than insist on following the practitioner's advice (Clifford and Burke 2005). Should the client express no concern for which he or she wants help, the practitioner should leave, having assisted the client in informed consent through awareness of options and consequences.

Ms. Donat was understandably suspicious of an offer from a person who she suspected had power to take away her freedom. She said that she did not want to be put in a hospital and made to give up her home and her cats. Ms. Jones clarified that there was not sufficient danger to make Ms. Donat leave her home and she could choose to continue at home without services. She asked Ms. Donat what she thought might happen to her and her cats if there were insufficient heat or if she became ill from contaminated food. To avoid such a situation, Ms. Jones was willing to help her become safer in her home. In this regard, she mentioned SSI (Supplemental Security Income) benefits and emergency fuel assistance as resources that might help Ms. Donat provide better food and heat for herself and her cats.

3. *The practitioner can offer an incentive to influence a client choice.* Incentives are consequences that are used to strengthen or increase a behavior (Simons and Aigner 1985). Use of incentives is more intrusive than persuasion but less so than coercion. Inducement should not be used to barter for basic necessities but rather as an *additional* benefit that the client can choose to select or ignore. In this regard, informing Ms. Donat about her possible rights to SSI benefits should not be used as an incentive. Ms. Jones might, however, offer to accompany her to Social Security or to have her talk with other clients who received SSI benefits without having to go into the hospital.

4. *Finally, the practitioner can advocate that the legal threshold for harm should be expanded.* If the practitioner thinks that client safety is in fact endangered despite not reaching legal thresholds for coercive intervention, he or she can advocate that the legal threshold be changed.

Cell 4: Limitations on Client Freedom Are Neither Legal Nor Ethical

Situations occur in which practitioners are pressured to intervene with clients who have neither done anything illegal nor endangered their well-being or that of others. For instance, while Alice's current situation was assessed as not presenting an immediate danger to her, her choice to live with twenty cats in a dirty home conflicted with community sensibilities.

In such situations, commitment to the principle of *negative self-determination* applies first. Voluntary choices that neither cause serious danger to self or others, nor physical or economic dependency, nor violate laws, should not be subject to undue influence. As stated earlier, the practitioner may register her disagreement with a plan and help the client explore alternatives, but the client ultimately has the right to decide. Hence, Alice could be reassured that she has the right to determine where and how she will live and is not required to accept services so long as those decisions do not harm her or violate laws.

Second, *positive self-determination* should be considered. In addition to not opposing or coercing client choices, how can those choices be positively supported? Ms. Jones could offer a contract to Alice to help her maintain her independence, protect herself and her cats through the winter, or attain other goals that Alice desired. Part of self-determination is respecting that Alice has every right to decline this offer, however well intentioned and potentially supportive of Alice's interests it may be.

This chapter has described legal and ethical foundations for work with involuntary clients. While legal and ethical issues with involuntary clients deserve books of their own, practitioners have limited time to review the relevant issues thoroughly in a turbulent, demanding environment. Confronted with decisions that need to be made quickly, and reports that must be written, practitioners need flexible guidelines for making decisions. The proposed guidelines are not precise prescriptions but move beyond impotence and indecision in the face of dilemmas.

While these guidelines should assist practitioners in making difficult decisions and improving local conditions, they cannot provide the kinds of changes needed to ameliorate prejudicial societal conditions, such as inadequate resources, which may engender deviance and hence produce involuntary clients. Entire treatment institutions have been found to violate both legal rights to adequate treatment and the most basic ethical standards of respect for human dignity. While practitioners do not have the legal power to close down such institutions, they can advocate for better conditions, greater access to resources, and more fair treatment for clients. It may feel safer for practitioners to report illegal or unethical methods in *another* institution rather than their own. While it may be harder for an employee of an institution to risk his or her job security to report unethical or illegal methods, work with institutional ethics committees can reduce the risk to an individual who reports such matters.

Should practitioners ignore issues of prejudice and unfair conditions in the larger society, they run the risk of providing social control with a smiling face: using otherwise ethical means to pursue unethical goals. Many practitioners resolve these conflicts by following orders and leaving concern for law and ethics to others, while others attempt to resolve the tension by "fleeing" to private practice. Consent under duress, however, is a pervasive problem that will still follow them in work with nonvoluntary clients despite the setting.

The choice to pursue legal, ethical practice means making judgments and decisions committed to both law and ethics. Pursuit of such a course does not avoid conflicts; involuntary clients have negative reactions when freedoms are limited, however ethically or legally done. Similarly, pursuit of such a legal and ethical course may conflict with agency practices that are unduly paternalistic, which include corrupt contracts or notices of consequences rather than legitimate contracts. Such pursuit may also mean advocating that legal thresholds be changed to include more people who are in clear and present danger. While pursuing a legal and ethical course will bring conflict, it may also ensure personal self-respect and integrity as no small benefit. In addition to legal and ethical practice, effective practice is the third foundation for work with involuntary clients. Hence chapter 3 reviews evidence about effectiveness in work with involuntary clients.

Discussion Questions

1. What is your agency's position on client rights, legal responsibilities, and actions related to confidentiality and privileged communication? Are these positions clear to clients? How do you know?
2. What are agency policies relating to alerting clients to their rights regarding access to records?
3. Under what conditions is client self-determination supported in your agency?
4. Some practitioners have negative conceptions about paternalism, and yet they and their agencies often act to protect their perception of client best interest. Are you clear about the lines that can be drawn around appropriate paternalism and beneficence and unethical intervention into client choice?
5. Can you apply the legal ethical matrix to help guide decision making?
6. Are informed consent forms explained in such a way that they support genuine informed consent or are they merely procedural guidelines?

Chapter 3

Effectiveness with Involuntary Clients

With a basis in the legal and ethical foundation, we move to consider the foundation of effectiveness. We discuss the evidence-based practice movement and its implications for work with involuntary clients, ethics of research with involuntary clients, and reviews of effectiveness with involuntary clients including summary generalizations. Finally, we review the transtheoretical model of stages of change and motivational interviewing to work with two involuntary populations: sexual offenders and domestic violence perpetrators.

Evidence-based Practice

Helping practitioners should make practice decisions and recommendations to clients based on the best available information (Sackett et al. 2000). This tenet of the evidence-based practice movement, originating in medical and nursing fields, is designed to ensure that clients and patients receive diagnoses and treatment guided by the best available information. Consequently, evidence-based practitioners would help clients in making informed decisions by sharing what is known about the efficacy of different treatment options (McNeece and Thyer 2004; Adams and Drake 2006). Such practitioners would be most influenced in their treatment recommendations by evidence generated through randomized, controlled trials. Even when such studies are lacking, practitioners should persist in seeking the best available information to guide decisions and recommendations. Evidence-based practice values informed consent in assisting clients in assessing alternatives in reaching their goals (Gilgun 2005). Many of the assumptions about evidence-based practice appear to assume that the client is voluntary. Involuntary clients have fewer treatment choices (ibid.). When involuntary clients have acted to harm or endanger others, the community is entitled to be informed about the evidence on whether interventions are likely to be helpful in making society safer (Bloomberg and Wilkins 1977). Consequently, there is a role for evidence-based practice with involuntary clients as well. Even when client choices are limited, those treatment options should be based on the best available evidence (Golder et al. 2005). Meanwhile, involuntary clients are entitled to know that the methods used with them are effective and humane.

Intervention effectiveness has been studied in several fields of practice and problem areas in which we can assume that many clients are involuntary. For example, in studies of intervention with domestic violence perpetrators, probationers and parolees, recipients of child welfare services, and persons with substance abuse issues, we can safely assume that most clients have not sought services of their own accord. However, such studies usually focus on the particular problem and client group and rarely on the clients' involuntary status. Despite these limitations, it is essential that we probe for the best available information to guide interventions with involuntary clients.

The Ethics of Research with Involuntary Clients

A fundamental tenet of research ethics is that human subjects should be protected from harm caused by participation in research (Kelty 1981). Consequently, research with human subjects is governed by the principles of informed consent described above in chapter 2. There are special problems in the application of informed consent principles to involuntary clients since their ability to provide consent without force or duress cannot be assumed. Concern for dignity and respect of individual participants in research is central to research ethics (Antle and Regehr 2003). Informed consent is hence central. Researchers must consider conceivable risks for participants such that they do not face harm or undue hardship. If inclusion in experimental treatment is one of the benefits, participants need to be assured that they would have equal access to that treatment whether or not they consent to participation in the research. Other kinds of benefits could include monetary compensation or covering babysitting and transportation costs. The

concept of beneficence requires that the potential benefits outweigh potential harm (ibid.). Research on effectiveness can, for instance, determine
whether restriction of freedom is necessary to reach desired outcomes or is
actually cruel and unusual punishment. Hence, research on effectiveness
may both protect clients from serving as "guinea pigs" for untested interventions and aid institutions and agencies in discovering effective and eliminating ineffective interventions. Research with involuntary clients must address
costs and benefits and define acceptable risk for individuals and society
(Bloomberg and Wilkins 1977). These questions need to be addressed in a
way that protects both involuntary clients from danger and also society's
right to discover methods that are safe, humane, and effective. Guidelines
that consider both costs and benefits to involuntary clients and to society are
suggested below.

1. *Informed consent must be sought from persons competent to provide
   it.* When competence is questionable, then consent must be sought
   from surrogates such as parents, guardians, and legal representatives (Reynolds 1982). The request for consent must include an
   appraisal of possible discomforts, risks, benefits, and alternate
   procedures.
2. *Consent must be voluntary, free from coercion or undue influence.* A
   review panel should assess potential for duress in securing consent
   in both mandated and nonvoluntary settings. Such an assessment
   should include the following:

   a) Use of inducements must avoid an unwarranted effect on the
      decision to participate.
   b) Implied influence should be avoided by making sure that the
      person requesting research participation does *not* have an au-
      thority relationship with the client.
   c) It should be explicit that the treatment will not be more favor-
      able for those who agree to participate in research or unfavorable
      for those who decline (Kelty 1981).
   d) Participants must be free to withdraw consent at any time.
   e) Confidentiality of information shared in research must be
      guaranteed.
   f) The research should yield results not obtainable in less obtrusive
      ways such that any discomfort or risk to participants must be
      outweighed by benefits to society (Bloomberg and Wilkins 1977;
      Reynolds 1982).
   g) Deception should be avoided or minimized by debriefing par-
      ticipants after research participation.

Employment of these guidelines should provide involuntary clients with a fair opportunity to decide whether to participate in research or not. Since involuntary clients perceive restriction of freedom as part of the definition of involuntary status, it should be expected that many involuntary clients may exercise one of their limited freedoms by sometimes choosing *not* to participate in research. Hence, involuntary clients who voluntarily choose to participate in research may *not* be representative of the population. As Videka-Sherman noted in her review of social work effectiveness in mental health settings, "It is also true that involuntary social services are underrepresented in this sample since human subjects review and the ethics of social research depend on clients' willingness to participate in the research. This willingness is, in all likelihood, associated with willingness to participate in treatment" (Videka-Sherman 1985:40).

Studies of Effectiveness with Involuntary Clients

It has been conventional wisdom in social work; other helping professions; and fields such as corrections, treatment of alcoholism, and child maltreatment that outcomes with involuntary clients are less successful than those with voluntary clients. The social work profession's pessimism about the effectiveness of work with involuntary clients was partly based in broader reviews of social work effectiveness. When Fischer examined experimental studies of social work practice conducted between 1930 and 1972, he found that none of the eleven studies reviewed clearly showed positive, significantly measurable changes, and concluded that "at present, lack of evidence of the effectiveness of professional casework is the rule rather than the exception" (Fischer 1973:19). While Fischer's review is well known in social work, the fact that five of the eleven studies reviewed were conducted with predelinquent, probably involuntary clients is less so. None of the five studies suggested that social work services prevented delinquency (Powers and Witmer 1951; Miller 1962; Craig and Furst 1965; Berleman and Steiner 1967).

Katherine Wood reviewed the studies of Fischer, as well as eleven additional studies that included quasi-experimental designs. She concluded that "the outcomes of these studies indicate that group work or psychotherapeutically oriented casework used alone or as the major intervention, have not been effective in preventing or ameliorating delinquency" (Wood 1978:438). Wood also identified a major clue to effectiveness in work with involuntary clients: lack of fit between client and practitioner motivation as a factor in the low outcomes of earlier research. Since the studies did not begin with the adolescent's perceptions of their own concerns, the intervention did not come from a contract about issues of concern to the adolescents. Consequently, there was little motivation to work on goals determined by others (ibid.).

The negative findings concerning delinquency prevention in social work were similar to other findings on treatment of delinquents such that it became conventional wisdom that "nothing works." This contention was further supported by Martinson's conclusion in his 1974 review of 231 research studies completed before 1967 that with few exceptions, efforts at rehabilitation had little effect on recidivism (Lipton, Martinson, and Weeks 1974; Martinson 1974). Shireman and Reamer objected to Martinson's conclusion that nothing works since many programs with at least quasi-experimental designs had been shown to be effective (Shireman and Reamer 1986). While the "nothing works" conclusion might have been overdrawn, there was little reason to believe that a clear way had been found to reduce recidivism among delinquents. Shireman and Reamer echoed Wood's theme about a lack of motivational fit: "Subjects have quite commonly been drawn into programs intending to produce change in their attitudes, behaviors and life styles and life situations without regard as to whether they wished to be targets of intervention. We are only now beginning to realize the frequent futility of such endeavors" (Shireman and Reamer 1986:88).

Summary Generalizations Regarding Effective Interventions with Involuntary Clients

Summary generalizations about research evidence regarding involuntary clients include: (1) court-ordered clients can achieve as successful results as legally voluntary clients can; (2) pro-social modeling has been associated with positive outcomes in corrections; (3) voluntary clients are rarely distinguished from nonvoluntary clients in data collection; and (4) clues to more positive outcomes appear to be based in client–practitioner interaction including *motivational congruence*. Interventions toward motivational congruence include: (1) enhancing choices and sense of personal control, (2) enhancing socialization into appropriate roles, (3) use of behavioral contracting, and (4) facilitating treatment adherence through client commitment to goals and participation in task design and selection. Each of these generalizations is examined in more detail.

1. *Court-ordered clients can achieve as successful outcomes as legally voluntary clients can.* Some authors have suggested more positive outcomes with court-ordered clients than the generally gloomy predictions expressed earlier. For example, Videka-Sherman found in her review of social work studies in mental health that "clients' motivation for intervention as indicated by

voluntary participation was not associated with differential outcomes as indicated. . . . In fact, studies of clients with mixed or involuntary motivation yielded higher . . . effect sizes for the more severely impaired population" (Videka-Sherman 1985).

Brehm and Smith came to a similar conclusion in their review of involuntary outcomes in the psychology literature: "Though many therapists and counselors are firmly convinced that successful therapeutic outcomes are substantially more difficult to achieve with nonvoluntary client populations, the results of applied (and therefore, necessarily correlational) research on this issue have not provided support for this belief" (Brehm and Smith 1986:88).

It has been long thought that some form of coercion can be useful to motivate change among drug users (Rosenberg and Liftik 1976; Flores 1983). It was, however, believed that coercion should not be overemphasized since longitudinal studies suggested that mandated alcohol abuse patients often ceased treatment when their court orders ended regardless of how favorably they may felt about the program (Ben-Arie, Swartz, and George 1986; Foley 1988).

More recently, problem-solving courts have been developed to address psychosocial issues around problems that bear significant costs to the community (Casey and Rottman 2005; Tyuse and Linhorst 2005). For example, such courts have been developed to address diverse social problems such as domestic violence, use of illegal drugs, and hazardous mental health conditions. Such courts have been hailed as a means for getting drug offenders to seek and benefit from treatment whatever their original motivation for seeking help. The court's coercive power is used to induce "participants" to take part in rehabilitation to avoid incarceration (Hennessy 2001). Typically the drug court program requires regular court dates, random drug testing, and full treatment compliance. Graduation can occur after twelve or more months of program attendance and sobriety. Failure to comply fully with the program can result in fines, additional court appearances, or incarceration (ibid.).

Drug courts have had promising program completion rates, including graduation from the court process and retention in treatment programs (Sanford and Arrigo 2005). For example, in a review of thirty-seven programs, Belenko found that the average program graduation was 47 percent and retention in treatment was on an average of 71 percent (Belenko 2001). Such measures of progress through the program are important because the rates of recidivism for graduates and nongraduates differ: 37 percent for drug court graduates and 75 percent for nongraduates (Peters and Murrin 2000). However, even those who do not complete programs but participate for extended periods have lower re-arrest rates than those who participate more briefly (Peters, Haas, and Hunt 2001). The level of threat of coercion measured by expected incarceration time has been associated with treatment retention and engagement (Rempel and Depies-Di Stefano 2001).

Offenders participating in the drug court programs have been described as voluntary, while acknowledging that avoiding incarceration is a strong incentive (Goldkamp 2000). We would describe such clients as nonvoluntary given the balance of available punishers and incentives for compliance. Court participation is, however, considered collaborative in that all parties work together to seek treatment and avoid incarceration.

Problem-solving courts have also been developed for dealing with domestic violence. Such courts are unlike the drug courts in that they are adversarial. In domestic violence courts, judges may confront violent perpetrators when they perceive them to be avoiding responsibility by assigning blame to victims (Levey, Steketee, and Keilitz 2001). Use of courts with domestic violence perpetrators has been useful in inducing them to seek treatment; however, treatment results themselves have been equivocal (Jackson et al. 2003). As with drug courts, program completion is key, as dropout rates are high and recidivism high among dropouts. As Chovanec notes in chapter 12 of this volume, women can be put at risk if they choose to stay with partners on the basis of the latter enrolling in a treatment program (Gondolf 1988).

In conclusion, in some problem-solving court situations, the threat of coercion and the inducement of avoiding prison and receiving treatment appear to have been effective means for helping some involuntary clients to engage in treatment. Reduced recidivism rates over one to two years are promising but more follow-up study is needed to determine whether changes achieved through "coerced voluntarism" last for a longer period.

2. *Pro-social modeling has been associated with improved outcomes with involuntary clients in corrections.* Pro-social modeling refers to reinforcing and modeling noncriminal values such as support and care for others and not supporting criminal or antisocial values (Trotter 2006). Practitioners supporting this principle would clearly identify the values they support and encourage them through modeling and praise. Conversely, they would challenge antisocial or pro-criminal values. For example, in drug abuse treatment, this refers to explicitly rewarding nonuse of chemicals (Barber 1995). Identifying inappropriate parent–child interaction and rewarding positive interaction has bee a consistent factor in child protection programs based on social learning theory (Gough 1993). Andrews et al. (1979) found that when probation officers modeled and reinforced pro-social comments and were empathic, their clients offended less frequently than the clients of other

probation officers (Trotter 2006:20). Similarly, Trotter found that the clients of volunteer probation officers who were more pro-social offended less than did clients of less pro-social volunteer officers (Trotter 1990). A later study also found that professional officers who used pro-social modeling were more effective than those who did not use the approach (Trotter 1993, 1996). The clients of practitioners using the pro-social approach were half as likely to be imprisoned over four years than those who used the approach infrequently (ibid.). Similar positive results were reported for use in child protection (Trotter 2002).

The pro-social modeling principle fits best with settings that have a clear educative mission about client values. Such a goal is prominent in education and corrections work with sexual offenders and perpetrators of domestic violence. The argument that client failures occur as a result of not internalizing pro-social values appears less applicable to some populations. For example, it appears the designers of welfare reform in the United States assumed that the values and beliefs of unemployed persons were a major obstacle toward their obtaining and keeping employment (Anderson, Halter, and Gryzlak 2004). Research has suggested, however, that many recipients of TANF services already shared pro-social values about employment, in part, and training attention to such values did not address contextual variables such as availability of support, health insurance, and job availability. Thus, while inculcating pro-social values could be seen as a useful tool to help TANF recipients in acquiring and keeping jobs, additional factors were also important (ibid.).

The pro-social modeling principle focuses extensively on an internal change of orientation on the part of the client. Such a focus may be particularly useful in settings in which there is a consensus about pro-social values. Practitioners using this principle should be mindful of contextual variables in addition to pro- and antisocial values in less educationally focused settings.

3. *Voluntary clients are rarely distinguished from nonvoluntary clients in the conduct of research.* Research on treatment effects has evolved from concerns about whether intervention is generally effective to more specific questions about which form of intervention works with which sort of client and problem under which conditions (Reid and Hanrahan 1982). Reid and Hanrahan reported that the proportion of social work effectiveness studies based in public settings, and hence more likely to include involuntary clients, decreased from an earlier review by Fischer in 1973 (Reid and Hanrahan 1982). In 1985, Videka-Sherman noted in her review of 142 studies of social work intervention in mental health that client characteristics tended to lack adequate description (Videka-Sherman 1985:188).

Even when client voluntarism is considered as a variable, comparisons are usually made between court-ordered clients and legally voluntary clients whose participation in treatment has been coerced. These "voluntary" clients may in fact be the nonvoluntary clients described in chapter 1. Comparisons between involuntary and voluntary clients in settings such as psychiatric hospitals and residential treatment might be better seen as comparisons between mandated and nonvoluntary clients who may have received services as a result of constrained or coerced choices.

There are similar comparisons between court-ordered clients and legally voluntary clients in studies of coerced intervention in alcoholism, drug treatment, and child maltreatment. For example, Flores notes in his study of the effectiveness of coercion with DWI participants that "voluntary clients" in the study were influenced by coercive, but nonlegal pressures: "unhappy spouses, worried friends, concerned doctors, and disgruntled bosses all make up a contingency that often uses subtle pressure to force individuals with different types of problems into counseling when those individuals do not agree that they have a problem" (Flores 1983). Similarly, Irueste-Montes and Montes note that the so-called voluntary clients in their study of court-mandated service for child maltreatment were all involved with child protective services. The clients did not have legal consequences, but they were "encouraged or pressured to attend" (Irueste-Montes and Montes 1988:38).

In addition, other studies of voluntary clients may, in fact, include many nonvoluntary clients. For example, Edleson reports that men participating in a study of a domestic abuse program were voluntary while also reporting that all came in at a time of crisis, frequently involving a separation from the spouse (Edleson et al. 1985). As discussed earlier with reference to participants in problem-solving courts, "choosing" the incentive of avoiding jail time is "coerced voluntarism." That is, when involuntary clients enter a voluntary drug treatment system with a status that is officially voluntary, yet always subject to recall by the social control system if clients fail to comply, their voluntarism is coerced (Waldorf 1971; Peyrot 1985). Such programs as well as treatment programs for domestic violence perpetrators might be more accurately considered as typically involuntary, containing in some instances men mandated by courts and many nonvoluntary clients pressured by formal or partner-mandated, informal sources and situations.

A first step to a more solid empirical base with involuntary clients in the future will be to clarify client referral status. Referral through legal mandates should be noted as such. Clients who enter contact through formal or informal pressure such that the decision to seek treatment was coerced or constrained rather than self-motivated should be noted as nonvoluntary.

4. *Motivational congruence between client and practitioner is an important clue toward effective intervention with involuntary clients.* Reid and Hanrahan describe this fit between client motivation and what the practitioner attempts to provide as motivational congruence. They updated Fischer's earlier review by assessing twenty-two additional studies conducted between 1973 and 1979 and reported "grounds for optimism" based on their finding that positive outcomes were reported in eighteen of the studies reviewed (Reid and Hanrahan 1982). They suggested that such congruence may be a factor in the more positive results found in their review of social casework effectiveness. The lack of fit between practitioner and client goals had also emerged earlier as an explanation for client dropout from casework and other forms of treatments (Mayer and Timms 1969; Maluccio 1979). Videka-Sherman explores motivational congruence as a possible explanation for her findings of similar outcomes between involuntary and voluntary clients and suggests that "the interaction between practitioner and client once the client (captive or not) arrives for treatment better captures . . . motivational congruence than whether the client was voluntarily or involuntarily referred" (Videka-Sherman 1985:40).

How can such motivational congruence be attained or enhanced? A further review of the literature suggests that congruence can be enhanced by (a) emphasizing choices and a sense of self-control, (b) socialization to role expectations, (c) behavioral contracting, and (d) supporting treatment adherence by facilitating client commitment and participation in task design and selection.

a. *Enhancement of choices and sense of control.* Perceived lack of voluntarism can be reduced by emphasizing choices and a sense of control. Brehm and Smith suggest that: "[T]hus while the specific determinants of perceived choice to receive treatment are far from clear and may not parallel official status as voluntary and nonvoluntary, there is some support for the inference that once perceived, personal choice to remain in treatment has a beneficial effect on treatment effectiveness" (Brehm and Smith 1986:88). Mendonca and Brehm conducted an experiment in a clinical setting designed to test the impact of perceived choice (Mendonca and Brehm 1983). One half of the children enrolled in a weight loss program were randomly assigned to a "take control" condition in which choices were enhanced. The control group in fact received the same treatment program as the "enhanced choice" group but without being offered choices in the structure of the program. At the termination of treatment, children in the enhanced choice group had lost significantly more weight than the children in the no-choice group. Mendonca and Brehm concluded that this was the strongest evidence to date of treatment benefits accrued through providing clients with their choice of treatment (Mendonca and Brehm 1983). In fact, studies have indicated that gains can be accrued though the illusion of control as well as the reality (Langer 1975). That is, the perception that one is in control can be beneficial, even when the reality would suggest much less actual control. Since the research suggests that a client does not have to actually *be* in control in order to perceive control, should the practitioner stimulate an *illusion* of control while maintaining control over outcomes with involuntary clients? Some therapists advocate encouraging an illusion of control while maintaining real control over the process themselves (London 1969; Wathney and Baldridge 1980). I believe that real choices need to be separated from outcomes that the client cannot influence. For example, while mandated clients may not be able to avoid treatment, they may be able to make choices about the type of treatment they receive. For example, Miller notes that court-ordered status is not inconsistent with choices for participants in alcoholism treatment programs: "Even with a population required to seek treatment (e.g., drunk driving offenders), it is feasible to offer a choice among a variety of alternative treatments and to foster the perception of personal control over the change process" (Miller 1989:72).

Sense of control can be enhanced with nonvoluntary clients by reminding them that they do not have to choose to be in treatment. Personal control and a sense of personal responsibility should be encouraged when such client efforts are likely to succeed. Even in potentially successful situations, enhancing responsibility can have negative side effects such as increased anxiety if clients are not confident of their ability to choose. In addition, should their choice fail, self-esteem can suffer.

b. *Socialization methods may assist in enhancing motivational congruence.* Socialization for treatment has been found to be a powerful intervention. Videka-Sherman found such socialization methods to be the one intervention technique predicting better outcomes in all subsets of her review of social work mental health studies: "The better-informed the client is concerning what will occur during treatment and what the client should be doing for his or her part of the treatment process, the more likely the client is to derive benefit from the experience" (Videka-Sherman 1988:328). Similarly, pretherapy training to clarify expected behavior has proven to be a solution to the problem of premature termination in psychotherapy (Heitler 1976).

Socialization methods have received less study with involuntary clients but results are promising. Brekke found that men in a domestic abuse treatment program who attended an intensive workshop at the beginning of contact were more likely to stay in treatment than were men not attending the workshop (Brekke 1989). Similar to socialization, role clarification has been proposed as a key principle in work with involuntary clients (Trotter 2006). Practitioners who are specific about client and practitioner expectations are likely to have more success than those who are not specific. The research on socialization methods reinforces the earlier findings about the efficacy of pro-social modeling by practitioners working with involuntary clients.

c. *Behavioral contracting enhances motivational congruence.* Contracting refers to an agreement between the client and practitioner that sets forth the purpose of the interaction and processes through which the goal is to be achieved (Kravetz and Rose 1973). Similar to pretherapy training and social-ization, contracts have been suggested as a means of preventing premature dropout (Mayer and Timms 1969). Reid and Hanrahan identified behavioral contracting as an important variable explaining the more positive results in their review of casework effectiveness: "The technique of behavioral con-tracting has shown considerable potential . . . in which the practitioner se-cures from clients commitments to undertake specific problem-solving action" (Reid and Hanrahan 1982:338). Rubin echoed this conclusion in his updated review of the next five years: "A prominent commonality among the studies was the use of highly structured forms of practice that were well-explicated and specific about the problems the social workers sought to resolve, the goals they sought to accomplish and the procedures used to achieve these ends" (Rubin 1975:474).

Nonvoluntary clients in the child welfare system were included among the studies that led to these conclusions. For example, Stein, Gambrill, and Wiltse found that parents receiving a behavioral contracting approach were significantly more likely to have their children returned to their custody than families receiving traditional child welfare services (Stein, Gambrill, and Wiltse 1978).

Seabury suggested, however, that involuntary clients are among the most difficult groups with which to establish a contract (Seabury 1976). Seabury concluded that it is more difficult to establish common agreement when the client fails to recognize a problem or does not view the worker as a person who can help. In addition, he suggests that the rational competence required to engage in contracting may rule out extremely disturbed, retarded, or brain-damaged clients and young children, though secondary contracts may be negotiated with family members and advocates (Seabury 1979). Seabury considered contracting to be problematic but possible with involuntary cli-ents: "It is crucial that the terms of the legal arrangement be distinguished from the stipulations of the social work contract" (ibid.:36). Hence, we find a similar theme to the recommendation above related to enhanced choices that it is *critically important to separate negotiable from non-negotiable items.*

d. *Treatment adherence can be facilitated through client participation in goal and task selection.* Adherence is defined as the extent to which patient behavior corresponds to medical advice (Weiss 2003). The term *adherence* is often preferred to *compliance* because it implies greater patient autonomy in following treatment regimens (ibid.). Meichenbaum and Turk suggest that the term noncompliance means failing to follow through with the practitioner's instructions (Meichenbaum and Turk 1987). It implies that the patient or client is at fault. Adherence is more likely with chronic conditions than with diet or behavioral changes designed to reduce risk. Most specifically, adherence with medication for psychiatric disorders often begins at a low rate and declines over time, contributing to relapse (ibid.). A positive, collaborative relationship between doctor and patient including information about medication and its side effects is associated with greater adherence (Weiss 2003).

Meichenbaum and Turk suggest that nonadherence may refer to a variety of types rather than a single problem behavior: those who never adhere may be different than those who do so occasionally and also from those who adhere, but do so inappropriately (Meichenbaum and Turk 1987). Whatever the cause, nonadherence is a very frequent occurrence among the seemingly voluntary population of persons with physical illnesses. Six factors have been suggested as helpful in increasing treatment adherence: (1) specific requests instead of vague ones, (2) overt commitments from clients to comply, (3) training in performing the task, (4) positive reinforcement of the task, (5) tasks that require little discomfort or difficulty, and (6) client participation in the selection and design of tasks (Levy and Carter 1976).

Given such high rates of nonadherence on the part of voluntary patients, nonadherence with involuntary clients can be expected to be as high. In the absence of studies about facilitating treatment adherence with involuntary clients, the aforementioned factors are suggested as provisional guides to enhancing treatment adherence.

In the following section, we explore the stages of change approach and motivational interviewing as particularly promising sources of future adaptation to work with involuntary clients.

Application of Stages of Change and Motivational Interviewing to Involuntary Clients

The transtheoretical model of stages of change attempts to explain how people consider changing behaviors without therapy. The model initially addressed cigarette smoking and later was adapted to alcohol use, overeating, and safe-sex practices (Wahab 2005). The model proposes that there are predictable steps in the process of making intentional changes (Prochaska, Norcross, and DiClemente 1994; Hanson and Gutheil 2004). Specifically, it is posited that most people do not immediately identify a need for change and readily adopt life style changes. Rather, they progress through stages including appearing oblivious to the problem, awareness of a concern but undecided about whether to take action, deciding to act but not knowing what action to take, and so on.

The *precontemplation* phase sounds familiar to much of what is experienced with and by involuntary clients. Persons in this stage do not link their behavior to adverse consequences, do not consider their behavior a problem, and may not be confident that they could change should they choose to do so (Hanson and Gutheil 2004). A person in the *contemplation* stage takes the problem seriously but has not determined to act to change the behavior. Persons in this stage may have begun initial steps on their own to modify or change a behavior, such as reducing drinking. In the *preparation or decision making stage*, a person is taking small behavioral and mental steps necessary to begin a change (Peterocelli 2002). In the *action stage*, a person is taking more decisive action over a period of time to address the problem behavior. Efforts then follow in the *maintenance stage* to solidify gains and prevent a lapse to earlier problematic behavior.

While the transtheoretical model assumes voluntary change efforts, stages such as precontemplation and contemplation have ready applications to clients who approach contact under mandated or nonvoluntary pressure. As noted earlier, involuntary clients frequently have problems attributed to them that they do not acknowledge as legitimate, similar to the behavior described as *precontemplation* in this model.

Awareness of the stage of change of the client-can be useful to the practitioner in determining how they might best direct their efforts. For example, frequently practitioners have assumed that clients were at the action phase and were ready to modify their behavior when in fact they had neither decided that they had a problem nor decided that they wished to change it.

Motivational interviewing is a client-centered intervention method designed to assist the client in exploring ambivalence about change and enhancing commitment to taking action (Miller and Rollnick 2002). Through empathic listening, the practitioner helps the client assess behaviors and consequences and consider options for change. Even in precontemplation, an involuntary client pressured to explore treatment can be made aware of choices made. For example, a practitioner might say, "Considering the pressures you are facing, you decided to come in and take a look at what was available: I am impressed that you made that choice" (Peterocelli 2002). Before further consideration of the promise of stages of change and motivational interviewing for involuntary clients generally, we first explore their application to specific involuntary problems and populations.

Treatment of Sexual Offenders

Sexual offenders are usually legally coerced to participate in treatment, hence are legally mandated clients (Glancy and Regehr 2002; Knox 2002). Given the harm to victims and society, the community is often considered the primary client rather than the sexual offender with primary goals of preventing future victimization and ameliorating harm caused by offenders (Colorado Sex Offender Management Board 1999). Consequently, treatment has often focused on confronting offenders with errors in thinking, developing empathy with victims, and with taking responsibility for the consequences of their actions. Groups have often been used to assist in confronting secrecy and denial (McGrath 1995; Knox 2002). Treatment may also attempt to redirect sexual arousal toward appropriate partners and activities, to improve social competence, and to address potential for relapse. Finally, there is often a clarification process whereby the offender is led to accept full responsibility for his or her actions, often in the form of a letter to the victim (Knox 2002).

Treatment effectiveness has been measured in terms of recidivism. Results of a meta-analysis of studies found that 19 percent of treated sexual offenders became sexual recidivists compared to 27 percent of untreated offenders (John Howard Society of Alberta 2002). Alexander (1999) reported that offenders who had received treatment became recidivists at a rate of 7.2 percent compared to 17.6 percent of those not receiving treatment. However, recidivism, defined in terms of re-arrest for sexual offenses, may underestimate the incidence of actual sexual offenses (Geffner, Crompton Franey, and Falconer 2003). With this proviso, the majority of sexual offenders are not adjudicated as repeat sexual offenders, and participation in treatment programs appears to reduce the likelihood of recidivism.

Kear-Colwell and Pollock (1997) have suggested that a treatment style that aims to confront offenders and seek admission of guilt and penetration of defenses does not engage the offender as an active participant in his treatment. By adapting the stages of change approach, offenders can be met at their stage of motivation and engaged in a decision analysis of alternatives in situations of risk (Kear-Colwell and Pollock 1997). Similarly, Yates suggests that a punitive style focusing on having the offender take responsibility for his or her actions results in an aggressive style of relating to the offender and creates power struggles (Yates 2003). This style makes it less likely to engage clients, and those who do not complete treatment are more likely to re-offend. Yates suggests that a style of work that emphasizes active listening, pro-social modeling, and reinforcement allows practitioners to challenge offenders around risk areas and also to engage them actively in positive self-management, not just attempting to avoid relapse.

These developments suggest that even when the community can be considered the primary client, engaging sexual offenders as persons capable of making decisions that help or harm them through adaptations of motivational interviewing and recognition of stages of change can make motivational congruence more feasible and choices can be emphasized.

Work with Domestic Violence Perpetrators

Persons who commit violence on others are not necessarily involuntary clients. However, it would appear that most treatment participants are at least nonvoluntary in the sense that they respond to pressures to enter treatment. According to Chovanec in chapter 12 of this volume, approximately 60 percent to 80 percent of men who complete violence treatment programs end their violent behavior; a smaller number reduce their threats and verbal abuse (Gondolf 1997). However, the dropout rate is at least 22 percent (Daly and Pelowski 2000), and women who remain with partners expecting them to complete programs may be in greater danger (Gondolf 1988).

While intervention models have often emphasized confrontation and taking responsibility for one's behavior (Chovanec, chapter 12 of this volume), concerns have been raised about whether confrontational models may inadvertently reinforce beliefs about power and control that those with more power may exert their will over those with less power (Murphy and Baxter 1997). According to van Wormer and Bednar, the assumption that power and control is the sole or primary motivation for domestic violence is now under question (van Wormer and Bednar 2002). Such an approach may marginalize other concerns raised by men.

As with sexual offenders, some are now suggesting that assaultive men can better be addressed at their stage of change. Perpetrators who find that the goals of treatment do not match their own goals are likely to drop out (Cadsky et al. 1996; Daniels and Murphy 1997). A recent study of assaultive men suggests that the majority are in precontemplation or contemplation in which efforts to engage will be crucial (Eckhardt, Babcock, and Homack 2004).

The Contribution of the Transtheoretical Stages of Change Model and Motivational Interviewing to Work with Involuntary Clients

Critics suggest that people may not progress through the stages in the orderly way suggested by the model (Davidson 1998; Littell and Girvin 2002). That is, they may move forwards and backwards and jump stages rather than progress in the orderly fashion implied by the model. Also, involuntary clients may have multiple issues or concerns such that they are at different stages on different issues. For example, a parent may be taking action on securing better child care at the same time as he or she may be in precontemplation related to the consequences of his or her own child care under the influence of drugs. In addition, Littell and Girvin suggest that involuntary clients may have a vested interest in portraying themselves as ready for change when in fact they see no reason for it, but rather understand the consequences of failure to acknowledge a problem (Littell and Girvin 2004). For example, if a child has been removed from the home related to failure to protect the child and a parental chemical problem, parents would be unlikely to deny that they had such a problem if they wished to regain custody of the child. Finally, there are concerns about full application of the approach to social problems that are broader than health decisions. For example, child welfare concerns may include health care issues but often include other concerns related to environmental resources and lack of support.

The stages of change model and motivational interviewing do not directly address involuntary clients but instead have significant implications for involuntary clients who face health decision issues. Specifically the motivational interviewing approach is designed to guide the practitioner in making interventions that fit where the client is now in terms of motivation for change. The model does not directly approach the issue of the role of the practitioner when that practitioner has mandated responsibilities to protect clients, dependents, and the community. That is, the approach appears to assume that the practitioner's role is to help clients with health care issues to consider alternatives and to make decisions. Sometimes mandated practitioners have to act to protect clients, dependents, and the community whether or not the involuntary client acknowledges the problem and indicates willingness to work on it.

Both the stages of change model and motivational interviewing are explored more thoroughly in part 3 of this volume. Section A presents applications of stages of change and motivational interviewing to three problems and populations. James Barber explores the utility of the approaches for work with chemically dependent clients in chapter 10. Chris Kleinpeter and Melinda Hohman then apply the approaches to work with adolescents in health safety issues in chapter 11. Finally, Michael Chovanec applies the approaches for work with men who perpetrate violence in chapter 12.

Discussion

The knowledge base for work with involuntary clients has been limited by lack of focus, varied quality of studies, and less than conclusive results. These limitations may in part reflect appropriate protections for mandated clients from participating in research against their will. Further studies are needed that specify the level of voluntarism, the extent of choices and their implementation, the nature of the treatment and involuntary client responses to it, as well as more specific applications to problems and populations. In this chapter we have suggested that intervention with legally mandated clients can achieve successful results. However, coerced intervention often produces *time-limited* benefits that do not last beyond the use of the external pressure. In addition, comparisons between involuntary and "voluntary" clients often appear to be comparisons between mandated and nonvoluntary clients. Further clues to effectiveness suggest that interaction between practitioner and client plays an important part in achieving these improved outcomes. Specifically, interventions designed to enhance motivational congruence between practitioner and client are promising sources for effective intervention. Motivational congruence should not, however, be construed as easily achieved with involuntary clients. Many choices are so constricted as to be negligible. In addition, as treatment adherence has been shown to be problematic with voluntary clients, there is little reason to expect it to be less so with involuntary clients. Mandated service agencies and institutions have community protection goals that impose obstacles to the pursuit of high congruence. Even when the setting affirms goals of congruence, time, resources, and practitioner discretion is needed to implement those goals. Such pressures often create a reactive stance that impedes the extra efforts required to seek congruence. In addition, public opinion often pressures agencies into punitive approaches and away from approaches seen as "coddling" wrongdoers. Despite these reservations, the pursuit of motivational congruence is promising toward a goal of legal, ethical, and effective practice with involuntary clients. Such efforts deserve experimentation and study to enhance compliance while respecting involuntary client legal rights and their self-determination.

Several clues to effectiveness in the pursuit of motivational congruence have been suggested. Enhancement of perceived choice is the first such clue. Since nonvoluntary clients can legally choose to refuse treatment, notification of such freedom is recommended for work with all nonvoluntary clients. As such a choice may bring some negative consequences as well as benefits, the consequences should be explored in assisting nonvoluntary clients in making such decisions. Perceived choice can also be enhanced with mandated clients when they are encouraged to make constrained choices between acceptable options, including the choice to accept legal consequences rather than participate in treatment programs. Manipulation of the *appearance* of choice for clients while withholding actual choices conflicts with guidelines suggested in chapter 2 regarding honest communication and restricting unethical paternalism. A more ethical choice is to make very clear the distinction between those issues that are required and non-negotiable and distinguishing them from issues in which clients have free choices or choices among constrained alternatives. We note that with some populations such as sexual offenders and domestic violence perpetrators, the community is often considered the primary client. However, by adapting a stages-of-change approach, it is possible to seek motivational congruence.

Additional clues include socialization and behavioral contracting methods that clarify such distinctions between the negotiable and the non-negotiable. Finally, guidelines for increasing treatment adherence including soliciting specific commitments and client participation in task selection were suggested.

At this point, there is no overarching theory or model about what works with involuntary clients. Intervention methods are reported that have different targets of intervention and different assumptions about the change process. Pursuit of ethical effective practice would suggest continuing the same methods in the face of less than uniform success may make less sense than exploring hypotheses from other methods and populations. Ultimate questions of whether some persons have committed crimes of such a despicable nature that they have forever forfeited the right to be treated as a client entitled to self-respect and some engagement in problem solving are not now answerable. We need to monitor the consequences of our assumptions about client status.

The stages of change approach and motivational interviewing are useful tools for addressing health care behaviors with involuntary clients with the proviso that adaptations have to be made. Motivational interviewing addresses the conundrum that involuntary clients in many fields are often less immediately concerned about their problem behaviors than are others. Rather than try to pressure or influence them to take action on problems that they do not acknowledge and ending in a confrontation–denial cycle in which clients are confronted about their irresponsible behavior, they defend themselves and are labeled as in denial, leading to more confrontation, this method focuses the practitioner on assessing the level of acknowledgment of the problem and inclination to action. A number of techniques are available for helping clients to assess the costs and benefits of their behaviors, and the costs and benefits to considering change.

The clues to intervention effectiveness developed in this chapter are transformed into more specific practice guidelines in chapters 6 through 8. We move next in chapter 4 to review practitioner influence methods such as use of rewards, punishments, and persuasion.

Discussion Questions

1. To what extent have you seen such guidelines as seeking motivational congruence and enhancing choices promoted in practice with involuntary clients?

2. Since practitioners with involuntary clients frequently interact with clients who do not perceive themselves as having the problems that others see them as experiencing, how useful is a conception of precontemplation and contemplation to such work?

3. To what extent have you seen efforts to seek congruence with clients such that their own goals are pursued rather than focusing on others' goals for them?

4. What is your experience with the concept of pro-social modeling as a conscious method for influencing involuntary clients?

Chapter 4

Influencing Behaviors and Attitudes

In chapter 2, we reviewed the circumstances in which practitioners with involuntary clients have ethical or legal grounds to attempt to influence behavior. In chapter 3, we saw that problem-solving courts are among the coercive interventions that can be effective with involuntary clients. In this chapter, we will explore methods designed to influence behavior and attitudes.

Practitioners working with voluntary clients sometimes see themselves as helping those clients make informed choices, or facilitating their growth, rather than influencing their behavior and attitudes. The latter has connotations of manipulation that may not fit the self-image of voluntary practitioners. Such practitioners may not be aware of or acknowledge that they and their clients are engaged in attempts to influence the behavior and attitudes of one another (Perloff 1993). However, denial or unconscious use of influence by practitioners is particularly problematic in practice with involuntary clients since that influence is often evident to the involuntary client if not the practitioner and may constitute an unethical use of power. Hence, we proceed in this chapter with the view that influence attempts do occur and that practitioners are better served by being conscious of power so that such efforts to influence behavior and attitudes can be ethically guided and evaluated.

Compliance-oriented methods are at the high end of a continuum of intrusiveness into client behavior, since they attempt to influence actions and attitudes directly through punishing undesirable events and rewarding desirable events. *Persuasion methods* are less intrusive as they influence actions and attitudes through providing information rather than manipulating rewards and constraints. Both compliance-oriented and persuasion methods have important roles for involuntary clients, with relatively more frequent use of compliance methods with mandated clients and more frequent use of persuasion with nonvoluntary clients. The characteristics, advantages, disadvantages, and guidelines for legal, ethical, and effective use of each form of influence are presented in this chapter. More attention is devoted, however, to persuasion methods, since their inappropriate use raises fewer ethical problems and practitioners and programs tend to be less knowledgeable about them (see figure 4.1).

Compliance-oriented methods are introduced with the following case study.

Gerald, sixteen, lived in a small residential facility for adolescents with behavior problems. As frequently occurs in such settings, the treatment program included a specific set of rules and procedures, such as rewards for approved behavior and penalties for disapproved behavior. A *token economy* system was used in which Gerald could earn points for good behavior that would accrue toward obtaining rewards (Morisee et al. 1996). For example, Gerald could earn one point for each hour in which positive behaviors, such as paying attention in school, were demonstrated. The system also included penalties for infractions. For example, swearing, acting in a way considered rude or sarcastic by a counselor, or

Figure 4.1   Coercion methods

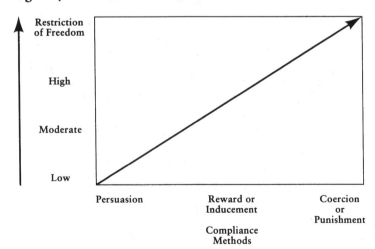

failure to comply with a counselor's request would result in a warning. After three such warnings, a punishment in the form of a half-hour of work such as scrubbing windows would be administered.

If, however, the form of negative behavior included aggression toward self or others, attempts to run away, property destruction or use of alcohol or drugs, the half-hour penalty was immediately administered. In addition, residents who were being disciplined were to "process" their punishment by discussing the reasons for the penalty with the counselor. While a punishment was being processed, residents were not allowed to watch television, interact with peers, use the telephone, or smoke.

Gerald had been in the setting for three months and had been earning steady rewards as well as a normal amount of penalties for his behavior. On one occasion, however, Gerald returned to the group home under the influence of marijuana after a weekend visit with his parents. The counselor on duty noted his dilated pupils and the distinctive odor of marijuana. When asked, Gerald acknowledged that he had been smoking marijuana. Returning to the group home under the influence of alcohol or other drugs was a clear rule violation. Gerald was told that the processing of the appropriate penalty would occur the next afternoon when he returned from school.

The next afternoon, Gerald did not "process" the discussion of the rule violation calmly. He was described as sarcastic by the counselors and was assessed a time-out to calm himself. Gerald was still irate after the ten-minute time-out and a half-hour restitution penalty was inflicted. Gerald refused to comply with the penalty and threatened staff members. When staff attempted to restrain Gerald, he broke free and broke a panel in a door. After he was successfully restrained and first aid applied to his cuts, two more penalties were issued. At this point, Gerald had lost 1,000 points for aggression toward self and others, had earned five hours of restitution, and further unsupervised home visits were now suspended. In addition, he was now suspended from outings with peers for six months. Staff told Gerald that he had hurt his parents by violating the rules: they could no longer have unsupervised home visits with him. Gerald became angry and had to be restrained once again.

Reminiscent of a lyric sung by Janis Joplin, "freedom's just another word for nothing left to lose," Gerald had lost so many rewards and accrued so much punishment at this point, that there was little incentive for him to try to succeed in the program. With little left to lose, and the program designed to influence his behavior in a positive fashion appearing to have a boomerang effect of escalating negative consequences, a reevaluation of procedures was called for. We will explore in the following sections how a compliance-oriented system can both work effectively and ethically to limit behavior but can also go wrong, as in this case, to acquiring its own momentum and producing results worse than the behavior that they were designed to curb. We will also explore how a better understanding of compliance methods might have permitted a different result.

Compliance-Oriented Methods

Compliance behavior occurs when a person accepts influence in order to escape a punishment or achieve a reward or approval (Feld and Radin 1982). Such methods can be appropriately used to protect others and to modify behavior dangerous to the client. The principle of pro-social modeling was described in chapter 3 as a clue for effectiveness involving a conscious, consistent plan for modeling and reinforcing behavior and attitude change (Cherry 2005; Trotter 2006).

The residential program where Gerald was placed attempted to use compliance methods to reach individual and institutional goals. While compliance-oriented methods are ethically neutral and are sometimes used with clients who have little input into goals and methods, use of contracts that specify negotiable and non-negotiable items is preferred (Stolz, Wienckowski, and Brown 1975). Compliance-oriented approaches make important assumptions that can be helpful in involuntary situations. By considering behavior as learned, attention can be focused on changing contingencies, observing models, avoiding dangerous situations, and rewarding alternative behaviors rather than dwelling on unchangeable past events (Cherry 2005). While it is beyond the scope of this book to examine compliance-oriented approaches in detail or to include all the involuntary populations with which they have been used, key concepts for use with involuntary clients are reviewed.

Punishment

Discussion of use of punishment and coercion takes place in a context in which extreme forms of coercion best classified as torture or what has been described as "tough techniques with the worst of the worst" have become an instrument of national policy in the war against terror. Waterboarding, which induces a sense of imminent drowning through strapping persons to boards and pouring water over the nose and mouth, has occurred as an instrument of policy (Warrick and Pincus 2008). Whatever the justifications for such usage for national defense, particularly problematic has been the compliance of medical personnel contrary to the Hippocratic Oath in collaborating in the design of torture and monitoring health so that health endangering methods can be used (Dossey 2006; Miles 2006).

Coercive methods have frequently been used in the context of human services with mental patients ostensibly to protect them and others, both with legally involuntary clients and ostensibly voluntary clients (Iversen, Hoyer, and Sexton 2007). Coercion has been studied to include both objective coercion which is intentional and can be observed and perceived coercion which includes the patients perception that it has occurred; 80 percent of patients in one study, whether mandated or voluntary, reported that they perceived coercion to have occurred (ibid.). In addition to objective coercion, implicit coercion can occur by failing to notify patients of rights. For example, voluntary patients on an in-patient unit have been stalled or delayed when they express a desire to leave if their departure was considered dangerous (Sjostrom 2006). Coercion occurs despite data to suggest that it arouses negative feelings, creates negative expectations about outcomes, impedes a trusting relationship, and makes many patients less open to services (Kaltiala-Heino, Laippala, and Salokangas 1997). The following presentation and discussion of coercion therefore takes place in a context of dangers as well as potential benefits.

Punishment or constraint is the most intrusive compliance method. It refers to methods intended to stop or reduce an unwanted behavior through administration of adverse consequences or withholding positive consequences (Rose 1998). There are five major types of punishment. *Positive punishment* refers to the use of an aversive consequence when an unwanted stimulus occurs (Thyer and Myers 2000). For example, requiring a delinquent youth to wash windows as a consequence for swearing is a form of positive punishment (ibid.). In the preceding example, when Gerald became violent, staff attempts to restrain him were designed to constitute positive punishment. It should be noted here that the term "positive" should not be construed to mean that this form of punishment is pleasurable or appropriate. *Response cost* refers to withholding positive reinforcements when an unwanted behavior occurs (Rose 1998). Hence suspending Gerald's outings with other residents and unsupervised home visits was a form of response cost. *Negative reinforcement* refers to the removal of an aversive consequence in order to stimulate a behavior (Thyer and Myers 2000). Hence, negative reinforcement is a coerced choice because some responses *are* rewarded. If Gerald could have immediately begun to acquire positive points toward regaining privileges following response cost, negative reinforcement would have been used more appropriately.

Overcorrection methods can be used to teach alternative behavior incompatible with the unwanted behavior. For example, restitution can be used to both provide an appropriate punishment and also reinforce pro-social behavior. Restitution is used in some victim–offender reconciliation programs that involve meetings between property offenders and their victims in which the form of restitution for damage done is negotiated between the two parties. Such methods may meet some of the real purposes of punishment by putting the offender in touch with the harm he or she caused (van Wormer 2004). Since the drug violation occurred while Gerald was under his parents' supervision, a meeting with Gerald and his parents might have more directly addressed the causes of the rule violation and assisted in the construction of an appropriate response. If Gerald and his parents had been consulted in the choice and design of appropriate penalties, their belief in the appropriateness of the penalty might be greater. Finally, *time-out* can be used as an extinction method by withholding reinforcement in a nonpunitive environment (Rose 1998). When Gerald was sent to his room for ten minutes, this was considered time-out. Each of these five punishment methods can be used legally, ethically, and effectively in certain situations.

Legal Use of Punishment

As described in chapter 2, use of coercion is legal when the practitioner has a mandated responsibility, client behavior falls within the domain of that mandate, and criteria for employment of punishment are clear and appropriately followed. Appropriate oversight boards must develop and periodically review use of intrusive procedures such as the use of restraints (Stolz, Wienkowski, and Brown 1975). In this case, the circumstances of the use of restraint with Gerald should have been reviewed by an oversight board to determine whether in fact there was immediate danger to Gerald or others.

Ethical Use of Punishment

Use of punishment is ethical when harmful behavior or behavior at high risk of injury to the person or others occurs, when less intrusive methods are ineffective such that few alternatives can be reinforced or reinforcers removed and when there is a panel to review appropriate use of the method regularly (Simons and Aigner 1985). There is question here whether there was risk of any immediate injury to Gerald or whether less intrusive methods such as consultation with Gerald and his parents about restitution could have been attempted. As noted in chapter 2, punishment and other paternalistic behaviors often emerge to meet the needs of the institution rather than more limited, situation-specific penalties. It may be easier for staff to administer punishments than rewards, and an ineffective punishment system can be established that unfortunately models the inappropriate aggressive behavior it intends to change (Rose 1998).

In addition, nonvoluntary clients in residential institutions have fewer legal protections from inappropriate use of punishment than do legally mandated clients (Iverson, Hoyer, and Sexton 2007; Surgenor 2003). Practitioners should act to protect client rights when compliance-oriented methods are used to regulate social deviance in matters that are neither dangerous to others nor illegal. Such methods are in particular danger of overuse with members of oppressed groups. For example, more punitive sentences for use of crack cocaine rather than other forms of cocaine disproportionately penalize African Americans (Sterling 2004).

Effective Use of Punishment
The effective use of punishment assumes that the practitioner has access to aversives powerful enough to stop the behavior, that the punishment is administered quickly and consistently, and that the practitioner is prepared for the drawbacks that frequently accompany its use (Simons and Aigner 1985). Punishment works most effectively when it is used to stop or reduce a harmful behavior in the short run (see figure 4.2). Hence, the penalties that Gerald received might have had an effect of immediate, though short-term, reduction in use of marijuana. Punishment tends, however, to suppress the harmful behavior rather than eliminate it and usually does not change attitudes (ibid.). Since aversives work best when they are powerful and consistent, the lack of power or consistency too often results in the client learning how to avoid getting caught for a similar offense rather than questioning the offense. If punishment is not combined with other forms of influence with Gerald, the most important thing he may have learned from this incident is to stop smoking marijuana earlier in the day before returning to the facility, to avoid detection, rather than change his beliefs about use of the drug.

Additional problems occur when aversives are neither powerful nor consistent. When this occurs, clients may learn to avoid punishment by lying, deceiving, or acting in an ingratiating fashion. Further, client beliefs in punishment as a solution to interpersonal problems may be inadvertently reinforced. They may believe that "might makes right" and punishment of them may lead to a displacement of aggression onto others outside the situation. Use of punishment is also frequently associated with increased fear,

Figure 4.2   Punishment

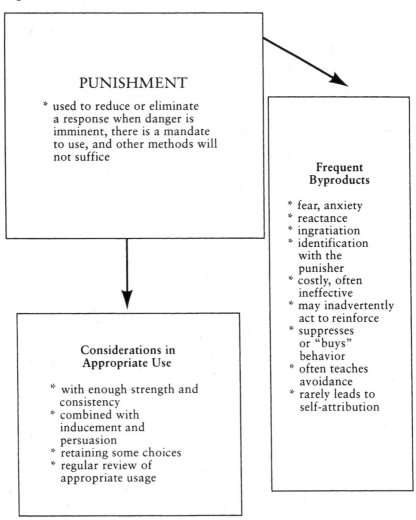

PUNISHMENT

* used to reduce or eliminate
  a response when danger is
  imminent, there is a mandate
  to use, and other methods will
  not suffice

**Frequent
Byproducts**

* fear, anxiety
* reactance
* ingratiation
* identification
  with the
  punisher
* costly, often
  ineffective
* may inadvertently
  act to reinforce
* suppresses
  or "buys"
  behavior
* often teaches
  avoidance
* rarely leads to
  self-attribution

**Considerations in
Appropriate Use**

* with enough strength and
  consistency
* combined with
  inducement and
  persuasion
* retaining some choices
* regular review of
  appropriate usage

hostility, and feelings of powerlessness and helplessness. In addition, punishment does not necessarily reduce attraction to prohibited behavior but may, in fact, cause it to be more valued (Brehm et al. 1966). Finally, if the reason for punishment is not clear, it may inadvertently punish other positive, desirable behaviors (ibid). In this case, Gerald's desire to smoke marijuana *again* when unsupervised may have increased and his general collaboration in the positively oriented token economy system may have decreased.

Effective use of punishment requires control of sufficient aversive resources. These resources may need to be used indefinitely if alternative behavior does not become reinforcing. Further, when a relationship begins on the basis of punishment, it is difficult to change to a relationship based on reward or persuasion as the practitioner and agency may be associated only with punishment.

However, access to sufficient coercive resources contains its own dangers. Availability of coercive resources encourages their use to exercise control and exert retribution (Kipnis 1972; Stolz, Wienckowski, and Brown 1975). Continued use of punishment can contribute to alienation and distancing from clients, including labeling and blaming those clients for negative responses to its use. There is little doubt that in the circumstance described, staff response focused primarily on Gerald's negative response to sanctions rather than questioning the appropriateness of their use.

Finally, punishment may continue to be used despite evidence that undesirable behavior is not stopping and that the punishment may in fact be reinforcing behavior. Despite ineffective use, practitioners and agencies may be inclined to use "more of the same" punishment strategies as a relief of tension for the punisher. Hence, punishment once used may be continued habitually without reexamination of its appropriateness or effectiveness (Milgram 1963). In Gerald's case, we saw punishment escalate to produce a worse outcome than the infraction. A review should have been conducted when a clearly undesirable result had occurred from following procedures. In Gerald's case, the immediate escalating administration of punishment with little opportunity to return to the generally positive behavior that had characterized his stay before the infraction should have been reviewed.

Punishment in corrections is designed to act as a deterrent. Specific or simple deterrence refers to a sentence that makes it unlikely that an offender is likely to recidivate (Bartholomew 1994). A general deterrent is one designed to deter the general population through its harshness or other special features. Correctional boot camps were designed, for example, to be specific deterrents through exposing participants to a brief, quasi-military experience. While such boot camps may have alleviated overcrowding, questions are raised about how much it has assisted with other rehabilitative goals given the emphasis on unquestioning obedience and aggression. In any event, dropout from the experience has been reported as nearly 50 percent (Welch 1999). An eight state comparison of boot camps showed that nonparticipants had comparable outcomes to participants (MacKenzie et al. 1995). Part of the problem with the design of sentences as deterrents may have been assumptions that decisions to commit offenses occur rationally rather than impulsively and that potential offenders perceive other alternatives to a path that leads to incarceration as readily available (Austin, Irwin, and Kubrin 2003).

Meanwhile restorative justice offers promise as an option that benefits victims and fosters human dignity and mutual respect (Sullivan and Tifft 2004). It has been characterized by the offender and the victim or a representative meeting during which the offender listening respectfully while the harmed describe how they have been affected, the offender apologizing and undertaking a reparative task as an effort to make amends at least partially through a positive act (Johnstone 2004). The principles of restorative justice have been used outside of the legal system to include the educational system with participation by students and teachers (Sullivan and Tifft 2004). Restorative justice has been described as featuring at its best a reintegrative shaming process in which the offense rather than the offender is shamed with a goal of reintegrating the offender into society (Maxwell and Morris 2004). Stigmatic shaming, conversely, often occurs as a result of punishment efforts in which an offender is made to feel that he or she is a bad person. Such stigmatization does not reduce recidivism but rather may contribute to further offending (ibid.).

Inducement

Inducement is a second compliance-oriented method that occurs when a person is influenced by the hope of receiving a reward (Kelman 1965). Inducement is used to increase a behavior by providing rewards contingent on performance of that desired behavior (figure 4.3) (Simons and Aigner 1985). Use of inducements is discussed below based on consideration of the following case study.

> Nathan Brown had a serious and persistent mental illness. To receive public assistance, Nathan had to demonstrate reasonable efforts to gain employment. While Nathan was faithful in making the required number of job applications, he was never selected for a job interview. One reason was the fact that Nathan did not take regular baths, wash his clothes, or shave. His public assistance worker proposed that for a one-month period he be offered the option of working on hygiene instead of completing job applications.
>
> Nathan acknowledged his problem regarding hygiene and wanted to get a job, but had not succeeded on his own in improving his hygiene. He agreed to a plan that called for a gradually increasing number of shaves, showers, and launderings before job interviews. He understood that at the end of this trial period he would be expected to try to maintain the new cleanliness habits in a renewed job search. Nathan's hygiene tasks were now successful and his resumed job search began to

Figure 4.3   Inducement or reward

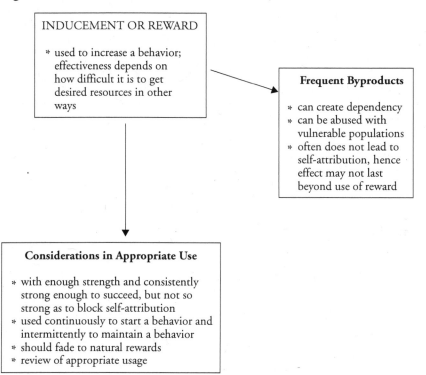

INDUCEMENT OR REWARD

* used to increase a behavior; effectiveness depends on how difficult it is to get desired resources in other ways

Frequent Byproducts

* can create dependency
* can be abused with vulnerable populations
* often does not lead to self-attribution, hence effect may not last beyond use of reward

Considerations in Appropriate Use

* with enough strength and consistently strong enough to succeed, but not so strong as to block self-attribution
* used continuously to start a behavior and intermittently to maintain a behavior
* should fade to natural rewards
* review of appropriate usage

result in actual job interviews. In addition, Nathan reported that friends had begun to compliment him on his cleanliness.

Inducement can be less intrusive than coercion by providing a choice to begin a behavior influenced by available rewards rather than stimulated by avoidance of punishment. Hence, Nathan's task to develop good hygiene habits was reinforced by the reward of public assistance and the temporary suspension for job search expectations.

However, such choices are typically constrained by limited access to alternative resources. A decision to not try the behavior desired by the persons controlling the resources often means choosing to live without the desired resource. Nathan had a constrained choice of continuing to carry out job interviews or participating in the alternative hygiene program, or choosing not to apply for assistance. In the sections that follow, guidelines for the legal, ethical, and effective use of inducement are explored.

Legal Issues in the Use of Inducement

Institutional programs such as the one in which Gerald was placed have long used token economies in which residents can earn tokens or points toward larger rewards though performing desired behavior (Rose 1998). Courts have ruled, however, that some penal programs have started at such a low baseline level that the program was in fact punishing rather than rewarding. Specifically, programs that used sleeping quarters and adequate food as rewards were found to constitute cruel and unusual punishment (Alexander 2003). Hence, the legal guideline here is that *inducements are not to be used to negotiate or bargain for basic rights and necessities. Inducements should be an additional resource such that a person could choose not to accept the resource* (Simons and Aigner 1985).

Rewards are often used in nonvoluntary conditions with fewer checks and balances. The same legal guidelines for mandated clients should apply for the protection of nonvoluntary clients in institutional and other settings. Nathan could at least choose to continue to receive public assistance by rejecting the hygiene option and proceeding with job search requirements.

Ethical Issues in Use of Inducement

While superficially inducement poses fewer ethical problems in work with involuntary clients than punishment, ethical problems also arise. As suggested previously, inducements can be used appropriately to support alternatives when behavior harmful to the self or other is occurring. Too often, however, inducements are used to exploit vulnerable clients and reinforce dependency. For example, rewards will be more effective if clients do not have ready alternative access to them. Hence, financial rewards are effective for clients who do not have ready access to money. Consequently, rewards are more effective with vulnerable clients with limited resources.

Such limited alternative access can lead to misuse and abuse of the power to dispense the resource.

Does control of such resources lead to abuse with vulnerable clients? It has been suggested with behaviorally disordered schoolchildren that docility is the implicit goal (Winett and Winkler 1972). Agency or practitioner control, or a monopoly of scarce resources means that compliant behavior may be elicited through discriminating or even indiscriminate use of such resources. It should also be considered that clients who are subject to a unilateral monopoly of scarce resources may attempt to restore the balance by "cheating," gaining access to the resource in other ways, and making coalitions with others in the same situations (Cook and Emerson 1978). Mary's wish to consider career plans was not a threat to either her well-being or that of others and hence led to an inappropriate use of the power to reward. Extracting more change than is necessary to meet agreed-on treatment goals violates professional values (Simons and Aigner 1985). Hence, the ethical guideline in use of inducements is that this use *should empower the person and reduce dependency.* Too often, however, continued dependency-on the practitioner and rewards from the program occur.

Effectiveness Issues with Inducement
Inducement can be effectively used to begin a behavior. For that behavior to be maintained, however inducement should be phased out and replaced by natural reinforcers and combined with other influence methods such as persuasion. *Continuous reinforcement* refers to the provision of an inducement *each* time a desired event occurs and is the best way to support a new behavior (Rose 1998). The inducement must be strong enough to reinforce the behavior and applied consistently. Continuous reinforcement is often begun by rewarding successive approximations or shaping the desired behavior. For example, starting with requests for a small number of hygiene activities from Nathan that gradually increase follows this principle.

Inducement is similar to punishment in that it is more successful at initiating a behavior than maintaining it after rewards have been discontinued. Behavior is best maintained by intermittent reinforcement schedules in which artificial rewards are decreased and natural rewards are substituted (Rose 1998). Behaviors are most likely to be maintained if the person attributes to him or herself the reasons for continuing the reward (Kiesler 1971) However, rewards can be used to enhance intrinsic interest or valuing of activities (Cameron and Pierce 1996). This can be done by identifying naturally occurring rewards while extrinsic rewards are still in effect.

Should rewards be too strong, attitudes toward the changed behavior are unlikely to change because the person is likely to perceive his or her compliance as forced by the promise of gaining a reward. The person likely may not take responsibility for his or her own change because the person may perceive that his or her behavior was "bought" (Kiesler 1971). For example, while Nathan was aware that his original compliance with the new plan was "bought" with the promise of continued assistance for this behavior, the behavior was maintained by natural reinforcers when he reported that others were complimenting him on his change. The practitioner in this case had begun with an approximation of a continuous reinforcement schedule, and lessened that reinforcement as natural reinforcers began to have an effect. While programs should work toward reduced use of inducement, frequently they are continued without appropriate phasing out (Simons and Aigner 1985).

If Nathan should now say to himself and others that he was carrying out a different hygiene program because it helped him get job interviews, and other people complimented him about the change, then the change would be self-attributed and would be more likely to be maintained than if he said that he persisted in the new behavior because his financial assistance was dependent on it. Following the principle of supporting self-attributed change, practitioners should use small inducements where possible, and practitioner support, praise, and encouragement for behavioral changes should not be overemphasized such that personal responsibility for changes can be supported (Simons and Aigner 1985).

We have seen that punishment strategies can be used effectively in combination with inducement in negative reinforcement. In Nathan's case, the choice to accept neither a job search nor the option of completing hygiene tasks would have resulted in denial of assistance.

When the use of inducement is contemplated, the following questions are considered:

1. Does the situation involve such danger to self or others that a form of punishment would work more quickly and safely?
2. Is inducement used to exploit clients who are in vulnerable state?
3. Has it been applied in a "package deal" to reinforce attitudes, behaviors, and beliefs that are neither illegal nor dangerous?
4. Is inducement applied to limited behaviors that are clearly supportive of treatment goals agreed upon in a contract?
5. Is inducement used to reward empowerment and reduce dependence?

Use of Cognitive Methods with Involuntary Clients

Cognitive methods have frequently been employed as part of efforts to influence the attitudes and behavior of involuntary clients. Such methods view behavior as influenced by mental images of the world. That is, persons are seen as not only reacting to objective events but rather to how those events are processed through mental images or schemas of those events (Berlin and Barden 2000). Cognitive methods are used to identify self-defeating or illogical or automatic patterns of thinking that inhibit pro-social problem solving (Rose 1998).

Cognitive methods have been used with many involuntary populations including persons with severe and persistent mental illness, men with battering problems, parents with problems of child abuse and neglect, alcoholism, cocaine addiction, delinquency, sexual offenses, drug court services, and school services (Linehan 1993; Kaplan and Carter 1995; Allen, Mackenzie, and Hickman 1998; Carroll 1998; Rose 1998; Thyer and Myers 2000; Bouffard and Taxman 2004; Bradshaw and Roseborough 2004; Stalans 2004; Murphy and Eckhardt 2005).

Cognitive methods are frequently part of treatment packages with juvenile sexual offenders (Craig, Browne, and Stringer 2003). Such packages have been associated with deterrence without specifying exactly what parts of treatment contribute to effectiveness (Efta-Breitbach 2004). Cognitive methods have been found in up to 75 percent of adult sexual offender programs (Stalans 2004). Such programs have included modules on anger management, enhancing empathy for victims and prevention of relapse (Yates 2003). Most specifically, they teach awareness of thoughts surrounding offenses and employ cognitive restructuring to challenge self-statements that excuse behavior (Efta-Breitbach 2004). A qualitative study of sexual offenders found that at least in the short run, such challenging of what are perceived as cognitive distortions may lead the offender to conclude that the therapist did not believe them, and they reported learning to say what the therapist wanted to hear (Drapeau et al. 2005).

Cognitive methods have been used with adult offenders to enhance the ability to reason morally using moral reconation therapy as well as a reasoning and rehabilitation program that challenges thoughts and attitudes considered dysfunctional. Moral reconation therapy has been found to be at least minimally successful in reducing recidivism (Allen, McKenzie, and Hickman 1998).

Persuasion

Persuasion methods are used to influence behavior and attitudes by providing additional information or reasons for making particular choices (Simons 1982). Persuasion can include guiding a person toward an attitude through familiarity with their values and goals, presenting alternatives and evidence to support them, and supporting choices (Reardon 1991). Persuasion need not include manipulation for the benefit of the persuader, hiding crucial facts and available choices, or coercion involving threat or force (ibid.).

A theme of this book has been that involuntary transactions occur between practitioners, representing agencies and legal systems, and clients. It is important to recognize that such transactions contain efforts by practitioners to influence client behavior and attitudes, and efforts by clients to influence practitioners. Such efforts occur whether or not the practitioners or clients are consciously aware of them (Frank 1973). The practitioner may consciously or unconsciously attempt to influence attitudes and beliefs by selecting certain statements to comment upon and reinforce and ignoring others (Reardon 1991). As we saw in chapter 3, the principle of pro-social modeling is one that supports being quite conscious of these efforts to support some attitudes, beliefs, and behaviors and discourage others. Persuasion methods can often be less intrusive and more helpful in promoting self-attributed change than compliance-oriented methods. In the sections that follow, principles for attempting persuasion and legal, ethical, and effectiveness implications of persuasion with involuntary clients are explored. These principles are explored in the case study of Wilmer Jones.

> Wilmer had a serious and persistent mental illness that had earlier resulted in involuntary hospitalization but taking antipsychotic medication now allowed him to live in the community. There was a continual struggle with his community care practitioner, Anne, about taking his medication. She was concerned that failure to take the medication would result in a return to the hospital. Wilmer resisted persuasion attempts, saying that the medication gave him a dry mouth, grogginess, fuzzy perception, and that it deprived him of religious experiences. Anne first referred Mr. Jones to a physician for a possible change of medication and dosage. However, Wilmer continued to dislike and distrust medications. Several persuasion principles were useful in working with Wilmer.

Factors in the effectiveness of influence attempts include intimacy, dominance, benefits, consequences for the relationship, and resistance to appeals (Reardon 1991). The *intimacy factor* entails how well the person attempting influence knows the recipient of the attempt and what they value. That is, the more the person attempting influence knows about those values, the more likely he or she is able construct a persuasive appeal. For example, a research finding suggests that women who have suffered from domestic violence often place diminished value on their own safety, yet they often draw the line when they believe that their childrens' safety is endangered (Syers-McNairy 1990). Hence, if this value was salient for a particular victim of domestic violence, efforts to explore positive and negative consequences for children might be a more effective strategy than appealing to their personal welfare. Based on her level of intimate knowledge of Wilmer, Anne knew that he greatly valued living independently in the community. Taking antipsychotic medication that had many unpleasant side effects was by no means highly valued.

Dominance is a second factor in the effectiveness of influence attempts and the degree to which threats permeate the discussion. Persuasion strategies designed to enhance compliance have been cast on a matrix that include reference to positive or negative consequences for the recipient and variation in the employment of dominance (Marwell and Schmitt 1967). Promise strategies are ones in which the essential argument is that, if the client complies, he or she will be rewarded by natural events, other people, or the person attempting influence. Threat strategies, meanwhile, suggest the opposite: if the client does not comply, other persons, events, or the person attempting influence will punish him or her (Reardon 1991). A third strategy is known as pregiving, whereby a recipient is rewarded by the person attempting influence before a request for compliance occurs. For example, taking a client with serious mental illness out for coffee before a discussion about taking medication would employ this principle (Angell, Mahoney, and Martinez 2006). The opposite of pregiving is a debt strategy in which it is suggested that the recipient should comply because of past favors paid by the person attempting influence. For example, some agencies ask that practitioners gather information from clients that the clients do not want to provide. For example, unwed mothers are often asked the names of the fathers of their children. They may wish to protect their secrecy and do not see a benefit to themselves or their children to provide this information. Couching such a request in a duty to repay prior favors such as providing transportation or getting clothes for the children would employ the debt strategy. This example suggests some ethical issues with a debt strategy if it is used to cause a client to deny what they consider to be their best interest because of a debt. A more ethically sound method for discussing this need for information would be to present the request in the light of potential positive consequences for their children to be assured of more financial support.

A self-feeling positive strategy is one in which the person attempting influence argues that the recipient will feel better if he or she complies. Similarly, an "altercasting positive" strategy is one in which the persuader maintains that a person with positive qualities such as a caring parent, would comply (Reardon 1991). Practitioners working with involuntary clients may be inclined to employ threat or debt strategies. In chapter 5, we explore reactance theory (Brehm et al. 1966) and how appeals based on threats to freedom sometimes result in a "boomerang" effect of less effectiveness.

A third factor is the degree to which the client would experience *personal benefits* or whether the persuader would experience them from the influence attempt (Reardon 1991). Practitioners working with involuntary clients should explore personal benefits for the client and avoid such benefits for themselves. Anne discovered that Wilmer's driver's license had been suspended when he was hospitalized and not renewed on his release. She recognized that Wilmer was more likely to take the medication as a means toward personal benefits such as staying out of the hospital, living independently, and being able to drive a car than valuing the medication for itself. Consequently, Anne and Wilmer revised the service agreement to describe agreed-upon goals of "staying out of the hospital" and "working to regain my driver's license." In their revised contract, taking a different dosage of the medication in the effort to reduce side effects became an instrumental task toward reaching personal benefits that were highly valued by Wilmer. As Anne did not have the power to restore his license, she committed herself to advocating on his behalf based on his past record of safely and evidence of regular mediation. Her recommendation would be included when he would apply for a reinstated license. This agreement resulted in greatly increased regularity in taking the mediation and a successful effort to regain his driver's license for use in restricted circumstances.

A fourth factor refers to the short- and long-term consequences for the relationship of the influence attempt (Reardon 1991). This is an important factor in which use of deceptive methods may diminish trust in the long term and inhibit pro-social modeling. Resistance refers to what will happen should the first influence attempt be rejected, as recipients of influence attempts often do not agree on the first presentation of the request. Indeed some influence approaches are predicated on assuming that the first appeal will be rejected. The "foot in the door" method implies that a person will be more likely to comply with a second request after complying with a first one, especially when there are few external rewards associated with the attempt (Reardon 1991). For example, Alice Donat, the client in chapter 1 with a mental handicap who lived at home with twenty cats, believed that if she applied for Social Security benefits, SSI officials might attempt to hospitalize her. The practitioner agreed with her goal of keeping her independence. She asked Ms. Donat for a one-time commitment to go together to the Social Security office for the sole purpose of gaining information. Accompanying Ms. Donat to the SSI office was a form of the "foot-in-the-door" method of securing agreement to try a new behavior in a small, experimental fashion without making a long-term commitment. By going on this visit with the practitioner, Ms. Donat could check out her beliefs in a safe way. While the offer to accompany her might be seen as a small inducement, it falls short of heavy-handed efforts to force her compliance.

The "door in the face" method refers to starting with a large request and, after it is rejected, returning with a smaller request. For example, a drug dealer may provide a free sample to a potential new user/addict, employing the "foot in the door method," in hopes that if the new "client" accepts, the way is prepared for paying for the drug and becoming "hooked." Meanwhile, a practitioner attempting to influence such a client later in the cycle when he or she has become hooked, might use the door in the face method to make a request that the user enter an intensive, inpatient treatment program. If that request were rejected, the practitioner might return with a request to consider a less intensive outpatient program.

The practice of *low balling* refers to offering a bargain and after it is accepted, adding other costs (Reardon 1991). The low balling method may unfortunately be used by practitioners working with involuntary clients if they hide less pleasant factors when suggesting a choice. For example, when suggesting that a victim of domestic violence consider movement to a shelter for protection, low balling could mean not calling attention to shelter rules such as no contact with the perpetrator while in the shelter.

The long-term effects on the relationship are especially important for practitioners working with involuntary clients because of the emphasis on modeling pro-social values. Hence, methods such as low balling raise serious ethical issues for helping professionals as they would not enhance trust and pro-social modeling.

Clients are inclined to adopt the same attitudes as people they like, consider expert, and trust, and oppose attitudes of persons not considered to possess these attributes (Heider 1958). Research on cognitive balance theories suggests that people are inclined to adopt the same attitudes as people they consider credible, likable, expert, with their best interests at heart (Osgood and Tannenbaum 1955). Conversely, they are unlikely to adopt the attitudes of persons they dislike or find lacking in these attributes. In Wilmer's case, Anne had a positive reputation in the community as a supporter and advocate for persons with serious and persistent mental illness, one who treated them with respect as people rather than as targets who were not taking the right medications. These attributes undoubtedly made her more persuasive with Wilmer than might have been the case had the same arguments been made by persons he did not consider credible nor having his best interest in mind.

Legal Use of Persuasion

Informed consent was described in chapter 2 as a guiding legal principle in work with involuntary clients. Since informed consent requires that the client have access to information that would permit an informed choice, appropriate use of persuasion methods can assist in providing knowledge of available alternatives and their potential costs and benefits.

Ethical Use of Persuasion

Persuasion attempts can range in pressure from education to brainwashing (Singer and Lalich 1996). Hence, some persuasion methods may be effective but are ethically questionable (Perloff 1993). Deceiving clients by "hooking them" based on hiding critical facts or using inaccurate "straw man" arguments about alternatives runs the risk of modeling manipulative behavior that is the opposite of pro-social modeling (Roloff and Miller 1968).

Persuasion can be used unethically around issues that are neither illegal nor harmful but violate the sensibilities of the practitioner or community. Hence, an important issue in ethical persuasion is drawing the line between behaviors that the practitioner can ethically attempt to influence and those that he or she should not. For example, the fact that Alice Donat, the client introduced in chapter 1, lives with twenty cats is not a legal issue as long as laws are not violated, nor an ethical issue unless her health or the health of others is seriously endangered. She might experience pressure from her neighbors, but it could be emphasized to her that she can choose to do something about that pressure or not. She can choose to do something about the number of cats when she is given access to accurate information about alternatives and consequences. She might be told that the number of cats was not illegal at this point. Similarly, she could be informed that if there was a danger that they could become a serious health hazard, another investigation might ensue. Such influence would be ethical. The practitioner may be tempted by pressure from the neighbor and/or supervisor to prey on Ms. Donat's fears by using unethical persuasion with exaggerated, inaccurate threats of harmful consequences. Hence, threats that the health inspector would probably exterminate her cats if she did not comply would prey unethically on her fears.

Ethical persuasion is very much like the conditions required for true informed consent reviewed in chapter 2: all alternatives should be explored, not just those favored by the practitioner, and the advantages and disadvantages of each should be accurately reviewed. Ethical persuasion is consistent with commitments to honest communication and is likely to be associated with greater effectiveness over time should the practitioner come to be considered likable, trustworthy, and expert. Ethical persuasion entails assisting the client in determining his or her own goals, increasing rather than decreasing options for meeting those goals (Wallace 1967). Steps toward ethical persuasion would include attempting to understand the client's logic and rationale for his or her choices of attitudes and behaviors; identifying ways in which there is consistency between the reasoning and values the practitioner is presenting and ones the client now holds; empathizing with the client's emotions; and then gently probing inconsistencies in logic or inconsistency of behavior toward those goals (Gardner 2004). As values are slow to change, a reasonable goal might be to continue to explore possible resolution of inconsistencies rather than assume that the client will make an immediate change of behavior or attitude.

For example, it is not uncommon for men alleged to have assaulted women to defend themselves by noting that they have always been good providers for the family (identifying client values). Practitioners might then affirm how significant such a role is for the welfare of the family (identifying consistency in practitioner and client values). The practitioner might note that given the value the client places on supporting the family, how troubling an accusation of assault must be (empathizing with client values). The practitioner might then gently probe how causing one's partner to go to the emergency room is part of that goal of being a stable, reliable source of support for the family (probe inconsistencies of behavior and values). Such a question might begin to stimulate dissonance or concern with consistency of values. This might then lead to exploration of other ways of providing overall support for the family, a central value, and also avoid harm to others (Gardner 2004) (see figure 4.4).

Dissonance may be stimulated if a central value is identified that is violated by the client's behavior. For example, when Wilmer Jones complained of the side effects of the medication, Anne empathized with these uncomfortable experiences and asked him to describe other consequences in the past when he stopped taking his medication. Mr. Jones remembered that not taking his medication resulted in an involuntary hospitalization. Anne then asked whether Wilmer wished to risk another hospitalization.

Involuntary clients can be helped through *inductive questioning* to see unanticipated or self-defeating consequences and to consider other alternatives in meeting their own goals. Decisions are often made because alternatives and unanticipated or negative consequences of actions have not been considered. Inductive questioning can be used to explore such alternatives and unanticipated negative consequences (Simons and Aigner 1985). The Socratic method is one form of indicting questioning. Using the Socratic method, a belief or assumption considered irrational can be challenged by asking a series of questions that explore exceptions to that irrational belief. The method can also be used to help clients clarify obstacles to goals and plans. The client is first asked to describe the goal he or she seeks and then to look at possible unanticipated consequences in questions such as "What do you think might block your plan?" Similarly, clients may be asked if they might have considered other ways of reaching their goals. The Socratic method is unlikely to cause much negative response when the practitioner's own suggestions are added after the client's own views have been heard. As the Socratic method can help

Figure 4.4   Ethical persuasion principles

1. Seek to understand client's values, goals, and logic for actions in pursuit of those goals.
2. Use knowledge of client's values to frame appeals to values.
3. Draw attention to behavior and attitudes inconsistent with client values.
4. Seek to help client identify own goals and how behaviors and attitudes are consistent or inconsistent with them.
5. Clients are likely to adopt the same attitudes as persons they like, trust, and consider expert, and to oppose the attitudes of persons not considered to have these attributes.

clients be aware of the consequences of their choices, it can also increase the self-attribution of those choices.

For example, when Anne discovered that Mr. Jones did not have his driver's license and wished to regain it, she engaged in a series of inductive and Socratic questions such as: "What might prevent you from regaining your driver's license?" When he was informed that he would need a doctor's recommendation that he could drive safely before the suspension would be lifted, Anne asked, "What do you think will influence the doctor's recommendation?" When Wilmer suggested that his safe driving history prior to hospitalization would be one such factor, Anne agreed. She then asked, "What about how you act now is likely to make a difference in your safety as a driver?" While Wilmer continued to note the negative side effects of medication, he did think that taking the medication might contribute to his safety as a driver and that it might influence the recommendation.

As noted in this example, the practitioner may add other consequences and alternatives to the client's list. These consequences may include informing the client of potential punishing or rewarding consequences such as rehospitalization and alternatives such as requirements for lifting the driving suspension. Information about alternatives and consequences make it possible to make constrained choices. Information about potentially punishing consequences is not itself punishment when the punishing contingencies are not manipulated by the practitioner, and the choice, however constrained, is left to the client about modifying central values. Practitioners should first attempt to identify those central values. We noted that Anne was able to identify that Wilmer highly valued staying out of the hospital, living independently in the community, and regaining his driver's license.

Clients who are undecided or have an opposing viewpoint are more likely to be persuaded by a two-sided argument than by persuasion that emphasizes only the view held by the practitioner (Simons 1982). Steps in the two-sided argument include: (1) empathizing with and showing understanding of the viewpoint or preference of the client first; (2) acknowledging the limitations of one's own position; and (3) considering the benefits and costs of these and other viewpoints. Presenting the client's viewpoint first with the favored viewpoint last is likely to be seen as more objective by those who hold an opposing viewpoint. Use of the two-sided argument can inoculate the client against counterarguments that might be given by other influential persons in the environment (ibid.).

This method is used effectively in motivational interviewing to assess the advantages and disadvantages of changing behavior in assessing decisional balance (Miller and Rollnick 2002). For example, if a client were considering the possibilities of reducing or stopping drinking, he or she might be assisted to list the advantages of continuing to drink ("it helps me relax, I enjoy drinking with friends") as well as the costs ("it harms my health, it is a bad example for my children, it is a source of stress in my marriage"). From this point, the practitioner might assist the client to assess the advantages of making a change in drinking behavior (less family stress, more time with my children, better example for my children, more money available for other things) as well as the potential costs (I would lose something I enjoy, I might lose my friends, I might not be able to cope with stress) (ibid.). Exploring only the positive reasons for making a change runs the risk of enhancing reactance and a boomerang effect of greater attraction to drinking by taking away a valued free choice.

Situations in Which Persuasion Methods May Be Used
with Involuntary Clients
Persuasion methods are recommended to help mandated clients who have violated the rights of others to accept services. Acknowledging reluctance, conveying empathy, citing instances of success of involuntary contact, or identifying undesirable consequences of continuing present behavior can all be ethical influences toward accepting mandated contact (Simons and Aigner 1985). As nonvoluntary clients fall between the extremes of voluntary and mandated contact, they are entitled to make decisions about accepting service based on information about the costs and benefits of service. Such choices are frequently constrained by the decisions of others and institutional policies. Helping nonvoluntary clients assess these real-life punishing and rewarding contingencies in making their constrained choices can be an ethical influence as long as those influences are not in fact controlled by the practitioner (Simons 1982). Hence, much of Anne's efforts to influence Wilmer toward the regular taking of his medication came from assisting him in examining the costs and benefits of the medication in light of his own perceived goals.

Persuasion is most appropriate in work with nonvoluntary clients since it is a less intrusive method of influence with fewer ethical and legal concerns. Persuasion can also contribute to maintenance of changes by facilitating self-attribution. Practitioners and agencies disillusioned with the lack of staying power of forced compliance might explore the combination of persuasion with other compliance methods in promoting longer-lasting change. Finally, persuasion does not use up scarce resources and can increase as the practitioner becomes a more credible source of influence.

Persuasion cannot be the only or primary mode of influence with mandated clients, though it can play an important complementary role in enhancing attitude change and maintaining behavioral change. The effectiveness of persuasion also depends on the client's ability to manipulate and process information in order to make a decision informed by knowledge of potential costs and benefits. Hence, clients who have limited ability to process information may be less influenced by persuasive methods.

Compliance methods, including coercion and inducement, and persuasion methods have been presented along a continuum of intrusiveness into involuntary client choice ranging from coercion at the high end, inducement in the middle, and ethical persuasion at the low end. Since compliance methods often have short-term success in promoting behavioral change, their disadvantages in maintaining behavior or changing attitudes are often ignored. Rather than exploring less intrusive methods, agencies and practitioners often use "more of the same" compliance strategies by increasing their strength if they fail to reach their goals (Raynor 1978). When law violations and/or danger to self or others are involved, the practitioner may be ethically required to use coercive means. While inducement is a less intrusive method, circumstances in which it is not used to empower the client but rather to maintain dependence with powerless clients from oppressed groups were also discussed. Hence, efforts to use inducement in ways that empower rather than weaken clients must be emphasized. Finally, the chapter has advocated use of ethical persuasion as the primary form of influence with nonvoluntary clients and as an important supporting form of influence to enhance the possibility of self-attribution for mandated clients. The possibilities for use of unethical, coercive persuasion are many, however, as practitioners are pressured or tempted to withhold information about choices and create incomplete arguments for less preferable choices. The practitioner should use legal, ethical, and effective forms of both compliance and persuasion methods as situations arise, appropriate to each, and frequently simultaneous use of several forms of influence is appropriate.

Discussion Questions

1. Which assumptions do you and/or your program make about how behavior is changed?
2. Which assumptions do you and/or your program make about how attitudes are modified?
3. What is the practitioner's role in terms of modification of attitudes and behaviors in your agency?
4. What is the role of practitioner confrontation in your program and what is assumed about its effectiveness?
5. What is assumed about how clients change over time in your program?

6. What are the practitioner roles in your program as the clients change over time?
7. What is your view and that of your agency about using ethical means of persuasion?
8. Have you witnessed use of "hooking" or "low ball" persuasion methods that mislead a client into making a choice without full information of the consequences of the choice?
9. What are the implications for development of a trusting relationship when using less ethical means of persuasion?

Chapter 5

Assessing Initial Contacts
in Involuntary Transactions

Review of the legal, ethical, and effective framework with involuntary clients provides a basis for planning work with them. However, use of these principles often takes place in difficult flesh-and-blood encounters in which the practitioner feels attacked or irritated. Principles of intervention may be far from the practitioner's mind as he or she focuses on the immediate task of conducting an initial assessment. This chapter introduces deviance, resistance, reactance, and strategic self-presentation as four perspectives or alternative lenses to aid in "seeing" this interaction. The four perspectives are assessed according to how well they fit a transactional view, their empirical and theoretical bases, how parsimoniously they explain observable facts, and how well they contribute to proactive practitioner responses. Three case studies are provided as an aid in exploring these concepts.

Assessment with Involuntary Clients

Assessments are working explanations of persons, problems, and situations, and their dynamic interaction. They are developed to aid the client and practitioner in formulating a plan of action (Epstein and Brown 2002). Since assessments should aid the client and practitioner in formulating a plan of action, they must focus on key issues and their use rather than gathering facts for their own good. Guides for assessment often emphasize the synthesis of objective and subjective facts from a variety of sources such as background sheets, verbal reports, direct observation of nonverbal behavior and interaction, collateral information, use of psychological testing, and the personal experience of the practitioner (Hepworth et al. 2005). Such guides further recommend focus on the person, his or her coping capacity, strengths, role transitions, needs and resources, aspirations and opportunities, problem sequences of antecedents, behaviors, consequences, and also an analysis of impinging systems, which can be peer or work environments that contribute to difficulties (ibid.).

While guides have been developed for the assessment process with voluntary clients, no such guides have been available for involuntary clients (Specht and Specht 1986). Involuntary assessment differs in at least four major ways from voluntary assessment. First, in legally mandated transactions, the practitioner is required to assess the client's situation according to legal mandates and agency guidelines, whether or not the involuntary client sees this assessment as useful. Results of that assessment may include actions against the client's wishes. Second, there are often conflicting expectations about who has a problem and who wants help; an nonvoluntary client experiences formal and/or informal pressure since assessments are often done at the request of a third party to inform a plan *for* a nonvoluntary client. Such assessments frequently start off on the wrong foot with confused and conflicting expectations on both sides (Cingolani 1984). Influenced by these conflicting expectations, involuntary assessment often takes place in the "heat of battle" with high client and practitioner tension. This emotional intensity can create further problems because practitioners are often urged to note their subjective responses to client behavior as part of the assessment. Responses of involuntary clients at a point of conflicting expectations, perceived limitations on freedom from coercion or constraint, and high emotion may not be representative of their behavior in other settings and might best be seen as a sample of client behavior under pressure (Epstein and Brown 2002).

Assessment tools exist within a framework of gathering information to promote decision making. They vary in the extent to which would be clients are afforded the opportunity to tell their own story, participate in the assessment, and seek solutions (Iversen, Gergen, and Fairbanks 2005). In many situations, their behaviors are assessed for potential to take responsibility for actions while assessing denial and minimization as defensive maneuvers (Frost 2004; Kroner and Mills 2004; Henning, Jones, and Holdford 2005).

Elaborate assessments may be of little value if they do not engage the nonvoluntary client to remain in counseling. Similarly, required assessments with mandated clients may have little lasting value if plans are made *for* them without their commitment to implement the recommendations. Assessment formats are developing that seek to both present danger and protective factors and engage family members accounts of what has occurred and their participation in the development of solutions (Akamatsu 1998; Parton and O'Byrne 2000; Lohrbach and Sawyer 2004; Lohrbach et al. 2005). The challenge for assessment with involuntary clients is to both assess danger and risk and also engage potential clients in developing solutions.

This chapter presents four perspectives to aid in assessment with involuntary clients. We begin with a case vignette as the basis for examining the first perspective, social deviance.

> As a teen, Molly experienced considerable family conflict and she called a social service agency requesting placement outside of the home.* It is unusual for a child or adolescent to be the initiator of such a report. The child welfare agency made an assessment of abuse and neglect and determined that the strife between adolescent and family did not constitute abuse or neglect such that she was endangered and a case was not opened. Soon thereafter, Molly ran away from home. She was now placed out of the home in a variety of placements ranging from shelters to group homes.

Deviance as an Assessment Perspective

Deviance is commonly considered to be behavior that requires social agencies to take action (Erikson 1964). In this case, both child abuse and neglect and running away are considered deviant acts such that social service agencies are required to intervene to investigate. Involuntary clients are frequently labeled deviant. For example, Cingolani describes involuntary clients as "persons who must deal with a helping professional because they have behaved in ways annoying or troublesome to society" (Cingolani 1984:442) and deviants have been described as persons who "come to the agency coerced by state, community or family." These sources of pressure cover the range of mandated and nonvoluntary pressures described in chapter 1.

This view of deviance as behavior requiring the attention of social agencies is one of several definitions of deviance. This view has been described as an *individual pathology* definition because of its focus on abnormal behavior of individuals that should be corrected by social control agents and therapists (Kirk 1972). The causes of deviance in this view are typically sought in the

---

*A videotape in which Dr. Rooney interviews Molly Morgan (disguised name) about her history as a client of several involuntary systems is available from www.insight-media.com as *Work with Involuntary Clients: The Consumer's Perspective*. A full listing of videos is available in the appendix.

personal history of the deviant with relatively little attention to the social causes or the practitioner's role in detecting and labeling deviant status (Nooe 1980).

The individual pathology view may be prevalent in social control and helping agencies assigned to work with persons labeled deviant. An individual focus is compatible with the therapy training of counselors and the individual focus of service delivery efforts by many agencies. Following this view, it might be useful to have explored Molly's developmental history as well as the escalating family tensions in her household that precipitated her running away.

While the individual pathology view is compatible with the services offered by many practitioners and agencies, it also has major blind spots. According to Kirk, persons holding an individual pathology view of deviance are likely to approach clients "as if they suffer from a defective self, which leads them to come voluntarily to the agency; as if the contact with the agency and the contact with the [practitioner] is always benign and as if the relationship exists in a social vacuum" (Kirk 1972:23). As Molly put it in a videotaped interview many years after the running away incident, "I was seen as the problem." The social service system focused on the running away event and her as the problem. The individual pathology view may lead to errors in ignoring nonvoluntary pressures, including very real dangers to the freedom of the persons labeled deviant, and, finally, may overemphasize individual causes of deviance while underemphasizing social or interactional causes.

There are several alternative perspectives on deviance that can supplement the strengths and correct for some of the blind spots in the individual pathology view. The *structural* model of deviance suggests that while goals of wealth, power, and status may be common across a society, access to opportunities and resources needed to reach those goals is often impeded for lower socioeconomic segments of the society (Merton 1980). Deviants may be seen in this view as frustrated in their attempts to use legitimate means to reach social goals and therefore are driven rather than attracted to illegitimate means. The structural model sensitizes us to the role of access to resources and opportunities as a factor in creating circumstances that lead to deviance. Following this view, we might hypothesize that more involuntary and deviant clients are *created* in times of economic hardship and lack of resources, should access to societal goals by legitimate means be blocked. Following a structural view, it would be considered significant that Molly as a teenaged female runaway had less access to resources and support than did her family. Fewer societal resources were expended on protecting adolescents who presumably are more able to protect themselves physically than more vulnerable children are.

The structural approach suggests society-wide prevention efforts to distribute resources and opportunities such that the conditions leading to deviance are reduced. The structural view has its own blind spots because of inattention to individual choice and action. Not all individuals in similarly deprived conditions use deviant means. Nor does the structural view explain the behavior of white-collar criminals such as inside-information stock traders who would appear to have high access to societal rewards (Thio 1978).

The *social labeling* perspective is particularly relevant for analysis of the involuntary transaction. In this perspective, no behavior is considered inherently deviant. Society is seen as *creating* deviance by setting rules that define it. These definitions have considerable cultural variation in the behavior defined as abnormal with, for example, subcultural differences in beliefs about the appropriateness of physical violence in child discipline (Robin and Spires 1983). Consequently, from the social labeling perspective, a deviant is one to whom the label has been successfully applied and deviant behavior is behavior people so label (Becker 1963). The response of society may interact with the response of the person labeled deviant to create and maintain a deviant role.

The social labeling perspective shares a blind spot with the structural view in ignoring the choice to participate in the act labeled deviant. It is not necessary to take the position that social reaction *causes a* person to take on a deviant role to recognize that the practitioner and the agency can play an interactive role in contributing to a deviant identity. Roger Nooe suggests that the individual pathology and structural and social labeling views can be combined such that the blind spots of each can be reduced and proactive practice guidelines that focus on actions in the practitioner's control can result. The discussion below draws heavily on Nooe's analysis to present that integration and practice guidelines.

A key concept in the social labeling perspective is *primary deviance*, which is defined as acting to violate social norms without being observed by others and hence not labeled as deviant by them. The particular cause of the original deviant act is not specified and can be influenced by organic, psychological, and environmental causes (Nooe 1980). Persons committing the violation may be aware that their behavior is somewhat different from others, may or may not see the behavior as a problem, and may decide to seek help. At the stage of primary deviance, persons generally do not take on a deviant role or label themselves as deviant (figure 5.1).

For an example of primary deviance, we return to Molly. When she ran away from home as an adolescent, she saw herself as escaping from an untenable family situation after making appropriate efforts by asking for placement to remedy the situation. At a later point, she has a child, becomes seriously depressed and receives a psychiatric hospitalization. Over the next several years, Molly experienced several lengthy hospitalizations.

Figure 5.1   Integrative model of deviance

Individual Pathology Model
* focus on abnormal behavior of individuals to be corrected by therapy and rehabilitation
* tends to ignore structural, social reaction and labeling effects

Structural Model
* focus on restricted access to resources needed to achieve goals
* tends to ignore choice and rule breaking by more powerful persons

Social Labeling Model
* focus on social response contingencies in creating deviant role through labeling
* tends to ignore role of choice and blames the social labelers

Social labeling theory next focuses on *social reaction* to the primary deviant behavior, suggesting that rules for identifying deviant behavior are inconsistently applied with many intervening factors influencing labeling. For example, when, where, and by whom the deviant behavior was identified becomes important. Age, race, sex, social distance, power, and social status are among the factors influencing who will be identified as deviant and who will not. Evidence for the mitigating factor of these variables includes the fact that low-income minority clients are frequently overrepresented in criminal justice and other service juvenile institutions (Council on Crime and Justice 2006).

The social labeling perspective suggests that persons labeled deviant often respond to protect their identity, to avoid isolation and stigma. Included among the responses to deviant labeling are rationalizing, minimizing, or denying harm, overgeneralizing, dissembling, blaming others, discrediting the alleged victim, arbitrary interpretations, selective abstractions, and magnification (Sagarin 1975). These defensive response patterns have been identified as occurring with those labeled as deviant, ranging from teenaged delinquents to those prosecuted for insider stock trading. The defensive, alienated responses are often interpreted as further evidence of pathology and deviance rather than as a response partially generated by the labeling process. Research on persons with disabilities has shown that persons can respond to the stigma of the label and perceived discrimination with illicit drug use considered by them as a small compensation for suffering that stigma (Li and Moore 2001).

Defensive reactions by the person labeled deviant can then interact with the social response to create a vicious cycle that can reinforce the primary deviance and become *secondary deviance*: when a person labeled deviant responds to that labeling by acting to take on a deviant role. In 1993, I had the opportunity to interview Molly about her lengthy career as a client of several involuntary systems. She spoke about labeling in relation to a hospitalization ten years earlier.

MOLLY: My prognosis in 1983 was guarded and that's about as low as you can get. That's where you get put on the maintenance program . . . and that essentially means three square meals, a roof over your head.

ROONEY: And at the time how did that feel to you?

MOLLY: I think it felt pretty hopeless. They were telling me for the rest of my life someone is going to put a roof over my head and I'm not going anywhere and I believe I saw a therapist at that time, but I don't know why. If no one believed I was going anywhere, why see a therapist? But they just believed . . . that's the most anyone could expect out of me. I would live where someone would put me or feed me or whatever.

ROONEY: And you didn't have much hope for your own future then?

MOLLY: No, I didn't. A doctor told me that that was the prognosis and told me what it meant and I kind of lost all kind of hope that I was going to do anything, so I didn't really try. I just laid around in bed and did what's expected of a hopeless person I guess . . . nothing.

It would appear that Molly was describing a process similar to secondary deviance whereby she was reacting to the diagnostic label and what she understood it to mean. The transition to secondary deviance is not inevitable. It may be influenced by the role of human service practitioners and agencies who act to normalize and defuse labeling or to reinforce a stabilized deviant role. Practitioners may reinforce secondary deviance by discrediting the client's own explanations for the incidents, by excluding them from treatment planning, by confessing, and taking on a sick role while protesting such a label may be seen as further evidence of resistance and sickness.

How can practitioners and agencies assess individuals while reducing their contribution to labeling and secondary deviance? Agencies can act through alternative programs developed for diverting many first-time juvenile offenders from formal court processing. Practitioners can be sensitive to the *specific* contingencies surrounding events leading to identification of deviant activity. Finally, the practitioner can act preventively to alleviate conditions that led to the primary deviance. In this case, it is possible that more assertive exploration of family difficulties when Molly asked to be placed out of the home including exploration of kinship alternatives for alleviating family stress might have been helpful.

While the social labeling perspective is useful in exploring the impact of labeling and the reaction to it on behavior, it is no longer credible to assume that labeling alone is sufficient to produce behavior labeled as mentally ill (Gove 1970). That is, social labeling is not a sufficient explanation for what results in hospitalization, but it may delay progress if the client is not empowered to participate in recovery. Persons are often aware of deviant labeling and appear to strive to avoid such labels (Link 1987). For example, for many people it is less stigmatizing to describe one's behavior as having had a "nervous breakdown" rather than suffering from a mental illness (Gove 2004). Indeed voluntarism can often be considered as a more positive status rather than being legally involuntary. In the next section of the transcript, Molly emphasizes her voluntarism, appearing to wish to separate herself from the stigma of having a court order into psychiatric treatment.

ROONEY: Can you tell us something about your experiences in being hospitalized?

MOLLY: I have never been court ordered, there has never been any court action for me to be hospitalized but I have been in locked units. That's where everything your tableware, clothing and everything is locked up. The staff and doctors control your every move. You lose every move.

ROONEY: Tell us . . . you were not court ordered into that situation, so how did you come to be in it?

MOLLY: Most of the time I was in a locked unit to be self protected . . . so I could be protected from myself because that's why I ended up there.

ROONEY: Had you signed a release to enter the hospital?

MOLLY: I think I signed standard admission papers, consent to treatment papers. You don't sign specifically what they're going to do to you. You just sign a blank- or a standard-consent to treatment.

ROONEY: You're telling us that part of your placement was voluntary in that you thought you needed help and probably needed to be in a safe environment.

MOLLY: Right, right. I talked with my doctor, or in some cases, my doctor suggested it or my therapist suggested it, but it was voluntary and I walked in the door.

Resistance

Martin, nineteen, applied to become a resident of a supportive living community for homeless men and women. He had just been released from a hospital suffering from pneumonia and had been living on the streets before his hospital admission. Since Martin had been a resident twice before and had been expelled for fighting with other residents, his application was discussed heatedly at a staff meeting. Staff hesitated about readmitting him, describing Martin as hostile and resistant, a person who might abuse resources that others could use more productively. Staff finally recommended to the intake interviewer that Martin be admitted *if* he agreed to the following conditions: (1) no overnights away from the community for two months, (2) attendance to a GED class on time every day, (3) full participation in the program structure of the center, and (4) obtaining a mental health and chemical dependency assessment.

When the conditions were presented, Martin sat staring into space without speaking for several minutes, and then said: "I agree to all of it . . . but I don't like the no overnights. . . . But I have no choice if I want to move back here, do I?" The interviewer agreed with Martin's assessment but urged him to think about his decision for a day. Martin declined to wait, saying he would agree to the conditions. As Martin's alternative was living on the streets, he could be said to have made a coerced choice influenced by formal agency pressure to abide by the community rules.

In the weeks that followed, Martin followed the rules to the letter . . . but not the spirit. While he took no overnights, Martin stayed awake all night many nights *and* persuaded other residents to keep him company! After sleepless nights, he slept through GED classes that he attended every day and on time. Martin would also become ill or forget to arrange to get bus passes for his assessment appointments. Meanwhile, he continued to press for permission for overnights, saying he was "obeying the rules."

Many would consider Martin as not only engaging in deviant behavior but also demonstrating resistance. Evidence for this assessment might be Martin's varied, ingenious efforts to undercut the rules. In fact, while deviant labeling and involuntary status overlap, resistance and involuntary status are often considered synonymous (Nelsen 1975). This is understandable since the behaviors and attitudes often grouped under the resistant label are familiar in the responses of involuntary clients: provocation, intellectualization, projection, verbosity, seduction, withdrawal, passive compliance, martyrdom, flight from the scene, refusal to answer, lateness for appointments, and changing the subject (Gitterman 1983).

What do these varied behaviors and attitudes have in common? They may be considered resistance if we define resistance as client behavior that the practitioner considers inappropriate and not in line with the plans the practitioner has for the client (Turkat and Meyer 1982). This definition can be considered from the perspective of deviant labeling. I define *resistance as a label assigned by practitioners to clients who have not acted to the practitioner's satisfaction.* It is not typically applied by practitioners to their own behavior, their agency policies. Use of the term constitutes pejorative labeling; hence, it may have consequences for subsequent secondary deviance through reinforcing a resistant role.

Current usage of resistance differs greatly from the original meaning of the term in psychoanalytic theory. Resistance originally referred to the analytic patient's unconscious use of defenses when subjects threatening to the ego were uncovered (Fenichel 1945). Hence, in this original definition, resistance was considered normal and expectable, unlike the current view emphasizing abnormal behavior. Second, resistance was considered to be unconscious, hence not under the client's control, while current use includes conscious opposition to plans. Third, the original use implied that the practitioner's responsibility for control or reduction, while current uses emphasize client responsibility and blame. Finally, the original use assumed application to voluntary analytic patients who, at least consciously, agreed to the goals and methods of treatment while current use routinely applies to involuntary clients (Nelsen 1975). Consequently, since involuntary clients neither seek treatment nor agree to the means by which it is conducted, their opposition is a conscious refusal to participate, and hence resistance in the original sense should not be used to describe their behavior since they have not agreed to goals (Ewalt 1982).

What are the consequences of current usage of the term? On the one hand, describing a client as resistant provides a shorthand way of describing difficult, uncomfortable behavior in a way that often enlists support from colleagues. On the other hand, resistant labeling as one form of expressing practitioner discomfort becomes part of the client assessment and may form a stigmatizing label that will have repercussions far beyond the instance in which it is first applied. This form of client labeling locates the cause of disturbance within the client rather than examining the transaction with the agency or the worker (Ewalt 1982). Having labeled the client as resistant, practitioners often feel discouraged and may project this helplessness onto the client. Instead of leading to positive steps, this use of the term absolves practitioners and their settings from responsibility for reducing the tension in the transaction and contributes to a self-fulfilling prophecy of failure. By locating the tension in the client, the question "resistant to what?" to guide intervention plans is not answered (Reid 1982).

There are several alternatives to the use of resistance as a form of deviant labeling. First, the term could be dropped from parlance as an undefined, pejorative term. The possibility of banning word usage among practitioners is limited, however, and such elimination might lead to "term substitution" to find another way to express practitioner exasperation for lack of compliance. Second, the term could be reserved for use in its original sense by psychoanalysts describing a phenomenon occurring in their particular form of influence. The advantage of such a move would be to reduce the pejorative connotations and not misapply to circumstances beyond the original meaning. This solution carries some of the problems of the first, however, as there is little way to monitor inappropriate usage. Third, the term could be specified and studied more objectively and operationally defined with focus on specific behaviors and influences rather than blame (Mahalik 1994).

Fourth, the term could be reframed and used in a transactional, normalizing context. Carel Germain suggests that there may be hope for resistance as a concept if it is applied to the *whole* transaction rather than to the internal processes of the client alone. She suggests that resistance should be considered *a natural* reaction to unwanted change that occurs to clients, practitioners, and their agencies (Germain 1982). Following this perspective, sources of unwanted change would be explored including the very real possibility that the involuntary client response stems at least in part from pressures brought by the practitioner or agency. Practitioners would be alerted to recognize their discomfort with involuntary client opposition without labeling it as the client's internal problem. Practitioners might then not only consider client hesitation as normal but might also acknowledge their own hesitance to see a potentially hostile client as exhibiting normal resistance.

This expanded usage of the term could also be applied to agencies and other parties to the transaction. Agency resistance can be identified when agencies set up unnecessary client hurdles and when they hesitate to change service hours to make them more convenient to clients.

Reframing resistance is unlikely to occur on a widespread basis unless there is a shift in focus from explaining behavior as primarily internally motivated to examining its transactional aspects. Should a reframing approach not be adopted, we return to a social labeling definition of resistance as applied to client responses when practitioners are dissatisfied with less than full compliance. Application of that label has consequences, however, for reinforcing a secondary deviant role as "resistant client."

Most theories of helping acknowledge that some form of opposition often occurs in treatment whether as an enduring client oppositional characteristic or as a transactional phenomenon that occurs during sessions (Beutler et al.

1996, 2001). However it is described, there is general agreement that its presence does not bode well for productive outcomes. Client hesitation to try out suggestions and explore new beliefs might better be reframed as an expectable ambivalence about making change. That is, an ambivalence in which the client is caught between a desire to change and fearfulness or beliefs that change is inappropriate or not possible should be normalized (Arkowitz 1996; Miller and Rollnick 2002).

In the interview with Molly after discussing her long period of hospitalization, we discussed events in her life after leaving the hospital.

ROONEY: Something changed? What has occurred since then?

MOLLY: It was about 6 years being hopeless and being on maintenance and doing essentially nothing. I was in a residential program and they had just started the community support and part of the program was that I was in a home that had outside programming and they told me after 6 years I had to do something 10 hours . . . I didn't think I could do it. I entered what is now called a kind of a community support day program kind of a thing.

ROONEY: So you were scared that you couldn't do it?

MOLLY: I was terrified! I was terrified to do it. I was scared I would somehow lose the house I was living in, if you can call it that, it was a group home. I was terrified I would lose that house because it was a condition that I do something if I would live there. In a way I was terrified that I could do it, too.

ROONEY: Because? What would that tell you, that you could do it?

MOLLY: Um, it would just . . . It scared me because it would create so much confusion. After so many years of being told I would go nowhere by people that were supposed to know what they were doing, or saying, it would just create too much confusion. If I could do something ten hours a week, that would mean all these people all these six years were wrong.

ROONEY: That they made a mistake.

MOLLY: They had made a mistake.

Molly describes a state of ambivalence, caught between desires to change and fear of changes. Rather than describe such as state as resistance, the motivational interviewing concept of contemplation captures this ambivalence more positively. That is, contemplation (Di Clemente and Velasquez 2002) captures the idea of a mental state in which a person is considering change but is not ready to make a commitment to action.

Other behaviors often grouped under the term resistance may in fact be quite different from one another. For example, having no desire to change, as is often the case with the involuntary client, can be different from not knowing how to change. Similarly, a negative reaction to pressure from others or a referral source may be more focused on that pressure than it it is to the actual behavior. Finally, there may be a negative response to the form of treatment or the helper but not about the focus of the change effort. Each of these can be experienced as contrary to desired outcomes by a practitioner but can functionally indicate quite different phenomena (Arkowitz 1996).

Finally, the psychological literature has dealt almost exclusively with resistance as a negative set of behaviors that a practitioner strives to overcome. A strikingly different perspective is one that describes some behavior often labeled resistant to be indicative of coping and surviving an oppressive environment (Robinson and Davis-Kennington 2002). For example, having a negative attitude about the potential for change, being inclined to grasp onto quick relief to escape chronic problems, and expressing an external locus of control in the sense of a belief that events control you more than you control events can all be seen as ways people cope with a hostile, unsupportive environment. That is, this view validates that it is not just "all in the head" of the involuntary, resistant client, but rather possibly in part a natural response to an unsupportive environment.

Reactance Theory

The experienced practitioner knows that by whatever name it is called, opposition from involuntary clients frequently occurs and that opposition is uncomfortable for the practitioner. While one might admire the ingenuity of Martin's efforts to bend the rules, one might also wish to wring his neck. Concepts are needed that describe responses to involuntary situations under the pressure of coerced and constrained choices. These concepts need to acknowledge practitioner discomfort while moving beyond blaming the client to suggest positive resolutions to expectable tension. Reactance theory provides an empirically based description of the behavior of persons in pressured situations that can serve as one major source.

I often introduce reactance theory in classes and workshops with the following exercise. Think about a situation in which you have been forced to do something against your will. Now, write down your thoughts, feelings, and actions in that situation as you remember them.

What do practitioners and students report? The most frequent thoughts about the coerced situations are: "Why me?" "I don't deserve this." "How can I get out of this?" "What are my rights?" "Can I appeal to a higher authority?" "This isn't fair." The feelings most frequently reported are: "I felt powerless . . . angry . . . frustrated . . . vengeful . . . confused . . . self-doubting." The most frequent actions reported are: "I did what was required *but* I sabotaged the requirement." "I complied verbally, but didn't follow through." "I did just enough to get by." "I delayed, procrastinated." "I went along passively, without sharing my true feelings." "I complained bitterly." "I talked to others and tried to get them to rebel." "I went along and tried to make the best of it." "I did what I wanted within their boundaries." "I took out my anger on someone outside the situation." "I refused to do it and took the consequences."

After this exercise, practitioners and students are often struck with how much negative thinking, feeling, and half-hearted compliance, and how little "positive experience with authority" is reported. They also note how similar their responses are to involuntary clients. I do not consider their responses to be unusual because reactance theory has led me to consider that responses to pressured situations may be more normal, predictable, and nonpathological than is often thought.

Reactance theory assumes that we each have behaviors that we are free to exercise (Brehm et al. 1966). Should some of these free behaviors be threatened or eliminated, the theory suggests that a person will experience *reactance*. Reactance is often expressed as one or more of five different direct or indirect response patterns designed to regain those freedoms (Brehm 1976).

1. Direct efforts are those in which the person attempts to recapture the freedom directly in spite of the consequences. We see this effort to restore freedom directly in Martin's brief attempt to negotiate overnight privileges.

2. As many freedoms cannot be restored directly, efforts may be indirect. For example, a person may try to restore freedom *by implication* through violation of another of the same class of behavior: "finding a loophole" or breaking a norm without technically violating the rules. Martin appeared to be a master at the "loophole" strategy. While he followed rules about overnights to the letter, he undercut the spirit and purpose of the rules by staying up all night and sleeping in class. This loophole pattern was also frequently reflected in practitioner responses such as: "I did what was required but I sabotaged the requirement." When practitioners use this strategy, they may consider it clever. When clients use it, practitioners may consider it less clever and label it passive–aggressive.

3. Another form of indirect restoration occurs when reactance is reduced by observing another person attempt to restore their freedom or attempt to incite others to perform forbidden behaviors. Martin may have reduced his reactance by convincing fellow residents to bend the unwritten rules about getting adequate rest; their reactance may have been reduced by watching Martin's antics.

4. If a person is blocked from expressing their reactance either directly or indirectly such that they have to "sit" on their reactance, their desire for the forbidden behavior increases (Brehm 1976). Readers who have given up an

addictive habit such as smoking can attest to a rise in the attraction of the prohibited behavior. Martin's preoccupation with overnights may be explained by this pattern. The preoccupation ended when he was given permission to take them: yet he rarely used the privilege after it was earned!

5. Reactance may also be expressed in the form of hostility or aggression toward the source of the threat, even when it is unlikely to restore freedom. The practitioner response that "I complained bitterly" might fit this pattern. Reactance research suggests that adolescents may be more likely to use this than their elders.

The five reactance patterns are familiar and sound like many of the behaviors grouped under the pejorative definition of resistance. Reactance theory, however, is similar to the reframed definition of resistance in describing responses to unwanted change in a normalizing fashion. It goes beyond the reframed view of resistance to provide a base of theory and empirical study that helps predict when reactance will occur and how it might be reduced.

Whether reactance is likely to occur and to what extent can be predicted by five factors. First, a person must have expected that they had the freedom to begin with and felt competent to exercise that freedom. Reactance occurs in relation to threats to free behavior. In the videotaped interview with Molly Morgan, she describes her response to the institutionalized living environment.

ROONEY: So among the things you found there, went along with, what I call the package deal of being in the safe environment was that you were in a locked ward. What were other things you found?

MOLLY: Well my freedom was taken away from me . . . even what to do with my time. At one hospital with adults, we had nap time. Everyone had to go in these small little rooms for a certain amount of time.

ROONEY: How did that make you feel?

MOLLY: It made me feel angry. What if I don't want to nap, or I don't feel tired? There wasn't a choice. You just had to do it as part of being a patient.

Molly is describing the freedom to decide whether you wanted to take a nap or not as an expected freedom as an adult. Over time, Molly's reactance to events such as required nap time diminished. A second factor is that repeated efforts to restore freedom that do not succeed may lead to learned helplessness. That is, a person may learn not to try in response to uncontrollable outcomes (Wortman and Brehm 1975). Earlier in the discussion about secondary deviance, Molly was quoted as saying:

I think it felt pretty hopeless. They were telling me for the rest of my life someone is going to put a roof over my head and I'm not going anywhere and I believe I saw a therapist at that time, but I don't know why. If no one believed I was going anywhere, why see a therapist? But they just believed that until my doctor or whatever . . . that's the most anyone could expect out of me. I would live where someone would put me or feed me or whatever. . . . A doctor told me that that was the prognosis and told me what it meant and I kind of lost all kind of hope that I was going to do anything, so I didn't really try. I just laid around in bed and did what's expected of a hopeless person I guess . . . nothing.

The first response to a loss of control is an attempt to reassert control. If those efforts are not successful over a period of time, efforts to reassert control are curtailed (Wortman and Brehm 1975). Such learned helplessness appears to be stimulated in a variety of environments in which such efforts to assert oneself are unlikely to succeed. For example, a study of unemployed persons compared the responses of chronically unemployed to more recently unemployed persons in their attempts to solve a difficult puzzle. The chronically unemployed were less likely to persist with the puzzle and experienced physiological changes associated with arousal while the more recently unemployed continued to work for a longer time on the puzzle (Baum, Fleming, and Reddy 1986).

Third, reactance occurs in relation to the importance or unique value of threatened behaviors to fulfill needs. If valued freedoms can be maintained with means still available, then the threatened freedom may not have unique value. It is not unusual for child welfare workers to be working with a female single parent who is attached to a male who is considered to represent a risk for her and/or her children. Efforts to persuade her to shed or loosen ties to the male often act to raise reactance and reinforce how important he is to her. It he finds her attractive, provides adult company, and assists with children, these factors may eclipse his deficits in her eyes. Should he represent a risk to her and her children, it is important to acknowledge the attributes he represents for her as well as those risks. She might be helped to consider how else she could get her and her children's needs met should she choose to distance herself from him.

Fourth, reactance will be high if a person loses even a few freedoms should those freedoms be one of few that the person has left. Reactance occurs in relation to the *proportion* of freedoms threatened or eliminated. If the number of choices is small, removing any one will cause considerable reactance (Brehm et al. 1966). Martin's strong response to the withdrawal of freedom to have overnights might be explained by overnights being one of few valued freedoms left to him. Group home staff members have mentioned that withdrawal of telephone privileges is perceived as a very severe penalty by group home residents. This may be explainable in terms of the limited number of free behaviors available.

Fifth, reactance is higher if there is an implied threat to other freedoms beyond ones immediately threatened. For example, overnights may symbolize a continuation of a private social life for Martin, a connection with friends, and threat to the overnights may stimulate reactance more because of the implied threat to other freedoms than for the loss itself.

These factors then help predict whether reactance might occur and how strong it will be. Can reactance then be predicted primarily through situational variables? What about individual differences? Martin appeared to experience every kind of reactance. Could some persons experience more reactance than others? While reactance theory comes from a social psychology tradition that does not emphasize individual differences, there are indications that some individuals are more likely to experience reactance than others. Reactance has been studied as an individual variable that is stable over time and associated with behaviors that are not promising for the process and outcome of psychotherapy (Dowd, Milne, and Wise 1991). For example, Dowd has developed a Therapeutic Reactance Scale (TRS) that measures reactance as a relatively enduring characteristic across situations. Those high on the scale also scored high on dominance, autonomy, aggressiveness, and minimal concern for impressions on others. They were also more likely to be dominant, quick to take offense, and frequently in conflict with authority. Finally, persons scoring high on the TRS were relatively careless of obligations, intolerant of beliefs, inclined to resist rules, and likely to express strong emotions (Dowd et al. 1994). In a study in which therapists rated improvement in functioning and compliance with medication, reactance was negatively associated with global improvement and positively associated with premature termination (Seibel and Dowd 1999).

Reactance theory has many practice implications including strategies designed to reduce it and others to increase it or take advantage of the fact that it is high. Sharon Brehm describes many ways that reactance can be reduced. First, a client can be aided in directly restoring his or her own freedom (Brehm 1976). This can be done by avoiding giving directives to the client, contracting to restore freedom, and clarifying available choices. When the intake worker at the homeless community center suggested that Martin think it over before deciding whether to enter the program, this might have reduced reactance.

Second, attributing behavior to the situation rather than the person reduces reactance. If Molly's guarded prognosis had been interpreted to her as a current situational assessment rather than a permanent judgment of her capacities, hope for possible improvement might have been stimulated. Third, emphasizing the freedoms still retained should avoid reactance. If Molly's nap time had been presented as a quiet time in which she could choose to sleep, read, or do whatever she wished quietly, she might not have experienced reactance. Fourth, avoiding dependency implications and avoiding linkage to other behaviors reduces reactance. Consequently, reactance is reduced when behaviors to be changed are highly specific rather than broad. For example, a directive to Robert (the delinquent young man from chapter 1) that he needs to "find a new peer group" is a global requirement that might be predicted to cause high reactance since it means the loss of much freedom. If this requirement were modified to "stay away from James and John," while free to maintain friendships with others, reactance might be reduced. Hence, the implied threat to other freedoms is reduced by separating requirements from what remains free. The staff may have reduced Martin's reactance by contracting with him to restore his freedom to take overnights and emphasizing the choices he could make within constraints, that is, by emphasizing specific rather than global changes such as "attending and participating in class daily" rather than "earning your GED."

Fifth, reactance can also be reduced by minimizing the strength of persuasion efforts. Providing more than one alternative should be considered since one-sided persuasion tends to increase reactance. When Molly experienced deinstitutionalization through a release to live in the community, she reported at first that she was fearful that she would fail in the requirement that she spend ten hours per week in outside programming and jeopardize her community living arrangement. She found, however, that there were many ways that she could fill those ten hours.

ROONEY: What happened then, when you went out, and did those ten hours?
MOLLY: I was scared for maybe a week. I got out and went out to a place called Vale Place and I loved it. I could be around people. I could help by writing a newsletter, or typing on the typewriter, and I learned I could do something. So I was really only scared for about a week. And I went from ten hours a week to almost ten hours a day.

The preceding example shows how clients may feel empowered through expanding choices. Clients may be more willing to try new behaviors if the practitioner does not overemphasize them. Greater pressure may be counterproductive and produce a boomerang effect. For example, in studies of reactance related to efforts to influence health choices, persuasive efforts that stimulated too much fear ran the risk of a boomerang effect of increased anxiety (Shoham-Salomon 1989).

Strategies are also available to *increase* reactance, or to take advantage of the fact that reactance is high. Reactance can be increased by heightening the importance of the free behavior and implying or stating threats to future freedoms (Brehm and Smith 1986). Stating the requirement of ten hours of outside programming as a condition for living in the community facility stimulated reactance in Molly. Practitioners working with involuntary clients in mandated situations may be forced by the responsibilities of their position to assess risks, danger, and law violations in such a way that reactance is likely to be heightened. Indeed "scared straight" educational programs for troubled youth were designed in part to increase reactance by making future losses of freedom due to incarceration evident.

When reactance is high, it has been suggested that defiance-based paradoxes may be appropriate. Such a paradox means that one prescribes *the opposite* of what is desired (Rohrbaugh et al. 1981). The strategy would suggest that if reactance is high such that suggestions are not likely to be followed, a boomerang effect is to be expected, then one might take advantage of this by making a prescription that you don't want or expect to be followed. Studies with students with problems such as procrastination and insomnia found that those with high reactance responded better to paradoxical instructions than they did to straightforward directive advice in resolving the issue (Shoham-Saloman, 1989). For example, directives to make a record of the procrastination or insomnia without trying to change it actually resulted in more successful efforts to change the behavior than straightforward advice for those with high reactance (ibid.). Other studies have been less supportive of the positive effect of defiance-based paradoxes with reactant persons (Dowd et al. 1988).

Shoham and Rohrbaugh have studied the interaction of couples in which one partner had a drinking problem and the spouse made persistent efforts to persuade the partner to quit. Well-intentioned efforts to resolve problems sometimes make them worse. Persisting in those efforts despite their failure has been called an ironic process (Shoham and Rohrbaugh 1997; Wegner 1997; Rohrbaugh and Shoham 2001). For example, a spouse may use nagging to influence a partner to reduce harmful drinking. If, however, the nagging itself produces a boomerang effect of increasing attraction for drinking, then it has become an ironic process (Rohrbaugh and Shoham 2001). Reducing the demand for change and emphasizing freedom of choice was more successful in reducing spousal drinking (Rohrbaugh 1999). Similarly, clients high in reactance have been shown to be more likely to reduce their smoking after muted advice while those with less reactance could tolerate more advice and effectively reduce smoking (Graybar et al. 1989). Practitioners working with involuntary clients should readily see the dangers of ironic processes in their work. They are called on to enforce laws and alert clients to dangers. The monitoring of the problem and attention to it may act, ironically, to reinforce it (Wegner 1997). Awareness of such a process in work with involuntary clients is paralleled in solution-focused methods in focusing attention on goals rather than on problems (De Jong and Berg 2001).

Assessment of the Value of Reactance Theory to
Work with Involuntary Clients

Reactance theory makes a major contribution to understanding work with involuntary clients from a transactional perspective. It makes a very good fit with the three-dimensional version of involuntary client status proposed in chapter 1. It suggests that pressures generating reactance can be personal or in response to direct coercion (like coerced choice), impersonal or constraining barriers that make engaging in a behavior more difficult or impossible (like constrained choice), or even self-imposed. Reactance theory helps unlock the puzzle of how some persons can lose many freedoms yet not seem very involuntary, while others may lose what appears to be insignificant freedom and yet experience a great deal of reactance. As Sharon Brehm notes: "Thus what may look to the observer like a mild threat directed at what appears to be an insignificant freedom on other grounds, such as importance or proportion of freedoms threatened, may to the person appear to be a threat of considerable magnitude, especially when other freedoms are implicated" (Brehm 1976:19). Reactance theory appears to be a very promising source of hypotheses for intervention and research with involuntary clients. Debate continues in psychology about the extent to which reactance occurs as a response to threatening situations as opposed to existing as a continuing personality characteristic across situations (Shoham 1989). However, its pertinence in situations in which choices are limited is clear. Work with involuntary clients may often bring together both conditions for reactance. Sharon Brehm suggests that "the more people who pose threats to a person's freedom and the more situations in which such threats occur, the more generalized and diffuse a person's anger may be" (Brehm 1976:21). That is, many involuntary clients in settings such as corrections and domestic violence treatment may be likely to score high on instruments such as the Therapeutic Reactance Scale such that reactance across situations may be predicted (Chovanec 1995). On the other hand, such settings are likely to stimulate reactance in many recipients of service whether or not they are likely to experience reactance in other settings. Consequently, increased attention to reactance theory in relation to involuntary populations, problems, and settings is in order. In fact, failure to attend to the promise of reactance theory in such circumstances may approximate an ironic process whereby methods are repeatedly used with involuntary clients that are intended to reduce the problem but may result instead in heightened reactance and aggravation of the problems.

Strategic Self-Presentation

Clients are often urged to be absolutely candid to get the most benefit from treatment. In fact, there is evidence that suggests that clients often attempt to put their situation in the best light by selective reporting so that the therapist/ expert will look favorably on them. Meanwhile therapists may not be entirely candid, for example, in sharing their clinical diagnosis for fear that the client might think less well of them (Kelly 2000). *Strategic self-presentation* refers to efforts to manage the impressions others have of us in order to better reach our goals (Friedlander and Schwartz 1985). Self-presentation efforts are most likely when the stakes are high. We introduce our consideration of this concept with a third case study.

> Irv and Joan were originally voluntary clients in the sense that there was no external pressure for them to get a divorce. As a precondition for granting the divorce, they were court-ordered to participate in mediation about visitation and custody for their two children, ages four and five. Should mediation fail, the court would appoint a professional to make a custody recommendation. Both Irv and Joan were hesitant about court-ordered mediation and had even more reservations when they were assigned to a mediator who was a social work student in a field placement. While both wanted the divorce, the court-ordered mediation and assignment to the student mediator came as a less desirable part of a "package deal." Irv and Joan can be considered to have chosen participation in mediation as a constrained choice from a formal pressure source.
>
> Joan, as the primary care provider, was concerned about the children's safety when they were with Irv since he had unsuccessfully completed alcoholism inpatient treatment twice, did not want to return for more treatment, and did not see drinking as a problem affecting custody. Meanwhile, Irv insisted on joint legal custody with primary physical custody remaining with Joan. Joan said that she would consider joint custody only if Irv would agree *to not drink* before or during visits.

The student mediator's supervisor felt that Irv's alcoholism would prevent him from keeping his promise not to drink. Hence, she recommended to the student that no mediation be attempted until Irv agreed to complete chemical dependency treatment once again. The student mediator, however, wanted to explore mediation with stipulated conditions about drinking and later wrote: "The more I was told to discontinue working with this couple, the more attractive the other alternatives became." The student mediator persisted in the negotiation of an agreement in which Irv would lose joint legal custody if he violated the agreement about drinking before or during visits and attorneys for both parents supported this recommendation.

The student mediator wrote later that during the sessions "Irv seemed to readily accept what I said, agree with my advice, observations, and interpretations. If he didn't agree, he avoided the issue or changed the subject. Perhaps this influenced my desire to work with them."

Irv's behavior may strike us as less than candid. Just as the student mediator and other practitioners may try to create a particular impression such as empathy, competence, and fairness, involuntary clients may present selected parts of themselves in order to achieve particular goals, as in this case in which visitation of children and a possible return to chemical dependency treatment are the goals. Irv might have chosen to tell his wife and student mediator that he has no problems with alcohol, that they should mind their own business, or that he is entitled to visitation. While this response might have been candid, it might also have prevented Irv from reaching his goal of regular visitation. Irv's quick agreement with the mediator's advice, on the other hand, influenced the mediator's willingness to work with the couple.

The six self-presentation strategies include ingratiation, intimidation, facework, supplication, self-promotion, and exemplification. Irv may have used *ingratiation,* which refers to attempts to make oneself more attractive in order to influence a person in power to act favorably (Jones 1964). Ingratiation usually takes the form of flattery, public agreement with the opinions of the other despite possibly conflicting private views, overemphasizing one's own positive traits, and deemphasizing the negative. Ingratiation efforts are covert, since their discovery might interfere with the goal of a better impression.

Efforts to ingratiate are more likely to occur when one is in a dependent position and the stakes are high, when there are no onlookers who might spot the insincerity of the effort, and when the actors feel the circumstances of their dependency are unfair (ibid.). In this case, Irv's efforts might have been spotted as ingratiating by Joan. She may have chosen not to expose the ingratiation because she shared the goal of receiving mediation. There are also indications that ingratiation may be rewarded if a person in power is *simultaneously* being threatened by others in a similar lower power position (Jones and Pittman 1982). For instance, other more compliant, ingratiating residents of the homeless community might have indirectly benefited from the contrast to Martin's challenging behavior.

The student mediator noted after the case that "it took me awhile to figure out that I was not that good at my job but that he was just good at letting me think I was. Perhaps, without realizing it, his behavior influenced my decision to work with these clients and not follow the conventional treatment of chemical dependency in mediation." Are there some persons who are more susceptible to ingratiation than others? Higher-power persons who believe in cooperation, understanding, and cohesion with the lower-power person and have high self-esteem, may be *more* susceptible to ingratiation than others without these views and with lower self-esteem.

Not all clients or practitioners in involuntary situations ingratiate. *Intimidation is* often used to influence the target person by creating a fearful impression. Threats may be direct, or messages may be given such as "I can't tolerate stress" or "I am not responsible for what I do if I get angry." Intimidation is often used in involuntary situations when the intimidator has resources to which the target does not have access, when the target cannot easily retaliate, and when the intimidator is willing to forgo good will (Jones and Pittman 1982). Consequently, intimidation may be attractive to the practitioner. There are many practice situations, however, in which involuntary clients appear to use intimidation when they do not have resources and the practitioner can retaliate. Such strategies may be overlearned and inappropriately generalized from other situations in which they were successful.

A third strategy is *supplication,* in which clients point out their own negative characteristics, advertise their dependency and inability to cope, and throw themselves at the mercy of the higher-power person in an effort to acquire sympathy and support. Supplication is most likely to be used in crises, when the higher-power person controls key rewards and can use that power arbitrarily. Supplication may be costly to the self-esteem of the person using it and may not succeed with persons who do not recognize a responsibility to help the defenseless (Jones and Pittman 1982).

A fourth strategy common in involuntary situations is *facework* in which a lower-power person, anticipating blame from a higher-power person, may deny the charge, justify his or her actions, or selectively confess to particular problems in order to diffuse the impact of anticipated negative feedback.

Self-promotion is similar to ingratiation in emphasizing one's best qualities with the focus, however, on creating an impression of competence rather than liking. Self-promotion may be more likely in situations in which there are conflicting claims about competence. Finally, *exemplification* strategies refer to efforts to convey an impression of integrity and moral worthiness. Practitioners may be inclined to self-promote with clients in order to create an impression of competence and to use exemplification to point out one's best qualities (Friedlander and Schwartz 1985). Indeed most of us have probably utilized self-promotion and exemplification in job interviews when asked, for instance, to describe our weaknesses and responded with an admission that perhaps we work too hard and take the job home with us.

Impression management theorists suggest that these strategies may be used selectively, simultaneously, or not at all. They may not be used when a person is very involved with the task at hand and when the person is particularly motivated to be candid. Strategies are stimulated by desires to increase power. Two or more strategies may be used simultaneously such as ingratiation, self-promotion, and supplication. Use of particular strategies may be influenced by personality variables and may be fairly consistent across situations.

Strategic self-presentation is particularly pertinent for older adults in our society. Specifically, many feel that they must present themselves as competent, self-reliant, and fitting social norm or they may risk losing independence (Martin, Leary, and Rejeski 2000). Meanwhile other elders may exaggerate their complaints with apparent hypochondriasis in order to have their complaints taken seriously. They want to avoid the consequences of being seen as old and less competent. Self-presentation is often difficult to maintain in pressured situations (Vohs, Baumeister, and Ciarocco 2005).

While the strategic self-presentation strategies ring true with the responses of many involuntary clients, there is once again danger of creating new labels for "the ingratiator" and "the intimidator." Self-presentation strategies can offer normalizing explanations for irritating behavior that has often been labeled as a personality deficit rather than a situational response. Clarifying the realities of power, including how to regain lost power, may go a long way toward reducing their use.

This chapter has explored the assessment of initial interactions between involuntary clients and practitioners, suggesting that involuntary client behavior in first contacts may be a sample of behavior under high stress or response to authority. Consequently, efforts to generalize from those responses to behavior outside the assessment situation are of questionable value. Explanations of such initial session behavior that focus on internal causes have been overemphasized, while explanations focusing on transactional perspectives have been underemphasized.

Four such transactional perspectives have been presented in an effort to augment and correct for some of the blinders of the individual pathology focus. Social labeling theory has provided insights into the process of identifying persons who will be labeled deviant and the role the practitioner and agency responses may have in rewarding and maintaining that deviance. Describing involuntary clients as resistant is a frequent source of deviant labeling that might be reduced by reframing resistance to refer to normal responses to unwanted pressures to change that may occur to clients, practitioners, and agencies. Reactance theory concepts have been presented as rich sources of hypotheses in predicting when these oppositional responses may occur and specific strategies to reduce reactance have been described. Self-presentation strategies used by practitioners and clients have been explored for insights into behavior involving differences of power.

These perspectives have suggested proactive guidelines for increasing sensitivity to a transactional perspective:

1. Practitioners can be aware of their own settings and their own use of power as factors influencing the involuntary transaction.
2. Practitioners can be more aware of client responses in the involuntary transaction as explainable in part by the circumstances of the transaction and not necessarily as pathology or labeled as resistance. Normalizing explanations for client oppositional behavior can be used including responses to deviant labeling, reactance responses, and efforts to manage impressions.
3. Practitioners can reduce deviant labeling by sticking to the facts and the objective consequences of behavior.
4. Practitioners can reduce reactance and efforts to manage impressions by clarifying the requirements of the situation, specifying the limits to that power, specifying changes needed to regain freedom, emphasizing choices, and pointing out remaining free behaviors.

Discussion Questions

1. How is the term resistance used in your work setting? What are the implications for practice of its use?
2. What are the implications for deviant labeling and secondary deviance in the use of diagnostic and administrative categories for assessing clients in your setting?
3. What are the implications of expectations that both clients and practitioners might be expected to be less than fully candid with one another but rather to present themselves in the best light?
4. What is the value of viewing reactance as in part a situational variable? What are the implications of high ratings on reactance scales of many clients in your setting?
5. What are the implications for use of paradoxes or prescribing the symptom with reactant involuntary clients? For example, would you agree with a truant adolescent that attendance is out of his or her control?

Practice Strategies for Work
with Involuntary Clients

While part 1 has provided a conceptual basis and principles for legal, ethical, and effective work with involuntary clients, part 2 transforms these principles into concrete guidelines for practice through frequent use of transcripts of interactions between involuntary clients and practitioners. Chapters 6 through 9 present guidelines for mandated and nonvoluntary contact with individual clients. Chapter 6 presents initial phase strategies for socialization, negotiation, and contracting. Chapter 7 then provides ways to formalize contracts and develop initial action plans as well as guidelines for middle-phase work and termination. Involuntary contacts that begin in family or group settings are discussed in chapters 8 and 9.

Initial Phase Work with Individual
Involuntary Clients

Dora, twenty-nine, had a serious and persistent mental illness. While she had always lived with her parents, she now wished to leave home and move to a public housing project. The housing staff was requiring, however, that Dora either complete an independent skills program or live in a group home for three months before they would agree to let her live in their project. At her next meeting with the county social service case manager, the following transpired.

PRACTITIONER: Last month when we met with public housing, Dora, they suggested that before they could admit you, you would either have to live in a group home for three months.

DORA: No, I don't want to live in a group home.

PRACTITIONER: That was definitely an option you didn't want. The other option was to have somebody from the skills program work with you in your parents' house on independent living skills as a way of proving to them that you could make it in their apartment program. It's about time for me to make that referral since that is the plan that you agreed on. I'd like your okay to do that.

DORA: I know I agreed to work with skills, but after thinking about it these last few weeks, don't want to work with them. I don't want people . . . I'm dealing daily with my parents, that's two people and then to have six or eight other people telling me what to do, telling me how to clean, doing stupid little things that are an insult to my intelligence. I don't need people telling me how to clean.

PRACTITIONER: Right, but Dora you know the fact is you made that decision to apply for public housing and to agree to the skill program. And now you're changing that?

DORA: Well, I agreed to move into an apartment, I didn't agree to have all these people telling me what to do, breathing down my neck, making me do all these little daily things that I am capable of doing on my own.

PRACTITIONER: Yeah, I know. I know, Dora, that you want your own apartment. Right? But I think you are kind of making it harder on yourself to get that.

DORA: Harder on myself! (with anger)

PRACTITIONER: At this point, yes.

DORA: These people are making it hard on me. They are the ones making all the rules that I have to live by. No one else has to live by these damn rules. Why should I?

PRACTITIONER: Well, Dora, okay . . . rules are a way of life. I mean if you want something, you have to jump through some hoops to get there. That is just the way life is.

DORA: I'm not going to jump through hoops. I don't need them. I can just stay here in my parents' house, I don't need you. They are trying to tell me what to do and now you are doing it. Just get out of my house and leave me alone.

Is Dora a client? If so, what kind of client? Potential clients and practitioners begin the initial phase with different goals and perspectives. Expectations of clients can be cast on a grid representing an active-passive continuum on one axis and a positive–negative continuum on the other (see table 6.1).

So, for example, practitioners desire and prefer to work with clients who are cooperative and compliant or both active and positive (cell 1). They frequently encounter clients who are active–negative or hostile clients who are

Table 6.1   Continuum of participation

Demeanor toward interaction	Level of Activity and Cooperation	
	Active	Passive
Positive	Cooperative and compliant	Cooperative and noncompliant
Negative	Hostile and compliant	Passive and noncompliant

Adapted from Littell, Alexander, and Reynolds (2001), p. 4

actively involved with the treatment and practitioner, but not in a positive way, though they may be compliant (cell 2). For example, some involuntary clients see treatment as an invasion of their rights (Jones 1990). Practitioners also encounter clients who are positive–passive who appear acquiescent. That is, these clients may appear to be amenable to the practitioner's plans but are not actively involved in them (cell 3). Finally, some clients are passive–negative, such that they are not actively involved in treatment and oppose it in a passive way (cell 4). This has been termed a resistant response (Littell, Alexander, and Reynolds 2001). This matrix is useful in separating demeanor from activity. Practitioners may be inclined to favor positive demeanor and unfortunately be less sensitive to activity level. That is, involuntary clients who are vocal about being unhappy about a plan yet comply with it are preferable to clients who may superficially support a plan but not act to enact it.

Clients referred by others or legally mandated are already in a circumstance in which they are likely to minimize problems identified by others (O'Hare 1996). Dora is involved with the practitioner but not in a positive way. She would be classified as hostile based on this interaction. In this chapter, we will explore means of working with mandated and nonvoluntary clients such that the potentials for motivational congruence are explored. While Dora and the practitioner originally agreed on the goal of moving to public housing, they have become entangled in a struggle about how to meet her goal, with the practitioner feeling the pressure to accede to the demands of the agency and Dora rejecting that pressure.

Motivational congruence between client and practitioner on goals and methods of practice was presented in chapter 3 as an important clue for legal, ethical, and effective practice. Much contact between involuntary clients such as Dora and her practitioner lacks congruence, however, as practitioners pressure involuntary clients to accept responsibility for their actions, to accede to the wishes of others, to work on the "right problems" for the "right reasons." On the other hand, involuntary clients often appear equally determined not to acknowledge these "right" problems attributed to them by others (Reid 1992).

Conflict between practitioner and client perspectives often leads to efforts to manipulate one another: to "hook" the involuntary client and to avoid being hooked. The resulting deadlock often results in limited compliance with mandates, little self-attributed change, escalating frustration, and charges and countercharges. The cycle of charges, accusations, and defenses has been called the confrontation–denial cycle whereby charges are met with defenses. Those defenses are interpreted by practitioners as denial, leading to a further round of charges (Kear-Colwell and Pollock 1997). In this way, it is similar to ironic processes whereby the very means to explore the problem may stimulate reactance and through an ironic effect, worsen the problem (Shoham and Rohrbaugh 1997).

Socialization or role preparation for practitioner and client can begin to extricate the practitioner and involuntary client from this deadlock by separating the fixed and non-negotiable from alternatives in meeting requirements and identifying rights and free choices. Completion of socialization steps can increase voluntary aspects of contact and decrease coerced aspects while working for the lasting change that is likely to occur if change is self-attributed (see chapter 5). Such self-attribution of change can be pursued with both mandated and nonvoluntary clients.

Self-attribution with mandated clients occurs in a context in which compliance strategies of coercion and inducement are also employed around non-negotiable requirements. Hence, mandated practitioners must partly play an enforcer role (Cingolani 1984). Compliance with mandates and motivational congruence can be enhanced if the mandated practitioner also plays negotiator and compromiser roles (ibid.). Persuasion, negotiation, and bargaining skills can be useful tools for practitioners to assist mandated clients in making constrained choices.

Nonvoluntary clients such as Dora can be helped to make informed decisions to become voluntary clients, or at least semivoluntary, or not to become clients at all. Should the nonvoluntary client choose to accept services and become at least semivoluntary, the enforcer role should be limited to non-negotiable requirements of the setting. Greater emphasis should be placed on playing the negotiator and compromiser roles as well as sometimes acting as an advocate or coach. Hence, negotiating, bargaining, and persuasion should be used more frequently with nonvoluntary clients than compliance strategies.

This chapter presents (1) preparation for initial contact, (2) initiating contact, and (3) socialization steps as preparation for four negotiation and contracting strategies.

Preparation for Initial Contact

Practitioners can prepare for initial contact with involuntary clients by completing nine preparatory steps: (1) review available case information; (2) anticipate possible stage of change related to attributed problems; (3) identify non-negotiable legal requirements (if any); (4) identify non-negotiable agency and institutional policies (if any); (5) identify rights; (6) identify free choices; (7) identify negotiable options; (8) examine practitioner attitudes that may interfere with service; and (9) make arrangements for initial contact.

The extent to which each of these steps is completed depends on time available and caseload size, competing responsibilities, and amount of information available before initial contact. The sequence of these preparation tasks is depicted in figure 6.1.

1. Review available case information. Available case information should be screened for specific information to determine what brings this person in at this time. The practitioner should focus more on the specific behaviors and events reported that led to contact than on pejorative labels. For example, a supervisor might find written in Dora's case record following the above session that Dora was "resistant, hostile, and unresponsive." Such labels often come as part of a diagnosis focusing on client pathology without consideration of the degree to which they are based on behaviors that may be normal responses to involuntary situations. Without a description of what occurred, the accuracy of such labels cannot be assessed. We know, however, that Dora requested help in getting into an apartment. She did not request the group home living or skills program that came as a "package deal" from the housing agency. Her anger might be seen as normal given her view that she did not need to demonstrate readiness for such living arrangements. Practitioners frequently encounter such client labels in records without an account of the interaction that may have in part produced the label.

2. Anticipate possible stage of change related to attributed problems. Practitioners working with involuntary clients frequently encounter persons such as Dora whose acknowledged concerns differ from those attributed to her. Clients who come to treatment under pressure from others such as threat of

Figure 6.1 Preparation for involuntary contact

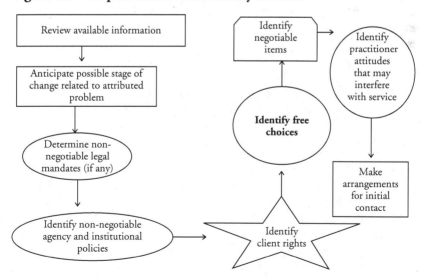

divorce, job loss, or court referral are likely to minimize problems that have been identified by others (O'Hare 1996). Much of the frustration of work with nonvoluntary clients stems from developing action plans based on the assumption that the client sees a need for change and is prepared to proceed. The stages of change perspective can help the practitioner to assess whether a problem is attributed by others or acknowledged (Corcoran 2002). For example, it appears that Dora wishes to live in an apartment. That is an acknowledged problem. She does not want to go through a training skills program in order to qualify for it. That problem is attributed. Should she not be willing to consider the value of the skills program, she might be said to be in precontemplation on this issue. That is, she does not know about or does not anticipate adverse consequences from failure to participate, she does not anticipate changing her mind or behavior about this in the near future, and she has no faith in the ability of the program to assist her with her concerns. If pressured to change, she might make token changes as a result of coercion but would be likely to resume her current attitudes when pressure is removed (Hanson and Gutheil 2004). It is common to anticipate that clients who are pressured to accept assistance or are court ordered are often in this stage related to the problem attributed to them (Peterocelli 2002). Were she willing to consider the problem, but ambivalent about its value, she would be in the contemplation stage. Persons in contemplation are more receptive to feedback as they are not yet convinced of the value of change.

Meanwhile, it should be noted that around the concern of getting her own apartment, Dora is probably in the preparation stage as this refers to having made a decision to change but not having sustained action beyond initial steps (Miller and Rollnick 2002). Meanwhile, in the action stage clients are prepared to make substantive changes over a more extended period and to plan and carry out exactly how to do it (ibid.). Clients who have made substantive changes over a period of time and are striving to maintain those changes and avoid a relapse are said to be in the maintenance stage (ibid.).

Stages of change are used here primarily for their heuristic value, as there are difficulties with broad application to problems that are outside the domain of the health-related concerns from which the stages of change model and motivational interviewing emerged (Littell and Girvin 2004). That is, many problems attributed to involuntary clients are not primarily or exclusively health related and action plans often require environmental modification, not just change of client behavior.

As the aforementioned example attests, it is not uncommon for involuntary clients to be in different stages related to different attributed concerns. Knowing this has value for practitioners in preparing for client response to problems they have not acknowledged: passive or hostile responses to plans to work on attributed problems about which they are in precontemplation can be anticipated. In addition, it has the value of drawing attention to problems that they acknowledge and about which they are often in the preparation stage and ready for action.

3. Identify non-negotiable legal requirements (if any). In reviewing case information, the practitioner should separate what must be done legally from what might be desirable but is not required. If legal requirements do not pertain, as in Dora's case, then the practitioner should proceed directly to step 4. What must be done legally frequently becomes confused with what the practitioner or referral source privately feels should be done. Failure to make this distinction may inadvertently sabotage the socialization and contracting process by using compliance methods on issues that are based neither on law nor on policy and may affect subsequent evaluations of effectiveness. Restricting requirements to a limited number of specific behaviors should also reduce client reactance (Brehm 1976).

Consequently, mandated practitioners need to identify the federal, state, and local legal parameters that limit and guide their work with involuntary clients. Practitioners employed in fields such as child welfare or probation must thoroughly understand those non-negotiable requirements that govern their behavior and determine the extent to which client behavior can be legally required to change (Palmer 1983). For example, a mandated client might be court-ordered to participate in a restitution program and the practitioner would be required to link the client to such a program.

When non-negotiable requirements exist, they should be made explicit so that areas for freedom of choice and maintenance of current behaviors can then be identified and clearly understood by the clients. The mandated practitioner needs to find out:

- What legal requirements apply here?
- What do those requirements indicate that the practitioner must do?
- What must the mandated client do?
- What recourse does the mandated client or the practitioner have in modifying the requirement?
- What are the consequences of noncompliance with the requirement for the practitioner and client?

4. Identify non-negotiable agency and institutional policies (if any). Practitioners working in agency settings are also influenced by policies that guide service delivery. For example, job descriptions for case managers may describe how frequently contact with clients must take place and priorities in carrying out their roles. Private agencies often have policies that include "package deals." For example, the housing agency may require that if Dora

"chooses" to apply for their housing, she must satisfy requirements such as an assessment that she be capable of living there safely. Similar guidelines to those developed for legal requirements then apply for non-negotiable agency or institutional policies:

- What non-negotiable agency or institutional policies apply here?
- What do those policies specify that the practitioner do?
- What do those policies specify that the involuntary client do?
- What recourse does the involuntary client or the practitioner have in modifying those policies?
- What are the consequences for noncompliance with the policies for the practitioner and client?

Preparation for work with involuntary clients in mandated and institutional settings too often does not progress beyond these four steps. To enhance motivational congruence, empower clients, and achieve greater success it is equally important to identify rights, free choices, and negotiable options.

5. Identify rights. Too often identifying rights is interpreted as handing involuntary clients a copy of legal rights without a dialogue about rights and options needed to pursue genuine informed consent (see chapter 2). Since the choice not to accept an offer of service is available for nonvoluntary clients, this most basic right should be clarified. For example, the practitioner could have prepared for the session with Dora by reminding herself that Dora could choose whether to pursue living in the housing project or not. Further, the practitioner should prepare to help the nonvoluntary client make an informed decision based on accurate information about the advantages and disadvantages of continuing that contact on a voluntary basis.

Presenting two sides to the decision about whether to participate and emphasizing choices should reduce reactance (Brehm 1976). Hence, the practitioner could think about advantages and disadvantages for Dora of choosing to work with the housing authority, and explore other available options as well. The practitioner should remember here that mandated clients can also choose to accept legal consequences if they refuse services.

The practitioner should also prepare to inform both mandated and nonvoluntary clients about their rights to confidentiality including any limitations to those rights, as well as available recourse to requirements or alternative services for which they may qualify.

For outside referrals, the practitioner should examine what the referral source is requesting in terms of rights the client has to accept or reject the recommended service. Nonvoluntary clients can often choose to work on a problem different than that attributed by the referral source (Epstein and Brown 2002). The practitioner might explore, however, the consequences for the client of making such a choice.

6. Identify free choices. It was suggested in chapter 5 that reactance may be decreased by clarifying behaviors that are not affected by requirements. For example, mandated clients can choose their attitude to the situation: whether to comply at all, to comply passively, or to make the best of the situation by working on some of their own concerns as well. Nonvoluntary clients can choose not to accept the service, or to accept it and work on their own concerns. Hence, Dora can choose to remain at home, to accept the housing authority's terms, to explore negotiation with the authority, or pursue another housing alternative.

7. Identify negotiable options. Reactance should also be reduced if options or constrained choices are available in the implementation of policies and requirements. The practitioner should be aware of discretion available in the interpretation of mandates and policies. For example, the practitioner might have explored whether there were alternative ways that Dora might be assessed for skills in living in the housing program without completing the skills program or living in a group home. Could she take a competence examination and, if she passed, obtain a waiver out of the program?

8. Examine practitioner attitudes that may interfere with service. Practitioners often come to shorthand predictions about what may occur with a client based on rapid assessment of available case information and comparisons with past experience of other clients with similar case information. While predicting the future is normal and unavoidable, prejudging has serious consequences. Such prejudging may occur when involuntary clients are accused of offenses such as child abuse or battering that are not only illegal but often personally offensive to practitioners. Practitioners' own personal history with the harm of such behaviors may cause them to prejudge if they do not strive to be aware of their own values about the alleged behavior that led to contact.

Avoiding prejudgment is important in order to make a legitimate offer of service that is not sabotaged from the outset. For example, practitioners in child welfare settings are often required to demonstrate "reasonable efforts" to help families stay together and avoid out-of-home placement (Stein 1987). Skepticism about the ultimate success of such efforts may be legitimate based on practitioner experience with similar cases. Failure to monitor this skepticism would be analogous to an instructor examining student transcripts and assigning a grade before the class begins. It is not in the best interest of either involuntary clients or agencies to "determine the grade" before the contact begins. Should the agency later need to move to permanently remove children, however, their documentation of genuine reasonable efforts will assist in their defense of those efforts.

While some referral information may trigger negative prejudgments from practitioners, positive prejudging can also occur. Practitioners might tend to discount illegal behavior that they think should not be illegal. For example, some practitioners have experimented with marijuana and other illegal drugs and may have come to personal opinions that such drugs are not harmful and should be legalized. That personal opinion might result in discounting the consequences for involuntary clients who might be misled in thinking that laws will not be enforced.

9. Make arrangements for initial contact. Involuntary clients, like voluntary clients, often pick up cues about what to expect from contact through the choices made available in arranging the time, locale, and physical arrangements of that contact. Timing choices may not be available in investigations of imminent danger or harm in which the practitioner may be required to make an unannounced contact. In such circumstances, potential protection needs may carry as an unavoidable byproduct a predictable sense of invasion of privacy and high levels of reactance. In most other practitioner-initiated contacts, however, the practitioner can call ahead or write to schedule an interview at the client's convenience.

The locale of that contact and the physical arrangement of the meeting place may also be modifiable. In many cases, the client may choose to meet in the office, in his or her home, or in a neutral location of his or her choice. Should the initial contact with the practitioner take place in an office, the practitioner can be aware of what nonverbal messages office interviews may suggest. For example, moving through a series of locked doors to an office may convey accurately that confinement is an issue here. A sterile environment without pictures and other amenities may convey threat. Seating arrangements can be made to create an expectation of collaboration by sitting to the side of a desk or arranging comfortable chairs or couches. Having toys and games available for children can communicate sensitivity to them and their parents. Some practitioners adorn their walls with attractive pictures or posters with positive motivational statements.

In some cases, practitioners may be unable to modify the physical arrangements of initial contact. Setting decor may be a low priority for the agency or institution, personal decorations may be prohibited, and chairs may be uncomfortable or unmovable. Rather than dwell on unchangeable physical arrangements, the practitioner is better advised to be aware of what those arrangements may communicate and to modify what they can.

Initiating Contact

Practitioners are often encouraged to initiate contact with voluntary clients by tuning in to what brings those clients in for contact (Shulman 1999). Outside pressures, including those represented by the practitioner, are frequently the reasons that contact is established with the involuntary client. The guidelines that follow differ according to whether the client was (1) self-referred, (2) referred, or (3) mandated (figure 6.2).

Figure 6.2   Initial phase steps

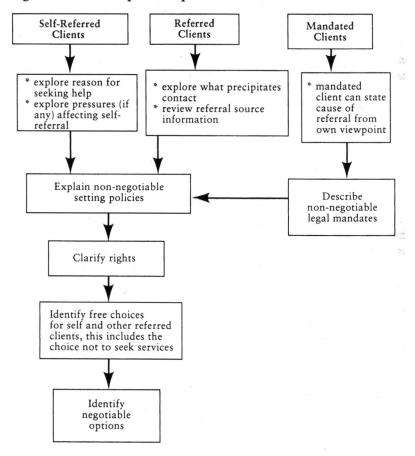

Self-Referred Clients

Contact with self-referred clients begins with: (1) exploring their reason for seeking help, (2) exploring any pressures effecting that self-referral, (3) explaining non-negotiable policies, (4) exploring negotiable options, (5) clarifying rights, and (6) clarifying free choices. Since many who ostensibly self-refer actually seek help as a result of pressure from others, practitioners should take seriously such self-referred clients' viewpoint that other things, people, and events brought them in. For example, when Ralph (introduced in chapter 1) met with a counselor from a mental health center for an intake interview, he said that he had no problems. The only reason he had come was that his mother threatened to make him move out of her house if he didn't stop the arguments with his wife. The counselor might consider that Ralph's own behavior probably played a part in stimulating the circumstances that led to contact, and indeed that Ralph's mother might be signaling the possibility of domestic violence in this case. It is also true that, from Ralph's viewpoint, he is responding to his mother's pressure. Rather than dismiss such an expression as a refusal to accept personal responsibility for "the problem," it is recommended that the practitioner accept that Ralph is expressing factually the problem as he sees it.

Should this initial assessment reveal external pressures that are not legal mandated, the practitioner can attempt to reduce reactance immediately and enhance voluntarism by acknowledging those pressures, helping the client assess the potential consequences of dealing with or ignoring those pressures, and clarifying rights, including the choice not to participate. The practitioner can proceed to explore the advantages and disadvantages of continuing that contact voluntarily.

For example, Keith ostensibly made a voluntary contact for admission into an alcoholism treatment center. The following exchange comes from his initial contact with Dick, his alcoholism treatment case manager.[1] Dick begins by exploring the reason for coming in to treatment from Keith's viewpoint, to suggest ways that Keith can reframe the decision to increase self-attribution, and explore his feelings about the pressured contact.

DICK: Keith, I believe this is your second treatment? What brings you in for treatment at this time?
KEITH: Yep. This is the second treatment. Ah, the family life just started blowing up again. Of course, using alcohol got blamed for everything, so I got kicked out of the house, and after about a week and a half of living in different places, I decided that I might as well come into treatment to see if I missed something the first time.
DICK: So it was really your decision to come in?

KEITH: Well, it was my decision to come in, but I was caught between a rock and a hard place, either come to treatment or lose my family.

DICK: Oh, I see. So it's pretty much the family says, do this or no family. I see. How do you feel about that?

KEITH: I feel that I'm taking the brunt of everything again. I feel like if I do this, everything else is going to be okay, and I don't think that's right.

Keith has produced a good operational definition of a coerced choice: being between a rock and a hard place! Dick could now move to explicitly acknowledge Keith's view of the cause of contact and clarify the choice he is making. For example, Dick could say:

DICK: So, Keith, it sounds as if you feel pressured by your wife and family to come in for more alcoholism treatment and that pressure doesn't feel good. Are you aware that you could choose to stay? I want to clarify that because it is important for people to make up their own minds about the program. Would it help if we were to explore the reasons why you might decide to stay here and make this work for you or to decide not to stay?

Dick should then go on to discuss the rights of patients and the non-negotiable policies and rules of the center, including policies for initiating discharge.

Referred Clients

Referred clients may be amenable to such referral or may feel pressured by it. The practitioner should (1) explore what brings the referred client into contact from their viewpoint, (2) review referral source information, (3) review advantages and disadvantages of doing what the referral source suggests, (4) identify rights, and (5) clarify options. The referred client is entitled to an explanation of the circumstances that have led to contact from the viewpoint of the referral source. This explanation should be objective, nonjudgmental, and concrete. As the referral may contain confidential information or diagnostic labels that may stimulate reactance, the information should be paraphrased to avoid either violation of confidentiality or inappropriate labeling. The practitioner might explore these issues with statements such as:

1. "I would like to know from your viewpoint what brought you here."
2. "I also have some information from the referral source. Would you like to hear it?"

3. "In the rest of our session we need to explore the choices you might make (develop agenda for session). The biggest one is whether you want to decide to become a client here or not."
4. "Would it help if we looked at the pluses and minuses of the decision to become a client here?" (Review advantages and disadvantages for deciding to become a client.)
5. "If you decide to become a client here, there are some agency policies that you should know about" (describe non-negotiable policies).
6. "You have certain rights (explain rights); and we also have several choices in what we do and how we go about it" (describe available options).

For example, Mrs. Simmons was referred to Walter, a county mental health counselor by her child welfare worker. Mrs. Simmons, accused of child abuse a year earlier, had agreed to a consent decree that stipulated that she would meet regularly with her child welfare worker around child management issues in exchange for the agency not taking her to court. Mrs. Simmons was not now attending those sessions and the working relationship between Mrs. Simmons and the child welfare worker was distant. Mrs. Simmons was in a nonvoluntary relationship with the child welfare worker because of the consent decree; her contact with Walter was not directly part of that agreement. Therefore, she could choose whether or not to become a client of the mental health center. The initial interaction between Walter and Mrs. Simmons is reproduced below.[2]

Walter begins with a description of the circumstances of the referral. His description is followed by a very negative response from Mrs. Simmons about that referral. This response might have been more muted had Walter first asked Mrs. Simmons to talk about her own understanding of the reasons for the referral.

WALTER: I'm meeting with you because the social worker involved with you and your son Jamie has indicated that there is a consent decree that says you have to meet with the social worker and follow through on recommendations. Apparently, there's some problem in terms of you keeping appointments, and I wanted to see if there was something I could do in terms of helping you look at what gets in the way, and see if we could plan some way around them.

MRS. SIMMONS: Yeah. You can get him off my case. He doesn't listen to me. It's got to be his way or no way at all. I'm sorry, but I think I know my little boy a little bit better than that, and I know my own mind.

WALTER: Well, what appears to have led to this consent decree is a petition that was brought by the social worker before the court, and the petition indicates that there's been a lot of problems in school with Jamie hitting other kids, kicking other kids, apparently throwing a piece of wood and hitting a kid in the eye. One time he was banging his head on the wall. Another time he was choking himself with some sort of a necklace, and I guess I'd like to know how you see these problems.

Walter clarified that he wanted to hear her side of the story and reported the intake information received in an objective and nonjudgmental fashion. He also requested her viewpoint. He might also have empathized here with Mrs. Simmons' anger about working with the social worker. This might also be the time to introduce her rights and choices, such as the following.

WALTER: I think it might help if we talked a little about your choices here. While you have to continue working with the social service agency because of your consent decree, you and I can decide whether we want to work together. If you decide to work with me, we can work on the things you are concerned about. We can also decide whether to take the social worker's concerns into account. You might also pursue getting reassigned to another social worker. We also need to look at what might happen if you decide not to become a client here and return to working with the social worker.

Mandated Clients

Mandated clients are entitled to (1) state the cause of contact from their viewpoint; (2) a description of legal, non-negotiable requirements; (3) a review of negotiable options, alternatives, and consequences; (4) an explanation of rights, and (5) a review of free choices. Since reactance can be expected to be high, available choices should be clarified from the beginning. Statements that the practitioner might make during this section of the interview might include:

1. "I would like to know from your viewpoint what brought you here."
2. "Let me share with you what I know about our contact."
3. "You and I need to meet because . . ." (objective description of cause of contact).
4. "What you and I have to do is . . ." (factual description of non-negotiable requirements).
5. "In the rest of our session we need to explore the choices you might make" (develop agenda for session).
6. "You are entitled to (explain rights)."

7. "You are free to (explain free choices and alternatives, and consequences)."
8. "We also have some choices in what we do and how we go about it" (describe available options).

The following dialogue takes place at the beginning of contact between Paul and Bill, his probation officer. Paul was preparing to enter an adult correctional facility, so the number of non-negotiable requirements was high.[3] Bill begins by respecting Paul's right to decide how he should be addressed and explaining why he needs to take notes. Bill then explains his own agenda for the session. He should also ask Paul for other things he would like to see covered in the session. Since Paul may be less likely to express high reactance if he describes the requirements himself rather than has them read to him, Bill asks Paul for his view of what he is required to do. Bill then continues to describe additional referral information that he has about non-negotiable requirements and explains the specifics of confidentiality.

BILL: Mr. Anderson, my name is Bill Linden, and I'm a probation officer. I've been asked by the court to supervise your probation. First of all, let me start off by asking what do you prefer to be called?

PAUL: Call me Paul.

BILL: Okay, Paul. Basically what we need to do today is to begin to gather some information to help me in supervising your probation as well as to get an understanding as to what the conditions are. As we talk today, I'm going to be taking some notes, so I can keep the particulars of your case separate from anyone else's. Do you have any problems with that?

PAUL: Go ahead.

BILL: Can you tell me what your understanding was of the sentence you received from the court?

PAUL: From what I understand from what my lawyer says, I'm going to have to go to the workhouse here on Monday, and I could have done a lot worse. But anyway, I've got to go to the workhouse, and I'm not quite sure what I have to do around that. They said something about four or five months, but I might be getting out early if I keep a clean act.

BILL: Let me then let you know the information I received from the court just prior to our meeting. Now my understanding is that you were initially charged with two felony counts. Count 1 was burglary, and count 2 was receiving and concealing stolen goods. In return for you pleading guilty to burglary, the state dismissed count 2, the receiving of stolen goods. The court sentenced you to thirteen months in prison with a stay of execution and five years of probation. Does that sound familiar to you?

PAUL: Yeah, that was it.

BILL: Now what that basically means is you're going to be on probation for five years. And as long as you follow the conditions of probation, you won't have to do the thirteen months of prison.

PAUL: What do they mean by probation? Do I have to show up and talk to somebody like you every month?

BILL: There are a number of conditions of probation, one of which is that you have to maintain contact with me and keep me informed as to where you're living and working.

PAUL: Do you come over and visit?

BILL: Sometimes. I do try and work the supervision around your work schedule, so that probation doesn't interfere with your working. I want to also let you know, Paul, that the information you provide is confidential. The only ones that can have access to that will be individuals with written permission from you, except for other people in the correctional community. Other courts can get it, other probation officers can get it. But anyone outside of the criminal justice system cannot have access to this information without your expressed approval or by court order.

While Bill reviews confidentiality rights here, he should go on to explore alternatives and free choices that Paul has. Paul could appeal the sentence, or decide how he was going to do the time including exploring how he could work on his own concerns.

Socialization Guidelines

Socialization, or preparation for assuming roles by practitioner and client, follows the steps in initiating contact. Socialization is another key clue in pursuing legal, ethical, effective practice with involuntary clients since clarity of expectations and roles is associated with better outcomes (Jones and Alcabes 1993). While one goal in mandated settings is to increase compliance with legal requirements, socialization efforts should also reduce reactance and respect self-determination in areas other than non-negotiable legal and agency requirements. The practitioner should carry out socialization by doing the following: (1) conduct any required assessment; (2) assess response to pressured contact; (3) express empathy for pressures experienced; (4) note values expressed; (5) employ selective confrontation around non-negotiable items; and (6) reaffirm choices and negotiable options (figure 6.3).

1. Conduct any required assessment. Assessment with voluntary clients typically involves exploration of strengths, weaknesses, goals, desires, and awareness of the systems of which the client is part. Such voluntary assessments often assume that the process is in pursuit of a mutual plan.

Figure 6.3   Socialization phase steps

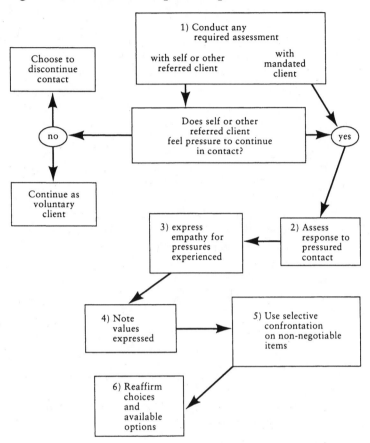

While mandated assessments may ideally end in a mutual plan, they must be conducted whether or not the involuntary client wants to participate. For example, when the practitioner is mandated to assess danger, the assessment itself may be a non-negotiable aspect of contact. In some cases, investigative protocols have been developed that aid the practitioner in assessing danger in a relatively objective manner (Stein and Rzepnicki 1983). In many others, specific protocols are unavailable and practitioners must craft their own.

Too often extensive assessments are developed for meeting an involuntary client's needs that far outstretch both legal requirements and the client's own perceived wishes. Hence, such assessments often provide a source of disappointment and frustration when the client is unwilling to pursue more than a required minimum. The general issues in conducting involuntary assessments are to determine:

- What information is the practitioner required to collect in order to make decisions or recommendations?
- What information might be useful for making required recommendations or decisions but is left to the discretion of the practitioner?
- What information is irrelevant to explicit or implicit requirements for assessment that might, however, be collected should the involuntary client give consent to pursue an issue voluntarily?

Assessment is an ongoing process that only begins at intake. The practitioner working with involuntary clients must be aware that initial assessment takes place in a context of pressured contact. Consequently, observations about client behavior might best be seen as a sample of how that client behaves under pressured circumstances.

2. Assess response to pressured contact. If the exploration of the cause of contact reveals outside pressures or mandates, no matter how tactfully or objectively such pressures are explored, many involuntary clients will respond negatively. A negative response is predictable in situations involving a threat to valued freedoms. Among the predictable responses are anger at imposed services or pressures from others, denial of wrong or harm, considering self as victim, blaming others as unworthy and deserving of harm, hostility toward the practitioner, passive indifference, and deception (Saltmarsh 1976). Practitioners have often interpreted these responses as evidence of internal dysfunction, guilt, or deviance rather than considering the possibility that they are normal responses to a situation stimulating reactance.

The practitioner can avoid premature labeling of such responses as evidence of pathology or resistance and consider that they may indicate reactance responses or the use of self-presentation strategies such as intimidation, supplication, selective confession, or ingratiation to defend against labeling. Even if negative responses are normal and predictable, they are usually uncomfortable for the practitioner. Such responses can often, however, be reduced by expressing empathy for pressures experienced.

3. Express empathy for pressures experienced. Such negative responses can be so strong that the involuntary client cannot "hear" what is being said or participate fully in the session unless those feelings are given attention. While the practitioner may privately suspect that some of the involuntary client's difficulties have been brought on by his or her own actions and hence not feel much empathy for the client's responses, the practitioner can be selectively empathic about the involuntary client's feelings of being forced or pressured

into contact against his or her will. It can be helpful to recall one's own reactions in coerced situations so as to better understand and empathize with the involuntary client's reactance. For example, a practitioner might say: "I'll bet it's hard coming in here when you didn't choose to be here. There are probably other things you'd rather be doing and other places you'd rather be."

4. Note values expressed. Involuntary clients often reveal their values and strengths in their response to pressured contact. The practitioner can note those values as ones to be aware of as positive motivations for later contracting and possible use in selective confrontation about how they may be jeopardized by client behaviors.

After Bill completed the summary of the many non-negotiable requirements involved in Paul's entry into the correctional system, Paul became angry about the many losses of freedom he was soon to encounter and denied responsibility for his actions. Bill responded to the reactance at this point, avoiding a power struggle, saving selective confrontation for later in the interview. He became aware through Paul's responses that he wanted to have money to pay rent, maybe a job, and freedom to have a good time.

BILL: Paul, you appear to be kind of angry at this point.
PAUL: Well, I don't know, it wasn't that much stuff. What the hell, they had plenty more stuff. I mean they had about five televisions and stereos. Hey, I needed the stuff, I needed some money. I've had three jobs in the last two years, and they all went to hell. I needed to get some money, I've got rent to pay and stuff. I want to go to a bar and have a good time just like everybody else, I'm entitled to it.
BILL: What I'm hearing you say, Paul, is that you are pissed off because you needed some money and don't feel you deserved the type of sentence that you got.
PAUL: Yeah. It wasn't that much. What the hell.
BILL: And I think most people would be mad in your situation about entering prison. But then I'd also ask you to take into account that you've got some choices to make and I hope you won't let your anger interfere with that. It is okay for you to be angry.

When Paul denies responsibility for the crime, denies harm to the victims, and suggests that they could spare the stolen goods he needed, it is as if there is a cartoon caption over his head saying "denial of responsibility." While many practitioners would confront Paul's refusal to accept responsibility at this point, Bill selectively empathized with the pressure experienced while not agreeing that the victims of the crime are to blame. The presence of denial does not suggest that confrontation will be effective at this point, since Bill is not yet likely to be a persuasive source of influence.

5. Employ selective confrontation around non-negotiable items. Many involuntary clients question the validity and interpretation of facts presented to them about the cause of contact or the fairness of requirements as Paul did. An escalation spiral of charges, defenses, and countercharges frequently ensues. We saw such a spiral occur in the beginning of the chapter in the interaction between Dora and her caseworker. Such escalation often contributes to a negative assessment by the practitioner. Practitioners often wish that involuntary clients would admit responsibility for their behavior or accede to the demands of others. It seems unlikely that many involuntary clients will have the communication skills to deescalate and move from a content to a process level by saying, "Hold on. It seems that we are in an escalation spiral here. I am angry and so are you and we are not listening to each other. Let's back up and start over." Hence, responsibility for such de-escalation rests with the practitioner.

Some believe that confrontation is necessary in some cases for clients to suffer enough discomfort that they will be motivated for change. Such a belief has been sustained in Scared Straight and therapeutic boot camp programs (Miller and Rollnick 2002). While there is evidence that information alone about the effects of drinking can be beneficial to drinkers (Juarez 2001; Burke, Arkowitz, and Dunn 2002), in fact a heavily confrontational style has been associated with increased drinking (Miller, Benefield, and Tonigan 1993).

How can mandated clients be presented with non-negotiable aspects of contact in a respectful, nonjudgmental fashion? Confrontation refers to techniques used to help a client discover blind spots, discrepancies, and inconsistencies between thoughts, feelings, attitudes, behaviors, and their consequences that perpetuate client difficulties (Hepworth et al. 2005).

Confrontation can also be seen as a persuasion method designed to affect attitudes, beliefs, and behavior. Many practitioners are unsure about when to confront or how to do so in ways that remain respectful and demonstrate caring. Confrontation is most appropriate when (1) a law or policy has been violated or a violation is imminent, (2) when danger or harm has occurred or is imminent, or (3) when a client's own goals are threatened by their behavior. Hence confrontation occurs most frequently with mandated clients who have violated laws. Confrontation with nonvoluntary clients is less frequent and occurs around conditions of danger, harm, or obstacles to their own expressed goals. Confrontation is rarely appropriate if beliefs or actions are not illegal, violations of policy, dangerous, or unrelated to client's goals.

Confrontation techniques range on a continuum of intrusiveness into personal choice from low intrusiveness to high. At the low end of intrusiveness, the practitioner can choose to not confront. Following the criteria for appropriateness of use of confrontation described in the preceding text, such a decision is appropriate if behavior is not illegal, harmful, or a threat to the client's goals. Following these guidelines, practitioners can choose to confront about some issues and avoid confrontation around others (figure 6.4).

The first level of appropriate confrontation is the use of self-assessment techniques to facilitate self-examination. Circumstances often exist in which behavior or attitudes may be interfering with client goals or legal mandates, or in which danger is possible but not imminent. In such circumstances, the completion of a written assessment of past behavior and attitudes relevant to the reason for contact can provide a relatively unobtrusive form of self-confrontation (Kopp 1988, 1989). Such a method promotes self-evaluation to facilitate change as a model for self-confrontation. Some involuntary clients may be stimulated to recognize dissonance between behaviors, attitudes, and goals without arousing much reactance. Self-assessment techniques may be most appropriate early in contact, prior to the development of an effective working relationship. The technique should not be used with the expectation that many clients will have an "ah ha!" experience in which they quickly become aware of dissonant behavior on their own. If the technique is expected

Figure 6.4   A confrontation continuum

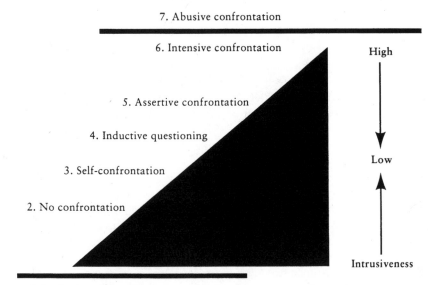

7. Abusive confrontation

6. Intensive confrontation

High

5. Assertive confrontation

4. Inductive questioning

Low

3. Self-confrontation

2. No confrontation

Intrusiveness

1. Lack of confrontation

Levels 2 or 6 can be appropriate uses of confrontation. Levels 1 and 7 are inappropriate.

rather to "plant a seed," little is lost in its use as it is relatively unobtrusive and hence provides little risk to the development of an effective working relationship. Such self-assessments should be phrased in objective, nonjudgmental terms.

Means of stimulating self-confrontation can be used much more frequently than is usually the case, with minimal risks. While such techniques may be insufficient for heavily defended clients, its use can provide information to guide higher levels of confrontation. If behavior includes law violations and imminent danger, self-assessment may be skipped or quickly followed with the next level, inductive questioning.

At a second level, practitioners can raise inductive questions that draw involuntary client attention to a potential discrepancy or inconsistency between behaviors, attitudes, beliefs, goals, and consequences. Discrepancies between verbal and nonverbal expressions or actions can also be explored in a questioning, tentative fashion rather than as statements of fact or interpretation (Draycott and Dabbs 1998). Inductive questioning is relatively unobtrusive and can hence be used effectively early in a relationship to plant a seed promoting self-confrontation without arousing much reactance. It may be used selectively around items in the self-assessment in which danger is probable or consequences are more serious. Inductive questioning can also be overused, and many clients will not respond to the tentative linkages suggested.

It is often appropriate to use inductive questioning with nonvoluntary clients to explore ways that behaviors may conflict with client goals. In the following section of the interview between Walter and Mrs. Simmons, he continues to gather information from her perspective about the previous allegations of child abuse and to provide selective confrontation. After exploring further what had occurred with Mrs. Simmons, the school, and Jamie, Walter moves to empathically confront and use an inductive question:

WALTER: Do you think sometimes Jamie's behaviors in the school are some of his own doing?

MRS. SIMMONS: I know he's not an angel. But he's not as bad as what they're making him out to be, either. He's just a typical, normal little boy that, yes, every once in a while, he does get into trouble. But not all of it is his fault.

WALTER: It's got to be pretty frustrating and very difficult for you to have this problem with Jamie and the school. I've seen you a couple of times with Jamie. And from what you're telling me now, and what I've seen in the past, I know you really love your son. And sometimes, as much as you love your son, it's got to be pretty difficult to deal with some of his behaviors.

A sequence of inductive questions can also be used to "plant seeds," to build dissonance or discomfort over a lack of fit between behaviors, attitudes, and goals or values. Bill had noted earlier that Paul did not believe he had a problem with alcohol and that he appeared frustrated over losing three jobs in the past year. After the series of inductive questions, Bill suggests that chemical abuse may be a problem that has gotten in the way of working. He also attempts a role reversal by suggesting that Paul see things from the employer's viewpoint. When Paul mentions that he was fired at his last job for being late, Bill asks:

BILL: Why was it that they said you were late?

PAUL: I had a hangover.

BILL: You had a hangover. Had you been out drinking pretty heavily the night before?

PAUL: Sunday night. Had to go to work the next day, thought what the hell.

BILL: Has that happened before?

PAUL: Sure.

BILL: How many times?

PAUL: Go out with all the gang. Lots of times.

BILL: Lots of times?

PAUL: Sure. Go out with the guys.

BILL: Have you had other employers say to you that you're not working up to par, that they feel like maybe you're drinking?

PAUL: No. They just say maybe I could do a better job next time. I think I do a pretty good job.

BILL: So they say that you could do a better job. You feel you're doing okay?

PAUL: I'm doing fine. I don't understand. Maybe I'm in the wrong field. But I like doing what I'm doing.

BILL: So you like auto body, you'd like to stay in that field?

PAUL: Sure.

BILL: Interesting enough, right there, you've presented some ideas where I can begin to see how the presentencing investigator did see the possibility of a chemical abuse problem. If you are working—now just think about this—and you're going out and getting drunk and that drinking affects your ability to work. What would you think if you were an employer paying someone thirty bucks an hour and they couldn't do the job?

Near the end of the interview, Bill again asks Paul to put himself in someone else's shoes.

BILL: I want to give you something to think about, and then during our next meeting, I want us to be able to talk about it. You are telling me that you want to stay out of trouble in the future. Let's say that you're staying out of trouble, and you do purchase a stereo and let's say, someone comes in and steals the stereo. I want you to then think about how you would react, and what you wound like to have happen to the individual that took your stereo. All I'm asking is that you think about that. I don't want an answer now, I want you to think about it. Okay? And also think about how that's in line with your goal of wanting to stay out of trouble in the future.

When behavior involves law violations or imminent harm, the practitioner must often progress to the next level: assertive confrontation.

Assertive confrontation refers to making specific statements in declarative form about discrepancies in thoughts, feelings, behaviors, and consequences rather than posing them as questions. Assertive confrontations should (1) include statements about proposed linkages between dissonant attitudes, behaviors, and goals based on specific instances; (2) separate free behaviors from requirements and constrained choices; (3) be conveyed in an atmosphere of warmth, caring, and trust in which concern rather than blame is communicated; (4) be presented tactfully but clearly enough that the client gets the point; (5) be well timed and focused on key issues; and (6) be followed with empathy.

A template of assertive confrontation is as follows:

I'm concerned because you (want/believe/are striving to)_____
(describe desired outcome) but your_____
(describe discrepant action, behavior, or inaction) is likely to produce_____ (describe probable negative consequence). (Hepworth et al. 2005)

Assertive confrontations are frequently employed with mandated clients around law violations, non-negotiable aspects of contact, and dangerous behavior and are also appropriate when client-expressed goals are jeopardized by behavior. When danger is high, lower-level confrontation steps are often skipped. Otherwise, assertive confrontation might follow unsuccessful attempts at inductive questioning. If, however, the behavior or attitude is neither a law violation nor a danger to self or others, nor a conflict with the involuntary client's expressed goals, it is questionable whether assertive confrontation should be used.

Confrontations are most likely to be successful when they come from a respected source who identifies specific problematic behaviors and consequences. As noted in the preceding interaction between Bill and Paul, the practitioner is at first unlikely to be a respected source. Consequently, confrontation is unlikely to be effective at the beginning of contact and hence should be used sparingly, concentrating on non-negotiable items.

The practitioner can sometimes empathize with the client's feelings about contact and then add the confrontation, using a linguistic sequence substituting and for but. This linguistic sequence affirms the validity of both the empathic statement and the confrontation rather than stating them in terms that suggest that they contradict one another (Saunders 1982). For example, the practitioner could say, "I hear your frustration that your child does not obey the way you feel he should and striking your child with a belt, raising welts is not a legal way to get him to obey you."

Child protective service investigations frequently require confrontation around non-negotiables. In the following interview segment, Betty, a child protection worker, is meeting with Diane, the single mother of two small children. Diane reported that she left her children in the care of a babysitter for an evening. Police, however, found the three- and five-year-old children playing unattended in a park at 3:00 A.M. across a busy street from the housing development in which they lived. Diane had completed an outpatient alcohol treatment program. This was now the third report of behavior assessed as neglectful since the treatment was completed. Additional reports indicated that Diane was not following the aftercare program and was again drinking.

Betty has to present the facts that led to the contact, explore Diane's explanation, and empathize with her response, while remaining firm about the agency's non-negotiable demands. She also identifies some common concerns, such as the children's welfare, and begins to explore options to meet requirements. Diane began by saying that she was not responsible for what happened to the children since she left a babysitter in charge.

BETTY: It does sound, Diane, as if you thought you were leaving your children in safe care. You are concerned about their welfare as we are. And one of the things that the law expects parents to do is make safe decisions in picking babysitters. So if kids were found alone wandering in a park late at night, the laws say that parents are responsible for that. And so that's why the police took them in.

DIANE: I'll never use her again. I'll never use her again.

BETTY: That would be a wise decision on your part. I think, Diane, if this were the first time that we had this kind of situation together, that would be the direction we would want to go. We would try to help you make better arrangements for babysitting. However, we need to look at the fact that this is the third time this year that the kids have been on a police hold.

DIANE: This wasn't my fault. This was not my fault. Maybe other times it was, but this was not my fault. You're just making a big deal out of this.

BETTY: Are you saying, Diane, that you feel blamed, that this time feels different to you since you had made what you thought were good plans for the children?

DIANE: Yes, I had a babysitter. It was her responsibility.

BETTY: While you feel this time was different, it is the third report we have received. So, we don't feel that it's safe for the kids to come home right now. There is another reason why we think that the children might be safer in foster care right now. We have also had a community report, Diane, that you have been seen drinking while with the children.

DIANE: It's not anyone's business if I drink! I already completed a treatment program. Who called in? I have enemies. You can't trust everyone who calls in.

BETTY: You are right that drinking is your own business, as long as your children are not in danger. You are also right that we can't always trust callers. It does seem as if drinking is playing a part in your childcare at this point. For this reason, I am going to recommend that if you want to regain custody of the children, that you complete another alcoholism assessment and any treatment they recommend. That may involve an inpatient treatment and a halfway house program. It may also be a return to an aftercare program. The assessment might also show that you don't need any kind of treatment now.

DIANE: I already did that once. I already did that.

BETTY: I know that you did. You successfully completed the program. But the problem is that your aftercare doesn't seem to be working.

DIANE: I think this is all a big exaggeration. The only thing that happened here is that the babysitter left, and that's not my fault.

BETTY: I understand that you feel that this is an overreaction, Diane. You do have some choices about what happens from here. One is that you can decide to work with us and to come to an agreement on a contract about completing an assessment, and the other is that you can decide to go to juvenile court and talk to the judge.

DIANE: I'm not going to court. I'm not going to court. You took my sister to court, and she doesn't have her kids anymore. I'm not going to court.

BETTY: So given those two options, you'd rather work with us than go to court.

DIANE: I don't have any choice. 'Cause I'm not going to court.

BETTY: Okay, it doesn't feel like much of a choice. You would prefer that we forget the whole thing. If you do choose to work with us rather than go to court, we expect you to complete the assessment and we will support the recommendations they make. I have a list of places that could provide an assessment for you. You can pick from this list or suggest another place that we might use.

Remaining empathic while being firm around non-negotiable requirements requires skill and patience. Betty presents options that Diane accurately perceives as coerced choices since the agency is unwilling to negotiate around an alcoholism assessment.

Negotiation and Contracting

The socialization steps presented above lead to negotiation and contracting. Contracting is designed to enhance motivational congruence and increase voluntarism through exploring available choices. We begin with an exploration of the distinction between the "good" relationship and the negotiated relationship. Four negotiating and contracting options with mandated and nonvoluntary clients are then presented, followed by a discussion of obstacles to negotiation and contracting.

The "Good Relationship" and the Negotiated Relationship

Most treatment approaches suggest that the development of a relationship is essential to productive change. Unfortunately, for the practitioner working with involuntary clients, the model for such relationships has been the voluntary relationship. This model "good" relationship assumes contact with clients who are willing to be engaged in a collaborative, contractual service and that practitioners can help by attending to client concerns in a warm, empathic, and genuine fashion (Cingolani 1984). Clients who oppose such collaboration are often labeled resistive. Consequently, practitioners working with involuntary clients often find that their relationships are not "good."

In fact, power and authority issues exist in all practitioner–client relationships, whether mandated or not (Palmer 1983). In addition to employing expert authority, which is invested in practitioners by client confidence in their ability, practitioners also employ legitimate power through the authority of their position, role, and agency. Finally, reward and coercive powers are also inherent in most practice relationships.

One can explore power relationships more directly by considering the negotiated relationship. The negotiated relationship acknowledges use of authority. For example, practitioners working with mandated clients use reward, coercion, and legitimate powers to act as enforcers to induce compliance. They can also act as negotiators who represent the agency in bargaining with the client, as mediators in the interaction between the client and society, as advocates who identify with client interests, and as coaches who collaborate with clients to enhance their capacity for dealing with the environment (Cingolani 1984).

To play the negotiator and mediator, Murdach suggests that practitioners must discover the bargainable, find areas of agreement, engage in critical bargaining, exchange counterproposals, and present the results of the negotiation in a public document (Murdach 1980).

Contracting is a negotiation process resulting in a mutual agreement that specifies client and practitioner roles, goals and target problems, client rights, methods to be used, time limits, tasks agreed upon, and criteria for deciding whether goals are reached (Seabury 1979). If mutual agreement on all goals, roles, and methods is an integral part of contracting, then contracts are rarely feasible for mandated and nonvoluntary clients (ibid.). Some question whether contracts are possible with "captured" clients who do not acknowledge problems nor see the agency or practitioner as a source of help (Rock and Collins 1987). In addition, involuntary clients cannot easily withdraw from the contract and often suffer consequences for failure to comply with its terms. Finally, mandated clients often find such contracts to include unbalanced accountability as the contract is often used more to hold them accountable to the practitioner and agency than vice versa.

Involuntary service plans are documents in which the agency spells out non-negotiable requirements, rights, and consequences for failure to meet requirements. While lacking mutual negotiation of goals, methods, and time limits, such involuntary service plans are necessary in many circumstances in which there are legal mandates and collaboration does not occur (figure 6.5).

Such involuntary service plans have distinct limitations. Some agencies do not require that such plans be signed, or that clients see or have copies of them. When plans are developed with minimal or no client contact, they might better be described as notices of agency intent that detail what the agency and practitioner wish to happen and consequences to the mandated clients for failure to follow these plans. Such notices are analogous to traffic citations that inform the motorist of charges, evidence, legal rights, and constrained choices such as making a court appearance or paying a fine. While situations exist in which such involuntary case plans and notices of intent may be unavoidable, such plans cannot be expected to contribute to motivational congruence or the self-attribution that would permit results to last longer than would the threat of punishment.

The semivoluntary contract is an alternative to the voluntary contract and the involuntary service plan. It acknowledges outside pressures and mandates by specifying non-negotiable requirements and policies, consequences for failure to meet them, and specifies client freedoms and rights. It also includes negotiable options and client-perceived problems. In such a perspective, conflict is defined as normal and the practitioner focuses on constructive ways to manage the conflict. Pursuit of semivoluntary contracts assumes that contracting is an intervention process that goes beyond fulfilling external

Figure 6.5   Voluntary contracts, semivoluntary contracts, and involuntary case plans

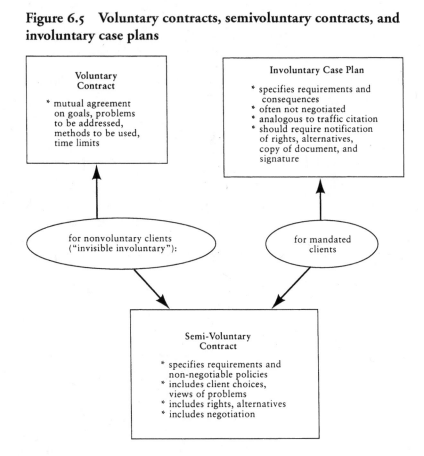

accountability requirements to become a powerful service method designed to enhance compliance, motivational congruence, and self-attribution.

Many mandated clients are able to work with practitioners on semivoluntary contracts when constrained choices are explored. Four strategies for exploring such choices are introduced briefly and then explained in detail below. Mandated clients can choose not to comply with legal mandates and non-negotiable requirements and accept legal penalties through an informed consent strategy. They can also choose to comply with legal mandates and non-negotiable requirements. The practitioner can help mandated clients find their own reasons for complying with mandates through a reframing or agreeable mandate strategy. Mandated clients and practitioners can also come to agreement through provision of an inducement in addition to working on non-negotiable requirements through a quid pro quo strategy. Finally, practitioners can acknowledge motivation to avoid punishing consequences by accepting compliance in order to get rid of the mandate.

Nonvoluntary clients can often move from semivoluntary to voluntary contracts through strategies parallel to those for mandated clients in which they explore constrained choices. The practitioner can first use the informed consent strategy to inform them of their freedom from legal requirements to accept or reject services based on an analysis of the costs and benefits of that service. Nonvoluntary clients can also choose to accept services for their own reasons regardless of outside pressure. They may choose to blend their own concerns with those of the outside pressure through the reframing or agreeable mandate strategy. Nonvoluntary clients can choose to accept services in order to receive an incentive through the quid-pro-quo strategy. Finally, they can choose to accept services in order to "get rid of the outside pressure." Though voluntary contracts remain preferable with nonvoluntary clients, semivoluntary contracts may be beneficial for many. For example, when the nonvoluntary client enters a program or institution with a host of requirements and policies as a "package deal" (i.e., accept these requirements and policies or "choose" to refuse services), such a semivoluntary contract may more accurately reflect the nature of the constrained choice the nonvoluntary client makes than a voluntary contract.

Steps in Negotiation and Contracting

Steps in the negotiation and contracting phase are: (1) explore the client's view of existing problems; (2) explore reframing for an agreeable mandate strategy; (3) explore a quid-pro-quo option; (4) explore a "get rid of the mandate or outside pressure" option; or (5) explore an informed consent option. These strategies may be used in a different order and varying combinations. Variations for work with mandated and nonvoluntary clients are presented.

1. *Explore the client's view of existing problems.* Many involuntary clients present their own views of problems during the socialization phase. Such client views are often missed because they are not the "right" motivations, hence labeled as lack of motivation, refusal to take responsibility, denial, or defensive behavior. The practitioner should listen carefully for expressions of client beliefs, values, and motivations during this phase without labeling them as expressions of no motivation, but rather understand them as expressions of current motivations, values, attitudes, and beliefs.

For example, when Mrs. Torres, a single parent with a full-time job, was in danger of having her child removed from an extremely cluttered home that was a serious fire hazard, she protested that she had already begun efforts to renovate her home. Jean, the child protective service worker, notes that Mrs. Torres has made efforts and compliments her. She will later suggest that Mrs. Torres' efforts may fit in part with the external pressure to make her home a safer place.

MRS. TORRES: These are my things, you know. I'm going to get around to it sometime. In fact, when we moved in, I got some stuff cleaned up right away. But I've really been busy. It's okay, it's good enough, it's better. We've got room here to get through now. And I do have a few more things to do.

JEAN: I know that these are your things. I can also see that you really have made some efforts. What have you worked on so far?

MRS. TORRES: Well, before we moved in we painted the cupboards in the kitchen. Can you see it out there?

JEAN: Yes, they look great. That room really shows that you have been making some efforts.

Rather than labeling Mrs. Torres' efforts as merely minimizing danger, Jean supports the efforts she has made. As Mrs. Torres may feel overwhelmed with the responsibilities of working at a full-time job, managing a house, and parenting a teenager, Jean should also have empathized with the feelings of being overwhelmed. She will also explore the provision of a homemaker to assist Mrs. Torres in her efforts.

Initial attitudes, beliefs, and concerns of mandated clients often include motivations that may be blended with mandates to enhance compliance. For example, Beth was an adolescent who had traveled widely through the child welfare system with stops in residential care, chemical dependency treatment, group care, foster care, and her own home. She had just worn out her welcome in a relative placement with her Aunt Barb. Nancy, her child welfare worker, was operating under a requirement that Beth needed to be living in a stable, permanent placement. While Nancy was exploring the circumstances of Beth's latest move from her Aunt Barb's, Beth said, "I don't want people telling me how to run my life. I don't want it no more. If it ain't my boy friend, it's Barb; if it ain't Barb, it's you; and if it ain't you, it's my parents. All of you guys are running my life and all you guys got me is nowhere."[4]

Rather than labeling Beth's expression as a refusal to accept responsibility for her own part in problems, Nancy might note Beth's implied motivation by suggesting, "It sounds like you have had it with other people making decisions for you."

If involuntary clients have not already expressed problems or concerns in the socialization phase, they are now asked for their views of problems that exist or situations that could be improved. The involuntary client can reply by describing a problem, stating that no problems exist, or make no reply. These responses can further be examined for fit with outside pressures or mandates. Such concerns may be similar to the mandate or outside pressure, unrelated to the mandate or outside pressure, directed at avoiding the mandate or outside pressure, or no response to pressures is expressed. Four contracting strategies will be described below to address these contingencies.

2. *Explore reframing for agreeable mandate strategy.* The practitioner can explore expressed concerns, values, or motivations for fit with outside pressures or mandates. The agreeable mandate is similar to reframing strategies in which practitioners are trained to join clients and families rather than insist that they work on the "right problems for the right reasons." In the solution-focused approach, this seeking of a goal which the involuntary client wishes to pursue is called co-construction of goals (Tohn and Oshlag 1996; De Jong and Berg 2001). One way of pursuing a reframe or agreeable mandate with physically abusive men is to explore a goal of talking about your anger without putting down or endangering others (Chovanec 2007).

a. *Variations for mandated clients.* Practitioners working with mandated clients seek to blend mandated concerns with client motivations such that mandated clients may choose to work on those required concerns for their own reasons. Use of this strategy does not mean that the practitioner joins or "hooks" the client without being clear about his or her own motivation. Mandated clients must be informed that mandated, non-negotiable concerns will be included. Three variations can be explored with mandated clients that blend client concerns with mandated concerns.

Mandated referrals often state or imply deviant labeling and an assumption of responsibility that involuntary clients are unwilling to accept. Mandated clients may, however, discover their own reasons for complying with the mandate. For example, when Jean was working with Mrs. Torres on the child protection issue related to a fire hazard, she found that though Mrs. Torres did not consider the state of her home adequate grounds for removal of her child, she acknowledged that she did not have enough help from her daughter in keeping the house clean. She wanted to have the house cleaned for the holidays, she wanted a safe environment for her child, and she wanted the child welfare agency to stop snooping on her. Mrs. Torres agreed to a contract when the practitioner pointed out that she had already begun making some efforts on her own to clean up, that she might be assisted with a homemaker, that she could get the agency out of her hair, and that she could also avoid a possible placement.

When mandated clients are faced with coerced choices about requirements, they can often choose the way they respond to those requirements. As contact often begins in crisis, the Chinese definition of crisis as a "dangerous opportunity" might be shared. For example, if involuntary clients note that the problem had been building up for awhile but they had not acted to change it, the practitioner might say:

> You have been wrestling with these issues for a long time. You may have thought about getting some help with these issues on your own and now something has happened that forced you to be here. You can make some choices in this situation about how you want to use your time and what you want to get out of this. You might choose to take your chances in court. You might choose to go along and ride it out, doing what you are required to do. You might also choose to use this opportunity to take a look at some of the concerns you have already been aware of.

Similarly, mandated clients might be asked to recall if there was ever a time in their past that something good came out of doing something they did not want to do. When had they made the most out of a bad situation? When had they made "lemonade out of lemons"? Could this be a time to make lemonade again?

Following this strategy, Bill, the probation officer, helps Paul explore possible problems he might choose to work on.

BILL: I want to find out if there are some things you would like to get out of probation, some things that you and I could work on together.

PAUL: Not to get in this situation again.

BILL: Okay, you don't want to be in this kind of situation again in which you are having to serve time for a crime.

PAUL: It doesn't work.

BILL: Okay. Is there anything else you and I can work on together that you would like to get out of probation? Not what the court is saying, but what you would like to get out of probation?

Some mandated clients perceive a concern similar to the mandated reason for referral without accepting responsibility for causing the problem. For example, many parents accused of child abuse think that their children are difficult to control (Rooney 1981). The practitioner could provisionally accept their view of the problem while stipulating that illegal forms of child discipline would not be used and legal, effective alternatives substituted.

Sometimes the mandated concern and the client-expressed problem can be reframed into a new statement that includes both by grouping them at a higher level of abstraction. For example, Beth, the adolescent who thought that "too many people are trying to run her life," was faced with a mandate that she live in an approved placement. Her concern and the mandated problem were blended in a reframed agreeable mandate: Beth thinks that too many people are trying to run her life. She wants to explore independent living. Such a reframing affirms the validity of the client's own concern without blaming or attaching a deviant label to it, while remaining firm about non-negotiable requirements.

b. *Variations for nonvoluntary clients.* Nonvoluntary clients can choose to avoid the outside pressure altogether, to work on their own concerns without regard for that pressure, or to work on a reframed view that includes both the outside pressure and their own concerns.

For example, Mr. Porter was an elderly patient hospitalized with a broken hip who wished to return to his home upon discharge. He was, however, locked in a struggle with medical staff about discharge plans. He did not accept the plans developed by hospital personnel and found ways to circumvent those plans he had not participated in developing. While medical staff members were reluctant for Mr. Porter to return to an unsafe environment and recommended nursing home care, Mr. Porter resented intrusions into his independence (Abramson 1981). In working with Mr. Porter, his hospital social worker presented several options. First, he could choose to avoid the outside pressure altogether. As there was no legal mandate at this point, the medical social worker reaffirmed that he could legally choose to return home against medical advice. She proceeded to present a two-sided argument to assist him in making that decision. Should he choose to return home without assistance, he would be taking chances that he might be reinjured and need to return to the hospital. The social worker also reminded Mr. Porter that he had expressed a wish to return home safely and not to return to the hospital. Hence, he could choose to work on his own concerns without regard to the outside pressure. The social worker then explored the possibility that his concern with returning home safely and not returning to the hospital could include the hospital staff's concerns about his safety. When his own goal of returning home safely was reaffirmed, Mr. Porter became more willing to consider staff advice about how to make that return. The staff meetings that had been structured to convince or pressure Mr. Porter to accept staff views were then restructured. When staff agreed to take the role as consultants to assist him in planning for a safe return and he was able to attend staffings, Mr. Porter and staff negotiated an agreement that included safety provisions he found acceptable, such as assistance in repair of a broken banister and arrangements for a visiting nurse.

The previous strategies assume that many involuntary clients do not wish to work on "the right problems for the right reasons" in the sense of acknowledging the problems attributed by others. This is of course not always true as some involuntary clients genuinely seek help despite the outside pressure or mandate, and accept responsibility for both the problem and the resolution of it (O'Hare 1996). Some involuntary clients readily acknowledge attributed problems, saying things such as: "I know that I need to get in touch with my inability to control my impulses"; "I need to accept my disability"; "I need to get in touch with my codependency issues"; "I need to pay attention in class"; "I need to keep a job"; and "I need to stay sober and accept my responsibilities." Such rapid acceptance, including all the right words and motivations, may indicate internalization, ownership of responsibility for the problem, insight, and confession.

If, however, the admission sounds too good to be true, it may be. Such admissions may be an ingratiating self-presentation strategy designed to reduce pressure through rapid, selective confession. Such expressions may reflect the possibility that the involuntary client is "bilingual" and speaks the jargon of the helping professions. However, rather than labeling such expressions as manipulative or passive aggressive behavior, the practitioner might consider less than full candor understandable and in fact reinforced in many settings. For example, involuntary clients experienced in residential, correctional, chemical dependency, or educational systems (among others) may have been rewarded for confessing or owning problems as seen by the staff that indicate that they are "getting in touch with their issues." There is no immediate way of knowing whether such admissions are genuine or, in fact, "too good to be true." Practitioners may accept such admissions at face value while suggesting that many in similar situations have mixed feelings about being pressured into contact.

The agreeable mandate option is the most positive of the four strategies to be presented and should be frequently explored. If agreement is reached, it should lead to greater compliance of mandated clients, empowerment through making at least constrained choices, self-attribution, and longer-lasting change. The option requires both practitioner time and skill in reframing. Time is, however, often very limited at initial contact and a crisis state may preclude extended negotiation. In addition, the practitioner may think that agreeable mandates effectively link concerns but the involuntary client does not see or accept the linkage.

Should the practitioner and the involuntary client settle on an "agreeable mandate," they can then proceed to elaborate upon a semivoluntary or voluntary contract. If the problems cannot be readily reframed, the involuntary client's expressed concerns do not fit the mandated or outside pressures, or the practitioner wishes to explore additional sources of motivation, the practitioner then proceeds to consider the other strategies presented below.

3. *Explore the quid-pro-quo or "let's make a deal" option.* Often no or weak intrinsic motivation for dealing with the mandated concern is found through the agreeable mandate option. In such cases, exploring use of inducements can strengthen compliance with mandates. In a quid-pro-quo version, the practitioner offers to supply an incentive to a mandated client to make compliance with the requirement more attractive. Deal making is a

commonly accepted practice in many cultures with popular quiz shows such as Deal or No Deal providing ready metaphors. The practitioner can supply an incentive to nonvoluntary clients in exchange for their choice to work on a problem attributed by others. If no acceptable deal is made, the practitioner can continue to explore the strategies that follow.

a. *Variations for mandated clients.* Since practitioners cannot barter on non-negotiable requirements with mandated clients, this option can be used to support mandated compliance by working on an additional voluntary concern, providing incentives, or supporting choices in the form of compliance with the mandate.

i. *Work on an additional voluntary concern.* When a problem is expressed that is unrelated to the mandated concern, practitioners can sometimes make a deal to assist with that concern in addition to work on the mandated problem. For example, Jean, the protective service worker, became aware that Mrs. Torres thought that her daughter was not helping her enough around the house and generally did not follow her rules. While these problems were not directly related to the mandated concern with safety, Jean offered to help Mrs. Torres work with her daughter around house rules and her role in helping make the home a safer place. In addition, Mrs. Torres expressed many times her concern that her valuable things not be discarded in an effort to make the home safe by the standards of others. Jean agreed to help her protect her valuable things as long as they were not a safety hazard.

ii. *Provide an incentive.* The practitioner can offer to provide an incentive to enhance compliance. For example, in a diversion program for prostitutes, a practitioner agreed to advocate for a reduction in loitering tickets contingent on the prostitutes' willingness to participate in treatment programs.

iii. *Support choice within the bounds of compliance.* Practitioners can support the selection of options in the way that requirements are implemented. For example, when Mr. James became aware that he was going to be involuntarily hospitalized, he became extremely agitated and struggled with mental health staff. A mental health aide then clarified for him that the permission for involuntary hospitalization had been gotten and Mr. James could not immediately change that. He could choose, however, how he would go to the ward, and he could be helped to initiate a legal appeal after he got to the ward. If he continued struggling, he would be forcibly restrained and taken to the unit. If he were able to become calmer, he would be able to walk up to the unit accompanied by mental health aides but without restraints. Mr. James calmed himself and chose to walk up to the ward, accompanied by the aides.

b. *Variations for nonvoluntary clients.* Use of incentives with nonvoluntary clients must not involve rights, entitlements, and basic necessities, but rather entail additional benefits that the practitioner or agency is not required to provide. The success of this option depends on the ease with which the nonvoluntary client can acquire similar incentives in other ways. Hence, the quid-pro-quo option is subject to abuse with vulnerable clients from oppressed groups. For example, a Native American woman from Minnesota left her child with relatives out of state. When she did not return at the agreed-upon time, the relatives contacted social services and requested that the child be placed. When the woman returned, she discovered that her child was in a white foster home. She was assessed as having a drinking problem and the agency did not agree to release her child to foster care in Minnesota or return the child to her until she completed a chemical dependency treatment program and got a job. These requirements were illegal as Native American children are entitled to placement in Native American homes as a first option, without condition (Indian Child Welfare Act). Similarly, transfer of the child to Minnesota was a right, not a privilege. In this case, establishing conditions for placement of the child in a Native American home and in Minnesota was illegal and an unethical abuse of a vulnerable client from an oppressed group. Capacity to parent the child might be appropriately assessed by social services in Minnesota in a way that did not violate these legal and ethical rights.

i. *Work on an additional voluntary concern in exchange for compliance with external pressure.* There are accounts of bartering with clients with severe and persistent mental illness in which community support practitioners agree to supply a benefit sought by a client living in the community in exchange for an agreement to regularly take prescribed medication (Angell, Mahoney, and Martinez 2006).

ii. *Provide of an inducement.* Alice Donat, the client described in chapter 1 who lived in a home with many cats and just above the threshold of legal danger, agreed to explore her eligibility for social security benefits if the practitioner would accompany her and arrange transportation to the office. In this case, since assistance with client transportation was not a client right, it might be provided as a legitimate inducement.

There are four concerns with the quid-pro-quo option. It is unethical to barter basic rights, entitlements, and necessities for compliance with mandated or externally pressured goals. Inducements must be an additional benefit beyond normal entitlements. As practitioners and agencies are sometimes tempted to cross this legal and ethical line, the strategy is subject to abuse with vulnerable involuntary clients from oppressed groups who have limited alternative access to desired resources. For example, adolescent parents who are themselves wards of the child welfare system have limited sources of income as they seek to complete school or GED and acquire job training while retaining their children (Teen Parenting Service Network 2005). The child welfare agency may well foster compliance with agency goals of supporting birth control with cash incentives beyond legal levels of support (ibid.).

Second, this option may "buy" behavioral compliance without changing attitudes or promoting self-attributed change. Some practitioners and settings may reject behavioral compliance without prior attitude change as "working on the right problems for the wrong reasons," insisting on acceptance of mandated or externally pressured changes for the right reasons. While such acknowledgment of attributed problems might be desirable, insistence on attitude change as a precondition for behavioral change is rarely successful. This option makes it more likely that behavior will change and attitude change may follow. However, compliance should not be expected to be maintained indefinitely unless that compliance becomes intrinsically rewarding or rewarded in the environment. To support self-attribution and longer-lasting maintenance, the inducements should be small and phased into natural reinforcement.

Use of this option also presumes that the practitioner has access to valued resources, is empowered with discretion to make deals, and has the time required to negotiate. Many agencies have policies that discourage making special arrangements on the grounds that they are unfair to other clients not offered such options. Hence, much of the legal reform in work with public agencies has focused on removing discretion and establishing uniform procedures. Even when negotiation is permitted, practitioners often lack access to incentives and have limited time for exploring them. With these reservations, the examples above suggest that with imagination and sensitivity, practitioners can be aware of issues that can act as ethical incentives for clients.

Finally, practitioners must learn how to negotiate. As negotiation requires the practitioner to engage in an exchange of proposals and counterproposals, practitioners have to learn how to continue negotiation without personalizing the problem even when an unacceptable counterproposal has been presented. For example, when Jean offered to advocate for the placement of a housekeeper to assist Mrs. Torres in cleaning up her home, Mrs. Torres responded that she wouldn't mind having a homemaker if she was under her control. Jean then clarifies the conditions under which a homemaker might be provided.

MRS. TORRES: You know, I wouldn't mind having a homemaker if I could tell her what to do. Now, I don't want you guys to be running my house. I mean this homemaker, I'd be in charge of her, I could tell her what to do, you guys wouldn't tell her to come and take all this stuff out?

JEAN: Well, that's a good question about who would be in charge. I am here to make sure that you and Julie are safe. So the homemaker would be working for the agency as part of our plan to help you get the house into a safe condition and not directly working for you. You could work with her in identifying the valuable things you want to keep and the things that you just consider junk.

4. *Explore the "get rid of the mandate or outside pressure" option.* Many involuntary clients express no concern or acknowledge only the pressure to see the practitioner as a concern: "Other than being here with you, I've got no problems." Such responses are often interpreted as denial, resistance, or failure to accept responsibility rather than accepted as an indication that the involuntary client does not acknowledge attributed problems. The practitioner can take the initiative by suggesting that facing a mandated situation or pressure from others may be a problem that the involuntary client might wish eliminated (Moore-Kirkland 1981).

In this "get rid of the mandate or outside pressure" option, the involuntary client may agree to contact in order to avoid or eliminate pressure rather than by acknowledging the validity of the outside pressure or mandate or through actions to receive an incentive. Hence, this option relies on punishment avoidance motivation, rather than the inducement and self-attribution motivations characteristic of the first two options.

If the involuntary client accepts this option, the practitioner can proceed to formalize a semivoluntary contract with the client. Should no agreement be reached, the practitioner can proceed to an informed consent strategy.

a. *Variations for mandated clients.* Mandated clients often respond to mandated pressure as if to punishment, whether or not that pressure is designed in part to help or rehabilitate the client. Rather than continuing to argue about the merits of work on the mandated problem, acknowledging a motivation of punishment avoidance or elimination can be a useful step toward some motivational congruence. For example, some involuntary clients find the option to end the contact early more acceptable than contracting around a problem they consider invalid. Since many adolescent clients on court-ordered supervision consider requirements for regular contact with a practitioner aversive, the practitioner can capitalize on this motivation by negotiating frequency and number of contacts based on compliance with a set of required tasks. This option can sometimes be used at a point in which more positive motivations have not been found. For example, after the home investigation revealed that Mrs. Torres would need to clean and remove boxes if Julie were to be safe, she did not respond placidly to this news.

MRS. TORRES: I don't know why you people are making such a big deal. The people down the street are yelling and fighting and I hear them screaming and playing music; and here I got a few too many boxes and you people come in here and tell me how to run my life. This is my house and these are my things, you shouldn't be able to tell me I have to get rid of them. Why don't you investigate those people, who are about three houses down, they've got trash out in their backyard and they are always yelling and screaming in the middle of the night. And here you are picking on some-body like me. I'm working, taking care of my kids, you guys make me sick.

JEAN: I can see that you are very angry because of my comments about the boxes in the other room.

MRS. TORRES: Well, of course I'm angry. You come in here, you high and mighty, you think you're so good. Why wouldn't I be angry, did you ever have anybody tell you about your house, that they don't like it?

JEAN: No, that has not happened to me, but I'm sure that I would be angry too.

MRS. TORRES: Well, I am. I am.

JEAN: I can hear that you are angry. If we had gotten a report on your neigh-bors, someone would have to conduct an investigation.

MRS. TORRES: Well, I ought to report them and get you off my back. I'm working hard.

JEAN: You want me out, huh?

MRS. TORRES: Yes.

JEAN: Well, again, I'm here because we need to make sure Julie is safe. And the way to do that is to help get the house into a safe condition. If you want me out, as soon as Julie is safe and the house is safe, I'm out.

This option may also be used simultaneously with other more positive contracting strategies. After the above exchange, a semivoluntary contract was agreed upon with Mrs. Torres including: (1) she wanted her home clean for the holidays and to retain custody of Julie (agreeable mandate); (2) she would receive the assistance of a homemaker for a time limited period; (3) Jean would work with Mrs. Torres and Julie to help them work together in cleaning up ("let's make a deal"); and (4) Mrs. Torres wanted to "get you people out of my hair" (get rid of mandate).

b. *Variations with nonvoluntary clients.* While nonvoluntary clients can choose to avoid working with the practitioner, they may also choose to work on ridding themselves of the outside pressure without acknowledging its le-gitimacy. For example, many schoolchildren are referred to counselors and social workers for a variety of attributed problems such as inattention, tru-ancy, and inadequate study skills. While they frequently do not acknowledge these teacher-attributed problems, they often acknowledge other problems: "Other students provoke me, get me in trouble with the teacher"; "The teacher picks on me." Hence, if the problem is framed according to an ac-knowledged problem such as "to get the teacher off my back," a semivolun-tary contract may be reached (Epstein and Brown 2002). For example, Walter summed up the situation with Mrs. Simmons, who was in a nonvoluntary relationship with the county worker over care of her child.

WALTER: From what you're telling me, you are pretty concerned about what's going on at the school. The school has concerns and you have your own concerns. You think that something needs to change between Jamie, the school, and yourself.

MRS. SIMMONS: Yeah, something definitely needs to change there.

WALTER: If we can get things changed at school, so that the other kids and teachers aren't picking on Jamie, and so that his behavior improves there, that will satisfy the court. If we start making some progress, the court would probably dismiss that consent decree early. You'll get them off your back. It will also get the school off your back. It also sounds as if Jamie's behavior at home could also be the focus of some attention. It can't be a lot of fun to go to work in a high stress job, then come home and have the teacher calling you and saying, "This or that happened today, and I want you to do something about it." And then for you to tell Jamie you want him to do something, and he tells you, "No." It's got to be frustrating. And I think that maybe we can look at that too, if you'd like.

Since this option focuses on removing a threat of punishment, it entails less positive motivation than the first two. Negative reinforcement strategies may enhance compliance without leading to self-attribution. Consequently, this option runs the risk of buying compliance only for the length of the contract and, like the "let's make a deal" or quid pro quo strategy, may be seen as working on "the right problems for the wrong reasons" by some referral sources and agencies. It does, however, connect with client motivation to restore freedom and hence may reduce reactance and enhance compliance. In addition, practitioners with access to coercive power may be tempted to overuse it. For example, practitioners working with mandated clients may frequently find punishment avoidance motivation immediately available and may be tempted to begin with it. In order to support motivational congruence and self-attribution, it should be attempted after or in conjunction with the more positive strategies described earlier.

5. *Explore the informed consent option.* Should none of the above achieve a level of motivational congruence, the practitioner can pursue a final informed consent option. Mandated clients can be reminded of their right to accept the consequences for failing to work on legal requirements or choose to comply with the minimum acceptable level to satisfy the requirement. Nonvoluntary clients can be reminded repeatedly through the contracting sequence that they can choose not to accept services. The decision not to accept services should, however, include information about potential consequences of that choice.

a. *Variations for mandated clients.* Some mandated clients experience such a negative reaction to forced contact that even agreeing to "get rid of the mandate" is not acceptable since it symbolizes some compliance in a disagreeable process. Hence, some mandated clients may choose to accept a legal penalty or the threat that a penalty will be imposed, or choose to comply with the bare minimum.

Those choices and their consequences can be clarified including the potentially self-defeating consequences of deciding not to contract. By refusing contracting options, the mandated client places most decision making in the practitioner's hands. For example, after having several contracting possibilities rejected by a teenaged client referred for delinquency, one practitioner proceeded to write her assessment in the client's presence. When the client asked what she was doing, the practitioner explained that since he had not chosen to participate in contracting, she was proceeding to carry out her job requirements and develop a plan without his input.

Some mandated clients reconsider when the consequences of failure to reach agreement are clarified and earlier options can be reexamined in search of a semivoluntary contract. If the mandated client does not reconsider contracting, the practitioner can empathize with pressures felt, and proceed to reaffirm the non-negotiable requirements of contact. The practitioner's role will essentially be one of enforcer at this point in contact, though more voluntary contracting may be possible later. Failure to reconsider may indicate high reactance and, if so, that assessment is based on attempting several strategies to reduce reactance rather than based on a premature conclusion at the beginning of contact.

Some writers have suggested that high reactance in the form of opposition to all practitioner initiatives may call for use of a defiance-based paradoxical strategy. For example, if lack of compliance with practitioner initiatives can be predicted, then the practitioner might prescribe the opposite of what is desired (Rohrbaugh et al. 1981; Shoham and Rohrbaugh 1997). Caution in use of defiance-based paradoxes is recommended with mandated clients. While evidence suggests that paradoxes can sometimes be effective in achieving compliance with practitioner goals, that achievement often occurs without self-attribution of gains. The short-term compliance gains may also jeopardize the potential for influence later in the relationship since persuasive influence may be more likely to occur if involuntary clients come to see the practitioner as trustworthy.

b. *Variations for nonvoluntary clients.* As the decision to accept or reject services is the legal and ethical right of nonvoluntary clients, any form of heavy-handed pressure is inappropriate. Hence, outreach efforts to potentially "at risk" clients such as teenaged single parents of newborns should provide information that can assist in making informed choices. For example, the practitioner might plant a seed with inductive questions about possible future difficulties experienced by others in similar situations and give the client information about resources they can seek should they come to have concerns in the future.

This section has presented contracting strategies designed to enhance compliance with mandates and non-negotiable requirements and also to facilitate motivational congruence, self-determination, and achievement of client-defined goals. Use of the contracting options should empower the practitioner and involuntary client toward more frequent semivoluntary or voluntary contracting solutions. Practitioners skilled in these strategies should be able to reduce client reactance in the initial phase of contact, increase compliance with mandated goals and non-negotiable policies, and achieve more frequent motivational congruence. While these hypotheses are based on theory and research reviewed earlier in the book, they will require further testing with specific target problems and client populations before they can be accepted as effective.

In addition, many obstacles to use of these strategies can be anticipated in advance. Obstacles coming from involuntary clients, practitioners, and agencies can be anticipated when there is lack of resources, competence, or skills, or adverse beliefs. Suggestions for dealing with these obstacles are also presented.

Lack of Resources, Competence, and Skills

Lack of adequate resources, competence, and skills can impede negotiation and contracting. Many involuntary clients lack competence, skill, or experience in contracting. Since contracting is largely a cognitive process, some clients lack the capacity to negotiate complex contracts. Further, practitioners sometimes consider that since some clients make impulsive decisions or ones based on factors the practitioners consider irrelevant, they cannot effectively participate in contracting. We noted in chapter 4 how Wilmer's decision to take antipsychotic medication was not based on an acceptance of its value for its own sake. Whether or not the client's decision-making process is one that the practitioner considers acceptable, clients continue to make decisions. Use of the options in simple, concrete form should produce greater motivational congruence and success than if such congruence is not pursued.

Lack of resources, competence, and skills can also occur with practitioners and agencies. Social services frequently struggle with limited resources, often resulting in large caseloads and limited attention to individual clients. Consequently, practitioners can sometimes barely carry out the minimum mandated requirements while keeping up their paperwork. They may have little time to work on problems other than mandated or required concerns. Such overload can lead to standardized rather than individualized case plans, crisis-driven work, and "going through the motions."

In addition, practitioners may not be permitted discretion to make deals such that they have little leverage over the packaging and form of requirements. Court orders and agency non-negotiable policies are sometimes written such that discretion in interpretation is unclear, or discretion is actively discouraged. Funding bodies may require mandated goals and not encourage individualizing those goals. For example, the frequency of contacts between a probation officer and client may be dictated by results of an assessment instrument rather than negotiated with the mandated client. Consequently, involuntary clients may desire a resource that the practitioner cannot provide and hence an acceptable exchange may not be attainable. Even when resources and discretion are available, effective use of the options requires practice and increasing skill in reframing and bargaining through separating the non-negotiable from the negotiable.

Use of the contracting options will not resolve resource deficits or increase discretion, and additional strategies are needed to influence such system needs. In the short run, the practitioner might be advised to attempt using the options as time permits. As experience and competence in use of the strategies increases, it should be possible to use them on a larger proportion of the caseload.

In addition, involuntary contacts often occur in a state of crisis such that involuntary clients fight with all their energies to preserve the status quo. Providing help with the perceived crisis is often an essential first step. Practitioners and agencies also have crises. For many key involuntary positions such as child protection work, turnover is high and new practitioners enter work with limited training. Sudden additions to an already pressured caseload may put the practitioner in a crisis state, whether or not the client is actually in crisis. Finally, agency resource limitations can create a crisis mentality in the agency. The strategies presented here are proactive and can, in the long run, reduce some kinds of client and practitioner crises by ensuring that there is motivational congruence with at least some clients.

Since even semivoluntary contracts involve an exchange of goods and services acceptable to all parties, sometimes an acceptable exchange is not reached. As involuntary clients may decide that requirements are unfair, unreasonable, or impossible to attain, they may decide to improve their situation outside of negotiation. When coerced choices entail "godfather's choices" between unacceptable alternatives such as accepting services or being prosecuted, many involuntary clients will not consider these as choices. Since perceived intrusiveness of a threat to freedom varies such that what is considered overwhelming by one person may be acceptable to another, agreements may be reached with some and not others. Practitioners should advocate for fair, nondiscriminatory options. If they do not succeed in modifying unfair options, then high client reactance, apathy, and powerlessness may result as a consequence of overwhelming unfair requirements.

Adverse Beliefs

The contracting process may also be inhibited by adverse beliefs, on the part of clients, practitioners, and agencies, including the need to work on the right problems for the right reasons, beliefs that contracts and case plans are paperwork formalities rather than inherently valuable intervention processes, that the other party to the negotiation cannot be trusted, that goals conflict, and that oppose negotiation.

Practitioners working with involuntary clients are often influenced by approaches that insist on early ownership of responsibility for harm caused and for the success of change efforts. While self-attributed change is desirable, insistence on early ownership of responsibility may produce counterproductive stalemate and prevent later influence. Consequences of such beliefs in required early ownership of responsibility may be a continued struggle to outsmart involuntary clients and ultimate reliance on power to reward and punish. Practitioners operating under such beliefs in the necessity of the right reason for the right problem may have to accept as inevitable that they will continue to pull teeth and to work harder than the involuntary client who may appear oblivious to problems or needs to change. Failure to produce coerced change may reinforce pessimism and contribute to beliefs that congruence is not possible, that clients are not changeable, and lead to further client labeling.

The options presented here suggest that while complete congruence is frequently impossible, some congruence is often better than none. Use of the strategies does not mean practitioner acceptance of responsibility for outcome but rather acceptance of responsibility for facilitating congruence. It may be easier for a practitioner to reach such a position if the agency has also come to terms with what can and cannot be changed. To use a baseball analogy, use of the strategies should increase the practitioner's batting average: skills in facilitating congruence does not mean that the practitioner will have a hit each time at the plate, but should connect more frequently. Averaging 3.5 hits in ten opportunities is often enough to win batting titles and may be a desirable goal for practitioners working with involuntary clients.

In addition, contracts and case plans are often considered paperwork rituals by both involuntary clients and practitioners. Practitioners may approach them as non-negotiable paperwork requirements completed to satisfy the needs of invisible state or agency auditors and visible supervisors. There may be few positive consequences for writing them effectively and negative consequences for lateness, checking the wrong box, or inconsistent use of the form. Practitioners may also have found that such paper transactions bear little resemblance to a reality in which involuntary clients sometimes provide superficial agreement, provide signatures without intending compliance, or may not even see the case plan. Similarly, involuntary clients may have experienced such "agreements" in the past as a railroaded formality. Use of semivoluntary contracts will hence require some belief in the value of the process by practitioners. Involuntary clients without prior experience in other systems may be more optimistic about their value.

While contracts should build trust, there are many reasons why practitioners suspect lack of candor from involuntary clients and involuntary clients have similar suspicions of the practitioner. As the practitioner is not the agent of the mandated client, those clients have reason to be careful in deciding what information they will share. Their own perceived problems may have appeared petty and were punished in the past as a lack of accepting responsibility for "the problem." As suggested earlier, early confessions may have been rewarded in the past, whether or not they were sincere. Such experienced involuntary clients may have found that you may not have to comply completely as long as you say the right words.

Similarly, involuntary clients have reasons to be suspicious of practitioner candor. Practitioners and agencies often do have hidden agendas. Mandated practitioners are not in place primarily to serve involuntary clients. Practitioners may practice manipulative, hooking strategies in which the axiom "start where the client is" is an instrumental technique used "to get them to where you them want to go." Hence, strategies of superficial agreement on one set of goals while in fact pursuing a hidden agenda to get at the "root problem" is common practice. Some writers have suggested that complete candor may impede effectiveness as the client system may oppose any overt change effort (Haley 1990). Similarly, service decisions are not always made on the merits of the case but according to agency policy and resources. For example, while reducing out-of-home placement costs has played at least a part in the current movement toward home-based services, this reason is not always shared with families.

In addition, agencies may not expect or wish for the contract to succeed. If they assess high probabilities of failure, they may be unwilling to take chances and in fact be prepared to go through the motions of making reasonable efforts. While greater candor on all sides might make for a better world, it would be more realistic at this point to accept lack of complete candor as expectable in involuntary transactions. Accepting such lack of candor without labeling it as a client characteristic then prepares for contracting that may empower both practitioners and clients by building dual accountability. Greater candor may be facilitated by modeling it: talking about power and its requirements and limits may increase trust. Such candor entails clarity about non-negotiables, consequences, and also practitioner hopes for changes beyond those required. While complete candor is probably impossible for either side of the transaction, the amount of energy devoted to hidden agendas should be reduced since modeling candor may facilitate greater effectiveness.

Lack of trust is also related to conflicting goals, both shared and unshared. Involuntary clients may agree to goals that they are ambivalent about reaching. For example, clients sometimes enter Alcoholics Anonymous groups with ambivalence about whether they wish to abstain from drinking. Similarly, agencies have multiple, conflicting goals in which they must simultaneously placate different constituencies such as taxpayers, supervisory boards, state oversight agencies, advocacy groups, and professional associations. Responsibilities to involuntary clients may play a small role in such considerations. In such circumstances, agencies may have given the message to the practitioner openly or covertly to make the involuntary client change by any means necessary, in which collaborative methods may be preferred but other means are approved if deemed necessary. The organization may believe that intervention can be used deterministically to change behavior and attitudes regardless of client wishes.

Such pressures often lead to involuntary service plans that include a large number of non-negotiable requirements designed to comply with the wishes of outside parties. Such service plans might be termed "cover your posterior" or "kitchen sink" contracts designed to demonstrate to outside constituencies that all bases have been covered, though there may not be enough hours in the day to touch all those bases. While such arrangements may appear to outside parties as thorough case plans, under the premise that the more treatment the better, they may in fact be doomed to fail. They may be used to demonstrate lack of client competence when in fact their purpose may be to demonstrate that an effort has been made, though in fact the effort may be primarily cosmetic.

Difficult issues are raised when such contracts are developed to protect involuntary clients and their vulnerable dependents. Compromises with the safety of others must not be made. Nor, however, should contracts that have no reasonable chance of succeeding be standard practice.

Clients, practitioners, and agencies may also be opposed to the negotiation process. Alienated involuntary clients may see practitioners with name tags as signals identifying them as members of occupation forces. Negotiation may be perceived as trickery to get them to do what they do not want to do. Negotiation may also be perceived as a sign of weakness that can be overcome with intimidating self-presentation.

Practitioners and agencies may also distrust negotiation. For example, it is sometimes believed that delinquent youth need a corrective experience with authority in which it is important to present a firm, fair set of requirements that cannot be undermined and overwhelmed. From this viewpoint, delinquent youth need and subconsciously want a structure that will hold them accountable. Consequently, negotiation might be seen as presenting a weak role model of authority, of coddling when firmness is required. Such beliefs imply that negotiation might give away critical power and authority, and model susceptibility to intimidation and manipulation. Constructive models of authority do not, however, require rigidity on all issues. Firmness on non-negotiable requirements and flexibility on negotiable items may be an alternative model of authority. Skills are then required in separating the non-negotiable from the negotiable.

Agencies and practitioners will need to explore the extent to which the obstacles described above occur in their practice. If such practice can be facilitated in its setting, the practitioner can proceed to develop a formal contract. Consequently, we proceed in chapter 7 to present guidelines for developing a formal contract and initiating mutually developed task plans for implementing that contract.

Discussion Questions

1. Socialization and contracting takes time. Practitioners often report that they barely have time to carry out essential elements of an assessment/investigation and that engaging potential clients is not a high organizational priority (Richards, Ruch, and Trevithick 2005). What are the implications of not engaging clients at this point?

2. It has been suggested from the stages of change perspective that many clients will be in the precontemplation or contemplation stage regarding their acknowledgment of attributed problems. What are the implications for the validity of action plans and contracts developed at this stage?

3. Practitioners attempting persuasion may represent agencies that some clients do not believe to be acting in their best interest. What are the implications for the potential success of such efforts?

4. What have you experienced related to organizational beliefs that involuntary clients need to work on "the right problems for the right reasons"? What are the implications of your beliefs?

Notes

1. This selection of dialogue is abstracted from a training videotape entitled *Socialization at Chemical Dependency Intake,* by Dick Leonard. This videotape is available from Ron Rooney at the University of Minnesota. See appendix for list of training tapes available and ordering information.

2. This tape, entitled *Nonvoluntary Client Contracting,* by Walter Mirk, is available from Ron Rooney at the University of Minnesota.

3. This dialogue is edited from a training videotape entitled *Socialization with a Probation Client,* with Bill Linden as practitioner. It is available from Ron Rooney at the University of Minnesota.

4. This interview segment comes from a training videotape entitled *Permanency Planning: Use of the Task-Centered Model with an Adolescent toward Independent Living. The Contracting Phase,* with Nancy Taylor. The video is available from the School of Social Work at the University of Wisconsin.

Chapter 7

Task-Centered Intervention with
Involuntary Clients

──

If application of the guidelines discussed in the preceding chapters results in a preliminary semivoluntary or voluntary contract, a variety of specific intervention models can be selected according to setting and type of problem. For example, particular chemical dependency treatment models or alternatives to aggression approaches might be selected for work with chemically dependent clients and men who have problems with violence. Some of these models are developed in part 3 of this book.

This chapter presents adaptations of one model, task-centered casework, that can be useful across many involuntary problems and populations. The foundation constructed in part 1 of this book is empirically based, drawing on theory eclectically and assuming a multisystems approach. Further, that foundation strongly emphasizes motivational congruence and careful limits on paternalistic prescriptions about client problems. Each of these features is a component of the task-centered approach, as described in the text that follows. Other task-centered features, such as time limits, are adapted only in part, since much work with involuntary clients is not short term. While the task-centered approach is not the only general model to serve as the basis for adaptations, it is hoped that the techniques developed here will be useful on their own and might also serve as a model for how other approaches might be adapted.

Based in the task-centered approach, techniques for *formalizing the contract* and *developing initial tasks* in semivoluntary contracts and involuntary service plans are presented. Four adaptations of the task-centered approach to work with involuntary clients are presented in specifying target problems, establishing clear goals, developing general tasks, and establishing time limits. The chapter continues with guidelines for developing initial client tasks, initial practitioner tasks, anticipation of obstacles, providing a rationale for task completion, necessary incentives, guided practice, and summarization of task plans.

Guidelines for middle-phase intervention follow. They include progress review, task review, assessment of obstacles, dealing with crises, and task plan revision. Special attention is devoted to *confrontation* because confrontation is more likely to be successful in the middle phase of work than earlier. The chapter concludes with consideration of issues in *termination* with involuntary clients.

Introduction to the Task-Centered Approach

The task-centered model is a time-limited, empirically based approach to intervention that focuses on the reduction of specific, agreed-upon target problems through the planning and implementation of client and practitioner tasks to be carried out in the environment (Reid 1992, 2000; Epstein and Brown 2002). The task-centered approach has been tested in work with the aging, family agencies, foster care, public schools, corrections, and mental health facilities (Epstein and Brown 2002). While the field studies testing the model vary in quality and rigor, they consistently report that clients appear to be helped with their primary target problems, especially when the problems are specific and relatively limited in scope (Reid 2000).

The task-centered model is based on two explicit values: (1) the client's expressed, considered wish is given precedence over other problems as defined by the practitioner, the agency, or significant others and (2) knowledge developed from empirical research is valued more highly than knowledge based primarily in theory or practice experience. As introduced in chapter 2, this approach distinguishes between problems *attributed* to the client by others and problems that the client *acknowledges*, with emphasis on the latter (Reid 1978). Such focus on acknowledged target problems minimizes deadlocks, is congruent with client interests, facilitates independence and right of choice, and maintains as much client control over fate as possible. Since involuntary clients are regularly faced with attributed problems, it is important to know that use of the task-centered approach does not prevent the practitioner from exploring attributed problems and needs as well as acknowledged problems and wants. The task-centered practitioner may work simultaneously on mandated and voluntary problems, and indeed mandated problems cannot be ignored when the consequences may be severe losses to client interest and well-being. Normally, mandated problems are agreed to on the condition that the client's own target problems are accepted by the practitioner (Reid 1978). The approach distinguishes between attributed problems that are legally mandated and those that are not. If an attributed problem is not legally mandated and the client's view appears incomplete, the task-centered practitioner may raise other problems or ways of looking at problems and attempt to make a persuasive case for those additional views. However, the client is free to reject the practitioner's suggestions *unless* the problem happens to be legally mandated. Exceptions to use of the approach occur when the client is currently incompetent, incapable, homicidal, or suicidal. In such cases, the practitioner may have to act to prevent clear and present harm (Epstein 1988).

Clients are aided in reducing target problems through the development of tasks that are activities planned in the session by the practitioner and client, to be implemented by the client or practitioner outside of the session. Tasks are further specified into general tasks that are broad plans of action and operational tasks that are the specific plans that a client might undertake between one session and the next. For example, completing job applications might be a general task and developing a first draft of a resume before the next session might be an operational task.

The normal time limit for the approach is six to twelve sessions, and clients can usually be helped to reduce two or three target problems within this time period. Since some clients have continuing longer-term contact with practitioners, the model includes provisions for recontracting, moving to a monitoring status, or linking to other forms of treatment.

The task-centered practitioner attempts to set change into motion in target problems through a self-understanding, verbal, reflective strategy (Reid 1978). Such work is enhanced by practitioners who convey acceptance, respect, and understanding to clients. Hence, task-centered practitioners try to actualize warmth, empathy, and genuineness within a problem focus (ibid.).

Adaptations of the Task-Centered Approach to Work with Involuntary Clients

The task-centered approach has been studied in a variety of mandated and nonvoluntary settings including child welfare, residential treatment, aging, probation, juvenile detention, chemical dependency, and public schools (Pazaratz 2000; Epstein and Brown 2002). While certain aspects of the approach fit well with involuntary work, other aspects are less compatible (figure 7.1).

Figure 7.1   Advantages and disadvantages of task-centered approach in work with involuntary client

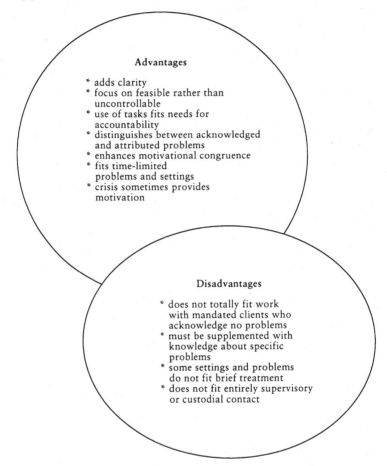

Advantages

* adds clarity
* focus on feasible rather than uncontrollable
* use of tasks fits needs for accountability
* distinguishes between acknowledged and attributed problems
* enhances motivational congruence
* fits time-limited problems and settings
* crisis sometimes provides motivation

Disadvantages

* does not totally fit work with mandated clients who acknowledge no problems
* must be supplemented with knowledge about specific problems
* some settings and problems do not fit brief treatment
* does not fit entirely supervisory or custodial contact

Several advantages of the task-centered approach for work with involuntary clients have been described in the literature. Foremost among these is *goal focus*, which helps practitioners focus on feasible action and reduces preoccupation with unattainable goals (Goldberg, Walker, and Robinson 1977). This goal clarity can help specify vague surveillance duties that otherwise often take the form of aimless visiting, "purposeless probation," and "hovering" over clients (ibid.). Work on limited goals is often also possible while at the same time progress on other problems may be slower. Finally, goal specificity matches social service trends emphasizing accountability and objective measures of service delivery.

The task-centered approach also assists in pursuit of *motivational congruence*. Emphasis on client-acknowledged problems moves away from preoccupation with totally imposed treatment plans by enhancing client collaboration and respect, clarifying expectations and rights, and distinguishing between mandated and voluntary problems. Third, *planned brevity* and *focus on client tasks* fits many involuntary settings that feature brief contact or require action to determine recommendations for terminating contact. Finally, the *crisis state* in which initial involuntary contact often takes place can provide at least temporary motivation to work on attributed problems through redefinition to include agreed-upon target problems. Such contracting around the crisis can then provide direction and assist in restoring equilibrium.

The task-centered approach fits less well with the needs for practice with involuntary clients in other areas. Since the task-centered approach is a model of voluntary, or at least semivoluntary, contact, it does not readily apply to work with mandated clients who do not acknowledge any problems or agree to work on tasks. In addition, time limits are not compatible with extended contact in settings such as residential treatment. Also, while studies conducted in public services have indicated that one-third to one-half of public social service clients could be served within the task-centered approach (Goldberg, Walker, and Robinson 1977), other circumstances remain in which contact is primarily supervisory, custodial, or supportive. Agency purposes can also be so problem focused that the scope of additional target problems that clients might wish to address is limited. For example, chemical dependency counselors may be instructed to address chemical use problems and provide outside referrals for additional client-defined problems. In addition, clients sometimes express target problems that conflict with the protection of the interests of others. Finally, the task-centered model is primarily a structure for providing service that must be augmented by information on particular problems and supporting theories.

Several adaptations to the approach have been developed to facilitate work in involuntary settings. First, in settings that have a particular problem focus, task-centered work can be facilitated by *limiting the permissible scope of target problems*. Second, the powerful role played by referral sources and mandated agencies with involuntary clients has resulted in guidelines to *maintain close involvement with referral sources,* informing them regularly of progress and agreements. Third, in long-term treatment settings such as community care of clients with serious and persistent mental illness, *continuation contracts* have been used in which a series of task-centered contracts may be completed with the same client. These sequences may occur one after the other or with breaks in which monitoring or non–task-centered contact continues. Fourth, *case management contracts* are sometimes developed that include tasks that link clients to other forms of treatment such as drug treatment. Finally, *specific information about particular target problems can be consulted in the development of tasks.* For example, task-centered work in foster care includes a focus on tasks to facilitate parental visitation that is informed by foster care research (figure 7.2).

Formalizing the Involuntary Contract

Additional guidelines for formalizing the involuntary contract adapting the task-centered approach are now presented. They include specifying target problem conditions to be changed, establishing clear goals, developing general tasks, and establishing time limits (figure 7.3).

Specifying Target Problem Conditions to Be Changed

Intervention plans can be more focused if the specific conditions of the problems to be rectified are identified. Target problem conditions include those

Figure 7.2   Adaptations of task-centered approach to involuntary settings

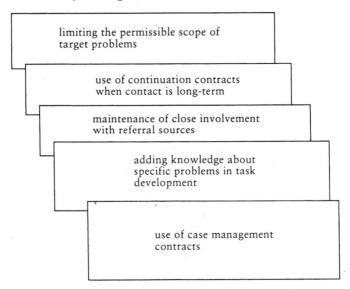

limiting the permissible scope of target problems

use of continuation contracts when contact is long-term

maintenance of close involvement with referral sources

adding knowledge about specific problems in task development

use of case management contracts

Figure 7.3   Task-centered contract

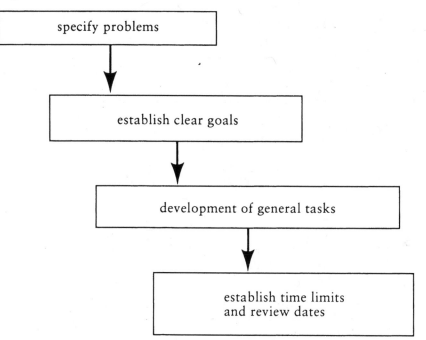

that occur with some frequency and those that are either present or absent. For example, the number of job applications completed, a condition that can be measured with some frequency while securing court permission for independent living, is a present/absent condition. In some cases, assessment tools are available that can be used to measure the extent of a problem (Okamoto and Le Croy 2004; Usher 2004). In other cases, practitioners may need to develop their own indicators of the problem conditions.

When conditions are identified, a baseline measure can then be taken of the current extent of the problem to develop a standard of progress toward resolution. For example, a client might have made three job applications in the past week as the baseline for a condition of job-seeking efforts. Similarly, the baseline for securing court permission for independent living might be that no such permission has been given.

Too often involuntary practice has included the unilateral establishment of target problem conditions by the practitioner rather than the mutual development of indicators. In the following section, Nancy and Beth, introduced in chapters 6, attempt to identify conditions around the target problem of "too many people are running my life," based on Beth's reports that her foster parent, her parents, her boyfriend, and Nancy herself too often told her what to do. Hence, how often people tell her what to do would be one target problem condition. They also previously identified exploration of independent living as a possible solution to this problem. An additional mandated problem was that "Beth does not now live in an approved placement that meets legal standards for permanency." This mandated problem led to a present/absent condition of approved placement.

In the following segment, Beth and Nancy identify that having a job or being self-supporting and having parental permission would all be conditions required for securing permission for independent living as one form of approved placement. Notice how Nancy elicits these conditions in part from Beth, rather than listing them herself. This technique should have a byproduct of reducing reactance, as adolescents frequently seem to trust their own explanations more than those of practitioners.[1]

NANCY: What do you think the requirements for getting independent living would be?

BETH: Finding a place, getting a job.

NANCY: So finding a place to live and getting a job would be required.

BETH: Yeah, household stuff.

NANCY: You mean like furniture?

BETH: Furniture, dishes.

NANCY: Do you know what the court would expect of you? Do you know what the law is as far as going back to the judge and saying, "I want independent living"?

BETH: I have to have a job.

NANCY: Yes, you have to have a job or a way that you can demonstrate that you're going to be financially independent of your parents. Right?

BETH: Right.

Less verbal or cognitively impaired clients may need more assistance in specifying problems and conditions. For example, Mike was an adult with a developmental disability who was living in an adult group home. As case management services were not mandated for Mike, he could choose whether to work with a case manager or not. Jane, a case manager for a county agency, met with him to explore whether he might wish to use her services. If he were pressured to work with Jane or work on problems that he did acknowledge, Mike would have become nonvoluntary. By focusing on Mike's concerns, Jane's contact with Mike quickly moved toward voluntary contact. Notice how Jane helps Mike be specific about problems in the group home.[2]

JANE: So, you have told me that things aren't going so well at Bertha's group home. Why don't you tell me a little bit more about what is not going so good?

MIKE: Everything's just going rotten.

JANE: Tell me some of the things that aren't going so well.

MIKE: Bertha ain't the best.

JANE: So you're not real happy with her right now?

MIKE: Nope.

JANE: What kinds of things is she doing?

MIKE: Everything.

JANE: Like?

MIKE: Hmmm.

JANE: What kinds of things is she doing that you're not real happy with?

MIKE: Only giving us five cigarettes a day.

JANE: Okay. So your cigarettes are getting limited.

MIKE: Right.

Jane is beginning to explore the target problem that "Mike is not happy living in his group home." Among the specific conditions identified are the limited number of cigarettes Mike can smoke a day. Later, curfew times and amount of spending money are also identified as conditions.

Establishing Clear Goals

Development of concrete, realistic, measurable goals assist in monitoring progress such that all parties can determine whether the conditions of the contract are met. Goals may be addressed toward reducing or increasing the frequency of target problem conditions. For example, Beth might want to decrease the number of times other people tell her what to do. For a present/absent condition such as a recommendation for independent living, receiving a positive recommendation might then be the goal. Goals may also include movement to a new situation in which the target problems are less likely to occur. For example, Jane and Mike developed a goal of living in a situation in which Mike felt more freedom.

Practitioners sometimes have reservations about developing specific goals or agreeing to goals that they consider unwise. For example, some practitioners hesitate to develop specific goals for fear that they will be locked in to goals that later prove to be either unworkable or too rigid if new circumstances arise. While new law violations may indeed influence recommendations about the conclusion of service, notifying mandated clients that this could occur is preferable to operating without goals. Vague goals often lead to vague efforts. More specific goals can empower the involuntary client by narrowing the scope of efforts.

In addition, involuntary clients sometimes express goals that the practitioner considers unfeasible or in other ways inappropriate. For example, when contacted by her parents, whose parental rights had been terminated, expressing a wish for their adolescent daughter Cheryl to return home, Cheryl told her foster care worker that she wanted to return to her biological parents and would undermine any foster placements or adoption planning. Simply rejecting or dismissing the goal on the grounds that it appears unfeasible or unwise may have little to do with Cheryl's commitment to the goal.

A wiser course might have been to ask Cheryl to list all the reasons why she would want to return home to her biological parents. Next, the practitioner might ask her to list any reservations she had about this idea and any obstacles to such a plan. The practitioner might add suggestions to both lists. Such efforts do not guarantee that the involuntary client's wish for an apparently unfeasible goal will change. They do, however, respect the involuntary client's right to express desires. Efforts can then be undertaken to explore their feasibility. When working as a foster care social worker, the senior author of this book once asked a twelve-year-old who was unlikely to ever return home to her biological parents where she would want to live. She indicated that she would be happy living with an aunt out of state. Her wish was not taken seriously. A year and a half later, she had indeed gone to the out-of-state aunt when other options failed.

In Beth's case, Nancy had reservations about the feasibility of her goal to achieve independent living. Rather than dismiss the goal, she was straightforward in helping Beth see the factors that would influence such a recommendation.

Development of General Tasks

While goals refer to the outcome sought, general tasks are the means to be used to reach those goals. It is important to distinguish between goals and general tasks for two reasons: (1) general tasks are sometimes completed while goals are not achieved; and (2) goals are sometimes achieved while general tasks are not completed. For example, a man participating in a domestic violence treatment program might carry out tasks to complete anger logs, attend sessions regularly, and practice relaxation. Despite completion of the tasks, he might also continue to be violent and the recommendation to the court is more likely to be influenced by the *outcome* of the efforts rather than completion of tasks. Clients may sometimes also reach goals by alternative means than those originally planned. For example, the Native American client introduced in the previous chapter who wished to regain custody of her child in foster care achieved success with controlling her alcoholism problem through work with a Native American religious group rather than through participation in a white aftercare program.

Beth's goal was to gain a positive recommendation for independent living and her general tasks included exploring housing possibilities, employment, schooling, and soliciting parental permission. Additional general tasks could have included acting in assertive ways that decrease the situations in which others were in a position to tell her what to do. Mike's goal of living in a situation with more freedom can be pursued by simultaneous exploration of ways conditions could be rectified in the current group home and exploring other living arrangements. Hence, arranging visits to alternative living situations was included, as well as discussions with Bertha about the current living situation.

Establishing Clear Time Limits

Much contact with both voluntary and involuntary clients occurs at times of crisis that frequently have a natural time limit of approximately six weeks. In addition, studies continue to show that whatever the planned length, service frequently lasts ten or fewer sessions (Wells 1982). Finally, establishment of time limits takes advantage of a goal gradient effect in which client and practitioner activities appear to increase near the end of a time-limited period.

Involuntary contact is sometimes necessarily long-term, as in the case of continuing case management relationships with clients with disabilities and serious and persistent mental illness, and in work with clients in institutional settings. Such long-term contact can lead to lack of focus and burnout on both sides of the desk. Both practitioners and clients can help maintain focus by cutting large problems and goals into smaller segments. Progress can then be evaluated at the completion of these break points and decisions made about continuing on the same goals, changing goals, changing forms of service, and terminating contact. For example, when the senior author of this book worked with a single-parent client who was attempting to regain custody of her eight children placed in foster care, achievement of this goal was not feasible over the short term. It was, however, feasible to establish an initial, renewable contract with the goal of securing unsupervised visitation with the children by the end of the first twelve-week contract. When that goal was achieved, the contract was renewed with a goal of regaining custody of one child in the next twelve weeks. Several additional time-limited contracts were negotiated over the subsequent one and a half years.

The Task Implementation Sequence

Developing a clear, specific strategy follows the formalizing of the contract around both mandated and agreed-upon target problems and goals. The task implementation sequence (TIS) was designed to guide practitioners in the development of a sequence of tasks to reduce the intensity of target problems (Reid 1978). Steps in the sequence to be reviewed and adapted here include development of initial client tasks, initial practitioner tasks, anticipation of obstacles, provision of a rationale, appropriate incentives, rehearsal, and task summarization (figure 7.4).

Development of Initial Client Tasks

Research on the task-centered approach indicates that client *expression of verbal commitment* to carry out a task is a stronger predictor of task completion than the source of the task, whether it was the client's or the practitioner's idea (Reid 1978). However, it might be expected in the pressured circumstance of involuntary contact that reactance would be reduced if the involuntary client's task ideas are considered first. Five factors should be considered in the development of initial client tasks: (1) determine which target problems the involuntary client would like to begin with; (2) find out how the client has attempted to resolve this problem in the past; (3) explore the involuntary client's ideas about what tasks might be attempted; (4) suggest client tasks; and (5) develop required tasks for mandated clients.

1. *Determine which target problems the involuntary client would like to begin with.* In general, the target problems that are approached first should be those that would make the most difference if resolved and those that can most feasibly be reduced. However, nonvoluntary clients have no legal constraints blocking their choice in the order of target problems they begin to work on. Mandated clients can often make constrained choices in selecting the order of work on problems. While mandated clients frequently have a list of non-negotiable tasks that they must complete if they are to avoid legal consequences, it is frequently impossible to undertake all of those requirements simultaneously, and mandated problems often have no required sequence. In such cases, involuntary clients may recommend an order of problems to address first. While some practitioners have suggested that given choice, involuntary clients will "start with the easy ones and avoid the hard ones," developing a momentum through successful completion of tasks can make it possible to complete more difficult tasks later. Unfortunately, there is often a negative generalization when the involuntary client is overwhelmed with competing requirements in the beginning. If there are compelling reasons

Figure 7.4   Task implementation sequence (TIS)

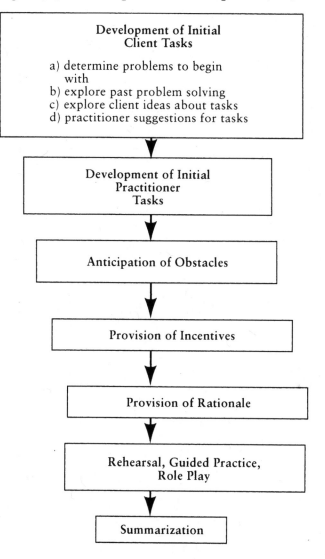

Development of Initial
Client Tasks

a) determine problems to begin
   with
b) explore past problem solving
c) explore client ideas about tasks
d) practitioner suggestions for tasks

Development of Initial
Practitioner
Tasks

Anticipation of Obstacles

Provision of Incentives

Provision of Rationale

Rehearsal, Guided Practice,
Role Play

Summarization

why some problems should be undertaken before others, joint or sequential selection might occur in which the involuntary client might pick the first problem out of a required list and the practitioner might pick the second, and so on.

In the following exchange, Jane (introduced earlier in this chapter) briefly describes what task-centered work would entail and helps Mike decide which problem he would like to begin work on.

JANE: You've told me that you're pretty unhappy about your living situation and where you're working right now. So it sounds like there's the possibility for us to do some work together on these problems.

MIKE: I agree.

JANE: We can work together around these two and try to figure out together how we could make them feel a little bit better for you. We can figure out what you can do, what I can do, and kind of piece by piece see if we can get this feeling better for you.

MIKE: Good.

JANE: What's the one that's making you most uncomfortable, what's the thing that you want to work on first?

MIKE: Moving.

JANE: Moving. You want a new place to live.

MIKE: Right.

Notice that Mike is already tipping his hand about his solution to the problem of being unhappy in his living situation: he wants to move. Jane notes this and will return to it, while exploring other solutions to his current unhappiness about his living situation as well.

2. *Find out how the involuntary client has tried to resolve this problem in the past.* The practitioner can then move to review prior problem-solving efforts. Such review sometimes uncovers good problem-solving skills that may have been impeded by a crisis. In other cases, the review may indicate that the problem is a new one that the involuntary client has little experience in resolving. After exploring possibilities for adapting to the current living situation and finding little promise in them, Jane begins to explore Mike's knowledge of alternative living arrangements.

JANE: Let me go back and make sure that I'm remembering everything correctly. When you moved up here, part of the reason that we said that you wanted to live here was that there weren't too many choices about where to live in the town where your folks were, and you wanted to be closer to work. And that's why you ended up at this particular group home. Right?

MIKE: Right, I agree.

JANE: So that's how you got here. Now it seems like we need to talk about what some of the other options might be about where to live. Have you thought about where else you might want to live?

MIKE: Not right off hand, no.

JANE: Do you know anybody else that's left the group home?

MIKE: No, I don't.

JANE: I was wondering, because if you knew somebody that left, we could talk about where they moved to. Do you know some of the other folks that you work with out at the plant, where do you live? What kind of places do they live in?

Jane continues to pursue Mike's knowledge of alternatives before moving to add her own knowledge of potential resources. In other cases, review of past efforts may uncover unsuccessful prior efforts. Such exploration may provide information about a lack of problem-solving skills or a misunderstanding of an otherwise effective method. For example, a client once told the senior author that she had tried time-out to discipline her child but it didn't work because after she would lock him up in his room for several hours, he would demolish his room! As he was preparing to suggest time-out as a method that she might try, he began to see how she might have misunderstood the specific, time-limited nature of the time-out procedure.

3. *Explore the involuntary client's ideas about what tasks might be attempted.* Practitioners should attempt to help clients develop initial tasks that are clear, specific, and likely to succeed. Successful completion of such initial tasks should help create a positive momentum that can contribute to completion of more complex tasks later.

After reviewing prior problem-solving efforts, the practitioner can initiate brainstorming about possible tasks to attempt. As reactance may be activated by starting with the practitioner's own ideas, the involuntary client's ideas about which tasks to attempt should be explored first. Involuntary clients frequently have good ideas about how to proceed or present ideas that can be made workable with a little revision. The practitioner should encourage any promising ideas and even those ideas that appear less promising give clues about the client's general problem-solving ability. In the following exchange, Nancy begins work to explore Beth's ideas about possible tasks to attempt toward achieving independent living and also clarifies what kind of job she wants to seek.

NANCY: On the problem of job seeking, what do you think would be a reasonable way to start between now and next week?

BETH: Go out looking for a job. And then there is the newspaper.

NANCY: Going out and making applications and getting a newspaper are good ideas. How else have you heard about jobs in the past? You've worked at a restaurant. How did you find that job?

BETH: Through friends.

NANCY: So you could talk to some friends about jobs that they might know of that would be available. Do you have any restrictions on the kind of jobs you want to get?

BETH: I don't want to work in no nut house like Randy's Restaurant.

NANCY: So you don't want to work in a place where there are a lot of difficult people to deal with?

BETH: Yes, a lot of drunks.

This exploration of possible client tasks should enhance involuntary client feelings of empowerment. By listening to Beth and supporting any promising ideas, Nancy is helping Beth figure out what she is willing to try. Sometimes practitioners have additional ideas that might revise client suggestions or expand their options.

4. *Suggest client tasks.* Practitioners often have useful ideas for client tasks based on empirical research, experience, and practice wisdom. Involuntary clients often reject these suggestions if they are pressured into the "best" solution rather than offered suggestions as part of a brainstorming process. The practitioner should become expert at *helping* involuntary clients solve problems rather than necessarily be an expert in solving all problems. At the same time, neither should the practitioner agree to work on problems blindly without consulting available sources. Practitioners should become familiar with evidence to support particular empirically supported task strategies (Corcoran and Vandiver 2004; Mullen 2004). In addition, practitioners can draw from their own practice experience with similar problems, and that of their peers, supervisors, and consultants.

As initial tasks should be clear, specific, and likely to succeed, practitioners can also use their expertise in fine-tuning client suggestions to make them more feasible. In the following section, Nancy suggests revisions to make Beth's job-seeking efforts more specific and feasible.

NANCY: What do you think about getting a couple of newspapers for a week? Does your aunt get a newspaper?

BETH: No.

NANCY: So you would have to go out and buy one. You might look through a newspaper at least every two to three days and circle the ads that look interesting to you. How does that sound?

BETH: Okay.

NANCY: So you have the money you would need to get a paper for a week or so?

BETH: Yeah, that's no problem.

NANCY: We could find a newspaper around here and circle some today if you want.

BETH: No, that's okay, I can do it at home.

NANCY: You might then also talk to some friends that might know something about job openings. I would suggest that you write down all the possibilities that you come up with and bring them in for us to look at. You could go ahead and apply for some if you want to, but it would be enough to get us started to have a list of possible jobs. How does that sound?

BETH: Okay.

5. *Development of disagreeable tasks.* Mandated clients always have required tasks to complete and nonvoluntary clients often encounter disagreeable tasks as part of a "package deal" of agreeing to be served even within a contract that includes some of their own concerns. If a mandated client does not object to completing a required task, then no special provisions beyond the above suggestions for client and practitioner tasks are needed. The broader problem, then, is assisting both mandated and nonvoluntary clients in completing tasks that they might consider disagreeable. The following six guidelines are designed to facilitate both treatment adherence and empowerment by offering at least constrained choices. It should be noted, however, that required or disagreeable tasks should be kept to the minimum and should not stretch beyond the guidelines for limiting self-determination and exercising paternalism (figure 7.5).

a. *Consequences of a choice not to complete the required task can be explored.* Even when choices are so constrained that failure to complete the disagreeable task is likely to lead to punishing consequences, the mandated client can choose *not* to complete the task and accept those punishing consequences. For example, eight children were removed from Mrs. Carter's home because of child neglect and a drinking problem. Mrs. Carter continued to maintain that her drinking was of no concern to the court and balked at following through with a chemical dependency evaluation and treatment program. Rather than continue in a stalemated position, the practitioner informed her that she could choose *not* to have the evaluation or treatment. She should know, however, that in the next hearing, the judge would be informed of progress with the required evaluation. She could choose to hope that her task completion in other areas would favorably impress the judge without work on the perceived alcohol problem. Mrs. Carter preferred for the time being to run the risk of a negative response in choosing not to follow the court order completely. Later in contact, she came to

Figure 7.5   Completion of disagreeable tasks

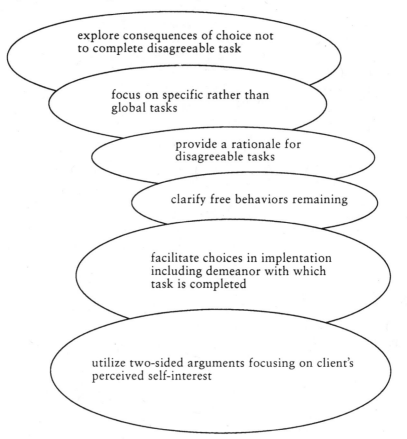

recognize a need for further alcohol treatment on her own and entry into treatment was facilitated.[3]

Nonvoluntary clients also often face disagreeable tasks that, while not legally mandated, exert an unwelcome pressure. For example, some clients find that agencies have policies requiring *all* family members to participate in treatment. If the family is unwilling or unable to comply with this requirement and if the agency policy is not negotiable, family members can be referred to other settings who do not have such policies.

b. *Focus on specific rather than global tasks.* Reactance is likely to be high if the involuntary client perceives there to be a global assault on valued freedoms. Reactance may be reduced by focusing on specific rather than global tasks. For example, Mrs. Torres (introduced in chapter 6) was angry about what she considered to be overwhelming and unjust pressures to clean her house. Her opposition was somewhat reduced by focusing on specific tasks to remove fire hazards such as garbage with a goal of eliminating five boxes a week, establishing clear walkways, and obtaining a separate bed for her daughter. Small, specific tasks were developed such as agreeing to sort ten boxes and discarding the contents of five by the following week.

c. *Provide a rationale for disagreeable tasks.* Involuntary clients are entitled to an explanation for *why* the task is required. It was explained to Mrs. Torres that minimum standards existed for determining fire hazards and client safety. Involuntary clients may continue to disagree with the rationale, but they are entitled to an explanation.

d. *Clarify free choices remaining.* Required tasks can be distinguished from other areas remaining in the free control of the involuntary client. For example, Mrs. Torres felt that the agency was pressuring her to discard valuable things she had inherited from her mother. The practitioner clarified that valued items from her mother were her own business and not the business of the child welfare agency. The agency was concerned only about safety hazards and would support her in keeping her valued inheritance if it did not continue to be a safety hazard. Indeed, the practitioner could assist her in seeking inexpensive storage facilities as a way of protecting her valuable things.

e. *Choices in implementation can be facilitated, including the demeanor with which the disagreeable task is completed.* Involuntary clients can have choices in the manner in which they implement disagreeable tasks. As described earlier in this chapter, practitioners can often negotiate the order of required tasks including which ones to begin with. For example, Mrs. Torres chose to begin by sorting her boxes and deciding what could be discarded, what could be given away or sold, and what could be kept. The practitioner assisted in securing a homemaker to facilitate this process. Obtaining another bed was postponed until these tasks were completed. Mrs. Torres was free to choose what materials would be kept, discarded, given away, or sold as long as five boxes full of garbage were discarded.

Practitioners sometimes contribute to their own and involuntary client frustration by expecting not only that the disagreeable task be completed but also that the involuntary client would appear to *enjoy it*. By separating the behavior from the attitude displayed in completing the task, the practitioner can restore some freedom while recognizing that behaviors often change prior to attitudes. This practitioner attitude implies some tolerance for involuntary client complaints about not liking the task. The practitioner can empathize with the feeling of not liking to be pressured to do required tasks, while remaining firm about the consequences of failure to comply. For example, Mrs. Torres continued to complain about not liking the housecleaning tasks while also continuing to complete them. She would often complete them with a new twist, such as selling some clothes, which had not been discussed but was her right and did not violate the agreement to discard a certain amount of items.

The practitioner can also solicit involuntary client input in fine-tuning required tasks. For example, alcoholism treatment programs sometimes require that clients read about alcoholism. There are often ways, however, that such required tasks can be tailored with client input. For example, Dick, the residential treatment counselor introduced in chapter 6, was able to negotiate with Keith about the amount of reading and the time frame for completing the required task of reading in the "big book."[4]

DICK: I'm sure you are familiar with the "big book," the Alcoholics Anonymous book, from your first treatment. Keith, I'd like to know, do you like to read?

KEITH: I hate it.

DICK: You hate to read. A lot of people do. I'm not a very good reader myself, and I can relate to that. The first five chapters in the big book are kind of a synopsis of what the whole program is about, where it started, why it was developed, what they wanted to do. There is a lot of reading in it; it is a big book. I wonder if 20 to 25 pages would be too much to read in a week? Do you think you could handle that?

KEITH: I think I can handle that.

DICK: Well, why not, instead of concentrating on all the first five chapters, concentrate on just chapter number five? I think it's only about twenty-five pages. Do you think you might have that done in a week?

KEITH: Sure, I'll do that.

f. *Two-sided arguments emphasizing client perceived self-interest can be utilized.* Practitioners may feel called upon to represent the community and others potentially harmed by the involuntary client's behavior. Persuasion efforts, however, are unlikely to be successful when they focus on values *not* held by the client that the practitioner thinks the involuntary client *should* have. The practitioner should avoid nagging, browbeating, or attempting to induce guilt around values that the client does not hold. Focusing on the values that the involuntary client openly expresses should be more productive. Hence, Jean emphasized Mrs. Torres' own expressed motivation to have the house clean for the holidays and the agency people out of her life. The consequences of choosing not to carry out the required task can be reviewed.

Potential costs and advantages of choosing to complete the required task can also be reviewed with the involuntary client who ultimately makes the decision.

Sometimes practitioners are unable to find values and motivations to support required changes for mandated clients. In such circumstances, practitioners can recognize problems in proceeding without motivational congruence by limiting their own expectations for progress beyond the impact of available compliance methods.

Development of Initial Practitioner Tasks

Explicit practitioner tasks can enhance a sense of partnership in resolving problems. Practitioner tasks should facilitate client efforts without doing things for involuntary clients that they can do for themselves. Hence, practitioner tasks are actions that the involuntary client cannot complete, would take too long for them to complete to be of value in addressing target problems, or those that are of no long-term value for the involuntary client to learn. The number of practitioner tasks depends also on available practitioner time and norms of the agency or setting. For example, practitioners often act to influence the social system to facilitate client action through arranging referrals and acquiring information (Reid 1978). If an involuntary client is unlikely to need such information or initiate such referrals on his or her own in the future, then the practitioner might offer to do it. The number of practitioner tasks may also decrease over time with increased client capacity.

There are also many intermediate steps between tasks that are undertaken either solely by involuntary clients or solely by practitioners that can be negotiated. Could the involuntary client complete the task with additional resources? Would skill practice or rehearsal help? Would it help if the practitioner or someone else performed the task together with the involuntary client or accompanied him or her (figure 7.6)?

For example, one of Beth's requirements for achieving independent living was to secure parental permission. In the following exchange, Beth and Nancy negotiate a joint client–practitioner task of contacting Beth's parents.

NANCY: How do you think we should let your mother and dad know about your plans?

BETH: That's left up to you. I don't want to talk to them.

NANCY: You don't want to talk to them alone. How would you feel about me accompanying you to talk to them?

Figure 7.6   Considerations in completing practitioner tasks

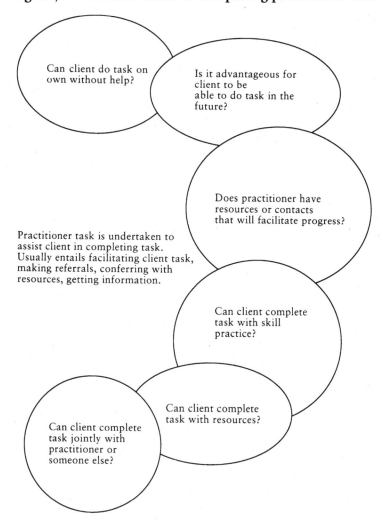

BETH: That would be okay. I'd like to find out before I go through all the hassle of doing it and then they don't want to give me permission.

NANCY: Okay, so my task between now and then is to get in touch with your mom and dad to set up a joint session.

Nancy might have explained her reasons for preferring to share the task rather than do it for Beth. If Nancy can assist Beth this time, she may be able to negotiate other things on her own next time rather than be dependent on Nancy.

Anticipating Obstacles

Task plans can be fine-tuned by anticipating obstacles to their successful completion. The questions suggested above for looking at possible joint client–practitioner tasks can also be adapted to tailor any client or practitioner task: What might interfere with task completion? Does the client have adequate resources to carry out the task? Does the client have adequate skills to complete the task? The practitioner can begin by asking the involuntary client to think of things that might get in the way of completing the task and then add his or her own ideas to the client list. Practitioners may find that they are more likely to identify obstacles to tasks suggested by clients than to tasks that were the practitioner's own idea. It would be wise for practitioners to ask involuntary clients for possible obstacles to practitioner-originated tasks as well as to those suggested by clients. If this review uncovers potential obstacles, then task plans can be revised to avoid them. For example, in the following exchange, Jane explores potential obstacles with Mike about a move from his current group home to Dexter, thirty miles away.

JANE: What do you think might get in the way of moving to Dexter?

MIKE: Maybe my buddies who I used to drink with.

JANE: So, the fellows you used to drink with live in Dexter. How might you handle their asking you to drink with them?

MIKE: Refuse them.

JANE: You sound pretty definite about that. Have you been able to see them without drinking with them in the past?

MIKE: Yes.

JANE: So, you have been able to do that already. We might have to keep checking on that one since I know that you have told me that you don't want to go back to drinking.

MIKE: I agree.

JANE: I can think of a couple of other things that might get in the way. I wonder if the transportation back up here to work every day would be hard for you since you would have that extra half-hour ride each day.

MIKE: I agree.

JANE: Let me just sum up where we are with thinking about a possible move. On the plus side, we've got the fact that you know more people in Dexter and you're closer to your folks, which is important. On the down side, you might have to worry about some of your old buddies trying to get you back to drinking.

MIKE: Right, I agree.

Jane and Mike have identified being around Mike's buddies who continue to drink and the ride to and from work as obstacles. Additional tasks might then follow to prepare Mike for telling his buddies that he does not want to drink with them. He might also experiment with the bus ride a few times to see if he could handle that.

Practitioners' tasks can also result from obstacle analysis. For example, John lived in a community residence for homeless persons. One condition of this residence was that he actively seek employment and eventually other housing. His job seeking efforts had been partly impeded by limited access to the community phone in the residence. In the following exchange, John and Cheri, his case manager, explore ways to facilitate his job-seeking tasks.[5]

JOHN: I made some applications but they haven't been calling me back yet. I wonder if I will even get a message with that phone out there in the Center.

CHERI: It is a busy phone. We've talked about getting another line here at the center. We have talked about your taking the initiative to call them back to check on your application. If you were going to make those phone calls this week, can you think of anything that might prevent you from completing the calls?

JOHN: Well, the noise out there. It gets pretty rowdy out there, sometimes. But other than that, no.

CHERI: Well, I was wondering about that. Depending on what time of day that you called them, I'd be willing to let you use my office phone here if that would be helpful.

JOHN: Sure, it would.

CHERI: I know that you also said that you were not quite sure of what to say to them on the phone, not wanting to sound too "needy." We could talk over what you want to say to them and maybe practice it a little before you call.

JOHN: I don't feel comfortable making the calls out there, that's for sure.

CHERI: What about if we practice here and then you could make the call here with me present or by yourself, however you want to do it?

JOHN: It would be okay to practice. I would rather make the calls then by myself, though.

CHERI: Okay. Let's try that.

Cheri and John have explored two options to making the call alone on the community phone. John has expressed preferences for how he would like to make the calls and Cheri has offered support in practicing the skills needed to make the call and feel more comfortable doing it. She might also move ahead to advocate more strongly for increased access for other residents to a more private phone.

Provision of Rationale

Self-attributed change may be enhanced if the involuntary client has a clear idea of the specific reasons for how carrying out the task would be a step toward reducing the target problem and reaching the goal. As with exploring task ideas and identifying potential obstacles, practitioners can empower clients and support self-attribution by asking the involuntary client for the connection between the task and the agreed-upon problem before supplying their own ideas. If involuntary clients cannot think of reasons to complete the task, then they may be unlikely to complete it or do so only under pressure to comply. Similarly, if involuntary clients originate the task idea, they may be more likely to understand the rationale for the task than if the task idea came from the practitioner. As with anticipation of obstacles, practitioners frequently forget to explore the rationale for ideas they originated since that rationale is usually obvious to the practitioner, if not to the involuntary client. This may be particularly true when the task is a required one for mandated clients or part of a "package deal" for nonvoluntary clients. In the following exchange, Dick reviews Keith's required task for completing a self-inventory of prior drinking behavior and bringing the answers into the treatment group.

DICK: When you fill out the answers to the questions about your past history in the book, you will have something to share in common with the other men in the group. We find that men can often learn from each other's past experiences through this kind of sharing in the group.

KEITH: Okay. But some of those questions go way back to where you can't even remember.

DICK: That's true, they do go back quite a ways. How about going through the book and answering those questions that are really important to you, that promote feelings, and answer those questions first? Then come and talk to me about it, and we'll see how far you want to go. Because in two weeks, I'd like you to tell the group some of the highlights of your life. Would you be willing to do that?

KEITH: You have to tell them *all* the highlights?

DICK: That sounds like you think it could be embarrassing to share some parts of your past with people you don't know very well.

KEITH: Yeah, I don't know these people.

DICK: You can make that decision as to what you want to tell them. By the time you do this, maybe the group will become more familiar with you and you will be better able to decide what you want to tell them. Okay?

KEITH: Okay.

While Dick has provided the program's rationale for completing the self-history for sharing in the group, Keith raises reservations about sharing potentially embarrassing information with people he doesn't know. Dick has attempted to empathize with that concern and clarified the choices Keith has in deciding what to share.

Provision of Incentives

Some situations require the involuntary client to carry out initial tasks that may be anxiety-provoking or have some punishing elements. In such circumstances, providing a concrete or symbolic incentive can be helpful in stimulating new behavior that is not at this point inherently reinforcing. However, in order to support self-attribution, concrete rewards should be only large enough to succeed and should be phased out early and replaced by symbolic rewards.

In the following exchange, Joan, a social worker in an outpatient mental health center, is working with Jim, a depressed nonvoluntary client, who has targeted the problem of "not being motivated to do anything." It is interesting to note that while Jim had a clinical diagnosis of depression, he does not acknowledge this attributed problem but focuses on the more specific acknowledged problem of lack of motivation. They have together identified washing his clothes, which had been piling up for weeks, as a desirable task in beginning to alleviate his lack of motivation. Earlier in the session, they decided to break up this large, depressing task into a series of steps including obtaining enough tokens for the washers and dryers, sorting the clothes on one day, and taking down a first load on the next day. In the following exchange, they review possible obstacles to finishing this task and explore possible incentives to enhance completion of a disagreeable task.

JOAN: Okay. So I will write down here that you plan to wash your clothes by Sunday. Can you think of any other things that might get in the way of your washing these clothes?

JIM: I hate washing clothes. It is one of the things I hate most.

JOAN: So your head tells you, I hate to wash clothes. Is there something that can help you get over that, something you can tell yourself that might help you feel better about doing it?

JIM: Not that I know of. Not right offhand.

JOAN: You mentioned earlier that you want some clean clothes in order to go back to school.

JIM: That whole issue is separate. I don't see it as part of the same issue.

JOAN: Okay, thinking about how you could use the clean clothes isn't a helpful idea for you. Would it help if I give you a call maybe on Friday to see how things go with the first step of separating the clothes?

JIM: Yeah, that would be all right.

JOAN: I also wonder if there is something special you can do for yourself when you try this hard first step.

JIM: You mean like a reward or something?

JOAN: Yes, what would be something you could do to reward yourself for separating the clothes?

JIM: Maybe I could go out to a movie or something.

Rehearsal

Some tasks are of such complexity that breaking them down and rehearsing parts can assist in task completion (Bandura 1971). For example, Nancy could have practiced looking through the want ads and making a list of job possibilities with Beth during the session. In addition, interactional tasks can be practiced in role plays. The practitioner can model how to complete the task, assist the client in practicing, assess together the strengths and weaknesses of that modeling, and then rehearse the desired behavior again (Reid 1978). For example, it was suggested that Cheri and John might have rehearsed the phone call to a potential employer. As adults are sometimes more hesitant than children are in carrying out role plays, a modified form of role play can be employed in which the practitioner walks the client through the task with questions such as "What do you plan to say? What do you think he/she will say back to you?"

Task Summarization

Practitioners frequently end a session by reading a list of client tasks and asking the client for affirmation that the list is accurate. Practitioners often interpret "uh-huh" responses as indications of understanding and commitment. Such practitioner recitations may indicate only that the practitioner understands what the task agreements are. In some instances, task summaries may be enhanced by use of a written task-sheet with copies for both the client and practitioner (Rooney 1981). Such a sheet can be completed by either the client or practitioner, listing who will do what by what date. Using such a task list, the practitioner might begin to summarize by saying, "These are the tasks I have agreed to complete. What are the ones you are planning to do?" If involuntary clients can then recount tasks, compliance may be enhanced. If, conversely, the involuntary client leaves a task off the list, it may indicate reservations about completing the task. The practitioner may then add to and amend the summary provided by the client, exploring any reservations. For example, Cheri reviews tasks with John at the end of their session.

CHERI: So to review, I said that I would make my phone available for you to call potential employers and possible references before our next meeting. What were the things that you're going to work on before we meet on Friday?

JOHN: I'm going to call Brown Tank tomorrow morning. And then I'll put out a couple more job applications. I don't know if I'll have to call for references until I talk to them.

Middle-Phase Change Principles

Chapter 4 described the use of influence methods including punishment, reward, and persuasion to enhance treatment adherence, self-attribution, and empowerment. It was noted that while reward and punishment methods can be used to support the development of a new behavior or reduce an undesirable behavior, continued use of such methods is unlikely to produce the self-attribution needed to support the maintenance of behavioral change. Consequently, middle-phase work should include reduced reliance on compliance-oriented methods and increased use of methods that enhance self-attribution such as facilitating expression of verbal or written commitment by involuntary clients to task completion, facilitating choices in task selection and enhancing freely chosen behavior, and increased attention to natural rather than artificial rewards.

As behavioral change often precedes attitude change, the socialization and contracting guidelines presented in chapter 6 emphasized behavioral changes more than attitudinal changes. Attitudinal change may, however, be more subject to influence in the middle phase if the practitioner has come to be considered a persuasive source of influence. Hence, selective practitioner confrontations may become more effective in the middle phase than was typically the case in initial contact. Attitudes and beliefs may be further influenced in the middle phase through trying out new behaviors on an experimental basis via the "foot-in-door" method in which the involuntary client may agree to try out a new behavior on an experimental basis. Should the new behaviors succeed, they may become naturally reinforcing and also challenge prior beliefs that they would be unsuccessful. Further references will be made to these principles as they apply to practice guidelines later in the chapter.

Case Management

Many practitioners who work with involuntary clients do so as case managers. The case manager assesses need, links clients to needed resources, assumes responsibility for service coordination, monitors progress, and advocates to ensure that the client receives appropriate services in a timely fashion (Johnson and Rubin 1983; O'Connor 1988).

Case management is typically provided to clients with multiple attributed problems such as those with serious and persistent mental illness and those with disabilities. General goals of case management often include reduction of inappropriate utilization of services, increased continuity of care, and empowering clients through access to service. Individual case goals often relate to attaining adequate levels of client functioning in areas such as independent living and vocational skills.

Definitions of case management functions vary, which contributes to confusion in implementation. Job descriptions have tended to focus on organizational arrangements defining what agency is responsible for arranging what service with relatively little emphasis on practice techniques. For example, there is little agreement on how much of the role is administrative and how much relates to client–worker interaction (O'Connor 1988). There are further variations in the autonomy and responsibility accorded the case manager and the complexity of the tasks to be assumed by him or her. Is the case manager primarily responsible for coordinating care provided by others or providing direct service? Case managers are frequently enjoined not to "do counseling" with their clients but rather to link them with others who will provide such resources. In other circumstances, case managers may be permitted to counsel or intervene as problem solvers yet find that large caseloads and heavy paperwork requirements often limit them to coordinating paper more than actual services.

Further, case management with clients such as those with severe and persistent mental illness has been considered difficult, unglamorous, and unrewarding. The emphasis on psychotherapy in community mental health centers has often meant that case managers have lower status and prestige than psychotherapists and consequently many case managers appear to be indifferent to intervening in the social system as it is lower-status work than seeking insight with psychotherapy clients (Johnson and Rubin 1983), though others suggest that case managers can play important roles in advocacy and empowerment with these client groups (Rose and Black 1985).

Case managers can work with involuntary clients in at least three ways. First, some clients may be mandated to work with a case manager in the community as part of an involuntary outpatient commitment (Wilk 1988). Second, many clients have no legal mandate but may experience nonvoluntary pressure to work with a case manager as a precondition for receiving another service. For example, a client with serious and persistent mental illness such as Dora (introduced in chapter 6) may find ongoing contact with a case manager to be a precondition to independent living. Finally, some clients may be willing to work with a case manager but feel constrained when such work focuses on attributed needs rather than client wants.

Case managers working with involuntary clients can act to empower them by advocating for their choices using the guidelines provided for negotiating and contracting. For example, when Mike first became Jane's client when he moved into the community after living in a residential institution, he came with recommendations from that institution that he "needed" to work on his impulsive expression of anger. Jane considered his expression of anger not to be a legal mandate but rather a possible obstacle that might interfere with his achievement of his own perceived goals. She chose to focus on what Mike was angry about, such as unhappiness with his living arrangement, rather than his expression of anger as a primary focus. Within this focus on an acknowledged target problem, Mike became voluntary. The processes of task development may, however, focus more on linkages with other resources rather than on tasks to be completed directly with the case manager.

Linking Clients with Resources
Involuntary clients frequently identify problems that would involve utilizing other services. Research on the linkage process suggests that often fewer than half of clients referred for services are actually linked with the designated resource (Kirk and Greenlee 1974). The resource linkage process varies according to the source of the suggestion and the strength of the pressure. The involuntary client can perceive the need for the resource first, the need can be identified by the practitioner or a referral source, or the resource may be required as part of a legal mandate.

The practitioner should attempt to help the client make an informed choice about pursuing the linkage by sharing available knowledge about the quality of services. If the client perceives the need, the process includes a straightforward assessment of whether an adequate resource might be available from within the agency. If that resource is available internally, then the linkage might be made directly. For example, Jane provided Mike with information about the living possibilities available and facilitated visits in which he could make his own assessment.

Should an appropriate resource be identified, a sequence of steps can be followed to facilitate the linkage. Simple directions in providing a name and address are sufficient for clients who are motivated to receive the service and capable of following the directions (Epstein and Brown 2002). Providing the name of a contact person makes the linkage easier in circumstances that might involve a complicated intake process. Similarly, providing the client with a letter of introduction that describes the problem and what the client would like to have done can facilitate the linkage. The practitioner can also help by making a phone call to the desired resource. Finally, facilitating in-person contact can occur by accompanying the client or arranging for a friend, relative, or case aide to accompany the client to the resource. These more complex means of facilitating linkage are useful with clients who cannot follow complex directions or have some ambivalence about pursuing the resource.

If the practitioner or another referral source initiates the suggestion for a resource that is recommended but not legally required, then a possible source of nonvoluntary pressure has been initiated. In this case, persuasion methods, including two-sided arguments, assessment of potential benefits and costs of pursuing the resource, or choosing not to pursue it can be used. Since the source of pressure is nonvoluntary, the client's right *not* to pursue the resource should be emphasized. For example, Jane encouraged Mike to enter an independent living skills group that might help him prepare for living outside the group home. She emphasized that he could choose *not* to join this group; however, acquisition of those skills might make a move to new housing easier.

Should the resource linkage be mandated, a similar sequence to nonvoluntary pressure can be followed with the added emphasis on legal consequences should the resource not be pursued. Even in such mandated situations, the involuntary client can choose not to pursue the resource and accept the consequences, as did Mrs. Carter when she chose not to get a chemical dependency evaluation while aware of the fact that chemical use would be reported to the court.

Should the client agree to pursue the resource, connections can be "cemented" through one of four methods. The client can: (1) report back to the practitioner after contact; (2) the practitioner can contact the client after the connection; (3) the practitioner can also schedule sessions before and after the contact; or (4) referral visits can be interspersed with the practitioner's own sessions with the involuntary client (Weissman 1976).

Guidelines for the Middle Phase

The task development process often kindles hope in the involuntary client and practitioner that progress can be made. These hopes are often dashed in progress review sessions in which the best laid plans have gone awry. Successful completion of *all* tasks should be considered the exception, however, rather than the rule. *Task failure* should not be interpreted as *person failure*. Focus on failure contributes to disillusionment, blaming, and reinforcement of helpless, powerless feelings. Hence, building positive momentum and avoiding blaming is a critical goal in the middle phase. The guidelines that follow can be employed by both case managers and practitioners who have more frequent and intensive client contact.

The following guidelines are designed to build positive momentum through: (1) reviewing progress on target problems and mandated problems, (2) reviewing task progress, (3) identifying obstacles to progress, (4) dealing with crises, (5) employing appropriate middle-phase confrontation, and (6) revising and summarizing task plans (see figure 7.7).

1. *Reviewing progress on target problems and mandated problems.* Task-centered work focuses on reduction or elimination of agreed-upon problems. Legally mandated clients are also engaged in reviews of progress on mandated problems, whether agreed upon or not. Review sessions should begin with a review of how these mandated, semivoluntary, or voluntary target problems appear to be changing or not changing according to the conditions of the problem identified in the contracting stage. It is useful to separate review of the problem conditions from the completion of tasks since problems sometimes change without task completion and, conversely, tasks may be completed without improvement noted in the problem conditions. For example, Beth reported that no one was now telling her what to do (a condition of her target problem) since her aunt kicked her out of the house! This was obviously not a task, but did temporarily reduce that pressure. On the other hand, tasks may be completed without change in conditions. In the example below, John has completed some of the tasks related to pursuing a job without yet actually getting a job. The involuntary client's assessment of change in conditions can be probed for specifics and practitioners should then add their own assessment of changes.

In the following exchange, Cheri has a mid-phase review meeting with John, the nonvoluntary resident of a homeless program. John has missed two

Figure 7.7   Guidelines for the middle phase

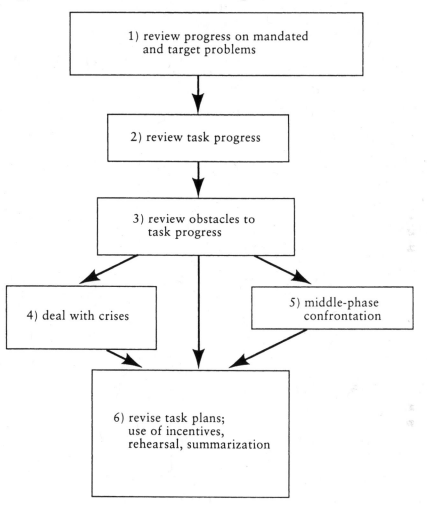

appointments with Cheri and does not appear eager to talk about his job-seeking efforts. Such apparently irrelevant discussion often occurs when clients are either having difficulties with their tasks or are not really sure they wish to work on the target problem. Cheri reviews that the last appointments were not kept in a matter-of-fact way without blaming. She supports his initial efforts while also noting John's reservations about talking about job seeking. She empathizes with his discouragement.

CHERI: Hi, John, I'm glad that we could finally get together. It's been a while. It's been three weeks since we've met.

JOHN: Has it been that long?

CHERI: Yes, it has. Originally we decided to meet at least once a week. How's it going?

JOHN: Well, it's going okay. I've got a lot of time on my hands. It's been kind of fun spending some time down at the Dome with all the excitement down there. It's been a lot of fun.

CHERI: Well, I'm glad to hear that you're having some positive things happen in your free time.

JOHN: I've got a lot of that.

CHERI: Let's just back up a minute, because I know that after we first met and went over what you were going to do about finding a job, we scheduled another appointment, and then you said you couldn't come because you had another job interview. We both thought that that made sense to miss that meeting, because getting a job is the main thing that we're working on together. I didn't hear from you after that, we rescheduled and you didn't come, and I'm wondering what happened.

JOHN: Well, I had the job interview and it went okay. And then he told me he was going to give me a call on Wednesday, and that's the reason that I didn't come in, and I hung out in the lobby out here waiting for him to call and waiting for him to call. And I just said the heck with it. And he didn't call, so I just split. I went down to Frank's and had a beer.

CHERI: I see. So you made an application and were waiting for a call. And you felt discouraged because you didn't get the call. I can understand that it is hard to just be waiting. I'm glad you made the call and am sorry it hasn't worked out yet. It will probably take a lot of applications, as you know, before we are successful with this. Maybe today we can work on ways to be more active in contacting the places where you have made applications. In the future, I would also appreciate it if you would let me know in advance if you can't come to one of our scheduled meeting.

2. *Reviewing task progress.* The practitioner can now review task efforts, including both involuntary client efforts and practitioner tasks. Sometimes clients immediately report on task completion as part of the target problem review step. As tasks are often not fully completed despite diligent efforts, task efforts can be praised. Praise should not, however, be overemphasized, as too much praise may undercut self-attribution of changes. That is, involuntary clients might come to feel that they are completing tasks to please the practitioner rather than doing them because they will produce some personal benefit. Since task review often leads directly to review of obstacles in completing tasks, an example combining the two steps is provided below.

3. *Identifying obstacles to progress.* When tasks are initially developed, anticipating that some tasks probably will not have been completed successfully is one way of avoiding preoccupation with failure. In addition, after the practitioner praises task efforts, he or she can explore obstacles that blocked success on some tasks. Such obstacle exploration should focus on *what* got in the way rather than *who.* Examining a variety of possible causes for task failure can prevent the practitioner from prematurely concluding that tasks were not completed because of a lack of involuntary client motivation. Lack of incentive or rationale for a task is indeed a possible explanation for task failure, but several other possibilities should also be examined (see figure 7.8).

The most basic question in obstacle analysis and identification is to find out whether obstacles have blocked the specific tasks or whether the problem is one that motivates the involuntary client, or both. If obstacles have blocked a specific task while the client remains committed to working on the target problem, the following include many of the possible explanations for the blocked effort: (a) lack of client skill, (b) lack of client capacity to complete the task, (c) lack of practitioner skill in task development, (d) the task was not adequately specified, (e) inadequate resources, (f) occurrence of an emergency or crisis, (g) inadequate rationale for the task, (h) lack of reinforcement, (i) debilitating fear or anxiety, and (j) adverse beliefs (Epstein and Brown 2002).

If the problem does not motivate the involuntary client, the practitioner can examine whether: (a) the involuntary client might have been pressured to acknowledge a problem attributed by others; (b) the involuntary client is unaware of consequences of failure to work on a mandated problem; (c) the involuntary client has conflicted wants such that work on this problem might jeopardize other benefits; or (d) the involuntary client has little hope that the problem can be resolved.

If obstacles have arisen that block a specific task, the practitioner can proceed to revise tasks mindful of those blockages. If the problem is not motivational, the practitioner can attempt to reframe the problem or examine incentives and consequences in the case of mandated problems.

In the following exchange, Cheri reviews and praises task effort with John and probes for obstacles. She discovers both obstacles related to the specific task and the whole target problem.

CHERI: What else did you agree to do?
JOHN: Well, I agreed to look for job ads in the newspapers. But that's real hard.
CHERI: How have you been going about that?
JOHN: I go through the newspapers. It's not hard to do. But it's like you sit down and read the newspapers, and I just feel this same kind of feeling

Figure 7.8   Obstacle analysis

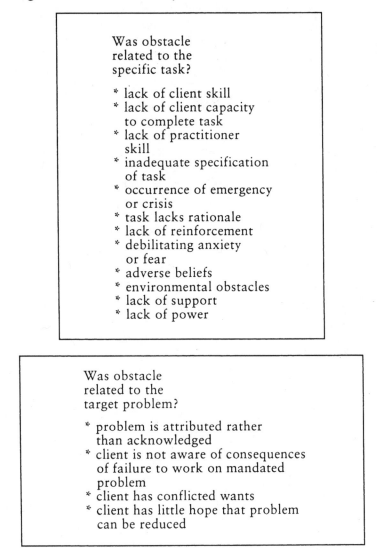

Was obstacle
related to the
specific task?

* lack of client skill
* lack of client capacity
  to complete task
* lack of practitioner
  skill
* inadequate specification
  of task
* occurrence of emergency
  or crisis
* task lacks rationale
* lack of reinforcement
* debilitating anxiety
  or fear
* adverse beliefs
* environmental obstacles
* lack of support
* lack of power

Was obstacle
related to the
target problem?

* problem is attributed rather
  than acknowledged
* client is not aware of consequences
  of failure to work on mandated
  problem
* client has conflicted wants
* client has little hope that problem
  can be reduced

when I'm waiting for the phone. I just want to crumple the thing up and throw it away.

Several obstacle possibilities emerge here. The task of looking in the newspapers might have been inadequately specified and he may lack skills in reviewing the ads. Most pertinent are his mention of feeling discouraged that suggests that the task is not rewarding and that he has doubts about whether it will be successful.

JOHN: But there was an ad in there that I responded to.
CHERI: Oh, you did?
JOHN: Down at Brown Tank. Yeah.
CHERI: Great.
JOHN: I filled out an application and mailed it into them. I mailed it into 'em, and there I wait. So I haven't heard from them. It would be a good job. I'd like to have it.
CHERI: I'm glad to hear that you made an application. I also hear that just waiting and wondering is something you are frustrated about.
JOHN: This is not a pleasant place to be here. I don't want to be here, but here I am.
CHERI: You really have been active before this in efforts to find a job and you've done a great job in the things that you agreed to do. And I can also tell that you're feeling frustrated and overwhelmed about the situation and not real optimistic. I think it's important to keep working at it and to keep doing the small things because that's how you do get a job. I think that's great that you sent in that application to Brown Tank. So now you're waiting for them to call you?
JOHN: Yeah. They didn't want people coming up there, so you had to mail in the application. So I mailed in the application, and there's nothing else I can do except wait for them to call me or not call me.
CHERI: What is it that you would like to know about Brown Tank right now, as far as where you stand with them?

Obstacle analysis now appears to be centering on lack of resources as John has not heard from Brown Tank. Cheri has praised John's efforts and empathized with his frustration. His lack of hope may be realistic if he lacks skills or jobs are unavailable. Specific job readiness skills might be explored here. We will return to this exploration with John below in the sections on appropriate middle-phase confrontation and task revision.

4. *Dealing with crises.* Crises within the task-centered context are large-scale obstacles that block all task efforts. They are also defined as stress problems

touched off by disruptions such as substantial change in the environment, loss of physical functioning, accident, or other losses (Epstein and Brown 2002). Involuntary clients are often members of oppressed groups with low incomes, inadequate housing, and limited access to health care such that environmental crises frequently occur. Rather than prematurely concluding that involuntary clients are crisis-ridden and disorganized, serious exploration of the nature of those crises is in order. Task-centered research in foster care indicated that clients experienced an average of three or more crises in twelve-session contracts yet were still able to have at least partial success in fulfilling the contract (Rooney 1981).

Consequently, practitioner response to crises is important in not losing hope for further progress. Several possibilities can be explored when crises occur: (a) Can the crisis be handled through focusing problem-solving efforts in one session? (b) If the crisis is unlikely to be quickly resolved, should target problems be revised to include it or should it become a new target problem? (c) If the crisis can be resolved within the session, can task work continue simultaneously on targeted problems? (d) When crises are generated by client decisions, the practitioner can clarify consequences of those decisions without blaming.

In the following exchange, Nancy discovers that a crisis has occurred. She helps Beth assess the extent and consequences of the crisis, revise the target problem, and make plans for next steps. Nancy clarifies the new circumstances without judging or blaming Beth. Instead, she describes consequences that have resulted from choices Beth has made.

NANCY: It seems that a lot of changes have happened since the last time I saw you; why don't you fill me in?

BETH: Well, Barb called the cops four times since you've been on vacation. The fourth time she had me and Jimmy removed from her premises by the cops and she wanted me to be taken up to juvenile hall and the cops said they couldn't do it. And they let me go on my own until you got back. Just that I had to contact your supervisor.

NANCY: Which you did, I know that.

BETH: And here I am.

NANCY: So you're out of Barb's and you feel that there is probably no chance that you'll be able to go back there?

BETH: I heard that she wanted me to come back but I don't want to go back.

NANCY: So, you want to change your plan, which was to stay at your aunt's until the hearing in June. The problem you wanted to work on of getting along with your aunt until you could get out on your own and support yourself on your own isn't appropriate anymore?

BETH: Right.

NANCY: So we will need to retarget and think about the problem you have now in your living situation. You don't have a job yet and I know that that has been something that has been very difficult for you to find a job. The other change is that you'll have to go to court earlier since you are not now living in an approved placement. I will have to notify the judge that you have moved out of Barb's and he will have to approve or disapprove of the new arrangements.

5. *Employing appropriate middle-phase confrontation.* Within the task-centered framework, confrontation can be considered a special form of obstacle identification undertaken by the practitioner. A continuum of confrontation was introduced in chapter 6, ranging from no confrontation through assertive confrontation. Assertive confrontations should be more successful in the middle phase if the practitioner has come to be trusted as a person who has the involuntary client's interest at heart, is expert, and is likable. Even when assertive confrontations are carried out following the guidelines for use of descriptive, nonblaming statements described earlier, such confrontations are still frequently interpreted as a put-down, verbal assault, or inappropriate criticism. As assertive confrontation is more intrusive than inductive questioning, higher levels of reactance can be expected to be generated by its usage including possible boomerang effects in which behaviors and attitudes solidify rather than change. It often provokes anger, helplessness, anxiety, fears, or remorse.

In the following exchange, Cheri combines use of inductive questions and assertive confrontation in her responses to John's concerns about the program and his frustration with it. Notice that she empathizes with his feelings of frustration but does not confront them, focusing confrontation rather on the requirements of the program and obstacles to John's own goals.

JOHN: Well, yeah, you know. And it's not my fault. I'm not like these guys that sit out in the lounge. They are half loaded, they get in the bag, and they're gone. I was a good worker up there in the mines. I was a good worker. It's just—I just get so frustrated, because I'm down here. I went to the school, get laid off, I go to the school, they tell me, take the school. You can be a welder, you can do okay. Go down to the cities, make some money. So I take the school. I do all the things that I'm supposed to do, but it just doesn't work out. I get pretty pissed off about what's going on. 'Cause they tell you to do this, and you do it. They tell you to do that, you do that. And then you shake your head, and I'm supposed to go out, and this lady's going to help me here. I'm still stuck here. What am I supposed to do? I don't want to be here. This isn't my idea of a picnic, here.

CHERI: I can see that you would rather be someplace else. You're feeling like I'm here telling you what you need to do, too. Nothing seems to be helping.

JOHN: Well, it seems to me that I'm supposed to be here.

CHERI: You mean here, in my office?

JOHN: I mean like, what happens if I don't come here?

CHERI: Well, that was one of the first things about your participating in this housing program that we talked about, when we first met. There were a couple of things, for you to be here, to live here and eat here, that you needed to agree to do, which you did do. Do you remember what those were?

JOHN: I agreed when I came here that I would do some of the handiwork around here in exchange for room and board. That I'd take care of myself. Well, mostly that I would do the odd jobs around here, some of the small maintenance things.

CHERI: You've done a great job, by the way. You've been the first one that's been able to fix that window. That's great.

JOHN: Well, thanks. And the other part is that I agreed that I'd come in here and see you. And that I would be active in my job search.

CHERI: Right.

JOHN: Which I did—I've been out there doing my stuff.

CHERI: Yes, you have been. One of my main roles here is to work with the people that are participating in this program to help them find employment and to be kind of a support person and to help get the ball rolling. It is important that you see me regularly.

JOHN: I hear that.

CHERI: I know that you don't really like being here, and I don't want you to have to be here either. I want you to have a full-time job so you can be on your own.

In the next exchange, Nancy carries out a series of assertive confrontations with Beth about not carrying through with plans to contact an alternative school. She makes the confrontations with specific facts followed by expressions of empathy.

NANCY: So you wanted to contact the high school to see if you could enroll this quarter and get one more credit and have that for when you want to take your GED test and want to get a high school diploma, right?

BETH: Right.

NANCY: What about GED studying, are you thinking about doing that now or are you thinking about doing that in the future sometime?

BETH: I could do it now.

NANCY: What do you know about where you could study for your GED?

BETH: I could try to enroll in Fresh Start. I could take my GED but then I couldn't get the credit that I need. All I get is my GED and not my diploma.

NANCY: Beth, when we started four sessions ago, you were talking about Fresh Start at that point and you didn't contact Fresh Start, and we talked about it at the second session and you said you had forgot and that you had been real busy, so you said you would contact them again, and you didn't contact them the second week. Is there something about Fresh Start that is holding you back?

BETH: Right now I want to get that one credit because then I can get that diploma instead of just a plain old GED. And if I go to Fresh Start, I can't get it because they don't give credits at Fresh Start.

NANCY: Are there any other things about Fresh Start that turn you off?

BETH: The work, I don't really, I don't think I could get into building houses, or apartment houses.

NANCY: The construction work doesn't appeal to you.

BETH: Not really.

NANCY: Did you say that to them when you were interviewing there? That it wasn't work you thought you could really get into?

BETH: No, I didn't say much of anything when I went there.

NANCY: Oh. Why didn't you say anything to them about that?

BETH: 'Cause I wasn't really sure.

NANCY: You were under some pressure to come up with a plan too, I know, at that time for the court.

BETH: Yeah, I was.

NANCY: It just seemed to me when you kept putting off contacting them that there must be something going on then. It just didn't fit with the way you saw yourself. Or the way you wanted your life to turn out, so I think it's a good idea but I don't want you to come up with that idea just to have one more idea for me. I want the ideas to be ones that are important to you.

Consideration of confrontation so far has concentrated on use of inductive questions and assertive confrontation. In some circumstances, intensive confrontation that is longer-term and from multiple sources is appropriate. Intensive confrontations sometimes can be utilized when illegal behavior has occurred of a very serious nature or when serious harm to self or others has occurred or is imminent. If the concern is about self-harm, evidence should demonstrate that without intensive intervention harmful, irreversible consequences are likely to follow. In circumstances that fail to meet these levels of harm or danger to self and others, involuntary clients should be able to choose to receive the intensive confrontation or avoid it.

For example, the intervention techniques used to persuade persons with chemical dependency problems to consider accepting treatment can be considered intensive confrontation. In such circumstances, intervention is defined as presenting reality in a receivable way to a person out of touch with it (Johnson 1976). Many experts consider chemically addicted behavior not to be "free" behavior under the control of the normal powers of will, but rather a driving physical and emotional need. According to this view, the driving need arouses a set of rigid defense mechanisms that are impervious to normal means of persuasion (Johnson 1980).

Such interventions may take the form of a professionally guided intensive confrontation in which a group of family and friends meet for an extended period of time with the chemically dependent person to express both caring and concern. Persons considered likely to be influential with the chemically dependent person are asked to compose letters that recall specific situations of loving and concern and specific instances of the harm caused to self and others by the chemically dependent person's behavior. Letters are edited to describe specific instances of harm without shaming or blaming. The chemically dependent person is asked to listen to the group while they read their letters before responding. After the response, specific options for dealing with the chemical dependency problem are strongly recommended.

Variations of such intervention methods have included preparation of the spouse of the alcoholic to carry out the confrontation. In Thomas's unilateral family therapy model, the spouse specifies a directive to enter treatment or decrease consumption and includes a consequence such as marital separation if the alcoholic refuses (Thomas et al. 1987). Preliminary model testing of this form of Thomas's unilateral family therapy method, including this programmed confrontation, has been supportive of the effectiveness of the technique. Thomas notes that while agreement with the programmed confrontation would be desirable in all cases, it is sometimes necessary to settle for less. In all cases, however, the spouse may be helped to consider his or her options if the intervention does not succeed and the chemically dependent person may move closer to acknowledging the problem. Sometimes alcoholics respond to the programmed confrontation by choosing to reduce consumption on their own. In this event, the practitioner attempts to gain a commitment from the chemically dependent person to enter a treatment program if reduction does not reach specific levels within a specific time limit (Thomas and Yoshioka 1989).

It is interesting that Thomas reports that chemically dependent persons sometimes select an alternative that would address the alcohol problem but that is *not* the specific recommendation made by the intervener and spouse. For example, some clients insist on finding their own treatment program rather than the one recommended. One explanation for these responses can come from reactance theory. Presenting one option may stimulate more reactance than presenting two or more, including those generated by the chemically dependent person.

Some treatment programs for persons who have committed crimes of physical violence, including sex crimes, make frequent use of intensive confrontation rather than a situation-specific approach. In such settings, discussions of use of intensive confrontation frequently focus on the type of persons who "need" intensive confrontation, those who are highly defensive, resistant, and sociopathic. Repeated use of intensive confrontation is sometimes based on beliefs that clients who commit crimes have erroneous thinking styles that maintain illegal, deviant behavior (Yochelson and Samenow 1985). These thinking styles are considered to include pervasive self-deception, refusal to take responsibility for actions, and a manipulative orientation that is impervious to all but the most intensive confrontation. Hence, it is argued that confrontation should not necessarily be in short doses or surrounded by messages of caring and acceptance. Rather, the dose must be large and the impact of the confrontation not dulled by acceptance of manipulative or self-deceptive behavior.

Intensive confrontation is sometimes used in ways that conflict with the guidelines for confrontation presented earlier. Those guidelines suggested that: (a) confrontation should meet specific circumstances of law violation, harm, or danger or choice to receive it by the involuntary client; (b) it is most effectively and ethically delivered when it includes specific examples and is conveyed with caring, respect, and support by a person respected by the involuntary client; and (c) that it is unlikely to be either ethical or effective when it emanates from the frustration of the practitioner rather than from client circumstances. If confrontation is done inappropriately, it can lead to fear, anxiety, resistance, and heightened defensiveness (Reid 1986).

Assertive and intensive confrontations can also lose their situation- and behavior-specific, caring qualities and become *abusive confrontations* in which the client is subjected to a blaming, uncaring onslaught. Factors influencing inappropriate usage of confrontation can include program and client variables, situational variables, and practitioner variables.

a. *Program and client variables.* Confrontation is sometimes used in frequent, intense doses as the method of the program rather than as a confrontation for specific clients and circumstances. Such usage is described by those programs as necessary to influence particular kinds of clients. Such high-frequency usage of intensive confrontation can have expectable consequences in involuntary client behavior. Efforts to protect oneself from intensive confrontation may be interpreted as further evidence of resistant behavior with little attention to the degree to which intensive confrontation *contributes to* behavior that is labeled defended and resistant. This interaction has been called the confrontation–denial cycle (Miller and Rollnick 2002). This cycle should be expected to generate high reactance as a byproduct of its usage. Further, if intensive confrontation is not carried out with accompanying messages of support from persons considered likable and trustworthy, the influence can easily be perceived as punishing rather than persuasive. If the influence method is perceived to be abusive, then it *may reinforce* the belief that might makes right by modeling intrusive behavior on the part of the practitioner. There is further concern about overgeneralizing the use of intensive confrontation methods beyond the circumstances that call for it. For example, frequent use of attacking methods that pressured encounter group members to change quickly led to a higher number and proportion of group casualties than in groups in which leaders employed more selective confrontation (Lieberman, Yalom, and Miles 1973). Inappropriate overuse of intensive confrontation methods might be avoided through increased use of self-assessments, inductive questions, and assertive confrontation early in contact.

b. *Situational variables.* When motivational congruence with involuntary clients has not been achieved, practitioners often experience frustration with involuntary client failure to complete required tasks. While the intention may be to jolt the involuntary client in the interest of his or her ultimate well-being, there is little reason to believe that an uncaring onslaught will change attitudes or provide more than a brief release of tension for the frustrated practitioner. When frustration is vented with the practitioner acting as prosecutor or critical parent, change may occur but only through fear of punishment and enhanced dependency. Further, such undifferentiated use may make clients *less* voluntary by ignoring areas of possible motivational congruence, contributing to distancing from involuntary clients, and labeling them resistant.

c. *Practitioner variables.* Finally, it has been suggested that some practitioners overuse or inappropriately use confrontation when they lack other helping skills. For example, Forrest suggests that some practitioners are consistently angry, manipulative, exploitative, and pathologically confrontive (Forrest 1982). Practitioners lacking empathy skills may try to overcome such lack of skills with overly reactive, negative confronting styles. Rather than assume that overuse of intensive confrontation is primarily a result of personality deficits of practitioners, the continuum of confrontation skills in the context of other helping methods may be more useful in extending the practitioner's skill repertoire. The real issues, then, are flexibility in use of confrontation methods, the ability to determine when confrontation is appropriate, and if so, the intensity and a sense of the expectable consequences. Practitioners who rigidly use particular modes of confrontation might explore a more flexible use of confrontation, including in some cases less frequent use so as not to diminish the effect of appropriate assertive confrontation.

Underuse of confrontation is also a problem. Practitioners trained to work with voluntary clients who value the "good relationship" may be hesitant to use confrontation for fear that it will damage the relationship. Remembering that involuntary clients who find themselves in a position of low power may be inclined to use self-presentation strategies and act with less than full candor can help in preparing for appropriate use of confrontation. Such practitioners should remember that the *lack* of confrontation in circumstances of potential harm, danger, law violation, or behavior that conflicts with client goals can be as damaging as inappropriate overuse. They can then experiment with increased use of inductive questions and assertive confrontation as appropriate, respectful methods that can enhance the working relationship.

6. *Revising and summarizing task plans.* The purpose of obstacle analysis and appropriate middle-phase confrontation is to improve the chances for more successful task plans. As in initial task planning, rationales for completing the tasks, possible incentives or rewards, and use of simulation or role play may be considered. Practitioner tasks may also be useful here in facilitating client action. In the following exchange, Jean and Mrs. Torres are making plans about the next steps in their work together related to making her home safer place. Notice how Jean is both specific and picks up on Mrs. Torres' ideas about how to limit the tasks. Mrs. Torres also puts her stamp on the particular ways she intends to carry out the tasks.

JEAN: Okay, how many shelves do you plan to clean?

MRS. TORRES: Well, I think those three that are right by the cupboards where I want to keep the extra groceries are probably the most important.

JEAN: Okay, that makes sense, since you will use them the most. So you plan to clean three?

MRS. TORRES: Yeah, I'll do that bunch right next to those cupboards, I'll do those, because a lot of that I think can be thrown away.

JEAN: That makes sense to do those three.

MRS. TORRES: But I'll have Julie help because some of that stuff she might want to keep. It's a lot of spare parts, and stuff.

JEAN: Yes, that would help.

MRS. TORRES: If I'm going to do the shelves first, I think that I should only try to do four boxes.

JEAN: Okay, I think that sounds good. If for some reason you get really ambitious, you know, and you really are on a roll, you can do more than what we agree on, you don't have to stick to this. It sounds as if you and Julie worked well together doing the boxes and a lot of things got done during that time. So, if you decide to do more, you might try that.

MRS. TORRES: Besides that, then we mark on the outside of the boxes what I've got in there. We got a marker and then we marked it down. Because since we moved then I forgot what is in what box, you know.

JEAN: Yeah, that can get very confusing if you do that.

MRS. TORRES: Okay, I'll start writing down, I'm going to make a list of things, I think I'll put that on here. Yeah, because I'm going to make a list of all the different kinds of things that Julie could help me with and then she'd be able to choose.

JEAN: That works well for you when Julie has a say in what parts she helps with.

The Termination Phase

Approaches to work with voluntary clients often consider termination with trepidation and predict that many clients at this stage will feel abandoned and regress to earlier stages. If the client has come to depend on the practitioner as a major source of support and problem-solving expertise without having enhanced his or her own skills and support systems, then such feelings of abandonment are both understandable and predictable.

Involuntary clients are less likely to experience such regrets. Since they did not seek contact, termination may be approached with relief that an unsought pressure will be removed. In fact, regrets may be a *good* sign since involuntary clients are likely to feel them only if contact had ultimately come to be valued. In fact, one family that that the senior author worked with as a result of required contact with an adolescent who was absenting from school noted as he finished his last session that the family sessions were "not so bad"!

Termination with mandated clients often involves practitioner decisions and recommendations about when to let go of contact. Such decisions can be difficult because rarely are all problems resolved. In addition, some clients continue to have frequent crises or do not have access to ongoing support.

Decisions about termination can be made more easily when specific goals were established during the contracting phase. In the absence of such specific goals, the involuntary client is maintained in a relatively powerless state without a focus for energies and reactance may be reinforced. When such criteria focus on essentials rather than on the ideal, termination is more likely to be successful.

The practitioner using the task-centered approach begins to prepare for termination in the first session by focusing clearly on the schedule of sessions, by reminding the client of the number of sessions completed and the number remaining. This focus on available time makes use of the "goal gradient" effect in which client and practitioner activities can be expected to pick up in pace when the end of a time-limited contract approaches. Second, practitioners can also gradually become less active in task formulation and obstacle analysis, expressing confidence in the client's ability to resolve problems. Practitioners can also limit the scope of work undertaken in later sessions by narrowing or reducing goals to more feasible levels.

It is often hoped that work done in time-limited contact will generalize to situations after contact is ended. Beth was interviewed after her contact with Nancy had ended and she had been approved for independent living. Below, the interviewer explores the possibility that task-centered work on her own target problems may have also taught a problem-solving process that might generalize when Beth approaches new situations.[6]

INTERVIEWER: You had been working with Nancy for quite a while but in February, she changed gears and worked a little differently with you. Did you notice any differences?

BETH: Yes, I wasn't arguing with her as much. I felt that she was letting me take charge of my life and letting me make the decisions and not her. Which helped me a lot because I realized that it was all on my hands and nobody else and that made me sit down and think that I better get my stuff together and that helped a lot.

INTERVIEWER: Over the last couple months you've done quite a few tasks or things that you worked out with Nancy. I'm wondering if you've learned anything about not just carrying out those tasks but solving problems on your own that you've been able to take to other problems, other than the ones you talked to Nancy about?

BETH: Well to me at first when I did have Nancy, they all just seemed like a pain in the butt, but now they have become more real that they are a problem, that they can be worked out in time. That you just have to spend a little bit more time on each one of them and not try to solve them all in one day because it just doesn't work.

INTERVIEWER: So one of the things you do differently is you don't try to solve them all in one day?

BETH: Right. I take one step at a time if it takes a week for one problem, then it's a week I have to spend on it. If it takes more, then it has to take more, but some can take just one day, but others take a month to figure out. And I learned from my problems, not to make mistakes twice.

INTERVIEWER: I understand that you got a notebook of your own and you were writing down some of your own tasks for yourself.

BETH: Yeah, after me and Nancy had gone through the eight-week sessions I started writing down tasks that I thought were important to myself, that I had to do to succeed. And I still do that and I write down the daily things of what I have to do and the end of the day before I go to bed I'll check them off. What I didn't do goes on the next day's list.

It appears that Beth was quite aware of making more decisions and taking more personal responsibility for issues in her life. She has a grasp of prioritizing problems in order to reduce the feeling of being overwhelmed by them and she generates tasks for herself. Successful efforts in this time-limited contact do not mean that her life will continue without setbacks nor that she will never again have contact with social services. How can the practitioner working with involuntary clients prepare for termination in such a way that such self-attribution is encouraged? Four options can be considered in the final phase: (1) termination, (2) extension, (3) recontracting, and (4) monitoring.

Termination

When the end of the time limit is reached, many involuntary clients and practitioners will be ready to terminate because problems are substantially reduced or a preset limit of sessions has been reached. *Extensions* can be negotiated if substantial progress has already been made and more can be expected with a few more sessions. For example, a client who wanted to increase her job-seeking skills extended her contract for two sessions when an important job interview was scheduled for a week after the scheduled final session. The extension was planned to prepare for that interview and to review the interview and the total contract in a final session. *Recontracting* refers to the development of an additional contract on new problem areas if the client and practitioner both expressly wish to continue and there is good reason to believe that substantial progress will be made on the same or additional problems. Recontracting assumes that the agency will permit more lengthy contact. Recontracting may also be done when a large problem has been broken down into smaller time-limited sequences. Hence, the client may proceed to a second sequence if the first has been productive. It is often the case that case management contact continues after a period of more intensive contact has ended. Such *monitoring* works best when it is carried out for a specific, contracted purpose rather than waiting for something to happen or go wrong. Monitoring can take place through brief in-person and telephone check-up sessions. It can be useful to assess the maintenance of gains after a period of more limited contact. Monitoring may also occur to support linkages made to other resources (Epstein and Brown 2002).

When a decision to terminate services or shift to a different mode of contact has been made, a termination or transition session can include the following steps.

1. *Review problem reduction on each target and mandated problem by examining change in conditions.* Concrete data for assessing change can be shared. For example, Beth and Nancy reviewed Beth's work on conditions that would be reviewed in court when the recommendation for independent living would be considered. Specifically, conditions of parental permission, having a place to stay and a source of income, or participation in an educational program were reviewed. In addition, Beth's feeling that too many people were telling her what to do was also reviewed, finding that completing tasks had moved her to a more independent place in which there were fewer people in a position to tell her what to do.

2. *Review tasks completed and obstacles encountered, focusing on successes and learning obtained from that process.* Beth and Nancy reviewed her efforts to get a job and enter an educational program and the obstacles related to both.

3. *Review the general steps in problem solving used in the case as a reminder of methods that can be used with remaining problems.* For example, it can be recalled that steps included: (a) identifying specific concerns or target problems, (b) prioritizing mandated problems and voluntary problems that might make the most difference, (c) considering task possibilities and anticipating potential roadblocks, and (d) reviewing progress and attempting to "fix" tasks that did not work based on obstacle analysis.

4. *Consider remaining needs on targeted problems and other problems of concern to the client.* The practitioner helps the involuntary client to plan how he or she might go about maintaining changes. The practitioner should also help the involuntary client anticipate potential obstacles to this plan and to consider how those might be overcome. For example, Nancy and Beth discussed several problems that might occur after she was in independent living and how she might pursue help for them.

This chapter has provided specific guidelines for carrying out task-centered interventions with involuntary clients. As a general rather than problem-specific model with an eclectic theory base, the task-centered approach has several elements that are compatible with involuntary client work. Use of the adaptations suggested should enhance motivational congruence and promote self-attribution. The adaptations should reduce reactance by breaking down large problems, which often make both involuntary client and practitioner feel helpless, into smaller components. The specificity of task development also enhances clear record-keeping and assists in developing mutual accountability. Adaptations have also been suggested for working with time-limited subcontracts when involuntary client contact is not brief.

The task-centered approach is not a panacea for the problems of work with involuntary clients. It provides no magical answers in working with mandated clients who cannot agree on any concerns with the practitioner. Choices in the form of implementation and timing of required tasks have been suggested. Such techniques may assist some involuntary clients in coming to greater motivational congruence over time. Otherwise, as stated earlier, involuntary work supported primarily by fear of punishment and promise of reward often achieves results that last only as long as those compliance methods are available. There is little substitute for motivational congruence in achieving self-attributed change.

The chapter also presented the middle phase in which the review of initial task efforts takes place. However carefully developed, initial tasks often fail. Ways to review progress that focus on maintaining momentum and using selective confrontation were presented. Finally, guidelines for conducting termination that focus on objectives accomplished and linkage to additional resources for further work were provided.

Discussion Questions

1. Initial action plans often fail. How often do you find that such failures are assigned to lack of client effort or motivation instead of an objective review of obstacles?

2. It is suggested in this chapter that confrontation is frequently overused and also underused. That is, some agencies and settings may use it in nonproductive ways and others may not use it when the situation requires. What are your attitudes and beliefs about use of confrontation? Can the continuum of confrontation ranging from self-assessment to intensive confrontation be useful as a guide?

3. This chapter introduces the concept of the disagreeable task. However well intentioned and potentially useful, some tasks feel arduous to clients. What is the value of acknowledging that the task may not be pleasant?

4. Practitioners and agencies sometimes have difficulty letting go of involuntary clients, thinking that if they were maintained in contact a little longer, more progress could be achieved. How do you and your agency decide when enough is enough?

Notes

1. This dialogue segment is from a videotape entitled *Permanency Planning: Use of the Task-Centered Model with an Adolescent toward Independent Living. The Contracting Phase.* Ordering information is available in the appendix.

2. This videotape entitled *Task-Centered Case Management* with Jane Macy as the practitioner is available from www.insight-media.com.

3. A videotape of actual work done in this case entitled *Return from Foster Care* by Ron Rooney was made by the School of Social Service Administration, University of Chicago.

4. This selection is from a videotape entitled *Socialization at Chemical Dependency Intake* with Dick Leonard as practitioner. It is available from Ron Rooney at the University of Minnesota.

5. This selection is from a training videotape entitled *Work with Involuntary Clients in the Middle Phase* with Cheri Brady as the practitioner. The videotape is available from Ron Rooney at the University of Minnesota.

6. This interview is included in a videotape entitled *Permanency Planning: Use of the Task-Centered Model with an Adolescent toward Independent Living: The Middle Phase.* 475-1-c. The videotape is available from the videotape resources department of the School of Social Work, University of Wisconsin, Madison. (See appendix.)

Chapter 8

Work with Involuntary Families

Most practitioners working with families would probably prefer YARVIS clients: persons who are young attractive, rich, verbal, intelligent, and sane (Franklin and Jordan 1999). Many family members possess few of these attributes and, further, at least one would rather not be present. That reluctance may occur in response to pressure from the larger community for family members to change because of identified dangers to the family and the community. A continuum of involuntary contact is presented in this chapter, ranging from little or no pressure (voluntary treatment) through nonvoluntary to mandated pressures. Exemplars of family-centered practice in child welfare and adolescent delinquency are presented next including a description of common factors in these approaches and guidance for engagement. While beyond the scope of the chapter to develop a fully elaborated model for involuntary family work, specific guidelines for the contracting phase are provided.

We begin with an interaction between a practitioner representing family-centered, home-based services and Mrs. King, single parent of sixteen-year-old Christine. Mrs. King called a public child welfare agency requesting that Christine be removed from her home because she was not obeying house rules, skipping school, and likely using drugs. Mrs. King and Christine were then referred for a home-based service assessment. Such services often require as a precondition that family members agree to work to remain together as a unit rather than separate, as some family members might prefer. Hence, while an offer of home-based service is welcomed by many as a better alternative than placement out of the home, some are court-ordered to receive services. Others may receive an offer of service as an alternative to an involuntary investigation (Alternative Response in Minnesota 2006). The following exchange occurred during an initial home visit to explore the situation and make an offer for home-based services. While the practitioner and Mrs. King talk, Christine sits staring into space, portable-radio earphones planted firmly on her head.

PRACTITIONER: I explained to you briefly about home-based services on the phone. Home-based services is a program that the county offers for families who are having difficulties similar to what you described to me. A team of workers would come into your home to meet with your family for at least an hour a week for six to nine weeks. In that time, we would talk about what's going on and try and find some resolution to some of the difficulties that are going on in your home.

MRS. KING: You know, when I called Child Welfare, I thought that you were going to come and get her out of here. I just thought that you were going to come and tell me the procedure for getting her out of the house. We can't have her here.

PRACTITIONER: So, you thought that I'd be putting Christine into placement.

MRS. KING: I think, you know, that's pretty much what I said over the phone . . . I'm telling you what I need.

PRACTITIONER: I can understand that you are disappointed that we can't offer the placement out of the home you wanted. We place children and adolescents out of the home in fairly restricted circumstances. We have found in the past that if the problems aren't worked on in the home, the child often returns after placement to the same situation. So, we are now offering in-home family-based service to help you with the problems that caused you to want to get her placed out of the home.

MRS. KING: So you're telling me how I'm going to be able to solve my problem, and I'm telling you what my problem is, and I know how to solve it. And that's to get her out of the house here. I mean this stuff of having her still live here, I mean she's just causing too much trouble.

Though Mrs. King made a voluntary request for service, she can hardly be described as voluntary during the above conversation. She discovers that the out-of-home placement service she requested is not available and experiences pressure to accept home-based services as a substitute. Further, sixteen-year-old

Christine has not yet been addressed and hence at this point may be considered more as an involuntary target than a client.

Practitioners frequently have involuntary contact with families, including persons such as Mrs. King and Christine. They often draw on family therapy perspectives in planning what to do with such families. Such perspectives permit analysis of family communications and role structures that have been found useful far beyond their original development in voluntary family therapy. Similarly, family therapy techniques for assisting families in making behavioral changes have been attractive alternatives to methods that focus primarily on seeking cognitive or emotional insight.

Family therapy perspectives, however, require many adaptations for work in involuntary family situations. In addition, many practitioners work with families regarding issues such as discharge planning and concern with the welfare of an elderly relative, in which family therapy is neither the service offered by the practitioner's setting nor sought by clients (Reid 1985).

How Are Families and Family Members Involuntary?

It is typical for some family members to be more eager to participate in therapy than others, raising the issue of voluntary participation for the latter (Margolin 1982). In fact, family contact often begins with an interview with one or more family members who are concerned about the problems of an absent family member (Reid 1985). That family member is frequently a child or adolescent and the problem is often viewed as their troublesome behavior. "Identified targets" such as Christine frequently participate minimally, occasionally rousing to defend themselves against parental accusations.

In other situations such as alleged child abuse or neglect, the practitioner initiates contact. In such situations, the family does not seek help and may not be willing to reveal problems. For example, when a child is at risk of placement, the only problem the family sees may be keeping the child at home and family contact is considered primarily as fulfilling requirements. Such families are often perceived to be dysfunctional; and practitioners may attach labels such as rigid, confounded problem-solving methods, conflictual, enmeshed, prone to externalize, with serious problems of multiple or long duration, with little executive capacity, overwhelmed, crisis-oriented, with critical communication, depleted goals, unempathic, either abdicating responsibility or too focused on the child (Weitzman 1985).

With such negative practitioner perceptions, it may not come as a surprise that "the therapist often meets a barrage of angry feelings, particularly before members are actively engaged" (Schlosberg and Kagan 1988:3). Such families are described as fearful, angry, distrustful, viewing helping professionals as intimidating parent figures who will not seek or accept their views and who are insensitive to their needs for privacy (ibid.). Similarly, families are described as feeling victimized by the court, schools, and social service staff, and are often seen as resistant to change despite orders, pleas, exhortations, and the combined efforts of many agencies. The practitioners assigned to work with them often feel frustrated and exhausted. The fact that such families are often headed by harried, low-income, single-parent mothers from oppressed groups is often neglected in the literature.

Professionals often perceive such families as if their primary problem were lack of insight into the problems in the situation as seen from the outside by practitioners. If only they would acknowledge the same problems that we see them as having, and do so without being pressured to do it, there might be progress. There has been interest in fields such as child welfare in finding assessment clues from early contact that would predict which clients might later succeed (Yatchmenoff 2005). Having a reliable set of such clues could help agencies target scarce resources to those who can make best use of them.

This quest for reliable diagnostic indicators has in part led to interest in the Stages of Change approach with its predictable phases and clear guidance to practitioners about how to respond in each phase (Littell and Girvin 2002 2004). However, there are complications with overly broad application of an approach that was developed to explain health-related change for voluntary individuals to families meeting under pressure and facing multiple difficulties, only some of which may be health related (ibid.). Application of the Stages of Change perspective to a child welfare sample revealed, for example, that some groups of child welfare clients appear to be immobilized. Though they acknowledged a need for change, they appeared overwhelmed by circumstances and not hopeful about change (Girvin 2004). Still others did not acknowledge a need for change yet reported they were actively engaged in a process of change (ibid.). These seem to be contradictory findings unless one considers the situation of families who have been pressured to accept a particular problem. For example, some mothers with child welfare issues are pressured to "stay away from a dangerous man" or "avoid drugs" if they wish to regain custody of their children before mandatory time limits are reached (*Adoption and Safe Families Act* 1997).

Such parents may have considered that it was in their interest to avoid seeing the man or avoid drugs, whether or not they agreed that these were dangers to them or their children, because they perceived the problems as mandated steps toward regaining custody of their children.

Involuntary work with families occurs in settings and problem areas as diverse as drug and alcohol abuse, delinquency, home-based services, spousal abuse, and in prisons (Showalter and Williams 1980; Weidman 1986). For example, the utility of work with families of chemically dependent persons has been described as including an examination of the functions that drugs serve in the family, the ways use is overlooked, treatment is sabotaged, and how significant others can influence maintenance of drug use (Stanton 1980). Similarly, when family methods have been used in the treatment of alcoholism, alcoholics are said to sometimes experience less isolation, feel gratified by the spouse's participation, and feel less need to be defensive and responsible for the entire problem (Janzen 1977). More recently, Shoham and Rohrbaugh have demonstrated how spouses may ironically reinforce the very substance abuse they wish to reduce (Shoham and Rohrbaugh 1997). By working with the spouse's response, they have been able to more effectively assist the spouse in reducing the substance abuse (Rohrbaugh and Shoham 2001).

A Continuum of Involuntary Family Contact

An involuntary family transaction refers to contact between a helping professional and two or more family members in which at least one participant experienced external pressure to participate in that contact. This definition focuses attention on the presence of factors outside the person as influencing initial contact. The pressures range from formal and informal nonvoluntary pressures to mandated pressures. The family as a total unit may fit on a continuum of external pressure. In addition, individual family members may be scattered throughout the continuum, with some experiencing nonvoluntary pressure, some experiencing mandated pressure, while others may be voluntary. Further, families and family members may become more or less voluntary during contact. For example, Mrs. King may have begun the request for service as a voluntary client while Christine experienced informal nonvoluntary pressure from her mother to participate in that contact. Voluntary, nonvoluntary, and mandated points on the continuum are elaborated in the following paragraphs.

The *voluntary family* is one in which family members *seek assistance from a helping practitioner without outside pressures from legal, formal, or informal sources.* For example, a couple may seek marriage counseling without either formal pressure or informal pressure from one spouse who is more committed to seeking help than the other. If the resource sought comes without strings attached by the agency or practitioner providing the resource, or if informal pressures are not present, then the family unit may be voluntary. As

Mrs. King's situation suggests, some family members may be voluntary as long as the problems they perceive are addressed and they do not experience mandated, formal, or informal pressure. The dilemma for family practitioners is that accepting the agenda of one person such as the parent often implies work with another family member as involuntary target. Hence, circumstances in which all family members are voluntary are probably the exception to the rule.

Nonvoluntary family contact occurs when at least one family member experiences a coerced or constrained choice from formal or informal pressure to participate in contact. Formal pressure may take at least five forms: (1) a desired service or resource is not available; (2) family service is presented as the only alternative to a punishing option; (3) family contact may be a precondition or *perceived to be* a precondition for receiving a desired resource; (4) the original request for individual treatment is reframed by the practitioner as a family problem; and (5) family service may be the policy of the agency. Each of these forms of formal pressure is presented separately with examples to illustrate them.

1. *Desired service or resource is not available.* Clients such as Mrs. King who may make a voluntary request may become involuntary when that request is not accepted. If their other options are limited, they may experience a constrained choice.

2. *Family service is presented as the only alternative to a punishing option.* Some families may experience a coerced choice to seek family counseling influenced by the expectation of avoiding major punishers controlled by outside agencies. Hence, juveniles and their families are sometimes presented with the coerced option of accepting family treatment or entering a residential treatment program.

3. *Family contact is a precondition or is perceived to be a precondition for receiving a desired resource.* Such preconditions may be intentional or unintentional, explicit or implied. For example, families seeking approval to become adoptive parents often find that a thorough family assessment is an intentional explicit precondition. Similarly, couples seeking divorce may find that the services of a mediator are a required precondition for judicial approval of their divorce request (Sprenkle and Storm 1983). Family members may encounter agency expectations that they attend counseling in support of the residential treatment of a family member.

In other cases, family contact may be *perceived* as a precondition when the suggestion that it take place comes from a powerful person or agency that controls major resources. The precondition may be implicit. For example, some referral sources such as foster care workers may recommend family therapy with the implied message: "Take six months of family therapy and we will review your plans to regain custody of your child."

That message may be unintentional. Unless free choices are clarified and the consequences for complying or not complying with the suggestion are clarified, family members may take the suggestion from a powerful person as an implied requirement. For example, Mrs. King may receive the impression that she must agree to home-based services as a necessary hurdle to show that lesser methods have not succeeded in their attempts to have out-of-home placement considered.

While families experiencing a coerced or constrained choice to "seek treatment" may have little doubt about its involuntary nature, practitioners receiving the "request for service" may be less aware of the coerced or constrained nature of the request if they are unaware of the benefits and punishers controlled by the referral source. Similarly, the referring practitioner may be unaware that the family is responding to a suggestion as if it were an implied requirement.

4. *An original request for individual treatment is reframed by the practitioner as a family problem.* As noted earlier, family members frequently come for help with concerns about another member of the family who is not present. They may voluntarily seek help to have a troublesome person "fixed." If the practitioner agrees to "fix" the identified target, the family members initiating contact remain voluntary. Practitioners with a systems view of family problems may, however, search for indicators for how the family system supports the identified target person's symptoms. If such practitioners attempt to reframe problems to the family system level, family members may experience a constrained choice to accept a "package deal" in order to receive attention on the problem that led them to seek help. Reluctance of family members to accept such a reframe is explained by Anderson and Stewart:

> Most families are at least skeptical about, if not overtly resistant to, the concept of family therapy. The anxiety-producing experience of beginning any kind of therapy becomes complicated by the seemingly illogical request that the entire family come in to be seen when the problem clearly resides in one member. Why should the family be seen when it is Johnny who doesn't like school or Mary who is "acting up." (Anderson and Stewart 1985:31)

Finally, there are many circumstances beyond family treatment in which a practitioner may suggest that other family members need to be consulted in order to resolve the problem presented. For example, adults sometimes seek help when they are concerned about the living conditions of their frail relatives. The practitioner may well seek to include those relatives rather than operate on them as targets.

5. *Family service may be the policy of the agency.* Some agencies may have a policy of refusing to see the family unless all family members are present or strongly suggest family involvement. Family members should be informed that other agencies and therapists may not have the same preference and assistance should be offered for such a referral (Margolin 1982).

In addition to formal pressures or situations in which no formal pressure from the practitioner or agency has been applied, family members often experience informal pressures from the rest of the family. For example, siblings may initially attend sessions because "Mom and Dad made me come" or because family therapists requested that they attend in order to see the "identified client" in the context of family interaction.

While nonvoluntary contact is probably the most frequent form of family contact, mandated family contact also occurs. For example, persons who have abused or neglected their children are sometimes court-ordered to receive family counseling (Irueste-Montes and Montes 1988). The involuntary nature of such an arrangement is usually clear to the family and the family practitioner carrying out the court order. Expectations for reporting on family progress to the court are often discussed and the power issues involved are often considered openly. Consequences, however, of failure to complete treatment or change in specified ways are often unclear.

Practitioners may also initiate an involuntary investigation. According to Reid, "many of these cases involve 'mandated' problems which essentially are problems that are defined not by the family but by the community and its representatives including the practitioner. . . . The social worker needs to reveal to the family at the outset the general shape of those mandated problems" (Reid 1985:37). In some cases, practitioners are able to work with the family and relevant community agencies in an effort to negotiate definitions of the problem acceptable to those involved.

Issues in Adapting Family Treatment Perspectives to Work with Involuntary Families

While family treatment approaches have made important contributions to work with persons in less than voluntary situations, there have been difficulties in exclusive reliance on family treatment for guidance in such work. These problems include (1) lack of fit with setting, (2) lack of attention to other systems levels, (3) goal conflict, (4) the resurrection of resistance, (5) issues in definition of practitioner role, and (6) ethical issues.

1. *Lack of fit with settings.* Many practitioners have contact with families in settings where the function is not family treatment (Tolson 1981). For example,

social workers often deal with practical problems such as assistance in finance and housing, dealing with illness, disability, locating and linking clients with resources, and acting as public agents for the well-being of children. Practitioners may work in discharge planning, consulting in an emergency room, returning children from foster care, and mediating conflict in which problems of illness and poverty often predominate. Caseloads may vary from small to hundreds. Clients served in such community organizations are often "not seeking the help offered." Yet while such work "in the trenches" may be the mission of fields such as social work, prestige is often accorded to practitioners based on their distance from such work.

The practice of helping professionals in such settings is shaped by factors such as their function in the organization, the kinds of problems and clients served, and their level of training. William Reid suggests that a framework for work with families is needed that includes both conventional forms of family treatment and other kinds of intervention, which is adaptable to work in the community, and which fits with an ecological problem-solving view in which the family is one of several systems (Reid 1985). We see below in the discussion of family preservation services in child welfare and adolescent delinquency that this framework is now under development.

2. *Lack of attention to other system levels.* While family therapy has been greatly influenced by systems perspectives, there are great variations in the way those perspectives are applied. For example, some approaches suggest that families are homeostatic systems that only superficially invite change while in fact they struggle with great determination to maintain the status quo (Haley 1963). Other family theorists suggest that family systems are not always static opponents of change. In this cybernetic view, families are seen as simultaneously engaged in efforts to change and also to maintain systems integrity (Luckhurst 1985). However, according to Pinsof, "unfortunately, in much of the family literature, system has become virtually synonymous with family" (Pinsof 1983). Harriet Johnson further suggests that while family approaches are often presented as systems approaches, they often redefine environmentally generated emotional distress as inadequate family or interpersonal functioning (Johnson 1986).

In general, however, family systems theorists treat the family as a closed system, omitting from their assessment any meaningful investigations either of the biological subsystems of individual family members or the social, economic, and organizational factors that may be suprasystems in which the family is enmeshed. Instead, there is a tendency to focus almost exclusively on interpersonal transactions rather than on systems (Johnson 1986).

William Reid suggests that overabsorption with family dynamics to the neglect of individual and environmental causes creates problems for social work similar to the absorption with intrapsychic processes that reflected the psychoanalytic emphasis of an earlier age (Reid 1985). More current approaches have attempted to redress this balance with greater attention to extrafamily systems.

3. *Goal conflict.* Sturkie suggests that family therapy methods can be conceptualized according to the goals of treatment (Sturkie 1986). Goals vary from seeking to enhance personal and interpersonal awareness to altering functioning through changing the family's organizational structure and sequences of interaction. Some approaches suggest that family conceptions of problems may be caught up in problem definitions that will not actually permit change. For example, they might suggest that "getting Christine out of the house" is a view of the problem that will not permit real change. Until the focus is shifted to "second-order" change directed to the way the family defines and solves problems, real change will not occur (Watzlawick, Weakland, and Fisch 1974). They suggest that practice with a restricted problem focus and explicit priorities may lead to "symptom chasing" (Sturkie 1986:620). These second-order change goals may include attempting to restructure roles in the family and adapting communication patterns, including methods of resolving conflict; assisting in the differentiation of roles; and examining patterns across generations (Laird and Allen 1983).

Working on these second-order goals does not preclude agreement with families on working to achieve some resolution of the problems that they brought to treatment. Some question whether families need to be aware of these second-order goals. According to Anderson and Stewart: "It is not necessary or desirable that family members agree with all of the therapist's goals for the family, particularly such general ones as 'less enmeshment'" (Anderson and Stewart 1985:64).

Tolson suggests, however, that if practitioners conclude that there are necessary preconditions to work on client-defined problems, then they must be careful to ensure "that the outcome goal is indeed achieved. Furthermore, they must effectively educate and persuade their clients that work toward theoretically derived goals will produce an important end point for the client" (Tolson 1981:340). Hence, she urges that the family-perceived goals not be misplaced in an attempt to address underlying issues. Work on theoretically derived goals may be an important step toward resolving family concerns. If so, that connection should be explained to them.

A further issue arises when the goals of the setting for the provision of service conflict with the goals of the families who receive the service. For example, family-based services to families is often described as having the goal of "empowering families." Yet the funding for such services is usually at the public expense and not intended for reaching family goals per se but at least in part influenced by societal goals of reducing costs of unnecessary out-of-home placement. Evaluation of the effectiveness of family-based services in the 1980s tended to focus on counts of unnecessary placements prevented more than on measures of family functioning (Frankel 1988). Hence, empowerment might occur if family goals are agreed upon that are compatible with a larger system goal of preventing unnecessary out-of-home placement. Many clients of family-based services may be readily convinced that in-home services are a means to reaching their goals and hence may not be nonvoluntary, or only temporarily so. Parents of teens, however, frequently seek out-of-home placement and may accept home-based services as a second-best alternative.

4. *The resurrection of resistance.* Conflicts between client-perceived goals and hidden second-order goals held by the practitioner can resurrect resistance. Perhaps because of the interactional nature of family work and the influences of a systems perspective, family practitioners have been more likely to consider family resistance in terms of interactional phenomena and less likely to attribute resistance to individual pathology. Consequently, use of the term *resistance* has had less negative connotations, including less blaming and more consideration of resistance as an expected phenomenon that is the practitioner's responsibility to address. For example, in the cybernetic view, the practitioner's role is both to support a need for stability and to ally with efforts to change (de Shazer 1982).

de Shazer suggests that the concept of resistance is a byproduct of a homeostatic systems view in which resistance is seen as an individual condition opposed to change rather than a product of therapist–family interaction (de Shazer 1982). de Shazer reframes resistance as the family's unique way of cooperating. In this view, the family tries to resolve problems in the best way they know how. This form of cooperation is seen as a process rather than a condition (ibid.). The resistance concept, according to de Shazer, locks practitioners into a relationship in which, like opposing tennis players, they need to win in order to control the relationships. de Shazer's reframed view positions both the practitioners and the family on the same side of the net, trying to defeat the problem (de Shazer 1984).

In contrast, Stewart and Anderson argue that the resistance concept does not imply a homeostatic system, nor is it located only in the family, as resistance can also occur to practitioners and the agency as well (Stewart and Anderson 1984). They define resistance as all those behaviors in the therapeutic system that interact to prevent the therapy system from reaching the family's goals for therapy. The authors include behaviors across the system as resistance including families missing appointments, practitioners not checking back when they miss appointments, and agencies not opening their doors after 5 P.M. or having adequate meeting space.

5. *Role conflicts.* The role of the practitioner varies with the system he or she represents. For example, the purpose for public agency contact may be different than in child guidance and hence the practitioner may be power broker or part of the system of power. Anderson and Stewart suggest that larger systems make family therapy difficult because they place therapists in the position of both therapist and policeman.

> When the practitioner is asked to do family therapy while simultaneously playing a role in which they must hold a threat over the family's head that their income may be withdrawn or one or more family members will be placed in a foster home or institution. . . . Families are understandably hesitant to admit a potentially threatening professional into their confidence. They really would have to be crazy to welcome such an intrusion into their lives . . . conducting any kind of therapy under these conditions must seem rather like trying to slay a very large dragon with a very short sword. (Anderson and Stewart 1985:223–224)

These role conflicts are further complicated when the practitioner's agenda differs from the family's. Practitioners frequently perceive dangers and feel more commitment to change them than do families (Schlosberg and Kagan 1988). When the practitioner takes on the role of the mastermind searching for leverage in changing a recalcitrant system, families may feel discounted. If the family's view is discounted, the relationship can quickly become adversarial (Wile 1981). For example, while use of deceptive means may be effective in the short run, families may eventually conclude that the therapist views them as too inept or childlike to be dealt with in a straightforward manner (Reid 1985).

Further role conflicts occur when practitioners assume multiple roles with different family members. Practitioners may be engaged in individual treatment with residents of treatment institutions at the same time as they are family therapists with other members of the family. Anderson and Stewart suggest that it may be possible to play such dual roles if the family is positively motivated for the contact, if the practitioner can mobilize adequate support systems, if caseloads are small enough to permit frequent contact, and if the practitioners can manage to demonstrate to families that they genuinely care about what happens to family members (Anderson and Stewart 1985).

6. *Ethical issues.* As suggested in the preceding text, much work with families starts with a request that the behavior of one family member be "fixed." If in fact that person's behavior is the target for work, then it is misleading to

suggest that the focus is work on a relationship (Margolin 1982). Margolin suggests that when one person such as a child is opposed to treatment, there are many advantages to including an advocate for that person and negotiating goals (ibid.).

Second, informed consent can be difficult with families in nonvoluntary situations. Pursuit of informed consent, including explanation of roles, possible discomforts, and risks, as well as benefits, may greatly assist the engagement process. However, if the practitioner is inclined to use methods that rely on secrecy for their success, failure to describe them limits true informed consent. Such secrecy may be useful with voluntary families who have agreed upon the goals for treatment since they have the option of leaving if they are opposed to the methods. Additional ethical issues are raised when families are court-ordered to receive treatment on issues that differ from those that arise through the practitioner's own assessment. Manipulation of involuntary families who pay a cost for withdrawing from treatment violates the limited provisions for paternalism described in chapter 2.

Emergence of Family-Centered Interventions for Involuntary Families

Service delivery interventions designed to address families in a broader systems perspective have emerged that address many of the concerns raised earlier about involuntary work with families. Such family-centered services have focused on work with families in which either child safety or community safety related to adolescent delinquency is one of the goals of service delivery.

Child Welfare

Child welfare services are engaged when a child's safety is endangered due to alleged child abuse or neglect (Turnell and Edwards 1999; Popple and Vecchiolla 2007). A child safety assessment is required intervention when a report suggests that a child may be at risk. While child safety is the highest priority for assessment, a prominent alternative for consideration is whether children can be safely maintained in their homes with the provision of services and supports (Pecora et al. 2000). A family preservation movement developed influenced by approaches such as the Homebuilders Model that focused on the delivery of intensive services in the home or at a place convenient to families (Kinney, Haapala, and Booth 1991). Child safety concerns are seen as existing in a larger systemic context of stresses on caregivers such that counseling services are matched with concrete or hard services. The movement gained considerable prominence with the promise that such services could successfully avoid unnecessary out-of-home placement while strengthening families. Early evaluations bore promising results but later studies reported that the provision of such services did not necessarily predict lower rates of placement than traditional investigative and case management services did (Scheurman, Rzepnicki, and Littell 1994). Reviewers have suggested that these disappointing results were in part due to low overall rates of out-of-home placement even among the traditional services and mixed results with different subpopulations such that families with some kinds of issues did better than families with other issues (Littell and Scheurman 2002). For example, families in which child abuse was a factor responded better to such services than did families in which neglect and/or substance abuse was a factor (ibid.).

Additional services that embody similar principles have followed. For example, family group conferencing draws together family members, agency officials, and support persons designated by the family to develop a plan to address family concerns (Marsh and Crow 1998; Burford and Hudson 2001). This approach has shown promise for cultural sensitivity, as it allows family members to designate the persons most significant to their problem-solving and considered resources as well as incorporating family rituals meaningful to the family (Waites et al. 2004).

Alternative or family assessment response (AR) is another service in which families with a lower priority of danger are given the option of having an AR worker assist them in identifying and addressing family needs (Alternative Response in Minnesota 2006). Similar to earlier family preservation services, AR focuses on working together with families in their own homes to reduce child safety dangers. Early results have been promising (ibid.).

Adolescent Delinquency

An intervention based on similar systemic principles has emerged to serve the families of adolescent delinquents (Henggeler et al. 2002). Based on the premises that adolescent delinquency relates significantly to interactions with four systems (intrafamily, school, peer, and community systems), multisystemic therapy (MST) provides intensive, in-home services addressed to family concerns and focused on negotiating interactions with the key systems maintaining the problem (ibid.). Research on MST has accumulated evidence that delinquency is reduced for several years after intervention (Henggeler, Melton, and Smith 1992; Henggeler et al. 1997). Critics suggest, however, that the MST intervention, however powerful with the microenvironment, still encounters families struggling to survive in hostile neighborhood and community environments (Littell 2006a, 2006b).

Common Factors in Family Systemic Interventions

The approaches described in the preceding text have implemented similar principles. They posit that adolescent behavioral problems and parenting issues are best understood in a larger systemic context. Families in these circumstances should be joined around issues of common concern, drawing on strengths and resources identified by the family. Services need to be delivered in a manner convenient to the family and include prompt access to emergency services.

Engagement

Critical to each of the preceding approaches is the manner in which they engage family members. Each attempts to join families in areas of common concern. However, some family members are unlikely to see problems in the same way that other family members do. For example, in MST adolescents often see the problem as "getting off probation" or "get Mom off my back" (Henggeler et al. 2002). Engaging adolescents around these concerns makes it more likely to that they will become at least nonvoluntary. Proponents of the approach, however, candidly note that some adolescents will find the agreement of other family members around curbing their behavior to mean, at least in the short term, losing many things they value and gaining little (ibid.). For example, there may be consensus among other family members around curbing contact with certain peers, attending school, and avoiding drug usage. Each of these goals may represent a loss of freedom for the adolescent, at least in the short term.

Overview of Adaptation for Work with Involuntary Families

Earlier practitioners who worked with involuntary families had to choose among three alternatives: approaching involuntary families within a voluntary family therapy format; rejecting family treatment perspectives in involuntary settings and roles; or blending family therapy perspectives with involuntary work on a case-by-case basis. The family-centered alternatives in child welfare and adolescent delinquency have provided a fourth alternative that includes family treatment perspectives within a larger ecosystemic perspective in which the family is one of several systems. This alternative includes work with individual family members, work on environmental problems, and includes settings and roles in which family therapy is not the service offered.

Guidance for specific steps in the engagement phase with involuntary families are presented here since many approaches suggest that negotiation should take place, yet fail to show how to negotiate or persuade family members to engage in contact. Interventions beyond the engagement process are described more briefly because it is assumed that the primary issue with involuntary families is achieving at least semivoluntary status. When semivoluntary status is achieved, a variety of voluntary approaches may be consulted for further guidelines. Primary assumptions underlying work with involuntary families include:

1. A *relevant systems perspective encompasses not only the practitioner and family but also the forces that impel the family into contact with the practitioner.* It is useful in most initial contacts between families and helping practitioners to assume that one or more family members have been impelled into contact at least in part by mandated, formal, and informal pressures. Such a perspective would include exploration of the pressures felt by Christine and Mrs. King in initiating contact.

2. *The practitioner and/or agency may become a source of formal pressure when attempts are made to redefine or reframe voluntary requests to focus on family issues.* It is useful to recognize that when the family-based service practitioner made an offer for service that differed from the request made by Mrs. King, formal nonvoluntary pressures were being exerted. Further, if the practitioner works on a hidden agenda to effect change in problems that family members have not chosen to work on, the practitioner may be creating additional pressures for families.

3. *Role conflicts can occur between family wishes and practitioner responsibilities to outside constituencies.* For example, practitioner responsibilities to make recommendations on such issues as child placement can create role conflict. In the aforementioned example, family-based services are often offered as part of an agency policy of preventing unnecessary out-of-home placement. This policy can be compatible with family wishes or contrary to them.

With these assumptions as a basis, guidelines are provided for initial work with involuntary families, including (1) initiating contact, (2) pursuit of informed consent, and (3) contracting.

1. *Initiating contact.* Guidelines for initiating contact vary according to whether the family is ostensibly self-referred or referred by others. Contact with families who are not self-referred begins with Step A while contact with self-referred families begins with Step B (figure 8.1).

> Step A. *If the family is not self-referred, family members are entitled to an account of the circumstances that have led to that contact.* For example, any requirements or information from the referral source about suggested issues should be shared. Second, client options, rights, and choices in response to this referral should be clarified. Hence, family members need to be made aware of their choices and the potential consequences of such choices. Family members should

Figure 8.1   Initiating contact in a potentially nonvoluntary situation

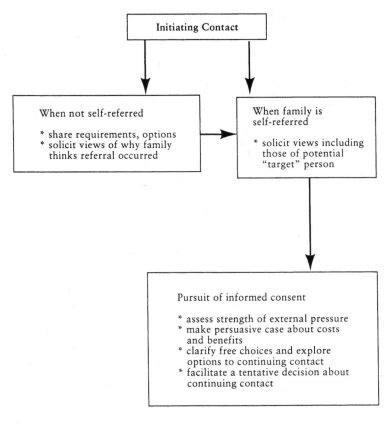

also be asked about their views of the circumstances that led to contact. When contacts occur through outreach, there is need to respect and validate the family system, identify positive aspects of behavior, recognize dilemmas faced by family members, respect cultural values, and support networks (Schlosberg and Kagan 1988). When this step is completed, the practitioner can proceed to Step B with families who are not self-referred. For example, in the following exchange, a family-centered service team follows up on the initial contact made at the beginning of the chapter.*

PRACTITIONER: I am glad that you both were willing to meet with us today. I understand that you met with Karen last week to talk about some of the concerns that you were having about how things were going here in the home. Betty and I are a home-based service team and we came here today to talk to you more about your situation and the choices that you have as you and Christine decide whether you want to continue with this. I understand that you had some reservations about whether you thought this was the best thing for you to do. You talked with Karen about having explored things on your own. You've gone to a number of other counselors, and you haven't felt as though things have lasted, so you have some reservations. I would think, Christine, you may have some reservations about how this might work for you as well.

> Step B. *If the family is self-referred, the practitioner begins by soliciting the views of family members about what they see as concerns and eliciting their views about what they would like to see accomplished.* Practitioners should be sensitive to suggestions of pressured contact in their presentation of concerns. If the request includes a desire that a family member be "fixed," this step includes asking that "target" person to state their view of concerns. This may also take the form of separate interviews with adolescents or children if they are unwilling or unable to share those concerns with the family.

2. *Pursuit of informed consent.* On hearing the circumstances that have led family members into contact, the practitioner can attempt to enhance voluntarism by pursuing informed consent. This involves several steps: (a) assessing the strength of pressures and requirements; (b) making a persuasive case about the benefits and costs of continuing with the practitioner; (c) exploring

---

*A videotape of the interview in which this dialogue takes place, entitled *Contracting for Home-Based Services,* is available from www.insight-media.com. See appendix for details.

options to continuing contact; and (d) facilitating a tentative decision about whether to continue.

a. *Assessing the strength of external pressures.* If the above steps have un-covered pressures experienced by one or more family members, then the scope of those pressures can be assessed. For example, if contact is court ordered, then the specific requirements of that order for the family and practitioner should be clarified. The consequences of noncompliance with court orders should also be reviewed (Gourse and Chescheir 1981). Similarly, any non-negotiable agency policies should be shared. For example, in the case of family-based service, the ground rules of working within a frame-work of time-limited contact toward the goal of preserving the family sys-tem would be described. In the case of a family treatment program for spousal abuse, the preconditions and beliefs of that program are shared. As the family is considered to be living in a currently or potentially dangerous situation, concurrent or completed individual or group treatment for the abusive person may be required. Similarly, the belief of the program that family violence is never justified is shared here as an agency belief (Weidman 1986).

When there is informal family pressure on a reluctant individual, coerced participation by the practitioner is unethical. The practitioner can, however, strongly encourage a family member to attend at least one session to discover what contact may offer. The practitioner can also explore the reasons contrib-uting to that person's reluctance. Finally, the practitioner should clarify the extent of involvement expected. In some cases, this may require only partici-pation as an observer so as not to impede progress (Margolin 1982).

b. *Making a persuasive case about the benefits and costs of continuing with the practitioner.* Families often feel ambivalent about service. Families seek-ing residential placement for their troubled adolescents want problem relief and often see placement as the only alternative. Yet they often feel pain, guilt, and a sense of failure in pursuing this alternative. Family-based services can be presented as another option (Henggeler et al. 2002).

Family members can be assisted in making an informed decision by knowing about the costs and benefits of the service that the practitioner can offer. For example, Weidman suggests that abusive partners be told that on the one hand, the abusive partner may not always get what he or she wants by participating in the program. On the other hand, if the violence continues, the relationship is likely to be lost (Weidman 1986).

Arguments are more likely to be persuasive when they relate to values, at-titudes, or goals that family members already hold. For example, in the case of family-based services, connection of the service offer to the problem expressed by the family should enhance its acceptance. Since out-of-home placement was a solution to a problem seen by Mrs. King, the practitioners can share Mrs. King's concern with the problem without agreeing with her solution. They can empathize with the family duress that led to the request for help and offer to provide help with those problems.

Other potential benefits of the service can also be explained. For example, in the case of family-based services, it can be explained that such services are provided in the home at times agreeable to the families, without financial cost, that practitioners are available on a twenty-four-hour emergency basis, and that relief is often provided in a relatively brief time period.

Potential costs and drawbacks of work with the family option should also be explored. For example, non-negotiable policies of the agency or service would be reviewed here. Circumstances in which confidentiality would be violated, such as in mandated reporting of suspected abuse or neglect, should be shared. Similarly, policies in some settings that require work with all members of a family should be explained and possible referral to settings with less restrictive policies considered.

Practitioners are advised not to oversell the family option that they represent. For example, family suspicions of the effectiveness of family-based services in resolving *all* their problems are well founded and their disappointment at not receiving immediate relief from all concerns they raise should be acknowledged. The time-limited nature of that work should also be explained. Later in the session with Mrs. King and Christine, the practitioner comments in support of realistic expectations:

PRACTITIONER: There wouldn't be tremendous changes overnight. We would be working on making some changes, such that Christine might do some things differently, and you would also do some things differently. You would notice some little changes, at first. Our experience is that over time those changes can build up, so that the situation that brought you to the point a week ago where you thought you really couldn't stay together with Christine wouldn't be there anymore. On the other hand, I don't think it's realistic to expect that all of the concerns that you and Christine have about each other are going to be cleaned up if we were going to work together ten weeks.

c. *Exploring options to continuing contact.* Alternatives to family contact should be explored. In the case of legally mandated contact, families can be advised that they may return to court to attempt a change in the order. In nonvoluntary cases, other options, including *not* working with the practitioner, should be explored. Such options might include dealing with the problems on their own and exploring other forms of help. In the initial session between Karen and Mrs. King, alternatives to home-based services were explored.

KAREN: I want to make sure that you are clear that you do *not* have to accept our service. You can look at other possibilities. While foster placement by the county is not now an option, you could choose to explore private placement. If you feel as if you might do a better job working on these issues on your own, you would also be free to choose to do that. You could call parental stress lines for assistance. You might also get some respite help from a friend or relative.

   d. *Facilitating a tentative decision about whether or not to continue family contact.* A power struggle and adversary relationship often occurs at this point, as the practitioner increases pressure in response to family opposition (Schlosberg and Kagan 1988). Reviewing options as above and facilitating a decision about whether to continue with contact demonstrates respect for the family process and does not proceed without their approval. Sometimes family members need time to make this decision. Family commitment to explore continuation even on a trial basis should be respected and seen as at least slightly increasing voluntarism. The option to pursue other directions should also be respected, however. For example, later in the follow-up session with Mrs. King and Christine, the practitioner asks the family for direction in considering their decision.

PRACTITIONER: We are at a point now where you need to consider whether you want to continue working with us or go in another direction. We've identified some issues each of you have individually and then together. If we agreed to go ahead, then we would probably pick a specific issue to start with and see if we can get something going on that right away. I don't know if it would be worthwhile for either of us to go much further in discussing home-based services until you decide whether you want to give this a try or you want to go another direction.

   3. *Contracting.* Should the family be willing to pursue further contact at this time, the development of a contract can be explored. In the case of emergencies, such as a lack of basic necessities for food, shelter, or safety, the practitioner would proceed to help the family acquire needed resources before pursuing more formal contracting. The contract should include any nonnegotiable requirements such as provisions about confidentiality and sharing information, problems to be worked on, goals set, time limit, and methods to

be used. Such contracting should enhance voluntarism and prevent focus on hidden agendas.

a. *Non-negotiable requirements.* Provisions for confidentiality and sharing of information should be included with all families. More specific requirements related to legal issues and requirements of the service provision should also be clarified. For example, in the case of marital work in spouse abuse, the agency goal of maintaining the family when this can be done without further risk of abuse or danger would be shared (Weidman 1986). Specific methods such as the development of a violence avoidance plan and anger diary required for work toward this goal would also be shared. Also, in family-based service, if service is delivered under the overall premise of avoiding unnecessary out-of-home placement, that condition is shared in contracting, as well as any other legal requirements. For example:

PRACTITIONER: We need to be clear that the service together needs to take place within a goal of keeping Christine from having an unnecessary out-of-home placement. In addition, there are laws about attending school and truancy that will influence what we do.

b. *Explore agreed-upon problems.* Having set parameters of requirements and non-negotiable conditions, the practitioner can proceed to pursue semi-voluntary or voluntary status by assisting family members in identifying problems that family members now agree exist. This method is advised even in instances in which practitioners feel that *reframing*, or movement to another problem that the family has not expressed, will be useful. The process should first follow original family conceptions of the problem in pursuit of problems that all family members now agree exist. Such original conceptions often locate the source and solution of the problem in the behavior of one person or a system outside the family. For example, parents tend to see the child as at blame and feel blamed by other counselors, court, or probation officers. On one level it is possible to join families on some concerns similar to the "get rid of the pressure" contracting strategy presented in chapter 6. Similarly, families who had expressed no other goals often agree to the goal of getting the court out of their lives (Schlosberg and Kagan 1988).

However, when family members locate the blame in the behavior of one person, the practitioner may accept that this is their view while ensuring that all family members can state their views. For example, when Mrs. King and Christine were asked for their views of problems, Mrs. King included that Christine was truant and did not obey curfew; she had a "nasty attitude;" she had "bad friends"; and she did not take care of her younger brother or do other chores. Christine responded that her mother yelled and tried to control her too much, did not respect her friends, and did not pay her for taking care of her younger brother. Mrs. King and Christine did not readily frame issues as family problems and blamed one another for problems that existed. The practitioners might look here for problems that both Mrs. King and Christine agree now exist. For example, both mention problems with her friends and with taking care of her brother. Hence, a first attempt at stating these problems in a more useful, nonblaming way would be to ask whether they would agree that "disagreement on Christine's friends and her responsibilities in taking care of her younger brother" were concerns both shared.

Reframing is used to recast problems in an interactional form or to define the problem in a slightly different way (Reid 1985:36). Reframing is useful in constructing workable realities that make change possible (Watzlawick, Weakland, and Fisch 1974). Practitioners sometimes reframe by identifying patterns of interaction or other problems that the family has not considered. They may also attempt to cast problems in a more favorable light. For example, Schlossberg and Kagan describe a case example in which parents describe their child as "horrible, terrible." The practitioner recognizes the family's efforts and suggests that they have become exhausted by working so hard (Schlosberg and Kagan 1988). On the other hand, when parents feel as if they have been inadequate because they should know how to deal with their child, Tavantsiz suggests reframing their view to suggest that they are "good parents who need all the help they can get" (Tavantzis et al. 1985). In the following exchange, the practitioner working with Mrs. King and Christine attempts to reframe issues expressed by them as a lack of trust.

PRACTITIONER: I'm wondering if trust and not knowing what to believe is an issue with both of you. You don't know when you can trust Christine, and you're feeling that your mother doesn't trust you about your friends. Is the lack of trust between you something you are concerned about?

One danger that practitioners need to be aware of in reframing by casting difficulties at a higher level of abstraction is that it may not capture what the family sees. They may reject the reframing or agree only superficially. Consequently, the practitioner should phrase the reframe tentatively to determine whether it is relevant to family members.

b. *Explore reciprocal or individual problems.* Some families do not accept such reframing and persist with noninteractional views. This is particularly frequent in instances in which adolescents have a history of law violations, and blaming of the adolescent may have been reinforced by corrections systems. It is sometimes possible in such instances to pursue reciprocal or quid-pro-quo exchanges. In the above instance, Mrs. King considered trust to be a lesser issue than obedience to house rules and school attendance. Meanwhile, Christine continued to be concerned about freedom to see her friends and respect for them. An exchange was established in which Christine could earn time with her friends in the home and noninterference with them if she would increase her school attendance to three times in the next week.

Some problems relate primarily to one individual. However, these individual concerns may have a major impact on the concerns of the family and the system as a whole. For example, Bob, a stepparent, did not feel respected by his stepson who had returned home recently from foster care. Aggravating the problem was the fact that Bob had lost his job and hence was around the house more. Bob now felt more called upon to take a disciplinary role that had previously been played by the mother. Instead of dismissing the problem of employment, session time could be taken to assist Bob in making plans to seek employment and supporting his efforts.

This chapter has suggested that nonvoluntary work with families occurs more frequently than is usually thought to be the case. While family therapy perspectives and treatment methods can be useful in work with involuntary clients, we have suggested that greater attention to the role of pressures impelling family members into contact is needed to enhance effectiveness and ethical contact. Many families are approached with family therapy concerns that do not fit their request and they are not persuaded that their concerns will be met through reframing. Problems can occur if alternative choices are not emphasized at the beginning of contact and when theories of underlying family dynamics lead the practitioner to focus on issues that have not been agreed upon with family members.

Evaluation of family outcomes becomes a critical issue when the practitioner is attempting to achieve goals other than those agreed upon. Some suggest that the practitioner has an ethical responsibility to place high priority on the assessment of desired change as seen by family members. There is a range of opinion about the importance of such change. Some see resolution of the family-defined problem as the sole criterion for assessing outcome; others see it as the most important, while others consider such resolution as one criterion among many (Gurman, Kniskern, and Pinsof 1986:609). Work on hidden agendas may lead to confusion in outcome should the family receive a negative evaluation if they did not stay on the boat when the practitioner changed course. While practitioners and families engaged in voluntary family treatment can perhaps afford less specificity in goals, vague goals in involuntary contact are likely to be costly to the families.

This chapter has made beginning steps in constructing an involuntary perspective for work with families by expanding the systems perspective to include the pressures that impel family members into contact and the practitioner or setting pressures that occur after contact is initiated. Practice guidelines have been suggested that are designed to assist in more informed choices in continuing family contact and enhancing voluntarism. Guidelines have not been provided for contact after the engagement phase, since many voluntary approaches can be useful at this point with originally nonvoluntary families. The guidelines do not resolve continuing issues in the potential conflict between attention to second-order change goals such as assisting a family in becoming less enmeshed or more individualized and commitment to the goals that the family explicitly agrees to. Should such commitment to second-order goals conflict with agreed-upon goals, family opposition may be an expected byproduct. At worst, families may be illegally and unethically forced to work on problems that are neither their concern nor legally mandated. Practitioner insistence on goals that are not legally required, setting requirements, or family concerns is unethical and likely to be ineffective. There is unlikely to be motivational congruence in such situations and insistence on practitioner-defined goals that exceed appropriate limits to self-determination and restricted use of paternalism is unethical (see chapters 2 and 3). While practitioners working with voluntary families can be somewhat sure that those families will raise objections or withdraw from contact if their own identified goals are not addressed, practitioners working with nonvoluntary and mandated families have no such assurance.

While specific examples have been provided for settings such as family-based service, more specific adaptations are needed for other potentially nonvoluntary settings such as discharge planning. Chapter 9 will continue adaptations of the involuntary perspective for work with groups.

Discussion Questions

1. How often do you find that meeting with families entails negotiating different viewpoints? Are identified clients entitled to their viewpoint?
2. Family services frequently entail a parent bringing in a child or adolescent to be "fixed." That child or adolescent may be treated as an

involuntary target of change unless there are systematic, open efforts to include their viewpoint. What practices have you seen to acknowledge and integrate work from the viewpoint of the persons brought by others to be "fixed"?

3. How extensively do you consider alternatives with individuals and families including rejecting services?

4. Common factors in family approaches to work with families in nonvoluntary situations have included increasing accessibility of services and coordinating with hard or concrete services. Are these part of your service delivery plan?

Chapter 9

Work with Involuntary Groups

A dozen women offenders file into the meeting room of the halfway house where they live. The program director has contracted with group leaders from an outside agency to lead a group. They describe the purpose of the group as helping the women deal with issues of abuse and violence in their lives and emphasize that this is to be *their* group.

As the leaders have led many such groups with women who were eager to attend, they are dismayed to discover the women sitting in baleful silence. After awhile, the women interrupt the presentation to say, "This is a bunch of bull. Why do we have to be here? Can we smoke? What I care about is getting a job, going back to school, not talking about this violence bull."

Finally, after several attempts to get the group away from these "distractions" and back to its purpose, the women sink back into a bored, detached silence, gazing out the window, checking their cell phones, sending text messages, and commenting that this had better be over soon because they have places to go.

These women are participating in an *involuntary group* in which members feel external pressure to participate. Involuntary groups are often led with persons with problems such as abuse and neglect, domestic violence, chemical dependency, sexual offenses, delinquency, and youth gangs (Tuszynski 1985; Milgram and Rubin 1992; Yu and Watkins 1996; Buttell and Pike 2003; Cameron and Telfer 2004; Levinson and Macgowan 2004). It is often assumed that grouping clients with the same situations and problems will provide a ripe arena for modifying behaviors and attitudes. And yet such groups are often equally ripe for learning antisocial behaviors, include high dropout rates, and persist with seemingly endless conflict or sullen, passive aggressive behaviors.

There are two kinds of involuntary groups. *Mandated groups* include legal external pressure, such as occurs with imprisoned sex offenders. *Nonvoluntary groups* are distinguished by nonlegal external pressure from family, friends, agencies, and referral sources. These pressures often create a feeling of coerced or constrained choice such that many choose attendance as a lesser evil. For example, Berliner notes when introducing groups for drivers convicted of driving while intoxicated (DWI), "You are here because you would rather try this than go to jail" (Berliner 1987). Similar nonvoluntary group transactions can occur between students and instructors in required courses and between agency staff and trainers brought in as "hired guns" to modify practitioner attitudes, beliefs, and behaviors.

Degree of voluntarism also varies *within* groups. For example, the women offenders group described earlier may include some women who consider talking about abuse to be beneficial while others react to the group discussion as an unnecessary imposition. On the other hand, some ostensibly voluntary groups for teaching parenting skills often include both highly voluntary clients and others who attend "because my child welfare worker said it would be a good idea." Such groups often include so-called hard-to-reach members who attend irregularly or participate minimally. Such "hard-to-reach" members may not agree with the purpose of the group, doubt its effectiveness, and attend as lesser of evil (Breton 1985).

This chapter presents guidelines for legal, ethical, and effective practice with involuntary groups. We begin by considering the decision to form an involuntary group in light of the formidable challenges expected in such groups. Application of these guidelines is designed to enhance commitment to both non-negotiable goals and voluntary group concerns. Guidelines are provided for *pregroup planning* and *beginning involuntary groups*. While specific guidelines are not provided for postcontracting intervention with involuntary groups, four frequent phases of such work are identified. This guidance is designed to facilitate movement through stages of group development and fostering individual growth and change.[1]

Introduction to Involuntary Groups

Clients labeled hard-to-reach, resistant, and unmotivated are often referred "for their own good" to groups with the notion that they can learn new behaviors with and from one another. At the beginning of such groups, such potential members often share a reluctance or ambivalence about receiving help (Behroozi 1992). Men in particular, who are socialized to be stoic and express few emotions, often find themselves pressed to share embarrassing aspects of their private lives in a public arena with strangers (Whatules 2000). The ideal client in an involuntary group enters the group acknowledging responsibility for problems and ready to pursue change. More frequently, prospective group members are pessimistic about the possibility of change or deny a need for it (Behroozi 1992).

Garvin defines *social control groups* as characterized by a lack of consensus on goals between members and the agency such that participation is often resisted for a long time or a common purpose is never reached (Garvin 1981). Mandated groups, as defined above, are social control groups. Despite the lack of legal mandates, nonvoluntary groups too often begin and end as social control groups. Participants often react to the purpose of involuntary groups as *mala prohibita* or wrongs due to law or statute rather than wrongs in themselves (Smith 1985). For example, men with domestic violence problems rarely enter groups thinking that violence is unjustified but rather acknowledging that it is illegal. They are rarely motivated to stop the abuse itself but rather to placate the court or their partners. These men are characterized as tending to externalize and blame others, to believe little can be done to change them, to doubt the severity of the problem, and to doubt the efficacy of services (Brekke 1989). Similarly, members of substance abuse treatment groups often begin by expressing open or passive hostility, by externalizing their alcohol and drug use, and by feeling that they can handle problems on their own (Milgram and Rubin 1992).

Hence, a challenge of involuntary groups is to assist members in coming to recognize problems such as violent behavior or alcohol and drug abuse as *mala in se* or bad in itself (Smith 1985). Many involuntary groups never advance beyond a *mala prohibita* motivation and persist in a power and control phase marked by continual vying for control. A coercive symmetry sometimes referred to as the "confrontation–denial cycle" occurs with members whose behavior is described as resistant, denying the need to change while irritated leaders alternately resort to threats, cajoling, shaming, confrontation, and preaching in efforts to encourage participation (Murphy and Baxter 1997). The challenge for involuntary group leaders is to both meet the societal and institutional purpose of the group and also assist participants in addressing their own concerns in socially acceptable ways (Behroozi 1992).

Involuntary groups have both advantages for work with involuntary clients and also potential disadvantages and dangers.

Potential Advantages of Involuntary Groups

The following are seven potential advantages of the group modality for ethical and effective work with involuntary clients (figure 9.1):

1. *The group can be a source of support.* Involuntary clients pressured to join involuntary groups frequently feel isolated, ashamed, and embarrassed by that pressure. The group setting can be less threatening than individual contact for many and support can be experienced by meeting others who share a similar situation. For example, many DWI clients share multiple crises such as loss of a driver's license, pressures to enter alcoholism treatment, legal involvement, attorney and treatment fees, increased insurance premiums, as well as family and social problems. The common mandated condition can create a useful crisis that can be reframed as a challenge in place of the original perception that it is a threat or loss (Panepinto et al. 1982).

2. *The group can provide an opportunity for "in vivo" learning.* New skills, knowledge, and attitudes can be learned through instruction and practice

Figure 9.1   Advantages of groups for work with involuntary clients

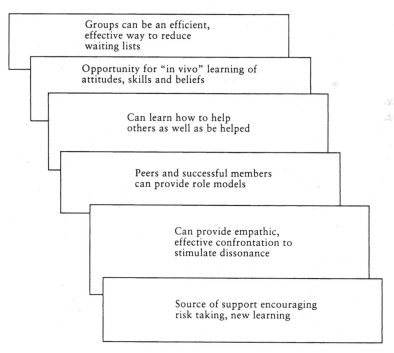

Groups can be an efficient, effective way to reduce waiting lists

Opportunity for "in vivo" learning of attitudes, skills and beliefs

Can learn how to help others as well as be helped

Peers and successful members can provide role models

Can provide empathic, effective confrontation to stimulate dissonance

Source of support encouraging risk taking, new learning

and vicariously through observing the problem solving of others. A learning atmosphere can be stimulated that promotes both acceptance and risk taking. As members consider plans for change, they can be helped to reality test those plans in the group before trying them outside.

3. *In addition to being helped, members can learn to be helpers.* Involuntary group members can move into a helping role in which they provide support, challenge, and modeling for other members. They can become more aware of their strengths and growth as well as pursue improvement in their individual problems.

4. *Peers and successful former members can provide role models.* Since attitudes and beliefs are more likely to be changed when the person attempting influence is considered likable, trustworthy, and expert, peers can often exert a more powerful influence than professional leaders. For this reason, many involuntary groups are "seeded" with successful former members or others further along in the change process (Garvin 1981).

5. *Involuntary group members who have harmed others can meet with victims.* Since involuntary group members who have acted to harm others are often unable to relate to harm caused, live presentations by victims can create empathy and acceptance of responsibility for harm. For example, presentations by victims of domestic violence can make denial of harm more difficult (van Wormer and Bednar 2002).

6. *Group members can provide empathic, effective confrontation to stimulate dissonance.* Groups can provide empathic confrontation when behaviors and attitudes persist that conflict with laws, policies, or client goals (Reid 1986). For example, when men with domestic violence problems continue to encounter circumstances in which they are tempted to use violence, peers can help them explore alternative ways for dealing with such situations (see chapter 12 by Chovanec in this volume).

7. *Groups can be an efficient, cost-effective way to reduce waiting lists.* The larger staff/participant ratio in groups allows settings to serve a larger population and hence reduce waiting lists. Indeed, orientation groups are sometimes helpful for those involuntary clients with domestic violence problems who are waiting to be served (Brekke 1989).

Many involuntary groups never reach the goal of providing ethical, effective help that meets both societal and individual needs. In fact, groups can be noxious as well as beneficial (Schopler and Galinsky 1981). Most of the aforementioned advantages can be reversed to describe six dangers of involuntary groups (figure 9.2).

1. *Involuntary groups often proceed with a completely imposed, unshared agenda.* Too often, involuntary groups proceed with an externally imposed

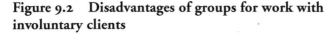

Figure 9.2   Disadvantages of groups for work with involuntary clients

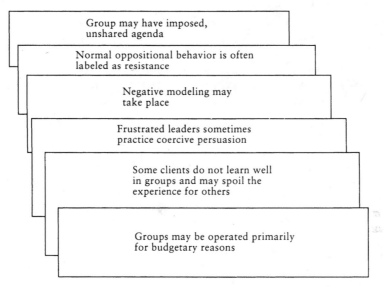

Group may have imposed, unshared agenda

Normal oppositional behavior is often labeled as resistance

Negative modeling may take place

Frustrated leaders sometimes practice coercive persuasion

Some clients do not learn well in groups and may spoil the experience for others

Groups may be operated primarily for budgetary reasons

agenda in which compliance is maintained by fear of punishment rather than by positive attraction to benefits of the group. Common goals and group process are often ignored in pursuit of individual change. Mixed messages are communicated through suggestions that "this is *your group*," as in the women offenders group at the beginning of the chapter, while in fact the agenda is not open for negotiation. When group purpose, methods, and rules are entirely predetermined by the agency and the leaders, many varieties of overt and covert oppositional behavior are a predictable result.

2. *Oppositional behavior is often labeled resistance.* Evasive behaviors and challenging leaders' direction often occur in involuntary groups. Oppositional behavior is often interpreted as pathological resistance without examining such behavior in the context of group interaction (Hurley 1984). For example, vocal opponents of the group's direction may in fact be potential group leaders who are attempting to help make the group worthwhile by focusing it on personally meaningful goals. In this way, their oppositional behavior may be more useful to the group than passive, compliant behavior that may not reflect a commitment to change in the group.

3. *Peer modeling is often negative.* While group members often learn from peers, such learning may be contrary to the goals of the group leaders. Group cohesiveness may develop the form "us against the leaders" in which the very

kinds of antisocial behavior that the group is designed to reduce may be reinforced. Members may *learn* from peers how to cope with involuntary groups in manipulative, deceptive ways.

4. *Frustrated group leaders sometimes practice coercive persuasion.* Faced with so-called resistive behavior, preaching and shaming may be used more frequently than focusing on positive attractions of the group. In their eagerness to help, group leaders can violate the dignity of individual members, demand participation, and resort to a form of coercive persuasion or brainwashing (Cushman 1986). Involuntary group methods that assault individual identity, provoke shame, demand pure and rigid adherence to an absolute standard, and include endless public confessions are comparable to brainwashing.

Lifton uses the term thought reform for coercive persuasion and identifies eight characteristics: (a) the person is placed in a disorienting situation; (b) a clear simple answer or goal is provided; (c) guilt about past transgressions is induced; (d) new beliefs and behaviors are modeled and rewarded; (e) the individual is exposed to others who have accepted new beliefs; (f) the individual has little opportunity for private thoughts and sharing of doubts with other group members at the same point; (g) the individual learns first to behave in an approved way (when he or she is rewarded for this, then the behaviors become ritualized); and (h) it is believed that the separation between private beliefs and public beliefs breaks down through repeated confessions (Lifton 1961). The conditions that best prepare one for thought reform have been called dependency, debilitation, and dread (Schein, Schneier, and Barker 1961). Hence, if involuntary group members are highly dependent on the leaders and institution, deprived of adequate exercise and food, and maintained in a highly punitive environment, the conditions for thought control exist. With perhaps exceptions for access to exercise and food, similarity between the characteristics of thought reform and the characteristics of treatment groups designed to influence behaviors labeled as deviant are striking.

Thoughts, attitudes, and beliefs that are neither illegal nor related to a client-defined goal are sometimes assaulted by group members or leaders. For example, an overweight member of an incarcerated sexual abusers group was verbally assaulted for not caring enough about himself to reduce his weight. While behaviors and attitudes related to sexual abuse are appropriate for such groups, weight problems are not an appropriate subject for coercive intervention if they do not endanger self or others, or are not a voluntary concern of the individual. Attack on attitudes, beliefs, and thoughts may be illegal under laws to protect mentation, or the right to one's own thoughts (Alexander 1989). Hence, a major legal and ethical issue in involuntary groups is determining the boundary between what is "fair game" for the group and what issues are matters of privacy and personal choice.

5. *Some clients do not learn well in groups and may spoil it for others.* Group composition is often a key variable in the success of groups. Yet many clients are sent to groups "for their own good," whether they learn well in groups or not. As a result, those persons may not learn and also make the experience more difficult for others.

6. *Groups may be operated primarily for budgetary reasons.* Staff in institutions may be unable to consider appropriate group composition because staffing limitations require that residents be in groups for most of their time. Hence, while groups can be an efficient, effective means for service delivery, they are often required even when not effective because they keep staffing costs down. At worst, group methods become used as a form of "cheap warehousing."

Pregroup Planning

Given the preceding discussion of the benefits and potential drawbacks of involuntary client, the following discussion considers first the decision of whether or not to form an involuntary group. Second, we consider how to prepare individuals for membership in such a group. Next, the concepts of stages of group development as applied to involuntary groups are presented. Finally, we follow with an integration of the earlier presented material on the stages of individual change to stages of group development.

Should an Involuntary Group Be Formed?

Following the advantages and disadvantages described in the preceding text, an agency and practitioner considering such a group should ask first whether such a group should be formed. A group that is unlikely to progress toward treatment goals but rather become a hotbed for learning and practicing antisocial behavior should not be formed. Hence, there should be genuine, tangible benefits available to members from participation. Second, leaders are needed who can model a supportive, empathic, respectful attitude at the same time as they can reinforce pro-social modeling through empathic, respectful confrontation (Trotter 2006). Seeding the group with successful graduates can increase this possibility.

It is recommended that the group have a clear, predictable structure that can be explained to prospective members. Some have suggested that lack of structure in a group generates tension that causes members to express or expose defenses that can be useful to treatment (Empey and Ericson 1972). Others note that members of unstructured groups are often blamed for this tension and, if chemicals or violence have been used in the past to cope with anxiety, such tension can inadvertently reinforce inappropriate behavior (van Wormer 1987). Prospective members want to know: "Why am I here? Are others here for the same purpose? What can I expect of the leaders and the group? What is expected of me?" (Shields 1986). The more specific the offer of service, the more the group members have to hold onto and the clearer the boundaries, the less the energy has to go into figuring out the worker, testing the boundaries, and searching out hidden agendas. Ambiguity creates anxiety that in turn intensifies defensive behavior.

Similarly, so-called hard-to-reach clients are motivated to maintain control, minimize risk, and avoid failing (Breton 1985). The rule of least contest can be used to address these motivations. Specifically, the practitioner can permit groups to start on their own turf, work with an intermediary person already trusted by group members, respect the values of the group, and give members an opportunity to state their own goals (ibid.).

Pregroup planning of involuntary groups raises special ethical issues and responsibilities for practitioners. Compulsory attendance in a group is like compulsory education: students can be compelled to attend but not to learn (Corey et al. 2004). If there are special limitations on informed consent and confidentiality for members of involuntary groups, then group leaders are responsible to fully inform potential members about requirements and rights. They are entitled to know about the nature and goals of the group, required procedures, as well as their rights and responsibilities (ibid.). Potential members need to know about the potential impact of behavior in the group on decisions that occur outside the group such as judicial recommendations or recommendations about program termination. Hence, ways their behavior in the group can affect their own goals should be emphasized.

Consequently, a challenge with involuntary groups is to provide both clear structure about non-negotiable conditions of service *and* clear opportunities for sharing in developing the processes of the group in negotiable areas. Opposition to threats to valued freedoms can be usefully reframed as expected reactance. Providing structure can reduce reactance by (1) clarifying boundaries by describing specific non-negotiable requirements; (2) clarifying available freedoms and choices, even though constrained; and (3) clarifying areas open for negotiation. Prospective group members are entitled to information about the goals of the group, basic rules, qualifications of the leaders, techniques to be employed, and their rights. Such information can be disseminated through preparation of written descriptions of the group, meeting with prospective members individually, or through informational group sessions.

For example, if the women offenders described at the beginning of the chapter could have received a flyer describing the group and had been invited to an informational session in which required purposes and negotiable possibilities for the group would be discussed, the initial level of opposition expressed might have been reduced (figure 9.3).

Meeting with Individual Prospective Members in Pregroup Orientation

1. *Clarify non-negotiables, focusing on specific requirements.* Reactance is likely to be high if members perceive that they will be powerless in the group.

Figure 9.3   Pregroup preparation

1) Clarify non-negotiables focusing on specific
   requirements
   * is there a choice to participate?
   * rules about attendance, participation

2) Be clear about rights and choices, including
   constrained choices

3) Expect oppositional behavior
   * clients frequently motivated to avoid stigma,
     taking risks, or failing
   * reframe oppositional behavior as expectable

4) Identify current motivations and attempt to link
   to them
   * members want to know: why am I in this group?
     are others here for same purpose?
     what can I expect of leaders?
     what is expected of me?
   * identify current values, wishes and goals

5) Identify positive skills and knowledge to be
   gained in group

6) Identify and seed with positive role models

Unnecessary reactance can be reduced by specifying basic ground rules of group participation and consequences for failure to follow those rules. When clients may be in a mandated status, their requirements, choices, and alternatives regarding participation in this group need to be clarified. If membership is required, basic member expectations regarding attendance and participation need to be clear. In addition, requirements of leaders that they report attendance and assess participation should also be clear.

Prospective members of nonvoluntary groups always have the right to choose *not* to participate in the group. If they choose to participate, they will need to be aware of the ground rules for group membership. For example, prospective members of a parenting group may need to agree to discuss at least one problem in parenting with which they are concerned.

2. *Clarify rights and choices.* Reactance is likely to be reduced if members are clear about their rights and can make at least constrained choices. The most basic right or choice is whether the prospective member can choose to be in this group or not. For example, unnecessary reactance among many of the woman offenders might have been reduced if they could have *chosen* to participate in the abuse group or a group devoted to another issue. If membership in the group is not a choice, then members need to know their rights and choices within the group. For example, in some mandated groups, members are permitted a limited number of excused absences. They can make a constrained choice for how and when they take those absences. Members also need to know their rights and choices about participation in group activities. Can group members participate in the selection of agenda items? Can they participate in the selection of the order for presentation of any required items? Can they pick a problem or goal they want to work on? In some cases, members can choose whether or not to participate in particular group activities or can choose the time for such participation (Corey et al. 2004).

3. *Expect oppositional behavior.* Membership in an involuntary group often represents a stigmatized status that members respond to with denial, shame, guilt, anger, and embarrassment. If motivations to avoid stigma and risks of failing in order to maintain a sense of personal control are to be expected, then opposition to external direction can be reframed as reactance to threatened freedoms. Group leaders can empathize with this feeling of pressure and reinforce available choices, opportunities for learning skills, and knowledge consistent with at least some of the group members' current motivations.

4. *Identify current motivations and attempt to link to them.* For involuntary group members to move from a *mala prohibita* (bad because illegal) to a *mala in se* (bad in itself) motivation, they will need opportunities to identify their own goals. Too often, those individually expressed goals are rejected by group leaders as inappropriate. For example, when clients in residential settings say that they want to "get out of here," this motivation is often rejected

as inadequate. While group leaders might wish that members begin with *mala in se* motivations, beginning with current *mala prohibita* motivation is better than with none. Linkage with current values and goals can enhance the possibility of at least semivoluntary motivation. For example, recognizing that men about to enter domestic violence groups are unlikely to want to be there and wish to get out of the court system is one way of acknowledging *mala prohibita* motivation.

5. *Identify positive skills and knowledge that can be learned as an alternative to illegal or disapproved behavior.* The involuntary group is likely to be more successful if members can expect to have some of their own concerns met. Such skills and knowledge are more likely to be accepted if they will probably be rewarded such that members can see progress in a time-limited period. Leaders can prepare by "tuning in" to the concerns of the population. For example, awareness of adolescent desires to be autonomous and avoid stigma can assist in linking with expectable motivations (Shields 1986). Similarly, leaders of domestic violence groups can be aware of motivations to avoid loss of control (Milgram and Rubin 1992). The group can be described as a place where men can choose to learn manly ways to deal with disputes without resorting to violence. In fact, the positive focus for the group can be reinforced with a name such as "alternatives to aggression."

6. *Identify possible role models to "seed" in the group.* As involuntary group members are more likely to be influenced by peers than by group leaders, finding role models is recommended. Former members who have completed the group successfully or are further along in the intervention process might assist in recruitment for and operation of the group. For example, the senior author found that group enrollment and attendance for groups of potential high school dropouts increased when "junior leaders" were recruited to assist in running groups (Rooney 1977).

Stages of Group Change for Involuntary Groups[2]

Stages of change were originally posed as applying to most kinds of groups (Bennis and Shepard 1956; Garland, Jones, and Kolodny 1965). These applications have tended to assume that clients are voluntary. The pregroup orientation is not included in those voluntary models. Potential members of involuntary groups make critical decisions about whether to join the group and how to engage in the group process prior to the first session.

Involuntary groups include a *pregroup planning phase,* in which potential leaders and organizations decide whether and how to form groups. The leaders try to enhance choices, however constrained, and to stimulate self-motivation for participation rather than relying exclusively on threats of punishment or promises of reward. Potential members are familiarized with rules, non-negotiable policies, and choices available in the group.

Most stage models assume that in the *beginning stage* of group development, new members are anxious about what they do not know and issues of trust and distrust are prominent (Kurland and Salmon 1998). Thus major tasks in the beginning stage include orientation to the group, clarification of group purpose and norms, and linking commonalities between group members to build cohesion. Trust is even more of an issue in the beginning stage of involuntary groups, since potential members often do not see themselves as like others nor that their difficulties are like those of others in the group (Berman-Rossi and Kelly 1998). Thus avoidance behaviors are more likely to be emphasized by group members. For example, in domestic abuse groups, men often present themselves in a wary, noncommittal fashion. Providing an opening statement that anticipates and addresses some of the initial concerns that potential members typically present is useful in reducing these avoidant behaviors and engaging participants in the group process. It is also important when clarifying norms that group leaders make explicit which norms are negotiable and which are not as a way of reducing reactance.

In addition, group members often express anger and frustration early on in the development of involuntary groups. Reactance theory suggests that those who feel coerced into joining the group are more likely to express their frustration and anger toward the group leader. Group leaders are tested early and need to respond to the men's complaints in an empathic and respectful way without condoning their problem behaviors. By articulating group members' anger and frustration early on, it avoids opposition from continuing or being driven underground by threats of retribution and members become engaged in the group process. When the group leader can respond to anger respectfully rather than cutting off or avoiding the issue, he or she can model a way of dealing with anger without putting others down. Many involuntary (and voluntary as well) groups never seem to progress beyond this beginning stage. Consequently, many techniques focus on ways to enhance cohesion and identification with the group. There is some empirical support for the notion that individual growth is enhanced through participation in a cohesive group (Levinson and Macgowan 2004).

As noted in the preceding text, many involuntary groups never appear to reach the *middle stage* of group development (Kurland and Salmon 1998). Characteristics of this stage are that the group leader's role is less central with more appearance of leadership and support between group members. Group members should be familiar with the group process by this point and well able to assess how they are similar and different from other members. The power of the group leader in an involuntary group may diminish in this stage as it is shared, but it does not disappear.

In the *ending* stage, group leaders help members to describe changes made and connect with supports outside the group (Kurland and Salmon 1998). How ending is experienced depends on whether the group is closed or open ended. In open-ended groups, the ending process is less intense since members are leaving at different times. There are typically completion requirements that determine when a group member ends participation, adding more structure to the ending process.

Integrating Stages of Individual Change with Stages of Group Change[3]

The beginning stage is critical with involuntary groups. Dropout or minimal participation is a frequent problem since many lack belief in the utility of the group or their view of the problem does not match the focus of the group (Eckhardt, Babcock, and Homack 2004). The transtheoretical model of change and motivational interviewing (MI) are helpful in addressing these issues since motivation is considered transactional rather than a character trait (Prochaska, Norcross, and Di Clemente 1994; Miller and Rollnick 2002). While developed for voluntary clients with self-identified health issues, several aspects of the approach are useful in work with involuntary clients on other than health issues. Motivational interviewing has been applied to involuntary clients with a variety of problems such as sexual offending (Mann and Rollnick 1996), domestic violence (Taft et al. 2001), as well as in work with offenders on probation (Harper and Hardy 2000).

Rather than viewing beginning involuntary group members as unmotivated, the MI perspective would view them as *precontemplators* who do not now see a need for change or as *contemplators* who have not yet decided to take action. From this perspective, many involuntary groups fail because they presume that members begin the group in the *action* stage in which they are ready to begin to make changes to address their own acknowledged concerns. The precontemplation phase sounds like *mala prohibita* motivation in that the problem focus of the group is not acknowledged as valid in its own right, but accepted because of its consequences. Thus, it would be expected that most involuntary clients would begin work in the group desiring to fulfill obligations and avoid punishing consequences rather than seeking a change for their own benefit.

For example, substance abuse treatment groups often assume that members are ready to change at the point they begin a group (Lincourt, Kuettel, and Bombardier 2002). Since legally mandated members are often likely to feel coerced and be unable to identify a problem or develop a treatment goal, Lincourt reports adding six sessions at the beginning of the group to enhance motivation. In the first session, members were encouraged to share pros and cons of beginning to deal with substance use. In the second session, they were introduced to the idea of decisional balance through reviewing what had tipped the balance toward their taking action with other behaviors such as smoking. In the third session, members were introduced to the concept of stages of change and asked to identify their current stage. In the fourth session, they completed a drinking profile with an assessor and were asked to present the results to the group. In the fifth session, members would brainstorm options for dealing with their situation and the pros and cons of each choice. Finally, in the sixth session, they would once again rate their stage of change. The additional sessions were effective in stimulating greater attendance among legally mandated members as well as completing treatment and reducing dependence on substances (ibid.). These techniques are incorporated below in the guidelines for increasing group participation.

Beginning Involuntary Groups

Involuntary groups often start, end, or persist indefinitely in power struggles between leaders and participants. Such participant efforts to regain control are to be expected in involuntary groups. While leaders of voluntary groups can share agenda setting on most issues with the group, many issues in involuntary groups may not be subject to negotiation. Yet even mandated groups often include at least constrained choices such that activities to pursue in the group can be selected from limited alternatives. Too often, involuntary groups struggle over non-negotiable requirements and never explore the negotiable.

The goal for the beginning session is to establish a basis for collaborative work that is at least semivoluntary, and includes both a framework of non-negotiable expectations and choices that individuals and the group as a whole may make. This goal is pursued through negotiation of a contract that is the convergence of agency-mandated purposes and rules and goals expressed by participants. Seven steps in the initial session are suggested: (1) arrange the meeting room; (2) make an introductory statement that clarifies non-negotiable issues and rights and negotiable issues; (3) initiate discussion of pros and cons of deciding to change; (4) solicit member goals and attempt to link to group goals; (5) negotiate some group process rules; (6) use tactful, experiential confrontation; and (7) clarify expectations and choices for the next session.

1. *Arrange the meeting room.* Involuntary group members want to know what to expect from the group and what is expected of them. They gather answers to some of these questions through pregroup individual sessions and handouts. They probe for further answers both from what is said in the

Figure 9.4   Initial session of involuntary group

Setting preparation
↓
Welcome members
↓
Initiate discussion of pros and cons of deciding to change
↓
Solicit goals
↓
Clarify negotiables and non-negotiables
↓
Negotiate process rules
↓
Tactful experiential confrontation
↓
Clarify expectations for next session

group and through nonverbal messages conveyed by leaders including the physical arrangements of the group setting. If member participation is to be reinforced and status hierarchies diminished, then leaders should consider arranging chairs in a circle and not separating themselves from the group. Refreshments might also be made available. Posters welcoming participants and handouts with the agenda can also clarify structure and choices.

2. *Make an introductory statement that begins to establish realistic expectations.* Leaders can begin to establish realistic expectations by: (a) welcoming the group; (b) searching for common concerns; (c) clarifying circumstances of the referral; (d) clarifying non-negotiable expectations of leaders and members; (e) clarifying rights, freedoms, choices, and areas for negotiation; and (f) empathizing with pressure experienced. Leaders can suggest common concerns in a matter-of-fact, nonjudgmental tone and empathize with feelings of pressure experienced by some without supporting the behavior that may have led to the referral. For example, many members may be expected to be ambivalent about group membership. They may have conflicted wants that include both attraction to the group and desires to avoid it. To address such conflicted wants in a group of persons who are together because they drove while intoxicated, that statement can be

- No one wishes to be here *(commonality)*.
- We all would like to stay out of trouble, but we may not wish to stop drinking *(conflicted wants)*.
- You are here because you decided you would rather try this than go to jail *(choices)* (Berliner 1987).

The latter statement implies that people are responsible for what happens to them, that choices can be made between undesirable alternatives (ibid.). "No one wants to be here" as an area of commonality and identifies wishing to stay out of trouble but not wishing to stop drinking is also a commonality that is noted without judging it. In addition to stating in advance what the commonalities might be, the group leader can ask members to introduce themselves including describing why they have come to this group. The leader can then note the similarities that emerge from those introductions. For example, they will often include an observation that other persons or events pressured the client to come to the group. The leader can note the similarity that no one chose to join the group freely, which can be difficult. Still, all members are similar in choosing to participate rather than accept other consequences. In addition to identifying common concerns and emphasizing choices, leaders can describe circumstances of the referral and expectations of the group and the leaders. Shields reports an introduction made by the leader of a group with drug-dependent adolescents in high schools as follows. The group leader identifies drug use leading to hassles with parents and teachers as common concerns, that members will not be judged and will have to make their own choices about drug use, and begins to identify expectations of the leader and of members (Shields 1986).

This is what I know: all of you are in trouble here in school because of drugs. The principal has spoken to all of your parents and has told them that you are all one step from being expelled (the students all agree) *(commonality)*. Now the principal asked me to meet you *(circumstances of referral)*. I've been thinking about what I can do to help. I think your drug use, whether a little or a lot, has gotten you into trouble with your families and here in school *(nonjudgmental description of commonality)*. Now, I know I can't stop you from getting high, and I'm not going to preach about drugs *(emphasizes choices and nonjudgmental attitude)*. You've heard all that. I know you make your own decisions about getting high *(emphasizes choices)*, since all of you are facing similar hassles—like probation here in school, feeling everybody is watching you, hassles with your parents, decisions about drugs *(areas of commonality)*—I think you can help each other work these things out, and I can help you do that *(what leader can do)*. You've all told me you want to stay in school *(commonality)*, and I'd like to help you do that, but it will mean work—looking hard at how you make decisions about getting high in school, how you handle the restrictions of probation and problems that arise with teachers here at school *(what members can do)*. Now, I think we can work these things out together—I can help you work together on these issues here in group. I can help you talk to teachers and maybe parents or I can even talk to them with you *(what leader can do)*, but you have to be willing to really share and work together here on the hassles you're facing if group is going to help *(what members can do)*. *How* about it? Can we do it? *(emphasizes choices)* (Shields 1986)

The introduction is also a time to describe beliefs and philosophies of the program. For example, many domestic abuse programs believe that the abuser is responsible for his or her own violence, is not provoked to use violence, chooses violence as a way of coping, that abuse rarely stops spontaneously, and that abuse is learned behavior (Purdy and Nickle 1981). While involuntary group members cannot realistically be expected to accept these beliefs as their own at the beginning of the group, they must be aware of the program's rationale.

Some mandated groups contain many non-negotiable rules. Even in such groups, constrained choices can be emphasized. For example, such groups often entail attendance requirements while permitting as many as two absences. Members can be encouraged to use their choice of absences judiciously as but two are permitted. Similarly, members may be required to select a personal goal to work on. They may select one from an approved list such as "improve employment skills, improve communication skills, improve health and nutrition."

Group leaders sometimes become involved in defending the fairness of the non-negotiable rules. It is important to keep these rules to the minimum necessary and be prepared to offer a rationale for them. Leaders can reduce the arguing and clarification by sharing a written list of non-negotiable expectations with prospective members *before* the first session. The leaders can recognize member discomfort with or disagreement with the rules while affirming that members have a choice about whether or not to join the group. If they choose to join the group, they are implicitly choosing to comply with the rules of the group.

Leaders should move as soon as possible to identifying rights, free choices, constrained choices, and areas for negotiation. Alternative ways to meet group goals are clarified next.

Nonvoluntary groups include more emphasis on choices to participate than mandated groups. Empathy with feelings of pressure experienced by nonvoluntary members in otherwise voluntary groups can be expressed. For example, in a parenting skills group, including some who joined the group voluntarily and others who came through pressure from their child welfare worker, the leader assures any members feeling pressure to attend that such pressure is external to the group. A reframing to identify what the prospective member would like to receive from the group rather than a focus on the referral source's agenda is suggested.

Some of you have come to this group because you think that it can help you with some parenting issues you are concerned about. Others may be here because someone suggested that you come and you felt as if you had to take their advice *(identifies areas of commonality)*. It can be difficult when you feel as if you don't have a choice *(empathizes with feelings of pressure)*. I want to make it clear to any of you who feel as if you don't have a choice that we are not requiring that *you* be here. You can decide not to come to the group and go back and talk it over with the person who referred *you*. *You* can also decide to remain and see if the group meets some of your own concerns. If you are unsure, *I* would suggest that you avoid making a decision until today's session ends. *You* might want to think about what you could get out of this group *for yourself,* not for the person who sent you *(emphasizes choices)*.

3. *Initiate discussion of pros and cons of deciding to change.* Members can be assumed to vary in their readiness to engage in change. Rather than punish members for being in the precontemplation or contemplation stage, acceptance of the likelihood that members have not yet decided to change is recommended. Members can be encouraged to make lists of all of the reasons why they may not now see a need to make a change. Then members make additional lists of reasons that would incline them to choose to make a change. Group leaders can emphasize that no one can make members choose to make a change, but the group can assist members in gathering the information they need to decide whether or not to change (Lincourt, Kuettel, and Bombardier 2002).

4. *Solicit member goals and attempt to link to group goals.* Self-attributed changes in behaviors and attitudes tend to last longer than changes produced primarily via reward or punishment. For members to self-attribute change and become at least semivoluntary, their own goals need to be explored. As considered above, many members can be expected to be in the precontemplation or contemplation stage, so their expression of goals is likely to be tentative. It should be expected that many of their goals at this point will be of the *mala prohibita* sort. Leaders can accept some of these motivations while beginning to encourage members to explore additional goals of their own. For example, members of one reported adolescent drug use group originally expressed motivations such as wanting to end involvement with the criminal justice system, to be released from the facility, or fear that further drug use would lead to incarceration while other members suggested, probably quite candidly, that they wanted to continue to use drugs and avoid getting caught (Smith 1985)!

The leaders can attempt to link individually expressed goals of the former kind with the mandated goals of the group. They can also identify common themes as group goals. For example, the leaders of the drug alternatives group could suggest that by learning about the dangers of illegal drug use and alternatives to it, members could also learn ways to avoid further involvement with the criminal justice system. Additional goals may be shared by members but be unrelated to the group mandate. For example, one such common goal in drug abuse groups for adolescents could be dealing with feeling stigmatized by others (Shields 1986).

As members express goals, leaders can support those goals or parts of them and, in some cases, reach for goals slightly beyond the *mala prohibita* level. For example, "it sounds as if most of you want to get out of this group successfully and to finish school. If you can learn some skills here that might help in school and in relations with your parents, all the better."

5. *Negotiate some process rules of the group.* If some rules for the group are non-negotiable, as in the attendance policy stated for this group, it is important to state these first before the floor is open to discuss other group-generated rules. Involuntary groups often have unexplored possibilities to share power in the process of the group. For example, within an overall non-negotiable framework of exploring issues in drug education, group members can identify the topics of most interest to them (Smith 1985). Knowing their preferences can then influence the order of presentation.

Agreements can be negotiated about expectations for member participation and group decision making. For example, rules about times for breaks, when and where members might smoke, and bringing in food might be negotiated in the group.

6. *Use tactful experiential confrontation.* Guidelines were suggested in chapter 3 about the use of confrontation with individuals that are also relevant for work with groups (Reid 1986). Confrontation is appropriate when behavior or attitudes are expressed that are illegal, dangerous, violate group rules, or are inconsistent with the person's own goals. Inconsistency with a member's own expressed goal is most likely to be effective, since dissonance may not be stimulated if the person does not consider the behavior or attitude in question to be *mala in se*. Since clients are more likely to be persuaded by persons they like, trust, and feel to be expert, leaders are unlikely to be sources of powerful influence in early group sessions if they are not yet seen by members as possessing these attributes.

Confrontation in groups is often initiated by group members and may lack the characteristics of specificity and empathy identified in chapter 3. On the other hand, other members may be more likely to be seen as similar and hence more powerful sources of influence. Therefore, confrontation in groups can be a powerful source of influence. It can also be a source of abuse when the member cannot choose not to receive it, when empathy is not expressed, and when choices are not available. Group leaders can shape, take the edge off of confrontation, or in fact sharpen it to make the point clear. They can also model how to confront in a nonjudgmental fashion.

7. *Clarify expectations for the next session.* Expectations of any tasks to be completed outside of the session should be reviewed before the session ends. Where possible, members should select such tasks from several possibilities, or should be encouraged to generate their own tasks. For example, the members of the prostitution group might have been asked to think of topics they would like to have discussed in the group. They might also examine the alternative programs for individual goals such as pursuing further education, acquiring job skills, getting a driver's license, or bringing in their own alternative ideas for an individual plan. In chemical dependency groups, members may be asked to read specified chapters of a text and bring in questions. As suggested in chapter 7, such initial tasks should be specific and highly likely to succeed such that a positive momentum might be generated.

Techniques for Enhancing Attendance, Participation, and Cohesion

For involuntary clients to benefit from group membership, they need to attend sessions, participate in activities, and experience some cohesion with other group members. Cohesive groups are more likely to have engaged members (Levinson and Macgowan 2004). Members have to come to see a need for change and develop an alliance with group leaders (Taft et al. 2004). Research on sexual abuse treatment in groups suggests that engagement is related to group progress, which in turn reduces recidivism (Hanson et al. 2002; Levinson and Macgowan 2004). Successful groups with sexual offenders with children are cohesive, promote responsibility, and foster a positive rather than confrontative style (ibid.). Members who make progress are more likely to be engaged and less likely to deny responsibility (Hanson and Bussiere 1998).

Members are more likely to value the group if their attendance and participation is valued. Since attending to the potential of dropout in domestic violence groups is critical, sending a handwritten letter or making a phone call inviting the member to return had been shown in one study to reduce dropout from 30 percent to 15 percent and increase attendance by 10 percent (Taft et al. 2001). Such respectful attention to attendance is recommended.

Asking members to self-assess their reasons for considering to change or not to change was described above as part of the first session as a way to begin supporting ownership of the decision to change. Subsequent sessions can introduce the concept of decisional balance, and examining what moved members to change around other problems they have identified such as smoking or weight loss can convey the idea that they acted to make positive changes in the past (Lincourt, Kuettel, and Bombardier 2002). Dissonance can be aroused by keeping a visual record of inconsistencies between goals and behaviors as a way of influencing the decisional balance (Draycott and Dabbs 1998).

Skills for enhancing member participation in involuntary groups are critical. Thomas and Caplan (1999) describe several techniques for enhancing participation. At one level, the leader is advised to pay attention to process or themes underlying the surface of the conversation. For example, the leader might say "it sounds as if many of us are raising some issues about how much they want to disclose in this group, how safe is it going to be for me to trust."

In addition, the leader should make explicitly empathic statements that indicate understanding of what the member is trying to convey. For example, if a member notes early on that he hesitates to share his views because he is quite sure that others won't agree, the leader would want to assure him that he would be listened to even if not all would agree with him.

Linking interventions are ones in which the concerns of one participant are connected to those of another (ibid.). For example, "Frank, when I hear you talk about wanting to be a good father for your sons, I am reminded of what George said last week about wanting to be a good role model."

Finally, inclusion techniques are used to encourage a member to increase his or her participation and note how participation so far has addressed treatment goals. For example, "Walt, I noticed that you brought in your anger diary. You appear to be taking it all in, thinking about what might work for you" (ibid.).

With involuntary clients in prison, efforts are sometimes made to engage members by exploring cognitive patterns and beliefs in a safe manner in which they will not be criticized. Using the sophistry technique, members are assigned to make a case pro or con for a particular belief without owning the belief necessarily as their own. For example, "If I am treated unfairly, I have the right to be unfair back" or "a strong person demands respect from others." After the positions in favor and opposed to the belief are expressed, members can be encouraged to make their own decisions about how the belief serves them (Evans and Kane 1996).

Solution-focused methods have also been successfully used to engage groups of domestic violence male offenders (Lee, Greene, and Rheinscheld 1999). Group leaders seek to explore exceptions, when the problem did not occur, and build on the exception. For example, the leader might explore instances in which the client had resolved disputes without resorting to verbal threats or violence.

Postcontracting Work with Involuntary Groups

Once a working contract is established that meets both non-negotiable purposes and individual goals, many forms of continued work are possible. Too often, involuntary groups never reach this stage. Activities after the contracting phase become much more specific to the type of group and problems addressed.

However, some general differences occur between open-ended and closed groups. For example, open-ended groups continue to add members and are ongoing, while other groups have closed membership and may last for a specific time-limited period. Open-ended groups offer members the opportunity to move through stages in the group from initiate to role model and are easier to staff, since the same group is used for persons at different stages. However, open-ended groups often have difficulty in maintaining a sense of forward progress, since attention must continually be given to orienting new members. Longer-term members, however, can often assist in this orientation process by describing their experience in the group and sharing group norms.

Closed, topic-oriented groups have the advantage of grouping persons according to where they are in a predictable sequence of change processes. For example, some writers propose that different group purposes are needed for the changing needs of alcoholics at early, middle, and ongoing support stages of the recovery process (Cohen and Sinner 1981).

Whether a single group or a sequence of groups is planned, a series of four phases is often found. Involuntary groups begin with an *orientation phase* in which information about the problem area is shared, followed by a *skill-learning phase* in which alternative behavioral skills are learned and practiced. Groups then often move to an *examination of attitudes and beliefs,* followed by attention to *preparation for experiences after the group ends.* These phases are described in more detail below (figure 9.5).

Orientation Phase

After the initial meeting described above, many involuntary groups continue with an orientation phase that is aimed at providing information and assisting members in making decisions about how they will use the group experience. For example, a study of rankings of therapeutic factors by male participants in groups for men who batter found that the participants ranked prominently issues related to self-understanding and understanding of the problem (Roy et al. 2005). Thus an emphasis on education early in the group helped the participants feel that they were not alone in dealing with the problem (Roy et al. 2005).

Figure 9.5   Phases of involuntary groups

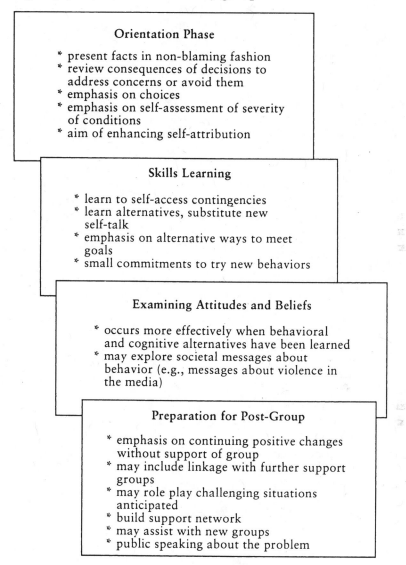

Orientation Phase

* present facts in non-blaming fashion
* review consequences of decisions to address concerns or avoid them
* emphasis on choices
* emphasis on self-assessment of severity of conditions
* aim of enhancing self-attribution

Skills Learning

* learn to self-access contingencies
* learn alternatives, substitute new self-talk
* emphasis on alternative ways to meet goals
* small commitments to try new behaviors

Examining Attitudes and Beliefs

* occurs more effectively when behavioral and cognitive alternatives have been learned
* may explore societal messages about behavior (e.g., messages about violence in the media)

Preparation for Post-Group

* emphasis on continuing positive changes without support of group
* may include linkage with further support groups
* may role play challenging situations anticipated
* build support network
* may assist with new groups
* public speaking about the problem

The orientation phase works best when members are presented with information in a factual, non-blaming fashion, assisted in self-assessment of problem behaviors, and encouraged to make proactive choices. Cognitive dissonance may be stimulated by the provision of information that indicates dangers to meeting the member's own goals (Draycott and Dabbs 1998).

1. *Presentation of problem behavior in factual, nonblaming ways.* As involuntary groups usually begin with greater concern for the *mala prohibita* goals, the orientation phase often includes a presentation of problem behavior in a matter-of-fact, nonjudgmental way. Hence, in DWI and alcoholism treatment groups, tapes and films examining the consequences of drunken driving or physical consequences of drug abuse are often shared at this point. Experts are also used to provide information. For example, Smith reports using credible, outside experts to describe effects of chemical use with chemically dependent adolescents. The experts discussed problem drug use in two-sided arguments (see chapter 4) and did not pressure the adolescents to change beliefs or behavior (Smith 1985). At this point, members are not pressed to take personal responsibility for having "a problem," but rather are asked to be open to hearing information about the consequences of such behaviors.

2. *Facilitate decisions about dealing with problem behavior.* Building on the decisional balance exercise described above, members can be encouraged to make a decision about whether or not to attempt change for their own reasons, not just because of outside pressures (van Wormer 1987). Contact with persons who have successfully completed the group often assists in this decision-making process (Citron 1978; Panepinto et al. 1982).

Decision making is often facilitated by asking members to complete a self-assessment of their own problem behavior. For example, Smith reports that adolescent drug users were helped to construct a behavioral definition of dangerous drug usage followed by completing an individual assessment of their own danger using the group-constructed definition (Smith 1985). To facilitate such self-assessment, members of alcoholism treatment groups are often asked to complete a written self-assessment of dangerous drug usage. Citron recommends that these questions be asked in a matter-of-fact, nonjudgmental fashion, avoiding value-laden questions such as "Are you powerless over alcohol?" (Citron 1978).

Involuntary clients might be expected to respond more to factual questions about behavior and consequences than to take on self-blame for the problem, especially when they are unaware of other alternatives in getting needs met.

Skills Learning

Change in orientation from *mala prohita* to *mala in se* motivation is more likely to occur if members become aware of alternative ways to meet their own goals. Hence, instruction in developing alternative behavioral, affective, and cognitive responses to problem situations often follows the orientation phase. For example, skills groups for domestic violence often include instruction in relaxation methods, substitution of positive self-messages for negative self-talk, and practice of alternative behavioral responses such as taking time-outs and making assertive requests (Saunders 1984). Teaching men to observe their own cues that indicate a potentially violent or anger-provoking situation is particularly important. When such situations occur, men are taught to record both positive and negative self-talk and to generate behavioral alternatives (see Chovanec, chapter 12 in this volume).

Similarly, in alcoholism treatment, assertiveness training groups can focus on alternative ways of dealing with situations that have led to drinking in the past (Brody 1982; see chapter 10 by Barber in this volume). In the S.O.B.E.R. program, members are taught to slow down, relax, analyze the behavioral exchange, and recognize the methods they use to deal with situations that in the past have led to alcohol use (Brody 1982).

Exploration of behavioral alternatives is more likely to be successful if there is emphasis on trying a new behavior with little external reward, with some emphasis on the difficulty of the task, and with anticipation of obstacles (Smith 1985).

Examining Attitudes and Beliefs

It is often the hope in involuntary groups that members will change not only behaviors but also beliefs and attitudes supporting those behaviors. Members of involuntary groups may be more likely to consider change in attitudes and beliefs if completion of the two previous phases has stimulated dissonance and alternative means of reaching goals have been learned. Domestic violence groups often address attitudes and beliefs at this stage by presenting violence as learned behavior frequently reinforced by society. Men who batter are seen as partly victims themselves of domestic violence through their lack of skills, fear of intimacy, and dependency on women (Purdy and Nickle 1981). They are seen as the products of a society that often teaches men to be unaware of their feelings, to have an action orientation, and to see less than perfect performance as failure.

Such normalizing and nonblaming attention to attitudes and beliefs may assist in the modification of values. However, the process is not smooth and many members continue to express values or carry out behavior that is contrary to group purposes. Some members leave the group during this phase. Group leaders eager to change a person's attitudes and behavior at this point are susceptible to a member's use of abusive confrontation that violates individual dignity, or a member's right not to participate and to withdraw within him- or herself (Bratter, Bratter, and Helmsberg 1986). Bratter suggests that unless the individual retains the right to self-determination in choosing whether and how to change behavior and attitudes, group leaders can become tyrants (ibid.).

When denial persists, Purdy and Nickle suggest asking direct factual questions about time and information gaps in reports of violence and asking about discrepancies in reports (Purdy and Nickle 1981). Emphasis on choices and consequences of behavior and attitudes that are obstacles to members' *own goals,* followed by empathy, are more likely to be successful forms of confrontation than assaults on attitudes and behavior (Roffers and Waldo 1983). In particular, confrontation around values and attitudes that the member does not have are unlikely to be successful. Without such self-attribution, members are likely to change overt behavior and attitudes only under the pressure of threatened punishment or tangible rewards. Evidence that such self-attribution is difficult to attain is suggested in domestic violence treatment research reports that men completing the program were more likely to reduce physical violence while maintaining or increasing psychological violence (Tolman and Bhosley 1987). This finding suggests that while physical violence remained *mala prohibita,* psychological violence did not become *mala in se.*

Preparation for Post-Group

If involuntary groups are to assist members in maintaining changes after the group ends, generalization to other settings and linkage with other resources must be facilitated. For example, role plays of situations in which peers attempt to influence a member to engage in renewed problem behavior can be helpful in preparing for difficulties. Planning for possible setbacks and regression in which a crisis plan, including means of maintaining an ongoing support plan, is developed can be beneficial. In addition, some members may move on to join ongoing support groups or assist in running new groups. Support for choices should be especially encouraged since self-attributed change is more likely to persist in the absence of the kinds of rewards and punishments that were available in the group.

Summary

This chapter has suggested that involuntary groups can be ethical and effective sources of influence that meet both societal needs and individual goals. Dangers of abuse of group leader power have also been described. Hence, a major issue is the determination of whether the specific purposes of a mandated or nonvoluntary group are legal and ethical. Questions to ask when an involuntary group's purpose are to be supported include: What role can individuals play in meeting their own goals? How can they participate in structuring the group? If structure is so rigid that neither leaders nor members can modify it, member efforts to regain some control can be expected, or, if they are unsuccessful, mute, passive acceptance. Are members required to participate who do not benefit and inhibit the benefit that others might obtain?

The chapter has also suggested that attitudes and beliefs may be more subject to change in groups through the influence of peers than is normally possible in work with individuals. While that influence can be ethical and effective, the danger of abusive confrontation in the group was also described. Remembering that confrontation is more appropriate as a persuasion method than as a method of punishment, questions should be asked about its use in the group. What choice does a member have in receiving confrontation? Corey suggests that members should be free to decline participation (Corey, Corey, and Callanan 1979:144), that groups are "not appropriate for endless interrogation . . . beating into submission. How is confrontation related to the members' own goals? To what extent is confrontation used as a means of venting frustration over progress perceived to be too slow by the leaders?"

Discussion Questions

1. This chapter has emphasized joining and linking methods designed to make the involuntary group a safe, cohesive place to try out new behaviors and attitudes. To what extent have you seen such methods used with involuntary groups?

2. Should groups have open membership with members joining and leaving at different times? What are some of the ways the benefits of the group can be maximized?

3. This chapter has suggested that members of oppressed groups may feel disproportionately singled out by a majority society for involuntary treatment. How can group leaders acknowledge disproportionality and also support member choices?

4. Confrontation from peers can be a powerful source of attitudinal influence. How can members be assisted to deliver and receive such confrontation in useful ways?
5. Some involuntary groups seem to persist in an unresolved power and control stage. What methods can leaders use to assist groups in addressing their growth as a group?

Notes

1. This chapter draws extensively from Rooney, R. and M. Chovanec. 2004. Social Work with Involuntary Groups. In *Handbook of Social Work with Groups,* eds. C. D. Garvin, L. M. Gutierrez, and M. J. Galinsky, pp. 212–226. New York: Guilford.

2. This section is largely drawn from Rooney, R. and M. Chovanec. 2004. Social Work with Involuntary Groups. In *Handbook of Social Work with Groups,* eds. C. D. Garvin, L. M. Gutierrez, and M. J. Galinsky, pp. 212–226. New York: Guilford.

3. See also chapter 10 by Barber and chapter 11 by Hohman and Kleinpeter in this volume.

Practice Applications with Involuntary Problems and Settings

Part 3 is divided into four parts. Section A contains three chapters that address the implications of motivational interviewing for work with involuntary clients (Miller and Rollnick 2002). Chapter 10 by James Barber applies a "stages of change approach" to work with substance abusers. Chapter 11 by Melinda Hohman and Chris Kleinpeter applies motivational interviewing to engaging adolescents related to health behaviors. Finally, chapter 12 by Michael Chovanec applies the approach to work with domestic violence perpetrators.

Section B applies solution-focused treatment to clients in two populations (De Jong and Berg 2001; Tohn and Oshlag 1996). Chapter 13 by Cynthia Franklin and Laura Hopson applies solution-focused methods to work in public schools, and chapter 14 by Julie Altman and Debra Gohagen applies those methods to child welfare.

Section C addresses applications to particular settings and populations. In chapter 15, Glenda Dewberry Rooney explores the interaction between members of oppressed groups and involuntary status. Chris Trotter examines the involuntary perspective in corrections settings in chapter 16. Next, in chapter 17, Tony Bibus applies the perspective to settings designed to enhance workforce participation.

Section D addresses applications to roles beyond direct practice and returns to a larger systems perspective. In chapter 18, Tony Bibus and Carol Jud present applications of the involuntary perspective to the role of supervisors in public social services. Finally, chapter 19 explores the involuntary practitioner and the system.

Part 3, Section A

Chapter 10

Work with Substance Abusers

James Barber

There are two fundamental reasons why any book on involuntary clients needs to deal with the issue of drug abuse. The first is that the misuse of drugs is arguably the single most important reason for clients becoming involuntary in the first place. Drug offenders now account for around two-thirds of all U.S. federal prisoners, for example, as well as 20 percent of all state prisoners (Office of National Drug Control Policy 2003). Furthermore, almost two-thirds of all violent offenses are committed while the victim or the perpetrator is under the influence of drugs or alcohol (Bureau of Justice Statistics 2002), and between one in ten and one in five prisoners had committed their offenses to obtain money for drugs (Bureau of Justice Statistics 2002). This nexus between crime and drugs has been drawing closer for decades. Between 1981 and 1991, for example, there was a 360 percent increase in the number of suspects prosecuted for drug offenses in the United States (Bureau of Justice Statistics 1994). In addition to the criminal justice system, drug abusers are very likely to turn up as involuntary clients within the child welfare system as well. All child protection risk assessment instruments today contain items on parental substance abuse (e.g., Ministry of Community and Social Services 2000) because it has been shown repeatedly that all forms of child abuse are much more likely to occur when one of the child's caregivers is addicted to drugs. Each year, more than one million American children are confirmed as victims of child abuse and neglect, and surveys of state child welfare records indicate that about one-half of these are directly associated with parental alcohol or drug abuse. Indeed, substance abuse is one of the two major problems exhibited by parents in about 80 percent of child welfare cases generally (Child Welfare League of America 1997). The drug–crime relationship needs to be interpreted carefully, of course, both because some of the relevant data are self-reported and also because it would be simplistic in the extreme to suggest that drugs alone are responsible for child maltreatment and crime. Criminal behavior is driven by numerous factors and drug abuse is only one of them. There is conclusive evidence nevertheless that psychoactive drugs are causally connected with violence and antisocial behavior, not merely correlated (Krivanek 1982).

The second reason why a book on involuntary clients must deal with substance abuse is that at any given time, the vast majority of addicts are resistant to change. It has been estimated that some 14 million Americans abuse alcohol (National Institute of Alcohol Abuse and Alcoholism 1994) and 12 million use illicit drugs (U.S. Department of Health and Human Services 1995), yet only a very small percentage of these individuals are in treatment. The U.S. Office of National Drug Control Policy (2003) recently estimated that approximately 4,000,000 of the individuals screened by health and human service providers in the year 2000 required but either did not receive or did not accept treatment for their drug addiction. In a recent British study, about 49,000 people were screened between October 2000 and September 2001 under the arrest referral scheme, in which suspects are asked by police if they would like to get help with drug problems. Nearly 24,800 of the individuals screened agreed to be referred but only 5,520 actually entered treatment, and the majority of those dropped out (Hough et al. 2003). While it would be unfair to suggest that all of those outside treatment are actively resistant to change, it is safe to assume that many or most are at least reluctant to do so, and that among those who do enter treatment, there are at least some who would rather not be there.

In short, then, not only is addiction involved directly or indirectly in behaviors that lead to involuntarism, but the most addicted individuals are also the least likely to volunteer for treatment. Social work is more likely than any other helping profession to deal with precisely such involuntary substance abusers (Barber 2002, 2003) because social workers staff the public service departments that deal with the consequences of drug abuse: the prisons, the child welfare departments, and the emergency relief agencies. Social workers rarely have the luxury of working with drug users who are highly motivated to change; such individuals are referred (often by social workers) to specialist treatment centers staffed by physicians, clinical psychologists, and nurses. Social workers are represented in such places, of course, but the overwhelming majority of us encounter drug abuse in the context of some other, often more pressing, social problem such as homelessness, child abuse, suicide, domestic violence, or relationship breakdown. For this reason, social work, more than any other helping profession, requires proven methods for dealing with resistant drug abusers. Moreover, since the presenting problem is often something other than addiction, these methods need to be brief and capable of being integrated into a larger case plan. The purpose of this chapter is to outline the principles involved in constructing such a plan.

Addiction Defined

Given the prevalence and intractability of drug addiction, it is ironic that there should continue to be such acrimonious debate among experts over exactly what it is (see Barber 2002 for a review of this literature). Much of this debate comes down to a clash among medical, psychological, and sociological ways of looking at the phenomenon (Barber 1994). The debate is not purely academic, however; there can be profound differences in treatment approach depending on which definition is preferred. All protagonists do agree that addiction is expressed as a behavioral compulsion or "preoccupation with the use of a drug and the securing of its supply" (Krivanek 1982:83). A drug addict can therefore be defined operationally as one who is involved with drugs to the extent that it is a major, and at the extreme, *the* major focus of his or her life. More specifically, the DSM-IV (American Psychiatric Association 2000) defines addiction as a maladaptive pattern of substance use leading to failure to fulfill one's obligations in life and/or to social, legal, or interpersonal problems. A great deal of subjectivity is clearly involved in making a judgment like this, but DSM-IV specifies the presence of three or more of the following seven criteria, occurring in the same twelve-month period:

1. Tolerance
2. Withdrawal
3. The consumption of larger amounts over a longer period than was intended
4. A persistent desire or unsuccessful efforts to cut down or control substance use
5. Long periods of time spent in activities intended to obtain the substance, use the substance, or recover from its effects
6. Abandonment or reduction of important social, occupational, or recreational activities because of substance use
7. Continuation of drug use despite recognition by the user of persistent physical or psychological problems caused or compounded by the substance.

As DSM-IV criteria make clear, the concept of addiction requires an understanding of the key terms *tolerance* and *withdrawal*. Put simply, tolerance means that with repeated use, the desired effect of the drug will diminish over time unless the dosage is increased. A drinker will need to drink more to get drunk and a heroin user must increase the dose to get high because the addict literally *tolerates* the drug better than the non-addict does. The notion of *withdrawal* refers to the subjective experience of suffering the countervailing effects of a drug after terminating its use. For example, heavy users of speed (amphetamine or methamphetamine, for example) will experience fatigue and depression when they stop using, while users of sedative-hypnotics like alcohol and heroin are likely to experience agitation and hyperexcitability, among numerous other unpleasant symptoms. It is the need to avoid or alleviate these withdrawal symptoms that causes drug users to take the sometimes extreme measures they do to procure drugs. In other words, habitual drug use is negatively reinforced by withdrawal symptoms (see Solomon 1977 for a physiological explanation of this point). An understanding of tolerance and withdrawal also helps to clarify the remaining criteria in the DSM-IV definition. The third criterion—ingestion of larger amounts over time—is a direct consequence of tolerance, while criterion four—repeated unsuccessful attempts to cut down or quit—is a consequence of withdrawal. Criteria five through seven are merely behavioral manifestations of tolerance and withdrawal since they all demonstrate the user's preoccupation with the drug to the exclusion of competing physical and social imperatives.

Toward an Integrative Theory of Change

In recent times, the psychosocial treatment of drug abuse has been dominated by the "transtheoretical model" (DiClemente and Prochaska 1998), which is a heuristic rather than empirically derived theory of change. Under the model, addicts are said to pass through five stages on their way to an addiction-free lifestyle. According to its proponents, the model is transtheoretical in the sense that it owes allegiance to no one theory of human behavior or school of therapy but provides an integrative framework that is capable of guiding practice irrespective of the therapist's preferred approach. Figure 10.1 conveys the essence of the model.

Under the model, addicted drug users pass through five stages on their way to resolving the problem. As the diagram shows, the stages occur in an iterative fashion represented by the spiral. The first stage is known as "precontemplation," which refers to the period that is the subject of this book: the stage when the individual is using and is unwilling to consider change. By definition, a precontemplator is one who would submit to treatment only

Figure 10.1   The "transtheoretical model"

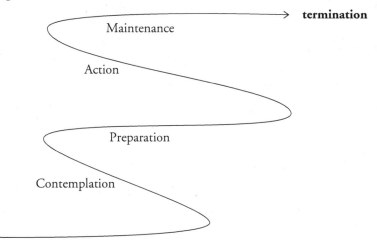

involuntarily. Next follows the "contemplation" stage during which the user begins weighing the pros and cons of change and experiences the discomfort that accompanies self-doubt and irreconcilable goals. Contemplators are dissatisfied with life but have not yet resolved to change. If the discomfort of contemplation becomes acute or persistent enough, the contemplator is predicted to enter the "preparation" stage, which involves both intention and action. The drinker may pour the bottle down the sink or the smoker toss away the cigarette pack. Whatever the action, it tends to be both sudden and symbolic. There is not yet a coherent change strategy or even a well-defined criterion for success. The "action" stage follows and refers to the use of deliberate strategies to modify the drug-taking behavior. During the maintenance stage, individuals have already made significant progress but they are still drawn to using. Vigilance is needed and the struggle against the urge to use must continue. The transtheoretical model recognizes that most individuals do not progress through these stages in a neat, linear fashion. For most, there is relapse, a return to the precontemplation stage and further cycles through the stages. In fact, in its original form the transtheoretical model conceived of the struggle to change as a cyclical process. The more recent spiral version presented here is intended to convey that with each journey through the stages, users are likely to learn something or acquire some new skill that makes success more likely in the long run.

Stated in terms of the transtheoretical model, then, the question before us here becomes: what is the most effective strategy or set of strategies for coaxing precontemplators toward contemplation? Phrased in this way, the question serves as a reminder of the time-honored social work injunction to "start where the client is." Not all habitual drug users are at the same point in their readiness to change, so both the methods and the objectives of treatment need to include cognizance of the client's disposition at the time we encounter them. For example, a precontemplator and a contemplator may both be engaging in the identical behavior (habitual drug use) but their openness to treatment is very different. Similarly, the challenges on entering treatment (action stage) are different from those on completion of treatment (maintenance stage). Prochaska, DiClemente, and Norcross (1992) point out that different change processes become important at different stages of change. This aspect of the transtheoretical model emanates from Prochaska and DiClemente's (1984) comparison of twenty-nine leading systems of therapy, which resulted in the identification of the following ten basic change processes:

1. Consciousness-raising
2. Self-liberation
3. Social liberation
4. Counterconditioning
5. Stimulus control
6. Self-reevaluation
7. Environmental reevaluation
8. Contingency management
9. Dramatic relief
10. Helping relationships

Generally speaking, as users move through the stages of change, they are predicted to move from cognitive processes like consciousness-raising and self-liberation to behavioral strategies like stimulus control and contingency management. It should be noted that the transtheoretical model has been subjected to vigorous critique on conceptual and empirical grounds (see Barber 2002 for a review), but the general framework provides a number of useful guides for practice in spite of its limitations. One such implication is that there is no point applying action stage processes to precontemplators because the very idea of behavior change is not under serious consideration.

While the treatment objective of turning precontemplators into contemplators is easily stated, it is no easy feat to achieve. According to Prochaska and DiClemente (1984, 1988), most drug users move from precontemplation to contemplation either because of maturational or environmental forces. Examples of the former include subjectively important milestones such as a fortieth birthday or the birth of a child, while examples of the latter include work and family pressures. Maturational forces are difficult if not impossible for helping professionals to orchestrate but the principle of environmental pressure opens up potential avenues of intervention. It is this strategic manipulation of environmental contingencies that is the fundamental principle behind the Pressures to Change Approach discussed below.

Precontemplation is by far the most under-researched stage of change. Treatment methods (some would say bandwagons) abound for all other stages despite the fact that individuals at more advanced stages of change are infinitely easier to deal with than are precontemplators. It is sometimes argued by its proponents that the motivational interviewing technique developed by William Miller and his colleagues (Miller 1983; Miller and Rollnick 2002) qualifies as a precontemplation strategy because it does not assume that the user is ready to change. Motivational interviewing is built on the proposition that motivation is a state rather than a trait. In other words, it is a product of the interaction between therapist and client rather than something that the client either does or does not possess. Motivational interviewing eschews labels like "alcoholic" and "drug addict" while placing responsibility on the client to make informed decisions about the seriousness of the problem and the need for change. It is not for the counselor to confront the client with "the truth" as the counselor sees it. Because the goal of counseling is to increase the client's intrinsic motivation for change, the strategies of motivational interviewing are more supportive than argumentative. Client resistance is met with empathy and reflection rather than with confrontation, both as a means of displaying respect for the client and of creating an atmosphere that is conducive to change. A detailed examination of motivational interviewing is provided in many texts that have been written on the subject (e.g., Coombs 2001; Peters 2001; Miller and Rollnick 2002). The important point for our present purposes is that motivational interviewing fails to qualify as a precontemplation technique for two major reasons. First, precontemplators will not attend counseling unless they are forced to, and it is not always possible or desirable to compel people into counseling. Indeed, compulsion is antithetical to the motivational interviewing technique itself. Second, motivational interviewing seeks to exploit any latent ambivalence within the user but precontemplators, by definition, have no ambivalence to exploit; if they did, they would be contemplators.

In order to work with precontemplators, then, we require strategies that do not expect drug users to attend for counseling and that can be applied in spite of client resistance. Interventions of this kind rely on the principles of operant conditioning, the most fundamental of which is that behavior is shaped by its environmental consequences. It follows that any given behavior should be capable of modification by altering the consequences that accrue to it. The worker's task is conceptually, if not operationally, simple: it is a matter of assessing the usual consequences of drug abuse and ensuring that the abuse is not inadvertently rewarded. On the contrary, the secret is to find ways of rewarding the incompatible behavior of moderation or abstinence. Because client cooperation is not an essential requirement for the strategy to work, environmental interventions are perfectly suited to resistant drug users. In the sections that follow, an environmental strategy for enticing precontemplators into treatment is described, followed by a strategy for negotiating with resistant clients once they arrive there.

"Pressures to Change": An Environmental Contingencies Approach to Precontemplation

The Pressures to Change (PTC) approach was developed by Barber and colleagues (Barber and Crisp 1995; Barber and Gilbertson 1996, 1997, 1998) as a method for the systematic manipulation of environmental contingencies. In essence, PTC seeks to train significant others to identify the environmental contingencies over which they have control and to use this control to bring maximum pressure on the user to change. Since it was originally developed, PTC has been applied to individual counseling (Barber and Gilbertson 1996), as well as in group work settings (Barber and Crisp 1995) and was recently committed to a self-help manual format (Barber 2002). In all of these forms, randomized controlled trials have shown PTC to be more successful than no-treatment or Al-Anon in coaxing previously resistant users into therapy. PTC has also been shown to improve the morale and coping skills of the drinker's friend or partner in the process. Depending on format, PTC requires between one (self-help format) and six (group format) sessions.

PTC is a didactic treatment approach that suggests to those who are adversely affected by someone else's drug abuse that while they are not responsible for the behavior, this need not mean that they are powerless to do anything about it. Thus, PTC is like Al-Anon (Al-Anon 1984) in insisting to family members that they must not blame themselves but is radically different from Al-Anon in its efforts to train family members as change agents. More specifically, PTC has three fundamental objectives. (1) It aims to provide family members and close associates of substance users with a greater measure of control over their lives and their relationship with the user. (2) The program explicitly aims to change the user's consumption habits. (3) PTC aims to bring the user into treatment.

PTC applies five levels of pressure on the user. The levels are arranged hierarchically from least to most assertive, and family members are encouraged to move from one level to the next if it becomes apparent that more pressure is needed. Each level is accompanied by a set of structured activities to be tried in the period between sessions. Family members can pause at any level if they have achieved their objective or if they do not feel comfortable proceeding further. In this context, it is worth noting that PTC goes to considerable lengths to ensure that female clients are safe from the prospect of domestic violence. All clients are carefully assessed on intake and referred to domestic violence services where there is either a history of violence in the relationship or where the client judges that PTC could place her in a dangerous situation.

The first level of pressure in PTC is *Information and Preparation*. At this point in the program, the client is presented with standardized instruments assessing his or her level of dependence and the effect of the user's behavior on the client. The primary purpose of this part of the procedure is to validate the client's experience and to maximize motivation for treatment by having the client review all of the ways his or her life is being diminished by the user. Level 1 also includes an outline of the stages of change described above and prepares the client for the possibility that initial progress toward moderation or abstinence by the user may be followed by relapse. As previously suggested, this is true even for individuals who successfully overcome their addiction and is therefore not necessarily a sign that the strategy is failing. Finally, Level 1 introduces clients to the notion of environmental contingencies and explains that in future sessions, we will work together to identify aspects of the user's environment over which the client has control and we will explore ways of using this control to increase environmental pressure to change.

The second level of pressure is called *Incompatible Activities* and it asks the client to reflect on all of the benefits the user is deriving from drug use. This is often experienced by clients as an odd question because all they can see is the damage that drinking or drug-taking is doing. The turmoil wrought by drugs was, of course, recognized in Level 1, so PTC does not deny that drug use is harmful. Rather, the purpose of Level 2 is to demonstrate that users must be deriving some very highly valued benefits from their behavior to be prepared to suffer all of the consequences identified in Level 1. Once we know what those benefits are, we may be able to figure out alternative ways of achieving at least some of these ends without resorting to drugs. For example, the drinker who uses alcohol to relax or to deal with social anxiety can be trained in other forms of relaxation or assertiveness or can be encouraged to engage in behaviors that are incompatible with drinking but that partially deal with the problem, such as vigorous exercise or some other form of cognitive or behavioral distraction.

The third level of pressure is called *Responding* and it begins by requiring clients to go back over the most recent occasions when they witnessed the user drunk or high. By completing a "drug diary," the client identifies the precise day and time of day, and briefly describes the situation and, most importantly, the way the client responded at the time. This exercise also asks clients to reflect on the occasions when the user was *not* under the influence of drugs. PTC then asks the client how his or her own behavior differed in those two very different circumstances. This question often reveals to clients that they have become so familiar with the situation that their behavior is relatively unaffected by it. As a result, the drug user is neither rewarded for abstinence nor punished for drug abuse by the client's behavior. This exercise bridges into the next part of Level 3, which invites the client to reflect on all of the benefits the drug user derives from their relationship. What exactly does the user get out of the relationship? Why does the user remain in the relationship? When these benefits have been identified, treatment focuses on how these potential reinforcers can be provided contingently in future.

Level 3 also considers the question of how to respond when a crisis occurs. In PTC, a crisis is defined as any behavior by the user that is a matter of regret to users themselves and that is a direct or indirect result of their substance use. A user may embarrass him or herself, have a brush with the law, or hurt a loved one. Crises like these are always a possibility for drug abusers, of course, but the increasing pressure that Level 3 now brings to bear makes such occurrences even more likely. Clients are therefore coached in how to exploit such occasions to advance the user toward change.

Level 4 raises the pressure further by introducing the idea of *Contracting* consumption levels that are acceptable to the client. Up to this point, it has been possible for the client to employ strategies that have not necessarily required an explicit commitment from the user to cut down or stop. However, Level 4 pressure involves negotiating with the user to make a contract with the client about drug use in the coming week. This strategy increases the pressure because it commits the user to a specific behavioral target. The details of the contract will obviously vary according to client circumstances but the general principles are:

1. The contract should target a "high risk time" when it is highly likely that the user will use.
2. The contract should set a precise behavioral target, such as total abstinence or the number of standard drinks allowed.
3. The target behavior should be difficult but not impossible to achieve.
4. The contract should involve two parties, not just one. In other words, if the user agrees to certain limits, the client must be prepared to offer something in exchange. Since PTC invested considerable effort in identifying potential reinforcers during Level 3, what the client has to offer in exchange is normally quite clear by this stage.

Once a contract has been made, there are only two possible outcomes: either the contract will be honored or it will not be. If the user honors the contract, he or she will have overcome a high-risk situation and started the process of change. This places the client in a position to negotiate a new contract for the week or month ahead. Conversely, if the user breaks the contract, it will precipitate a minor crisis of the kind referred to in Level 3 and the client has by now a carefully rehearsed strategy for dealing with such crises.

Level 5 pressure is called *Involving Others*, and, as its name suggests, it encourages clients to extend the principles they have been using to others in the users' social network. Clients are instructed to select only those individuals who satisfy all of the following criteria:

1. The person must have the love and respect of the user.
2. The person must care deeply about the user.
3. The person must be capable of understanding and applying the foregoing PTC strategies.
4. The person must have ample opportunity to interact with the user.

With the help of the PTC self-help manual (Barber 2002), clients are assisted to train such individuals in PTC techniques so that the user will be exposed to a consistent reinforcement regimen. If after some weeks of pursuing a concerted strategy the user's behavior is still unaffected, the client is coached in the use of "personal statements." Personal statements are essentially letters that are read or delivered to the user by all of those now involved in the PTC procedure. The letters are in three parts:

1. A simple and sincere expression of the author's love or affection for the user
2. A description, with examples, of the ways in which drug use is diminishing the relationship
3. A gentle but firm request for the user to do something about his or her drug use

At its most confronting, the personal statement strategy involves calling a meeting between the user and all of the authors and having each participant read their letters one by one. As previously indicated, PTC is designed so that clients can stop raising the pressure at any point where they judge that sufficient progress has been achieved or where they feel too uncomfortable to proceed. In our clinical experience to date, we have encountered very few clients who have been willing to proceed to this final point with PTC of publicly reading personal statements.

In controlled trials of PTC, we have found that approximately two-thirds of the precontemplators exposed to the procedure will eventually agree to attend at least one interview at a specialist drug treatment facility (Barber and Crisp 1995; Barber and Gilbertson 1996, 1998). Clearly, such individuals often attend only under sufferance but for those who by then have any misgivings at all about their drug use, the motivational interviewing technique referred to earlier is the best supported technique currently available. For drug users who remain in opposition, however, I have proposed an alternative technique known as "negotiated casework" (Barber 1991, 1995).

Negotiated Casework with Resistant Drug Users

In the case of individuals who enter treatment resentfully, either because of environmental pressures like those described above or because of legal sanction, there are obviously formidable obstacles to the therapeutic alliance necessary for change. Generally speaking, social workers engaged in casework with involuntary clients have three broad practice options open to them. The first, and because of our current practice models, most common approach is to seek to bury the political dimension of the work and avoid conflict wherever possible (see Barber 1991). Against all the odds, workers committed to this approach will try to create an atmosphere of affirmation and warmth. Such workers are likely to feel uncomfortable, even apologetic, about the external pressures on the client and will make various concessions in an effort to reduce client hostility. I have referred to the strategy of trying to buy cooperation in this way as "casework through concessions" (Barber 1991) and the fundamental problem with the approach is that it fails to acknowledge the inherent conflict between worker and involuntary client. A second and antithetical casework option can be referred to as "casework by oppression," under which the worker accepts, even embraces, the conflict and fights hard to ensure that the worker's own terms are complied with. From the outset, the worker lays down the law about what will happen if the client does not change. As described earlier in this book, workers who adopt such a stance undermine the prospect of change by creating reactance in the client, which has the paradoxical effect of buttressing the client's resistance to change. I have called the third option "negotiated casework" in an effort to convey the idea that it is possible to achieve some degree of client empowerment and thereby to maximize the prospect of lasting change while also acknowledging that the client is constrained. The technique is intended for clients who attend treatment only because of environmental pressures like those described earlier or because of court orders like those frequently imposed on parents whose children have been taken into care.

Negotiated casework involves six discrete steps (see Barber 1991, 1995 for a fuller description with case examples):

Step 1: Clear the air. When an individual attends for treatment because he or she feels she or she has no choice, the worker's communications are likely to be filtered through a haze of mistrust, suspicion, and hostility. This haze must be cleared away and channels of communication opened up for any progress to be made. To begin the process, the worker needs to direct the client's attention to the factors that have brought them together. Where applicable, it can be useful to bring a copy of a court order to the first meeting, for example, and read it through with the client, or to discuss openly the external pressures that have forced him or her into treatment. This step not only sets the terms of the relationship but it also reminds both parties of the external forces that are ultimately responsible for the limits placed on the worker's and the client's behavior. While the worker should anticipate, even invite, some expression of antipathy in the early stages, it is important that the conflict not be allowed to degenerate into a personal dispute between the two parties. In a very real sense, the worker's role is to negotiate a settlement between the client and external parties; it is not a dispute between the worker and the client. This is not to suggest that the worker should apologize for their work or seek to dispense with client resentment by hiding behind external parties. Indeed, after restating the terms of the work, the worker should openly acknowledge the ambiguity of the relationship and invite the client's reaction. Where appropriate, this can also mean that the worker expresses his or her own discomfort in the relationship. Step 1 of the negotiated casework procedure involves setting the stage for a negotiated settlement by restating the order under which the work is being conducted, encouraging the client to air his or her feelings about the situation, and allowing the worker to emerge as a real and active participant in the problem: one who is in the position of mediator between the external parties and the client.

Step 2: Identify legitimate client interests. When client and worker have expressed their feelings about the situation, the negotiation process can proceed to the next stage, that of identifying the reasons for client resistance to treatment. The ultimate aim of this step is to list the legitimate client interests that appear to be threatened by treatment. Thus, the focus of attention is not so much what needs to be achieved before treatment can be terminated, as what lies behind the client's objection to treatment in the first place. Very often, the difficulty experienced by workers treating involuntary clients arises because treatment plans are decided upon prematurely. When the worker can see only one treatment objective (e.g., total abstinence) or only one treatment strategy, the major task ahead can only be to ensure client compliance. However, although there will often be some non-negotiable components of intervention, there is usually some part of the treatment plan that is open to negotiation, and much of the art of involuntary work boils down to creating as much freedom of choice as possible within the limits that apply. To avoid foreclosing on the intervention plan, then, the worker needs to know with considerable clarity just what the client stands to lose through involvement in treatment. In the beginning, this may not be clear even to clients themselves, who can be so preoccupied with the fact that they are being constrained that they fail to explore how their lives are actually being diminished. The general rule here is always to look behind the client's opposition and focus instead on the interests that they are fighting to protect. Clearly, the most fundamental interest being threatened is the client's right to self-determination and, just as clearly, this is a legitimate interest that the worker must not only acknowledge but also take seriously when formulating treatment plans. As well as this fundamental objection to involuntarism itself, there will often be a number of secondary interests that are under threat. Secondary objections could include not wanting to be labeled a junkie, for example, or not having access to child care. Once again, these are legitimate objections that need to be identified and integrated into the case plan.

Step 3: Identify negotiable aspects of the treatment plan. Whereas step 2 in negotiated casework involved opening up possibilities for case planning, the next step involves the honest acknowledgment of any constraints that apply. As previously suggested, specific treatment objectives may be mandated by a court, or non-negotiable terms may be laid out by an employer or partner. Whatever these non-negotiables are, they must now be identified and worker and client need to agree on precisely what conditions are not open to negotiation by them. It is important to note that this step is not always as straightforward as it might appear at first. Since workers can frequently see only one way of executing an official directive, they may consign more to the realm of non-negotiable than is justified. For example, the non-negotiable component of a child protection order may be merely that the client enters treatment; everything else including time, place, method, and frequency could potentially be negotiated. Despite this, workers and clients often draw preemptive conclusions about what is implicit in court orders. For this reason, it is imperative that both parties be prepared to question their interpretations of all treatment conditions and come to agreement on what constitutes the "bottom line." The aim of the exercise is twofold. First it sets the inevitable limits of negotiation and so prevents the kind of self-destructive "casework by concessions" approach referred to earlier. Second, by examining and eliminating needless assumptions about what is implied in each clause of an order or ultimatum, the process of empowering the involuntary client gets underway.

Step 4: Identify potentially negotiable aspects of intervention. Having agreed on the non-negotiable components of treatment and so set the parameters within which compromise is possible, the next step is to identify all possible clauses in the case plan whose negotiation can be left to the worker and client. The skills required to complete this task successfully are the antithesis of those required in step 3. Whereas in step 3 worker and client are engaged in a process of careful definition requiring precision, attention to detail and careful scrutiny of presuppositions, step 4 requires creativity and imagination as well. Worker and client now think as broadly as they can about the situation in an effort to generate as many life domains as possible over which the client can exercise some freedom of choice. To achieve this, it can be useful to employ a structured problem-solving technique, such as the "brainstorming" procedure described by D'Zurilla and Goldfried (1971) and by Rawlinson (1970).

Step 5: Construct the case plan. The next step in the negotiation process is where the details of the treatment plan are decided upon. The aim is to combine all the negotiable components of the plan identified in step 3 with the non-negotiable components identified in step 2. By the end of step 3, all that has been agreed is what is potentially negotiable in the treatment plan. No decisions have yet been made about the terms of the agreement itself. Thus, for example, step 3 would conclude when client and worker agree that time, place, method, and frequency of contact are all potentially negotiable aspects of the treatment plan. Now, in step 5, the aim is to make decisions about all these issues. To facilitate the process it can be useful if a written list of client interests has been produced during step 2 of the negotiation. This list can now be used to guide decisions about specific clauses of the intervention plan.

Step 6: Agree on methods for monitoring progress. Although it might seem obvious that worker and client should agree on what they will accept as sufficient progress to justify renegotiating and perhaps even terminating their relationship, it is surprising how frequently this step is overlooked. Conversely, until there is a crisis it is common for workers to ignore the issue of what should be done if the client breaches one of the terms of the agreement. Such oversights on the worker's part make it likely that the worker will resort to unilateral action when and if treatment gets into trouble. Inevitably, the end result of such action will be bitterness on the client's part as they would rightly see this as a denial of all the principles of negotiation that had been professed up to now. It is essential, therefore, that a negotiated treatment plan incorporate specific criteria for monitoring progress. Before intervention begins, worker and client should discuss each aspect of the plan and decide on how it can be monitored. How will we know that intervention is working? How much progress is enough? What should happen if the client fails to comply with one or more of the terms negotiated? Such questions must be asked at this point and detailed, behaviorally specific answers must be found.

The procedures involved in negotiated casework are designed to maximize client power in the involuntary casework relationship and to satisfy as many of the client's legitimate interests as possible. Nevertheless, the very concept of negotiation presupposes that not all client interests can be met fully. For the client as well as the worker, some concessions are inevitable. In step 5, we looked at the need to assess fairness in negotiated settlements, but where it is not possible to attain a result which is satisfactory to the client, the worker may resort to bargaining to prevent negotiations from breaking down entirely. For example, the child protection worker might compensate the client attending treatment by agreeing to increase contact visits with children in care or to work on another problem that the client is keen to resolve. Despite the worker's best efforts, however, there will always be some clients who steadfastly refuse to work toward a negotiated settlement. Such individuals cannot get past their hostility at having to submit to treatment and will simply restate their opposition despite efforts to direct attention to the interests underlying their hostility. In such cases, the worker can embark on steps 3 to 6 in the presence of the client but without the benefit of client input. Thus, with the client sitting through the process, the worker can identify all the non-negotiable and negotiable aspects of the case plan, construct the plan and decide on procedures for monitoring progress. More often than not, the process of thinking aloud through these steps will be enough to entice the client into negotiating. But where even this tactic fails to engage the client, at least the worker will have demonstrated a willingness to negotiate and a desire to take account of the client's right to influence the terms of the relationship.

The principles involved in working with precontemplative substance users can, of course, be extended to any client who is an involuntary recipient of social work intervention. In the final analysis, people become involuntary clients because a behavior or set of behaviors is unacceptable to others, whether that behavior be substance abuse, domestic violence, or dangerous psychotic behavior, for example. And by definition, it is these "others"—the state or subjectively important individuals—not the involuntary client, who sees the need for change. In view of social work's stated commitment to self-determination and anti-oppressive practice (NASW 1999), many social workers will feel uncomfortable being an instrument of the state or another person's desire to prevail over another. Just as surely, however, such work must be done if the self-determination of others is to be protected. Taken together, Pressures to Change and Negotiated Casework are procedures for empowering others to set limits on the suffering they will endure from precontemplators, while seeking to maximize the precontemplator's freedom within limits. And freedom within limits is all that is available to anyone who lives a social existence.

Practical Exercises and Discussion Questions

1. With the help of a child protection worker, either construct or obtain an example of a court order compelling a drug-addicted parent to receive treatment before a child is released from care. Use this scenario to role play a negotiated settlement according to the steps described in this chapter.
2. Can you think of other behaviors to which the Pressures to Change procedure could be applied? Construct a PTC case plan around one such behavior.

Chapter 11

Bringing Up What They Don't Want to Talk About: Use of Brief Motivational Interviewing with Adolescents Regarding Health-Related Behaviors in Opportunistic and Other Settings

Melinda Hohman and Chris Kleinpeter

Frequently, social workers and other practitioners encounter adolescents in a variety of settings, including schools, medical clinics, emergency rooms, or drop-in counseling centers. Often these settings provide an opportunity to screen for and address high-risk health-related behaviors. These settings are identified as "opportunistic" in that the client may actually be requesting services for some other problem or concern (Heather 1998). While clients may not necessarily be considered involuntary, the social worker may utilize this as a chance to address sensitive topics.

Motivational Interviewing (MI) is a technique that aims to encourage people to commit to goals for change, which was originally developed for engaging substance abusers in treatment (Miller and Rollnick 2002). Evidence for the effectiveness of MI has accrued with meta-analysis of treatment outcomes supporting its use, both as a stand alone treatment and a prelude to more intensive interventions, particularly for alcohol and drug use (Burke, Arkowitz, and Menchola 2003; Vasilanki, Hosier, and Cox 2006).

Brief Intervention Therapies

Brief interventions are specific, structured interventions that are provided to clients in typically one to five sessions (Bien, Miller, and Tonigan 1993). They are often indicated for those with mild or moderate problems, allowing the individual to change his or her problem behavior through specific strategies. Clients may also be motivated to seek further in-depth treatment, if that is indicated (CSAT 1999; Miller, Turner, and Marlatt 2001).

Brief interventions have been found to be beneficial to clients, including adolescents (Dunn, DeRoo, and Rivara 2001). Their advantages include that they can be implemented in the client's setting or environment, that clients do not have to have an investment or desire to change, and that lifelong change is not required. Furthermore, clients can set their own change goals and take responsibility for achieving those goals (Miller 2001; Monti, Colby, and O'Leary 2001). Brief interventions are also a way to reach those who would not typically present themselves for treatment (Barnett, Monti, and Wood 2001; McCambridge and Strang 2004).

Because brief interventions are often conducted in opportunistic settings, their overall goals may be to raise the awareness of a problem and to motivate the client to either change the behavior or seek treatment (CSAT 1999). Miller and Sanchez (1993) use the acronym FRAMES to define the elements of brief interventions for alcohol problems: (1) *F*eedback of personalized assessment results; (2) *R*esponsibility for change resides with the client; (3) clients may be given *A*dvice about change; (4) this advice can include a *M*enu of options; (5) Counselor use of *E*mpathy and nonjudgmental listening allows clients to think about options; and (6) counselor's support of client's *S*elf-efficacy to change provides encouragement. CSAT (1999) recommends that this outline be implemented in five steps, particularly in opportunistic settings: (1) introduce the behavior in the context of the client's health; (2) assess and evaluate the behavior; (3) provide feedback to the client about the behavior; (4) discuss possible changes and set goals; and (5) summarize and close.

Motivational Interviewing

Motivational Interviewing (MI) is defined as "a client-centered, directive method for enhancing intrinsic motivation to change by exploring and resolving ambivalence" (Miller and Rollnick 2002:25). MI posits that clients are ambivalent about making behavioral changes and may become stuck in negative behaviors, such as substance use or high-risk sex activities, because it is difficult to imagine making the necessary behavioral changes. Motivation to make changes, in the positive direction, comes from an interaction between a client and counselor whereby the discrepancy in desired values and actual behaviors is highlighted. Clients are encouraged to participate in "change-talk" (Miller and Rollnick 2002) in that they are the ones to discuss the benefits of changes for themselves. Clients who receive support and encouragement to make changes that they have selected are more likely to follow through.

MI is also described as a "style," not a mixture of techniques (Miller and Rollnick 2002). Social workers are to respectfully understand the client's view of the problem, and do this by using open-ended questions, listening reflectively, and avoiding arguments with the client or becoming directive or confrontational. The directiveness of the intervention comes in what the social worker chooses to reflect back to the client, highlighting client ambivalence and discrepancies in behavior and values, for instance. The social worker continually assesses the stage of change of the client, based on the transtheoretical model (Prochaska, DiClemente, and Norcross 1992). Change is not to be pressed for prematurely but only as the client begins to move in that direction. Clients are continually reminded that only they can make the choices for change, however, the social worker's task is to support self-efficacy to make these changes.

Brief Motivational Interviewing with Adolescents

MI, and particularly brief motivational interventions, may be particularly appropriate for work with adolescents. MI addresses the stage of change of the client, not making assumptions that the client is interested in changing, as is often the case with skill-based interventions (Barnett, Monti, and Wood 2001). Adolescents, when compared with adults, have been found to have lower levels of motivation to change substance use behavior (Melnick et al. 1997). MI is not confrontational, and social workers treat clients as "partners" in the change process, thus avoiding power struggles that adolescents have experienced in their other interactions with adults, particularly regarding high-risk behaviors. Acknowledging ambivalence about changing as well as choices about change helps to give adolescents support for their own autonomy (Baer and Peterson 2002; Tevyaw and Monti 2004).

Brief interventions for adolescents that have been implemented, with the use of a Motivational Interviewing approach have at least six components: (1) the client receives personalized feedback from assessment instruments; (2) the client, in discussion with the social worker, interprets the feedback; (3) the client is provided information by the social worker; (4) the client is asked to envision the future with and without the behavior change; (5) the client establishes a plan that includes strategies for making the behavior change; and 6) the client is asked to anticipate and plan for barriers in the change process (Monti, Colby, and O'Leary 2001; Miller and Rollnick 2002). Other variations of this model that have recently been tested have included the addition of hypothetical situations if the client was not ready to address risky behaviors and/or the use of some sort of decisional balance (McCambridge and Strang 2003).

The following sections provide is a literature review of empirical work regarding health-related brief motivational interviewing (BMI) with adolescents.

Tobacco

Stephens (2001) utilized a brief motivational intervention with adolescent smokers. High school students were recruited from a teen tobacco court in Pocatello, Idaho, and were asked to participate in this study. Fifty-six teens were randomly assigned to one of three conditions: to the Adolescent Smoking Check Up (ASCU), to an educational group that provided information and discussions on smoking, or to a waiting list. Measures included smoking quantity/frequency, motivation to quit smoking, and abstinence self-efficacy. Those in the ASCU were also given a forced vital capacity lung function test. Social workers met with the students in the ASCU condition on an individual basis, to provide feedback (one session) and to complete a decision-making matrix (second session). Results indicated that those in the ASCU cut their number of cigarettes smoked per day in half, while those in the educational group increased their smoking. Adolescents in the ASCU condition also increased their self-efficacy scores to quit and to maintain abstinence as well as their motivation to change.

Colby and her colleagues (1998) found that adolescent smoking could be reduced through a brief motivational intervention in an opportunistic setting—a hospital emergency room. Adolescents who were being treated for various health reasons and had smoked in the past thirty days were recruited to participate, and were randomly assigned to the brief motivational intervention or to a brief advice condition. Those in the brief motivational intervention were given an individualized assessment of their smoking and received a half-hour interview that focused on feedback of the assessment data, along with a discussion on the consequences of smoking, advice, and encouragement, and a setting of goals for abstinence. The patients were followed up at three months, and it was found that those who received the BMI were more likely to report smoking abstinence over the past seven days as compared to those in the advice condition.

Not all brief interventions need to be conducted in a face-to-face interview. Woodruff and colleagues (2001) provided a brief motivational intervention for teens located at six rural school sites through a virtual world chat room. Teens "chatted" with a smoking counselor for one hour per week over a seven-week period. Pre- and post-measures (one month follow up) were compared, and it was found that the subjects made significant changes in quitting, intentions to quit, and the amount smoked.

Substance Use

Walker, Roffman, and Stephens (2004) have developed the Teen Marijuana Check-Up II, which is based on the Drinker's-Check-Up (Miller, Sovereign, and Krege 1988) and the Marijuana Check-Up (Stephens et al. 2004), both for adults. The project targets teens who are not seeking help for their marijuana use but may be interested in discussing it. Participants from four high schools are recruited through an educational class on marijuana or through ads and posters. Students may also be referred to the project through a teacher or parent. Interested adolescents are informed about the study and are screened for eligibility. Those who are eligible are randomly assigned to either the intervention group or the delayed treatment control group. Subjects complete an assessment regarding their use of substances, the positive and negative consequences of their use, attitudes that support and are a barrier to change, barriers or supports to changing marijuana use, and goals for the future.

Two feedback sessions are held after the assessment. The counselor provides an individualized feedback report that is reviewed with the adolescent. Using motivational strategies, the counselor elicits and reinforces reasons for change. If the adolescent is interested in change, the counselor works with him or her to set goals and change strategies. Each session lasts about one hour. Follow-up assessments are held at three months. The data gathered include the adolescents' substance use, including marijuana, positive and negative consequences of use or nonuse, and if any help-seeking behavior was implemented. Almost 100 teens participated and initial results indicated both the intervention and the control group reduced marijuana use at the three-month follow-up, particularly if they had initially been assessed to be in a later stage of change. Those who were initially assessed to be in an early stage of change and were in the intervention group were more likely to decrease their use when compared to those in the control group.

McCambridge and Strang (2004) tested the efficacy of a single session of motivational interviewing with 200 late adolescents (ages sixteen to twenty) who were multiple substance users. Half were seen for a brief intervention by a trained peer counselor and the other half received education-as-usual. Participants were students at Further Education colleges in England, which are described as "non-traditional educational and training institutions for those of postcompulsory schooling age" (McCambridge and Strang 2004:41). These students had to have used marijuana or stimulants at least weekly for the prior three months. For the intervention, participants were asked to fill out questionnaires regarding their drug use. They were then presented with a menu of topics that could be discussed. Typically their range of drug use was discussed as were their concerns or areas of risk. Participants were asked to discuss the benefits and negatives of their use along with risks and ideas of options for change. If students decided to make a change, change plans were discussed. Results indicated that those who received the MI approach were more likely to reduce their use of tobacco, cannabis, and alcohol, as compared to those who received the educational component. The effect was greatest among the heaviest drug and tobacco users.

Baer, Peterson, and Wells (2004) conducted a study of the use of BMI in an outreach to homeless youth who were substance abusers. The researchers felt that MI may be effective with street youth who are less likely to be engaged in traditional counseling settings and may be more open to harm reduction efforts, not substance use cessation. Through their Project STARRS (Street Teen Alcohol Risk Reduction Study) outreach was made to homeless teens who were not interested in treatment to participate in a research study. The intervention produced mixed results (Baer, Peterson, and Wells 2004).

While the intervention model followed the steps outlined earlier regarding brief interventions, the researchers discovered several areas that they needed to modify. These modifications are now being implemented in the STARRS II study. These included the need to make the assessment briefer, that polysubstance use must be assessed, and more than one single intervention session utilized to facilitate engagement. Because it was hard for the youth to sit through a longer feedback session, feedback sessions have been shortened and increased to four twenty-minute sessions. Finally, because of the multitude of services that were needed by street youth, the intervention sessions are now given in the context of a social service agency to facilitate linkage. Current evaluation of pilot data from the STARRS II study shows reduction in thirty-day substance use.

Alcohol

Marlatt and colleagues (1998) utilized BMI in a sample of college students. Students completed assessment information regarding their alcohol use and received individualized feedback that included a comparison of their drinking with normative college student drinking. Expectancies regarding the effects of drinking were discussed as well. Subjects were also assessed again at six and twelve months. At the end of the twelve months, they were mailed individualized feedback reports. Those who were classified as high-risk drinkers received a telephone call that utilized a motivational approach, offering further contact and encouraging drinking reduction. Outcomes from this study found that both groups decreased their consumption of alcohol, however, the intervention group was significantly different from the control group in the decrease of alcohol-related consequences.

Adolescents (thirteen to nineteen years) who were seen in either a pediatric or adult emergency room for an alcohol-related problem were recruited to participate in a study of their alcohol use (Barnett, Monti, and Wood 2001). Patient assessment measures included alcohol consumption, alcohol-related injuries, other alcohol-related problems, risk-taking behavior, readiness to change drinking behavior, pros and cons of drinking, depression, and demo-graphic information. Once assessed, patients were randomly assigned to either the motivational interviewing condition or to standard hospital care. The standard care group received educational information regarding alcohol use and a referral list of local treatment agencies.

The motivational interview was divided into five components. In the first part, the adolescents were asked to discuss the event that brought them to the emergency room, with the counselor emphasizing the nonjudgmental aspect of the interview. In the second component, the adolescents were asked to describe pros and cons of drinking and drinking and driving, in order to assess his or her Stage of Change. Subjects were also asked to describe family and friends' attitudes toward drinking and drinking and driving. In the third part of the interview, the adolescents reviewed a computer-generated feedback form of the assessment data with the counselor. Data reviewed include own alcohol use compared to social norms and blood alcohol content, with educational information regarding impact on behavior and metabolism, to identify misperceptions regarding tolerance. Normative information regarding alcohol-related consequences is also compared with the adolescents' own personal consequences.

Next, adolescents were asked to imagine the future if their drinking were to stay the same and if it were to decrease. In the last phase, the adolescents identified goals for behavior change while exploring barriers to the change.

The subjects received follow-up interviews at three and six months post-ER visit. Both groups had reduced their drinking at the three-month interview. At six months, those in the motivational interviewing intervention group were, however, significantly less likely to report drinking and driving as compared to the control group. Injuries and alcohol-related injuries were reported significantly less by the intervention group at six months.

In a similar study, Johnston and colleagues (Johnston et al. 2002) conducted brief twenty-minute motivational sessions with 300 injured adolescents in an emergency room, who were randomly assigned to either the intervention or standard emergency room care. Six high-risk health behaviors were addressed: binge drinking, driving after drinking, riding with a driver who had been drinking, not wearing seat belts, not wearing bike helmets, and carrying a weapon. Subjects were contacted at three and six months post injury. At six months, those who had received the brief intervention were more likely to wear seat belts and bike helmets than those in the control group.

High-Risk Sexual Behavior

To date, no studies regarding the use of BMI with adolescents for reducing high-risk sex behavior has been reported in the literature, however, there has been some work with conceptual applications (Brown and Lourie 2001). Effective interventions for adolescents at risk for HIV have included an attempt to increase perceived susceptibility to HIV, to enhance favorable attitudes toward condom use, to build social skills, and to improve self-efficacy (Kalichman, Carey, and Johnson 1996). Motivational interviewing techniques attempt to increase the adolescent's perception of the risks associated with unsafe sexual behaviors and explore the barriers to behavior change (Tober 1991). An approach that matches the intervention to the adolescent's readiness for change makes the application of motivational techniques to sexual behavioral change particularly relevant (Schultz, Brown, and Butler 1996). The goal of the motivational approach among sexually active adolescents is not sexual abstinence but rather, taking a harm reduction approach aimed at reducing unprotected sex (Baker and Dixon 1991). This empathetic approach sets the groundwork for increasing perceived susceptibility by illustrating the incongruence between the adolescent's stated desire for safety and actual risky actions (Brown and Lourie 2001). Techniques for increasing perceived susceptibility include (1) open-ended questions, (2) affirming language, (3) reframing, and (4) a menu of strategies.

Cowley, Farley, and Beamis (2002) combined MI with Narrative therapy for a brief intervention with forty adolescent females to discuss contraceptive use. The participants in the study had presented to a reproductive health clinic seeking health services. They were considered high-risk for early childbearing as they were ambivalent about contraception or had positive attitudes toward pregnancy. The authors indicated that the use of MI may be particularly beneficial for this group of teens as they are not particularly interested in receiving information on contraception and family planning, which is the typical intervention. BMI, as used in this study, asked the adolescents to determine their goals within the context of their lives and to think through the benefits and concerns of pregnancy and of postponing pregnancy. The teens also received feedback of their current health status and their probability of getting pregnant in the months ahead. While this was not an outcome study of the efficacy of BMI, it was found that 38 percent of the adolescents decided to use some sort of hormonal birth control, and did so for an average of four months.

Case Vignette

While the use of BMI has not been studied with eating disorders in adolescents, this is an area of health behavior change where it may also have an impact. Eating disorders in adolescents are characterized by issues of power and control (Rose and Fatout 2003). BMI is nonjudgmental and does not seek to change or persuade a client to change behaviors but attempts to motivate clients by addressing their ambivalence.

The following dialogue is set in a general hospital emergency room where a fifteen-year-old female has been brought in by ambulance for passing out. Her mother found her unconscious in the bathroom and called for help. She has been examined by the medical team and it has been determined that she has low potassium levels and indication of self-induced vomiting. The preliminary diagnosis is Bulimia. The social worker has been asked to do a psychosocial evaluation and determine the best treatment option for this adolescent.

SOCIAL WORKER: Hello Susan. I am a social worker here. My name is Maria. I have been asked to meet with you by the medical team to discuss your situation and find out more about what happened that led to your hospitalization. Would you share with me what happened this morning? (Greeting and introduction; open with a general question.)

SUSAN: (Sighs.) I really don't know what happened to me. I woke up on the bathroom floor and my Mom had called 911 because she was scared. I had been sick and was vomiting before I passed out. (Problem exploration; gain understanding and definition of the problem from the client's point of view.)

SOCIAL WORKER: That must have been very frightening to you also. I have the results of your medical tests; would you like me to share with you what the doctors have learned so far? (Gain client's permission to offer information and direction for the conversation.)

SUSAN: Ok, I guess.

SOCIAL WORKER: See this number here on the report? It means you have a low potassium level, which can cause the passing out. It usually happens when people have a great deal of vomiting or diarrhea and can be very serious. In some cases it can lead to a heart attack or even death. What do you make of this? (Provide feedback from assessment and ask the client for his/her interpretation of the results.)

SUSAN: Well, I had used some medication that day in hopes of losing weight. It causes me to get very sick, but yesterday I lost about 5 pounds when I took it. I need to lose about 10 pounds, so I thought that if I could take it two days in a row I could lose the weight I need to lose. . . . Maybe I should have waited another day or so before I took it again. But it hasn't really been that big of a deal in the past. (Client interprets the feedback.)

SOCIAL WORKER: The medication was used for weight loss, you haven't had problems with it before, however this time it caused a serious health risk in your case. Can I ask you, when you look ahead in the future, what do you see happening to you should you stop using medication for weight loss? (Client is asked to envision the future without the current behavior.)

SUSAN: (Makes a face.) Oh boy! I would get fat really fast without using the medication. I can't control my eating, so without the vomiting I would be huge! I am too big now, and that is with the medication. I can't even imagine how big I would be without it. No way could I not use it.

SOCIAL WORKER: You can't even imagine how you would control your weight without the medication and yet you have had a serious health complication by using the medication. That must be a very difficult problem to face. (Highlight the ambivalence; demonstrate empathy.)

SUSAN: You don't even know the half of it! I have always had trouble controlling my weight. I have been teased at school and am just not willing to get fat again. I have more friends now since I lost weight, and guys are now looking at me. If I gave up the medication, I would go back to being ignored, I would have no friends, and no boyfriends, that's for sure!

SOCIAL WORKER: And if you keep using the medication to control your weight, do you have any concerns about your future? (Explore the option of no change looking into the future; see if the client has concerns about the behavior.)

SUSAN: Yeh! I was really hurting this morning. The vomiting is very painful when it goes on so long. I also felt so worried that my family would find out. Well, they certainly did this time and it has freaked my mother out. They don't know about the pills. They just think I lost weight by dieting. I knew that they would be upset with me if they knew I was taking pills to throw up. My friends would be grossed out if they knew. I don't want anyone to find out about this.

SOCIAL WORKER: It must have been very hard to keep a secret like this one, and worry that if anyone knew they would disapprove. On one hand you want to lose weight, and on the other hand you need a method that will not make you sick or afraid that others will find out. (Reframe the problem and reflect ambivalence; validate her goal, explore other methods of obtaining her goal.)

SUSAN: Well, maybe . . . If I could find another way of dieting that would work for me, I would try it. I don't want to be fat, but I am scared that if I keep taking the pills they will make me pass out or worse in the future. I am really tired of this secret too. It makes me feel guilty to keep this from my Mom and best friend.

SOCIAL WORKER: Sometimes people who come here for this kind of problem go to a treatment program to get some help. There are treatment programs to address just what you are struggling with. Would you like information on how to get help with this problem? (Offer information; don't tell client what to do.)

SUSAN: Yes, sort of. I just don't know how I am going to tell my mother about this.

At this point in the dialogue, the client has become open to advice about referrals for treatment. The social worker would then work with her and her family toward choosing a treatment option that would be best for her. The referrals are provided at her request. Using the BMI model, she must be the one to choose which treatment is best for her. The social worker offers referrals, but the final treatment decision is left to the client. The client chooses the goals and the treatment strategies in the BMI model. The client does not have to accept the label (i.e., Bulimic) in order to access treatment or to have positive treatment results. The therapeutic work is framed in terms of behavior changes that are desired by the client. The progress is measured by looking at where the client is currently, and where the client would like to go in terms of behavior changes outlined. The client and the social worker would also need to discuss barriers that might get in the way of entering and staying in treatment.

Discussion

Eating disorders have the potential to have a major impact on the health and well-being of adolescents. Youth with eating disorders are afraid of gaining weight (Rose and Fatout 2003). Disturbances in the perception of body size underlie the development of eating disorders. Adolescents who have anorexia nervosa eat too little and are put at risk for starvation. About 1 percent of adolescent girls and a small number of adolescent boys suffer from anorexia. In a twenty-year follow-up study of forty patients with long-standing illness, 63 percent recovered, 20 percent were still chronically ill, and 15 percent had died of anorexia (Ratnasuriya et al. 1991). A second long-term study that spanned thirty-three years reported a slightly higher death rate at 18 percent (Theander 1985).

Adolescents with bulimia nervosa eat too much food at one time and to prevent weight gain they get rid of the food by taking enemas or laxatives, exercising incessantly, and vomiting (Rose and Fatout 2003). Estimates are that about 2 percent of youngsters have bulimia nervosa. Providing mental and physical health care to adolescents involves the dual tasks of treating immediate health problems and influencing habits and life-style choices that will have far-reaching consequences throughout adulthood (Snyder 1989). MacKenzie (1991) views medical problems that develop as a result of eating disorders as situational expressions of maturational crises such as adolescence and young adulthood. In this view, eating disorders may be seen as a response to puberty that challenges the individual's sense of control. According to Miller and Carlton (1985), control is a central issue, with the power struggle projected onto food and fought with the family and within the self. Behaviors that underlie symptoms of disordered eating may serve an adaptive function that is viewed by the adolescent as a solution rather than a problem, making them very difficult to change (MacKenzie 1991).

MI may be helpful in the treatment of adolescents with eating disorders due to its nonconfrontational style of relationship, and focus on goals and treatment strategies that are chosen by the client. This approach may assist clients to feel more in control and less likely to engage the social worker in a power struggle. The exploration of ambivalence may be an important approach to demonstrate that the social worker appreciates the conflict that the client is experiencing. The resolution of ambivalence may be the key to making changes in eating behaviors.

Adolescents are often referred by others to get help and may be very angry with adults generally, and the source of the referral particularly (Rose and Fatout 2003). Exploring these feelings helps to open communication and begin to establish a helping relationship. The social worker may begin by exploring the adolescent's view of the problem or why he or she has been referred for help. Techniques for engaging adolescents in the helping process are to ask about a typical day in their life, and to encourage them to talk about their concerns even if they seem unrelated to the presenting problem. Allowing adolescents to make choices in the direction of the discussion gives them a sense of empowerment and autonomy. Broad treatment goals may be a place to begin, as the social worker and client gain a mutual understanding of the purpose and process of meeting. The social worker brings a body of knowledge, access to resources, methods, and skills of helping. The helping relationship serves as a context for treatment and as a dynamic element of treatment.

Opportunistic settings can be successfully used to address health-related concerns in adolescents. As has been demonstrated in this chapter, brief MI has been shown to be effective in motivating clients to reduce high-risk behavior and/or to seek out treatment services. BMI is nonthreatening to adolescents and allows them the choice to address behavior change. It may be used as a primary intervention, or in combination with other treatment approaches. BMI respects the client's right to self-determination by using the social worker's skill to assist clients through the decision-making process by helping clients to identify the positive and negative consequences of various alternatives.

Discussion Questions

1. What are some of your concerns about using opportunistic settings to discuss health-related behaviors with adolescent clients?
2. What might be some of the benefits that you see for using BMI with adolescents?
3. What might be some of the drawbacks?

Chapter 12

Work with Men in Domestic Abuse Treatment

Michael Chovanec

The purpose of this chapter is to introduce innovations in domestic abuse treatment that better engage men in the treatment process in an effort to reduce attrition and improve treatment effectiveness. First the extent of the problem is introduced. Next, I will make a link between domestic abuse treatment and involuntary clients. I will then review treatment effectiveness and influencing factors including methodological flaws, the attrition problem, and the use of the confrontational model. I will then apply innovations from Reactance Theory, Stages of Change, Motivational Interviewing, and the Caplan and Thomas Process model to domestic abuse treatment. Finally, I will present future treatment and research implications of these innovations.

Introduction to the Problem of Domestic Abuse

Domestic abuse is a social problem that impacts women and their families and the community. At least eight million women of all races and classes are battered by an intimate partner each year and current patterns predict that between 20 percent and 50 percent of women will be a victim of domestic abuse at some point in their lives (Roberts 1998). The National Institute of Justice found that domestic violence costs $67 billion per year in property damage, medical costs, mental health care, police and fire services, victim services, and lost worker productivity (Miller, Cohen, and Wiersema 1996).

Group work has traditionally been the treatment of choice to address this significant social problem (Healey, Smith, and O'Sullivan 1998) and is recommended by the majority of state standards (Austin and Dankwort 1999). By the mid-1980s approximately 195 programs had been developed (Pirog-Good and Stets-Kealey 1985). Group programs range from process oriented (Jennings 1987, 1990; Caplan and Thomas 1995, 2002, 2004; Stosny 1995; Dutton 2007) to the more structured approach, integrating cognitive behavioral, social learning, communication, and feminist theories (Edleson and Tolman 1992; Russell 1995; Babcock and Taillade 2000). The Duluth model, based on the psychoeducational program developed in Duluth, Minnesota (Pence and Paymar 1993; Pence and Shepard 1999), is probably the most widely applied in domestic abuse programs. The model defines abuse broadly to include emotional and economic abuse and the use of intimidation, coercion, and/or threats. The basic assumption is that men abuse women primarily to maintain power and control. The facilitator role includes holding men accountable for their abuse; keeping the group discussion on issues of violence, abuse, and control; and challenging, not colluding, with men's abusive belief system.

While this confrontational model has been the treatment of choice for addressing domestic violence, its effectiveness in addressing domestic violence has been challenged. Approximately 60 percent to 80 percent of program completers end their violent behavior and fewer reduce their threats and verbal abuse (Gondolf 1997b, 2004). However, methodology used to assess effectiveness has been questioned. In addition, high dropout rates of between 22 percent and 99 percent (Daly and Pelowski 2000) not only cloud the effectiveness issue but also create safety concerns for women whose partners are in domestic abuse treatment. Women often remain with partners who enroll in domestic abuse programs expecting them to complete the program and no longer abuse them (Gondolf 1988). Yet, dropouts are more likely to re-offend than program graduates, putting their partners in dangerous potentially abusive situations (Dutton 1986; Shupe, Stacey, and Hazelwood 1987; Edleson and Grusznski 1988; Palmer, Brown, and Barrera 1992; Gondolf 1997c).

Groups and Involuntary/Nonvoluntary Participation

Group facilitators have the daunting task of working with this population of men who at least initially are to some degree involuntary. Rooney (1992) breaks down involuntary clients into those who are formally mandated into programs through court orders and nonvoluntary clients that are pressured into attending. Men referred to domestic abuse treatment fit both categories. Court-ordered programs for domestic abuse have multiplied since the early

1980s (Ganley 1987; Gondolf 1991). Roberts (1982), in his national survey, reported that 66 percent of programs surveyed received 40 percent to 95 percent of referrals from a court system. In 1997, 136,000 men were arrested on charges of domestic violence with 86 percent ordered into counseling (Hagen 1998).

Other men are nonvoluntary clients. These men are not formally court-ordered; however, they are pressured to attend either by a partner threatening divorce, significant others pleading with them to get help, or professionals who influence their ability to access their family. In a qualitative study of men who had completed treatment, 90 percent had requested help only after their partner had left or had threatened to leave (Gondolf 1985). Thus, even if the potential client is not court-ordered, they encounter a variety of pressures to stop their abusive behaviors.

The visibility of involuntary status with domestic abuse clients varies depending on whether men are mandated or nonvoluntary. Men who are formally mandated into a program are visible to the practitioner and agency. Nonvoluntary men are less visible, with sources of pressure to attend unknown unless men are specifically asked about their pressures in the intake process.

Involuntary status is fluid as the client's perception of coercion changes over time. Court-ordered men whose involuntary status is most visible are more likely to be labeled as resistant to change, yet individual changes occur from the time of arrest to entering a domestic abuse program. For example, the court and/or jail experience can increase mens' motivation to change. O'Hare (1996) found that in a sample of court-ordered mental health clients, 28 percent were already making efforts to change their behavior. This is important information for group facilitators who can easily ignore these individuals if they have a static view of involuntary status. Identifying men who have progressed further in the change process are valuable resources, both for group facilitators who can support changes made and for other group members in the program who are struggling with the change process.

Effectiveness of Domestic Abuse Treatment

While outcome studies suggest high numbers of treatment completers ending physical abuse, methodological flaws and treatment attrition challenge the validity of these findings. Five published reviews of approximately thirty single-site evaluations reported approximately 60 percent to 80 percent of program completers end their violent behavior (Eisikovits and Edleson 1989; Tolman and Bennett 1990; Gondolf 1991, 1997a, 2004; Rosenfeld 1992).

Outcomes measures have included reduction in the conflict tactics scale as completed by participants, their partners, or both; post-treatment contact with police; and court records of posttreatment convictions. A variety of methodological flaws have been identified in these evaluations including low response rates (30 percent to 45 percent), self-report measures, short-term follow-up (generally six months), lack of control groups, and failure to account for intervening variables such as accounting for program dropouts (Gondolf 1997b).

A limited number of studies have attempted to address the lack of control groups in domestic abuse treatment evaluation, finding mixed results in regards to treatment effectiveness. Davis, Taylor, and Maxwell (1998) found significantly fewer re-arrests for a six-month program, but with no differences in victim reports of new abusive incidents between program participants and control group members. Palmer, Brown, and Barrera (1992) found significantly fewer re-arrests for the treatment group (10 percent) compared to the no-treatment controls (31 percent). Feder and Forde (2000) found no differences between program and controls in men's arrests, probation violations, attitudes, or male and female reports of abuse. The low numbers of women reporting partner abusive behavior and limited data on the partner's relationship with the man at follow-up weaken these studies. Also, dropouts in these experimental designs are considered part of the program, although they may have had either limited or no contact with the program.

Attrition, as mentioned earlier, is a major factor impacting the effectiveness of domestic abuse treatment. Gondolf and Foster (1991), examining attrition from initial contact to treatment completion, reported only 10 percent of men completing the program. In addition, court orders used to retain men in the treatment process report mixed results (Daly and Pelowski 2000). High rates of attrition, with dropouts left out of the outcome analysis, can seriously inflate treatment success.

While many studies examining attrition in domestic abuse treatment have focused on demographic variables, violence-related factors and client pathology, only a limited number of studies have examined men's level of motivation or commitment to attend (Daly and Pelowski 2000). DeMaris (1989) found that men who rated highly the importance of stopping their violent behavior were twice as likely to complete the program. Cadsky et al. (1996) found that men with higher treatment congruence, who were willing to report abusing their partner in the intake, were more likely to complete the program. A few qualitative studies have examined the change process from the men's perspective in domestic abuse treatment (Gondolf and Hanneken 1987; Pandya and Gingerich 2002; Brownlee and Chiebovec 2004; Silvergleid and Mankowski 2006). The strongest theme identified in all of these studies regarding individual changes men identify was the process of recognizing their abusive behavior and taking responsibility for it. Given the safety issue for partners whose men drop out of treatment, ways to better engage men in the treatment process needs to be part of the discussion on best practices in domestic abuse treatment.

Standard Confrontational Approaches Impact Attrition

Historically, due to safety concerns of the victims, batterer programs focused primarily on stopping physical abuse with little attention to the change process. The Duluth model focuses on confronting men's rationalizations and challenges them to acknowledge responsibility for their abusive behavior (Pence and Paymar 1993). While the goal of helping batterers to accept responsibility for their abusive behavior is common in most treatment programs, the means to accomplishing this goal is controversial.

While the effects of confrontation used in domestic abuse groups have not been researched, adverse effects can be found in other settings. Confrontational approaches were introduced in the chemical dependency field in the 1970s and 1980s (Thomas and Yoshioka 1989). Research in chemical dependency treatment support the use of empathic rather than confrontational interventions for successful outcomes (Miller 1985; Miller and Rollnick 2002). Lambert and Bergin (1994) found that clients most at risk of deterioration within group treatment were those with low self-esteem and impaired self-concepts. High-risk clients fit the description of many batterers (Hamberger and Hastings 1991; Dutton and Starzomski 1993). Personality disorders and men with history of severe child abuse are common in this population (Hamberger and Hastings 1989; Faulkner et al. 1991; DeHart et al. 1999; Hamberger, Lohr, and Gottlieb, 2000).

Using a confrontational approach without acknowledging clients' readiness for change limits engaging men in the treatment process. Murphy and Baxter (1997) question how well this confrontational approach supports the goals of safety and justice for battered women since research mentioned earlier suggests increased risk for partners whose men drop out of treatment.

The confrontational approach also calls into question what facilitators are modeling for abusive men when using confrontation to change behavior. With increased resistance to confrontations, the issues of power and control are more likely to be present between therapist and client. This mirrors the dynamics many men have grown up with who enter domestic abuse treatment and contradicts the goal of moving men from inequality in power and control to more equality in relationships (Pence and Paymar 1993).

Evidence for Best Practices

In recent years there has been a call for guidelines for empirically based treatment in clinical practice (Howard and Jenson 1999; Howard, Edmond, and Vaughn 2005). In domestic abuse, guidelines for best practices are in demand as states develop standards for treatment (Austin and Dankwort 1999). In the domestic abuse treatment literature, there is no empirical evidence to support greater effectiveness of one modality over another (Tolman and Bennett 1990; Saunders 1996; Gondolf 2000; Babcock, Green, and Robie 2004). However, variations in format appear to have some effect on treatment effectiveness. Groups offering more structure within a didactic format are more effective than didactic and discussion and self-help groups (Edleson and Syers 1989; Gondolf 1999). Also, short- and long-term treatments produce similar reductions in assault (Edleson and Syers 1989; Gondolf 1999).

Innovations in Domestic Abuse Treatment

Given the high attrition rates found in the literature, best practices need to include ways to better engage men in the treatment process in addition to abuse reduction. Several program components have been examined that have been found to reduce program attrition. Tolman and Bhosley (1987) and Brekke (1989) found the use of orientation groups reduced attrition. Stosny (1994) used a video in a domestic abuse program that dramatized spousal abuse from the perspective of a young boy, which significantly increased attendance and group participation.

A more systematic approach to examining the engagement process in domestic abuse treatment would include application of four key theories/practice models including reactance theory, stages of change, motivational interviewing, and the Thomas and Caplan Group Process model. These theories and practice models have yet to be examined as to their impact on attrition and reducing abuse. While more research is needed, practice knowledge suggests these theories and practice models deserve attention as potential best practices.

Reactance theory applied to domestic abuse treatment suggests that men court-ordered or pressured from others to attend have lost the freedom to leave treatment without negative consequences. The theory suggests that men court-ordered or pressured into a program should demonstrate high levels of reactance or motivational arousal that is presented through an array of predictable behaviors, that is, hostility toward group leader or passive participation (Brehm and Brehm 1981). Chovanec (1995) confirms the assumption of high levels of reactance in men entering a domestic abuse program. A variety of interventions have been suggested to either reduce or increase reactance with individuals (Rooney 1992; Norcross, Beutler, and Clarkin 1998) and more recently with groups (Rooney and Chovanec 2004). For example, acknowledging pressures men experience and providing choices in programming help to reduce reactance on entering a program.

Assessing reactance early in the treatment process has been found useful in engaging general practice clients early on in the treatment process and increasing the chances for successful outcomes (Prochaska et al. 1994; Beutler and Berren 1995; Beutler et al. 1996; Groth-Marnat 1997). However, little attention has been given in examining Reactance in the domestic abuse setting.

The Stages of Change model (Prochaska, Norcross, and DiClemente 1994; Norcross, Beutler, and Clarkin 1998) is another promising framework for addressing the attrition problem through examining the process of change men go through as they enter domestic abuse treatment.

Motivational Interviewing is another useful framework evolving out of the chemical dependency literature. The framework developed in work with chemical dependency clients who were opposed to entering treatment (Miller and Rollnick 2002). Resistance is reframed as ambivalence and explored with the client. For example, clients are asked to identify negative and positive consequences of changing their behavior. Client *self-motivating statements* toward change are identified and supported. If not elicited by the client, the worker initiates these statements through self-reflective questions asked the client.

The model has been combined with the stages of change and applied to work with domestic abuse clients. Daniels and Murphy (1997) point out that while most domestic abuse programs assume an unmotivated client who is coerced into treatment, the majority of domestic abuse treatment interventions work best with men who have accepted they have a problem and *want* to work on it. For example, in the Duluth model the facilitator role includes facilitating reflective and critical thinking, providing new information, and teaching noncontrolling relationship skills (Pence and Paymar 1993). Murphy and Baxter (1997) focus on the process men go through of weighing the pros and cons of changing their abusive behavior. They provide an array of interventions that more accurately pace with men as they move through the stages of change. They also validate the value of open-ended groups in which men at later stages of change can inform and challenge men who also are unwilling or ambivalent about changing their abusive behavior.

The Thomas and Caplan (1999) Group Process model is included as an innovation since its emphasis is on process rather than on psychoeducational programming and it provides a variety of strategies for engaging men in the change process, potentially reducing the risk of dropout. Group techniques are categorized into process, inclusion, and linking interventions. The group facilitator uses *process* interventions to identify the emotional message behind the client's statement and reflects the client's worldview. Common emotional themes found in domestic abuse clients' stories include betrayal, abandonment, and powerlessness. *Linking* interventions are used to connect client individual issues with others in the group and allow the group leader to make generalized statements about the group itself. *Inclusion* interventions encourage uninvolved group members to join the group discussion and include didactic and projective exercises that allow group members to voice their opinion without being singled out. These interventions have been explored as to how they can be used to help facilitators stay in the moment in uncomfortable exchanges with clients to further growth and avoid a confrontational impasse (Caplan and Thomas 2002).

Specific Application of Innovations for Domestic Abuse Treatment

The remaining pages of this chapter offer suggestions and examples on how the identified innovations are applied to domestic abuse treatment throughout the stages of group development while examining men's anticipated stages of change. Figure 12.1, adopted from Rooney and Chovanec (2004), links interventions to group stages and to stages of change and provides a useful guide as we proceed through the treatment process. The Kurland and Salmon (1998) model of group development is used since it includes a pregroup planning stage, a crucial element in domestic abuse treatment when examining ways to better engage men in treatment.

Pregroup Planning

Pregroup planning is important in developing a program that responds effectively to men initially resistant to treatment and anticipates the varying degrees of readiness for change men present. Reactance theory suggests that increasing choices and clarifying negotiable and non-negotiable rules reduce reactance (Brehm and Brehm 1981; Wright, Greenberg, and Brehm 2004). Thus it is important to identify in the program where choices can be offered and to clarify negotiable and non-negotiable elements. For example, court-referred men can be encouraged early in the intake process to check out other programs with regard to cost and time available before committing to one program. Men who are required to complete various tasks/exercises required for completion of the program (i.e., control plan, empathy exercise) may be given choices in terms of when they complete them. Applying the stages of change model to domestic abuse treatment suggests that men will be at varying stages of change when entering the program. While a majority of men

Figure 12.1 Interventions and stages of change and development

Interventions	Group Stage	Anticipated Level of Individual Motivation for Change

1) Decide on the non-negotiable and negotiable elements of the program.
2) Pre-group orientation
  a. Initial orientation of group
  b. Anticipate resistance and reframe as ambivalence.
  c. Clarify and validate choices.
	Pre-group planning	Pre-contemplation

3) Emphasize joining and inclusion
  a. Provide opening statement addressing client's initial concerns/fears.
  b. Clarify non-negotiables.
  c. Support positive choices made to date.
  d. Provide emotional support.
  e. Explore ambivalence.
  f. Identify self-motivating statements.
  g. Stimulate non-threatening attention to issues.
  h. Use inclusive group exercises to pull in disengaged members.
  i. Support self-evaluation regarding possible problem.
  j. Review formal testing to provide information on potential problem.
  k. Use videos that dramatize impact of abuse.
  l. Continue to clarify non-negotiables.
  m. Continue to clarify choices.
	Beginning	

4) Deciding to make a change
  a. Assist in assessing costs and benefits of change.
  b. Provide information about choices.
  c. Provide videos that dramatize the consequences of not changing.
	Middle	Contemplation

5) Support in planning actions; preparation for action, i.e., role-play, buddy systems. 6) Gather feedback on change attempts.		*Preparation* Action
7) Utilize clear criteria for group completion a. Plan for maintenance; prepare for lapse via role-play.	**Ending**	Maintenance

Adapted from Rooney and Chovanec (2004).

can be anticipated to be in the precontemplation stage (not see a problem), a number of men may not (O'Hare 1996). Facilitators need to ask early on about the client's perception of the problem, motivation to change, and the pressures to change they enter treatment with.

Another important element of pregroup planning is the development of a prepared opening statement that is presented to men in either a first group or an orientation meeting with one or more men. Originally developed to anticipate client concerns and fears in contracting with voluntary groups (Schwartz 1976; Shulman 1999), the opening statement allows the facilitator to join with the potential group members by anticipating some of the major questions and concerns men bring with them as they enter the program. The statement can also be used to reduce reactance and support men's preliminary efforts toward change. The following is an example of an opening statement one could use for men entering a domestic abuse program:

Welcome to the program. I know many of you may feel you have been forced to come here. Many men who are in similar situations never make it to orientation. I support your choice in attending the program. (Validate choices made.) You may be anticipating that we will try to force you to change. The reality is that no one can make you change. (Comment on change process.) All we ask is that you listen to what we have to say and take the bits and pieces of the program that make sense to you and that can help you avoid future problems and/or contact with the court system. You may also be fearing that you will be judged as guilty, or worse, shamed for the incident that brings you in. Many of you have already gone through the court system. We are not here to judge you as guilty or innocent for the charges you bring with you. Our focus is on helping you learn from whatever incident brings you in. Our task is to create a safe environment for men to examine their actions and learn from their mistakes. I will not tolerate physical or verbal abuse within group sessions. Those men who are abusive within the group will be asked to leave. In regard to confidentiality, we ask that all men keep confidential what is said within group. I cannot force group members to do this but expect men will do this in respect for others within group. (Clarify non-negotiable group rules.) The exception to confidentiality for me as the facilitator is that if you tell me that you are in danger of hurting yourself or others I need to by law, report that information to other professionals or the authorities.

Beginning Stage

In anticipation of precontemplators, the focus is on exploring the change process of men entering treatment. Prochaska, DiClemente, and Norcross (1992) suggest the change process has both an experiential and behavior component. In the beginning of treatment, the focus is on the experiential that includes men thinking about or reacting emotionally to abusive behavior they have been accused of using. Facilitators use reflective listening skills and encourage self-evaluation of the situation. The goal is to move men from not seeing a problem to considering they may have a problem and might want to address it. Negative consequences of using abusive behavior are explored, that is, court and jail experience and the impact the abusive incident had on significant others in their lives, that is, children or parents. Men are asked to self-evaluate the degree to which they feel responsible for the abusive incident. Including other group members in the discussion who may be further ahead in the change process is useful, as they many times can identify with the men who don't see a problem and can offer ideas that helped them in the change process (i.e., talking to others, taking responsibility for self). In addition, the use of inclusive group exercises, that is, check-in/out, pull in disengaged group members in a nonthreatening way, asking for their input on group topics. The following is an example of work with a precontemplator in an early session.

> Joe is a twenty-seven-year-old who has been in and out of chemical dependency treatment. He reports that he was charged with fifth-degree assault when his partner of several years and he got into an argument over an old boyfriend of hers whom they had seen at the bar that night. Joe reports they were both drunk and the argument escalated to Joe shoving his partner, claiming he had no other choice. "I was trying to get her out of my face." She promptly called police. Joe and his partner are no longer together.

JOE: I don't know why I am here. She is the one that needs an anger program. Besides I am no longer with her and I have not drunk since this happened so this problem will never happen again. I don't consider myself to have an anger problem.

LEADER: Sounds like you are feeling forced into being here (Reflective skills). Given that you have come tonight tells me that at least part of you wants to figure out what happened to make sure it never happens again (Assuming ambivalence). A lot of men decide not to attend this group and go to jail instead so I support your choice (Validate choice to attend treatment). Even if you don't reconnect with this partner you want to make sure this type of situation doesn't happen (Possible client goal). Looking back on the incident, what part do you take responsibility for from 0 percent to 100 percent? (Encourage self-evaluation). Sounds like this argument caught you off guard and that things happened pretty quickly.

JOE: I take maybe 40 percent responsibility for what happened. I did shove her, but she forced me to do it.

LEADER: Joe, it takes courage to take responsibility for your part in the past conflict. That 40 percent is what we will focus in on in this program since that is the part that you have control of. Who else in this group can identify with the struggle to take responsibility for their part in past abuse? (Linking other men farther ahead in the change process.)

Using the Duluth model, a group facilitator would work to avoid colluding with Joe, view his description of the problem as denial, and challenge his perception of the problem. In contrast, applying these innovations, the facilitator avoids challenging beliefs too early in the process and looks for change efforts to validate. The discussion of taking responsibility for abusive behavior is brought up early and is seen on a continuum, with men taking more responsibility as they feel validated, separate from their abusive behaviors.

Contemplators may also be present in the beginning of group as earlier research suggests (O'Hare 1996). The focus in domestic abuse treatment is on exploring the pros and cons of ending abusive behavior. Encouragement of self-evaluation continues gathering information on consequences of continuing abusive behavior, like the effects of anger on one's physical health or the impact of their children witnessing the abuse. Video that dramatizes the impact of abuse on victims and their family members is also useful when men are in this stage (Stosny 1994). The goal is to help the client resolve their ambivalence about ending abusive behavior. The facilitator supports any attempts at change and helps them evaluate them. Group members again are extremely helpful providing information on the impact of abusive behavior and how they went about resolving their ambivalence toward the problem. The following is an example of work with a contemplator in an early session:

JOE: After a few sessions I have decided that I can't do anything about that court order now so I might as well make the most out of it. I still think my ex-partner should have a group like this but I know I did shove her. I am realizing that I was a jerk at times. Things just started building up and when she got in my face and told me she didn't love me anymore I couldn't handle it.

LEADER: It takes a lot of courage to look at oneself and take responsibility. What helped you do this? (Praising strengths.)

JOE: I don't know, I just didn't want to waste any more time; I just want to get it over with.

LEADER: Sounds like you want to make sure this type of incident doesn't happen again. Tell me more about how things started to build up.

JOE: Well like I said we were just talking and then things got a little out of hand and she got up in my face and was showing me up, saying she didn't love me.

LEADER: That must have been hard to hear. What things can you do to avoid this type of build up in the future?

JOE: I don't know, maybe not respond right away when she mouths off at me.

LEADER: So you have some choices about how you choose to respond to her. (Reinforcing choices.) Can you identify other things that might have set you off?

JOE: I had a bad day at work with my boss giving me a hard time. When I got home I started to get upset with the little things she said and before you know it we were screaming at each other. It happened so quickly. I'm not sure what I can do to avoid the pressure build up. All I know is that I don't want to ever experience that again.

LEADER: How many men can identify with Joe's pattern of getting angry? [Many hands go up.] What have others done to deal with this pattern?

Several other members now tell their story of how they have gotten angry.

LEADER: The challenge is how to speak up [about concerns] without putting others down before things get out of hand. (Linking to other group members who have addressed this pattern of anger build up.)

Middle Stage

In the middle group stage, with the earlier efforts of engaging men in the change process you will have men in the preparation and action stages of change. The stage fits well with a majority of teaching interventions identified in a traditional domestic abuse program. For example, the Duluth model identifies one of the roles of the facilitator of providing information on relationship skills and encouraging critical and reflective thinking (Pence and Paymar 1993). Teaching counter conditioning, finding alternatives to abusive behavior is focused on in this stage, as well as offering reflective listening skills and I messages to improve communication in relationships. Role-play and modeling behavior is useful in building men's confidence to try out skills/information learned in the group. The goal of the facilitator is to support change efforts of the men and encourage self-evaluation and feedback from others to help refine their efforts to change. Daniels and Murphy (1997) encourage the use of "buddy" systems for social support as men try out various change efforts among their family and friends when men are in the action stage.

Ending Stage

In the ending group stage, most men are building confidence in changing their abusive behaviors and ready to examine ways of maintaining their changes after group is completed. On a program level, it is important that there are clear criteria for treatment completion, such as number of tasks/sessions. This not only reduces reactance of men entering the program but also provides clear feedback to participants about their progress in the group. Clear criteria for program completion also is helpful to partners, family, and probation workers who are interested in the participant's progress.

Relapse is a particularly dangerous problem in domestic abuse treatment as it leads to re-assault of partners. Useful relapse prevention strategies have been developed for domestic abuse treatment (Jennings 1990). Daniels and Murphy (1997) make a distinction in domestic abuse treatment between a "lapse" that results in verbal and psychological abuse and a relapse that results in a re-assault. They recommend focusing on lapses in men's change efforts to reduce the risk of relapse. Men can be asked to identify situations that test their ability to be nonabusive. Once these situations are identified, men can brainstorm alternative strategies with the group to reduce their risk of becoming verbally or psychologically abusive. Requiring men while in the program to connect outside the group for a series of meetings to discuss ways to maintain their changes can also be helpful. The intent of the meetings is to increase the chance of men using former group members as support as they run into challenges once they have completed the program.

This chapter focused on the application of Reactance theory, Stages of Change, Motivational Interviewing, and the Caplan and Thomas Process model to domestic abuse treatment. These innovations consist of program recommendations and interventions that facilitators can use to better engage men in the treatment process and to reduce the risk of future abusive behavior. While practice knowledge suggests these innovations can improve domestic abuse treatment, research is needed to confirm this. Research on these innovations and their impact on attrition and treatment effectiveness will lead toward more respectful and effective treatment of men and increased safety for women, children, and the community.

Practical Exercises and Discussion Questions

1. Reflect on your current involuntary group program. What elements of your program are negotiable/non-negotiable with the group members? What elements in the program currently offer choices for the group members? What elements in the program could be modified to increase choices for group members?

2. What are the kinds of pressures you anticipate men having as they enter a treatment program?

3. Reflect on an involuntary group you will or are currently running. What are the important issues/questions you anticipate your group members will be having in the first session? Include issues of authority, that is, acceptance by the group leader, and intimacy, that is, acceptance by the group members and issues specific to your group. Write out an opening statement for the first session that addresses these concerns/questions.

4. Reflect on the stages of change (precontemplation, contemplation, preparation, action, and maintenance). Identify individual and group interventions that best fit each of the stages of change.

5. Reflect on the following process themes and how they might be presented in an involuntary group: marginalization, lack of respect, intimacy, avoidance of responsibility, incompetence, loss/grief, betrayal, abandonment, powerlessness.

6. Develop a collection of potential high-risk situations that could lead to relapse of the problem behavior your group focuses on. Have group members rate them on a one to five scale. Each member presents his or her most at-risk situation and uses the group to brainstorm strategies to address the situation.

Part 3, Section B

Chapter 13

Involuntary Clients in Public Schools:
Solution-Focused Interventions

Cynthia Franklin and Laura Hopson

Intrinsically, public schools have characteristics that make them involuntary settings. Laws that govern compulsory education and truancy of adolescents are special features of public schools that make them mandatory and not voluntary in their characteristics. Mental health providers such as school social workers who practice in public school settings often work with adolescents who are involuntarily referred for services. In a school setting, for example, a small percentage of adolescents who receive treatment are self-referred (Kuhl, Jarkon-Horlick, and Morrissey 1997). Students are typically referred for counseling by school staff for emotional or behavior problems in the classroom (Weist et al. 2003). Adolescents may be reluctant to engage in mental health services for a range of reasons that include developmental, social, and environmental issues. This chapter examines the nature of involuntary clients as it relates to adolescents in a school setting, the mental health needs of adolescents, and approaches that are likely to be helpful with this population. Particular attention is given to solution-focused therapy interventions and research support for solution-focused therapy with adolescents in a school setting.

Mental Health Needs and Services in Schools

Surveys estimate that 20 percent of adolescents have mental health issues that would benefit from treatment (CHHCS 2000). Only about one-fourth of students in need of mental health care receive appropriate services. Adolescents are likely to be exposed to many stressors in their environment, such as violence in school, gang activity, and pressures to engage in drug and alcohol use and sexual activity (Putnam 1995; Jobes, Berman, and Martin 2000). Engaging in treatment is especially important for this age group because suicide is the third leading cause of death among teenagers and results in the death of 8 of every 100,000 teens between the ages of fifteen and nineteen. Nineteen percent of teens in grades 9 through 12 reported that they had considered suicide, and 8.8 percent reported that they had attempted suicide in 2001 (National Center for Health Statistics 2002).

While many children's mental health needs go unaddressed, more than 70 percent of those receiving care obtain services at school (CHHCS 2000). Approximately 60 percent of schools have mental health professionals on staff, and more than 80 percent of schools report providing case management services for students with behavioral or social problems (CHHCS 2000). Intervening with teens in a school setting is important because teens may experience many stressors while at school. According to survey data collected by the National Center for Educational Statistics in 1999, 8 percent of students in grades 6 through 12 reported criminal victimization at school, 8 percent of students in grades 9 through 12 reported being threatened or injured with a weapon on school property, and 5 percent of students ages twelve through eighteen reported that they had been afraid of being attacked or harmed on school property during the past six months (Kaufman et al. 2001). Adolescents may respond to stressful environments and situations with a range of behaviors that include fluctuations in mood, impulsivity, inattention, aggression, poor eating and sleeping habits, decreases in academic achievement, preoccupation with sexual issues, school absences, and substance use or abuse (CMHS 2003).

Providing services at school increases the chances that services will benefit students because they are highly accessible. Increased access to services is especially important for the most at-risk youth. Hispanic and African American children have the highest rates of need for mental health services and are most likely to go without care. Hispanic youth are the least likely group to access mental health care (RAND 2001). Minority children also receive poorer quality mental health care (CHHCS 2000). Many homeless teens, immigrants, teen parents, and gay and lesbian youth are also in great need of mental health services and may receive care only through institutions such as public schools, the criminal justice system, or health care organizations. Public schools may be one of the best points of entry for at-risk youth because most have some contact with the public school system (Harris and Franklin 2003).

Another reason for intervening with students in a school setting is the relationship between unaddressed behavioral and emotional needs and poor academic performance. Roans and Hoagwood (2000) conducted an extensive review of school-based mental health services and found positive outcomes for children participating in interventions addressing emotional and behavioral problems, depression, conduct problems, stress management, and substance use. When these issues are successfully addressed in schools, students are better able to meet their academic goals (Roans and Hoagwood 2000). School-based mental health services are important because teachers and other school staff observe and interact with students for extended periods of time and are often in a good position to detect mental health problems in children (Werthamer-Larsson 1994). One intervention fact is certain: any effective model of intervention in a school setting requires as its base skills for collaboration and cooperation among many different service providers. The treatment approach discussed in this chapter, solution-focused therapy, is one approach that offers many skills for helping practitioners develop collaboration in school settings.

Working in a school requires close collaboration to ensure that the students' needs are met, but it also requires collaboration among teachers, counselors, social workers, and other staff. Each staff member may have different understandings about the best approach for the student, which can lead to conflicts or even to situations in which no one addresses the adolescent's problem appropriately (Poland 1994; Kline, Schonfeld, and Lichtenstein 1995). It is often not enough for staff to be located within the same school and update each other on their work with students. To maximize their effectiveness with students and create a supportive school climate, all staff will need to share information, respect the knowledge and skills of other disciplines, and be flexible in integrating others' ideas into their interventions (Streeter and Franklin 2002). The challenges of collaboration and cooperation among the adult providers of mental health services are complicated further by the involuntary nature of school-based mental health services and the perceived resistance of adolescents by school mental health professionals.

The Developmental and Contextual Issues Leading to Perceptions of Adolescent Resistance

Developmentally, adolescents are striving to achieve independence. Because they are struggling with a desire for more autonomy while continuing to want guidance, adolescents may have strained relationships with adults that result in reluctance to engage in adult guidance activities, including mental health services (Aguilera 1990). Another potential perception that aids resistance concerns confidentiality. Adolescents are highly sensitive to issues of confidentiality and are less likely to seek treatment if confidentiality is not guaranteed by the practitioners. Adolescents may avoid counseling because they feel their problem is too personal, they prefer to handle the situation on their own, or they feel that another person will be unable to help (Dubow, Lovko, and Kausch 1990). Basic issues of trust have to be bridged as well as a basic understanding of differences between generations and the limitations of the structure of schools as institutions that do not maintain confidentiality very well. The more the practitioner can bridge the perspective of the adolescent and mediate the basic issues around confidentiality and respect between the school and the adolescent the more likely he or she is to gain the trust needed for the helping relationship. Adolescents may also be reluctant to engage with a mental health provider because of the stigma attached to mental health treatment. Stigma can result in poor access to at-risk adolescents because those who avoid seeing a provider due to stigma may be most likely to need services (Tatar 2001). The better the practitioner can normalize instead of pathologize adolescents' experiences and empower them to solve their own problems, the more trust is likely to be gained toward the mental health services. Solution-focused therapy encourages practitioners to take such a perspective with adolescent clients.

Another potential perception of resistance is the frequency of referrals to school mental health staff for disciplinary purposes, such as reducing behavior problems in the classroom and truancy. School mental health staff may become highly involved in discipline of students. A survey of school counselors in three states indicated that when asked about the most common reasons for referral, 41 percent of counselors said they were referred students for disciplinary reasons, 54 percent were asked to counsel students by the principal, and 62 percent were asked by teachers to provide counseling to students who were disruptive in the classroom. Students may have a difficult time viewing mental health providers as helpers. This does not mean, however, that mental health staff should not be referred students for disciplinary reasons, because the behaviors that lead to such referrals may be associated with serious mental health issues (Skickel and Satchwell 1991). Truancy, for example, may be a symptom of conduct disorder, anxiety and school phobia, or bipolar disorder (CMHS 2003).

Changing the Viewpoints of Helping Adults Toward Adolescent Resistance

Even though adolescents are often perceived as involuntary clients in a school setting, mental health practitioners cannot assume that every adolescent will be difficult to engage. Adults often view adolescents as difficult clients and may treat them as resistant. This view not only strains the relationship between adolescents and adults providing mental health services, it may also be unwarranted (Tatar 2001). Research suggests that resistance from students in a school setting may be more attributable to the organizational structure of the classroom than to individual student characteristics (McFarland 2001). The assumption that the adolescent client is uncooperative is contrary to the assumptions of the solution-focused intervention approach that is discussed later in this chapter. The solution-focused approach assumes that all clients are social beings with strengths and that they want to get along with people. It is up to the practitioner to begin where the adolescent client is in his or her unique social context and developmental level and to cooperate with him or her in a change process (De Jong and Berg 2001). The research suggests that the common adult perception that adolescents avoid talking with adults about their problems has little empirical support (Kuhl, Jarkon-Horlick, and Morrissey 1997). A study of adolescent help-seeking behavior found that adolescents identified guidance counselors, mothers, and teachers as good sources of help. Gender and ethnic differences were associated with variations in views about help seeking. Females had more positive attitudes toward seeking help than did males, and Asian Americans had less positive attitudes toward seeking help than did adolescents of other ethnic groups (Kuhl, Jarkon-Horlick, and Morrissey 1997). To be effective with adolescents in a school setting, school mental health staff need to assess each adolescent individually and examine and change their own attitudes about adolescent resistance.

Strengths-Based Approaches with Involuntary Clients

Strengths-based approaches developed within family therapy traditions are helpful with adolescent populations. These approaches include but are not limited to brief solution-focused therapy, structural/strategic, and the multisystemic models. This chapter focuses on methods developed within the solution-focused therapy model. Franklin (2002) lists the following practices that can be effective with involuntary clients:

1. Communicate a nonjudgmental acceptance of the client's perspective on the problem.
2. Discuss the demands placed on involuntary clients.
3. Help the client define goals for the sessions even if the client's goals are different from the reason for the referral.
4. Define the therapist's role so that it is congruent with the client's goals for the sessions.
5. Use reframing to help the client find similarities in his or her goals and the reasons for the referral.

6. Give the client as much choice as possible to minimize feelings of helplessness.
7. Educate clients about what to expect from therapy sessions.
8. Set specific, small, well-defined goals with the client.
9. Define goals that are not negotiable from the perspective of the referral source and discuss potential incentives for compliance.
10. Use the client goal of reducing negative interactions with the referral source to increase cooperation in sessions.
11. Be neutral in representing the viewpoint of the referral source and the client.
12. Take a nonconfrontational approach and ask questions that help the client to understand their feelings about what they are expected to accomplish.

Solution-Focused Therapy with Involuntary Clients

Brief solution-focused therapy is a model that is particularly helpful in practicing these techniques with involuntary clients. Solution-focused therapists work to demonstrate great respect for the client and belief that the client is the expert in resolving their problem. They assume that clients have the knowledge, strength, skills, and insights to solve their own problems (Berg 1994). Four underlying assumptions guide solution-focused therapy sessions:

1. Every client is unique.
2. Clients have the inherent strength and resources to help themselves.
3. Change is constant and inevitable, and small change can lead to bigger changes.
4. Since it is not possible to change the past, the session should concentrate on the present and future (Lipchik 2002).

Involuntary clients may respond well to a solution-focused approach because it views the client as expert (de Shazer 1988). Solution-focused therapists define resistance as a message from the client that the intervention is not helpful. Yet, the approach acknowledges that clients have different levels of motivation for change. They do not label clients as resistant because it can result in an antagonistic relationship between the client and therapist (de Shazer 1988). Solution-focused therapists discuss the difference between a customer, a complainant, and a visitor (Berg 1994). A customer is motivated to change and is, most often, willing to engage in a mutual, helping relationship. But, at other times, this may not be the case. A complainant is a person who complains about someone else and wants that person to change. Complainants are often the referring agencies or the loved ones who socially coerce the other person to come for the interview. They are often not motivated to change themselves but want the practitioner to change the person referred. A visitor is someone who comes to sessions and provides information but is not motivated to make any changes.

Most mandated clients are visitors and their greatest motivation may be for the visit to end. Even though this may be their initial intrinsic motivation, this does not nullify the client's level of motivation as an important entry point for cooperation with the client because for the mandated or involuntary client to be able to gain permission to stop the services, this assumes that they may be willing to participate in life-changing behaviors in order to see that this happen. In other words, I am willing to do X, Y, and Z to get them off my back, although some may see this as a temporary and convenient means of escape by escape artists. Others with more creative and discerning minds can quickly comprehend the relational nature of this process. As the client changes and cooperates with the practitioner to get the people off their backs, surprising outcomes can sometimes occur. Positive feedback will be the result of positive behavior and more motivation and change will be the result and so forth. We are entering with the client into a positive, amplifying behavior, feedback loop. This is why focusing on the strengths and entry point for change instead of the resistance is the strategy that the solution-focused therapist follows with the adolescent client.

Solution-Focused Therapy with Adolescents

Some of the techniques used in solution-focused therapy that are especially helpful with adolescents include taking a not-knowing approach, finding exceptions to the problem, scaling questions, goal-setting, delivering compliments, and behavioral tasks. Applications of these techniques to work with involuntary adolescents are described below.

Taking a Not-Knowing Approach

The solution-focused therapist takes the position of "not knowing" by laying aside all preconceptions about the problem and its potential solutions (Berg 2002). The therapist allows the client to define the problem and does not impose his or her own ideas about the problem and its potential solutions (Franklin and Moore 1999). A respectful, not-knowing approach may decrease any feelings of distrust the adolescent may feel toward the therapist. The therapist accepts the client's definition of the problem and demonstrates a commitment to understanding the client's perspective (Berg 2002). Therapists can build rapport with an involuntary client by acknowledging the client's feelings about participating in counseling. This approach leaves the client feeling that the struggles and concerns leading up to the counseling referral are legitimate and can demonstrate the therapist's belief that the client has the ability to resolve the presenting problem (Osborne 1999).

Finding Exceptions to the Problem

To find exceptions to the problem, the therapist asks about times when the presenting problem could have happened but did not. By discussing examples of times when the problem was absent and how they prevented the problem, clients may feel that they already have the skills and knowledge to succeed (de Shazer 1988; Berg 1994). When a client is having difficulty in thinking of exceptions to the problem, the therapist can ask for times when the problem was less severe or less frequent (Berg 1994).

Finding exceptions to the problem gives clients a sense of hope that things will get better. With adolescents, this can be especially helpful because they have difficulty seeing beyond the present situation and believing that things will improve (Jobes, Berman, and Martin 2000). Finding exceptions to the problem encourages students to think of ways they have coped with similar problems in the past, and they can imagine a future without the problem. They may also see that the problem could possibly be worse.

Scaling Questions

Scaling questions are used for assessment in many areas, such as self-esteem, prioritizing problems, perceptions of hopelessness, and progress toward achieving goals. Scaling questions typically ask clients to rate their situation on a scale from 0 to 10, with 0 the worst/lowest and 10 the best/highest. Scaling is a versatile technique that most clients easily understand and can be especially helpful when clients are having a difficult time seeing their progress (Berg 1994; Sklare 1997).

Scaling questions work well with adolescents because they can relate to the idea of rating something on a scale from 1 to 10 (Berg 1994). They also help the student to identify potential solutions to a problem. If a student ranks the situation as less problematic in successive sessions, the therapist asks about the behaviors that cause the improvement (Greene et al. 2000; Berg 2002). This technique places the responsibility for evaluating progress toward achieving goals on the adolescent (Corcoran 1998).

Setting Small Achievable Goals

Adolescents often define their problem in vague, ambiguous terms and may need help creating manageable goals (Corcoran 1998). Solution-focused therapy emphasizes the importance of setting small, specific, achievable goals. Working toward small goals can help the adolescent feel that the problem is within their control (Roberts 2000). Goals are also stated in positive terms indicating what clients want to be present in their lives instead of what they want to be absent. This is important in engendering hope and creating goals that clearly define actions the client can take to improve the situation (Berg 1994).

Solution-focused goals are based on the client's ideas about potential solutions and are expressed in their own words. When clients develop their own goals, they are more motivated to achieve them (Greene et al. 2000). With involuntary clients, the therapist can clarify the client's role in identifying goals to reinforce their ownership of the goals (Osborne 1999). Even if an adolescent states a goal as getting the assistant principal to leave him or her alone, the adolescent works with the therapist to identify steps toward reaching that goal. The therapist can often reframe the requirements of the referral source as consistent with the client's goals for therapy.

Delivering Compliments

The solution-focused therapist delivers genuine compliments based on the client's strengths. Delivering compliments helps clients see their own strengths and increases their awareness that they have the ability to solve their problems. With an adolescent, genuine compliments can continue the process of identifying client strengths and resources that they already have. The therapist should use only genuine compliments based on session content and should not overcompliment adolescents because they are likely to view this behavior as insincere. The counselor can compliment students for choosing to engage in counseling, which reinforces their decision-making power. Even if the choice is made to avoid a negative consequence, such as school suspension, the student has made a choice to participate (Osborne 1999).

Behavioral Tasks

The solution-focused therapist and client also set a behavioral task for the client to complete before the next session. Tasks may be defined by behaviors the client has indicated as helpful through exception questions. The therapist will give the client the talk of "doing more of the same" for behaviors that clients have described as helpful. Clients will be directed to "do something different" when they indicate that they have tried one way of coping numerous times with no success (Berg 1994, 2002). Such strategies result in concrete tasks that the adolescent may be likely to complete, because they are based on strategies that the client has defined as helpful or not helpful. With involuntary clients, it is important that therapists present recommendations for tasks as options, not prescriptions. Clients will take more ownership of a task if they feel they had some decision-making power in defining the task (Osborne 1999).

Solution-Focused Therapy in School Settings

Brief solution-focused therapy is a model that increasingly demonstrates its effectiveness in school settings. The model is well suited for school settings because of its emphasis on brief treatment and interdisciplinary collaboration (Murphy 1996). Solution-focused therapy works well in a school setting because of the emphasis on active listening and focusing on strengths, which facilitates collaboration with others involved with the student. The solution-focused approach encourages use of tools from other models if they are used thoughtfully to accommodate the student's goals. Solution-focused therapists in a school setting collaborate with students, parents, and teachers in developing interventions. The therapist adopts the stance that there are many approaches that may result in solutions and respects the unique ideas, beliefs, and styles of students, parents, and teachers. The solution-focused practice of defining small, concrete goals is also more realistic is a school situation in which those involved have limited time and resources (Murphy 1996).

Efficacy of Solution-Focused Therapy with Adolescents

Although more research is needed on the efficacy of solution-focused therapy, a growing number of studies demonstrate its effectiveness with adolescents (Kelly, Kim, and Franklin 2008). Findings suggest that solution-focused therapy results in positive outcomes for adolescents on self-esteem measures and coping measures (LaFountain and Garner 1996), a reduction in acting-out behaviors and other behavior problems (Franklin et al. 1997, 2001; Corcoran and Stephenson 2000; Newsome 2004; Franklin and Hopson 2007), reaching goals (Newsome 2004; Littrell, Malia, and Vanderwood 1995; LaFountain and Garner 1996), improved social skills (Newsome 2004), and improved grades and attendance in schools (Newsome 2004; Franklin et al. 2007). A meta-analysis of studies on solution-focused therapy indicates that the approach has small but positive treatment effects and has demonstrated greater improvements in internalizing behavior problems than alternative treatments (Kelly, Kim, and Franklin 2008). Students participating in solution-focused therapy have also demonstrated significant improvements in drug use, as well as attitudes and knowledge about drugs (Froeschle, Smith, and Ricard 2007).

Other studies demonstrate that further research is needed to understand the efficacy of solution-focused therapy. Although they found that students receiving solution-focused therapy experienced improvements in self-esteem, Springer, Lynch, and Rubin (2000) found no significant differences between those receiving solution-focused therapy and students in the comparison group. Similarly, Corcoran (2006) found that students receiving solution-focused therapy made significant improvements in behavior but students did not improve more that those in the comparison group who received cognitive behavior therapy. Several of these studies were conducted with adolescents in school settings (LaFountain and Garner 1996; Springer, Lynch, and Rubin 2000; Franklin et al. 2001).

Working with adolescents in a school setting requires that mental health staff be effective with involuntary clients. This does not mean that practitioners should approach adolescents with the assumption that they are resistant. The solution-focused approach can be successful with adolescents who are referred for treatment because it does not treat adolescents as resistant and allows them to feel in control of the goals and tasks of treatment. By respecting the perspective of all clients, whether involuntary or not, the therapist helps adolescents develop a sense of self-efficacy and empowers them to achieve their own goals.

Practical Exercise and Discussion Questions

Myra is a seventeen-year-old girl referred to see the school social worker because she punched her friend Elizabeth in the face during her English class. Before meeting with Myra, the social worker speaks with several teachers and other school staff to gather information. Myra has never been involved in a physical fight on school grounds and her teacher is concerned that she may have gotten involved with drugs. The quality of her school work has declined during the past six weeks, she often arrives late, and she has missed several classes. Myra is generally well liked at school and has two close friends, Elizabeth and Tonya. Myra lives at home with her mother and younger brother. She has recently started dating an older boy who does not attend her high school. The fight began when Elizabeth told Myra she should stop seeing her boyfriend because he was no good for her. During the session, Myra responds to the social worker but does not speak unless questioned. Her answers are brief and she often responds with "I don't know." When the social worker asks her why Myra is there to see her, Myra says that she may be suspended for the fight if she does not participate in counseling.

Questions for Discussion

1. How would you begin the session with Myra working from a strengths perspective?
2. Describe three techniques you would try and how you think Myra would respond.
3. How would you end the session with Myra?

Chapter 14

Work with Involuntary Clients in Child Welfare Settings

Julie Altman and Debra Gohagan

Nearly all child welfare clients can be considered involuntary or nonvoluntary clients. These individuals frequently have not asked for nor do they want services, and many do not see the need and/or value of the service for their families. They come to the attention of child protection through a judgment of their failures as caretakers, with goals too often selected and imposed on them by the child welfare system.

These clients become clients when they decide that it is possible to accept the terms of the help offered. They often enter the helping encounter with feelings of anger, anxiety, vulnerability, shame, fear, confusion, hostility, and suspicion. In many cases, participation occurs because of a real or perceived negative forced choice: their refusal to participate may result in the loss of custody of their children and/or increased pressures to accept outside help (Rooney 1992). Efforts to engage them in services are critical, and often require considerable worker skill (Altman 2005).

This chapter examines the context of client nonvoluntariness in the child welfare service environment, illustrated with a case example drawn from one author's recent research (Altman 2004). Systemic factors that impact child welfare service delivery at various levels of intervention are then highlighted, as is current research about best practices with involuntary clients. Models of child welfare service delivery that focus on client strengths and enhancing resiliency are emphasized, specifically family group decision making and solution focused treatment.

Case Example

Ms. J. is a thirty-eight-year old African-American woman living in an impoverished urban community, herself once a child in foster care. Her daughter, A., age seven, was removed from her care three months ago, after numerous substantiated reports for neglect. Ms. J. states that as the youngest of her three children and the only one she has attempted to raise on her own, A. presented some challenges. She often refused to go to school and Ms. J. found supervision of her during nonschool hours difficult.

Ms. J. had worked as a government employee for some time before A.'s removal, and is in a long-term relationship with the father of A., who works as a mechanic. Bouts of domestic violence, often fueled by alcohol, prompted Ms. J.'s arrest for assault on him recently, and the two have lived apart since. Ms. J. is making ends meet by going to a food pantry, though she worries about losing her subsidized housing.

She comes to the child welfare helping encounter involuntarily, though realizing that she must do what she has to in order to reunite her family. Efforts by the worker to work with Ms. J. have been uneven, as the worker has twenty-four cases, each as difficult as the next. While Ms. J. believes the worker is trying her best, she worries that the worker's inexperience and lack of clarity around expectations have hindered progress toward reunification. She also struggles with the worker's lack of a sense of urgency:

> And I don't want to say she don't do her job because maybe she's trying to do what she has to do but in my concern I think she need to follow-up more . . . we have a finite amount of time for me to get my child back . . . Just tell me what to do. She leave things vague . . . Who's the name of this person you want me to see? What room she in? What floor? What's her name? Come on; give me something to work with, you know?

Further complicating their work together are differences in age, parental status and ethnicity, and the perceived impact of those differences. Ms. J. reflects:

> . . . this is a f—ing heavy responsibility of a job. I'm surprised they got somebody that young working here. She is Puerto Rican and she's probably . . . I don't even know if she got kids . . . I don't think she has no idea of what I'm going through. No idea what so ever.

Desiring more than just a friendly relationship with the worker, Ms. J. wants her to be effective. In her view, this means the worker needs to be honest and straight with her, "to say what she means, and mean what she says":

> And she's very nice and she's, you know, she sits and stays with us and she joins in like a family, you know . . . but that ain't helping me get her back . . . don't tell me that you're going to come to my house and don't show up. Don't tell me that you're going to send me some mail and don't send it. Don't tell me that . . . that's the worse thing you can do. You know 'cause I don't know what to do and then I think I'm getting somewhere . . .

Ms. J. emphasizes her desire to do "whatever it takes" to ensure that A. will be returned to her care, and yearns for clear direction on what exactly that entails:

> I'm ready to piss them a river. They keep accusing me and it's not fair . . . you know, I don't care, I'll do it . . . whatever I've got to do. I really don't mind. But tell me. Don't just tell me the name of it, like anger management. Where can I go get some anger management? It's not like I'm shopping for it at Home Depot, you know what I'm saying?

She admits that she really wishes the worker had more time for her:

> I know she's busy, you know, and she's like she's got a million things to do but . . . you know if I could catch her face-to-face then we could talk, you know . . . This is a very serious situation and I know I'm just another caseload to you but this is serious shit to me. I need my child back, you know, don't just brush me off like that . . .

The Context of Involuntariness in Child Welfare

Working with child welfare clients in effective and efficient ways is critical to ensure child protection, enhance planning for permanency, or expedite reunification. As was illustrated through the case of Ms. J., a number of contextual factors significantly impact the helping process, including new federal law, cultural and other differences between workers and those they serve, and issues of power and authority.

The Adoption and Safe Families Act

One of the most significant legal interventions in recent years that has long-range ramifications for child welfare work is the *Adoption and Safe*

Families Act (ASFA; P.L. 105-89), which passed as an amendment to the Social Security Act in 1997. It requires that decisions about termination of parental rights be made within a twelve-month timeframe. It further explicitly permits that reasonable efforts to place a child for adoption or with a legal guardian may be made concurrently with reasonable efforts to make it possible for a child to safely return to their home. This reduction in the time the window of treatment is open to families with children in foster care adds to the stress the parents feel and no longer affords the system or the parents extended periods of time to establish worker–client relationships. It places engagement and subsequent treatment interventions on the fast track to an outcome of reunification and/or termination of parental rights. Workers need models for service delivery that allow them to work more quickly within the constraints of such policy, and caretakers such as Ms. J. are desperately asking for them as well.

Degrees of Difference

Another arena that significantly impacts work with child welfare clients is the area of culture, status, and value differences, as illustrated in the case example. These differences place distance between the worker and client and can make the process of providing services to involuntary clients complex. When clients perceive that they are being robbed of their cultural values, their resistance can be great. Cultural and family values and childhood experiences are powerful reinforcers that what one is doing is right; families may well resent intervention, and focus only on ways to escape from child welfare scrutiny.

Abney (2000) suggests that working with clients in child welfare settings requires critical worker skills and effort to reduce the distance of differences. Child welfare professionals, first, have a responsibility to be aware of their own individual and cultural values and biases, attitudes, and beliefs. It is also necessary that the worker know something about the client's worldview and to know strategies that are culturally relevant to working with this client (Miller and Gaston 2003; Yan and Wong 2005). In child welfare, it takes a skilled worker to work out compromises between client cultural values and legal standards of child and family caretaking. Collaboration with clients cross-culturally requires careful attention to traditional notions and impacts of empathy, mutuality, power and authority, use of self, and communication (Shonfeld-Ringel 2001).

Power and Authority

Child welfare practice is fraught with inequalities of power and authority, making the collaborative ideal difficult to achieve and the ideal of a worker–client relationship unlikely (Dore and Alexander 1996; Alexander and Dore 1999; Rooney 2000). Research has shown that the more clients feel that power and authority are shared, the more likely they are to form a positive working relationship leading to better outcomes (Horvath and Luborsky 1993). In child welfare work, effective collaboration rests on creative ways to develop and balance a sense of reciprocity, shared power, and responsibility (DeChillo, Koren, and Schultze 1994), working through what many define as resistance.

Resistance is a much debated, misunderstood, and, unfortunately, much used concept in child welfare environments. Guilt, anger, shame, and depression may lead some caretakers to appear reluctant, unmotivated, or unwilling, when, in fact, they may never have chosen to become clients (Rooney 2002). Likewise, it may be that the goals and services of the agency do not fit their needs, or their definition of the problem bringing them to the attention of child welfare authorities. It is suggested that outcomes of child welfare work are more likely to be successful if there is some overlap between the client's own perception of the situation that led them to the agency's attention, and that of the agency, or "motivational congruence" (Rooney 2000).

Involuntary clients in child welfare settings may not recognize the importance or necessity for change. They perceive themselves as being forced to see workers against their will, believe that the system is not just or fair, and often see the child welfare agency and its workers as unwanted intrusions into their lives, and the remedies recommended to them as meaningless or harmful (Miller 1991). Their reluctance to engage in services can be recognized as ambivalence, as a sign that the worker is pushing beyond the client's readiness for change, or that the agency' service arrangements are "inapt" (Ivanoff, Blythe, and Tripodi 1994).

Rooney (1992) believes resistance should be reframed positively as *reactance,* the normal, expected response to one or more of one's personal freedoms being threatened (Brehm 1976). In fact, reactance is often strongest when the threatened freedom was valued, thus causing the client to value the prohibited behavior more than before, such as temporarily increasing illicit drug use, or becoming hostile or aggressive toward child welfare authorities. Losing a child to foster care when you highly value parenting and the privacy of family life may prompt strong reactance. For example, child welfare clients may respond to reactance by attempting to restore the parenting role that has been threatened, such as by having another baby. They may reduce reactance by fulfilling the letter but not the spirit of the mandate, such as by attending counseling but not participating in it. They may also reduce reactance in more subtle ways, such as by observing another client restore freedom through participating in parent advocacy groups.

Workers in Child Welfare Settings

Providing services to involuntary and nonvoluntary clients requires specific knowledge and skills on the part of the child welfare worker and establishing the client–worker relationship is an important first step in the planned change process. There are perhaps no higher stakes for families than the threat or re-alization that someone wields the power to remove one's children from their care, or not return them, as was painfully illustrated in the case of Ms. J. and her daughter, A. The relationship between workers and clients in child welfare is intimate and can be highly charged. Clients' expressions of outrage at the child welfare system can be so extreme that at times the worker withdraws from the relationship before it gets a chance to develop into a partnership.

Workers working with involuntary clients in child welfare have demand-ing and stressful jobs. Knowing oneself is perhaps the most important but difficult challenge when working with families in these settings. Facing one's own beliefs, values, and feelings about clients and their behavior can curb worker tendency to blame or punish parents for their deficits and incapaci-ties. Working in a straightforward and nonblaming manner is difficult and can feel ambiguous, such as when conveying hope of progress without pro-moting false assurances of reunification. Yet, workers need to promote a sense for the client throughout that they are being heard and communicated to honestly about their circumstances, as Ms. J. repeatedly asked for. Establish-ing this kind of trust often comes through positive actions on the part of the worker, not words.

Helpful assumptions from which the worker may begin their work with child welfare clients include the following: (1) parents are not deliberately will-ful in their behavior, but rather are doing the best they can in response to the difficulties they face; (2) parents are unhappy about the situation, even though defensive, and really do care about their families; (3) if given the opportunity, families will demonstrate their strengths and positive attributes; (4) people are more alike than different; (5) parents are the primary influence in the lives of their children; (6) the first and best effort should be made to help ensure ade-quate care and protection of the child in their own home; (7) families today experience multiple and complex demands in their daily life; and (8) change is possible (Kadushin and Martin 1988; Kinney, Haapala, and Booth 1991).

Research on Strategies for Work with Involuntary Clients in Child Welfare

Increasingly, child welfare research values clients' perspectives on service delivery—what they perceive as helpful and what they perceive as barriers to change, such as what Ms. J. so willingly shared. Recent research has high-lighted elements of service delivery considered critical at four primary levels of client intervention in child welfare: (1) clients who are considered at-risk for child abuse and/or neglect, and offered services at the *prevention level*; (2) clients who have founded investigations of abuse and/or neglect are offered services at the *protective services level*; (3) clients considered at extreme risk for removal of their children due to abuse and/or neglect and are offered *preservation services*; and (4) clients involved in child welfare services because their children have been removed from their care *(family reunification services)* due to maltreatment.

Preventive Services

Altman (2003) researched how potential child welfare clients decide whether or not to accept agency-initiated services. These were families known to be high-risk for child abuse and neglect and who were offered early intervention, prevention-oriented home visit services. The aim of the research was to understand, from the client's point of view, what mattered most as they contemplated an offer of agency-initiated, supportive, home-based service. Using qualitative methods, five themes deemed most important to them when contemplating the offer of service were: (1) how clients viewed their own need for the service offered; (2) how they understood the potential fit of service to match those needs; (3) how effective they believed the potential service might be for them; (4) what the service would cost in exchange for the benefit they estimated it to be in their lives; and (5) how much choice they thought they had in freely deciding whether to accept or decline those offered services.

Protective Services

Yatchmenoff (2005) studied the engagement process of parents who had recently become child welfare protective service clients. Defining client engagement as "positive involvement in the helping process," she developed a measure that quantified what they found to be its five major dimensions: (1) receptivity, or a client's openness to receiving help; (2) expectancy, or the perception of future benefit clients see; (3) investment, or client commitment to the helping process; (4) working relationship, or the quality of the interpersonal relationship between worker and client; and (5) mistrust, the belief that the agency and/or worker is manipulative or malicious.

Intensive Family Preservation Services

Much work has been done studying client participation in intensive family preservation services (IFPS), a level of service offered to child welfare clients who are at extreme risk for placement of one or more of their children into foster care. Collaboration in treatment planning and compliance with program expectations are seen as key components of caregiver participation in services; greater collaboration is related to better compliance (Littell 2001). Caregiver and other factors such as substance abuse, mental health problems, severe childcare deficits, chronic child neglect, inadequate housing, minority status, and lack of extended family support impact those levels, as do strong deficit orientations of workers in IFPS, job clarity, quality of supervision, and worker autonomy (Littell and Tajima 2000). Programs that provided a wide array of concrete services and had an emphasis on advocacy were linked to high levels of collaboration.

Research on use of the stages of change model (Prochaska and DiClemente 1982) for work with child welfare clients in IFPS may or may not be useful (Girvin 2004; Littell and Girvin 2004), as more research on the context of motivation for these clients is needed. In recent work, problem recognition and intention to change on the part of caretakers were found to be associated with somewhat different case characteristics, and may be affected by child welfare worker experience levels (Littell and Girvin 2006).

Family Reunification Services

One study, using qualitative data from workers, supervisors, parents, and foster parents, examined effective ways of working together in family reunification services (Altman 2004). Seven common themes were identified as important in their efforts to work together toward positive family change: (1) the need for families and workers to set common and clear goals together; (2) the need for parents and workers to maintain a sense of hopefulness during the change process; (3) the need for parents to be aware, to acknowledge, and to understand their situations accurately; (4) the need for parents to be consistently motivated in their change efforts; (5) the need for workers to identify, understand, and respect cultural issues in their relationships with families; (6) the need for workers to communicate truthfully, honestly, and respectfully; and (7) the need for workers to be persistent, diligent, and timely in their efforts to help families.

Best Practice Models in Child Welfare

The child welfare service arena incorporates components of the strengths perspective, resiliency enhancement, and empowerment practice models in best practice approaches (Berg 1994; Petr 1998; Norman 2000; Pecora,

Reed-Ashcraft, and Kirk 2001; Walton, Sandau-Beckler, and Mannes 2001; Herbert and Harper-Dorton 2002). However, many of these treatment approaches have been slow to address the responsibility that child welfare practitioners have to apply these models specifically in the context of the development of the client–worker relationship with involuntary and nonvoluntary clients.

Yet, the research on client perspectives (cited earlier in this chapter) gives concrete evidence of the need to incorporate the principles and practice skills that are consistent with strengths perspective and empowerment practice. Further, empirical evidence is beginning to support the usefulness of practice and intervention approaches that integrate the best of these approaches. Two such models are family group decision making and solution-focused treatment.

Family Group Decision Making

Family group decision making (FGDM), originally developed to increase the culturally relevant services provided to ethnic populations in New Zealand, is increasingly being used as a service delivery model in child welfare agencies in the United States (Hassall 1996; American Humane Association 2000; Fulcher 2000). Its increase use in the United States is a response to the escalating number of children, disproportionately minorities, who are spending an extended length of time in out-of-home care settings or experiencing multiple out-of-home placements (American Humane Association 2000). This model, with variations, is known as family unity model, family group conferencing, and family decision meetings. FGDM practice is used in a variety of professional settings including child welfare, law enforcement, and restorative justice programs (Maxwell and Morris 1993; McCold and Wachtel 1998; U.S. Department of Justice 2007). In addition, given its historical roots in the Maori culture, it is being implemented with diverse populations (Vance and Elofson 1999) and in families experiencing domestic violence (Pennell and Burford 2000).

Research on the effectiveness of FGDM appears positive (Burford et al. 1996; Walton et al. 2004). Studies have shown that FGDM can be used with a variety of family situations, does not result in increased risk, produces high levels of satisfaction in the families who participate, and has positive effects on child placement outcomes (Burford et al. 1996, as cited in Walton et al. 2004). Further positive outcome indicators include a decrease in the number of children living in out-of-home care, and a decrease in the number of court proceedings, an increase in professional involvement with extended families, an increase in the number of children living with kin, an increase in community involvement among nuclear family members such as fathers and a decrease in recidivism among juveniles engaging in violent crimes (Burford et al. 1996; McCold and Wachtel 1998; Jackson and Morris 1999; Hudson, Sieppert, and Unrau 2000).

In this model, families and other concerned individuals join with the child welfare worker to share in the responsibility for developing plans that protect and nurture their children from further abuse and neglect. FGDM is a family-centered, family and community-strengths oriented, culturally competent, and solution-focused model that encourages family and community empowerment. FGDM is, in fact, a nonadversarial process that provides families with the opportunity to make these important decisions. It recognizes that families have the most information about themselves to make well-informed decisions and that individuals can find security and a sense of belonging within their families. It emphasizes that, first and foremost, families have the responsibility to not only care for, but also to provide a sense of identity for, their children. It encourages families to connect with their communities, and the communities to link with their families. It is typically implemented in stages, using group meetings in which a facilitator, whose level of presence and participation is negotiated, allows the family group conferencing participants to negotiate a plan of action. In our earlier case scenario, Ms. J. would have been considered for FGDM services, given the strengths that appear to exist in her personal and family life (i.e., extended family connections, work history, etc.). Members of her family as well as other interested parties would have been invited to meet to develop a plan to care for Ms. J.'s daughter, A.

Solution-Focused Treatment in Child Welfare

Another treatment model gaining attention for its usefulness in working with "treatment resistant" populations is solution-focused treatment (SFT). This section cannot provide a comprehensive review of all components of this model; rather, it provides an overview of the model and its appropriateness for use with involuntary/nonvoluntary clients, with particular reference to the core principles and techniques that relate directly to the development of worker–client relationships. SFT skills reflect the strengths perspective and empowerment practice approaches (Osborne 1999; De Jong and Berg 2001). This approach challenges the traditional problem-based, pathology-based, and deficits approaches to working with difficult families, requires workers to assess (or reassess) their personal value system, and provides a specific set of knowledge and skills in working with this population.

SFT is a brief therapy approach developed originally at the Brief Family Therapy Center in Milwaukee, Wisconsin (Dielman and Franklin 1998). It is being used with a variety of at-risk populations including addictions, domestic violence, marital, mental health, children and adolescents, and pastoral counseling (Adams, Piercy, and Jurick 1991; McFarland 1995; Nickerson 1995; Kok and Leskela 1996; Corcoran 1997, 1998; Eakes et al. 1997; Murphy and Duncan 1997; Corcoran and Franklin 1998; Dielman and Franklin 1998; Kruczek and Vitanza 1999; Rowan and O'Hanlon 1999; Selekman 1999; Turnell and Edwards 1999; Corcoran and Stephenson 2000; Todd, 2000; Gingerich and Wabeke 2001; Weiner-Davis 2001). One recent meta-analysis yielded favorable outcomes (Gingerich and Eisengart 2000), while Corcoran and Stephenson (2000) found some positive differences in short-term outcomes between treatment groups of children with behavioral disorders in which the SFT approach was used.

As was seen in the research reported earlier in this chapter, clients want to be respected for their capacities to act and change and for their knowledge about themselves and their family. SFT assumes that all clients have the resources and strengths to change and using the clients' life experiences makes them the expert on the problem or complaint. Change of any size or shape in emotions, behaviors, and perceptions is the goal of treatment. A small change in the complaint is all that is necessary as a change in one part of the system can affect change in another part of the system (Stalker, Levene, and Cody 1999). With SFT, rapid change and resolution is believed to be possible and normal. The child welfare worker believes that the client is competent to make choices that are good for her; thus, the worker avoids any language or behavior that suggests a condoning, enabling, or patronizing attitude. This positive focus on the change and strengths gives the client permission to assume or resume control of his/her life, i.e., "What happens when you are not leaving your child alone?" or ". . . when you are not letting your child stay home from school?"

In SFT the focus is on the solutions not the problems; thus, the worker does not focus solely on the problem or complaint that brought the client to the agency. Herbert and Harper-Dorton (2002) suggest that the "workers responsibility is to see the cup as half full rather than half empty" (p. 257). Client problems are no longer labeled as pathological and clients are not seen as having multiple deficits. Cowger (1994) suggests that the deficits approach has negatively defined and limited our perceptions, expectations, and interactions with clients. For example, in SFT behavior that does not fit the expectations of the treatment plan is not defined as resistance or noncompliance, but would be defined, as Rooney (1992) suggests, as reactance; thus, significantly decreasing the client's need to respond negatively to our actions and interactions. Therefore, the client's views and behaviors, when different from the child welfare professional's expectations, are considered quite valid and are not challenged or questioned. Workers are encouraged to deliberately appear "confused" about communication inconsistencies or gaps and not to rely on confrontation tactics. When confrontation is appropriate, workers are encouraged to use a curious tone of voice to avoid the use of an accusatory approach.

The use of SFT with child welfare cases does not imply that the child welfare professional does not have to complete required paperwork and follow legal procedures to protect the vulnerable members of their community; nor does the worker turn a blind eye to dangerous behaviors. In addition to gathering the information required during an investigation, workers can gather information about times in which this problem was not occurring.

Joining, the goal of which is to build a cooperative foundation, is a necessary ingredient for engagement with clients (Corcoran 1998; Corcoran and Franklin 1998) and is one of the key concepts in the SFT. It is believed that joining will result in cooperation which is likely to occur when the worker projects to the client a positive, warm feeling which then gives the client confidence in the worker's trustworthiness. In this approach, when the client perceives that the worker is sincerely interested in him or her, he or she is more likely to cooperate and work with you to make changes. This requires a change in the worker's mindset from the advice giving, lecturing, or nagging with clients whom workers have previously labeled as difficult or resistant. One very simple but powerful technique for enlisting cooperation is to compliment clients and to find areas in their lives in which they have been successful (de Shazer et al. 1986; Stalker, Levene, and Cody 1999). Finding areas in the clients' lives or environment to compliment them and searching for as well as recognizing successful periods in the client's life are useful approaches. Recognizing and honoring strengths the clients bring to the worker–client relationship is another option. For example, thanking clients for making the choice to attend a meeting or for completing a treatment plan activity can also enlist cooperation.

Communication skills for engaging clients in SFT are numerous. The purpose of solution-oriented interviewing is to direct the conversation toward the goal of enhancing the client's sense of competence and self-empowerment to find clues that lead to solutions (de Shazer et al. 1986; De Jong and Miller 1995; Berg and De Jong 1996; De Jong and Berg 1998). It is easier and more profitable to construct solutions by looking for successes in the past, and getting the client to repeat what he or she has been successful at in the past is easier than teaching new skills. The worker's task is to find, amplify, reinforce, look for exceptions, and help the client repeat any positive changes s/he has already made on his or her own. In addition, the worker asks and even insists that the client take part in the solution. This can begin by encouraging the client to imagine solutions.

While SFT provides multiple techniques for helping clients construct solutions, asking questions is the first step. Several question formats are available

(Dielman and Franklin 1998). These question formats, using our case scenario involving Ms. J. and her daughter, A., include: (1) *Survival questions* ask the client to explain how he or she did it, that is how do they survive under these circumstances. For example, "Ms. J., how do you manage to work full time, raise a daughter, keep the bills paid, and have a relationship?" (2) *Coping questions* ask the client to identify how s/he did it when the behavior they are concerned about was occurring. For example, "Ms. J., how do you do it when you were fighting with your boyfriend?" or ". . . when you were worried about everything?" or ". . . when you are feeling so alone?" (3) *Support questions* ask the client who helps him/her do this? For example, "Ms. J., who helps you to make decisions about your life?" or ". . . about your daughter's behavior?" (4) *Exception questions* ask the client for information about when this complaint or behavior does not occur. For example, "Ms. J., when are you not feeling overwhelmed?"; "What is different about those days, Ms. J., when your daughter, A., does attend school?" or ". . . when you and A. are able to spend time together that you both enjoy?" (5) *Possibility questions* ask the client to imagine what would it take for this change in behavior or attitude to happen and how would the client know this change occurred. For example, "What would it take for you to get back to work, Ms. J.?" or "If you decided to return to work, what would that be like?" (6) *Esteem questions* ask the client to imagine what would be different about him/her if this change occurred. For example, "What would be different about you, Ms. J., if you were able to make good decisions about your daughter and your life?" or ". . . if you were able to return to work?"

Scaling is another useful SFT technique (Corcoran 1998). Clients are asked on a scale of 1 to 10, with 1=low and 10=high, where they would rank themselves on a particular behavior. Workers can adapt this approach to ask clients to identify where they would rank themselves on their readiness to participate in services, their concerns about the process/legal situation, and so forth. Clients respond positively as this approach lets them quantify their reaction and lets them know that the worker is interested in understanding their "reactance." In our case scenario, Ms. J. could be asked to rank herself on a variety of areas including: How likely I am to make a decision to return to work? How much I want to work things out to have my daughter returned? or How I feel about my efforts to date to have my daughter returned home?

The focus of SFT on the positive, respectful, searching for success and strengths helps clients become hopeful, builds self-esteem, and encourages clients to take control and responsibility for their actions. The child welfare worker's primary task is to uncover forgotten problem-solving skills and to help clients find ways to adapt these skills to current difficulties by reminding clients of past successes and asking what it will take to repeat these successes now; thus, directing the client toward future action. It is the core of the solution-focused approach (Berg 1994; Corcoran 1998).

Working with involuntary or nonvoluntary clients in the field of child welfare is difficult and exacting. Challenges abound, not the least of which is the need to help families move forward within the short ASFA timeline. At the core of this work lies a worker's capacity to engage those clients who feel least like developing a working relationship. While building skills and using best practices are certainly important, equally so is the worker's ability to critically self-examine.

In this chapter, the ways in which the child welfare client population express themselves in the context of their nonvoluntariness were identified. Key contextual factors impacting service delivery at various levels of intervention were highlighted. Best practices for engaging these clients were offered, with an emphasis on two specific models: solution-focused treatment and family group decision making.

Discussion Questions

1. How can we adapt current social work training to allow for better service delivery to involuntary clients in child welfare settings?
2. What are critical differences in engaging families who are nonvolunarily receiving services in child welfare and those who are involuntarily mandated to receive child welfare services?
3. How might we work toward better cultural identification and respect for families engaged in involuntary child welfare services?
4. How might you envision the impact of policies that support inclusive and universal services to families with respect to child welfare?

Part 3, Section C

Chapter 15

Oppression and Involuntary Status

Glenda Dewberry Rooney

Clients who are racial and ethnic minorities are discussed in the social work literature as members of oppressed groups. Oppression is characterized as having limited power and limited resources and constrained choices (hooks 1984; Pharr 1988; Van Voorhis 1998). Its manifestations and effects are described as a matrix in which interlocking structures and conditions frame a life course where economic and social justice is a privilege (Gitterman 1995; Van Soest and Garcia 2003; Clifford and Burke 2005). The experience of oppression is often symbiotic with minority status.

There is also an emphasis in the social work literature on the extent to which power and the dominant political, social, and economic order are implicated in the array of problems experienced by those who are oppressed (Gil 1978, 1998; Dei 1996; Margolin 1997; Al-Krenawi and Graham 2001; Finn and Jacobson 2003; Stewart 2004). Social workers are also encouraged to consider the weight and impact that sustained oppression has on psychological functioning and the psychosocial self when assessing the behavior of members of oppressed groups (Williams 1994; Van Voorhis 1998; Finn and Jacobson 2003; Lum 2004; Stewart 2004). Despite a wealth of oppression-related literature as well as the person-in-environment focus, understanding the experience of oppression is often a difficult task for social workers and for the agencies in which they work. Funding priorities for social welfare programs add to this lack of comprehension as these resources have historically focused on rehabilitating or correcting individual maladaptive acts or behaviors in exclusion of changing the environment in which these behaviors have occurred.

Involuntary Status and Oppression

Is there a connection between involuntary client status and being a member of an oppressed group, in particular ethnic or racial minorities? Certainly, not all involuntary clients are members of oppressed groups, nor are they persons of color. Similarly, not all members of oppressed groups are involuntary clients. Figure 15.1 illustrates a point, nonetheless made by Rooney over a decade ago, that "members of oppressed groups are disproportionately represented among involuntary clients" (1992:21). This trend has not changed and it holds true for social work practice in both public and private agencies. In addition, although members of racial and ethnic minorities may be a smaller segment of the client population, they are a larger portion of clients who are involuntary. Also, these individuals and groups and indeed the communities in which they live are often targeted for rehabilitative or corrective intervention services. Although higher socioeconomic class is insufficient to blunt the scope of oppression, with few exceptions, the client base of social welfare organizations is poor and minority which further erodes their power and status.

Given the premise that ethnic and racial minorities are disproportional among those clients who are involuntary, is there a connection between involuntary status and oppression as illustrated in figure 15.2? This chapter explores the question, and proposes a definite intersection between involuntary

Figure 15.1   Client base and involuntary status

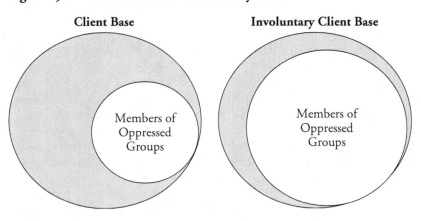

Figure 15.2   Intersection of involuntary status and oppressed groups

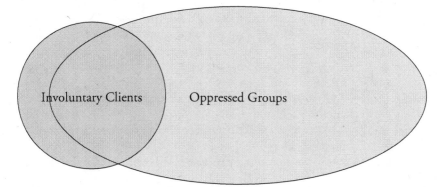

client status and racial or ethnic minorities as members of oppressed groups. It further explores similarities between the two. Involuntary clients become so, often as a result of pressure, a legal mandate to correct a behavior, or an act that is inconsistent with the norms and laws of society. What then are the acts or behaviors that place racial and ethnic minority groups in an involuntary transaction with society? Are there attributes that involuntary clients and racial or ethnic minorities have in common that have the potential to intrude upon the helping relationship?

Micro and Macro Nature of Oppression

The proposed intersection between involuntary client status and oppression can be understood by examining the reach of oppression at the individual and systems level. Oppression is to be without power, to be subjected to dominant preferences but without the resources to comply with the norms of the more dominant society (Pharr 1988; Freire 1998). In its scope, oppression occurs at the individual and systems level, and is not limited to any one minority group. In its multiple forms, oppression is an accepted, normative experience, deeply rooted in the social, economic, political, and cultural structure of our society. As such, oppression often frames the experience of those who are different, including individuals with different physical, emotional, or cognitive abilities, sexual orientation, economic status, and gender.

Over time, there have been attempts by various oppressed groups to rank their experience based on historical legacies. Rankings most often occurred as various groups compete for resources that have caused antagonism between oppressed groups as well with other groups who claim ideological oppression (Pharr 1988; Margoda 1995; Ogawa 1999; Melendez and La Sala 2006). Claims about who is oppressed as well as the ranking of oppression are counterproductive. An overarching measure of oppression is that irrespective of its pedigree, historically oppressed people share a common bond in that they have been acted upon by the dominant group (Pharr 1988; Margoda 1995; Freire 1998). This bond involves systemic implicit and explicit actions that govern or deny individual and group rights, a lack of power, autonomy, and self-determination. As such, oppressed people lack the opportunity to fully participate in the social, political, and economic processes guaranteed by right of citizenship and belonging. In essence, the failure to fit is the essential act that underscores the marginal status of those who are members of oppressed groups in society.

Lum (2004) articulates the reach of oppression in terms of process and structure. This framework aids our understanding of the circuitous interaction of micro and macro factors that are seamlessly woven into oppression and hence involuntary status. The process of oppression positions members of oppressed group in the lower ranks of society (Lum 2004). In tandem, the hierarchical structure of oppression creates and reinforces individual status at the lower ranks, and by extension, the groups to which they belong. In essence members of oppressed groups are "a part of the whole, but outside of the main body" (hooks 1984:ix). Being outside of the whole is evident in systems that obscure individual inequality which turn perpetuates group vulnerability. Gil (1978:61) described the tendency to locate and interpret problems as those of the individual as a "powerfully political act," in that this focus in fact distracts from the holistic nature of group oppression and vulnerability. The individual focus allows the dominant elite to pose such questions as "Why is this person so lazy, or unmotivated?" Instead the question could be framed as "What are the factors that inhibit the growth and success of entire communities?" Of course, this inquiry would require a different course of action-focused justice beginning first with an acknowledgment that people are oppressed.

Systems level oppression operates in concert with naming the individual as deviant. At the system's level, inequality and the accompanying social issues associated with oppression are rationalized as individual attributes rather than the structural arrangements of society that affect the group as a whole. The attribution bias undermines the capacity of the oppressed groups by portraying individual success or failure as a result of personal characteristics, cognitive abilities, motivation, and personal responsibility (Lopez, Gurin, and Nagda 1998). Empowerment championed as altering the circumstances of oppressed groups or communities by addressing inequality is akin to the attribution bias. Zappay (1995), in a critique of community empowerment, concluded that such initiatives were inherently political, in particular their outcomes. The fallacy lies in the premise that empowered groups and communities can against formidable odds marshal the resources and power to change their vulnerable life conditions.

Pathways to Involuntary Status

The circuitous and reciprocal nature of oppression is inherent in Lum's (2004) process and structure framework. Being positioned at the lower ranks of society almost guarantees that racial and ethnic minorities, especially those who are low income, will have contact with social welfare organizations or the courts. As members of a permanent underclass, oppressed groups have contact either as voluntary applicants in need of resources or more often than not, the result of a mandate that seeks to regulate their lifestyles and behaviors, and correct for deficits. The consensus perception is that involuntary status involves correcting the behavior of those who are court-ordered or under some form of legal action. The *silent mandate*, introduced later in this chapter, which is neither legal or court ordered, nonetheless is a common practice that represents another route to involuntary status.

Legal Mandate

Perhaps the most familiar course to involuntary client status involves the court order or legal mandate, in which the individual is required to seek help (Rooney 1992; Ivanoff, Blythe, and Tripodi 1994; Rooney and Bibus 2000). Court-ordered mandates are intended to alter or correct behaviors or actions that are outside of the realm of societal expectations which may also be the result of illegal acts.

Does the premise that there is a connection between involuntary status and oppression hold true for racial and ethnic minority individuals in this category of cases? Some would argue that involuntary status, for example, when a crime is committed, has little to do with oppression. This argument presumes equity within systems that are charged with ensuring and protecting the public good. Following this train of thought raises questions about drug eradication strategies that are directed toward a particular segment of the population, mainly poor and minority communities. In spite of the magnitude of the use and commerce of drugs in the United States, politicians, professionals, and the general public have been passive about the "no-knock" search and surveillance of illegal drugs activities in racial and ethnic minority communities. It seemed as if society accepted police activities that in fact infringed on the rights and privacy guaranteed under the

U.S. Constitution. Also in question are the mandatory sentencing laws that eroded judicial discretion as well as the harsher sentences for those who used or were in possession of crack, a derivative of cocaine, but not cocaine. In effect, this practice discriminated against poor minority men and women. In contrast, when methamphetamines became a major concern in white communities, politicians and professionals were immediate in their call for treatment programs, emphasizing that prisons were not a viable answer to this epidemic.

For others, the connection between involuntary client status and racial and ethnic minorities is the chicken or the egg argument. For example, does the omnipresence of the police in minority communities contribute to the perception that minority men and woman commit crimes more often? Or is it that the potential for arrests heightened by the aggressive presence and tactics of the police in these communities? Intense scrutiny of minority communities as an argument can also be applied to the racial visibility factor and the practice of zero tolerance for certain behaviors of minority males that results in a high number of school suspensions or referrals to specialized behavioral groups (Artiles and Trent 1999; Townsend 2000). Scrutiny is equally applicable to the child welfare system in which mandated reporting and decision making have in large measure led to families of color being overrepresented in the child protection system and juvenile and adult correction (Hsia and Hamparion 1997; Morton 1999; Ogawa 1999; Lane et al. 2002; Critical Resistance 2003; Derezotes, Poertner, and Testa 2005). The surveillance of certain group behaviors is also pervasive in the larger community. Minority youth, for example, express a mix of anger and humor, citing the irony of their being harassed by mall security and observed by store personnel because of their hip hop culture dress (a non–race-based phenomenon), when their clothes were purchased from the same stores that are affronted by their dress.

Irrespective of your point of view, in truth, we cannot dismiss the fact that racial and ethnic groups live under some form of surveillance albeit the police, professionals, public policy, or the media. Moreover, America has a lengthy social and political history of perceiving the cause and resolution of its social problems by focusing on those who are different. In essence, those who are different, and who reside at the margins of society, the outsiders, are thought of as deviant, lacking in competence, ungrateful and unmotivated, who must ultimately be controlled (Gil 1978; Freire 1998).

The argument here is not against community standards laws or rules of living or conduct that governs a civilized society. Instead, it takes exception to the discriminate manner in which rules and laws are applied and that have a disproportionate impact members of oppressed groups. Roberts (2002a) characterizes the disparate enforcement of laws and the intrusion into minority communities as a matter of basic rights and freedoms. Specifically Roberts believes that the excessive intrusion experienced by minority communities by child welfare and the police reinforces the oppressive notion that without supervision, minority individuals and communities are "incapable of governing themselves" (ibid.:20).

Silent Mandate

Rooney and Bibus (2000) have distinguished involuntary client status, citing the importance of the presence or absence of a legal mandate. Legally mandated contact with a professional is understood as requiring interaction with a professional for an identified problem that has been imposed by a sanctioned authority. An inherent tension occurs when a client has not sought the help that is offered and further does not agree with the imposed service decision. It is the absence of a legal mandate in which the transitory waters to involuntary client status becomes somewhat murky. I refer to this transition, which may involve informal and discretionary pressures, as the *silent mandate*. In some instances, this mandate may be intertwined with one that is legal.

Silent mandates, whether established in dominant societal preferences, public policy, or professional acts may assume a posture of best interest and good intentions, often with paternalistic overtones. On the part of the professional, the exercise of care can mimic oppression when well-intentioned instincts of what is best seem to imply that clients are incapable of correctly assessing their needs (Orme 2002). Lacking a focus on empowerment and participation, imposed services add to rather than diminish stressors and are perceived by the client as another level of oppression. The two cases discussed below illustrate the force and power of the silent mandate

The first case is typical of reports from minority parents about their interactions with educational systems in which the power of the silent mandate as exercised by professionals is reinforced at the institutional level.

> Jermaine attends middle school. He likes math and has frequently mentioned his dream of becoming an architect. But, his reported inability to sit for extended periods in two classrooms had resulted in a recommendation that he be placed in a classroom for students who are described as having emotional and behavioral problems (EBD). The majority of the students in this class are minority males.
>
> In the meeting with the EBD team, his parents having received no information about the school's concerns were angered by the team's recommendation and demanded to know, "Why can't you all teach our kids?" "What has been tried?" Why weren't we told that he had a

problem sitting in his seat?" "How does he act in other classes?" The parents believed that his placement in an EBD classroom was a drastic step to a behavior that could be modified. They described their meeting with the EBD team as "stacked against their son, because their minds were already made up." "When we entered the room, there were twelve people sitting in a semicircle around the table. A man introduced himself as the team leader and informed us of the team's decision. He then handed us parental consent papers to sign, like we agreed with what they were doing." Another team member read a lists of complaints from two teachers, "with my child sitting there listening to them, nothing positive was said; one of which was that Jermaine finds it difficult to sit for long periods." When asked which teachers had made these statements, "the team leader snapped his folder shut and said that the information was confidential." After observing the area of the school in which the EBD classes were located, the parents commented that the locked doors in this section of the school building "felt like a prison." When we said that "it seemed like we didn't have a choice and that we didn't like the recommendation," the team leader suggested that "Jermaine might be better served in an alternative school."

A professional's discretionary interpretation of public policy in the second case demonstrates the way in which an applicant for services can transition into involuntary clienthood. The case is also an example of how a professional's discretion can become a silent mandate in support of the prescriptive lifestyle of the more dominant society.

In this situation, an elderly minority female requested services from a publicly funded in-home health care service. Her request was denied by the social worker because her unemployed, single-parent daughter, and her four children also resided in the home. Instead, the social worker advised her that he would recommend that she move to a "more structured environment," in which the needed services were readily available. This recommendation was based on his observation that the apartment "appeared to be a gathering place for a host of relatives and their children." His described the "chaos and clutter in the apartment caused by so many people" as potential risks to the woman's well-being as the justification for the recommendation. Like Jermaine's parents, the elderly client was presented with a non-negotiable choice of the service believed to be appropriate by the professionals or no service.

I applied the term *silent mandate* to both case situations, rather than referring to them as nonvoluntary contacts. Using the Rooney and Bibus (2000) screen related to the presence or absence of a legal mandate, in each situation, a legal mandate is not involved, nor is there a court order for service. Thus, at first glance, each case resembles the pressured contact that is associated with nonvoluntary status. In nonvoluntary situations, however, the individual may choose to more or less accept help in which he or she may or may nor incur serious consequences. For example, an employer or a relative may pressure an individual to get help or else. Depending on the authority of the source, and the power of the individual, they may follow the recommendation or choose to endure the consequences.

Conversely, a *silent mandate* for those without power has the force and characteristic of one that is legal, in that it has a similar prescriptive power that is associated with constrained or coerced choice. For example, Jermaine's parents were given a choice of accepting the EBD class or an alterative school, neither of which was attractive to them. There are policy guidelines related to EBD placements, but not a law that dictates that the inability to sit for long periods should result in a remedial education class. In reality, Jermaine was entitled to have an advocate present in the meeting as well as a documentation of intermediary interventions before the decision was made to place him in an EBD classroom. For example, when the parents asked "What has been tried?" the team should have been able to cite at least one intervention that addressed the situation. Nor in the case of the elderly woman is there a law that determines the number of people who should live in a household, or the quality of that experience, unless there is evidence of a health hazard, neglect, or egregious harm.

The silent mandate is supported by the authority of an organization as well by the status of the professional. In contrast, clients recognize the fragility of their power and their innate vulnerability. In most instances, it is the centrality of the power that resides in the professional's authority that will ultimately influence a client's response (Orme 2002; Clifford and Burke 2005). Thus, it is highly unlikely that vulnerable and oppressed clients who are involuntary will cognitively differentiate between the presence and absence of a legal mandate. Although the silent mandate lacks a legal basis, and on the face of it resembles a nonvoluntary contact, it has implications that are much more powerful.

Constituents of Social Work Practice

Many social work professionals are engaged in practice with individuals who by and large are members of oppressed groups. Although their status as outsiders may differ in degree, on the whole they are outsiders by virtue of being different, by virtue of their behavior or lifestyle, or by their failure to fit into the dominant societal schema. Racial and ethnic minorities served by social workers are further disenfranchised by the framing of social issues. Enabled by political debates, media coverage that negatively profiles them as disadvantaged further contributes to their social, psychological, and economic marginalization. Televised segments on welfare initiatives are examples of the discourse on social problems in which the media has had a powerful role. For example, one representative prime time news segment and interviewer posed questions of a minority woman, "Why haven't you found full-time employment? How long have you been looking for work?" In response, the woman replied "about four months." "Why has it taken you so long to find a job?" As the woman launched into an explanation about available jobs being primarily seasonal or part-time work and without benefits, and that she would like to complete a nurse practitioner training program, the interviewer smiled, looked directly into the camera, and stated, "Back to you Jim and Terri." Caught off guard, the woman continued to talk. The auditory portion of the interview faded and the segment ends with her looking embarrassed, confused, and ultimately angry. The viewing public is left with an image of the unmotivated and hostile welfare recipient who is content to live off the earnings of an innocent hard-working public. These segments play to the social categorization of *we–they* in which "they are portrayed as all alike, while the "we" have attributes that are more favorable to the dominant group. This portrayal effectively controls the image of those with less power.

Oppression as Political

Oppression is hierarchical, pervasive, systematic, and inherently political. Public policy is political. To assume otherwise suggests that the system works equally for all people is tacit acceptance of the established order (Galper 1975; Gil 1978; Mullaly 1997; Vodde and Gallant 2002). Influenced by the Puritan ethic of good or bad, policies are not neutral, nor do they in most instances seek the input of or collaborate with those affected or seek to understand their circumstances. For the segments of the population who are positioned at the lower ranks, public policy, as reflected in the dominant narrative, in many respects is akin to social control (Gil 1978; Mullaly 1997). Whyte (1956) referred to the controlling dominant narrative in organizations as the *social ethic.* The social ethic in essence established a set of values that became morally legitimate in the form of pressures of society against the individual (or groups).

As social workers, we have tended to embrace the notion of political neutrality in our relationships with our clients, even those who are voluntary. Professional standards reinforce this notion by emphasizing a nonjudgmental attitude, human dignity, and worth and self-determination. Political neutrality is not possible with members of oppressed groups or with involuntary clients. For both groups the helping process is co-managed by a legal mandate, the preferences of the dominant viewpoint, or a more restrictive distribution of resources and public policy than occurs for the elite. Note for example the stringent work requirements for welfare recipients, but not for the employers with political leverage. Some employers were awarded federal funds to hire welfare recipients even though they did not make a commitment to provide long-term employment. In fact, in many instances when the federal supports were exhausted, the employers discontinued the employment of welfare recipients.

Social workers are confronted with a dual responsibility: to the client, and to the authority of the legal mandate and dominant societal preferences, the latter of which may often represent the agenda of moral entrepreneurs (Weinberg 2006). More often than not the scope of relationships and professional responsibilities with involuntary clients and members of oppressed groups are codified in the rules, policies, and procedures of public policy and laws. When confronted with the responsibility of the regulation, rehabilitation, and discipline, social workers in the context of caring are caught between balancing tensions as agents of good and a preoccupation with their accountability to a legal mandate and to society (Reamer 1994, 2005; Reid 2002; Orme 2002; Weinberg 2006). In fulfilling their dual responsibility, social workers can become entangled in the process and structure that is oppressive, especially when a legal rather than a problem-solving and relational remedy is emphasized. In the former, the common life circumstances of oppressed people is ignored or dismissed.

While individual social workers may be unable to dismantle oppression, they can acknowledge and seek to neutralize its impact. This work is presented in the following case example. The social work must reconcile a policy that defines parental behavior as a problem, with an intervention manages and improves the oppressive circumstances of the family's life.

The Ruiz Family and Educational Neglect

The Ruiz family is Mexican-American consisting of a father and mother and four children. They live in a small rural Midwestern community where both parents are employed at the poultry processing plant. Some weeks the parents work on the same shift, while at other times their assigned shifts vary. Work schedules are posted at the end of the week, which makes it difficult for the family to plan ahead. They lack the seniority that would allow them to have predictable and desirable shifts.

The family's involuntary entry into the child welfare system and conflict with the educational system occurred because the two older children were responsible for caring for their two younger siblings when both parents were scheduled for the day shift. Each child had missed more than thirty days of school at various times throughout the fall term. A teacher reported that the children appeared to have "lacked an understanding of the issue" and were "vague about whether their parents were sufficiently concerned about their absences to meet with the teacher." In addition, the teacher reported that the reticence of the children to talk about their parents was strange. The school (as legally mandated) reported the absences to child protection services, which intervened on the basis of educational neglect.

What were the initial assumptions in this case? Under education and child welfare policies the parents were negligent. In seeking to protect and ensure the rights of children, the policies have an explicit assumption and bias. Specifically, child welfare policies assume that some parents are unwilling or incapable of parenting, thus casting the state in the role of the ultimate parent. Educational policies assume that there are certain parents who do not value education. In both instances, a corrective intervention is required and the focus is on parental behavior. Neither policy discriminates with respect to individual circumstances. Rather, when public policy or societal rules are violated the outsiders must be sanctioned. Policies do not examine the reasoning behind acts that an individual commits nor the circumstances in which those acts occurred. In consequence, the application of rules and related sanctions becomes oppressive (Day 1981). The Ruiz's decision that the older children miss school had violated a rule created by societal institutions for the education and protection of children. In their failure to abide by the rules, the parent's decision was deemed to be an act of neglect that requires an intervention.

Procedural Justice

Involuntary clients are rarely involved in the decisions or mandates that affect their lives. As such, like Mr. Ruiz, they are more likely to perceive the outcomes of policies as unjust. People seek to have direct and indirect control over their own lives and react with strong emotions to appraisals of their behavior, actions, and decision making as deviant. Unlike distributive justice which addresses fairness in the allocation of resources, procedural justice involves the client's perspective and participation and they assess the fairness of an intervention relative to the situation (Greenberg and Tyler 1987; Folger 1987; Tyler 1989; Beitin and Allend 2005). Procedural justice is compatible with the just practice framework articulated by Finn and Jacobson (2003), in particular the ethic of participation. As does procedural justice, the just practice framework considers the big picture, examining the overall context of a client's life. By incorporating procedural justice into their work with oppressed groups, specifically by inviting the client's story, the social worker can gain access to a client's perspectives and experience. Procedural justice and just practice questions facilitated engaging the Ruiz family as illustrated by revisiting the case.

Engaging the Ruiz Family Using the Just Practice Framework

In meeting with the family, the social worker encountered reactance, expressed in the family's hostility, shame, anger, fear, and confusion. De Jong and Berg (2001) and Rooney (2000) suggest a first step in engaging clients that is consistent with procedural justice is to allow mandated clients to tell their story, describing their understanding of the mandate or referral. Questions posed by Finn and Jacobson's (2003) "just practice" framework with regard to participation and power are also applicable. In this framework, an essential component of creating an atmosphere in which the client is invited to talk responds to the question, "How do people give meaning to the experience and conditions that influence their lives?" The question essentially extends power to the client as an equal participant in both the process and the outcome. The question further elaborates procedural justice in that it inserts the voice and experience of the client who has not been involved in the policy debate or its formulation. A second question directs the social worker to query, "How do I apprehend, interpret, and appreciate the contextual nature of human experiences and interactions?" (hence diminishing the opportunity for judgment and bias, and also moving the contact beyond the conclusions of a policy and the language of the mandate or referral).

When asked about his understanding of the intervention by child protective services, Mr. Ruiz explained that a friend had told him that it was because "we kept the children at home to baby-sit." As a migrant worker, he felt he had few protections, which added to his confusion about the school's intrusion into the family's life and the authority of child protective services. In exploring context, as discussed by Finn and Jacobson (2003), in particular the circumstances and conditions that influence and surround particular events and situations, Mrs. Ruiz spoke about the conflict with their work schedules and the need for childcare. Glancing at Mr. Ruiz as if seeking his confirmation she said, "we want education for the children so they can be better off." Having heretofore worked as migrants, they had welcomed the opportunity for permanent employment and the stability it provided their children. Moving to the community also had disadvantages. They were strangers. Having the older children provide childcare was the only alternative that they believed to be available to them given their status in the community.

Throughout the interview, Mr. Ruiz expressed anger toward child protective services. "Yes," he understood the explanation provided by the friend. But, he said "we are honest, hard working and we don't cause trouble for nobody." At one point, he became so frustrated that he demanded that the social worker leave the home. In staying the course, the social worker understood that Mr. Ruiz perceived the intervention as punitive. "No one has tried to help us, so we do the best we can." He demanded, "Where were child protective services when my children were working in the fields, working long hours and living in bad conditions?" In fact he held the aspiration that is common among all people, that of having control over their personal lives. Further, he felt punished because he and Mrs. Ruiz believed that they had made "the best decision," given their circumstances. His anger was somewhat diminished when the social worker explained her role, the intent of the policies that had led to the intervention, and the potential choices available to them. She then empathized with his situation, including the experience of being a stranger in the community, and acknowledged his comment about being "hard working people, who did not want to cause trouble." She then moved to reframe the issue to a need of childcare, rather than that a case of neglect. Both Mr. and Mrs. Ruiz subsequently agreed to work with the social worker.

What makes this case different? Had this been a less visible, nonminority family with ties to the community, would the situation have been handled differently? At first glance, it appears to be a fairly straightforward case of educational neglect resulting from a decision made by the parents. How was the decision by the social work to reframe the case as a lack of child care rather than that of neglect made? What are the dynamics of oppression and vulnerability that suggest a link to involuntary client status?

Mr. Ruiz explained that there are few people in the community "who look like us," and therefore finding childcare had been difficult. Although there are other Mexican American families in the community, they work at the poultry plant and as new employees they had similar schedules. Many of these families had experience with child protective services for reasons that few understood. In addition, while the other people in the community had not been openly hostile, they had not been particularly friendly either. In fact, during the previous two weeks, the local newspaper had published the results of interviews with local residents about the presence of the "Mexican families in the town." Sentiments expressed referred to the families as "the newcomers," "those people," and that it would take some time for "folks around here to get use to seeing them on a regular basis." Another resident asserted, "But we shouldn't have to get use to them." While few people had noticed or objected to these families as transitory migrant workers, the idea that they would "settle in the community was another matter."

Some residents voiced the familiar charges, such as "they are taking our jobs," and "their children are a burden to our school system." There were also complaints about Cinco de Mayo celebrations and the display of the Mexican flag. When interviewed, the plant manager stated "they are good, reliable workers, despite their problems." The vague notion of "their problems," as articulated by the plant manager, speaks to the family's vulnerability. In characterizing the families as problems, the community and the manager were absolved of any responsibility for their well-being. An interpretation of their problems was rationalized as characteristics of the individual families, absent of their position in and interaction with the community. The very fact that community residents were asked to comment on the "newcomers" was symbolic of the vulnerable status of the oppressed. The responses of the community illustrated both the process and structure of oppression, in which the hierarchy assigned the newcomers to membership at a lower rank of the community. How might the newspaper story been different if the Mexican American families had been given the opportunity to comment on their experience?

Let's assume benign intent on the part of the newspaper. Perhaps the article intended to introduce the families to the community. It is possible that the residents were simply responding to the questions that they were asked. Nevertheless, by focusing on the Mexican American families and eliciting community opinions about their being in the community effectively elevated the power of the non-Mexican American residents, and reinforced a hierarchy of ranking. Their responses indicated that they held the power to decide whether or not Mexican American families were accepted as members of the community. Some residents would no doubt say that this is much to do about nothing. Realistically, the statement that "it will take some getting use to," perhaps is a norm that is applied to all new residents. Yet it is unlikely that the focus would have been on families whose demographics were consistent with those of the majority residents.

This case further illustrates that oppressive circumstances can be instrumental in facilitating involuntary client status. The Ruiz family responded to a public policy about the education and care of children even though no court order had been imposed. The power of the silent mandate is manifested in the authority of the teacher's interpretation of the children's response. The children had not been a problem at school, they did not appear to be in distress, nor was there a report that they their grades were a concern. The intervention occurred because they had missed school. Initially, the reason for their absences was unclear. The social worker learned, however, that school attendance was commingled with the family's need for child care, specifically the irregularity of the parent's work shifts. The school, in accordance with their responsibility, responded to the situation and the Ruiz's involuntary contact with the child welfare system. Without the context in which school attendance was located, along with the family's vulnerable status in the community, the situation could have been judged as simply a matter of failure of parental responsibility and hence neglect. It was the social worker's diligence in framing her inquiry to include the circumstances of the family's status that enabled her to seek agreement from the family about resolving their child care needs rather than pursue the sanctions associated with educational neglect.

Competence in Culture and Oppression

In working with oppressed groups, in particular clients who are ethnic and racial minorities, the social work literature has emphasized cultural competence. Culturally competent social workers are attuned to and respectful of differences, aware of their own bias, and seek to understand the client's behavior, values, and lifestyles from their cultural vantage point. Further, culturally competent professionals avoid judging and labeling differences that perpetuate oppression based on differences (Holland and Kilpatrick 1993; Dei 1996; Arrendondo 1999; Vera and Speight 2003).

Cultural nuances in the Ruiz case supported a culturally competent emphasis. Note for example that it was the father who primarily spoke for the family. According to Lum (2004:167), "it is his role as the head of state." In this role, it is to be expected that the intervention by child protective services and the school would be perceived by Mr. Ruiz as a "direct assault on his authority." Recall that at one point in asserting his authority and family autonomy, he ordered the social worker to leave the home. His reaction of course was not culture specific. Rather, it represented the moral outrage that may be expressed by involuntary clients in response to an intervention believed to be unjust. In the case of Mr. Ruiz, the response was related to his belief that the school and child protective service lacked an understanding of the family's circumstances. The mother, when speaking about the value of education, looked at Mr. Ruiz. Her doing so could have been construed as her seeking his permission. Her behaviors may have represented a cultural relic, a personality trait, or simply an arrangement in this particular family. Culturally competent practice would suggest exploring any conclusions about her behavior, rather than measuring it against stereotypical roles in Hispanic families. An understanding of culture is also indicated in the teacher's report regarding the hesitancy of the older children and their "vague" response when they were asked about their parent's availability to meet with school officials. Their reluctance, however, to discuss their parents is not uncommon in the many cultures in which children are forbidden to comment on the affairs of adults or the home situation without permission.

Observing culture in this case was important, especially for understanding the role and reaction of Mr. Ruiz. Indeed, solely emphasizing models of practice that preclude culture is one form of oppression (Dei 1996; Arrendondo 1999; Vera and Speight 2003). But this emphasis alone would have been insufficient to explain or resolve the family's situation. In fact, culture and the Ruiz's beliefs and values were not central to their contact with the social worker, nor was their childcare decision culturally based. Instead, it was the circumstances of oppression relative to power and the family's marginal status as Mexican Americans in the community that had precedence. As such, problem solving with this family indicated a need for competence in the residue of oppression, especially the way in which power and privilege translate into the experience and capacity of clients who are members of oppressed groups (Dei 1996; Van Voorhis 1998; Al-Krenawi and Graham 2001; Weaver 2000, 2004; Vodde and Gallant 2002). In the absence of knowledge of about the family's circumstances, you may want to argue that neither the residents nor the newspaper can be faulted for the childcare decision. Nonetheless, the Ruiz's decision cannot be adequately assessed or resolved without considering their reality-based perception and experience that constrained their resource choices. Thus, in much the same way that cultural competence should be an evolving goal (Dean 2001), social workers must strive to a level in which they are attuned to systemic oppression and its relationship to involuntary client status. In this case, the social worker's focus on family need demonstrated sensitivity to the multiple forms of oppression that the family had experienced, especially that of marginal status and vulnerability. Her doing so was critical to engagement and eventually problem solving.

Attributes of Oppression and Involuntary Status

At the beginning of this chapter, I raised the question of whether members of oppressed groups and involuntary clients share in common the potential to intrude upon the helping process. As social workers, we are educated to assess clients' situations using both a person-in-the-environment and a human behavior-in-the-social environment framework. Our assessments are also informed by both the cultural and strengths perspectives. Even so, there are challenges in working with involuntary clients from oppressed groups. First, despite the apparent overlap between involuntary status and oppression there is limited literature that directly connects these populations to each other.

Thus there is a void in practice that assimilates and is capable of providing guidance. Second, as professionals, we understand oppression yet we lack the guidance to incorporate the complexities of this understanding in our work with clients. Nagda and colleagues (1999), in articulating this dilemma, suggest that concerns related to oppression are stalled at the intuitive and emotional level. Clifford and Burke (2005) point to yet another difficulty: that of the profession's ethical principle of having respect for differences. Specifically, respect for another individual becomes much more of a challenge when the individual is of a very different social standing.

In examining the attributes of involuntary clients and members of oppressed groups. Table 15.1 lists specific attributes that are common to both involuntary clients and members of oppressed groups. Perhaps the most prominent attribute is that of being an outsider which perpetuates marginalized status. In addition, as an outsider, one's self-image and problems are largely shaped by others who are unfamiliar with or disinterested in their circumstances. As a result, both the involuntary client and the client from an oppressed group are respondents to a perceived deficit and are judged. Historical legacy, that is, a long-term involvement with social welfare organizations is not indicated for the involuntary client. It is, however, often a factor for racial and ethnic group members. When these attributes take on the added dimension of the vulnerability this triangulation has the potential to converge into a forceful and intrusive dynamic in the helping relationship.

Table 15.1   Shared attributes of oppressed groups and involuntary clients

	Involuntary Clients	Oppressed Groups
Compliance	X	X
External locus of control	X	X
Distrustful	X	X
Constrained self-determination	X	X
Historical legacy		X
Powerlessness	X	X
Marginalized	X	X
Outsiders	X	X

Status

An unexplored dimension of involuntary status relates to the involuntariness of individuals who merely by their birth acquire membership into an oppressed group. These individuals are decidedly involuntary in this status. The depersonalized and stigmatized rubric of being different is hardly erected or sustained by those who are affected. Oppression in this regard is an involuntary transaction with society because members of oppressed groups do not willingly seek a status that has limited power and resources, and in which there is a high potential for being marginalized. The exchange between society and members of oppressed group resembles the involuntary transaction in which the client experiences the dynamic of a legal and normative imbalance of power. For example, the involuntary transaction between the Ruiz family which contributed to their vulnerability was enlarged by a community that "embraced the notion of other" (Freire 1998:38). In much the same way as the involuntary client would prefer to be somewhere else (Rooney 1992), oppressed individuals left to their own volition would hardly choose to be different and disenfranchised. Nor would the majority use language that is associated with being oppressed.

Oppression in the classic sense is the language of professionals and social scientists who study the structural arrangements of a society. Individuals who are members of oppressed group would more likely describe their personal circumstances as realized in the macro content of their lives. For instance, rather than perceiving themselves as deficient or unmotivated their stories might speak to their lack of sufficient resources, of being visible and invisible, the experience of discrimination, bigotry, and their familiarity with the day-to-day tasks of coping without the status and privilege that is available to others.

Similarly, because of their status, involuntary clients believe themselves to be vulnerable and to lack power. They also appropriately view themselves as being different from clients who on their own accord seek help. In much the same way as the stories told by oppressed individuals would differ from the dominant perceptions, the involuntary client's story would not embrace the professional paradigm that summarizes their attributes. For example, professionals may view an involuntary client as uncooperative, unmotivated, angry, or hostile and the client may express anxiety, discouragement, and fear that stems from their lack of power or resources.

Both the social worker and the client experience the descriptive language, both societal and professional, that marginalizes the client status and that magnifies the power and the social distance between the dominant and the dominated. The remnants of oppression may be observed in the often deficit-oriented and depersonalized professional language used to describe the involuntary client and members of oppressed groups. The fact that clients are for the most part not privy to this language in their face-to-face interactions with professionals does not diminish its potency. In fact, clients experience and are subjected to the residuals of language when professionals respond to their status rather than to the person.

Compliance

Compliance is a factor for both groups. Involuntary clients are expected to show evidence of compliance by completing the requirements of their case plans that has been set forth by legal or silent mandate. They are also required to accept the authority that has defined their problem. Similarly, it is the responsibility of the oppressed to adapt and to comply with the mandates inherent in dominant societal realities, social order, behaviors, lifestyles, and values. Both involuntary clients and oppressed people have limited choices that are inherent in their involuntary status. For oppressed groups choice is often limited by access to resources, including desirable housing, employment, and education. Constrained self-determination is central in that there is a real or perceived feeling of powerlessness and vulnerability. For involuntary clients the imbalance of power in the relationship is reinforced when the professional's power is acknowledged in the mandate. Compliance as a coercive dynamic creates tension and conflict and diminishes trust when the professional authority to ensure compliance is emphasized. Further, clients are likely to perceive the professional role as indicative of their collaboration with the mandate authority.

External Locus of Control

In describing the experience of oppression, Frye (2004:176) contends that oppression is "the living of life," in a manner that is "confined and shaped by forces and barriers that are not accidental and hence avoidable." Oppression is akin to "being caged in, feeling that all avenues in either direction are blocked or booby trapped." For the involuntary client the expectation to behave in a certain way, to comply with a requirement or a mandate to seek help is analogous to feeling experienced by those who are oppressed. Given the experience of oppression, which when joined by involuntary status, a member of an oppressed group is apt to be hypersensitive, distrustful, and suspicious. In many instances, such clients perceive contact with a professional, especially when the contact has been mandated, as oppression disguised as helping. When confronted with situations in which they feel powerless, clients may view themselves as victims of an oppressive system created by the authority that exerts control over their lives. External control combined with compliance become counterproductive forces that cast an aura over the helping relationship.

Outsiders and Stigma

The social work relationship with the involuntary client from an oppressed group is a subjective experience. The behavior and attitude of both the social worker and client are informed by their experiential and cognitive worldviews. Members of oppressed groups, especially those who are low income have often experienced a social welfare legacy that positions them as "the problem" rather than receiving help focused on the problems that they experience. As outsiders, they are detached and isolated from a society and its organizations and their experience with oppression is rarely acknowledged (Freire 1970, 1998; Van Voorhis 1998). In contrast, social workers hold a position of privilege. This privilege is derived from their status, power, and social class, all of which contribute to inequality in the contact with clients. In addition, social workers' worldviews are informed by the privilege and authority of educational status and in many instances that of race. Their status is further bolstered by policies and services that empower them to interpret and diagnose client problems.

Like oppressed racial and ethnic minorities, involuntary clients are outsiders. Involuntary status essentially ranks them in a hierarchy of the willing and unwilling, the latter of which is perceived to be outside of the norm. The dynamic of reactance may reinforce their marginal status, effectively separating them from clients who acknowledge their need and who are subsequently motivated to change related to goals of their own choosing.

Racial and class differences instigate yet another troublesome dynamic between the social worker and the client with whom they have contact. These differences are enlarged by a diverse experiential and social distance (Davis and Gelsomino 1994; Green, Kiernan-Stern, and Baskind 2005). Social distance in the social worker–client dyad between involuntary clients and racial and ethnic minorities is further exaggerated by a persistent stigma encoded with assumptions about deviance, health, personal responsibility, family, and life styles. The stigma attached to racial and ethnic minorities is in fact an oppressive double bind. They are in need of services and resources, yet are stigmatized by the language of organizations and professionals for seeking help. For example, they may be labeled at risk or high risk (Orme 2002; Weinberg 2006). The involuntary client is stigmatized for their acts or behaviors, for example, as perpetrators in the case of men who batter or neglectful or abusive in the case of parents who fail to ensure their child's well being. In any case, neither the involuntary client nor a member of an oppressed group is unlikely to willingly become involved in an asymmetrical relationship. As outsiders, they appropriately react to the professional with whom they interact and whom they perceive as lacking an understanding of or is disinterested in their circumstances.

Reactance

Reactance is a robust emotion that can be understood in the context of the psychosocial self, the origins of which are immersed in the historical and environmental experience with the social environment (Van Voorhis 1998; Walsh 2003). It may manifest as a reluctance to accept the reason required for seeking help. As a dynamic, reactance can also be relative to stigma, external control, and compliance because a sanctioned authority has identified the problem and the solution, thereby limiting self-determination and curtailing freedom. Emotions such as anger, fear, or anxiety evoke a psychosocial response to the perception of a threat. Clients' emotional responses in mandated situations are fueled by their perception of intrusion into their private lives and they may feel punished. Recall the manner in which Mr. Ruiz responded to what he believed was interference by child protective services and asserted the family's right to their autonomous decision making. He also expressed anger at being judged, and felt misunderstood, which prompted his demand that the social worker leave his home. His reaction perhaps was informed by the cognitive schema of many involuntary clients and oppressed people in which control and punishment rather than care are perceived as salient factors in their interaction with helping systems. Hence, they feel threatened and mistrust the capacity of social services to treat them fairly.

In many encounters, reactance becomes a circuitous dynamic in the social worker's response to the client's involuntary status. In brief, the involuntary client meets the involuntary social worker. When faced with client reactance, professionals may feel threatened. For example, when Jermaine's parents asked, "why can't you all teach our kids?" the team leader became uncooperative. The parent's questions and their statement linking the locked doors to a prison represented a message within a message. Their overall message expressed their worldview that involved the historical legacy of African American males incarcerated in U.S. prisons and the failures of an educational system to prepare them successfully for life. When presented with the parents' question and observation, the team leader suggested that Jermaine might "be better served in an alternative school." What the team leader heard was threatening to him and seemed like an indictment of the team's professional status and a critique of its judgment. In turn, he concluded that the parents were uncooperative, hostile, and that they misunderstood the team's best effort to help their son. Further, the tenor of the interaction underscored the social distance and differing worldviews of the parents and the professionals. Whereas the team leader acted from his position of authority, privilege, and power, the parents acted as members of a marginalized, alienated group in society.

The result was an impasse in which neither side was satisfied with the outcome. Hence no problem solving occurred because the team leader lacked an understanding of the power dynamics and the experience of the parents.

Crisis

Even voluntary clients tend to seek help when an event or situation has exceeded their capacity to manage. A crisis is generally thought of as an episodic event or situation in which relief will reestablish a previous level of equilibrium (James and Gilliland 2005). Members of oppressed groups, especially those who are poor, live with varying levels of crisis in their everyday lives in which stressors and strains exhaust their strengths and coping capacities. Their lives are permeated with high levels of psychological, social, and economic stressors that have strained their personal and community resources.

Regardless of how routine an encounter may be for the social worker, for the involuntary client the contact may evoke a crisis state. Involuntary contact may become entangled with and add to existing stressors and historical experiences and create a traumatic event. For Jarmaine's parents, the trauma occurred because their son was judged as inadequate and stigmatized by being placed in an EBD class. Likewise for the Ruiz family, responding to external demands created by contact with the social worker precipitated a crisis event. In crisis situations, comparable to the dynamic of reactance, the language of clients may have a tone that is emotionally focused.

Distrust

When racial and ethnic minorities are involuntary the dynamics of the relationship and the psychological contract with the expert authority assumes a distinctively different texture. Differences related to race, class, and world-view and unequal power are volatile ingredients that create a relationship that is void of trust, as was observed in the responses of Jarmaine's parents and the team leader. Distrust is a core dynamic when problems or needs have been determined either by a mandate or other means of coercion and authority. In addition, the helping relationship is overshadowed by fear, powerlessness, compliance, and control (Cingolani 1984; Hutchison 1987; Rooney and Bibus 2000; Reid 2002). The relationship of those who engage voluntarily with professionals is in contrast to one with an involuntary client. In the former, relational problem solving and collaboration and general goodwill are attributed to the professional, and a collaborative, reciprocal arrangement is nurtured. For the involuntary client who is also a member of a racial or ethnic minority group, the psychological authority of the professional occurs in a vastly different social context. For this reason, when the involuntary client is also a member of a racial or ethnic minority group the context in which the relationship is located requires attention, in particular the crisis associated with being judged.

Individuals from racial and ethnic minority groups often speak in the abstract of the entities they view as exerting control over their lives in the abstract, for example, *"they,"* or *"the system,"* or in the case of individuals *"he"* or *"she."* In the latter, the use of pronouns is indicative of an individual believed to represent the system. These expressions underscore the tension, distrust, and distance between themselves and the systems or individuals whom they perceive as having power. It is also a form of reactance to the imbalance of power in the relationship. Finally, in much the same way that professional and societal language may be depersonalized with respect to involuntary clients and members of oppressed groups, the impersonal language of clients when referring to professionals has similar undertones. The lack of trust is emphasized in the language and behaviors of both parties.

Mandates or court orders do not invite trust, nor do they allow for emotions. Mandates do, however, contribute to feeling real or imagined of being vulnerable to power and authority of the invisible and the unfamiliar. Moreover, trust is difficult to establish in an asymmetrical relationship where oppression and involuntary status resemble the structural arrangements in society that exist between the dominant, the dominated, the oppressed and the oppressor. It is useful to work through these waters in order to establish a working alliance. In the following case situations, many of the involuntary client and oppressed group attributes may be observed. The intersection of the shared attributes between involuntary status and membership in an oppressed group is an additional hurdle that must be crossed.

The Case of Mrs. W.

CLIENT: *They* told me to come and see you about getting my son back. It seems like with black people, we are always being told to go see somebody about something that *they* say ain't right. *They* [are] always messing with our kids and us.

SOCIAL WORKER: When you say *they,* it would be helpful for me to understand whom you are talking about.

CLIENT: I don't know, but you know *them.* All I know is *they* said I wasn't taking care of my son. When *she* came into my house with the police, I go was mad. I cussed *her* out. *She* don't know nothing about me, and here *she* is in my face talking s . . . . about neglect. Two big old policemen held me back while *she* took my child—he was crying and all *she* did was look stupid. Everybody was out in the hallway looking. Then, I got real scared. *They* ain't never gonna let me have my child, you know what I am saying. This is messed up!

SOCIAL WORKER: I understand your feeling scared and angry. I also imagine that it was traumatic for your child to be removed from your care. Would it be helpful for me to explain why you were asked to see me?

CLIENT: Well, maybe, but you know the *system* works this way. My sister, my cousin and one of my friends all had their children taken for crazy reasons. For us black people, *they* use any excuse to take our children. It's always some b . . . . s . . . about neglect, like we don't care about our kids.

SOCIAL WORKER: I hear that you believe that African American kids are removed from their homes and that the system is unjust. I also hear that you believe that your son was removed from your home because you are African American.

CLIENT: Yeah, how are you gonna help me get my child back?

SOCIAL WORKER: I work for Pegasus. This agency contracts with the county child welfare agency to work with parents so that they can complete their case plans and be reunited with their children. It would help me to understand your situation if you told me what happened.

CLIENT: I am sick and tired of *people* messing with me, you know what I mean. I work, try to keep my head up, but things just keep coming at me. My son Darnell has asthma. I stopped smoking because the doctor said this would help. One night he was really bad, so I took him to the emergency room. We had to take the bus. The doctor, *he* asked me a bunch of ignorant questions, like I didn't care about my child. (she mimics the doctor) "Mrs. W., why did you wait so long to bring your son to the ER?" I just stood there and looked at him like *he* was some kind of fool. Then *he* said that I would have to see the social worker and left the room. I was tired, cold and scared. All I wanted was for them to help my child.

SOCIAL WORKER: Then what happened?

CLIENT: *She* [the hospital social worker] came in and asked me more stupid questions, just like the doctor, and filled out this form. *She* said something about being required to complete a risk something or other.

SOCIAL WORKER: Yes, the social worker would complete a risk assessment. Perhaps I could explain this to you if you are interested, but first, tell me what happened next.

CLIENT: I got mad. When Darnell got better, I went into the room, took him, and left. Next thing I know, *they* were at my house to take him away, saying that I was neglecting him. Then *she* wrote a report saying that my apartment was unsafe because *she* saw the traps that I had for mice and roaches. Everybody in the building has rats and roaches. The garbage is always over flowing cause *he* [the landlord] don't pay the garbage people for regular pick up. I would not know the *man* if he was in this room; his name is Mister something or another. We send our rent to a post office box. I have called *him* to fix the water leaks—the building is a mess—where am I gonna go that's gonna be better?

The crazy thing is that I was doing the best that I could. I got a cat from a friend and that helped. I don't keep a lot of food in the house, that's why I go mad when to *they* [the police] opened my cabinets and said that there was no food in the house. Then, you know what *she* had the nerve to say—the cat was making my son sick. I tried to tell that b . . . . that his doctor said that a short-haired cat was okay. It's like they were looking for a reason. When we got to court, the judge said that I needed to find another apartment. When *she* talked to the judge, *she* didn't tell him nothing about me or what I had done, because she don't care or know nothing about me. Just playing games with me, and there is nothing I can do about it if I want to get my son back.

What are the connections between involuntary client status and oppression in this case?

First, throughout the client's narrative, she alerts the social worker to her lack of power, and that of people like her. For example, her comments that speak to her lack of power and that of an invisible power were, "It seems like with black people, we are always being told to go see somebody about something that *they* say ain't right." In addition, the issues of power and external locus of control are reflected in the client's dispirited statement, "I am sick and tired of *people* messing with me. . . . I work, try to keep my head up, but things just keep coming at me." Choudhuri (2005:133) proposed that in interactions with professionals that "it is in the spirit" that impact of oppression can be observed. When the social worker empathized with the client, she plunged ahead with her story, of being "caged in" as suggested by Frye (2004) and a victim the "roadblocks" of an unspecified system. Allowing the emotionally charged catharsis of the client is important as at this point in the contact, she is unwilling or unable to hear and to trust that the social worker understands. Despite the overtures made by the social worker, her statement is insufficient to persuade Mrs. W. of her interest in helping. Generally at this stage of contact, reactance is high, especially in response feeling of being judged and controlled and the loss of freedom, in this case, her status as a parent. Mrs. W. in fact amplified her feelings about being judged when she expressed anger that neither the social worker nor the judge knew anything about her.

Are there other aspects in this case that call attention to an overlap between oppression and involuntary status? As social workers, we are in contact with people who are vulnerable and overwhelmed by conditions of their lives that they feel powerless to control. In addition, the problems that low-income clients experience are often related to oppression and vulnerability.

The order from the judge to find a new apartment, for example, set forth a requirement that she feels is unjust, if not impossible, and further as she states, "where am I gonna go that's gonna be better?" Her question is valid. As a low-income, minority single parent, she is vulnerable. Vulnerability in that her economic status places her at the mercy of a housing market in which affordable housing is difficult to locate. Like most low-income minority individuals, her limited options tend to be concentrated in inner-city neighborhoods, in which the quality of the rental housing stock is questionable. As noted by Anderson and Collins (2001), inner-city neighborhoods tend to be politically isolated conclaves of poverty and subjected to crime and chronic neglect by those in power.

Anti-Oppression Problem Solving

Anti-oppression problem-solving requires a conscious commitment to social justice and to advancing professional knowledge about the weight of oppression in the lives of clients. This level of problem solving is best guided by structural thinking based on principles embodied in the structural approach. Principles of the Structural Approach encourage the social worker to assess the relationship between problems and oppression. In effect, structural thinking on the part of the social work expands the scope of the person in environment to include the influence and inequities of the dominant political and social order (Galper 1975; Carniol 1992; Mullaly 1997; Lopez, Gurin, and Nagda 1998). Also to be understood are the complex dynamics inherent in the professional–client dyad relationship fostered by the shared attributes of the involuntary client who is a members of an oppressed group. Therefore, the social worker must attend to the environmental, emotional, and historical context in which the relationship is located, especially the juxtapositions of the powerful and the powerless, and that of belonging and alienation.

Anti-oppression problem-solving guides the social worker to assess the situation relying in part on the realistic social context of clients' lives. For example, what is the capacity of Mrs. W. to comply with the court order? It is a fact of life that in poor neighborhoods landlords routinely ignore housing codes. Further, low-income people are subjected to code rules that they lack the power to enforce. While city codes require regular garbage collection, unscrupulous landlords are generally adept at managing the margins in which codes allow them to operate. Complaints must be registered, citations issued, and there is a grace period for correcting the situation before officials act. With this understanding, these landlords maximize to their advantage the lack of oversight by city or county officials as well as the complaint process. They also understand the dilemma faced by low-income tenants. Thus, the statement, "where am I gonna go, that's gonna be better," is a realistic assessment by Mrs. W. of her situation. In addition, landlords lack incentives to fix their problem properties. They are aware that for every resident who moves out, there are others who will take their place. The structural thinking that is relevant in this case would involve understanding the validity of the client's statement as well as a realistic appraisal of her housing options. Understanding and empathizing with Mrs. W.'s dilemma is a first step. But acting on this information requires that her situation is communicated to the court. Otherwise a lack of progress in finding a new apartment could result in the unjust permanent placement of her son.

Structural thinking is also indicated in response to the client's comment that "My sister, my cousin and one of my friends all had their children taken for crazy reasons. . . . *They* use any excuse to take our children. It's always some b . . . . s . . . about neglect, like we don't care about our kids."

Research findings are inconclusive about the extent that race and geography has a significant influence with respect to out of home placement (Garland et al. 1998). Nevertheless, it is not uncommon for clients who reside in a particular geographical population to articulate the "visibility hypothesis." Their assumption is based on the fact that in certain neighborhoods they have experienced proximity to others who have experienced intervention by child welfare authorities resulting in the placement of their children in foster care.

The social worker attempts to address the client's belief about the removal of African American children from their homes, as well as her belief that her son was removed "because he is African American." The client simply responds "Yeah, how are you gonna help me get my child back?" The client still lacks sufficient trust that the social worker understanding is to her benefit. In fact, when asked to identify *them* she responds to the social worker "*you know them,*" believing the social worker another agent of the system. The bottom line for her is getting her child back and further, will the social worker assist her in doing so? In essence this is her challenge to the social worker. Even so, because the social worker encourages Mrs. W. to tell her story, the fact that she does so is indicative of a beginning level of trust.

In this case, Mrs. W. is involuntary in her status as a minority and in her situation. Her situation has resulted in her becoming an involuntary client, and she believes that her status as an African American is equally relevant. She has attempted to problem solve and feels that she has engaged in behaviors that would improve her son's help. She stopped smoking. She obtained a cat to deal with the problem of mice in her apartment. Further, when her son's asthma was out of control, she took him to the emergency room. But in her mind, neither child welfare authorities, nor the doctor, nor the judge acknowledged her efforts. She is just another African American, without power, an outsider who has been judged and told what to do. The client emphasized this point when she stated, "When *she* talked to the judge, she didn't tell him nothing about me." Her feelings of powerlessness, distrust, and vulnerability are also evident in her statement, "[They are] just playing games with me, and there is nothing I can do about it if I want to get my son back." In essence, her statement highlights her distrust of the people and systems that she believes to have dismissed her as a person, with a particular set of circumstance and who had not taken the time to represent her reality. Several observations are relevant at this point. First, the life that Mrs. W. describes is reminiscent of Frye's (2004) description of oppression, of being "caged in" and of "road blocks." Second, her sentiments point to the lack of procedural justice, specifically, the opportunity to have a voice in the decision making and the absence of being considered as individual resulted in a lack of fairness. Finally, it would be useful to explain to Mrs. W. that it was unlikely that the judge was privy to her prior efforts, but that this information could be included in the report from Pegasus to the court.

Application of Attributes

This chapter began with a premise that social work practice in large part involves involuntary clients a significant number of whom are members of oppressed groups. Hence, the client base has dual status. The shared attributes of involuntary clients and members of oppressed groups as illustrated in table 15.1 can be summarized as environmental and behavioral. Environmental attributes, for example, include the oppressive forces of marginal status, external locus of control, and a lack of power. Attributes that are behavioral involve the emotions associated with a crisis, reactance, distrust, and compliance. Figure 15.3 proposes considerations parallel to the problem-solving process. The discussion highlights the behavioral and environmental attributes that are represented in phase using examples from the cases of the Ruiz family and Mrs. W.

Behavioral Attributes

The behavioral attributes of clients are likely to present themselves at the initial point of contact. Because the encounter with a professional for a reason other than one identified by the client may be threatening, the response is emotion focused. Faced with client emotions, the tendency may be to ignore them or use them as evidence to judge the client readiness for change. Crisis intervention strategies provide a guide for the social worker to gather information about the meaning of the contact for the client, as well as how to assess emotional state (James and Gilliland 2005).

Figure 15.3   Integration of attributes and problem solving

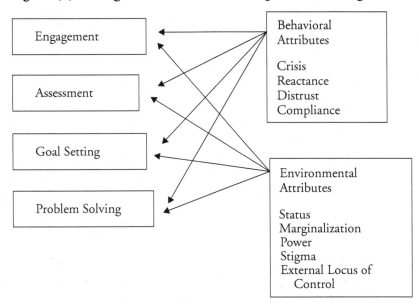

James and Gilliland (2005) provide a triage in which the emotional, cognitive, and behavioral state of the client is assessed. The engagement process is facilitated by sensitivity on the part of the social worker, reflective listening, and empathetic responses to the client's emotional state. The social worker, for example, acknowledged and validated Mrs. W.'s feelings, and "I understand your feeling scared and angry. I also imagine that it was traumatic for your child to be removed from your care." In her use of open-ended questions, for example, "It would help me to understand your situation if you told me what happened." With this statement, the social worker invited Mrs. W.'s participation as well as gained information about the meaning of the contact.

Vulnerable people are often overwhelmed by their life circumstances; thus the meaning that they attach to the contact with a social worker may heighten their existing stress level to traumatic stress Traumatic stress as defined by Okun, Fried, and Okun (1999) is prominent in imposed situations or circumstances beyond an individual's control. Mrs. W. had experienced a series of events that when combined were traumatic and over which she had little control. She was marginalized as a person and a parent in her encounter with the doctor and the hospital social worker, whose decisions questioned her ability to guarantee her son's well-being. Her privacy was violated by the child protection worker and the police and her subsequent emotional response in the presence of her neighbors. These accumulated events resulted in the ultimate trauma of her son's removal from her care.

Mrs. W.'s response centered around her preoccupation with the mandate as well as how she had been treated. The burden of compliance is evident in her statement, "*They* told me to come and see you about getting my son back." Although as an African American she distrusts the system to treat her with fairness, she is not unwilling to be involved with the social worker. Implicit in her statement is her reason for the meeting: specifically, regaining custody of her son, and further that she wants to know the benefit of the contact. Will her meeting with the social worker help her get her son back? In her lengthy monologue, her reference to the various abstract systems and players that brought her to the point of contact underscored her perception of the oppressive authority with power and her lack thereof.

The contact as an additional stressor can be recognized in her recounting of the things that she has done to keep going in spite of her life's circumstances. Stressors, when measured against Mrs. W.'s strengths, have exceeded her coping capacity, and she is troubled by the fact that her efforts to deal with her situation were unrecognized. A limitation of the strength perspective can be observed in this. The strengths perspective should not overshadow oppression and should take into account the constant struggles poor and oppressed people encounter in their daily lives (Saleeby 1996; Margolin 1997). A lack of recognition in fact distorts Mrs. W.'s strengths in dealing with constant stressors and the experience of oppression, focusing instead on her assumed deficits. She is especially angry that the child protection worker, in presenting her care to the judge, "didn't tell him nothing about me."

People are concerned about their direct and indirect control over their lives. In encounters with social workers as involuntary clients, emotional responses may be the result of how they have been treated, as well as the extent that they had control over the process that led to the contact. In general, they are not concerned with developing a long-term relationship with the professional or other third parties. But they are interested in having control over the process and the decisions that affect their lives. In the procedural justice literature, process control has to do with the evidence that is presented, and the belief that this information will influence the decisions made (Tyler 1989). In essence, the distribution of controls between participants and the third party is consistent with fairness. Thus, for Mrs. W. the judge's understanding of who she was, what she had done to keep her son safe, and her situation were important factors to be considered in the decision-making process.

Client Beliefs

Client's beliefs may be expressed in their behaviors and therefore they play a prominent role in the engagement process. Their life experiences and events cannot be separated from historical and social contexts (Clifford and Burke 2005). Because the socially constructed experiences of clients inform their cognitions and beliefs, exploring their beliefs provides insight in to their view of themselves and their place in the structure of society. Mr. Ruiz distrusts the motive for the contact and questioned, why now? For example, he demands to know, "Where were child protection services when my children were working in the fields, were working long hours and living in bad conditions?"

Mrs. W. is more explicit in her belief that racism played a role in her son's removal from her home. She asserted that black people are always being told what to do and critiqued "like we don't care about our kids." Further, her son's removal is an extension of the racism experienced by others like her. Her comments underscored the fact that she distrusts the system and its representatives to deal with her with fairness. In this instance, the social worker in her statement alerts the client that she understood her belief. In acknowledging her belief about racism the social worker could have probed further, but at the risk of further alienating Mrs. W. as well as allowing her beliefs to become a barrier to engagement. Instead, she posed a critical question, "Would it be helpful for me to explain why you were asked to see me?" The question of course could be perceived as circumventing the race question. More importantly, the social worker's acknowledgment of the client's belief about race validated Mrs. W.'s belief without losing focus. Her question also begins the process of building trust by explaining the reason for the contact. In doing so, she removes the uncertainty of Mrs. W.'s essential question of regaining custody of her child. In essence, the message that the social worker conveyed is, I will help you get your child returned home.

Clients' Stories

Listening to clients' stories is as integral to the engagement process as understanding behavioral attributes and their relationship to client's beliefs. Clients' narratives about life events and experiences provide insights into the impact of oppression on functioning (White and Epston 1990; Holland and Kilpatrick 1993; Saleeby 1996; Schmitz, Stakeman, and Sisneros 2001; Choudhuri 2005). Because clients' stories inform the professional of the environmental and their alienating experiences with oppression, they should be encouraged (Van Voorhis 1998; Guadalupe and Lum 2005). Allowing clients' stories is a means to engage them as doing so invites their participation as well as give them power. Note that the social worker asked Mrs. W. to explain what happened at the hospital. Irrespective the reason for the contact that has been described in the record, the social worker elicits Mrs. W.'s frame of reference. Participation by the client symbolizes democracy and self-determination in that the message conveyed is that through discussion, the inequalities experienced by the client can be understood. For example, the Ruiz family story became a key site within which the social worker understood the child care difficulties the family experienced as strangers in the community.

Environmental Attributes

Were Mrs. W. and Mr. and Mrs. Ruiz presenting themselves in a more positive light that was warranted? In both cases, the clients underscored their status and the circumstances associated with this status, rather than behaviors or acts that led to their involuntary contact. Each also emphasized that they had made the best decisions available to them, given their circumstances and resources. Self-presentation is not specific to involuntary clients, and it is used by most people in familiar and unfamiliar interactions. Yet, there may be a tendency on the part of professionals to judge involuntary clients based on their presentation of self. Not everything can be blamed on the system or oppressive forces. At the same time, oppression cannot be ignored. Carniol (1992) suggests, however, that in order to accurately assess the extent to which oppressive forces contribute to the client situations requires an "unmasking of the situation." This unraveling is most critical in the assessment process, goal setting, and problem-solving stages. However, as illustrated in figure 15.3, it is relevant to the engagement stage as well.

Assessment

Mandates, silent or legal and corrective in their intent, address a range of behaviors but not an array of circumstances. Therefore, client situations should be assessed from the standpoint of examining environmental attributes, for example, oppressive forces and the level of alienation they experience (Van Voorhis 1998). A pertinent question for the social worker to explore is, "Is there a relationship between the client's situation and oppressive forces?" For example, in the Ruiz family story, it would have been easy for the social worker to blame the family for their childcare decision rather than exploring their status as Mexican Americans who were strangers in a toxic community. Adaptation to unfamiliar environments involves reciprocity in human relationship. Reciprocity between the community and the Ruiz family was notably absent. Interactions between the family and the community were not openly hostile, but neither were they welcoming. As such, their ability to interact with the community and in the workplace as equals was curtailed, and they were viewed as in, but not a part of the community. In consequence, their marginal status limited their power and access to resources. The Ruiz case also prompts an assessment question related to the life transition and the degree of alienation experienced by the family. For example, they transitioned from a level of marginal status as migrant workers to further marginalization as outsiders status in the community, without particular ties to the community. Even so, the strength of the family is the fact that they had functioned, against formidable odds, until their decision about child care led to their involvement with child protective services as involuntary clients.

Clients' behaviors and their beliefs are not isolated actors from their environment. The interplay between behavioral and environmental attributes may be observed in the case of Mrs. W.'s status. She is subjected to an ongoing environment of less than desirable living conditions over which she has little control. She described a situation involving her and the other residents in the apartment building in which basic human dignity and health had been ignored by the landlord. The bureaucratic processes that are required in order for corrective action to be initiated by city officials added to their marginalized status. Mrs. W. made adjustments, for example, getting a cat, keeping little food in her house, each of which resulted in a negative appraisal of her as a parent. In addition to an environment in which she has little power to alter, specifically that of living in a rodent-infested building, she has maintained by attempting to deal with the daily struggles by trying to keep her head above water. Despite these adjustments, she is faced with an acute situation in which her son's asthma grew out of control. Her corrective action, specifically taking him to the hospital, contributes to an additional stressor that is compounded by his removal from the home. This destabilizing intervention added to the daily living, including the environmental crises, ultimately becoming the defining crisis in her life. She perceives herself and the other residents as powerless, and this perception is reinforced by the environment.

Goal Setting

In goal setting, social workers need to understand whether or not oppressive forces may in fact infringe upon a client's capacity to successfully achieve a goal. Environmental attributes can be formidable barriers to clients in achieving goals. Assuming, for example, that all parties involved want the Ruiz children to attend school regularly and the return of Mrs. W.'s child as goals, what were the potential barriers? In the case of Mrs. W., finding suitable and affordable housing as required by the court was a challenge. For the Ruiz family, given their status in the community, what is the likelihood of their finding an alternative child care arrangement? Addressing these questions relative to goal achievement requires additional effort on the part of the social workers.

Problem Solving

Problem solving begins with the recognition of who is the client, and what is his or her situation in light of his or her experience in the social environment. Effective problem solving is initiated by examining the goals of the intervention. Is the goal, for example, to resolve the identified concern, or to apply prescribed sanctions and rules to the situation? Moreover, which strategy involves the least harm? Problem solving rather than sanctions in fact attends to the needs of the client, by seeking to understand the reasons for their behavior. In essence, problem solving is combined with care and social justice (Orme 2002). It would be equally important to examine whether their status and beliefs pose a barrier to problem solving. Clients, because of their experiences, may in fact be immobilized, believing that little can change.

Helping clients to resolve their situation may involve the social work roles of advocacy, mediator, and education. Understanding the reality of Mrs. W.'s situation, the social worker could advise the court of her constrained housing choices, and the fact that limited options would delay or possibly prohibit her compliance with the court order. If corrective action beyond what the client had already done was indicated, the social worker could provide resources that would facilitate the return of her child. This action would require the negotiated cooperation of child protection services and the judge. The social worker could also work with her to file complaints with the city about the code violations in her apartment building.

For the Ruiz family, the social worker can meet with the plant manager and the school in an effort to restructure the environment into one that is nurturing and sustaining. With regard to child care, she can begin to help the family develop a network of support within their own community. When people are isolated and alienated and feel under siege, they may not recognize each other as resources. In addition, communities of faith could be explored as a source of support as well as for their potential as child care providers. Neither child welfare nor educational policies acknowledge the impact of employment scheduling on family life. The social worker in this case could also seek to alter the parent's work schedule with the plant manager, thereby including him as an agent in problem solving with the family.

Persons who experience environmental, structural, and personal stressors are more likely to come to the attention of authorities and institutions. They are also likely to be persons of color and their contact is more apt to be involuntary. Environmental, structural, and personal stressors are closely associated with the inequalities of oppressive forces. Oppressive forces described as "interpersonal–intrapersonal–environmental systems" that either intentionally or unintentionally reinforced dominance or subordination (Guadalupe and Lum 2005:85). The experience with domination and subordination was also evident in social policies that lack procedural, and in effect promote a hierarchy of oppression (Wambach and Van Soest 1997; Van Voorhis 1998; Lum 2004; Beitin and Allen 2005).

The circumstances of oppression can be made relevant by the professional by assessing its impact on the capacity and functioning of individual clients and actively soliciting and using this information in the problem-solving process. Doing so can circumvent the multiple-edged sword that racial and ethnic minority clients experience in their encounters with professionals and social welfare organization. Their encounters may involve problem-solving strategies that minimize oppression and perpetuate the dominant normative narrative (Pharr 1988; Guadalupe and Lum 2005). The dominant narrative represents an alienating force and includes decisions about their problems, acts, or behaviors; assigns stigma; and makes assumptions about deviance. Recall that Mr. Ruiz's statement, "we are honest, hard working and we don't cause trouble for nobody," was an attempt to counter the notion that the family was deviant. Clients' feelings about constrained self-determination and limited power in their everyday lives can be accelerated in response to interventions that imposed solutions. For them, the power to define and the power to control is flawed and unjust.

Another side to the dilemma for clients is that social workers when confronted with the oppressive content in clients' stories are often uncomfortable, relying instead on interpretations of deviance and pathology (Saleeby 1996). Saleeby (1996) and Freire (1970) liken this response to the interactions between the oppressor and the oppressed, in that the focus interventions are aimed toward assisting marginalized people to restructure their beliefs or lifestyles and conform to the dominant narrative.

Evaluative steps that can be taken by the social worker to reconcile the tensions between clients' experiences and accepted protocols include self-reflection, which is crucial. Self-reflection is guided by a willingness to explore biases, emotions, and reactions that are touched in the encounter with the client. An additional question to be included is a reflection: "How can I use my power and authority to resolve the client's situation?" In addition, "Am I confusing my legal obligation to protect from harm, thereby diminishing the problem solving objective of the profession?"

Consultations with supervisors are also integral to enhancing professional competence in work with oppressed groups. Supervisors in their review of case records can also be helpful in this regard. For example, a supervisor questioned the foster care placement decision of a staff person for a disabled child, which included respite care and other resources that aided in her ability to care for the child; however, the agency was unwilling to provide the same level of resources for the biological mother, who was a member of a minority group, so that she could keep her child.

Social work practice with involuntary clients from oppressed racial and ethnic groups is justice work. This work calls for expanding the person-in-the-environment focus to include human behavior in oppressive circumstances. This focus is consistent with the practice ethics and values that guide our moral, fiduciary, legal, and ethical obligation. Adjunct to this obligation is evaluating whether the mandates or policies are fair and that the requirements are within the client's resources. Pursuing the obligations found in ethical standards and the right for effective treatment and the social justice framework of fairness and equality. For example, the potential sanctions, if implemented, would have resolved the family's need for childcare. The social justice emphasis of the profession also guides us to consider whether the outcomes of processes that may be legal but unjust, and therefore harmful (Reamer 2005). The hospital social worker and the doctor in fact acted upon what they perceived to be neglect. Their actions, however, set in motion a series of events that resulted in further exacerbating the fragile life circumstances of Mrs. W. In both cases, the ethical obligation of effective problem solving resided with the social workers to whom the cases had been referred.

Reid (2002:7) traces advances in social work to "practice movements evolved from dissatisfaction with existing order." The existing order for working with involuntary clients who are racial and ethnic minorities should acknowledge that in many instances they are one of the same. Care should be taken by social workers to ensure that their practice does not replicate the experience of oppression.

Discussion Questions

1. Think about your own practice with racial and ethnic minorities. What do you know about the problems that they experience as a result of oppression?

2. Carniol (1992) suggests "unmasking" oppressive forces is an essential part of the assessment process. Discuss how you would assess both behavioral and environmental attributes with racial and ethnic minority involuntary clients.

3. Models of practice have tended to focus on personal problems or behaviors, instead of the social justice issues that may be present in

a client's situation. Given these two competing interests, how would you propose to reconcile the differences?

4. In the Ruiz case, the social work focused on childcare needs rather than educational neglect. What are the potential pitfalls of this shift in focus? Also, would you have handled the case in a different manner? Why or why not?

5. How would you respond to a client who raised issues about race and inequality?

Chapter 16

Work with Involuntary Clients in Corrections

Chris Trotter

Professionals work with involuntary clients in corrections in a variety of settings. Probation officers, parole officers, and community corrections officers supervise offenders in the community. They have a role in ensuring that the conditions of a court order are carried out and in helping those under supervision to stop offending. Professionals, usually probation officers, may also work with the courts undertaking assessments and providing advice regarding sentencing and treatment options.

Other professionals who work with offenders in the community have more specialized roles. They may be specialists, for example, in drug and alcohol treatment, in psychiatric or psychological treatment, in anger management, in dealing with domestic violence, in housing or emergency accommodation, in family support, or financial counseling.

In some cases the offenders who see these professionals may be on court orders that require them to attend appointments. In other cases the offenders may be referred by a probation officer for specialist treatment or assistance. In other cases the offenders may seek out the treatment on the advice of a lawyer or another professional or they may seek out assistance on a purely voluntary basis.

Professionals also work in the field of corrections in residential settings. Prison social workers and prison psychologists may offer individual counseling to adults or juveniles in custody. They may even be involved with prisoners' families. They may also offer group counseling in a range of areas, for example, substance abuse or anger management. Professionals working in halfway houses and in residential units also work with offenders often in order to help those offenders reestablish themselves in the community.

Involuntary Clients in Corrections

For the most part, clients in the corrections system are involuntary. Clients on the whole attend interviews with a probation officer because they are required to do so by a court order. They go to anger management groups or substance abuse treatment because they are directed either by a court order or someone in authority such as a probation or parole officer.

In my book *Working with involuntary Clients* (Trotter 2006), I defined involuntary clients in terms of a continuum. On one end of the continuum the clients (or recipients of welfare or legal services) can be described as involuntary because they have not chosen to receive the services they are being given. In fact, the clients may be actively opposed to receiving the service. They may believe that it is unnecessary and intrusive. The clients accept the service offered only because of a court order or the threat of some other legal sanction.

In some cases, however, clients who are on court orders are not entirely involuntary. For example, a dependent client who visits her or his probation officer without an appointment on a daily basis cannot be described a purely involuntary. What of the client who uses the problem-solving skills of her or his probation officer to work through problems? What of the depressed prisoner who asks for assistance from the prison psychologist or social worker? Most clients in the corrections system are involuntary inasmuch as they are required to attend interviews. For the most part, however, client worker interviews and interactions involve both voluntary and involuntary components.

One way of looking at the involuntary/voluntary issue in corrections is to see it as having two elements. The client is involuntary in terms of having to comply with the condition of a court order, for example, attend interviews or undertake a prison sentence. The client then has a choice, however, to use or not use the helping services that are offered by the professional worker.

Who Are Clients in Corrections?

In talking about clients in corrections I am referring to adults, young people, and children who have been found guilty of a criminal offense and have been placed on a court order that involves some sort of supervision or intervention by a professional service provider in the criminal justice system. The notion of client assumes that there is some sort of supervisory or treatment relationship. This could be offered by a probation or parole officer or one of the many specialist treatment workers whom I have referred to above. It could also be offered by a youth justice worker in a residential setting. The term *client* would not be used, however, to describe the relationship between a police officer and an offender or a prison officer and a prisoner unless that prison officer had a designated treatment or casework role. In this chapter I limit my discussion therefore to situations in which there is a worker and a client in some sort of a helping as well as supervisory or law enforcement relationship.

Effectiveness of Work with Involuntary Clients in Corrections

In the 1960s and 1970s practitioners and academics in the field of corrections often accepted the "nothing works" view in relation to interventions in corrections. An extensive literature review by Robert Martinson and his colleagues (1974) supported the view that casework and other interventions that aim to rehabilitate offenders seem to have little impact in terms of reducing re-offending rates. This view was supported by literature reviews about casework in general in the 1970s (e.g., Fischer 1973).

During the 1980s and 1990s the "nothing works" view was increasingly challenged. It was argued that rather than corrections interventions having no impact they in fact have an effect, but it can be both positive and negative. Some approaches or intervention methods lead to reductions in offending and some lead to increases in offending. More recently it has been argued that the more effective interventions can reduce re-offending by as much as 80 percent, with the average effective interventions resulting in 40 or 50 percent reductions in offending (Trotter 1996a; Gendreau, Cullen, and Bonta 1998; Andrews 2001). Since the early 1990s there have more and more publications that offer literature reviews and meta-analyses of the "what works" research. These reviews have argued on the basis of the research that corrections interventions can be successful in reducing re-offending (e.g., Andrews et al. 1990; Izzo and Ross 1990; McIvor 1990; McGuire 1995; Andrews and Bonta 1998; Dowden and Andrews 1999; Andrews 2001; Farrell 2002; Hopkinson and Rex 2003; McNeill 2003; Raynor 2003; Wing Hong Chui 2003; Trotter 2006).

The burgeoning "what works" literature has been accompanied by an increasing willingness in many places, in both community and residential corrections settings, to embrace rehabilitation alongside a law and order and punishment agenda. Correctional systems in Western countries seem to be increasingly punitive with rising numbers in incarceration, yet at the same time "what works" conferences and rehabilitation programs are increasingly part of the corrections landscape.

What do the traditional literature reviews and the meta-analyses tell us about what works? In discussing this I focus primarily on what works in the one-to-one supervision of offenders in community settings. The principles apply generally, however, to institutional work and to work with groups of offenders.

Pro-social Modeling and Reinforcement

I have conducted two studies in corrections, one with juvenile offenders and another with adult offenders, each of which found that probation officers and community corrections officers who scored high on the California Personality Inventory (CPI) Socialization Scale had offenders with lower re-offending rates compared with those who scored low on the inventory (Trotter 1990, 1993, 2000). The Socialization Scale measures the extent to which people have pro-social or pro-criminal attitudes. My studies suggested that the more pro-social officers were more inclined than the less pro-social officers to model pro-social behaviors, to focus on the pro-social behaviors of their clients, and to appropriately challenge the pro-criminal comments of their clients. These practices were directly related to lower offending rates. Similar outcomes were found in a Canadian study in the 1970s although the Canadian study suggested that it was also important for the probation officer to have high levels of empathy (Andrews et al. 1979).

Pro-social modeling and reinforcement has been shown to be effective in a number of other studies and it is included as one of the key components of what works in most of the "what works" reviews (e.g., Gendreau, Cullen, and Bonta 1998; Andrews 2001; McNeill 2003; Raynor 2003). One illustration of the power of simple modeling processes is seen in a study I recently completed in child protection (Trotter 2004). When child protection clients indicated that their workers returned their phone calls, kept their appointments, and did the things they said they would do, the outcomes for the clients were much better than when the clients believed that their workers did not do these things. Client satisfaction was greater, worker estimates of client progress were greater, and cases were closed earlier. The results could not be explained by client risk levels or other factors. It seems that the principles of pro-social modeling may be important not only with corrections clients but with involuntary clients in general.

Problem Solving

Effective interventions in corrections address the issues that have led offenders to become offenders. The literature reviews and meta-analyses often refer to the concept of criminogenic needs. Criminogenic needs are needs or problems that are related to offending but that it is possible to change. Obviously age, gender, and prior criminal history relate to offending. They cannot, however, be changed. On the other hand, employment, family relationships, drug use, peer group associations, housing, finances, and pro-criminal attitudes, may all relate to offending and can be changed. These are criminogenic needs. Criminogenic needs do not include intrapsychic issues such as anxiety, self-esteem, or depression, factors that cannot easily explain offending behavior (Gendreau, Cullen, and Bonta 1998).

There seems little doubt that effective practice in work with offenders involves addressing the clients' offense-related problems or needs. My research suggests also that the problem-solving process will be more successful in reducing offending if the workers and the clients reach agreement on the problems to be addressed and what is hoped to be achieved (Trotter 1996a, 2006). The general counseling literature is replete with research studies that point to the importance of working with the client's view of their problems (see, e.g., Hepworth et al. 2005 for further details on this issue). It may be perfectly clear to the worker that a particular young male client is persistently offending because of rejection by his family, because of drug use, or because of homelessness. However, until the client acknowledges that these are problems for him, it is very difficult to work through the issues. Effective work in corrections involves a collaborative approach that helps the client to acknowledge his or her offense-related problems.

It is also important in work with offenders to canvass a range of potential offense-related problems. Don Andrews (2001) suggests that the meta-analyses conducted by his colleagues and him point to much greater reductions in re-offense rates when as many as six problems are addressed in the intervention. I have argued elsewhere that holistic approaches work best with involuntary clients (Trotter 2006), and work in corrections is no exception to this.

Role Clarification
Much of the work with offenders involves what Ronald Rooney (1992) and Jones and Alcabes (1993) refers to as client socialization, or what I have referred to as role clarification (Trotter 2006), in other words, helping the client to accept that the worker can help with the client's problems even though the worker has a social control role. This involves exploring the client's expectations, helping the client to understand what is negotiable and what is not, the limits of confidentiality, and the nature of the workers authority. The stage is set for effective work once the client begins to accept that the worker can help and once the worker and client begin to reach agreement on the goals of the intervention.

A Balanced Approach: Social Control and Problem Solving

The research consistently suggests that interventions which focus exclusively on punishment or scare tactics lead to increased offending (e.g., Gendreau, Cullen, and Bonta 1998; Andrews 2001). Similarly interventions that focus exclusively on developing insight or that focus exclusively on the client worker relationship are unlikely to be helpful (Trotter 1990, 1996b; Gendreau, Cullen, and Bonta 1998). This was also evident in my recent child protection study: when clients described their workers as helpers and investigators the outcomes were substantially better than when they saw them as either a helper or an investigator (Trotter 2004). Again it seems that the principles of effective practice that apply to offenders may apply to work with other groups of involuntary clients.

Focus on High Risk

Much of the literature talks about the importance of focusing on high-risk offenders rather than low-risk offenders. It is argued that there is a relatively large group of offenders who are unlikely to re-offend and are unlikely to benefit from intensive intervention, whereas there is a smaller group of medium- to high-risk offenders who are more likely to re-offend and more likely to benefit from supervision (see, e.g., Gendreau, Cullen, and Bonta 1998). For this reason it is important to assess risk levels and to focus resources on medium- to high-risk offenders.

The issue of risk assessment is a complex one and it has its critics (see Robinson 2003 for a discussion about the issues). The primary criticism is that risk levels are often used as part of a sentencing process and as part of a postsentencing method to provide for varying levels of supervision. This can lead to offenders who are already disadvantaged getting harsher penalties. An offender who is homeless, without family support, with a drug or alcohol addiction, and without employment might receive a harsher sentence or intervention than someone else who does not have these problems but has committed a similar offense.

Nevertheless it does seem to make sense to concentrate welfare or human service resources on higher risk individuals who are likely to re-offend. To this end a number of risk assessment profiles have been developed for use by corrections services. One of the most popular ones is the LSIR (Level of Supervision Inventory Revised) developed over many years by Don Andrews and James Bonta (1998). It is in use in many probation and community corrections services in many English-speaking countries, for example, Canada, the United States, Australia, and the United Kingdom. The LSIR, as well as providing a risk assessment, also helps to identify criminogenic needs that can inform the problem-solving process.

Programs

A recent meta-analysis by Don Andrews and his colleagues suggests that structured learning programs may have the most potential for reducing re-offending (Andrews 2001). Community corrections services around the world offer group and individual programs based on the "what works" principles. These programs, in the words of Peter Raynor (2003:79), "put together a series of planned and sequential learning opportunities into a cumulative sequence covering an appropriate curriculum of skills and allowing plenty of opportunity to reinforce learning through structured practice." (The reader is referred to the Cognitive Centre Foundation Web site in the United Kingdom, www.cognitivecentre.com, for descriptions of a range of structured programs based on the "what works" principles.) Research on one of those programs, for example, the reasoning and rehabilitation, has shown promising results (Raynor 2003; Pearson et al. 2002).

Other Factors

This is not an exhaustive list of "what works" principles. The reviews refer to a number of other practices. For example, "multimodal" approaches, which rely on a range of intervention methods, are likely to be more effective than those that rely on only one method (Gendreau, Cullen, and Bonta 1998). This is supported by my study in probation, which found that re-offense rates among the clients of probation officers who used a range of skills, including modeling and reinforcing pro-social behaviors, role clarification, and problem solving were lower than in situations in which the workers made use of only one or two of the skills (Trotter 1996a).

There is also some support for working with families of young offenders (see Corcoran 1997 for a review of the evidence) for intervention methods that are implemented as they were intended and for matching workers and clients according to learning style and personality (Gendreau, Cullen, and Bonta 1998; Wing Hong Chui 2003).

Relationship skills are also referred to in some of the reviews (e.g., Gendreau, Cullen, and Bonta 1998). I have not identified this as a key skill or a key factor in effective practice because the evidence in relation to this area is somewhat equivocal. Studies I have undertaken in corrections with both juveniles and adults have found that probation officer empathy levels, for example, do not relate to re-offending rates (Trotter 1990, 1996a). Don Andrews and his colleagues also found that high-empathy workers did better with their clients only if they made use of the other skills (Andrews et al. 1979). On the other hand, my study indicated that when workers made judgmental comments about their clients (e.g., lazy, no hope) those clients were more likely to re-offend even after taking into account client risk levels. Certainly workers in corrections need to be able to listen to their clients and to model appropriate behavior. It seems that we cannot say much more than this about the value of the worker–client relationship.

An Application of Best Practice

The following two case studies present alternative ways of using a problem solving approach. The first interview focuses on what the worker believes is the primary criminogenic need, the client's drug use. The second interview focuses on working with the client's view of the problem but working toward helping the client to accept that her drug use is an issue that needs to be addressed. In the second interview the worker demonstrates the skills of role clarification, pro-social modeling and reinforcement, and problem solving.

The transcript is taken from a role-played video tape on Working with Involuntary Clients produced at Monash University. The probation officer was one of the probation officers in my corrections study who had clients with low re-offending rates. In the first interview he is drawing on information about the client's problems, which was written in the file at the time of the initial assessment undertaken for the court. The second interview reflects the way he usually works.

*Problem-Solving Interview 1**

PROBATION OFFICER: Jennifer, thank you for coming back. You've been to correctional services twice now, the first time when you came in they went through a number of forms, we explained to you what you had to, and when you have to come. When you saw me last time we talked about what my role will be and we started to look at implementing some of the conditions on your order. What I want to do today is speak to you about the problems you've got in your life and one of the things that you really need to address as a matter of urgency is the drug use because that will . . .

JENNIFER: Yeah, but I mean I don't think I've got a drug problem, I told you that when I first met you so, I mean I don't think it's necessary to go into that.

---

* I wish to acknowledge the work of Michael Scheel who plays the probation officer and Anna Tasevska who plays the role of client in the interviews presented in this chapter. The script for the role play was developed by them.

PROBATION OFFICER: You committed offenses and you committed offenses in the past and they're all drug related so I think you've got a problem that you need to deal with.

JENNIFER: Well, why do you think they're drug related? I mean, who told you that?

PROBATION OFFICER: Well the information that was provided that you gave to the court was that it was drug related and we need to deal with that fairly quickly. So, what I want to do today is look at that and start dealing with that in terms of getting the counseling arranged and getting the testing done and so on. Some of the other things that relate to your offending, that you've got problems with are the accommodation difficulties that you mentioned.

JENNIFER: Yeah, that's right, yeah.

PROBATION OFFICER: And the relationship with your boyfriend that you've had some difficulties with.

JENNIFER: Yeah.

PROBATION OFFICER: The other thing that was causing you difficulties was the relationship with your parents and you mentioned that you didn't have enough money to pay rent.

JENNIFER: Yeah, well I don't because I don't have a job.

PROBATION OFFICER: Yeah and employment's another one that we need to look at. So, what I want to do today is, maybe I'll just write those few things down so that we don't miss any of them and we'll talk about it in order of priority. Remember last time we sort of made reference to the problem survey where we look at all of the things that are really causing difficulties in your life.

JENNIFER: Yeah.

PROBATION OFFICER: And what I want to do today is talk to you about how we're going to do that and I've mentioned already that one of the more important ones is the drug use so I expect you to go to drug treatment.

JENNIFER: Yeah, I know you keep bringing it up. It seems to me you're calling me a drug user and you don't even know me. So, to me personally I think that finding a job is more important to me then what you're saying.

PROBATION OFFICER: Yeah and I think that it's great that accommodation and finding a job is important for you but whilst you're using drugs you're going to get in more difficulties and if you get into more difficulties . . . .

JENNIFER: Well you don't know I'm using drugs. How do you know that?

PROBATION OFFICER: I guess from the information that's on file at the moment and the order that you've got requires you to do it so you just have to do it. And the testing will then identify whether you're using or not and give me an indication anyhow. So once you've done a few tests we can see whether you're still using or not.

JENNIFER: What kinds of drugs do the tests show?

PROBATION OFFICER: They'll show up any drugs that you may be using. Prescribed medications, it might be cannabis, it can be alcohol, it can be heroin, speed, any of the drugs that are available out there at the moment. So, we'll need to deal with that as a matter of priority because I don't want you to get in further trouble with the law. And the other thing is the next one we're going to look at is the money side of it because you mentioned earlier that you haven't got enough money to pay for your rent.

JENNIFER: Well that's right. I don't.

PROBATION OFFICER: Yeah. So you mentioned you need to go to community work so you may have difficulties because you've got no money.

JENNIFER: Yeah, which will make it hard for me to complete this order anyway.

PROBATION OFFICER: What do you think you can do about that?

JENNIFER: About what?

PROBATION OFFICER: With the money side of it.

JENNIFER: Well I don't know. Hopefully find a job.

PROBATION OFFICER: Yeah, how would you go about doing that?

JENNIFER: Well, I don't know. I don't have much skills.

PROBATION OFFICER: Have you looked for jobs before?

JENNIFER: I've had a few jobs. Yeah. I haven't worked for a long time though.

PROBATION OFFICER: Can you tell me how you went about doing that last time?

JENNIFER: How to find a job?

PROBATION OFFICER: Yeah.

JENNIFER: Usually basically just people that I knew who already work there got me the job.

PROBATION OFFICER: Yeah. And I understand you have to go to centerlink on a regular basis as well and part of that is you need to look for work.

JENNIFER: Yeah.

PROBATION OFFICER: So I expect you to continue that and keep looking for work that way. You might want to look through the paper as well. We've got the local paper at the front in the interview room. You might want to grab that and have a look at the employment section in that.

JENNIFER: There's not many jobs there though.

PROBATION OFFICER: But if you don't go out and look though you won't find any.

JENNIFER: I don't think they'll hire me anyway.

PROBATION OFFICER: Why's that?

JENNIFER: I don't have any skills. I'm on this order so they're probably not going to want to hire a criminal even though I don't consider myself a criminal anyway. I mean I've never harmed anyone before in my life and I don't intend to.

PROBATION OFFICER: It would have caused some harm doing the burglaries because there would have been some victims in the process. You went in to somebody else's house.

The following interview represents a more collaborative approach to the problem-solving process. The probation officer is talking to they same client.

Problem-Solving Interview 2

PROBATION OFFICER: Jennifer, thank you for coming in today. You actually made it on time. We appreciate that.

JENNIFER: I tried to, yeah.

PROBATION OFFICER: That's good to see Jennifer. Just a recap from the last two sessions, the first time you came to correctional services was when I took you through the induction process, where you filled in a number of forms and got some clarification on what you need to do. And then you came back and saw me three days ago and we talked a bit about what my role is in terms of supervising you on your order and we talked about the two aspects of it. One part was that I supervised your order and made sure that you do the things you're expected to do and the other part that we talked about was that I'm also there to help you identify what issues are in your life and how you want to work through those. Do you remember that?

JENNIFER: Yeah.

PROBATION OFFICER: OK then. Jennifer what do you see are some of the issues that are impacting on your life at the moment?

JENNIFER: I guess a lot has changed in the last couple of months. My boyfriend's been put in jail. I think he'll be there for the next six or seven years.

PROBATION OFFICER: How do you feel about that?

JENNIFER: Well, quite upset about that actually. I mean I don't think he deserves such a harsh penalty for what he did.

PROBATION OFFICER: It was a serious offense, wasn't it?

JENNIFER: Well, I mean he shot the people whose house we burgled but he didn't kill them. I mean other people have murdered people and they've gone to jail for as long as him. I don't think that's the same thing.

PROBATION OFFICER: Still it's a very serious offense, isn't it?

JENNIFER: I don't think he meant to, you know, I don't think he wanted to kill them.

PROBATION OFFICER: That's probably reflected in the sentence as well. Because had the person died it would have been a lot more serious.

JENNIFER: Yeah, well it's just made it hard because I'm on this order and they won't let me see him at all and we've been living with these friends of his and ever since he's gone to jail I just don't feel comfortable living there any more but I don't really have much of a chance to leave because I don't have any money.

PROBATION OFFICER: So Jennifer, one of the things you've mentioned is not being able to get in touch with your boyfriend at the moment. Is that OK if I write that down?

JENNIFER: Yeah.

PROBATION OFFICER: Just so that we don't lose them all. We'll deal with all of the things that are worrying you. We'll write it down and identify what all of the issues are and so we don't forget any of them. OK what are some of the other things?

JENNIFER: Well, as I was saying I don't really want to live where I'm living right now but I don't have any money to find another place to live because it's for free but ever since my boyfriend went to jail I just feel like I'm not wanted any more because they're actually friends with my boyfriend. I just met them through him so I wouldn't mind finding somewhere else to live.

PROBATION OFFICER: Where have you lived in the past Jennifer?

JENNIFER: Well, I left home when I was about fourteen.

PROBATION OFFICER: OK. That's about four years ago now.

JENNIFER: Yeah and I went to live with a friend of mine and her family for a couple of months after that and then after that I sort of had an argument with her and I had to leave there and I lived on the streets for a while and then I met my boyfriend and he was living with these people and I moved in with them and that's where I've been ever since.

PROBATION OFFICER: And you need to look at some new place to live now, do you?

JENNIFER: Yeah, well I'd like to.

PROBATION OFFICER: So, we'll put that accommodation down as an issue that we might need to work on?

JENNIFER: Yeah.

PROBATION OFFICER: OK. What are some of the other things that are worrying you at the moment?

JENNIFER: Well I don't have a job so I guess that's the only way I can really get some money to find a place to live.

PROBATION OFFICER: Have you been employed in the past Jennifer?

JENNIFER: I have but I haven't had really good jobs they've just been, you know, working in a milkbar and waitressing and stuff like that.

PROBATION OFFICER: Yeah, but you have been able to get a number of jobs?

JENNIFER: Yeah, but they've never really lasted very long, only a couple of months.

PROBATION OFFICER: Is there any reason for that?

JENNIFER: Well, the first job when I was working in the milkbar, they thought that I was giving away free food and stuff like that and the second job as a waitress, they thought that I was stealing everyone else's tips which is not true but they fired me for that.

PROBATION OFFICER: So, we can say that at this point we've got three issues. The first one is in relation to your boyfriend, the other one was the accommodation and then you need to look at employment, finding a job possibly—Anything else that's affecting you at the moment Jennifer?

JENNIFER: No, not really, no.

PROBATION OFFICER: In relation to the court order, there's some suggestions about drug treatment and the offenses seem to have some relationship to drug use. What do you think about that?

JENNIFER: Well, when we were arrested apparently they found that I was under the influence of alcohol and drugs.

PROBATION OFFICER: What sort of drugs?

JENNIFER: Heroin.

PROBATION OFFICER: OK. And the offenses were they committed to purchase more drugs? That your boyfriend was involved in?

JENNIFER: Well, yeah. And to buy clothes and food.

Key Issues in Working with Involuntary Clients in Corrections

Perhaps the biggest issue for direct practice workers in corrections relates to the worldwide trend toward tougher penalties. Prison populations are increasing all over the world. At the same time more and more people are being placed on community-based corrections orders. This has led to ever increasing caseloads and increasing numbers of relatively low-risk clients finding their way into the criminal justice system. This in turn has fueled the development of risk assessment as a method of dealing with the increasing numbers and as a method of rationalizing scarce resources.

Yet at the same time, as I mentioned earlier, there appears to be increasing acceptance at least in some places that treatment and rehabilitation programs are important. The public may want tougher penalties but they also seem to want something done to prevent offenders re-offending (Cullen et al. 1990).

There is also a trend in many parts of the world toward case management. Therapeutic work that was once done by probation and parole officers is now contracted out to specialist workers. Individual offenders might be involved with numerous treatment agencies and workers. For example, they might be required as part of a court order to attend for anger management, for drug treatment, for psychiatric treatment, and for programs such as reasoning and rehabilitation. In addition to this, they may be referred to other agencies for housing, for family support, for literacy, or for assistance with employment. In some instances even risk assessment is contracted out. This process can lead a probation and parole officer to see him or herself as simply a referral agent and an agent of social control. It provides limited opportunity for the holistic and balanced approach to social control and helping that the research suggests is so important to effective outcomes. Similarly it is difficult for the specialist worker who has a treatment rather than a social control role to maintain a holistic and balanced approach.

Holistic and balanced interventions work best. Systems that facilitate this also are likely to work best. Unfortunately the organizational systems in many places mitigate against, rather than for, holistic and balanced approaches. In the meantime those who work within these systems will do better if they are aware of the "what works" principles and if they try to adopt a balanced approach to the work when they can.

Contributions of Work with Involuntary Clients in Corrections to Knowledge About Involuntary Clients

There are similarities in the issues that face those who work with involuntary clients whether in child protection, mental health, or substance abuse. The growth of risk assessment and the development of case management systems, for example, are not limited to corrections settings. Child protection, for example, has seen burgeoning numbers of referrals in the last ten years, and, like corrections, is increasingly concerned with risk assessment, often, it is argued, at the expense of treatment or helping interventions (Krane and Davies 2000; Parton and Byrne 2000). Case management is criticized in child protection circles for the same reasons it is criticized in corrections (Hood 1997; McMahon 1998).

Interest in evidence-based practice and concern about outcomes is common across work with a range of involuntary clients. It is perhaps an area in which corrections has led the way. Outcome measures are complex in child protection or mental health or work in schools. In corrections, however, the recidivism outcome measures are more straightforward. As I mentioned earlier, the technique of meta-analysis has provided information about which particular approaches or intervention methods have most impact on recidivism (e.g., Andrews 2001).

Recidivism research has shown, for example, that pro-social modeling and reinforcement is an important factor in corrections interventions. Pro-social modeling and reinforcement, however, has had little application in research with other groups of involuntary clients. Yet a study I have recently completed suggests that it is also an important factor in work in child protection (Trotter 2002, 2004). I referred earlier to the most simple modeling practices by workers having a substantial influence on child protection outcomes. It could also be that structured learning programs that have proved successful in corrections could be adopted with similar success in work with other groups of involuntary clients. Another area in which corrections may be leading the way in research with involuntary clients relates to the concept of "program integrity." In other words, are programs or intervention methods or risk assessment profiles being implemented as they were intended or is there a drift away from the theory or model on which they are based? It is argued that program integrity is an important factor in achieving positive outcomes (Gendreau, Cullen, and Bonta 1998).

Discussion Questions

1. To what extent do the effective corrections practice principles apply to work with involuntary clients in other fields?
2. Look again at the two case study scenarios and discuss which approach is likely to lead to the better outcomes.
3. Discuss the reasons for this.
4. Can you identify examples of role clarification or client socialization in the two scenarios?
5. Can you identify examples of pro-social modeling or reinforcement in the scenarios?
6. What is the difference between the way the problem survey or problem assessment is undertaken in the two scenarios?

Chapter 17

Involuntary Clients and Work in the Era of Welfare Reform

Tony Bibus

Headline:
Welfare clients get spur to work:
New program withholds cash in favor of four months of job-seeking
Hopfensperger 2004, p. B-1

With its tight time limits, eligibility restrictions, new work requirements, and punitive sanctions for noncompliance, welfare reform has intensified the involuntary dynamics for public assistance clients in the United States. People on welfare have historically experienced some degree of stigma, making their condition on contact with social services staff less than voluntary. Because all able-bodied adults are expected to seek work and to rely on work for income, health insurance, and other supports, the stigma associated with not working is pronounced (Dudley 2000; Katz 2001). Meanwhile, as parents with few barriers to work leave welfare, the proportion of those facing multiple barriers and remaining on welfare until their time limits expire increases (McDonnell 2004). "Ten years of research on welfare reform has produced a troubling but consistent finding: Welfare-to-work programs generally succeed with 'easy' clients—adults with diplomas, work experience, and stable home lives—but they often falter with more disadvantaged recipients—those with disabling illnesses, mental impairments, volatile families, or long histories of poverty" (*Star Tribune* 2005:A12; see also The Urban Institute's report "A Decade of Welfare Reform: Facts and Figures," June 2006).

Thus, there is a deepening concentration of desperate and highly vulnerable families who are likely to be involuntary to some extent as they meet or are referred to helping professionals. Social workers must become as well prepared as possible to anticipate the involuntary condition in which many of these families enter services and respond accordingly with approaches likely to improve outcomes such as access to income, health care, and social inclusion. This chapter applies the principles of work with involuntary clients to this urgent practice arena.

Case Example

When officials in Minnesota introduced the state's original experiment in welfare reform, the 1994 Minnesota Family Investment Program (MFIP), they recognized that its combinations of incentives and mandates for clients to move off assistance and into employment would present welfare workers with new challenges. Therefore, from the beginning, training in work with involuntary clients has been offered to MFIP staff. At one of these training sessions, participants enacted a typical interchange during the first meeting of a support group for parents seeking employment.

GROUP LEADER [as four members settle into their chairs in a semi circle]: On behalf of the Workforce Center, I'd like to welcome you to the first meeting of this Job Finders Club. My name is Tony Bibus, and I am a licensed social worker. MFIP staffers have contracted with me to facilitate this support group for job seekers. We'll be talking more about the group and your expectations, but as a starting point, let me say that the main goal will be to help each of you find employment so you can support your families. I hope this group will become a resource for ideas in your job searches. I believe that we each grow from strengths, so this group could be a chance to identify your strengths and build on them, learning new job seeking skills and sharing what you know with the rest of us. One possible outcome will be positive attitudes and traits that are attractive to employers so you are ready to meet their expectations and your own, too.

In a minute I'm going to ask you each to introduce yourselves and tell us how the group might help you and any concerns or fears you might have. First, let's set a couple guidelines: Whatever we share in this group should be kept confidential (unless it's information that would trigger a child protection report or something like that); so we all need to agree to keep what is said here in this group for our own purposes and not share it with others outside the group unless we have each other's permission—OK?

Great! That means I won't be reporting to MFIP staff anything that you say here. But I will be reporting who is in attendance at each session and if any one is absent. Clear enough? So, who would like to start?

LOUISE [in a sweet voice]: Should I stand up?

TONY: No—you can just stay where you are and tell us your name and what you hope to gain from the group and maybe a fear you have?

LOUISE: Well, I'm Louise, and I'm sort of a homebody. I haven't worked much outside the family since my youngest was born fifteen years ago. I hope this group will show me the way.

SHARON [with a gruff edge]: I can see why *you're* here—but I don't know why I've got to waste my time with this group when I'm already working. My name is Sharon, and I'm a cashier down at the Jiffy Market—by the way, my boss just scheduled me to work next week at this time, so I'm not going to be here.

TONY: Thanks Louise and Sharon for getting us started. Sharon, we might be able to arrange another time for the group, so some scheduling conflicts might be able to be accommodated. Let's see if we can negotiate this after the rest of the group has a chance to introduce themselves.

ANITA [animated]: I'll go next—I'm Anita, and I've got my days free for now, so I don't care what time this group meets. I just quit my job at this local law firm, where I was their secretary—actually their gopher! Couldn't see any future in it, so I quit.

SHARON: You're so young—you think everything is going to be possible—you should be thinking about your kids.

ANITA: You should mind your own business!

LEO [in a monotone]: Let's all take it easy, now—calm down. Tony's here to help us. I've been to a bunch of other groups like this, and you might want to check out all the resources in the Resource Room, where they've got computers for us to use. I've sent out my resume and contacted lots of employers and even had a couple interviews.

ANITA: Well, leave it to the man to act like he knows it all—if you're so on top of things, how come you're here?

In order to keep this first group meeting moving in a functional and potentially positive direction, Tony will need competencies in work with involuntary transactions. For example, he should listen carefully for each member's priorities and make tentative mental notes about possible areas to explore for motivational congruence. Each of the group participants is likely to be experiencing and expressing various degrees of reactance (Brehm et al. 1966). That is, members could have an acute sense of losing control over previously available resources (money, job, mobility, freedom to come and go); their hopes for benefits from participation in the group (improvements in income, work opportunities, other gains, or release from program requirements) could vary. While some appear to be entering the group under more voluntary conditions than others, each is likely to be experiencing some degree of formal and informal pressures; even Leo's apparent compliance and upbeat (though monotone) demeanor may mask uncertainty or actually be a strategy of giving a good impression and thus influencing those whom he perceives has having power, like the group leader. Sharon's antagonism may be an asset for bringing to the surface the underlying concerns that each member faces, so Tony will want to keep her engaged without derailing the group from its intended focus. Finally, he must recognize that each group member, as a welfare client, will be under the pressures inherent in the persistent stigma of using welfare in the United States.

Context of Practice

The climate of public opinion toward welfare clients in the United States continues to be accusatory and judgmental toward those who have not secured self-reliant means of support. Lawmakers have developed instruments to manifest stern public condemnation of parents who refuse to work, such as sanctions (reducing or completely cutting off assistance as punishment for parents not complying with rules): "The use of the work first philosophy is an example of the moral judgments of stakeholders influencing policy and programming. This philosophy values immediate workforce attachment over previous human capital investment strategies" (Mulroy and Tamburo 2004:119–120).

Extending this strategy, welfare policies at national and state levels have turned away from generous and successful incentives to work and eliminated exceptions to requirements for qualified clients who are abiding by the rules. For example, in 2003 lawmakers in Minnesota reduced cash grants to welfare clients if they were also receiving federal housing subsidies or Supplemental Security Income (SSI). In testimony before the Minnesota legislature (Lohn 2005), client Lynn Vincent, a mother of two, advocating for restoring these cuts in benefits, recounted how her family has suffered in having to find discarded food for meals: "I have to go through the spoiled food and cut off mold and such, which is really gross, but I was doing that . . . . This has just put us into a place where it's hard to live." In 2007 assistance for clients in Minnesota receiving SSI was restored to pre-2003 levels, but the penalty for receiving housing subsidies remained in place.

This suffering, often referred to historically as the spur of want (Trattner 1999), is precisely the outcome intended by welfare policies that structure aid to come up short and never fully meet needs; the idea is that the "stick" of these harsh consequences will punish laziness and push parents to comply with work expectations. However, as Trotter, who has researched work with involuntary clients, points out and as studies on use of negative reinforcement confirm: "Approaches which blame, punish and judge clients in the hope that their behavior will change seem doomed to failure" (Trotter:1999:40).

In a series of findings with ramifications for work with involuntary clients, studies of welfare reform indicate that parents who are sanctioned do not end up working as often as other parents leaving welfare for work (fewer than 40 percent of sanctioned clients working compared to more than 60 percent in some studies of welfare leavers working), and their earnings are substantially lower (Tweedie 2001; Weil and Finegold 2002; Lindhorst and Mancoske 2006; for analysis of sanction policy, see also Hasenfeld, Ghose, and Larson 2004). Families with parents who are sanctioned or with parents who have used all of their allotted benefits under time limits and exemptions are very vulnerable to stay poor or fall into poverty. Analyzing data from a nationally representative three-city sample, Lohman et al. (2004) concluded that "the experience of sanctions appears to be particularly problematic for young children's development" (p. 66). In another study covering twenty cities in fifteen states comparing the experience of mothers on welfare whose benefits were reduced by sanctions to those who were not sanctioned during the prosperous economy in 1998–2000, Reichman, Teitler, and Curtis (2005:226) found that:

> Sanctioned mothers are 85 percent more likely to report any material hardship than nonsanctioned mothers. They are 63 percent more likely than nonsanctioned mothers to report maternal or child hunger, 76 percent more likely to report having their utilities shut off, and 79 percent more likely to report being unable to receive medical care (due to cost) for themselves or a child.

In addition, these and other outcomes indicate that arbitrary and absolute time limits tend to harm rather than help improve poor families' economic status. Despite the assumption on the part of many that time limits have been successful, for some former recipients, employment is only part-time and leaves them poorer than when they were on welfare, as well as without health care coverage (Crichton 2003). In a Louisiana study examining the status of parents who were dropped from welfare involuntarily due to time limits or sanctions, the majority were not working, and their financial resources were significantly less than available to parents who leave welfare for work or who stay on welfare (Lindhorst and Mancoske 2006:110): "It appears that being involuntarily removed from welfare leads to increased economic stress, which is not resolved through greater labor force participation." Thus, parents who lose cash assistance due to time limits are likely to do less well (e.g., with housing and food) and to earn less than other parents leaving welfare voluntarily. Generally, parents leaving welfare for whatever reason may be employed (though in 2002 "work by welfare leavers declined to 57 percent from 63 percent in 1999," The Urban Institute 2006:2). However, they typically do not earn enough to raise their families out of poverty, and their incomes are usually lower than the total combined income of welfare assistance plus earnings before leaving welfare (Reichman, Teitler, and Curtis 2005). Even full-time employment may not raise families headed by poor single mothers out of poverty (Gabe 2003). And as we will see, this loss of income has detrimental effects on their children.

Racial disparities and discrimination also have harmful effects on welfare clients. Disproportionate negative impacts on families of color continue to show up in research studies nationwide (Finegold and Staveteig 2002; Wilder Research Center 2003; Minnesota Department of Human Services 2007). Clients report discrimination in job seeking; parents of color moving from welfare to work make substantially less ($2.00–$3.00 per hour in a Hennepin County, Minnesota study) than white parents (Hollister et al. 2003). Citing studies by Delgado and Gordon (2002) and by Newbeck and Cazenave (2001), Abramovitz notes that welfare caseworkers tend to treat "white women more favorably than women of color" and that sanctions are used more predominantly with people of color (Abromovitz 1988:176). In her integrative review of more than 50 studies of welfare reform in Minnesota, McDonnell (2004) documented a trend toward disproportionate sanctioning of clients from minority or oppressed groups: "African Americans had a 38.1 percent sanction rate and Native Americans 48.7 compared to a statewide average of 34.2 percent" (ibid.:26). She found similar disparities in the likelihood that families of color will lose welfare benefits due to time limits, with nearly half (43 percent) of timed-out families in Minnesota being African Americans, who comprise only 24 percent of the welfare caseload in the state. (For more details on these racial disparities, see also DeMaster 2007). While Reichman, Teitler, and Curtis (2005) found no differences associated with most demographic variables comparing sanctioned and nonsanctioned mothers, they did find "that being foreign-born substantially increased the likelihood of experiencing hunger, utility shutoffs, and any material hardship" for sanctioned mothers (ibid.:226). Upon reviewing extensive documentation of states' policies, Rodgers and Payne (2007) concluded that "states with the largest black populations and the highest rates of welfare use by blacks tend to adopt the most restrictive rules, provide the least generous welfare benefits, and the poorest support services" (ibid.:4). In contrast, "the states that have adopted the most generous, inclusive and supportive programs suffer less child poverty" (ibid.:12).

The Impact of Welfare Reform on Children

While caution in attributing causal relationships is in order (Besharov 2003), research on the effects of welfare reform on children's well-being suggests that strategies focusing on maintaining financial aid and resisting cuts in aid are justified. Public governmental assistance is critical to keep many families out of poverty, and the harm for children if parents lose income is real (Gennetian and Miller 2002; Zaslow et al. 2002; Dunifon, Kalil, and Danziger 2003; Morris and Gennetian 2003; London et al. 2004). Furthermore, recent studies show that increased family income leads to better outcomes for children. After reviewing research over the past seven years (McDonnell 2004), the University of Minnesota Centers for Urban and Regional Affairs and for Advanced Studies in Child Welfare concluded that more money helps; indeed, they found that increased family income is the most influential factor, rather than parents' work effort in improving children's lives. Other reviews of the literature nationally similarly observed that increased income is key (Bibus, Link, and O'Neal 2005; The Urban Institute 2006). Increases in family income either by encouraging parents' work and making it pay or by providing financial subsidies, or both, lead to improved well-being for children (better academic achievement, positive engagement in school, fewer problem behaviors, happier).

Conversely, cuts in financial aid place more children at risk. For example, in Wells and Guo's study (2004) in the Cleveland area comparing children in foster care before welfare reform (1995–1996) with those in foster care after welfare reform (1998–1999), there was a higher percentage of children in care after welfare reform who were considered neglected, a higher percentage in placement, and a higher percentage in placement longer with decreased speed in reunification.

The effects of requiring parents to work or seek work in order to receive public assistance are less clear (Dunifon, Hynes, and Peters 2006). Work requirements alone may neither help nor harm. Just mandating that parents work appears to have neither positive nor negative impacts on children's well-being, though there is some evidence that adolescents may suffer (e.g., see the summary of outcomes for adolescents in Lohman et al. 2004, and researcher Constance Williams' [2005] conclusions on the effects of inconsistent child care and lack of adult supervision in her ethnographic study in Boston). From research nationally to date, it appears that "parents with children age 6 to 10 who are struggling to balance new work responsibilities with child rearing may feel more stress as a result" (The Urban Institute 2006:5). Combining work requirements and incentives for work such as cash supplements and other benefits does lead to increased employment and reduced poverty. In addition, making work pay (either through parents finding well-paying jobs or by subsidizing earnings if necessary to raise family income above poverty) increases parents' participation in work and also lifts families out of poverty.

Despite these strategies, some families are worse off when they are no longer on welfare and are very vulnerable. Some parents (from 14 percent to more than 50 percent in some studies) who leave welfare are not working, do not have economic support from spouses, are likely to be exposed to violence, and do not receive other government benefits; these families are extremely poor, in ill health, and half or more of these families are unable to pay rent or utilities, and they often reduce or skip meals for lack of food. The more barriers to employment parents face, such as in mental health, learning disabilities, education, work history, physical health, children's difficulties, domestic violence, drug abuse, and alcohol abuse (see, e.g., Gorske et al. 2006), the less likely they are to be able to work even part-time. "As the number of barriers increased, the percentage of participants working at least half-time decreased" (Taylor and Barusch 2004:180).

Parents' Aspirations to Work and Experience with Welfare

Contrary to public perception, women relying on welfare tend to share the same degree of commitment to work, self-sufficiency, and high expectations for their children as the general public in the United States; they have "mainstream aspirations regarding work and exhibit strengths" (Anderson, Halter, and Gryzlak 2004:186); in general, they are pragmatic in adapting to their economic circumstances by turning to a variety of sources of income to meet the needs of their families (Almgren, Yamashiro, and Ferguson 2002). Depending on welfare when needed may even be associated with subsequent job satisfaction when parents find gainful employment (Scott 2006). Despite encountering multiple barriers to employment, welfare clients generally share the American dream for opportunity and freedom and believe they have talents to offer their communities.

While many clients have the same negative stereotypes regarding welfare clients as the general public, they tend to see themselves as unique compared to others on welfare. Their perceived strengths (measured after leaving welfare) include having a positive attitude toward working; some have improved economic circumstances in the workforce, are proud of modeling good citizenship for their children, and have enjoyed contact with and mutual support from others in similar situations. But this mainstream identity is challenged when, in contact with welfare service workers, instead of being seen as strong and resourceful, welfare clients experience disrespect and intrusion; they report often feeling trapped, and some perceive their work assignments as demeaning (Seccombe 1999; Lengyel 2001; Hays 2003; McPhee and Bronstein 2003; Hage 2004; Bibus, Link, and O'Neal 2005; Cleaveland 2005).

Less than adequate case planning, unresponsive services, and even hostility thus can mar interactions between welfare caseworkers and clients. Some caseworkers view clients stereotypically and denigrate them. Nevertheless, clients frequently perceive their workers as vital in determining what services they will receive; they encounter some supportive workers who become their advocates, but they see other welfare staff as deliberately withholding information. A client quoted in Lengyel (2001:147) stated: "My first caseworker was horrible. He didn't help, and I went to his supervisor, and she hasn't helped much either. She doesn't call or try to contact me if there are problems. She hasn't taken the sanction off yet, even with the [required] doctor's note." Another client quoted by McPhee and Bronstein (2003:38) described interactions with caseworkers as personally degrading: "It's the way they talk to you, the way they talk down at you that's humiliating. They're working for the government. 'You're here to get something from the government, so I'll talk down to you any way I want to.'" Similarly, members of a support group for mothers on welfare related to Bibus, Link, and O'Neal (2005) experiences of being treated rudely and "brushed off" when seeking help and of feeling forced to reveal embarrassing details of their lives.

In summary, like most Americans, welfare clients value independence and want to control their lives, and caring for their children is top priority (McPhee and Bronstein 2003). Some have been politically savvy in influencing expanded benefits and have mobilized to soften more punitive initiatives. Welfare's cash aid often represents for parents like those in the Job Finders Club the sole source of income and thus a vital and valued source of freedom to life and support for their families. Parents on welfare are likely to perceive agents of welfare reform as threatening the loss of valued freedoms including the ability to care for their children. Research on the outcomes of welfare-to-work policies validates parents' concerns that complying with mandates may not lead to improvements in family stability. Even if successful in raising family income, moving from welfare to work does not appear to produce improvements in parents' mental health (e.g., depression or low self-esteem) nor to improve household order, predictability, or routine as parents attempt to balance demands on their time at work and home. Other service interventions are needed. If a wide, comprehensive array of benefits, social services, and supports is available to parents in transition from welfare to work, they are less likely to return to public assistance programs. These services include access to education and training, housing subsidies, coverage for health care, financial aid for child care, expanded use of the Earned Income Tax Credit, food stamps, transportation help, support groups, mentoring (combined with concrete services, Ferguson et al. 2005), in-depth case management, and advocacy.

However, in many parts of the United States, social services are stretched beyond capacity (Abramovitz 2005). Social service agencies are seeing an increase in families' needs that exceeds agencies' ability to meet immediate demands, much less expand services. Abramovitz and others (e.g., Hays 2003) have noted that as welfare rules tighten and benefits dry up, the predictability of the work day for practitioners serving welfare clients has suffered: they have "less time to think and plan" (Abramovitz 2005: 180) in an environment where information and services are more scarce. Successful engagement between thus stressed practitioners and their clients who are possibly experiencing reactance requires a sophisticated level of competence and integrity. Welfare caseworkers should anticipate forms of reactance (from each other as well as clients) such as hostility, looking for loopholes, ingratiating, intimidating, escaping, or refusing to comply. They can help welfare clients by recognizing these normal reactions to the loss or threatened loss of valued freedoms and by joining with clients in developing a plan to meet clients' own goals as well as those mandated by welfare reform. As elaborated upon in the following guidelines, the parents' and practitioner's mutual interest in the children's well-being is a potentially powerful resource for planned actions to meet these goals.

Practice Guidelines

Considering approaches presented in this book and elsewhere (e.g., in Trotter 2006) that have been developed for effective work with involuntary clients in the context of contemporary welfare-to-work policies and building on research findings, we offer the following practice guidelines for practitioners serving clients on welfare. Permeating each are cultural competencies (see also chapter 15 by Dewberry Rooney on work with members of oppressed groups).

1. *Recognize and respond to reactance empathically and with cultural competence.* A key skill in cultural competence is the ability to generate a wide range of alternative explanations for behaviors that the dominant culture might label as deviant (Rooney and Bibus 1995; Green 1999; NASW 2001). Hence, when social workers first encounter clients who express reluctance to comply with welfare regulations, who appear apathetic, who are ingratiating in an apparently manipulative manner, or who show hostility toward the worker, they can recognize that such responses might be normal, natural reactions to the threats that requirements pose to their freedom to act on behalf of their family's well-being.

Of course, any preconceptions or assumptions about an individual's state of mind, perceptions, interpretations, health, or habits need to be tentative and cautious. And values associated with individual freedom (and threats to it) will be less prominently featured in some cultures than in others. Nevertheless, in the United States it is sensible first to consider reactance as a possibility. Clients should have the opportunity to elaborate on their views regarding the pressures and mandates they face, and social workers should listen empathically. As Green (1999:108) states, "empathy is a deliberative effort to learn what one's clients or patients are trying to convey, of adopting a learner stance toward their perspective and their words." This learner stance is life-long. "Cultural competence is not static and requires frequent relearning and unlearning about diversity" (NASW 2001, Standard 3 Interpretation). This learning must be specific to the influence of culture in one's own life and the strengths and vulnerabilities of clients' cultures (especially help-seeking traditions, experience of oppression, and worldview, e.g., toward work), and this learning must be specialized in the area of welfare history and policies and "how they serve or fail to serve specific client groups" (NASW 2001, Standard 3 Interpretation.)

For each of these practice guidelines, skills in cross-cultural communication are essential. In responding to possible forms of reactance, practitioners should evaluate clients' culturally based behaviors potentially "as strengths and differentiated from problematic or symptomatic behaviors, integrate the information gained from a culturally competent assessment into culturally appropriate intervention plans, and involve clients and respect their choices in developing goals for service" (NASW 2001, Standard 4 Interpretation).

For example, Tony could ask members of the job seekers group to share the value that each member's culture places on one or both parents' employment outside the home: how does each culture judge what is the proper gender or "bread winner" roles? What has been the culture's historical experience with job discrimination? Where have there been barriers to employment such as language or citizenship documentation? Is raising children considered valuable work? He should be aware of community resources that are culturally responsive and be ready to make referrals as appropriate.

2. *Explain the dual roles of the professional helper.* Practitioners should identify and explain clearly their often dual role on the one hand as helpers and on the other as agents of social control, and then focus change efforts on welfare clients' goals as well as the welfare program's mandated goals.

It is important to explain the workers' various roles, clarify expectations, and lay out explicitly the theoretical and empirical foundation of work. In his study in corrections, Trotter found that this approach reduced recidivism of probationers by half.

Having clarified the dual role social workers have with involuntary clients, practitioners must then focus on developing a culturally competent working relationship with the client: "Although it is important to learn about diverse cultures, a core skill in cross-cultural competence is the skill and ability to engage with others for the purpose of developing a working relationship. It is then that we can learn about others' meanings, values, and beliefs" (Van Soest and Garcia 2003:34). Tony's initial statement regarding the purpose of the group is a good way to start, but he would subsequently need to discover with each client their understanding of why they are attending, whether they are required to attend, and what are the consequences of not successfully completing the group.

3. *Reach for motivational congruence.* In developing their approach to working with clients who are welfare recipients, practitioners should take into account what we know about the importance of increased income for families and about the potential benefits and harms of policies associated with welfare reform and then combine that knowledge with what is known to be most effective practice with involuntary clients. As presented elsewhere in this book, research findings reveal that increasing motivational congruence will improve the likelihood that clients will achieve their goals. For a recent example, see Trotter's study (Trotter 2002) gathering information from 282 clients of child protection workers in Australia; he found that when clients rated workers high in skills such as understanding the client's point of view and discussing real problems as defined by the client, then client satisfaction and successful case outcomes increased significantly compared to when clients rated workers low in these skills.

Qualitative studies provide some clues for potential motivational congruence even given the desperate circumstances welfare clients often face (McPhee and Bronstein 2003; Anderson, Halter, and Gryzlak 2004; Bibus, Link, and O'Neal 2005; Cleaveland 2005). Clients' desires for income and commitment to their children's well-being partially overlap with the goal of welfare reform to move parents off welfare and into the job market. If jobs for which clients are prepared and trained are in fact available and pay above poverty wages, employment could become the most fruitful means for parents to ensure financial stability, safety, and health for their families. Parents on welfare often "are resolutely committed to the protection and welfare of their children. There is often little distance between the interests of the children and those of the parents" (Lengyel 2001:8). Impediments to work (such as lack of affordable child care that is available at the frequently odd times when parents are working) can coincide with threats to children's well-being (such as low quality child care). But many parents work hard to protect children from bearing the brunt of welfare reform. Practitioners can join with parents in buffering the impact of these barriers and sanctions. High potential exists for common ground between parents' desire to raise their children with income adequate to the task and the program requirements for parents to move from welfare to work. For some parents, because of the stigma associated with welfare and dependence on public assistance, being free of welfare is a top priority; and this goal coincides with policy targets to reduce the number of clients on welfare roles.

In the job seekers group, Anita hinted at a possible area to explore for congruence between her experience with a job that seemed to have no future and the program's intention to prepare group participants to move off welfare and into gainful and possibly more meaningful employment. However, Tony must be ready to advocate that the welfare program consider group members' need for more advanced training or education as a legitimate element in their work plans. Defining job training and higher education as "work" is more difficult under the welfare policies in some states than in others, but is subject to change (and thus influence) at the local level. Using skills in effective advocacy (Influencing State Policy 2005), Tony could mobilize the group to gather facts and figures on the impact of low wage, "dead end" jobs, study the legislative process, join coalitions, identify key players, communicate with them in a trustworthy manner, and remain persistent in the effort to have education count as preparation for work.

4. *Understand clients' perception of problem and clients' goals.* Observing that involuntary clients' goals may not always be appropriate (e.g., a client suffering from a dangerous mental condition that can be controlled only by medication might want to be free of drugs), Trotter (1999) asserts that "nonetheless, the research consistently points to the need to work with client definitions of problems and goals with both involuntary and voluntary clients" (ibid.:22). "Working with client goals is more likely to lead to positive outcomes" (ibid.:6). So a critical step in effective practice is to understand how the involuntary client defines problems, in the client's terms, and what solutions might be preferred to achieve particular client goals. Focusing only on workers' goals or program mandates will not work as well.

Applying this approach to practice with clients on welfare, practitioners should listen carefully, empathetically, and reflectively for the clients' perception of their situation. What problems, issues, or needed changes do they see in their lives related to being welfare recipients? Trotter provides an apt example of this approach to problem identification related to job seeking (ibid.:87): "In relation to a problem of unemployment, the worker might seek to clarify with the client how long she has been unemployed; how she feels about this; whether she has worked previously; how she fills her days."

Subsequent case planning should include careful assessment of employment skills and deficits, clear discussion of work and training requirements and options, and provision of information about services and benefits

(Anderson, Halter, and Gryzlak 2004). Tony could, for example, ask Leo to share what he has learned so far about the job-seeking process, which of the agency's resources have been most helpful, what he has done that has been most successful, and where he has run into barriers.

5. *Identify what is negotiable and what is not.* Because practitioners involved with involuntary clients often are required to help make changes in clients' behaviors that clients themselves do not recognize as problematic, it is critical to identify negotiable and non-negotiable concerns. Trotter (1999) suggests making two problem lists with the client: the client's list and the list of the problems seen by worker, agency, or those of the referring agent. Some actions to address problems will involve a range of options; for example, welfare clients may be allowed to choose among job training sites or they may be able to divide up their time between the job application process and job preparation activities such as education. To reduce reactance and reach for motivational congruence, practitioners should emphasize and strive to expand choices and options. Other actions will be constrained by mandated outcomes and deadlines. For example, welfare clients may be required to attend on time and participate for the full duration of an orientation workshop on how to find a job; if they are late, they might be locked out and their aid reduced. Again, to reduce harmful reactance, practitioners could help the client think through how attendance at the workshop limits their freedom for only that short portion of a day and will maintain their eligibility for financial aid and other services over many months. While delineating the Job Finders Club rule regarding confidentiality, Tony began to clarify that attendance would be monitored and reported, thus implying that it is not negotiable. On the other hand, when the group meetings were scheduled was evidently subject to some mutual negotiation.

6. *Rank problems and goals according to those most important to clients.* When clients generate a list of pressing issues, ranking concerns according to urgency and importance to the client is a useful way to begin service planning. Trotter adds: "It is important that the problems are listed in the client's terms and in the client's language. This is the client's list" (ibid.:87). So if one of the clients in the Job Finders Club says that her problem is "I don't have work," Tony should write that definition in those words and not substitute his own wording, such as "unemployment." Trotter adds though that it can be helpful to rephrase in order to clarify the meaning of a concern.

When practitioners and clients have agreed-upon problems in priority order, ranking goals respective to the top priority problem or two can proceed. The criteria for ranking goals would include their urgency, their immediacy, their likely success in the near future, and their meaning in the client's view. Practitioners should look for opportunities to pair clients' concerns with mandated problems and frame goals in specific and practical terms. For example, if Sharon wanted to pursue a promotion with higher salary and benefits so she might earn enough to raise her family off welfare, she could enlist the help of the group in developing and proposing her plan to her boss; with Tony coaching, group members could assist Sharon in composing a script of what she would say and then role play various reactions the boss might have and responses Sharon could productively make.

Trotter offers more useful guidance for exploring and formulating goals to address problems. If the client's top problem is being out of work, he suggests determining how long the client has been without work. Has the client ever worked? If so, what type of job was it? How long did the client work in a particular job? When the client left work, was leaving a voluntary decision or was the client fired? Is the client interested in seeking work now as her or his own goal or mainly because the welfare policies require unemployed parents to be job seekers? What job training, skills, or educational programs has the client completed?

The practitioner and client should generate as many specific details as possible on the client's work history, successes, and difficulties. What solutions emerged? What strategies to find and keep jobs were most useful? And what barriers got in the way? Defining goals specifically sets the stage for ironing out differences in interpretation between the client and practitioner. Trotter suggests that a client such as Louise will have more difficulties successfully meeting a general goal such as "to get a job" than a more specific one such as "to find part-time employment in a sales position within six weeks" (ibid.:92).

7. *Use task-centered contracting.* During the contracting phase of work with clients on welfare, practitioners should develop with each client specific mutual tasks, especially in the early stages (Reid 1992). If possible, first tasks should be clearly linked to reaching clients' goals; while mandated goals must also be attended to, tasks aimed at achieving them may be developed later as clients gain momentum in successfully completing their tasks. For example, if Louise contracts with the job seekers group to compose a draft cover letter and resume, Tony can facilitate assignment of a mentor from among the other group members to edit a first draft, and he can distribute several models of letters and resumes. Group time can be devoted to reviewing sample resume drafts or to rehearsing informational interviews with prospective employers. If practitioners refer clients to other services, they should plan to follow up with the client and referral source within days and offer to collaborate further as needed.

Some tasks required for welfare clients to remain eligible for benefits are likely to be distasteful. Because she has not been employed outside the home for a number of years, Louise might experience distress just thinking about interviewing for a job and possibly being rejected. As we have discussed earlier in the book (and in Rooney and Bibus 2001:401–403), there are several ways to assist involuntary clients to accomplish goals, even disagreeable ones, including *quid pro quo* and "getting rid of the mandate." Practitioners can support completion of disagreeable tasks by helping to break the task down into steps and inviting the client to choose the order in which they would take the steps. For example, Tony and the group could help Louise identify steps in planning for and conducting an informational interview, starting with generating a list of possible contacts by name, location, phone number, e-mail address, etc. Perhaps Louise would find it less distressful to have the name of an employer's secretary to call rather than the company's chief executive officer. The group could role play with her making this call and have some fun with the various permutations of business telephone conversations. Thinking through the worst that could happen (she would be put on hold indefinitely!) can be helpful.

8. *Confront ethically as appropriate or needed.* Welfare reform has presented social workers with ethical dilemmas in the areas of confidentiality, self-determination, and challenging injustice (Abramovitz 2005). These ethical issues are particularly pertinent as practitioners decide whether and how to confront involuntary clients on welfare. They must always be ready to honor parents' desire to provide for and protect their children. Social workers can credit and nurture aspirations for work and self-sufficiency as well as model and reinforce with genuine praise and encouragement parents' interest in education, training, work, or attending a group. But practitioners should also not hesitate to use effective, nonabusive confrontation of behavior that is not meeting a mandated goal. As discussed earlier in this book, the intensity of confrontation should be calibrated to the level appropriate to the harm or risk presented by the client's behaviors or decisions. For example, if Louise balks at taking reasonable steps to explore employment possibilities, Tony could help the group examine with Louise what effect the delays are having on her daily life and future opportunities. Inductive questioning could help clarify for Sharon some of the ways the job seekers group might be useful to her: "Are you satisfied that your current job as a cashier provides opportunities for advancement and perhaps more rewarding work?" If Leo continues to ingratiate or present himself as engaged in the group and fully accessing the resources of the agency but also is not successful in finding a job, a more assertive or intensive confrontation may be necessary. Tony could facilitate group members directly relating to Leo their concern that Leo appears to want to work, but going through the motions of job searching has not been successful so far, and he risks running out of eligibility time—the clock is ticking! Intensive confrontation would be appropriate if any group member decides to commit an act of fraud in falsifying work records, for example.

As with the other practice guidelines, confrontation must also be culturally competent. Proctor and Davis' studies (1994) on skills in cross-cultural practice are especially pertinent here. They found that clients from oppressed groups have three primary concerns in working with professional helpers: Is the helper a person of goodwill? Is the help offered valid and meaningful? Is the helper trained and skilled? So, before confronting involuntary clients who are on welfare, practitioners should have first established themselves as persons of goodwill by warmly greeting the clients, pacing interactions according to the clients' preferences (not rushing, for instance, to cover business), and being aware of physical cues or mannerisms and how they might be interpreted. For example, if Tony is white and the group members are African American, he should recall that group members likely have had troubling experiences with authorities during which they were stopped, interrogated, or required to reveal private information solely on the basis of their appearance or racial profile. Before asking questions, he should use a moderate, warm tone of voice with expressive "listening" eye contact (not staring or glaring), remain seated with relaxed open posture, explain the purpose of his inquiries, and give room for the clients to ask clarifying questions or decline to answer a particular line of questioning. If he has difficulty understanding what the clients say, he should acknowledge that immediately. And he should make it clear fairly soon in the first group meeting that any concerns clients have about the difference in race or cultural background between himself and any client are appropriate to raise and that he will try to understand and address them professionally. This will set the stage for successful later confrontations with clients to meet their own goals or to make changes required to meet mandates or comply with welfare program expectations.

9. *Review work so far and evaluate together.* Both during and at the end of work with involuntary clients on welfare, practitioners should take the initiative to set up with clients systematic and flexible processes for clients to comment upon what has been helpful or what could have been done differently: "Clients seem to know if they are being helped" (Trotter 1999b:144). Thus, Tony could ask at the end of each group session what has been most helpful and least helpful; he could have group members fill out an anonymous brief survey on what he should continue doing, stop doing or start doing differently; and he could have a final evaluation form for group members to fill out and send back to the agency. Group members could be invited to join in designing the evaluation and choosing the format with which they were most comfortable (e.g., online or in person or on paper).

When Bibus, Link, and O'Neal (2005) met with a support group for parents on welfare, they asked participants to describe the benefits and drawbacks of welfare reform; participants preferred to give their comments orally in focus group format or in anonymous written notes rather than on tape or on a more formal survey. Positive aspects of welfare reform in their experience included the availability of emergency cash assistance and medical assistance coverage at least for their children; they also highly valued the support group offered at the community agency. Participants agreed that explaining the tougher work rules was helpful (most saw a need for them), but they objected vehemently to the time limits, cuts and sanctions as arbitrary, discriminatory and harmful. Practitioners should keep in mind the implications from national research on the damage done by sanctions: "As applied, they appear to be punishing those who have serious difficulties adhering to program requirements due to limiting factors, such as poor physical or mental health. This finding suggests that individual circumstances should be strongly considered before sanctions are applied" (Reichman, Teitler, and Curtis 2005:233).

10. *Use supervision.* As discussed in the chapter on work in supervision, social workers practice most effectively and ethically by using supervision well. Because welfare clients are in particularly vulnerable circumstances both due to their low income and due to the cutbacks in public assistance, practitioners serving clients on welfare need to maintain as regular and competent supervision as possible. Trotter (1999b:148–149) recommends that supervisors and supervisees explore questions such as "What does/do the client/s understand to be the purpose of your work with them?" "How will you know if the client is successful in achieving his/her objectives?" "What positive actions did you praise or reward?" "What actions did you confront?" and "Does the client believe you are helping?"

Ideally, Tony's supervisor would have particular competency in supervising social work with groups and should be ready to help him sort out what's going well, how best to anticipate and facilitate the group members through developmental phases of their work, whether conflicts are surfacing and being managed, how well members are achieving their goals, and to what degree a climate of mutual aid has been growing (Anderson-Butcher, Khairallah, and Race-Bigelow 2004; see also chapter 12 by Chovanec in this volume).

11. *Advocate!* According to the *Social Work Dictionary* (Barker 2003:11), "advocacy" in social work is "championing the rights of individuals or communities through direct intervention or through empowerment" and is "a basic obligation of the profession and its members." In an influential cross-disciplinary and cross national essay on advocacy, social welfare scholar and activist David Bull (1989:52) from the University of Bristol distinguished between "advice" (go and get it) and "advocacy" ("I'll try to get it on your behalf.") Finally, based on an extensive literature review and thoughtful analysis, Schneider and Lester (2001:65) offer this *new* definition: "Social

work advocacy is the exclusive and mutual representation of a client(s) or a cause in a forum, attempting to systematically influence decision making in an unjust or unresponsive system(s)."

As suggested in this definition, two basic levels of social work advocacy are *Case* Advocacy and *Cause* Advocacy. *Case* (or client) advocacy focuses on securing "services that the client needs and is entitled to obtain on his or her own" (Sheafor and Horejsi 2003:414). *Cause* (or class) advocacy focuses on advancing "the cause of a group in order to establish a right to a resource or opportunity" (Sheafor and Horejsi 2003:438).

Advocacy is at the heart of social work practice with involuntary clients who are on welfare. In addition to advocating as part of direct services to clients, under responsibilities to the broader society, according to NASW's *Code of Ethics* (1999), "social workers should advocate for living conditions conducive to the fulfillment of basic human needs and should promote social, economic, political and cultural values and institutions that are compatible with the realization of social justice." Advocacy can take on a variety of dimensions including speaking on behalf of clients on welfare, accessing rights and benefits, and using legal bases and demonstrating political influence (Schneider and Lester 2001). In her study with more than 100 nonprofit human service agencies serving welfare clients in New York City, Abramovitz (2005) noted that staff engaged in three forms of advocacy: "*case advocacy,* or work on behalf of individual clients; *self advocacy,* encouraging clients to take more control of their own destiny; and *cause advocacy,* directed to policy change" (ibid.:185). Most agencies shared information about welfare reform and its effects, encouraged clients to attend community forums, and held educational meetings; fewer, but still many, encouraged clients to participate in rallies and demonstrations, partnered with advocacy groups, and met with or wrote city officials, legislators or policy makers. In the words of one of her respondents (ibid.:183): "It's like the babies are flowing down the river and we're pulling the babies out. At the same time we have to ask the question who's throwing the babies in up there?"

As he facilitates the group of welfare clients, Tony can advocate by encouraging the group to examine effects of sexism in the workplace and generate strategies to transcend discriminatory barriers. For example, he may wish to share information about the privileges men with educational opportunities and other resources enjoy in the job search process compared to women generally and to men who have not had educational opportunities. One group of welfare clients who met with Bibus, Link, and O'Neal (2005) included as most important in their list of recommendations for improving welfare reform that lawmakers take testimony from recipients. These mothers also recommended that more explanation be given for the new time limits and reductions of housing assistance and SSI and that staff enforce the work rules but lift the time limits. They added that increase in cash assistance and food stamps would help, and they asserted that parents should be able to make a living off welfare: that is, their jobs must pay at least $9.45 per hour before the parents could move off welfare. Child care should be available at more times, more flexibly, and for extended hours. And the parents valued any encouragement and support toward more and better education and job training.

Based on the evidence so far on outcomes of welfare reform, practitioners should advocate for improvements such as:

increasing the supply of jobs in inner-city and rural areas; expanding wage supplements, for example, the Earned Income Tax Credit, tax incentives for employers to "carefully incorporate TANF leavers into their businesses," and better wages for menial jobs (Cleaveland 2005:65);

raising the minimum wage;

securing access to food stamps;

providing universal health care coverage and expanding Medicare/Medicaid;

increasing public housing subsidies;

making high-quality child care available for working parents;

counting education or training for jobs that pay a living wage with benefits as work activities;

repealing arbitrary time limits on eligibility for public assistance; and

stopping sanctions that reduce family income and thus harm children.

Cash assistance should be sustained until parents' income is 130 percent or higher of the poverty level. (In 2007, 100 percent of the U.S. federal poverty level for a family of four was $20,650 per year or $1,431 per month; 130 percent would be $26,845 per year or $2,237 per month.) Culturally competent social services for families with parents who are unemployed must also be available including case management, crisis intervention, mentoring, support groups, legal and policy information, and human rights advocacy.

The author has been consulting with supervisors and staff in welfare reform programs, offering the strategies presented in this book as ways to cope and perhaps even help under these desperate circumstances. But the level of frustration that supervisors and staff feel parallels in severity clients' desperation. As we'll see in chapter 18, one said in anguish: "You can only be screamed at so many times—it's beginning to wear on us." Confronted with the double bind of striving to accomplish the mission of the agency to promote self-sufficiency in an environment of diminishing resources, practitioners face potential disillusion and discouragement. The creativity and energy needed to reach for motivational congruence with clients, to expand the range of choices within mandates, and to advocate can drain away. I hope that the practice strategies, ideas, and research presented in this chapter will be resources to cultivate hope for positive change and improved well-being.

Discussion Questions

If you were in Tony's place, how would you respond when Anita says, "Well, leave it to the man to act like he knows it all—if you're so on top of things, how come you're here?"

1. What step would you take first to reach for motivational congruence with each group member? Why?
2. Which of the clues for effectiveness in practice with clients who are on welfare might apply in your practice?
3. Reflect on your own preconceptions or stereotypes about welfare clients. Which have changed as a result of reading this chapter? How so?
4. Which of the advocacy activities do you plan to follow up on in your practice?

This chapter offers practice guidelines drawn from empirical research as well as ethical principles. Such "evidence-based practice" is ideal, but Kessler, Gira, and Poertner (2005:247) argue that "working with involuntary clients and the balance between individual choice and social control presents significant challenges to this effort." Among the challenges they note are parents presenting themselves as cooperative yet saying little and parents being outnumbered by professional helpers in service planning meetings. What other challenges to evidence-based practice with involuntary clients on welfare do you see? What benefits, on the other hand, would you anticipate from evidence-based practice?

Part 3, Section D

Chapter 18

Applying the Involuntary Perspective to Supervision

Carol Jud and Tony Bibus

This chapter applies strategies for work with involuntary clients to supervision. It offers both supervisors and supervisees useful practice guidelines based on the authors' experience and available evidence of effectiveness. Lawmakers' growing reliance on mandates, sanctions, time limits and other forms of pressure or coercion to enforce compliance is increasing the proportion of involuntary clients in public social service settings (McGowan and Walsh 2000; Pecora et al. 2000; Billings, Moore, and McDonald 2003; McPhee and Bronstein 2003; Salus 2004; Bibus, Link, and O'Neal 2005). Similarly, the movement to managed care and the crisis in financing health care have led to restrictions in treatment options and length of service available for practitioners and clients in both nonprofit and for-profit agencies (Munson 1995; Strom-Gottfried and Corcoran 1998; Kadushin and Harkness 2002). Mental health practitioners in a variety of settings more frequently face situations that require involuntary treatment or court-ordered interventions (Taylor and Bentley 2005).

Supervisors play a pivotal role in monitoring whether clients who did not request help still receive effective and ethical services. Since many practitioners have been trained under models of practice that presume their clients will be voluntary, supervisors and supervisees must together develop competencies in work with involuntary clients. Clients who feel forced under legal mandates or in other ways pressured to have contact with social workers are vulnerable to premature termination of services or exploitation of their low-power status for the purposes of social control. Given attentive, responsive, and expert supervision, practitioners can recognize these vulnerabilities and work to transcend adversarial dynamics, to reach past clients' initial hostility or apparent indifference, and to develop at least tentative agreements and working relationships with involuntary clients.

As mentioned in the previous chapter, the authors have been consulting with supervisors and staff in welfare reform programs. The level of frustration that supervisors and staff feel parallels in severity clients' desperation. As one said in anguish: "You can only be screamed at so many times—it's beginning to wear on us." Another supervisor added: "How can I help staff stay positive when I'm on the verge of burnout myself?" Striving to accomplish the mission of the agency while resources are diminishing, staff and supervisors face disillusion and discouragement in the creative and sustained effort needed to reach for motivational congruence with clients. Drawing from public social service and child welfare settings, the case examples in this chapter illustrate how even in this challenging context supervisors can still work to improve social work services with involuntary clients. These supervisory strategies are resources for dealing with a stressful work climate and coercive policy environment and for pursuing social workers' mission with a greater possibility of success.

Supervisory Strategies for Work with Involuntary Clients

Supervisors should encourage workers to plan for reactance, to use contracting to link clients' concerns with agency mandates, to address performance difficulties, and to apply the legal-ethical matrix in making decisions. Supervisors (and supervisees) can also use these concepts in dealing with managers and other professionals, particularly as mediators.

Reactance

The concept of *reactance* highlights predictable strategies that people turn to when valued freedoms are threatened. Supervisors should keep reactance in mind in their work with supervisees as well as with clients. For staff in public social service agencies, which are often subject to tumultuous turmoil and cascading crises, one valued freedom is some remnant of personal control over the routine of record keeping. Preserving this degree of predictability when so many other demands dictated by external pressures are being made on one's time and attention is often perceived as vital. In many social service settings, though, change is a constant—and some changes challenge practitioners' skills, philosophies, and abilities. The following example shows how understanding reactance helps predict and respond effectively to the inevitable periodic spasms of change or re-organization.

In 1999, the state of Minnesota required all county agencies to adopt a new statewide social service information system (SSIS). Social workers now had to enter all client contacts on the computer system. Handwritten notes were no longer allowed. In addition, tasks previously done with pen and paper must now to be done on the computer.

One of the authors (Jud) was involved in implementing SSIS, working with both Information Technology staff and social workers toward a smooth transition. In this role, I encountered *reactance*. Some staff had never used computers except for e-mail and had no desire to learn. Others could not imagine how they could keep up with case notes if they had to put them all into the computer. They could foresee having to sit at a computer all day and having no time to visit clients.

Staff responded in several ways. Some attempted to take freedom back directly. They would simply refuse to use the new system and made comments like "What are they going to do? Fire me? Well, let them!" Other workers tried to *find the loophole*. They would enter the minimum needed in SSIS and then do everything else the old way. Some workers began to *value the prohibited behavior more than ever*. They wanted the option to write notes by hand, stating they could never compose on the computer and still see clients. A few workers responded with *hostility or aggression*. Many people complained about the new system, and some workers were outright hostile, as if I had made the decision that they had to use SSIS. One social worker told me he was going to unplug his computer and destroy the whole system! (Clearly, his understanding of computers was rather limited.) A few workers tried to *incite others to restore freedom* by telling other workers: "We should all just refuse to use SSIS and see what they do. What will management do if we all refuse to use it?" Some workers dealt with their feeling of losing control by *watching others attempt to restore freedom*. These people enjoyed watching others complain and refuse to use the system or attend training, and they hoped their coworkers' efforts would be successful.

The system was introduced and now is used without question. During the entire process of learning the new system, it was important for supervisors and managers to understand that the responses social workers had were normal, and these workers should not be labeled "resistant to change" or "problem employees" because they were slow to adjust to the changes. Change is difficult for everyone, and some people just have a harder time adjusting. This characteristic does not make them "bad" social workers. The supervisor helped staff identify how the changes had the potential to ease their work load and serve clients more efficiently as well as hold the agency accountable to its mission, to which they had devoted their careers. The new information system thus became an agreeable (or at least tolerable) mandate.

Applying Contracting Principles

The supervisor's clarity about the purpose of supervision and the supervisee's understanding and mutual commitment to this purpose are keys to successful supervision. "As in work with clients, the lack of a clear contract will frustrate efforts at almost every turn" (Shulman 1993:43). When consulting with supervisors on particularly problematic situations or supervisees, we recommend that they "begin again" with crafting a contracting statement of the purpose of supervision. Asking the question: "What will we be working on in supervision?" can be fruitful, and focusing on clients' goals is essential, even when the primary services are mandated. Other supervisory questions that are associated with effective services (Harkness and Hensley 1991; Trotter 1999b:148–149) include:

- What do clients understand to be the purpose of your work with them?
- What have you done to reach agreement with your clients about purpose?
- How will you know if your clients are successful in achieving their objectives?
- Do you have a contract?
- What positive actions by clients have you supported or recognized?
- What actions or inactions by clients have you confronted?
- Do your clients believe you are helping?

Practitioners familiar with the body of knowledge regarding power differences within involuntary transactions are less likely to ignore clients' concerns that are not requirements or to approve unnecessarily coercive measures to resolve problems that their agency is required to address (Hasenfeld 1992). When clients express feelings of being invaded, trapped, or humiliated (Lengyel 2001; McPhee and Bronstein 2003), supervisors can guide staff to expect these normal reactions to being involuntary and avoid prematurely labeling clients as uncooperative or resistant. Faced with volatile adversarial interactions, supervisors and supervisees who use negotiating and mediating models encourage cooperation and expand the range of choices within mandates (Center for Advanced Studies in Child Welfare 2002).

Once practitioners are skilled in engaging involuntary clients and negotiating successful service agreements, their supervisors should continue to support and assist staff in maintaining competence. Moreover, supervision includes demand for work, holding supervisees' accountable for effective and ethical client services. The strategies developed for work in involuntary transactions can be particularly effective when confronting staff when their performance falls below standards.

Addressing Performance

There are two distinct strategies that a supervisor can choose in dealing with performance issues. Just as managers might dictate to their program staff how to solve a problem (instead of involving the program staff in designing a solution), a supervisor can tell a supervisee what the practitioner needs to do to solve a performance problem; or, instead, the supervisor can involve the supervisee in the process. As we will see in the following scenarios, the latter strategy is more likely to be successful. High quality supervision combines concrete suggestions for improving performance with respectful listening for the supervisees' point of view (Westbrook, Ellis, and Ellett 2006).

Scenario 1

SUPERVISOR: Hi Mary. I called you into my office today to discuss some concerns I have about your work.

MARY: Concerns? What kind of concerns? Has someone been complaining about me?

SUPERVISOR: I've received several phone calls from clients and collaterals who say they can't get a hold of you because your voice mail is full, and you do not return pages. I have tried to page you on numerous occasions and have not heard back. My second concern is that your paperwork is several months behind, and workers on coverage are not able to answer questions about your cases because your case notes are not up to date. Also, we have discussed you closing four cases on your caseload and they have not yet been closed.

MARY: I've been busy! I have fifteen cases and there is no way I can stay up to date with that many cases!

SUPERVISOR: I'd like you to take the next five days to catch up on all of your paperwork. I want all four cases closed and on my desk by Friday. Also, you need to clear your voice mail three times a day so clients can get a hold of you. I expect you to be up-to-date by next week. O.K.?

MARY: I guess so, but I don't know where I'm going to find the time to do any of this! I'll do what I can.

Scenario 2

SUPERVISOR: Hi Mary. Thanks for coming in to talk with me. You've seemed really overwhelmed lately, and I'm concerned. Are you feeling as overwhelmed as you look?

MARY: Yes! I am totally overwhelmed. I don't know what to do! I have fifteen cases, and I'm so behind on paperwork I don't know how I'm going to get caught up! I'm trying to see clients, but am having trouble keeping up to date with that! And every time I'm gone from my phone, the voice mail fills up. I just can't return all the calls I'm getting!

SUPERVISOR: Have you had a chance to close those four cases we talked about closing?

MARY: No. I've been spending my time dealing with crises, and haven't had a chance.

SUPERVISOR: Well, I think our first priority should be getting you caught up so you're not feeling so overwhelmed. How does that sound to you?

MARY: That would be great! But how?

SUPERVISOR: What do you think it would take to get caught up on your paperwork and close those four cases? I think if you could close the four cases, you'd feel a lot better since your caseload would be down to eleven.

MARY: If I could spend three days working only on paperwork and not have to see clients or answer the phone, I think I could get caught up. But how am I going to do that?

SUPERVISOR: How about if you take off three days next week, say Monday through Wednesday, just to do paperwork. Put a message on your voice mail that you will not be available on those days. If anyone needs anything, the coverage worker can contact me. Unplug your phone so you don't hear it ring. Reschedule any appointments you have on those days, and if an emergency comes up, I will take care of it. How does that sound?

MARY: That would be great! Would it be OK if I took a laptop home and worked at home for those three days? Then I wouldn't be so distracted by coworkers.

SUPERVISOR: Fine with me. Then, next week we can brainstorm some ways you could use to stay caught up. So, by Friday of next week, what do you think you can have done?

MARY: I'll have the four cases closed and on your desk. I will also be within two weeks of being caught up on the case notes for all my cases.

SUPERVISOR: Are you sure you can get all of that done in just three days?

MARY: Yes, I'm sure. I just need some time to do the work.

SUPERVISOR: O.K. So by Friday, I will expect the four cases to close on my desk, and your case notes to be within two weeks of being caught up. I'm writing this down so I remember, and I'll make a copy for you as well. Then, let's meet on the following Monday at 10:00 a.m. to talk about how things are going. O.K., Mary?

MARY: O.K. I'll see you next Monday.

Scenarios 1 and 2 show different ways to address performance. In the first scenario, the supervisor tells Mary what the problems are and what the solution is. Mary really doesn't have any say and isn't asked for input. In the second scenario, the supervisor focuses on concerns that Mary is overwhelmed. Mary then readily admits to being overwhelmed and defines the problem herself, asking for help. The supervisor reaches for motivational congruence so she and Mary are working together on a solution for the performance problems. Mary may be able to catch up, and then she and the supervisor can work on ways for her to stay caught up. In the second scenario, Mary could feel more supported by her supervisor and be less likely to react as if she had done something wrong or was "in trouble." She will be more open to her supervisor's helpful suggestions.

The two scenarios also use different ways to talk with the social worker about the work that needs to be done. In the first scenario, the supervisor just tells Mary what needs to be done and when the work must be completed. In the second scenario, the supervisor utilizes contracting with Mary by asking for her input in what tasks need to be done and what she can do by the following Friday. She uses a task-centered approach, specifically asking Mary what she thinks she can complete and then writing these tasks down so there are no misunderstandings (Caspi and Reid 2002). The supervisor then sets a follow-up meeting. Of the two scenarios, the first one is much less time-consuming for the supervisor. However, the second scenario may be more successful and also models techniques in working with involuntary clients.

Sometimes performance problems are chronic. In such situations, other concepts for working with involuntary clients can be used. For instance, if after several meetings Mary continues to be behind in court reports, case notes, and seeing clients, the supervisor should become more directive. A first step would be to identify what's negotiable and what's mandated, and the next step could be to expand choices. Scenario 3 illustrates how a supervisor might use this technique.

Scenario 3

SUPERVISOR: Mary, I continue to be concerned about how behind you are in your work. We've discussed these issues several times, and have tried some different techniques to help you catch up. However, you are still behind in your court reports, case notes, and client contacts.

MARY: I know. I just can't seem to get caught up. There are just too many reports to write and too many requirements!

SUPERVISOR: Well, I know this job has a lot of paperwork associated with it. However, completing court reports and case notes is a required part of the job. Seeing clients is also required and extremely important, as you know. Child protection workers are responsible for assessing risk to children on an ongoing basis—and we need to make sure you're seeing the families on your caseload regularly.

MARY: I know. I just don't have enough time! Can't I just see clients and not worry about the paperwork so much?

SUPERVISOR: Well, the paperwork that needs to be done is not negotiable. However, how you structure your time to get it done is up to you. We have discussed some different ways you could structure your time—has that been helpful?

MARY: Yes, I guess. I'm still working on figuring out a system to get my paperwork done. I just haven't figured anything out yet.

SUPERVISOR: Mary, I guess I'm not quite sure what is keeping you from getting caught up in your work. We've tried having you work for three days on paperwork at home, but I still haven't received the case closings I requested two months ago. You asked me to not assign you a case so you could catch up, and I did this. However, you still have not caught up. I guess I'm not sure what the problem is, and why you haven't been able to catch up. What do you think is keeping you from getting caught up?

MARY: I just have too much to do. It's impossible to do this job with so many cases. I want to get caught up, but just haven't been able to do so.

SUPERVISOR: I agree this job is difficult with so many cases. I have suggested trying to get your caseload down so that you have a more manageable caseload, and we have tried a few different ways to give you time to close the four cases that need to be closed. I still haven't seen these cases on my desk. What do you think it is going to take to get these cases closed?

MARY: I just need to finish catching up on the paperwork for the cases before I close them. I just need more time. Maybe if I work on Saturday I can get these cases closed.

SUPERVISOR: O.K. I need to let you know that if you continue to be so behind, I will have to start looking at disciplinary measures. I'd like to avoid this, and I know you would also. But I do have a responsibility to the clients we serve, and you have been consistently behind on your work for several months now, and none of the ideas we've tried has seemed to work. The bottom line is that you need to be seeing clients and staying caught up in your paperwork. I'm willing to have you work on Saturday to get caught up, but am wondering what will be different this time from the other times you've taken time to do paperwork.

MARY: I know I'll be able to do this Saturday. Everything that's due will be on your desk Monday morning.

In Scenario 3, the supervisor let Mary know that paperwork is required, clearly identifying what is negotiable and what is mandated in the job. Mary continues to be behind on her paperwork despite previous interventions by the supervisor. In the next step, the supervisor tries to find out what Mary's view of the problem is, and what are her goals. Mary asserts that she has too many cases, and her goal is to get caught up. Accepting her view of the problem is an important aspect of addressing the performance concerns. The supervisor has already joined with Mary to address these issues. However, these efforts have not been successful in solving the performance problems. The supervisor is ultimately responsible for clients' receiving the services they need and therefore must continue to address the performance problem. In the dialogue above, the supervisor tries again with Mary, responding to her view of the problem. She then reframes the problem as a win–win situation. Finally, using informed consent, the supervisor addresses with Mary the consequences of noncompliance in getting caught up in her work. Mary's performance problems have reached the point of possible disciplinary action, and the supervisor has the legal and ethical obligation to confront Mary forthrightly.

Use of the Legal–Ethical Matrix

The legal–ethical matrix facilitates making ethical decisions in involuntary settings (see chapter 2 of this volume). Social workers often have a sense that something doesn't feel right, but they may have difficulty verbalizing what exactly is bothering them or on what basis to proceed in a specific direction. The legal–ethical matrix provides supervisees and supervisors with a tool for discussing such situations, as the following scenario illustrates.

Scenario 4

Ron, a child protection social worker, comes into the supervisor's office to talk, following an earlier discussion in which the supervisor advised him to close the Teresa Wells case.

RON: I'd like to talk to you about the Teresa Wells case. I know we talked about me closing the case in supervision, but I just don't feel right about it.

SUPERVISOR: Do you know what's bothering you about closing the case?

RON: It just doesn't feel right. I know we consulted with the county attorney's office, and they said we did not have enough to file a petition, but I still don't feel it's a good idea to close the case.

SUPERVISOR: Well, Teresa Wells is refusing to work with you and has not taken advantage of any of the services you've offered her. Correct?

RON: Yes, that's true. I don't even know where she is half of the time.

SUPERVISOR: How are the children doing?

RON: They're fine. Their grandparents are caring for them most of the time and making sure they have enough to eat, and they are all making it to school on time. The grandparents are really committed to these children and are making sure they get proper care even when mom's not around.

SUPERVISOR: So the children are receiving adequate care, Ms. Wells is refusing to work with us, and we do not have any evidence of maltreatment on her part that would enable us to go to court to have her ordered to work with us. Is that right?

RON: That's correct. But it just doesn't seem right that mom is out using cocaine all the time, and we can't do anything about it. I think the children would be better off if mom transfers custody to the grandparents, or if she would get the help she needs to stop using drugs.

SUPERVISOR: True. Ethically, it makes sense to intervene in this family's life. You have tried to work with mom, and she's not interested in working with you. Legally, we do not have grounds to intervene by removing the children or taking mom into court. Therefore, since she's not working with you, we need to close the case. The children are being cared for adequately, and the mother is not cooperative with services.

RON: It still doesn't feel right, although I understand what you're saying. The grandparents don't want us to close either.

SUPERVISOR: I think your gut feeling that ethically the community and social services should be intervening more with this family is right on target. However, the agency doesn't have the legal right to continue our intervention, even though we'd like to. Mom has a right to refuse services, and as long as her children are doing OK, we can't legally do anything. I know it's frustrating, but that's part of this job. You could talk to the grandparents and let them know that if they stop bailing out Ms. Wells every time she goes out to use cocaine, there will be a maltreatment finding based on abandonment, and we would have a legal basis to intervene—but as long as the grandparents keep caring for the children when mom takes off, we can't do anything about it.

RON: OK—I'll talk to the grandparents before I close the case, and explain to them what you've explained to me. Thanks for your help in clarifying this for me. At least now I know why I'm feeling so uncomfortable with closing the case.

In scenario 4, the situation with the Wells family fit into Cell 3 of the legal–ethical matrix: intrusion is ethical but not legally based. Looking at the situation in terms of the legal–ethical matrix helped Ron understand why he felt bad about closing the case, but also why he still needed to end services. In other situations, such as in the following example, social workers may feel uncomfortable because an action on a case may be legal but not ethical.

Serena comes into the supervisor's (Jud's) office to discuss some concerns she is having with a new case she just received. Ms. Byers is nine months pregnant, and the case was opened due to prenatal exposure of the child to chemicals. Ms. Byers had several toxicology screens while pregnant that were positive for cocaine. She is currently committed to inpatient treatment until she has the baby. Ms. Byers has been doing well in treatment and plans to enter a halfway house with the baby after the child is born. Her parental rights to one other child were terminated two years ago due to her illegal drug use, and she is determined to keep this baby.

The child protection investigating social worker has filed a petition in juvenile court, an Order for Immediate Custody of the child is in effect, and the child is to be placed in foster care as soon as it is born. Ms. Byers has no knowledge that the agency is planning to take her child when it is born, and the investigating social worker did not want her to be told.

Serena expresses concerns with the decision not to tell the mother of the plans to remove her child when it is born. While this plan is legal, in that there is no obligation to tell the mother anything, it still did not feel right.

We discuss the case and whether it would be ethical to deceive Ms. Byers about the plan for the baby. If Serena didn't tell Ms. Byers, and then removed her baby from her, Ms. Byers might never trust a social worker again. If she did tell Ms. Byers, there was a risk that Ms. Byers would leave the hospital or treatment with the baby against advice, although based on her stated commitment to this unborn child and her sobriety, Serena judges that Ms. Byers would stay.

After discussing the case situation, we ultimately decide to tell Ms. Byers about the Order for Immediate Custody, and then work with her to get the child returned to her safely as soon as possible. Serena states that she feels a lot better about this course of action, and she predicts it will lead to a more successful working relationship with Ms. Byers.

In the above example, Serena was not comfortable with a plan made by another social worker because she didn't feel it was ethical. This situation falls into Cell 2 of the legal–ethical matrix: intrusion is legal but not ethically based. Discussing the case in terms of this framework helped clarify why the other worker was legally able to support the decision to remove the baby after birth without telling mom, and why Serena had an ethical rationale to object to a deceitful plan. This example also illustrates the influence that involuntary transactions can have on the work and service environment, a context that can be particularly stressful and conducive to unethical and abusive practices. The following section suggests supervisory strategies for effectively and ethically managing this context.

The Involuntary Context

Supervisors and supervisees need to understand the challenges of working in an involuntary context and to recognize ways social workers may handle their frustrations. In social service agencies today, difficulties such as those described above are commonplace. In the United States, society typically focuses on an individual pathology in addressing social issues. For instance, people tend to view family members who neglect their elders as "the problem." The societal factors that may have led to the neglect are largely ignored. Some examples of societal-based or structural factors include poverty, discrimination, drug abuse, neighborhood dangers, and lack of affordable childcare, housing, or health coverage. People of color are disproportionately subject to coercive and punitive rather than supportive or preventative interventions. Welfare-to-work programs use punishments to gain compliance, such as sanctions if clients miss meetings. They may not consider how poverty limits access to transportation or how difficult it is to carry several children onto the bus to get to a required appointment. Managed care policies may only fund short-term therapy for clients who would be better served by longer-term therapy. Often, it seems as if agencies are more concerned with processing people than meeting their needs. For example, some public social service agencies have adopted outcome-based programs to measure success. While there are advantages to such a focus, sometimes outcome statistics become ends in themselves, eclipsing clients' needs.

Studies have shown that clients will make longer lasting changes when they have self-attribution, that is, when they feel they made changes for themselves. However, heavy caseloads may not allow the social worker enough time to work with clients to gain self-attribution. According to Sherman and Wenocur (1983), social workers may cope in several different ways. They describe the *capitulator* response as resolving conflict by identifying with the organization. Using this strategy, social workers comply to minimal expectations, accept the current level of resources, and without guilt refrain from making any additional effort beyond routine services. Often they will stop advocating for change, shut down their empathy, and shuffle papers. The *noncapitulator* response, on the other hand, rejects complacency. Using this strategy, social workers will identify with clients' anger rather than powerlessness and may become isolated. Other practitioners may fall into the response of *self-victimization or martyrdom. Finding a niche,* such as a work unit whose supervisor is adept at buffering dispiriting stressors (Westbrook, Ellis, and Ellett 2006), usually works better. *Withdrawing* or leaving the agency is usually an option, though not without consequences. The *functional noncapitulator* strategy is a most promising response to frustration with the organization. Conflict is managed by acting responsibly to influence the organization. Using this strategy, practitioners form a supportive work group, pick their battles, and decide when to take calculated risks in negotiating the conditions of work.

Supervisors should watch for signs of all of these responses in staff. If any of the less functional strategies are evident, supervisors and supervisees should talk, identify specifically the pattern they noticed, and then work together to find more effective ways to deal with stress. Scenario 5 illustrates this work.

Scenario 5

SUPERVISOR: Hi Greg. I'd like to talk to you about some concerns I've had recently. Have a seat.

GREG: Thanks. What kind of concerns are you talking about?

SUPERVISOR: Well, you know we've been working together a long time, and I've always considered your work to be excellent.

GREG: Yes, I know you've told me that several times. Has something changed?

SUPERVISOR: Well, I'm not sure. I've noticed recently that you seem to be connecting less and less with clients, which isn't typical for you. You're always up-to-date in your paperwork . . . that's still true, but there is something different in how you talk about clients in supervision.

GREG: What exactly do you mean by "something different?"

SUPERVISOR: Well, you used to relate little anecdotes about each of your clients as you were talking with me about cases, and I got to know the clients through you as individuals. Lately, it seems as if you just group all the clients together, focus purely on what they have or haven't done, and your sense of hope seems to be diminished somehow. Does that make sense?

GREG: Actually, it does. I have been feeling really burned-out lately. I've been really angry since management refused to give us the additional staff we asked for, and I've been overwhelmed by the number of cases I've had. I guess I figured that if management doesn't care about the clients and maintaining a decent caseload size for workers, I don't need to care either. I told myself I'd just do the paperwork, which is what management seems to want, and try not to care so much about the clients. I don't think it's fair to them that I can't work with them the way I want to, so I guess I'm sort of just going through the motions.

SUPERVISOR: How does that feel to you?

GREG: Lousy! It's like part of me has shut down in doing the job, and I don't enjoy the work as much as I used to. I'm so angry still at management, because it seems that they don't care as much as I do, and that's frustrating.

SUPERVISOR: So you're not going to care either?

GREG: I guess.

SUPERVISOR: Greg, I know you well enough to know that you're not going to last in this job doing it the way you've started to do it lately. You won't be happy with yourself, and your clients won't be getting as good service as they should. Would you be willing to talk with me about some other ways to deal with your anger towards management, so you can be happier in your job and clients can get the service they deserve.

GREG: Yes, I would like to talk about that. I'm glad you brought it up—I know the way I'm dealing with this isn't working, so maybe we can figure something else out.

In Scenario 5, Greg was frustrated with management, and had begun to assume the role of *capitulator*. By bringing this issue out in the open, Greg is able to articulate how he feels about management's decision not to approve new staff for the department as well as how he's been coping with this anger. The supervisor and Greg can now talk about alternative coping strategies. By bringing the issue up early, the supervisor is also showing she values Greg's work and wants him to be happy in his job, as well as effective in his work with clients. The potential positive function of supervision in work with involuntary clients becomes evident in these examples and is also substantiated to an extent in research findings, as reviewed in the next section.

Functions of Social Work Supervision in the Context of Work with Involuntary Clients

Following the long tradition of social work scholarship devoted to supervision (Shulman 1993; Kadushin and Harkness 2002; Munson 2002; Tsui 2005), we think of supervisors as serving three primary functions: *administrative, educational, and supportive.* These functions interrelate to meet the primary goal of delivering services to clients effectively and ethically.

Exercising their *administrative* function, supervisors manage and direct supervisees' work, oversee the daily operations of their units or work teams, and carry out the agency's mission. The administrative function requires sophisticated skills in communicating, team building, leading, problem solving, managing conflict and crises effectively and diplomatically, networking within the professional community and at large, and other outwardly oriented strategic skills (Preston 2004). It also demands an increasingly high proportion of social work supervisors' time and attention (Collins-Camargo and Groeber 2003; Strand and Badger 2007). In some settings, such as those serving people facing difficulties with drugs or alcohol, supervisors may also carry a caseload, which while potentially valuable further limits their time for supervisory functions (Joseph 2006).

In contrast to administrative duties, supervisors often cite the *educational* function as more rewarding because they can focus on teaching supervisees and fostering their professional development. These teaching opportunities span the spectrum from informal orientation and on-the-job training to formal presentations modeling and demonstrating practice competencies (Caspi and Reid 2002). As their attention is absorbed in administrative duties, though, supervisors report that they have less time for teaching (Westbrook, Ellis, and Ellett 2006).

Similarly, supervisors value, but are often diverted from their *support* function. Ideally, in addition to instruction and education, social work supervisors should both support supervisees individually and as a group, thus cultivating both a nurturing work climate and service effectiveness (see, e.g., Yoo and Brooks 2005). Lawrence Shulman has extensively researched and elaborated upon the support function. Supervisees tend to rate their satisfaction with their supervisors as positive if their supervisor has created an "emotional atmosphere in which I feel free to discuss my mistakes and failures, as well as my successes" (Shulman 1993:137). Shulman's research over three decades in a variety of settings indicates that effective supervisors take advantage of a parallel process wherein their support of supervisees, including their demands for work, encourages support for clients which in turn leads to positive case outcomes.

Likewise, other scholars (e.g., Bednar 2003; Latting et al. 2004) have found that the success of supervisees' practice with clients is influenced by the quality of supervisory support: "If the supervisor works to empower and support the worker, so too will this be reflected in work with clients" (Kane 1991:20). Following a review of the empirical research on social work supervision by Ming-sum Tsui (1997), Bruce and Austin note that supervisees find the greatest satisfaction "(1) when the agency provides a supportive and clearly understood work environment; (2) when supervisors exercise leadership and authority based on competence and position; and (3) when workers feel supported by their supervisors" (Bruce and Austin 2000:87). In their review of the research on supervision, Kadushin and Harkness (2002:480) conclude "that supervision makes a significant contribution to worker's job satisfaction and that agency administration operates more effectively as a result of the availability of supervision." In a recent study of the factors leading to retention of competent social workers in child welfare, respondents described their most valuable managers "as being supportive and caring, trusting and trusted, and interested in the professional development of their employees" (Westbrook, Ellis, and Ellett 2006:52). In the absence of supervisory support, practitioners are likely to experience dissatisfaction with their work (Joseph 2006).

However, most of what we know about the effectiveness of supervision is dependent on the perceptions of supervisors or supervisees, so these research findings must be interpreted with caution. Few studies have been able to link supervisory activities with client outcomes (Bibus 1993; Tsui 1997). For his 2006 integrative review of the effects that managers and supervisors have on client outcomes, Poertner found just eleven studies, six focused on supervisory behavior and the rest on organizational climate, use of teams, and program impacts. Still, he concluded that "this body of research, while not experimental, provides evidence that supervisory behavior makes a difference to consumers. . . . Supervisors who are proactive, problem solvers who use effective interpersonal skills tend to have work units that produce more positive outcomes for consumers" (Poertner 2006:17–18).

Because supervisees may have been trained in practice models that presume clients have voluntarily sought their help, supervisors will need to offer *supportive* and *educational* supervision that is informed by models developed for involuntary transactions. Yet supervisors must now attend primarily to *administrative* duties responding to additional mandates, such as those imposed by welfare reform, and hence may not have time to provide direct support to staff. Anticipating trends that further focus social work supervisors' attention on external demands rather than internal relationships, Bruce and Austin (2000:102) write:

> Supervising staff under these new realities places increased emphasis on skills related to assessing outcomes, monitoring systems, and managing resources. . . . Welfare reform has shifted the focus from client dependency to client self sufficiency, placing new pressures on workers and supervisors to use interventions which empower clients to assume increased responsibility for their lives. Supervising staff in the welfare reform environment that is increasingly community-focused involves greater understanding of interdisciplinary and community practice.

Thus, social service settings today present uniquely complex and challenging environments for social workers and their supervisors. A variety of outside forces will continue to have an impact upon the focus of practice. Practitioners will continue to encounter radical shifts in their job descriptions based on legislative changes, media coverage, public opinion, internal policy changes, and budget cuts. Dominated by political pressures and interests, this practice arena often will be emotionally charged. Special interest groups may lobby for changes in policy, and social workers may face significant pressures to change their practice accordingly. Media coverage is another area that can be frustrating. Supervisors must become savvy in use of media so that supervisees' judgment and accountability can be appraised fairly.

Another challenge of practice in the public sector and in many private agency settings is the court system. In addition to the adversarial nature of the court process, judges and attorneys may disregard the opinions of social workers despite the fact that many are master's level clinicians. Also, judges may blame practitioners if the clients are not following the case plan. A cycle of coercion and blame often develops, as in the following case example:

> Rebecca, a child protection social worker, is working with the Jansen family. The court ordered Camilla Jansen, the mother of two young children, to undergo an assessment for substance abuse and follow all recommendations. Rebecca has worked hard with Ms. Jansen to set up appointments for the assessment. Ms. Jansen has failed several appointments, and always has an excuse why she could not attend. Rebecca has provided her with a bus card to get to the appointment, but Ms. Jansen said she lost it. Rebecca offered to drive Ms. Jansen to the appointment, and Ms. Jansen refused the offer, stating she could find her own ride. Then Ms. Jansen failed the appointment, claiming Rebecca told her a different time. Rebecca provided Ms. Jansen with phone numbers and addresses of several places where she could participate in an assessment of her dependency on alcohol, but Ms. Jansen has not followed through, stating it's too difficult to get to any with her two young children.

At court, Ms. Jansen claims her social worker hasn't helped her enough, and that's why she hasn't completed the assessment. Rebecca's court report outlines the efforts made to work with Ms. Jansen. The judge is clearly upset that her orders were not followed and believes the social worker is to blame. She therefore orders the social worker to schedule another appointment and take the client to the appointment. Rebecca is extremely frustrated because her hard work has gone unnoticed, and she appears to be blamed for the client's failure. In addition, she feels the judge has undermined her attempts to have clients assume appropriate responsibility. This frustration affects her relationship to Ms. Jansen, whom Rebecca blames for not getting to the appointment.

After the court hearing, Rebecca confers with her supervisor and recounts her frustration. The supervisor must be able to validate the supervisee's perceptions of events while at the same time help the supervisee think through effective next steps. For example, it can be helpful to suggest how the powerlessness that the social worker is experiencing in the court system may mirror the client's experiences with the agency.

Practicing in this conflicted, stressful, and pressured context, supervisors must develop expertise in administrative and community-based approaches based on evidence for effective supervision (Bunker and Wijnberg 1988; Shulman 1993, 1995; Tsui 1997; Kadushin and Harkness 2002; Munson 2002; Poertner 2006; Westbrook, Ellis, and Ellett 2006). Their position in their agencies mediating the boundaries between line staff and upper administration and between their work units and the community (resource agencies, courts, the general public) provides both a challenge and an opportunity to effect positive change. The following sections offer examples of and suggestions for supervisors' use of skills such as mediating, buffering or amplifying the dynamics of the service system, offering case consultation, building cultural competence, and attending to safety.

Mediating

One area in which successful supervisors develop competence is in mediation skills. When there are differences of opinions between social workers and other professionals, a sequence of strategies is typically employed. First, the supervisor needs to encourage the practitioner to deal with the problem directly with the other professional. When this strategy is not effective, supervisory intervention may be warranted. The supervisor can call a meeting between the supervisee, the supervisor, the other professional and that person's supervisor. The purposes of the meeting are to air each party's opinions and positions and to reach for consensus or compromise. Since social workers typically believe they are advocating for a client's welfare, their positions are heartfelt; supervisors should be ready to affirm the strength with which opinions are held without necessarily agreeing with their content. If a meeting at the supervisory level does not solve the problem, the supervisor should invite managers to help address the dispute.

Mediating also may be utilized with a practitioner and a client. Involuntary clients frequently complain that their assigned social worker does not understand them and is not adequately listening to or serving them. For example, as noted in chapter 17, Lengyel quotes a client: "My first caseworker was horrible. He didn't help, and I went to his supervisor, and she hasn't helped much either. She doesn't call or try to contact me if there are problems" (Lengyel 2001:147, from the testimony of a 21-year-old mother on welfare). The following case example illustrates use of mediating skills with clients and supervisees.

> As a supervisor, I (Jud) received a call from Ms. Johnson, a client of Rachel, one of my supervisees. Ms. Johnson was in tears, and requested a new worker because she couldn't work with Rachel anymore. She said Rachel wouldn't listen to her, and Ms. Johnson always ended up very upset after their meetings. When I checked this out with Rachel, she said she was never able to discuss the case plan and other pertinent issues with Ms. Johnson because Ms. Johnson would keep focusing on unrelated issues, become upset, and then start screaming at Rachel until Rachel would leave.
>
> I offered to meet with Rachel and Ms. Johnson to discuss their concerns and determine how they could better work together. Rachel made a written list of all of the things she wanted to tell Ms. Johnson but never was able to because Ms. Johnson would start yelling at her. I began the meeting by asking each what they would like to discuss, and made a list. I assured them both we would get to all the concerns, but that I also might move the meeting along in the interest of time.
>
> Ms. Johnson began by talking about her concerns that Rachel didn't listen to her and wasn't on her side. She talked about how frustrating it was with her child in foster care and Rachel in control of when the child would return. Rachel then explained that the court ultimately made the decisions regarding the return of the child, and Rachel provided the court with reports from the service providers. Therefore, if Rachel and Ms. Johnson could work together to make sure Ms. Johnson was successfully participating in programs such as her treatment, domestic abuse counseling and parenting classes, Rachel would have positive reports to provide to the court.

Rachel gave Ms. Johnson a sheet explaining in writing what she needed to do and how Rachel could help her. Ms. Johnson was given time to read the list and ask questions. She finally understood more about how Rachel could help her. Rachel had the opportunity to listen to Ms. Johnson and learned that when she was yelling and crying, she was expressing anxiety and sadness about her predicament and how frustrated and trapped she felt.

At the end of the meeting, Ms. Johnson decided she would continue to work with Rachel, now that she understood Rachel's role better and felt that Rachel heard her concerns. Rachel was also better able to work with Ms. Johnson now that she understood her anxiety and how putting items and tasks in writing worked well to keep their meetings on track.

Buffering or Amplifying Dynamics

Rather than regretting that they are often caught in the middle, supervisors can take advantage of their powerful mediating position "in the middle"— ideally able to influence both "above" and "below," either "buffering" or "amplifying" the messages and influence attempts of administrators or constituencies external to the work unit (Bunker and Wijnberg 1988; see also Westbrook, Ellis, and Ellett 2006:53, who refer to this skill as "running interference"). In actively buffering the work unit from pressures that threaten an empowering climate, supervisors assertively represent the needs of their workers to upper management while carefully and rationally interpreting the rules and requirements for their units, keeping focused on services in the best interests of vulnerable clients. For example, a supervisor can buffer fault-finding dynamics and focus instead on the supervisees' strengths in learning from mistakes. Westbrook and colleagues found that supervisors and managers play another important role as they buffer the effects of negative publicity that may arise from a tragic incident or scandal "by establishing and sustaining positive relations with local media and *by championing media coverage of local successes*" (ibid.:56, italics in the original).

Conversely, the supervisor can amplify dynamics that are more positive, such as interest in serving customers, being responsive to clients, creating a work climate that honors caring for clients as a priority, and enhancing the prestige of the agency by showcasing successful innovations or cost savings or by recognizing veteran staff. However, supervisors may also inadvertently amplify the cycle of coercion by uncritically passing through to staff coercive messages from upper management. Conversely, supervisors might excessively buffer messages from upper management (such as those meant to make services more culturally competent) to such an extent that staff members do not realize the full import of new expectations.

Building Cultural Competence

With the increasing diversity of communities that social workers serve and given the persistent disparities in outcomes for people of color and other oppressed groups (Rodenborg 2004), supervisees must build cultural competence. According to the National Association of Social Workers (NASW 2001:Section 1.04), "cultural competence is a set of congruent behaviors, attitudes, and policies that come together in a system or agency or among professionals and enable the system, agency, or professionals to work effectively in cross-cultural situations." The supervisors' role in holding themselves, their agency and their supervisees to standards of cultural competence is key. If an agency has been successful in recruiting a multi-cultural staff, supervisors also will encounter the challenges inherent in cross-cultural supervision (Kaiser, Kuechler, and Barretta-Herman 2000). Differences in cultural background and in degree of cultural competence can exacerbate the power imbalance between supervisors and supervisees. In work with involuntary clients, if the supervisor does not address this potential difference in power, as well as possible cultural differences explicitly and directly, inadvertent abuse of power can spill over and endanger both staff and clients (see chapter 15 by Glenda Dewberry Rooney on work with members of oppressed groups). In addition, when a supervisor explores with supervisees the possibility that clients' actions may be signs of reactance, the supervisees' capacity to use critical thinking skills grows as they generate explanations for clients' behavior that are plausible alternatives to those that first might come to mind from the supervisee's cultural perspective (Deal 2003).

Attending to Safety

Increasingly, social workers practice in settings where there is a palpable risk for violence (Spencer and Munch 2003). Whether in the public sector or in so called "voluntary" private sector, social service agency staff can be perceived as agents who are withholding desperately needed benefits and assistance or as investigators who are interfering with or spying upon citizens. Research in work with involuntary clients indicates that practitioners should be vigilant; even though they see themselves as well-intentioned helpers, clients may view them as threats to valued freedoms. Reactions ranging from intimidation and staring or stalking, to verbal attacks and destruction of property and even physical assaults are possible.

Supervision is critical for assessing the potential for violence both interpersonally and in the environment; this is especially important when staff are visiting with clients in their homes. Setting up teams for home visits and supplying cellular or mobile phones as well as having supervisors and support staff "on call" to respond to distress calls can reduce the risk for harm to staff and clients. "Training during the initial orientation, periodic in-service programs, and ongoing staff meetings should address risk factors [such as] . . . mandated treatment." (Spencer and Munch 2003:537). Westbrook and colleagues (2006:53) observed that "when a worker is sent out on a difficult case, a 'good supervisor' doesn't leave the office until the worker has returned safe and unharmed." Supervisors also should take the lead in developing agency policies and procedures that increase safety for staff and clients (Weinger 2001; O'Neill 2004).

If an attack on a supervisee occurs, supervisors must be ready to provide support personally "and ensure staff access to a full range of agency support, including their direct coworkers and agency administrators" (Spencer and Munch 2003:540). In addition, Spencer and Munch remind supervisors themselves to cultivate a support system to tap if they are called upon to manage an incident of violence toward a supervisee.

Practice Guidelines

The examples in this chapter have been drawn directly from the authors' practice as supervisors in social service agencies serving involuntary clients. We try to engage employees in making decisions and solving problems. When a unit is overwhelmed due to high caseloads, we will take this issue to agency managers or the governing board, but we also ask staff to brainstorm ways they can make their workload more manageable. So we will not promise to solve the problem—we do what we can (talk to management, rearrange workload, etc.), and supervisees do what they can (block off time to do paperwork, spend less time with lower risk clients, etc.). After reviewing research thus far on effective supervision and management, Poertner (2006) concluded that "managers who have more interaction with those in authority apparently acquire more resources and have units with services with more scope and sufficiency" (p. 19).

The supervisor's primary goal is helpful service to clients, and the usual means of achieving that goal is fostering the development of supervisees as professional practitioners. In a process parallel to effective and ethical direct practice, supervisors are most successful when they create a supportive atmosphere, based on trust in supervisees and building on strengths. They set clear expectations and don't check up on supervisees unless performance warrants. However, supervisors must always be ready to override considerations of supervisees' interests or needs in order to direct activities or attention to clients' interests and needs.

Scholars in social work supervision have noted that "there is a dearth of literature on the nature and effectiveness of supervisory practice" (Bruce and

Austin 2000:86), and very few studies link supervisory interventions to effects that benefit clients. Nonetheless, evidence from training supervisors and supervisees in work with involuntary clients supports the following guidelines (Bibus 1993:19):

1. Be honest, direct, and clear about your expectations of your staff, your own role, and what is required or what is negotiable in supervision; in case consultations identify mandates and what's negotiable in case plans.
2. Help supervisees generate solutions to problems in collaboration with you rather than telling them what to do.
3. Ask questions about clients' goals and keep the focus of case discussions on including the client's version in service plans along with agency mandates; look for any areas to explore potential motivational congruence.
4. Within limitations imposed by increasing administrative demands, be available to assist or direct staff with difficult case situations, encourage staff to build competence in use of supervision, and facilitate consultation and support groups.
5. Compare your views of the problems faced by supervisees to their views and seek partnership with staff in setting goals and tasks.
6. Expect staff and clients to have reactions when valued freedoms are threatened.

May you be undaunted in the realization of the vital importance of the supervisors' role in work with involuntary clients!

Practical Exercises and Discussion Questions

1. The authors state that involuntary clients are vulnerable to exploitation of their low-power status. Do you agree? Give an example of how involuntary clients are vulnerable to exploitation.
2. Practitioners in nonmandated settings may approach all of their clients as if they were completely voluntary, missing some of the nonvoluntary pressures and nonmandated expectations that result in clients being only semivoluntary or entirely involuntary. Think of a nonmandated situation that you are familiar with. What strategies would you use as a supervisor or supervisee to raise awareness and initial assessment of where each client might fall on the continuum from voluntary to involuntary?

3. From your experience, give a specific example for each of the kinds of pressures below as supervisors and supervisees might experience them:

   a) legal pressures
   b) media pressures
   c) court pressures

4. What are some of the most stressful aspects of social work practice in adversarial settings common in work with involuntary clients? Under what circumstances might a practitioner have exhausted appropriate internal avenues to reduce or buffer stress factors and then might consider leaving the post or agency?

5. What are some of the advantages of the supervisor's position "in the middle"? What are some of the disadvantages of the supervisor's position "in the middle"?

6. Give an example of one of the forms of reactance that you have observed in supervision. How can supervision best address reactance?

7. How can effective supervision increase motivational congruence during performance reviews?

8. What are some ethical dilemmas you face? How did you handle them? In the light of this chapter, would you handle them differently? If so, in what way? How might you have used supervision in your decision making?

9. How can supervision most successfully support a group of functional noncapitulators?

10. Give a specific example from your practice of the *administrative* function of supervision; try to describe in detail what you did or what you observed others do, how actions and statements were received, what happened, and how successful you or others were.

11. Give a specific example from your practice of the *educational* function of supervision; try to describe in detail what you did or what you observed others do, how actions and statements were received, what happened, and how successful you or others were.

12. Give a specific example from your practice of the *support* function of supervision; try to describe in detail what you did or what you observed others do, how actions and statements were received, what happened, and how successful you or others were.

13. What is the missing link in research on the effectiveness of social work supervision? How could it be best addressed?

14. What do you predict will be a major future trend in supervision in settings where there are involuntary clients?

15. What might you do as a supervisor in an agency with which you are familiar when you notice that a particular client or group is being stigmatized, marginalized, or in other ways not being served appropriately?

16. Read each of the standards of cultural competence developed by NASW and assess your level of competence so far related to each. What specifically can you do to maintain or reach the highest level of competence? How can you use supervision to grow in cultural competence?

17. Pick one of the practice guidelines at the end of the chapter (p. 446) and set up an action plan to implement that guideline in your own practice as supervisor or as supervisee. Contract with a colleague to check in on your progress.

Chapter 19

The Nonvoluntary Practitioner
and the System

The preceding chapters have applied concepts for working with involuntary clients to varied problems, populations, and settings. This final chapter focuses on the nonvoluntary practitioner across problems, populations, and settings. It suggests guidelines for reducing work-related stress and improving agency service conditions. Finally, a research and practice agenda for further development of strategies for work with involuntary clients and agencies is suggested.

Nonvoluntary Practitioners

Nonvoluntary practitioners are helping professionals serving involuntary clients who are themselves nonvoluntary. There is a parallel to nonvoluntary clients, as such practitioners consider themselves disadvantaged because desirable alternatives are believed to be available elsewhere and/or they feel forced to remain in their current positions because the cost of leaving them would be too high. Nonvoluntary practitioners make *constrained choices* to continue such work because of the threatened loss of other benefits such as income, pension plans, and convenience. Some public agency practitioners speak of well-paid work with involuntary clients as "golden handcuffs" since they might prefer working elsewhere but fear that they would have to do so with lesser pay. Hence, their motivation to remain in their jobs may be more influenced by extrinsic rewards rather than by the intrinsic valuing of the work.

Nonvoluntary practitioners often feel a lack of *motivational congruence* with the system. Many of the intervention guidelines suggested in this book are not currently compatible with the policies of organizations employing nonvoluntary practitioners. Hence, reading this book may in fact stimulate cognitive dissonance. Practitioners may come to doubt the legality, ethics, or effectiveness of the services provided in their settings. They may believe that an overemphasis on punitive options and a lack of choices and inducements might act to maintain behavior that comes to be labeled as reluctant, disgruntled, hard-to-reach, and resistant in involuntary clients. They may experience dissonance when their settings have beliefs that focus on client pathology and ignore situational explanations for client responses to involuntary circumstances. Cognitive dissonance theory suggests that if practitioners cannot change their behavior to fit their values, they may reduce dissonance by changing those values (Draycott and Dabbs 1998).

Practitioners may respond to nonvoluntary situations in ways that are similar to those patterns described for clients in nonvoluntary situations. For example, practitioners experiencing nonvoluntary pressure from persons perceived to have more power may use *self-presentation strategies* such as self-promotion, exemplification, and ingratiation when that higher-power person controls access to needed resources (Kelly 2000). Similarly, practitioners may experience *reactance* when valued freedoms are threatened. In such circumstances, practitioners often report procrastinating or "finding the loophole" in an unwelcome task by carrying out the required task in a narrow way while undercutting the purpose of the task (Brehm et al. 1966). Of particular concern is the pattern suggested in reactance theory that repeated failed attempts to reassert valued freedoms may result in learned helplessness (Baum, Fleming, and Reddy 1986). Hence, practitioners who seek to be resourceful and empowering in work with their clients may find obstacles if their own agency experience is less than empowering.

Job Stress, Burnout, and Compassion Fatigue

There is high turnover in many of the settings in which involuntary clients are encountered. For example, turnover rates in child welfare often run above 30 percent (Drake and Gautam 1996; Anderson 2000). Also, working conditions can be hazardous and job satisfaction lacking. Despite diligent efforts by practitioners, tangible positive results may be scarce with clients who have little commitment to goals set by agencies for them (Tam and Mong 2005).

Practitioners also self-select and are selected for such settings in part be-cause they can empathize with clients. However, such capacities can also lead to risk for experiencing *compassion fatigue* or an emotional burden experi-enced by helping professionals from overexposure to client traumatic events (Schwam 1998; Iliffe and Steed 2000; Figley 2002; Adams, Boscarino, and Figley 2006; Strom-Gottfried and Mowbray 2006). Staff in such settings need to be able to assess their own signs of stress and then to develop and ap-ply their own coping skills (Dane 2000). Debriefing and mourning or me-morial rituals can be helpful for workers suffering from secondary trauma related to client losses or death (Strom-Gottfried and Mowbray 2006). Prac-titioners experiencing compassion fatigue also at times experience compas-sion satisfaction or appreciation of their efforts that can mitigate burnout or compassion fatigue (Conrad and Kellar-Guenther 2006; De Panfilis 2006).

In addition to individual stress and compassion fatigue, a kind of practi-tioner disempowerment has been purported to occur in overloaded public welfare agencies (Sherman and Wenocur 1983). Agencies hard pressed to meet overwhelming demands are inclined to a kind of defensive, protective prac-tice, focusing on avoiding lawsuits rather than proactively attaining client goals (Turnell 2006). Sherman and Wenocur suggest that probationary staff in such organizations often start with *a skill and routine mastery* stage in which they become oriented to the job in the context of limited caseloads and access to frequent supervision, somewhat like internships and field place-ments in professional education programs. Such protected practice can en-hance skill and confidence that efforts with clients can be successful. However, in times in which resources are increasingly limited, even this pro-tected entry is often foregone in the interest of immediately reducing the caseloads and pressures on highly stressed staff members. So, if the protected period occurs, this "honeymoon" period is often followed by a *social integra-tion* stage in which the protections are removed: caseloads increase and access to supervision decreases. Practitioners may come to realize that no matter how hard and skillfully they work, the agency lacks sufficient resources for them to carry out their jobs as described. This realization is purported to lead to a *moral outrage* stage in which workers become angry and confront their supervisors with the incongruity of resources and demands. Too often, this complaint may be met with a double-bind response from supervisors: "your frustration shows us that you are the kind of conscientious person we thought you were when we hired you; we are confident that you will find the resources to cope."

Sherman and Wenocur suggest that this outrage is followed by feelings of guilt, frustration, repressed anger, and depression. Similarly, clients frus-trated by the lack of resources project anger on the practitioner held respon-sible for the lack of resources.

Sherman and Wenocur then suggest six ways of coping with this conflict between job descriptions and lack of resources. The *capitulator* resolves the conflict by identifying with the organization: do what is possible without guilt, stop advocating, shut down empathy, and shuffle papers. In contrast, the *noncapitulator* continues to fight by rejecting the values of the organization. Such practitioners identify with client anger rather than powerlessness. According to the authors, they also often become isolated, identified as mavericks and house radicals, such that they come to resign, are counseled out, or are fired. A third response is *niche finding* in which practitioners find a special position such as training director in which they can use their skills outside of the line of fire of high client contact and low resources. This solution can last as long as the person holds such a position. A fourth response is *withdrawal,* in which practitioners leave the job in hopes of finding a less constrained environment. Other forms of withdrawal can include psychological withdrawal or detachment, emotional distancing from clients, or a physical withdrawal. The latter can occur when practitioners have the opportunity to remove themselves, at least temporarily, from the pressure through long commutes or spending a day on paperwork. Sherman and Wenocur suggest that frustrations may recur within similarly constrained positions unless conflict management skills are learned.

Self-victimization or martyrdom occurs when the practitioner identifies with the powerless client and tries to overcome the guilt over ineffectiveness by overworking. Such practitioners may work evenings and weekends, accumulating overtime, often at the risk of alienating persons in their own personal lives and support systems. It should be noted that policies requiring extensive access of clients to practitioners through beepers may also produce this stress on personal support systems. Practitioners with high skills and client commitment may be particularly prone to this martyrdom.

While each of these five responses are understandable styles of coping with the dissonance over conflicting job descriptions and limited resources, Sherman and Wenocur describe *a functional noncapitulator* response as more functional. In this response, conflict is managed by acting responsibly to influence the organization. Functional noncapitulators pick their battles, deciding when to capitulate and when to take calculated risks in negotiating the conditions of work. This response also models a form of empowerment that enables them to negotiate with their clients within boundaries.

With the exception of the functional noncapitulator role, most of the remaining coping styles have negative connotations. Practitioners with experience in such overloaded settings have suggested that selective use of such responses such as withdrawal into paperwork for a day or looking forward to a long drive after a client visit can be productive coping methods. Other styles noted by such experienced practitioners include the *scrapper*, who models being pragmatic and making the best of bad situations, and the *cheerleader*, who praises peers and arranges for staff treats and lunches as a way of maintaining staff morale. The *pragmatist* emphasizes not getting deeply emotionally involved in situations but rather focusing on what the practitioner is required to do and the currently available choices rather than seeking to extend them.

High focus on individual styles of coping runs the risk of implying that individual practitioners can and should be able to regulate their own stress and their response to it through appropriate use of individual coping techniques. In fact, the working conditions in many involuntary settings are such that emotional exhaustion could be considered a normative response to extraordinarily adverse conditions (Lacoursiere 2001). Work stress increases for staff when clients suffer from a lack of resources (Lewandowski 2003). In addition to stress management training, organizational interventions such as increased worker autonomy and organizational support are needed (Mor Barak, Nissly, and Levin 2001).

If clients are to be assisted in experiencing more power and influence to improve their circumstances, then the workers who serve them also need to feel as if they also have an impact on their environment (Gutierrez, GlenMaye, and De Lois 1995; Kondrat 1995; Cohen 2002). Assessment of organizational performance should include input from staff members and recipients of service. Encouraging staff members to advocate for service improvements and with explicit commitment of top administrators to the work of staff are among the characteristics of empowering organizations (Hardina 2005).

Organizations have a variety of both internal and external methods that can assist in workers feeling valued and empowered in their employment. The organization can regularly solicit and utilize staff feedback, publicly express respect and appreciation for workers, promote a learning environment, include worker participation in planning of change efforts, and provide access to professional development (Turner and Shera 2005). Outside the organization, leadership can focus on acquiring increased resources for the population or domain of the agency and sponsor positive public campaigns about the importance of the work. They can also support legislative initiatives that promote greater social justice for users and collaborate in community research initiatives to enhance knowledge about effectiveness (ibid.). For such organizational support to occur, a transformational leadership style is recommended that provides intellectual stimulation and inspirational motivation and is not characterized by a reactive or laissez faire style of leadership (Mary 2005).

Flow

Antithetical to burnout and stress is the experience of *flow*, or the mental state in which a person is fully immersed in what he or she is doing. Csikszentmihalyi originally studied artists to discover what allowed them to persist in the absence of significant external rewards (Csikszentmihalyi 1975). He found that the artistic experience was intrinsically rewarding for them, and later found that this sense of intense involvement was also experienced by persons across professions and cultures (Csikszentmihalyi 1991). Further, the components of flow experiences can be described as including having *clear goals*, such that the goals are attainable and expectations are understandable. A person in flow is able to *concentrate and focus* by paying attention to key activities and avoiding distractions. While in flow, a person is *not self-conscious*. That is, the person is so deeply immersed in the acivity that he or she is not thinking about or worried about others' perceptions of them. While in flow, there is a *distorted sense of time*. For example, extended periods can pass and seem less because the person is so immersed in the activity. On the other hand, a person can be so engrossed in an immediate event that he or she can get a large amount of information out of it. For example, some helping professionals can become so engrossed in a crisis situation that they can describe in detail events that transpired in a brief period. Flow activities are usually characterized by *direct and immediate feedback* such that they can tell how successful they are immediately and alter course if need be. Flow occurs when there is a *balance between ability level and challenge*. So, for instance, when challenge is too high and you are overloaded, you experience frustration. On the other hand, if ability is higher than challenge, you experience boredom. Hence a person should seek a balance such that the challenge is formidable, attainable, but not too high and out of reach. Hence, the process of assisting clients in an empowering fashion to enhance skills should incorporate seeking such a balance by raising expectations to a level that is attainable but not easy. Persons in the state of flow have a sense of *personal control* over their actions such that they are focused on what they can do and not distracted by what is out of their control. The flow experience is *intrinsically rewarding* such that action does not appear effortful. Finally, focus while in flow is absorbed in the activity, called action awareness merging (Csikszentmihalyi 1975).

The linkage between flow and working conditions with involuntary clients can be summarized in the following way. Persons who become involuntary may experience a kind of psychological entropy in which their energy feels useless and they feel out of control, unfocused, and overloaded. Similarly, hard-pressed practitioners facing excessive expectations may also experience a similar entropy (Csikszentmihalyi 1991). Trying to reduce entropy suggests seeking to establish conditions that foster flow. Hence, practitioners might seek to develop clear, attainable goals with clients with ready feedback. They would seek to support enjoyable activities. Similarly, the practitioner would seek to focus on attainable goals and establish working conditions that support concentration, for example, finding ways to not be disturbed while concentrating on writing a report. Finally, a supervisor wanting to support flow-like conditions would seek to support the above principles by establishing clear attainable goals, providing ready feedback, and attempting to match skill with demand level.

Change Efforts with Involuntary Clients

Change efforts can occur at many levels in work with involuntary clients. Individual practitioners can utilize guidelines from this book to enhance their work with individuals, families, and groups. They can reduce stress and enhance flow by concentrating on specific goals. For example, they might be alert to mandated and nonvoluntary circumstances, empathize with reactance responses to unwanted pressure, utilize ethical persuasion, and contract with clients utilizing motivational congruence to pursue goals meaningful to clients. In so doing, they can seek to enhance meaningful choices. They can assist clients in making choices about which problems to explore first and which to table and make further choices in deciding which kinds of efforts and services to employ in seeking the goals. They can pursue pro-social modeling and clarify roles including boundaries between helping and protection roles. Such efforts should enhance working relationships with involuntary clients and reduce time spent on trying to out-manipulate clients who are attempting to manipulate them. Hence some stress reduction and flow enhancement is within the capacity of individual practitioners.

The solitary practitioner, however, works in an environment that operates under laws, policies, resources, and philosophies. Frequently such policies are engaged not in pursuing meaningful engagement with clients and seeking mutually defined success but rather in carrying out the letter of the law and demonstrating reasonable, reimbursable efforts. Hence the organizational climate is critical in enhancing the efforts of individual practitioners. Sending practitioners to training and bringing training in-house can be beginning parts of an effort to develop a supportive agency environment. Frequently, however, such efforts are planned top-down with agency administrators determining what is in the agency's best interest, paralleling an involuntary service agreement approach with clients that is unlikely to engage practitioners as active participants. Polling practitioners and working with a planning group of practitioners and supervisors is more likely to produce initiatives that will engage practitioners beyond the agency's capacity to reward and punish.

Developing initiatives with clearly defined goals and markers for measuring progress including supporting norms of not merely studying compliance but rather assessing together what is working and examining obstacles impeding goals (Turnell 2006). Instead of focusing exclusively on problems that are occurring, identifying and studying promising exemplars of practice can assist in empowering the organization to succeed more than focusing exclusively on reducing errors (Ferguson 2001, 2003). Hence identifying models of practice that appear to be done well can guide further initiatives (Ferguson 2001). For example, the senior author of this book conducted training in the methods described in this book with a group of urban child welfare workers. After the training concluded he met with each team of practitioners attending the training, asking them to bring one case each that they wished to consult about and one case whose success they were pleased with. In this fashion, the often-extensive focus on failure that occurs during consultations was avoided by devoting equal time to successes (Greene, Lee, and Hoffpauir 2005). Further, this identification of successes then led to the development of training videotapes in which agency practitioners were able to demonstrate promising models of practice. Hence, further training need not focus on what is wrong with agency practice but rather on how to increase successful practice.

A Research Agenda for Work with Involuntary Clients

Beyond individual and agency efforts, further studies of intervention with involuntary clients are needed. The areas in which further knowledge are particularly needed are delineation of ethical, effective practice; studies of influence and engagement; studies of practice with members of oppressed groups; studies of variation of influence methods across problems, groups, regions, and nations; studies of interventions such as Motivational Interviewing and Solution-Focused Brief Treatment; and exemplars of best practices at the individual practitioner and organizational levels.

1. *Ethical practice.* This book has advocated that practice with involuntary practice needs to be both ethical and effective. Practitioners need guidance about balancing responsibilities to involuntary clients, agencies, and social control. That is, they need to know how to include client goals and clarify limits and duties regarding privileged communication, confidentiality, informed consent, and social control responsibilities (Reamer 2005; Taylor and Bentley 2005; Burman 2004). Practitioners need guidelines for including clients in decision making (Adams and Drake 2006).

2. *Effective practice.* Practice must also be designed to be effective. That goal must consider a lens of evidence-based practice (EBP) in determining guidelines for practice. EBP refers to consulting appropriate research literature, and explicitly and judiciously using that evidence in making intervention decisions (Sackett et al. 1996). The evidence-based practitioner formulates questions that can be answered with data, assesses the reliability and validity of that data, and shares the conclusions with clients as part of informed decision making (Gambrill 2006; Gibbs 2007). Such descriptions of EBP explicitly support collaborative practice and involving clients centrally in decision making. As mentioned in chapter 3, those descriptions appear to assume that clients are voluntary and hence can be the final judges over interventions to be used with them. Decisions are made guiding practice with involuntary clients as well, and consulting empirical data is no less important. For example, Scared Straight programs were developed as an intervention designed to prevent juvenile delinquency by exposing youth to incarcerated criminals (Petrosino, Turbin-Petrosino, and Buechler, 2004). Later studies questioned the effectiveness of this method (ibid.). However, fields of practice such as child welfare often have a limited number of studies in which clients were randomly assigned to conditions (Thomlison 2003; Whiting-Blome and Stieb 2004; Kessler, Gira, and Poertner 2005). Consequently, practitioners and agencies need to consider the best available knowledge in their areas of practice in determining practice guidelines.

3. *Studies of influence and engagement with involuntary clients are needed.* Interventions that are coercive or exert a powerful source of influence require additional scrutiny in the decision to use them (Scheyett 2006). Hence, guidance for work with involuntary clients should include information about the ethical, effective use of influence to achieve individual and societal gains. In this regard, studies of the effectiveness of drug courts and other controls of drug use are important (Rempel and Depies-Di Stefano 2001; Brecht, Anglin, and Dylan 2005; Klag, O'Callaghan, and Creed 2005;). Such studies also examine the extent to which coercion has similar effects across nations (Stevens et al. 2005). In other arenas in which coercion is used, such as outpatient treatment of persons with serious and persistent mental illness, studies need to examine the quality of life of such patients (Swanson et al. 2003; Brophy and Ring 2004). Of particular interest are studies of the interaction between practitioners and patients living in the community in which efforts to utilize persuasion are featured (Floersch 2002; Angell, Mahoney, and Martinez 2006). Finally, since the first step in influence is engagement, studies of ethical, effective engagement are needed (Littell, Alexander, and Reynolds 2001; Yatchmenoff 2005).

4. *Studies of involuntary practice with members of oppressed groups.* We need to continue to study the disproportionate representation of members of

oppressed groups among the ranks of involuntary clients (see chapter 15 by Dewberry Rooney in this volume). For example, we need to know the extent to which race is a factor in the use of coercive means to control drug usage (Beckerman and Fontana 2001) and use of groups to control domestic violence (Buttell and Carney 2005). Guidelines for ethical, effective practice with involuntary clients who are members of oppressed groups are needed.

5. *Study variation in ethical, effective practice with involuntary clients across problem areas, populations, and countries.* In addition to focus on members of oppressed groups, studies are needed on the variation of effectiveness across problems, populations, and countries. For example, studies of drug courts with substance abusers need to consider variation in the substance used (Brecht, Anglin, and Dylan 2005). Studies on the variation in the engagement of women as clients are needed (Barlow et al. 2005; Clark et al. 2005). Finally, the incidence of involuntary status and variation in methods used are needed across nations (Ho and Chui 2001; Billinger 2005; Stevens et al. 2005; ; Chui and Ho 2006).

6. *Studies of the adaptation of interventions such as Motivational Interviewing and Solution-Focused Brief Treatment to work with involuntary clients.* As demonstrated in part 3 in the chapters by Barber (chapter 10), Hohman and Kleinpeter (chapter 11), and Chovanec (chapter 12), Motivational Interviewing and stages of change offer promising perspectives for engaging involuntary clients at their own stage of development. Similarly, Franklin and Hopson (chapter 13) and Altman and Gohagan (chapter 14) have demonstrated the utility of Solution-Focused methods in pursuing co-constructed goals and focusing on positive outcomes. Simplistic applications that ignore power differentials and the authority of mandated workers to operate under laws does not serve public agency workers. Hence, applications to the role of mandated worker are needed.

7. *Exemplars of best practices at individual practitioner and organizational levels are needed.* Beyond broad guidelines for practice, profiles of best practice under difficult circumstances are needed. Models of what such practice look like are needed to guide practitioners (Ferguson 2001, 2003; Turnell 2006). Guidelines for implementation at organizational levels (Whittaker et al. 2006) are needed including incorporation of the voice of practitioners and clients about identifying key ingredients of quality services (Dale 2004). Studies are needed of how to construct a climate of appreciative inquiry in which practitioners, clients, and agencies can explore together to find best practices (Turnell 2006; Wilson and Tiles 2006).

Discussion Questions

1. How do you see job stress as interacting in work with involuntary clients? What is the responsibility of the practitioner to protect against burnout? How can the agency support practitioners at risk of compassion fatigue?

2. How do practitioners in your agency cope with client and organizational pressures? How can they be replenished and at least occasionally experience flow in their work?

3. What are the assumptions in your agency about how and why involuntary clients change? Are they considered to be motivated primarily to avoid punishments and gain rewards? To what extent are their personal goals validated?

4. What is the value of cross-fertilization in research on involuntary clients? That is, what is the value of examining processes and outcomes with other involuntary audiences outside your own arena?

5. What do we know about the power of coercion to induce change? What assumptions are made in your setting about this?

6. How can your organization create a climate of appreciative inquiry that seeks to improve practice through incorporating the voices of clients and practitioners?

Training Videotapes on Strategies for Work with Involuntary Clients

Selections from several videotapes were used to illustrate the use of intervention methods in chapters 5 to 8. Three tapes are available from www.insight-media.com. Contact Insight Media directly for further information.

1. *Task-Centered Case Management.* Jane Macy-Lewis. 22 minutes. This tape depicts a recontracting session between a case manager for an adult, disabled, and mentally ill caseload in a small rural county and Mike, her actual client, who is unhappy in his current group home placement. Macy-Lewis specifies the problem, reviews options, and helps Mike make plans about future living arrangements in a clear model of commitment to client self-determination and normalization inherent in the task-centered approach (see chapter 7).

2. *Contracting for Home-Based Services.* Ron Rooney and Betty Woodland. 52 minutes. Family-centered, home-based services are a form of in-home assistance to families usually aimed at preventing out-of-home placement. This tape depicts contracting with a mother and daughter to reduce the problems that caused the mother to seek out-of-home placement. The tape models involuntary contracting strategies, persuasion, work with a highly oppositional client (the mother), and ways of bringing the situation to a productive focus (see chapter 8).

3. *Work with Involuntary Clients: The Consumer's Perspective.* Ron Rooney. This videotape includes a live interview with a consumer of mental health services. The consumer describes her history in hospitals, social services, and work with a variety of helping professionals. She describes respect, listening, and supporting choices, as professional activities that have helped her. This tape is referenced in chapter 5.

Two training videotapes were developed by the University of Wisconsin School of Social Work. DVDs can be ordered for $15 each from UW-Madison Learning Support Services, Mary Prochniak, Media Librarian, 1220 Linden Drive, Madison, WI 53706-1525.

1. *Permanency Planning: Use of the Task-Centered Model with an Adolescent toward Independent Living. The Contracting Phase.* Nancy Taylor. 4744-C. This tape demonstrates the contracting process with an actual adolescent client (see chapters 6 and 7).
2. *Permanency Planning: Use of the Task-Centered Model with an Adolescent toward Independent Living. The Middle Phase.* Nancy Taylor. 475-1-c. This tape demonstrates the six-week review session in which obstacles to original contracted goals are identified and new tasks are developed with an actual adolescent client. The tape includes a model of effective, middle-phase confrontation. It also includes a follow-up interview conducted by Ron Rooney (see chapters 6 and 7).

Four training videotapes were developed by the University of Minnesota, School of Social Work. Links to these videos can be shared by contacting Ron Rooney at the School of Social Work, University of Minnesota: rrooney@umn.edu.

1. *Nonvoluntary Client Contracting.* Walter Mirk. 25 minutes. This tape depicts an actual initial session between a county mental health worker and a nonvoluntary client pressured by her public agency social worker to seek help (see chapter 6).
2. *Socialization with a Probation Client.* Bill Linden. 26 minutes. Contracting with a mandated client about to enter prison presents a challenge for any practitioner. Linden demonstrates ways in which choice and respect for the client can be introduced into an otherwise highly coercive situation. Linden also demonstrates well-timed, respectful confrontation with this actual client (see chapter 6).
3. *Work with Involuntary Clients in the Middle Phase.* Cheri Brady. 22 minutes. This tape depicts a middle-phase session with a nonvolun-

tary client. The methods used draw heavily on the task-centered approach. The tape models methods for dealing with tasks that have not been completed, examination of obstacles, role plays, developing new tasks, appropriate middle-phase confrontation, and summarization (see chapter 7).

4. *Socialization at Chemical Dependency Intake.* Dick Leonard. 40 minutes. Chemical dependency settings have been associated with strongly confrontive methods designed to challenge and crack the defenses and denial of chemically dependent clients. Leonard models two different methods to approach intake situations in chemical dependency inpatient settings. The same intake interview is hence presented twice, using different methods in each. The tape was developed with an actual client (see chapters 6 and 7).

References

Abney, V. D. 2000. What Principles and Approaches Can I Use to Engage Clients Across Cultures? In *Handbook for Child Protection Practice*, eds. H. Dubowitz and D. DePanfilis, pp. 41–43. Thousand Oaks, CA: Sage.

Abramovitz, M. 1988. *Regulating the Lives of Women: Social Welfare Policy from Colonial Times to the Present*. Boston: South End.

Abramovitz, M. 2005. The largely untold story of welfare reform and the human services. *Social Work* 50(2):175–186.

Abramson, M. 1981. Ethical dilemmas for social workers in discharge planning. *Social Work in Health Care* 6(4):33–42.

Abramson, M. 1985. The autonomy-paternalism dilemma in social work practice. *Social Casework* 66(7):387–393.

Abramson, M. 1989. Autonomy vs. paternalistic beneficence. *Social Casework* 70:101–115.

Adams, J. F., F. P. Piercy, and J. A. Jurich. 1991. Effects of solution focused therapy's formula "first session task" on compliance and outcome in family therapy. *Journal of Marital and Family Therapy* 17(3):277–290.

Adams, J. R. and R. E. Drake. 2006. Shared decision-making and evidence-based practice. *Community Mental Health Journal* 42(1):87–105.

Adams, R. E., J. A. Boscarino, and C. R. Figley. 2006. Compassion fatigue and psychological distress among social workers: A validation study. *American Journal of Orthopsychiatry* 76(1):103–108.

Adoption and Safe Families Act. 1997. 42 U.S.C.@ 671(a)(15)(b). P.L. 105–189.

Aguilera, D. C. 1990. *Crisis Intervention: Theory and Methodology*, 7th ed. St. Louis: C. V. Mosby.

Akamatsu, N. 1998. The Talking Oppression Blues: Including the Experience of Power/Powerlessness in the Teaching of Cultural Sensitivity. In *Revisioning Family Therapy: Race, Culture and Gender in Clinical Practice* (2nd ed.), ed. M. McGoldrick, pp. 129–144. New York: Guilford.

Al-Anon. 1984. *Al-Anon Faces Alcoholism.* New York: Author.

Albert, R. 2000. *Law and Social Work Practice,* 2nd ed. New York: Springer.

Alexander, L. B. and M. M. Dore. 1999. Making the parents-as-partners principle a reality: The role of the alliance. *Journal of Child and Family Studies* 8:255–270.

Alexander, M. A. 1999. Sex offender treatment efficacy revisited. *Sexual Abuse: A Journal of Research and Treatment* 11:101–116.

Alexander, R. 1989. The right to treatment in mental and correctional institutions. *Social Work* 34(2):109–114.

Alexander, R. 2003. *Understanding Legal Concepts That Influence Social Welfare Policy and Practice.* Pacific Grove, CA: Brooks-Cole.

Al-Krenawi, A. and J. R. Graham. 2001. The cultural mediator: Bridging the gap between non-Western community and professional social work practice. *British Journal of Social Work* 31(5):665–685.

Allen, L., D. MacKenzie, and L. Hickman. 1998. The effect of cognitive behavioral treatment for adult offenders: A methodological, quality-based review. *International Journal of Offender Therapy and Comparative Criminology* 45(4):498–514.

Almgren, G., G. Yamashiro, and M. Ferguson. 2002. Beyond welfare or work: Teen mothers, household subsistence strategies, and child development outcomes. *Journal of Sociology and Social Welfare* 29(3):125–149.

Alternative Response in Minnesota 2006. American humane. *Protecting Children* 7(1):1.

Altman, J. C. 2004. Engagement in Neighborhood-Based Child Welfare Services. Final Report. Garden City, NY: Adelphi University School of Social Work.

Altman, J. C. 2005. A qualitative examination of client participation in agency-initiated services. *Families in Society* 84(4):1–9.

American Humane Association. 2000. Family Group Decision-Making National Roundtable and International Conference: Summary of Proceedings. American Humane Association, Englewood, CO. Children's Division.

American Psychiatric Association. 2000. *Diagnostic and Statistical Manual of Mental Disorders, Fourth Edition, Text Revision (DSM-IV-TR).* Arlington, VA: Author.

AmeriStat. March 2003. Diversity, poverty characterize female-headed households. Retrieved from http://www.prb.org/AmeristatTemplate.cfm?Section=MarriageandFamilyandtemplate=/ContentManagement/ContentDisplay.cfmandContentID=8277.

Anderson, C. and S. Stewart. 1985. *Mastering Resistance: A Practical Guide to Family Therapy.* New York: Guilford.

Anderson, D. G. 2000. Coping strategies and burnout among veteran child protection workers. *Child Abuse and Neglect* 24(6):839–848.

Anderson, M. L. and P. H. Collins, eds. 2001. *Race, Class, and Gender: An Anthology,* 4th ed. Belmont, CA: Wadsworth-Thomson Learning.

Anderson, S., A. Halter, and B. Gryzlak. 2004. Difficulties after leaving TANF: Inner-city women talk about reasons for returning to welfare. *Social Work* 49(2):185–195.

Anderson-Butcher, D., A. O. Khairallah, and J. Race-Bigelow. 2004. Mutual support groups for long-term recipients of TANF. *Social Work* 49(1):131–140.

Andrews, D. 2001. Effective Practice, Future Directions. In *Sustaining Effectiveness in Working with Offenders.* Cardiff: Cognitive Centre Foundation.

Andrews, D. A. and J. Bonta. 1998. *The Psychology of Criminal Conduct.* Cincinnati: Anderson.

Andrews, D. A., J. J. Keissling, R. J. Russell, and B. A. Grant. 1979. *Volunteers and the One-to-One Supervision of Adult Probationers.* Ontario, Toronto: Ministry of Correctional Services.

Andrews, D. A., I. Zinger, R. Hoge, J. Bonta, P. Gendreau, and F. Cullen. 1990. Does correctional treatment work? A clinically relevant and psychologically informed meta-analysis. *Criminology* 28(3):369–401.

Angell, B., C. Mahoney, and N. Martinez. 2006. Promoting treatment adherence in assertive community treatment. *Social Service Review* 80:485–526.

Antle, B. and B. Regehr. 2003. Beyond individual rights and freedoms: Metaethics in social work research. *Social Work* 48(1):135–144.

Arkowitz, H. 1996. Toward an integrative perspective on resistance to change. *In-session: Psychotherapy in Practice* 2(1):87–98.

Arrendondo, P. 1999. Multicultural counseling competencies as tools to address oppression and racism. *Journal of Counseling and Development* 77:102–108.

Artiles, A. J. and S. C. Trent. 1999. The overrepresentation of minority students in special education: A continuing debate. *The Journal of Special Education* 27:134–142.

Austin, J., J. Irwin, and C. Kubrin. 2003. It's about Time: America's Imprisonment Binge. In *Punishment and Social Control* (2nd ed.), eds. T. Blomberg and S. Cohen, pp. 433–440. New York: Aldine De Gruyter.

Austin, J. B. and J. Dankwort. 1999. Standards for batterer programs: A review and analysis. *Journal of Interpersonal Violence* 14(2):152–168.

Babcock, J. C., C. E. Green, and C. Robie. 2004. Does batterers' treatment work? A meta-analytic review of domestic violence treatment. *Clinical Psychology Review* 23:1023–1053.

Babcock, J. C. and J. Taillade. 2000. Evaluating Interventions for Men Who Batter. In *Domestic Violence: Guidelines for Research-Informed Practice,* eds. J.Vincent and E. Jouriles, pp. 37–77. Philadelphia: Jessica Kingsley.

Baer, J. S. and P. L. Peterson. 2002. Motivational Interviewing with Adolescents and Young Adults. In *Motivational Interviewing: Preparing People for Change,* eds. W. R. Miller and S. Rollnick, pp. 320–332. New York: Guilford.

Baer, J. S., P. L. Peterson, and E. A. Wells. 2004. Rationale and design of a brief substance use intervention for homeless adolescents. *Addiction Research and Theory* 12(4):317–334.

Baker, A. and J. Dixon. 1991. Motivational interviewing for HIV risk reduction. In *Motivational Interviewing: Preparing People to Change Addictive Behavior,* eds. W. R. Miller and S. Rollnick, pp. 293–302. New York: Guilford.

Bandura, A. 1971. *Psychological Modeling: Conflicting Theories.* Chicago: Aldine-Atherton.

Barber, J. G. 1991. *Beyond Casework.* London: Macmillan.

Barber, J. G. 1994. Alcohol addiction: Private trouble or social issue? *Social Service Review* 68:521–535.

Barber, J. G. 1995. Negotiated casework with involuntary clients. *International Perspectives on Social Work* 1:13–21.

Barber, J. G. 1995. Working with resistant drug abusers. *Social Work* 40(1):17–23.

Barber, J. G. 2002. *Social Work with Addictions,* 2nd ed. London: Palgrave.

Barber, J. G. 2003. *Social Work Through the Lifecycle.* Melbourne: Tertiary Press.

Barber, J. G. and B. R. Crisp. 1995. The "Pressures to Change Approach" to working with the partners of heavy drinkers. *Addiction* 90:271–278.

Barber, J. G. and R. Gilbertson. 1996. An experimental investigation of a brief unilateral intervention for the partners of heavy drinkers. *Research on Social Work Practice* 6:325–336.

Barber, J. G. and R. Gilbertson. 1997. Unilateral interventions for women living with heavy drinkers. *Social Work* 42:69–78.

Barber, J. G. and R. Gilbertson. 1998. Evaluation of a self-help manual for the female partners of heavy drinkers. *Research on Social Work Practice* 8:141–151.

Barker, L. 2003. *The Social Work Dictionary.* Washington, DC: NASW.

Barlow, J., S. Kirkpatrick, D. Stewart-Brown, and H. Davis. 2005. Hard-to-reach or out-of-reach: Reasons why women refuse to take part in early interventions. *Children and Society* 19(5):199–210.

Barnett, N. P., P. M. Monti, and M. D. Wood. 2001. Motivational Interviewing for Alcohol-Involved Adolescents in the Emergency Room. In *Innovations in Adolescent Substance Abuse Interventions,* eds. E. F. Wagner and H. B. Waldron, pp. 143–168. Amsterdam: Pergamon.

Bartholomew, A. 1994. Prisoners' perceptions of punishment: A comment on Indermaur. *Australian Psychologist* 31(1):60–62.

Barton, W. and G. Barton, G. 1984. *Ethics and Law in Mental Health Administration.* New York: International Universities Press.

Baum, A., R. Fleming, and D. Reddy. 1986. Unemployment stress: Loss of control, reactance and learned helplessness. *Social Science and Medicine* 22:509–516.

Becker, H. 1963. *Outsiders: Studies in the Sociology of Deviance.* London: Free Press.

Beckerman, A. and L. Fontana. 2001. Issues of race and gender in court ordered substance abuse treatment. In *Drug Courts in Operation: Current Research,* pp. 45–61. New York: Haworth Press.

Bednar, S. G. 2003. Elements of satisfying organizational climates in child welfare agencies. *Families in Society* 84(1):7–12.

Behroozi, C. S. 1992. A model for social work with involuntary applicants in groups. *Social Work with Groups* 15(2/3):223–238.

Beitin, B. K. and K. R. Allend. 2005. The multilevel approach to integrating social justice and family therapy. *Journal of Systemic Therapies* 24(1):19–34.

Belenko, S. 2001. Research on drug courts: A critical review 2001 update. New York: National Center on Addiction and Substance Abuse at Columbia University. http://casacolumbia/absolutem/articlefiles/researchondrug.pdf.

Ben-Arie, O., L. Swartz, and G. C. George. 1986. The compulsory treatment of alcoholic drunk drivers referred by the courts: A 7 to 9 year outcome study. *International Journal of Law and Psychiatry* 8:229–235.

Bennis, W. and H. Shepard. 1956. A theory of group development. *Human Relations* 9:415–437.

Berg, I. K. 1994. *Family-Based Services: A Solution-Focused Approach.* New York: W. W. Norton.

Berg, I. K. 2002. *Interviewing for Solutions,* 2nd ed. Pacific Grove, CA: Brooks/Cole.

Berg, I. K. and P. De Jong. 1996. Solution-building conversations: Co-constructing a sense of competence with clients. *Families in Society* 77:376–391.

Bergeron, L. and B. Gray. 2003. Ethical dilemmas of reporting suspected elder abuse. *Social Work* 48(1):96–105.

Berleman, W. and T. Steiner. 1967. The execution an evaluation of a delinquency prevention program. *Social Problems* 14:413–423.

Berlin, S. and J. Barden. 2000. The Cognitive-Integrative Approach to Changing a Mind. In *The Handbook of Social Work Direct Practice,* eds. P. Allen-Meares and C. Garvin, pp. 175–196. Thousand Oaks, CA: Sage.

Berliner, A. K. 1987. Group counseling with alcoholic offenders: An analysis and typology of DWI probationers. *Social Work with Groups* 10(1):17–31.

Berman-Rossi, T. and T. Kelly. 1998. Advancing stages of group development theory. Paper presented at the annual program meeting of the Council on Social Work Education, Orlando, FL, March 1998.

Bernstein, S. 1960. Self-determination: King or citizen of the realm of values. *Social Work* 5(1):3–8.

Besharov, D. J., ed. 2003. *Family and Child Well-Being After Welfare Reform.* New Brunswick, NJ: Transaction Publishers.

Beutler, L. E. and M. Berren (eds.). 1995. *Integrative Assessment of Adult Personality.* New York: Guilford.

Beutler, L. E., E. J. Kim, E. Davidson, M. Karno, and D. Fisher. 1996. Research contributions to improving managed health care outcomes. *Psychotherapy* 33:197–206.

Beutler, L., F. Rocco, C. Moleiro, and H. Talebi. 2001. Resistance. *Psychotherapy: Theory, Research, Practice, Training* 38(4):431–436.

Beutler, L., M. Sandowicz, D. Fisher, and A. Albanese. 1996. Resistance in psychotherapy: Conclusions that are supported by research. *In Session: Psychotherapy and Practice* 11:77–86.

Bibus, A. A. 1993. In pursuit of a missing link: The influence of supervision on social workers' practice with involuntary clients. *The Clinical Supervisor* 11(2):7–22.

Bibus, A. A., R. J. Link, and M. O'Neal. 2005. The Impact of U.S. Welfare Reform on Children's Well Being: Minnesota focus. In *Safeguarding and Promoting the Well-Being of Children, Families and Communities,* eds. J. Scott and H. Ward, pp. 59–74. London: Jessica Kingsley.

Bien, T. H., W. R. Miller, and J. S. Tonigan. 1993. Brief interventions for alcohol problems: A review. *Addiction* 88:315–336.

Biestek, F. 1951. The principle of client self-determination. *Social Casework* 32:369–375.

Billinger, K. 2005. A focus group investigation of care-provider perspectives in Swedish institutions for the coercive care of substance abusers. *International Journal of Social Welfare* 14:55–64.

Billings, P., T. D. Moore, and T. P. McDonald. 2003. What do we know about the relationship between public welfare and child welfare. *Child and Youth Services Review* 25(8):633–650.

Bloomberg, S. and L. Wilkins. 1977. Ethics of research involving human subjects in criminal justice. *Crime and Delinquency* 23(4):435–444.

Bouffard, J. and F. Taxman. 2004. Looking inside the "black box" of drug court services using direct observations. *Journal of Drug Issues* 34(1):195–218.

Bradshaw, W. and D. Roseborough. 2004. Evaluating the effectiveness of cognitive-behavioral treatment of residual symptoms and impairment in schizophrenia. *Research on Social Work Practice* 14(2):112–120.

Bratter, T., E. Bratter, and J. Helmsberg. 1986. Uses and Abuses of Power and Authority in American Self-Help Residential Communities: A Perversion or a Necessity? In *Therapeutic Communities for Addiction: Readings in Theory, Research and Practice,* eds. G. DeLeon and J. T. Ziegenfus, Jr., pp. 191–208. Springfield, IL: Charles C Thomas.

Brecht, M., M. Anglin, and M. Dylan. 2005. Coerced treatment for methamphetamine abuse: Differential patient characteristics and outcomes. *The American Journal of Drug and Alcohol Abuse* 31:337–356.

Brehm, J. 1976. *A Theory of Psychological Reactance,* 2nd ed. New York: Academic Press.

Brehm, J., L. Stires, J. Sensening, and J. Shaban. 1966. The attractiveness of an eliminated choice alternative. *Journal of Experimental Social Psychology* 2:301–311.

Brehm, S. 1976. *The Application of Social Psychology to Clinical Practice.* New York: John Wiley.

Brehm, S. and J. Brehm. 1981. *Psychological Reactance: A Theory of Freedom and Control.* New York: Academic Press.

Brehm, S. and T. Smith. 1986. Social Psychological Approaches to Psychotherapy and Behavior Change. In *Handbook of Psychotherapy and Behavior Change*, eds. S. Garfield and S. Bergin, pp. 69–115. New York: Wiley.

Brekke, J. 1989. The use of orientation groups to engage hard to reach clients: Model, method and evaluation. *Social Work with Groups* 12(2):75–88.

Breton, M. 1985. Reaching and engaging people: Issues and practice principles. *Social Work with Groups* 8(3):7–21.

Brody, A. 1982. S.O.B.E.R. A stress management program for recovering alcoholics. *Social Work with Groups* 5:15–23.

Brophy, L. and D. Ring. 2004. The efficacy of involuntary treatment in the community: Consumer and service provider perspectives. *Social Work in Mental Health* 2(2/3):157–174.

Brown, L. K. and K. J. Lourie. 2001. Motivational Interviewing and the Prevention of HIV Among Adolescents. In *Adolescents, Alcohol, and Abuse: Reaching Teens Through Brief Interventions*, eds. P. M. Monti, S. M. Colby, and T. A. O'Leary, pp. 244–274. New York: Guilford.

Brownlee, K. and L. Chiebovec. 2004. A group for men who abuse their partners: Participant perceptions of what was helpful. *American Journal of Orthopsychiatry* 74(2):209–213.

Bruce, E. J. and M. Austin. 2000. Social work supervision: Assessing the past and mapping the future. *The Clinical Supervisor* 19(2):85–107.

Bull, D. 1989. The social worker's advocacy role: A British quest for a Canadian perspective. *Canadian Social Work Review* 6(1):49–68.

Bunker, D. R. and M. H. Wijnberg. 1988. *Supervision and Performance: Managing Professional Work in Human Service Organizations*. San Francisco: Jossey-Bass.

Bureau of Justice Statistics, U.S. Department of Justice. 1994. *Substance Abuse and Treatment, State and Federal Prisoners*. Washington, DC: Author.

Bureau of Justice Statistics, U.S. Department of Justice. 2002. *Statistics on Drugs and Crime*. Washington, DC: Author.

Burford, G. and J. Hudson. 2001. *Family Group Conferencing*. New York: Aldine de Gruyter.

Burford, G., J. Pennell, S. MacLeod, S. Campell, and G. Lyall. 1996. Reunification as an extended family matter. *Community Alternatives* 8:33–35.

Burke, B. L., H. Arkowitz, and D. Dunn. 2002. The Efficacy of Motivational Interviewing and Its Adaptations. In *Motivational Interviewing: Preparing People to Change Addictive Behavior* (2nd ed.), eds. W. Miller and S. Rollnick, pp. 217–250. New York: Guilford.

Burke, B. L., H. Arkowitz, and M. Menchola. 2003. The efficacy of motivational interviewing: A meta-analysis of controlled clinical trials. *Journal of Consulting and Clinical Psychology* 71:843–861.

Burman, S. 2004. Revisiting the agent of social control role: Implications for substance abuse treatment. *Journal of Social Work Practice* 18(2):197–210.

Burstein, B. 1988. Involuntary aged clients: Ethical and treatment issues. *Social Casework* October:518–524.

Buttell, F. and M. Carney. 2005. A large sample evaluation of a court mandated batterer intervention program: Investigating differential program effect for African American and Caucasian men. *Research on Social Work Practice* 16(2):121–131.

Buttell, F. and C. Pike. 2003. Investigating the differential effectiveness of a batterer treatment program on outcomes for African American and Caucasian batterers. *Research on Social Work Practice* 13(6):675–692.

Cadsky, O., R. Hanson, M. Crawford, and C. Lalonde. 1996. Attrition from a male batterer treatment program: Client-treatment congruence and lifestyle instability. *Violence Victims* 11(1):51–64.

Cameron, H. and J. Telfer. 2004. Cognitive-behavioural group work: Its application to specific offender groups. *The Howard Journal* 43(1):47–64.

Cameron, J. and W. Pierce. 1996. The debate about rewards and intrinsic motivation: Protests and accusations do not alter the results. *Review of Educational Research* 66(1):39–51.

Caplan, T. and H. Thomas. 1995. Safety and comfort, content and process: Facilitating open group work with men who batter. *Social Work with Groups* 18:33–51.

Caplan, T. and H. Thomas. 2002. The forgotten moment: Therapeutic resiliency and its promotion in social work with groups. *Social Work with Groups* 24(2):5–26.

Caplan, T. and H. Thomas. 2004. "If we are all in the same canoe, Why are we using different paddles?" The effective use of common themes in diverse group situations. *Social Work with Groups* 27(1):53–73.

Carniol, B. C. 1992. Structural social work: Maurice Moreau's challenge to social work practice. *Journal of Progressive Human Services* Supplement (1):1–20.

Carroll, K. 1998. A Cognitive Behavioral Treatment Approach: Treating Cocaine Addiction. National Institute on Drug Abuse. NIH Publication No. 98–4308.

Casey, P. and D. Rottman. 2005. Problem-solving courts: Models and trends. *The Justice System Journal* 26(1):35–56.

Caspi, J., and W. J. Reid. 2002. *Educational Supervision in Social Work: A Task-Centered Model for Field Instruction and Staff Development.* New York: Columbia University Press.

Center for Advanced Studies in Child Welfare. 2002. Mediation Skills for Child Welfare. Practice Notes, Issue No. 11. St. Paul, MN: Author.

Center for Health and Health Care in Schools (CHHSC). 2000. Children's mental health needs, disparities and school-based services: A fact sheet. Retrieved from http://www.health-inschools.org/cfk/mentfact.asp (accessed July 9, 2008).

Center for Mental Health in Schools (CMHS). 2003. Guidebook: Common psychological problems of school aged youth: Developmental variations, problems, disorders, and perspectives for prevention and treatment. Los Angeles, CA: Author. Retrieved from http://smhp.psych.ucla.edu (accessed July 12, 2008).

Center for Substance Abuse Treatment (CSAT). 1999. Brief Interventions and Brief Therapies for Substance Abuse. Treatment Improvement Protocol (TIP) series, No. 34. DHHS Pub. No. (SMA) 99–3353. Washington, DC: U.S. Government Printing Office.

Cherry, S. 2005. *Transforming Behaviour: Pro-social Modelling in Practice—A Handbook for Practitioners and Managers.* Cullompton, England: Willan Publishing.

Child Welfare League of America. 1997. *Alcohol and Other Drug Survey of State Child Welfare Agencies.* Washington, DC: Child Welfare League of America.

Choudhuri, D. 2005. Oppression of the Spirit. In *Explorations in Privilege, Oppression and Diversity,* eds. S. K. Anderson and V. A. Middleton, pp. 127–135. Pacific Grove, CA: Brooks/Cole-Thomson.

Chovanec, M. 2007. Personal communication.

Chovanec, M. G. 1995. Attrition in the treatment of men who batter: A closer look at men's decision-making process about attending or dropping out of treatment. In Proceedings of the Eighth National Symposium on Doctoral Research and Social Work Practice, Ohio State University, November 3–4.

Chui, W. and and K. Ho. 2006. Working with involuntary clients: Perceptions and experiences of outreach social workers in Hong Kong. *Journal of Social Work Practice* 20(2):205–222.

Cingolani, J. 1984. Social conflict perspective on work with involuntary clients. *Social Work* 29:442–446.

Citron, P. 1978. Group work with alcoholic poly-drug involved adolescents with deviant behavior syndrome. *Social Work with Groups* 1(1):48.

Clark, C. 1998. Self-determination and paternalism in community care: Practice and prospects. *British Journal of Social Work* 28:387–402.

Clark, C., M. Becker, J. Giard, R. Mazelis, A. Savage, and W. Vogel. 2005. The role of coercion in the treatment of women with co-occuring disorders and histories of abuse. *The Journal of Behavioral Health Services and Research* 32(2):167–181.

Clarkin, J. F. and K. N. Levy. 2004. The Influence of Client Variables on Psychotherapy. In *Handbook of Psychotherapy and Behavioral Change* (5th ed.), ed. M. J. Lambert, pp. 194–226. New York: John Wiley.

Cleaveland, C. 2005. Fragile work attachment among a cohort of Philadelphia welfare recipients: Menial labor and its implications. *Aretê* 28(2):54–67.

Clifford, D. and B. Burke. 2005. Developing anti-oppression ethics in the new curriculum. *Social Work Education* 87(2):677–692.

Cohen, M. 2002. Pushing the Boundaries in Empowerment-Oriented Social Work Practice. In *Pathways to Power: Readings in Contextual Social Work Practice*, eds. M. O'Melia and K. Miley, pp. 143–155. Boston: Allyn and Bacon.

Cohen, M. and A. Sinner. 1981. A group curriculum for outpatient alcoholism treatment. *Social Work with Groups* 5:5–13.

Colby, S. M., P. M. Monti, N. P. Barnett, D. J. Rohsenow, K. Weissman, A. Spirios, R. H. Woolard, and W. J. Lewander. 1998. Brief motivational in a hospital setting for adolescent smoking: A preliminary review. *Journal of Consulting and Clinical Psychology* 66:574–578.

Collins-Camargo, C. and C. Groeber. 2003. Adventures in partnership: Using learning laboratories to enhance frontline supervision in child welfare. *Professional Development* 6(1–2):17–31.

Colorado Sex Offender Management Board. 1999. Standards and Guidelines for the Assessment, Evaluation, Treatment and Behavioral Monitoring of Adult Sex Offenders. Denver, CO.

Congress, E. P. 1999. *Social Work Values and Ethics*. Chicago: Nelson-Hall.

Conrad, D. and Y. Kellar-Guenther. 2006. Compassion fatigue, burnout, and compassion satisfaction among Colorado child protection workers. *Child Abuse and Neglect* 30:1071–1080.

Cook, K. and R. Emerson. 1978. Power, equity, commitment in exchange networks. *American Sociological Review* 73:721–739.

Coombs, R., ed. 2001. *Addiction Recovery Tools: A Practitioner's Handbook*. New York: Sage.

Corcoran, J. 1997. Solution-oriented approach to working with juvenile offenders. *Child and Adolescent Social Work Journal* 14(4):277–288.

Corcoran, J. 1998. Solution-focused practice with middle and high school at-risk youths. *Social Work in Education* 20(4):232–244.

Corcoran, J. 2002. The transtheoretical stages of change model and motivational interviewing for building maternal supportiveness in cases of sexual abuse. *Journal of Child Sexual Abuse* 11(3):1–17.

Corcoran, J. 2006. A comparison group study of solution-focused therapy versus "treatment-as-usual" for behavior problems in children. *Journal of Social Service Research* 33:69–81.

Corcoran, J. and Franklin, C. 1998. A solution-focused approach to physical abuse. *Journal of Psychotherapy* 9(1):69–73.

Corcoran, J. and M. Stephenson. 2000. The effectiveness of solution-focused therapy with child behavior problems: A preliminary report. *Families in Society: The Journal of Contemporary Human Services* 81(5):468–474.

Corcoran, K. and V. Vandiver. 2004. Implementing Best Practice and Consensus Procedures. In *Evidence-Based Practice Manual: Research and Outcome Measures in Health and Human Services*, eds. A. Roberts and K. Yeager, pp. 15–19. New York: Oxford.

Corey, G., M. S. Corey, and P. J. Callanan. 1979. *Professional and Ethical Issues in Counseling and Psychotherapy.* Monterey, CA: Brooks-Cole.

Corey, G., M. S. Corey, P. J. Callahan, and J. M. Russell. 2004. *Group Techniques,* 3rd ed. Pacific Grove, CA: Brooks/Cole.

Council on Crime and Justice. 2006. Final report: Reducing disparity and enhancing safety. Minneapolis, MN. Retrieved from http://www.crimeandjustice.org/.

Cowger, C. D. 1994. Assessing client strengths: Clinical assessment for client empowerment. *Social Work* 3:262–268.

Cowley, C. B., T. Farley, and K. Beamis. 2002. "Well, maybe I'll try the pill for just a few months . . ." Brief motivational and narrative-based interventions to encourage contraceptive use among adolescents at high risk for early child bearing. *Families, Systems, and Health* 20(2):183–204.

Craig, L., K. Browne, and I. Stringer. 2003. Treatment and sexual offence recidivism. *Trauma, Violence and Abuse* 4(1):70–89.

Craig, M. and P. Furst. 1965. What happens after treatment? A study of potentially delinquent boys. *Social Service Review* 39:165–171.

Crichton, L. I. 2003. The Welfare Time Limit in Minnesota: A Survey of Families who Lost MFIP Eligibility as a Result of the Five Year Time Limit. St. Paul, MN: Department of Human Services.

Critical Resistance. 2003. Bureau of Justice Statistics Prison and Jail Fact Sheet, Oakland, CA.

Cull, L. and J. Roche. 2001. *The Law and Social Work: Contemporary Issues for Practice.* New York: Palgrave.

Cullen, F., S. Skovron, J. Scott, and V. Burton. 1990. Public support for correctional rehabilitation: The tenacity of the rehabilitation ideal. *Criminal Justice and Behaviour* 17:6–18.

Cushman, P. 1986. The self-besieged: Recruitment, indoctrination processes in restrictive groups. *Journal for the Theory of Social Behavior* 16(1):1–32.

Csikszentmihalyi, M. 1975. *Beyond Boredom and Anxiety.* San Francisco: Jossey-Bass.

Csikszentmihalyi, M. 1991. *Flow: The Psychology of Optimal Experience.* New York: Harper and Row.

Dale, P. 2004. Like fish in a bowl: Parents' perceptions of child protective services. *Child Abuse Review* 13:137–157.

Daly, J. E. and S. Pelowski. 2000. Predictors of dropout among men who batter: A review of studies with implications for research and practice. *Violence and Victims* 15(2):137–160.

Dane, B. 2000. Child welfare workers. An innovative approach for interacting with secondary trauma. *Journal of Social Work Education* 36(1):27–38.

Daniels, J. W. and C. M. Murphy. 1997. Stages and processes of change in batterers' treatment. *Cognitive and Behavioral Practice* 4(1):123–145.

Davidson, J. 1998. The Transtheoretical Model: A Critical Overview. In *Treating Addictive Behaviors* (2nd ed.), eds. W. R. Miller and N. Heather, pp. 25–38. New York: Plenum Press.

Davis, L. E. and J. Gelsomino. 1994. An assessment of practitioner cross-racial treatment experiences. *Social Work* 39(1):116–123.

Davis, R., B. Taylor, and C. Maxwell. 1998. Does Batterer Treatment Reduce Violence? A Randomized Experiment in Brooklyn. Washington, DC: National Institute of Justice.

Day, P. R. 1981. *Social Work, Social Control.* London/New York: Tavistock.

Deal, K. H. 2003. The relationship between critical thinking and interpersonal skills: Guidelines for clinical supervision. *The Clinical Supervisor* 22(2):3–19.

Dean, R. G. 2001. The myth of cross-cultural competence. *Families in Society: The Journal of Contemporary Human Services* 82(6):623–630.

DeChillo, N., P. E. Koren, and K. H. Schultze. 1994. From paternalism to partnership: Family and professional collaboration in children's mental health. *American Journal of Orthopsychiatry* 64:564–576.

DeHart, D. D., R. J. Kennerly, L. K. Burke, and D. R. Follingstad. 1999. Predictors of attrition in a treatment program for battering men. *Journal of Family Violence* 14(1):19–34.

Dei, G. J. S. 1996. *Anti-racism Education.* Halifax: Fernwood.

De Jong, P. and I. K. Berg. 1998. *Interviewing for Solutions.* Pacific Grove, CA: Brooks/Cole.

De Jong, P. and I. K. Berg. 2001. Co-constructing cooperation with mandated clients. *Social Work* 46:361–374.

De Jong, P., and S. D. Miller. 1995. How to interview for client strengths. *Social Work* 40(6):729–736.

Delgado, G. and R. Gordon. 2002. From Social Contract to Social Control: Welfare Policy and Race. In *From Poverty to Punishment: How Welfare Reform Punished the Poor,* ed. G. Delgado, pp. 25–52. Oakland, CA: Applied Research Center.

Delgado, M. 2001. *Where Are All the Young Men and Women of Color? Capacity Enhancement Practice and the Criminal Justice System.* New York: Columbia University Press.

DeMaris, A. 1989. Attrition in batterers' counseling: The role of social and demographic factors. *Social Service Review* 63(March):142–154.

DeMaster, D. 2007, April. At the Limit: December 2005 Minnesota Family Investment Program (MFIP) Cases that Reached the 60 Month Time Limit. St. Paul, MN: Minnesota Department of Human Services.

De Panfilis, D. 2006. Compassion fatigue, burnout and compassion satisfaction: Implications for retention of workers. *Child Abuse and Neglect* 30:1067–1069.

Derezotes, D., J. Poertner, and M. F. Testa. 2005. *Race Matters in Child Welfare.* Washington, DC: Child Welfare League of America Press.

de Shazer, S. 1982. *Patterns of Brief Family Therapy: An Ecosystemic Approach.* New York: Guilford.

de Shazer, S. 1984. Post-mortem. Mark Twain did die in 1910. *Family Process* 23(March):20–21.

de Shazer, S. 1988. *Clues: Investigating Solutions in Brief Therapy.* New York: W. W. Norton.

de Shazer, S., I. K. Berg, E. Lipchik, E. Nunnally, A. Molnar, W. Gingerich, et al. 1986. Brief therapy: Focused solution development. *Family Process* 25:207–222.

Devore, W. and E. Schlesinger. 1987. *Ethnic-Sensitive Practice,* 2nd ed. Columbus, OH: Merrill.

Dewberry Rooney, G. 2002. Breaking the silence: A candid discussion on the disproportionality of African-American children in out of home placement. Retrieved from http://ssw.che.umn.edu/cascw/pdf/2001%20PROCEEDINGS.pdf.

Dickson, D. 1976. Law and social work: Impact of due process. *Social Work* 21(4):274–279.

Dickson, D. 1998. *Confidentiality and Privacy in Social Work.* New York: Free Press.

DiClemente, C. and J. O. Prochaska. 1998. Toward a Comprehensive Transtheoretical Model of Change: Stages of Change and Addictive Behaviors. In *Treating Addictive Behaviors* (2nd ed.), eds. W. R. Miller and N. Heather, pp. 3–24. New York: Plenum Press.

DiClemente, C. and M. Velasquez. 2002. Motivational interviewing and the stages of change. In *Motivational Interviewing: Preparing People for Change,* eds. W. R. Miller and S. Rollnick, pp. 201–216. New York: Guilford Press.

Dielman, M. B. and C. Franklin. 1998. Brief solution-focused therapy with parents and adolescents with ADHD. Practice highlights. *Journal of National Association of Social Workers* 20(4):261–267.

Doolan, M. 2002, October. Family group conferences and social work: Some observations about United Kingdom and New Zealand. Paper presented at Building on Strengths: International Perspectives on FGCs workshop sponsored by Family Rights Group, England. Retrieved from http://www.frg.org.uk/Conferences/conf081002 (accessed July 6, 2007).

Dore, M. M. and L. B. Alexander. 1996. Preserving families at risk of child abuse and neglect: The role of the helping alliance. *Child Abuse and Neglect* 20:349–361.

Dossey, L. 2006. Where were the doctors? Torture and the betrayal of medicine. *Explore* 2(6):473–481.

Dowd, E., S. Hughes, L. Brockbank, and D. Halpain. 1988. Compliance-based and defiance-based intervention strategies and psychological reactance in the treatment of free and unfree behavior. *Journal of Counseling Psychology* 35(4):370–376.

Dowd, E., C. Milne, and S. Wise. 1991. The therapeutic reactance scale: A measure of psychological reactance. *Journal of Counseling and Development* 69:541–545.

Dowd, E., F. Wallbrown, D. Sanders, and J. Yesenosky. 1994. Psychological reactance and its relationship to normal personality variables. *Cognitive Therapy and Research* 18:601–612.

Dowden, C. and D. Andrews. 1999. What works for female offenders: A meta-analytic review. *Crime and Delinquency* 45:438–452.

Drake, B. and Y. Gautam. 1996. A structural equations model of burnout and job exit among child protective service workers. *Social Work Research* 20(3):179–187.

Drapeau, M., A. Korner, L. Granger, and L. Brunet. 2005. What sex abusers say about their treatment. Results of a qualitative study of pedophiles in treatment at a Canadian penitentiary clinic. *Journal of Child Sexual Abuse* 14(1):91–115.

Draycott, S. and A. Dabbs. 1998. Cognitive dissonance 2: A theoretical grounding of motivational interviewing. *British Journal of Clinical Psychology* 37:355–364.

Dubow, E. F., K. R. Lovko, and D. F. Kausch. 1990. Demographic differences in adolescent health concerns and perceptions of helping agents. *Journal of Clinical Child Psychiatry* 19:44–54.

Dudley, J. R. 2000. Confronting stigma within the services system. *Social Work* 45(5):449–455.

Dunifon, R., K. Hynes, and H. E. Peters. 2006. Welfare reform and child well-being. *Children and Youth Services Review* 28:1273–1292.

Dunifon, R., A. Kalil, and S. K. Danziger. 2003. Maternal work behavior under welfare reform: How does the transition from welfare to work affect child development? *Children and Youth Services Review* 25(1/2):55–82.

Dunn, C., L. DeRoo, and F. P. Rivara. 2001. The use of brief interventions adapted from motivational interviewing across behavioral domains: A systematic review. *Addiction* 96:1725–1742.

Dutton, D. G. 1986. The outcome of court-mandated treatment for wife assault: A quasi-experimental evaluation. *Violence and Victims* 1:163–175.

Dutton, D. G. 2007. *The Abusive Personality: Violence and Control in Intimate Relationships,* 2nd ed. New York: Guilford.

Dutton, D. G. and A. J. Starzomski. 1993. Borderline personality in perpetrators of psychological and physical abuse. *Violence and Victims* 8:327–337.

D'Zurilla, T. and Goldfried, M. 1971. Problem solving and behavior modification. *Journal of Abnormal Psychology* 78(1):107–126.

Eakes, G., S. Walsh, M. Markowksi, H. Cain, and M. Swanson. 1997. Family centered brief solution-focused therapy with chronic schizophrenia: A pilot study. *Journal of Family Therapy* 19(2):145–158.

Eckhardt, C., J. Babcock, and S. Homack. 2004. Partner assaultive men and the stages and processes of change. *Journal of Family Violence* 19(2):81–93.

Edleson, J. L. and R. J. Grusznski. 1988. Treating men who batter: Four years of outcome data from the Domestic Abuse Project. *Journal of Social Service Research* 12(1):3–22.

Edleson, J. L., D. M. Miller, G. W. Stone, and D. G. Chapman. 1985. Group treatment for men who batter. *Social Work Research and Abstracts* 21:18–21.

Edleson, J. L. and M. Syers. 1989. *Domestic Abuse Project Research Update* (No. 2). Minneapolis MN: Domestic Abuse Project, Inc.

Edleson, J. L. and R. M. Tolman. 1992. *Intervention for Men Who Batter: An Ecological Approach.* Newberry Park, CA: Sage.

Edwards, K. and J. Sheldon-Wildgen. 1981. Providing Nursing Home Residents' Rights. In *Preservation of Client Rights,* eds. G. Hannah, W. Christian, and H. Clark, pp. 319–344. New York: Free Press.

Efta-Breitbach, J. 2004. Treatment of juveniles who sexually offend: An overview. *Journal of Child Sexual Abuse* 13(3/4):125–138.

Eisikovits, Z. C. and J. L. Edleson. 1989. Intervening with men who batter: A critical review of the literature. *Social Service Review* 37:385–414.

Emerson, R. 1962. Power-dependency relations. *American Sociological Review* 27:31–41.

Empey, L. T. and M. L. Ericson. 1972. *The Provo Experiment.* Lexington, MA: Lexington Books.

Epstein, L. 1988. *Helping People: The Task-Centered Approach.* Columbus, OH: Merrill.

Epstein, L. and L. Brown. 2002. *Brief Treatment and a New Look at the Task-Centered Approach,* 4th ed. New York: Macmillan.

Erikson, K. 1964. Notes on the sociology of deviance. In *The Other Side: Perspectives on Deviance,* ed. H. Becker, pp. 4–21. Glencoe, IL: Free Press.

Evans, T. D. and D. P. Kane. 1996. Sophistry: A promising group technique for the involuntary client. *The Journal for Specialists in Group Work* 21(2):110–117.

Ewalt, P. 1982. Understanding resistance: Seven social workers debate. *Practice Digest* 5(1):5–24.

Farrell, S. 2002. *Rethinking What Works with Offenders Probation Social Context and Desistance from Crime.* Devon, England: Willon.

Faulkner, K. K., R. Cogan, M. Nolder, and G. Shooter. 1991. Characteristics of men and women completing cognitive-behavioral spouse abuse treatment. *Journal of Family Violence* 6(3):243–254.

Feder, L. and D. Forde. 2000. A test of the efficacy of court-mandated counseling for domestic violence offenders: The Broward experiment. Washington, DC: National Institute of Justice.

Feld, S. and N. Radin. 1982. *Social Psychology for Social Work and the Mental Health Professions.* New York: Columbia University Press.

Fenichel, O. 1945. *The Psychoanalytic Theory of Neuroses.* New York: W. W. Norton.

Ferguson, H. 2001. Promoting child protection, welfare and healing: The case for developing best practice. *Child and Family Social Work* 6:1–12.

Ferguson, H. 2003. Outline of a critical best practice perspective for social work and social care. *British Journal of Social Work* 33:1005–1024.

Ferguson, M., J. Ritter, D. M. DiNitto, J. Kim, and A. J. Schwab. 2005. Mentoring as a strategy for welfare reform. *Journal of Human Behavior in the Social Environment* 12(1–2):165–183.

Figley, C. R. 2002. Compassion fatigue: Psychotherapists' chronic lack of self-care. *Psychotherapy in Practice* 58:1433–1441.

Finegold, K. and S. Staveteig. 2002. Race, Ethnicity and Welfare Reform. In *Welfare Reform: The Next Act,* eds. A. Weil and K. Finegold, pp. 203–233. Washington, DC: Urban Institute.

Finn, J. L. and M. Jacobson. 2003. Just practice: Steps toward a new social work paradigm. *Journal of Social Work Education* 39(2):57–78.

Fischer, J. 1973. Is casework effective? A review. *Social Work* 19(1):5–20.

Floersch, J. 2002. *Meds, Money and Manners: The Case Management of Severe Mental Illness.* New York: Columbia University Press.

Flores, P. 1983. The efficacy of the use of coercion in getting DWI offenders into treatment. *Journal of Alcohol and Drug Education* 28:18–27.

Foley, D. 1988. The Coerced Alcoholic: On Felons, Throwaways and Others. In *For Their Own Good: Essays on Coercive Kindness,* ed. A. Rosenblatt, pp. 115–148. Albany, NY: Nelson A. Rockefeller Institute of Government, State University of New York.

Folger, R. 1987. Distributive and procedural justice in the workplace. *Social Justice Research* 1(2):143–159.

Forrest, G. 1982. *Confrontation in Psychotherapy with the Alcoholic.* Holmes Park, FL: Learning Publications.

Fowler, J. 2003. *A Practitioners' Tool for Child Protection and the Assessment of Parents.* Philadelphia: Kingsley.

Francis, D. 2001. Bush tax cuts widen U.S. income gap. *Christian Science Monitor* May 23.

Frank, J. 1973. *Persuasion and Healing,* 2nd ed. Baltimore: Johns Hopkins Press.

Frankel, H. 1988. Family-centered, home-based services in child protection: A review of the research. *Social Service Review* 61:137–157.

Franklin, C. 2002. Becoming a strengths fact finder. *AAMFT Magazine.* Washington, DC: The American Association of Marriage and Family Therapists.

Franklin, C., J. Biever, K. Moore, D. Clemons, and M. Scamardo. 2001. The effectiveness of solution-focused therapy with children in a school setting. *Research on Social Work Practice* 11(4):411–434.

Franklin, C., J. Corcoran, J. Nowicki, and C. Streeter. 1997. Using self-anchored scales to measure outcomes in solution-focused therapy. *Journal of Systemic Therapies* 16(3):246–265.

Franklin, C. and L. Hopson. 2007. New challenges in research: Translating community-based practices into evidence-based practices. *Journal of Social Work Education* 43(3):377–404.

Franklin, C. and C. Jordan. 1999. *Family Practice: Brief Systems Methods for Social Work.* Pacific Grove, CA: Brooks-Cole.

Franklin, C. and K. C. Moore. 1999. Solution-focused Brief Family Therapy. In *Family Practice: Brief Systems Methods for Social Work,* eds. C. Franklin and C. Jordan, pp. 105–142. Pacific Grove, CA: Brooks/Cole.

Franklin, C., C. L. Streeter, J. S. Kim, and S. J. Tripodi. 2007. Using concept mapping to examine school dropouts: A solution-focused alternative school case study. *Children and Schools* 29(3):133–144.

Freire, P. 1970. A critical understanding of social work. *Journal of Progressive Human Services* 22:3–5.

Freire, P. 1998. *Pedagogy of the Oppressed.* New York: Continnum.

Friedlander, M. and G. Schwartz. 1985. Toward a theory of strategic self-presentation in counseling and psychotherapy. *Journal of Counseling Psychology* 32(4):483–501.

Froeschle, J. G., R. L. Smith, and R. Ricard. 2007. The efficacy of a systematic substance abuse program for adolescent females. *Professional School Counseling* 10(5):498–505.

Frost, A. 2004. Therapeutic engagement styles of child sexual offenders in a group treatment program: A grounded theory study. *Sexual Abuse: A Journal of Research and Treatment* 16(3):191–208.

Frye, M. 2004. Oppression. In *Race, Class and Gender in the United States* (6th ed.), ed. P. S. Rothenberg, pp. 146–149. New York: Worth.

Fulcher, L. C. 2000. *Cultural Origins of Contemporary Family Group Conferencing*. FGDM Roundtable. Englewood, CO: American Humane Association.

Gabe, T. 2003. *Trends in Welfare, Work, and the Economic Well-Being of Female Headed Families.* New York: Novinka Books.

Gadow, S. 1981. Advocacy: An Ethical Model for Assisting Patients with Treatment Decisions. In *Dilemmas of Dying*, eds. C. Wong and J. Swazley, pp. 135–142. Boston: G. K. Hall.

Galper, J. 1975. The *Politics of Social Services*. Englewood Cliffs, NJ: Prentice-Hall.

Gambrill, E. 2006. Evidence-based practice and policy: Choices ahead. *Research on Social Work Practice* 16(3):338–357.

Ganley, A. 1987. Perpetrators of Domestic Violence: An Overview of Counseling the Court-Mandated Client. In *Domestic Violence on Trial*, ed. D. Sonkin, pp. 155–177. New York: Springer.

Gardner, H. 2004. *Changing Minds: The Art and Science of Changing Our Own and Other People's Minds.* Boston: Harvard Business School Press.

Garland, A. F., E. MacLeod, J. A. Landsverk, W. Ganger, and I. Johnson. 1998. Minority population in the child welfare system: The visibility hypothesis reexamined. *American Journal of Orthopsychiatry* 68(1):142–146.

Garland, J. A., H. E. Jones, and R. L. Kolodny. 1965. A Model for Stages of Development in Social Work Groups. In *Explorations in Social Group Work*, ed. S. Bernstein, pp. 17–71. Boston: Boston University School of Social Work.

Garvin, C. D. 1981. *Contemporary Group Work*. Englewood Cliffs, NJ: Prentice-Hall.

Geffner, R., K. Crompton Franey, and R. Falconer. 2003. Adult sexual offenders: Current issues and future directions. *Journal of Child Sexual Abuse* 12(3/4):1–16.

Gendreau, P., F. Cullen, and J. Bonta. 1998. Intensive Rehabilitation Supervision: The Next Generation in Community Corrections. In *Community Corrections Probation Parole and Intermediate Sanctions*, ed. J. Petersilia. New York: Oxford University Press.

Gennetian, L. A. and C. Miller. 2002. Children and welfare reform: A view from an experimental welfare program in Minnesota. *Child Development* 73(2):601–620.

Germain, C. 1982. Understanding resistance: Seven social workers debate. *Practice Digest* 5(1):5–24.

Gibbs, L. 2007. Applying research to making life-affecting judgements and decisions. *Research on Social Work Practice* 17(1):143–150.

Gil, D. G. 1978. Clinical practice and politics of human liberation. *Catalyst* 2:60–69.

Gil, D. G. 1998. *Confronting Injustice and Oppression: Concepts and Strategies for Social Workers.* New York: Columbia University Press.

Gilgun, J. 2005. The four cornerstones of evidence based practice in social work. *Research on Social Work Practice* 15(1):52–61.

Gingerich, W. J. and S. Eisengart. 2000. Solution-focused brief therapy: A review of the outcome research. *Family Process* 39:477–498.

Gingerich, W. J. and T. Wabeke. 2001. A solution-focused approach to mental health intervention in school settings. *Children and Schools* 23:33–47.

Girvin, H. 2004. Beyond stage of change: Use of readiness for change and caregiver-reported problems to identify meaningful subgroups in a child welfare sample. *Children and Youth Services Review* 26:897–917.

Gitterman, A. 1983. Uses of resistance: A transactional view. *Social Work* 28(2):127–131.

Gitterman, A., ed. 1995. Introduction: Social Work Practice with Vulnerable Populations. In *Handbook of Social Work Practice with Vulnerable Populations*. New York: Columbia University Press.

Glancy, G. and C. Regehr. 2002. Step-by-Step Guidelines for Assessing Sexual Predators. In *Social Workers' Desk Reference*, eds. A. Roberts and G. Greene, pp. 702–708, 710–713. Oxford: Oxford University Press.

Goldberg, M., D. Walker, and J. Robinson. 1977. Exploring task-centered casework. *Social Work Today* 9(2):9–14.

Golder, S., A. Ivanoff, R. Cloud, K. Bessel, P. McKiernan, E. Bratt, and L. Bledsoe. 2005. Evidence-based practice with adults in jails and prisons. *Best Practices in Mental Health* 1(2):100–132.

Goldkamp, J. 2000. The drug court response: Issues and implications for justice change. *Albany Law Review* 63:923–961.

Gondolf, E. W. 1985. Fighting for control: A clinical assessment of men who batter. *Social Casework* 66(January):48–54.

Gondolf, E. W. 1988. The effects of batterer counseling on shelter outcome. *Journal of Interpersonal Violence* 3(3):275–289.

Gondolf, E. W. 1991. A victim-based assessment of court-mandated counseling for batterers. *Criminal Justice Review* 16:214–226.

Gondolf, E. W. 1997a. Expanding Batterer Program Evaluation. In *Out of Darkness: Contemporary Research Perspectives on Family Violence*, eds. G. K. Kantor and J. Jasinski, pp. 208–218. Thousand Oaks, CA: Sage.

Gondolf, E. W. 1997b. Batterer programs: What we know and need to know. *Journal of Interpersonal Violence* 12(1):83–98.

Gondolf, E. W. 1997c. Patterns of reassault in batterers programs. *Violence and Victims* 12:373–387.

Gondolf, E. W. 1999. A comparison of reassault rates in four batterer programs: Do court referral, program length, and services matter? *Journal of Interpersonal Violence* 14:41–61.

Gondolf, E. W. 2000. A 30-month follow-up of court-referred batterers in four cities. *International Journal of Offender Therapy and Comparative Criminology* 44(1):111–128.

Gondolf, E. W. 2004. Evaluating batterer counseling programs: A difficult task showing some effects and implications. *Aggression and Violent Behavior* 9:605–631.

Gondolf, E. W. and B. Foster. 1991. Preprogram attrition in batterer programs. *Journal of Family Violence* 6:337–349.

Gondolf, E. W. and J. Hanneken. 1987. The gender warrior: Reformed batterers on abuse, treatment and change. *Journal of Family Violence* 2:177–191.

Gordon, L. 1994. *Pitied but Not Entitled: Single Mothers and the History of Welfare*, pp. 1890–1935. New York: Free Press.

Gorske, T. T., C. Larkby, D. C. Daley, E. Yenerall, and L. A. Morrow. 2006. Childhood abuse and psychiatric impairment in a sample of welfare to work women. *Children and Youth Services Review* 28:1523–1541.

Gough, D. 1993. *Child Abuse Interventions: A Review of the Research Literature*. Public Health Research Unit, University of Glasgow, HMSO, London.

Gourse, J. and M. Chescheir. 1981. Authority issues in treating resistant families. *Social Casework* 62(2):67–73.

Gove, W. 1970. Societal reaction as an explanation for mental illness: An evaluation. *American Sociological Review* 35(5):873–884.

Gove, W. 2004. The career of the mentally ill, an integration of psychiatric, labeling, social construction and lay perspectives. *Journal of Health and Social Behavior* 45(4):357–375.

Graham, M. 2004. Empowerment revisited: Social work, resistance and agency in black communities. *European Journal of Social Work* 7(1):43–56.

Graybar, S., D. Antonnuccio, L. Boutilier, and D. Varble. 1989. Psychological reactance as a factor affecting patient compliance to physician advice. *Scandinavian Journal of Behavior Therapy* 18:43–51.

Green, J. W. 1999. *Cultural Awareness in Human Services: A Multi-Ethnic Approach*, 3rd ed. Boston: Allyn and Bacon.

Green, R. G., M. Kiernan-Stern, and F. R. Baskind. 2005. White social workers' attitudes about people of color. *Journal of Ethnic and Cultural Diversity in Social Work* 14(1/2):47–68.

Greenberg, J. and T. R. Tyler. 1987. Why procedural justice in organizations. *Social Justice Research* 1(2):127–143.

Greene, G., M. Y. Lee, and S. Hoffpauir. 2005. The languages of empowerment and strengths in clinical social work: A constructivist perspective. *Families in Society* 86(2):267–277.

Greene, G., M. Y. Lee, R. Trask, and J. Rheinsheld. 2000. How to work with clients' strengths in crisis intervention: A solution-focused approach. In *Crisis Intervention Handbook: Assessment, Treatment, and Research* (2nd ed.), ed. A. R. Roberts, pp. 31–55. New York: Oxford University Press.

Groth-Marnat, G. 1997. *Handbook of Psychological Assessment*, 3rd ed. New York: John Wiley.

Guadalupe, K. L. and D. Lum. 2005. *Multidimensional Contextual Practice: Diversity and Transcendence*. Pacific Grove, CA: Brooks/Cole.

Gurman, A. S., D. P. Kniskern, and W. M. Pinsof. 1986. Research on the Process and Outcome of Marital and Family Therapy. In *Handbook of Psychotherapy and Behavior Change*, eds. S. L. Garfield and A. E. Bergin. New York: John Wiley.

Gutierrez, L., L. GlenMaye, and K. DeLois. 1995. The organizational context of empowerment practice: Implications for social work administration. *Social Work* 40(2):249–258.

Hage, D. 2004. *Reforming Welfare by Rewarding Work*. Minneapolis: University of Minnesota Press.

Hagen, M. A. 1998, July. Bad attitude. *National Review* 50(13):38–39.

Haley, J. 1963. *Strategies of Psychotherapy*. New York: Grune and Stratton.

Haley, J. 1990. *Strategies of Psychotherapy*. New York: W. W. Norton.

Hamberger, L. K. and J. E. Hastings. 1989. Counseling male spouse abusers: Characteristics of treatment completers and dropouts. *Violence and Victims* 4:275–286.

Hamberger, L. K. and J. E. Hastings. 1991. Personality correlates of men who batter and nonviolent men: Some continuities and discontinuities. *Journal of Family Violence* 6:131–147.

Hamberger, L. K., J. M. Lohr, and M. Gottlieb. 2000. Predictors of treatment dropout from spouse abuse abatement program. *Behavior Modification* 24(4):528–552.

Hanson, M. and I. Gutheil. 2004. Motivational strategies with alcohol-involved older adults: Implications for social work practice. *Social Work* 49(3):364–372.

Hanson, R. K. and M. T. Bussiere. 1998. Predicting relapse: A meta-analysis of sexual offender recidivist studies. *Journal of Consulting and Clinical Psychology* 66(2):343–362.

Hanson, R. K., A. Gordon, A. Harris, J. Marques, W. Murphy, V. Quense, et al. 2002. First report of the collaborative outcome data project on the effectiveness of treatment for sex offenders. *Sexual Abuse: A Journal of Research and Treatment* 11:49–67.

Hardina, D. 2005. Ten characteristics of empowerment-oriented social service organizations. *Administration in Social Work* 29(3):23–42.

Harkness, D. and H. Hensley. 1991. Changing the focus of social work supervision: Effects on client satisfaction and generalized contentment. *Social Work* 36:506–512.

Harper, R. and S. Hardy. 2000. An evaluation of motivational interviewing as a method of interviewing with clients in a probation setting. *British Journal of Social Work* 30:393–400.

Harris, G. and D. Watkins. 1987. *Counseling the Involuntary and Resistant Client.* College Park, MD: American Correctional Association.

Harris, M. and C. Franklin. 2003. Effectiveness of a cognitive-behavioral, school-based group intervention with Mexican-American pregnant and parenting adolescents. *Social Work Research* 27(2):71–84.

Hasenfeld, Y. 1987. Power in social work practice. *Social Service Review* 61(3):469–483.

Hasenfeld, Y., ed. 1992. *Human Services as Complex Organizations.* Newbury Park, CA: Sage.

Hasenfeld, Y., T. Ghose, and K. Larson. 2004. The logic of sanctioning welfare recipients: An empirical assessment. *Social Service Review* 78(2):304–320.

Hassall, I. 1996. Origin and Development of Family Group Conferences. In *Family Group Conferences: Perspectives on Policy and Practice*, eds. J. Hudson, A. Morris, G. Maxwell, and B. Galaway, pp. 17–36. Monsey, NY: Willow Tree Press.

Hawkins, R., M. Almeida, B. Fabry, and A. Reitz. 1992. A scale to measure restrictiveness of living environments for troubled children and youths. *Hospital and Community Psychiatry* 43:54–58.

Hays, S. 2003. *Flat Broke with Children: Women in the Age of Welfare Reform.* New York: Oxford University Press.

Healey, K., C. Smith, and C. O'Sullivan. 1998. Batter intervention: Program approaches and criminal justice strategies. *Issues and Practices in Criminal Justice.* Washington, DC: National Institute of Justice.

Heather, N. 1998. Using Brief Opportunities for Change in Medical Settings. In *Treating Addictive Behaviors* (2nd ed.), eds. W. R. Miller and N. Heather, pp. 133–148. New York: Plenum Press.

Heider, F. 1958. *The Psychology of Interpersonal Relations.* New York: John Wiley.

Heitler, J. B. 1976. Preparatory techniques initiating expressive psychotherapy with lower class, unsophisticated clients. *Psychological Bulletin* 83:339–352.

Henggeler, S., G. Melton, M. Brondino, D. Scherer, and J. Hanley. 1997. Multisystemic therapy with violent and chronic juvenile offenders and their families: The role of treatment fidelity in successful dissemination. *Journal of Consulting and Clinical Psychology* 65:821–833.

Henggeler, S., G. Melton, and L. Smith. 1992. Family preservation using multisystemic therapy: An effective alternative to incarcerating serious juvenile offenders. *Journal of Consulting and Clinical Psychology* 60:953–961.

Henggeler, S., S. Schoenwald, M. Rowland, and P. Cunningham. 2002. *Serious Emotional Disturbances in Children and Adolescents: Multi-Systemic Therapy.* New York: Guilford.

Hennessy, J. 2001. *Drug Courts in Operation: Current Research.* New York: Haworth Press.

Henning, K., A. Jones, and R. Holdford. 2005. I did not do it but if I did, I had a good reason. Minimization, denial and attributions of blame among male and female domestic violence offenders. *Journal of Family Violence* 20(3):131–138.

Hepworth, D. H., R. H. Rooney, G. Dewberry-Rooney, K. Strom-Gottfried, and J. A. Larsen. 2005. *Direct Social Work Practice: Theory and Skills*, 7th ed. Pacific Grove, CA: Brooks/Cole.

Herbert, M. and K. Harper-Dorton. 2002. *Working with Children, Adolescents, and Their Families.* Chicago: Lyceum Books.

Heymann, G. 1986. Mandated child abuse reporting and the confidentiality privilege. In *Psychotherapy and the Law*, eds. L. Everstine and D. Ererstine, pp. 332–354. New York: Grune and Stratton.

Ho, K. and W. Chui. 2001. Client resistance in outreaching social work in Hong Kong. *Asia Pacific Journal of Social Work* 11(1):114–130.

Holland, T. P. and A. C. Kilpatrick. 1993. Using narrative techniques to enhance multicultural practice. *Journal of Social Work Education* 29:302–308.

Hollister, D., M. Martin, J. Toft, J. Yeo, and Y. Kim. 2003. *The Well-Being of Parents and Children in the Minnesota Family Investment Program in Hennepin County, Minnesota, 1998–2002*. St. Paul: University of Minnesota School of Social Work Center for Advanced Studies in Child Welfare.

Hood, S. 1997. The purchaser/provider separation in child and family social work: Implications for service delivery and for the role of the social worker. *Child and Family Social Work* 2:25–35.

hooks, b. 1984. *Feminist Theory from Margin to Center*, ed. M. Marable. Boston: South End Press.

Hopfensperger, J. 2004. Welfare clients get spur to work: New program withholds cash in favor of four months of job-seeking. *Star Tribune* 232(88):B1 and B5.

Hopkinson, J. and S. Rex 2003. Essential Skills in Working with Offenders. In *Moving Probation Forward: Evidence, Arguments, and Practice*, eds. Wing Hong Chui and M. Nellis. Essex, UK: Pearson Longman.

Horvath, A. O. and L. Luborsky. 1993. The role of the therapeutic alliance in psychotherapy. *Journal of Consulting and Clinical Psychology* 61:561–573.

Hough, M., A. Clancy, T. McSweeney, and P. J. Turnbull. 2003. *The Impact of Drug Treatment and Testing Orders: Two-Year Re-Conviction Results*. London: Home Office.

Howard, M. O., T. Edmond, and M. G. Vaughn. 2005. Mental Health Practice Guidelines: Panacea or Pipedream? In *Mental Disorders in the Social Environment: Critical Perspectives*, ed. S. Kirk, pp. 270–292. New York: Columbia University Press.

Howard, M. O. and J. M. Jenson. 1999. Clinical practice guidelines: Should social work develop them? *Research on Social Work Practice* 9(3):283–301.

Hsia, A. M. and D. Hamparion. 1997. Disproportionality in Minority Confinement. *Juvenile Justice Bulletin*, Washington, DC: U.S. Department of Justice.

Hudson, J., J. D. Sieppert, and Y. Unrau. 2000. Family group conferencing in child welfare: Lessons from a demonstration project. *Families in Society* 81(4):382–391.

Hurley, D. J. 1984. Resistance and work in adolescent groups. *Social Work with Groups* 1:71–81.

Hutchison, E. 1987. Use of authority in direct social work practice with mandated clients. *Social Service Review* 61(December):581–598.

Iliffe, G. and L. Steed. 2000. Exploring the counselor's experience of working with survivors and perpetrators of domestic violence. *Journal of Interpersonal Violence* 15(4):393–412.

Indian Child Welfare Act. 25 U.S.C. chapter 21. §1901 et seq.

Influencing State Policy. 2005. *Social Work Advocacy: The State Budget*. Video no. 5 available from R. Schnieder, P.O. Box 842027, Virginia Commonwealth University, Richmond, VA 23284.

Irueste-Montes, A. M. and F. Montes. 1988. Court-ordered involuntary treatment of abusive and neglectful families. *Child Abuse and Neglect* 12(1):33–39.

Ivanoff, A., B. Blythe, and T. Tripodi. 1994. *Involuntary Clients in Social Work Practice: A Research-Based Approach*. New York: Aldine de Gruyter.

Iversen, R., K. Gergen, and R. Fairbanks. 2005. Assessment and social construction: Conflict or co-creation? *British Journal of Social Work* 35:689–708.

Iversen, K., G. Hoyer, and H. Sexton. 2007. Coercion and patient satisfaction on psychiatric acute wards. *International Journal of Law and Psychiatry* 30:504–511.

Izzo, R. and R. Ross. 1990. Meta-analysis of rehabilitation programs for juvenile delinquents. *Criminal Justice and Behaviour* 17:134–142.

Jackson, S., L. Feder, D. Ford, R. Davis, C. Maxwell, and B. Taylor. 2003. *Batterer Intervention Programs: Where Do We Go from Here?* Washington, DC: National Institute of Justice.

Jackson, S. and K. Morris. 1999. Family group conferences: User empowerment or family self-reliance? *British Journal of Social Work* 29:621–630.

James, R. K. and B. E. Gilliland. 2005. *Crisis Intervention Strategies.* Pacific Grove, CA: Thomson-Brooks/Cole.

Janzen, C. 1977. Families in the treatment of alcoholism. *Journal of Studies on Alcohol* 38(1):114–130.

Jennings, J. L. 1987. History and issues in the treatment of battering men: A case for unstructured group therapy. *Journal of Family Violence* 2(3):193–213.

Jennings, J. L. 1990. Preventing relapse versus "stopping" domestic abuse violence: Do we expect too much too soon from battering men? *Journal of Family Violence* 5(1):43–60.

Jobes, D. A., A. L. Berman, and C. E. Martin. 2000. Adolescent Suicidality and Crisis Intervention. In *Crisis Intervention Handbook: Assessment, Treatment, and Research* (2nd ed.), ed. A. R. Roberts, pp. 131–151. New York: Oxford University Press.

John Howard Society of Alberta. 2002. Sexual offender treatment programs. http://www.johnhoward.ab.ca/PUB/respaper/treatm02.htm.

Johnson, H. C. 1986. Emerging concerns in family therapy. *Social Work* 31(4):299–306.

Johnson, P. and A. Rubin. 1983. Case management in mental health: A social work domain? *Social Work* 28(1):49–54.

Johnson, V. 1976. *Intervention: How to Help Someone Who Doesn't Want Help.* Minneapolis, MN: Johnson Institute.

Johnson, V. 1980. *I'll Quit Tomorrow.* San Francisco: Harper and Row.

Johnson v. Solomon, Fed Suppl 1979; 484:278–320.

Johnston, B. D., F. P. Rivara, R. M. Droesch, C. W. Dunn, and M. K. Copass. 2002. Behavior change counseling in the emergency department to reduce injury risk: A randomized, controlled trial. *Pediatrics* 110:267–274.

Johnstone, G. 2004. How and In What Terms Should Restorative Justice Be Conceived? In *Critical Issues in Restorative Justice,* eds. H. Zehr and B. Toews, pp. 5–16. Monsey, NY: Criminal Justice Press.

Jones, E. 1964. *Ingratiation: A Social Psychological Analysis.* New York: Appleton-Century-Crofts.

Jones, E. and T. Pittman. 1982. Toward a General Theory of Strategic Self-Presentation. In *Psychological Perspectives on the Self,* ed. J. Suls. Hillsdale, NJ: Erlbaum.

Jones, J. and A. Alcabes. 1993. *Client Socialization: The Achillles' Heel of the Helping Professions.* Westport, CT: Auburn House.

Jones, M. 1990. Working with the Unmotivated Client. National Criminal Justice Reference Service. In *Violence Hits Home: Comprehensive Treatment Approaches to Domestic Violence,* eds. S. Stith and M. Williams, pp. 115–125. New York: Springer.

Joseph, M. A. 2006. *Supervisory Effectiveness in Chemical Dependency Settings: The Impact of Organizational Conditions, Job Strain and Job Dissatisfaction.* Unpublished doctoral dissertation. Columbia University, New York.

Juarez, P. 2001. *A Randomized Trial of Motivational Interviewing and Feedback on Heavy Drinking College Students.* Unpublished master's thesis. University of New Mexico, Albouquerque.

Kadushin, A. and D. Harkness. 2002. *Supervision in Social Work,* 4th ed. New York: Columbia University Press.

Kadushin, A. and J. Martin. 1988. *Child Welfare Services,* 4th ed. Pacific Grove, CA: Brooks/Cole.

Kaiser, T. L., C. F. Kuechler, and A. Barretta-Herman. 2000. *Challenges in Cross-cultural Supervision.* St. Paul, MN: College of St. Catherine/University of St. Thomas.

Kalichman, S., M. Carey, and B. Johnson. 1996. Prevention of sexually transmitted HIV infection: A meta-analytic review of the behavioral outcome literature. *Annals of Behavioral Medicine* 18:6–15.

Kaltiala-Heino, R., P. Laippala, and R. Salokangas. 1997. Impact of coercion on treatment outcome. *International Journal of Law and Psychiatry* 20(3):311–322.

Kane, D. 1991. *Strategies and Dilemmas in Child Welfare Supervision: A Case Study.* Unpublished doctoral dissertation, City University of New York.

Kaplan, J. and J. Carter. 1995. *Beyond Behavior Modification: A Cognitive Behavioral Approach to Behavioral Management in the Schools.* Austin, TX: Pro-ed.

Katz, M. 2001. *The Price of Citizenship: Redefining the American Welfare State.* New York: Henry Holt.

Kaufman, P., X. Chen, S. P. Choi, K. Peter, S. A. Ruddy, A. K. Miller, J. K. Fleury, K. A. Chandler, M. G. Planty, and M. R. Rand. 2001. Indicators of school crime and safety: 2001. Washington, DC: U.S. Departments of Education and Justice. Available at http://nces.ed.gov.

Kear-Colwell, J. and P. Pollock. 1997. Motivation or confrontation: Which approach to the child sex offender? *Criminal Justice and Behavior* 24(1):20–33.

Keith-Lucas, A. 1972. *Giving and Taking Help.* Chapel Hill, NC: University of North Carolina Press.

Kelly, A. 2000. Helping construct desirable identities: A self-presentational view of psychotherapy. *Psychological Bulletin* 126:475–494.

Kelly, M., J. S. Kim, and C. Franklin. 2008. *Solution-Focused Brief Therapy in Schools: A 360 Degree Review of Practice and Research.* New York: Oxford.

Kelman, H. 1965. Compliance, Identification and Internalization: Three Processes of Attitude Change. In *Studies in Social Psychology,* eds. H. Proshansky and B. Sendenberg, pp. 140–148. New York: Holt, Rinehart and Winston.

Kelty, M. 1981. Protection of Persons Who Participate in Applied Research. In *Preservation of Client Rights: A Handbook for Practitioners Providing Therapeutic, Education and Rehabilitative services,* eds. G. Hannah, W. Christian, and H. Clark, pp. 401–414. New York: Free Press.

Kendall, K. and S. Pollack. 2003. Cognitive behavioralism in women's prisons: A critical analysis of therapeutic assumptions and practices. In *Gendered Justice: Addressing Female Offenders,* ed. B. Bloom, pp. 69–96. Durham, NC: Carolina Academic Press.

Kessler, M. L., E. Gira, and J. Poertner. 2005. Moving best practice to evidence-based practice in child welfare. *Families in Society* 86(2):244–250.

Kiesler, C. 1971. *The Psychology of Commitment.* New York: Academic Press.

Kinney, J., D. A. Haapala, and C. Booth. 1991. *Keeping Families Together: The Home-Builders Model.* New York: Aldine-de Gruyter.

Kipnis, D. 1972. Does power corrupt? *Journal of Personality and Social Psychology* 24(1):33–41.

Kirk, S. 1972. Clients as outsiders: Theoretical approaches to deviance. *Social Work* 17:24–32.

Kirk, S. and J. Greenlee. 1974. Denying or delivering services. *Social Work* 19:439–447.

Klag, S., F. O'Callaghan, and P. Creed. 2005. The use of legal coercion in the treatment of substance abusers: An overview and critical analysis of thirty years of research. *Substance Abuse* 40:1777–1795.

Kline, M., D. J. Schonfeld, and R. Lichtenstein. 1995. Benefits and challenges of school-based crisis response teams. *Journal of School Health* 65(7):245–250.

Knox, K. 2002. Juvenile Sex Offenders Risk Assessment and Treatment. In *Social Workers' Desk Reference,* ed. A. Roberts and G. Greene, pp. 698–701. New York: Oxford.

Kok, C. J. and J. Leskela. 1996. Solution-focused therapy in a psychiatric hospital. *Journal of Marital and Family Therapy* 22(3):397–406.

Kondrat, M. 1995. Concept, act and interest in professional practice: Implications of an empowerment perspective. *Social Service Review* 69:405–428.

Kopp, J. 1988. Self-monitoring: A literature review of research and practice. *Social Work Research and Abstracts* 24:8–20.

Kopp, J. 1989. Self-observation: An empowerment strategy in assessment. *Social Casework* 70:276–284.

Krane, J. and L. Davies. 2000. Mothering and child protection practice: Rethinking risk assessment. *Child and Family Social Work* 5(1):35–45.

Kravetz, D. and S. Rose. 1973. *Contracts in Groups: A Workbook.* Dubuque, IA: Kendall-Hunt.

Krivanek, J. A. 1982. *Drug Problems, People Problems: Causes, Treatment and Prevention.* Sydney, Australia: Allen and Unwin.

Kroner, D. and J. Mills. 2004. The criminal attribution inventory: A measure of offender perceptions. *Journal of Offender Rehabilitation* 39(4):15–29.

Kruczek, T. and S. Vitanza. 1999. Treatment effects with an adolescent abuse survivor's group. *Child Abuse and Neglect* 23:477–485.

Kuhl, J., L. Jarkon-Horlick, and R. F. Morrissey. 1997. Measuring barriers to help-seeking behavior in adolescents. *Journal of Youth and Adolescence* 26(6):637–650.

Kurland, R. and R. Salmon. 1998. *Teaching a Methods Course in Social Work with Groups.* Alexandria, VA: Council on Social Work Education.

Lacoursiere, R. 2001. Burnout and substance user treatment: The phenomenon of the administrator clinician's experience. *Substance Abuse and Misuse* 36(13):1839–1874.

LaFountain, R. M. and N. E. Garner. 1996. Solution-focused counseling groups: The results are in. *The Journal for Specialists in Group Work* 21(2):128–143.

Laird, J. and J. A. Allen. 1983. Family Theory and Practice. In *Handbook of Clinical Social Work,* eds. D. Waldfogel, and A. Rosenblatt. San Francisco: Jossey-Bass.

Lambert, M. J. and A. E. Bergin. 1994. The Effectiveness of Psychotherapy. In *Handbook of Psychotherapy and Behavior Change* (4th ed.), eds. A. E. Bergin and S. I. Garfield, pp. 143–189. New York: John Wiley.

Lane, W. C., D. M. Rubin, R. Monteith, and C. W. Christian. 2002. Racial differences in the evaluation of pediatric fractures for physical abuse. *Journal of American Medical Association* 288(13):1603–1609.

Langer, E. 1975. The illusion of control. *Journal of Personality and Social Psychology* 32:311–328.

Latting, J. K., M. H. Beck, K. J. Slack, L. E. Tetrick, A. P. Jones, J. M. Etchegaryay, and N. D. Silva. 2004. Promoting service quality and client adherence to the service plan: The role of top management's support for innovation and learning. *Administration in Social Work* 28(2):29–48.

Lee, M. Y., G. J. Greene, and J. Rheinscheld. 1999. A model for short-term solution-focused group treatment of male domestic violence offenders. *Journal of Family Social Work* 3(2):39–57.

Lengyel, T. E., ed. 2001. *Faces of Change: Personal Experiences of Welfare Reform in America.* Milwaukee, WI: Alliance for Children and Families.

Levey, L., W. Steketee, and S. Keilitz. 2001. Lessons Learned in Implementing an Integrated Domestic Violence Court: The District of Columbia Experience. Williamsburg, VA: National Center for State Courts.

Levinson, J. and M. Macgowan. 2004. Engagement, denial and treatment progress among sex offenders in group therapy. *Sexual Abuse* 16(1):49–63.

Levy, R. and R. Carter. 1976. Compliance with practitioner instigations. *Social Work* 21:118–193.

Lewandowski, C. 2003. Organizational factors contributing to worker frustration: The precursor to burnout. *Journal of Sociology and Social Welfare* 30(4):175–185.

Li, L. and D. Moore. 2001. Disability and illicit drug use. An application of labeling theory. *Deviant Behavior* 22:1–21.

Lidz, C., A. Meisel, E. Zerubavel, M. Carter, R. Sestak, and L. Roth. 1984. *Informed Consent: A Study of Decision Making in Psychiatry.* New York: Guilford.

Lieberman, M., I. Yalom, and M. Miles. 1973. *Encounter Groups: First Facts.* New York: Basic Books.

Lifton, R. T. 1961. *Thought Reform and the Psychology of Totalism: A Study of Brainwashing in China.* New York: W. W. Norton.

Lincourt, O., T. J. Kuettel, and C. H. Bombardier. 2002. Motivational interviewing in a group setting with mandated clients: A pilot study. *Addictive Behaviors* 27:381–398.

Lindhorst, T. and R. J. Mancoske. 2006. The social and economic impact of sanctions and time limits on recipients of Temporary Assistance to Needy Families. *Journal of Sociology and Social Welfare* 33(1):93–114.

Linehan, M. 1993. *Cognitive Behavioral Treatment of Borderline Personality Disorder.* New York: Guilford.

Link, B. 1987. Understanding labeling effects in the area of mental disorders: An assessment of the effects of expectations of rejection. *American Sociological Review* 52(1):96–112.

Lipchik, E. 2002. *Beyond Techniques in Solution-Focused Therapy.* New York: Guilford.

Lipton, D., R. Martinson, and J. Weeks. 1974. *The Effectiveness of Correctional Treatment.* New York: Praeger.

Littell, J. 2001. Client participation and outcomes of intensive family preservation services. *Social Work Research* 25(2):103–114.

Littell, J. 2006a. Lessons from a systematic review of multisystemic therapy. *The Children and Youth Services Review* 27:445–463.

Littell, J. 2006b. The case for multisystemic therapy: Evidence or orthodoxy. *The Children and Youth Services Review* 28:458–472.

Littell, J., L. Alexander, and W. Reynolds. 2001. Client participation: Central and underinvestigated elements of intervention. *Social Service Review* 75(1):1–28.

Littell, J., L. Alexander, and W. Reynolds. 2001. Client participation and outcomes of intensive family preservation services. *Social Work Research* 25(2):103–114.

Littell, J. and H. Girvin. 2002. Stages of change: A critique. *Behavior Modification* 26:223–273.

Littell, J. and H. Girvin. 2004. Ready or not: Uses of the stages of change model in child welfare. *Child Welfare* 83(4):341–365.

Littell, J. and H. Girvin. 2006. Correlates of problem recognition and intentions to change among caregivers of abused and neglected children. *Child Abuse and Neglect* 30:1381–1399.

Littell, J. and J. Scheurman. 2002. What works best for whom? A closer look at intensive family preservation services. *The Children and Youth Services Review* 24:673–699.

Littell, J. H. and E. Tajima. 2000. A multilevel model of client participation in intensive family preservation services. *Social Service Review* 74(3):405–435.

Littrell, J. M., J. A. Malia, and M. Vanderwood. 1995. Single-session brief counseling in a high school. *Journal of Counseling and Development* 73:451–458.

Lohman, B. J., L. D. Pittman, R. L. Coley, and P. L. Chase-Landsdale. 2004. Welfare history, sanctions, and developmental outcomes among low-income children and youth. *Social Service Review* 78(1):41–73.

Lohn, M. 2005. Senate bills target relief for welfare recipients, farmers. *Star Tribune*, February 4, 2005. Retrieved from http://www.startribune.com/stories/587/5221795.html.

Lohrbach, S. and R. Sawyer. 2004. Creating a constructive practice: Family and professional partnership in high-risk child protection case conferences. *Protection Children* 19(2):26–35.

Lohrbach, S., R. Sawyer, J. Saugen, C. Astolfi, K. Schmitt, P. Worden, and M. Xaaji. 2005. Ways of working in child welfare: A perspective on practice. *Protecting Children* 20(2/3):93–100.

London, A. S., E. K. Scott, K. Edin, and V. Hunter. 2004. Welfare reform, work-family tradeoffs, and child well-being. *Family Relations* 53(2):148–158.

London, P. 1969. *Behavior Control.* New York: Harper and Row.

Longres, J. 1990. *Human Behavior in the Social Environment.* Itasca, IL: F. E. Peacock.

Lopez, G. E., P. Gurin, and B. A. Nagda. 1998. Education and understanding structural causes for group inequities. *Political Psychology* 19(2):305–329.

Luckhurst, P. 1985. Resistance and the "new" epistemology. *Journal of Strategic and Systemic Therapies* 4(1):3–11.

Lum, D. 2004. *Social Work Practice with People of Color. A Process-Stage Approach,* 5th ed. Pacific Grove, CA: Thomson-Brook/Coles.

MacKenzie, D., R. Brame, D. McDowall, and C. Soural. 1995. Boot camp prisons and recidivism in eight states. *Criminology* 33:327–357.

MacKenzie, R. G. 1991. Foreword. In *Adolescent Health Care* (2nd ed.), ed. L. S. Neinstein. Baltimore and Munich: Urban and Schwarzenberg.

Madden, R. G. 1998. *Legal Issues in Social Work, Counseling and Mental Health.* Thousand Oaks, CA: Sage.

Mahalik, J. 1994. Development of the client resistance scale. *Journal of Counseling Psychology* 41(1):58–68.

Maluccio, A. 1979. *Learning from Clients.* New York: Free Press.

Mann, R. E. and S. Rollnick. 1996. Motivational interviewing with a sex offender who believed he was innocent. *Behavioral and Clinical Psychotherapy* 24:127–134.

Margoda, C. 1995. La Guera. In *Race, Class and Gender: An Anthology* (2nd ed.), eds. M. L. Anderson and P. H. Collins, pp. 15–22. Belmont, CA: Wadsworth- Thomson Learning.

Margolin, G. 1982. Ethical and legal considerations in marital and family therapy. *American Psychologist* 37(7):794–795.

Margolin, L. 1997. *Under the Cover of Kindness: The Invention of Social Work.* Charlottesville: University Press of Virginia.

Marlatt, G., J. Baer, D. Kivlahan, L. Dimeff, M. Larimer, L. Quigley, J. Somers, and E. Williams. 1998. Screening and brief intervention for high-risk college student drinkers: Results from a two-year follow-up assessment. *Journal of Consulting and Clinical Psychology* 66(4):604–615.

Marsh, P. and G. Crow. 1998. *Family Group Conferences in Child Welfare.* Oxford: Blackwell Science.

Martin, K., M. Leary, and W. Rejeski. 2000. Self-presentational concerns in older adults: Implications for health and well-being. *Basic and Applied Social Psychology* 22(3):169–179.

Martin, R. 1981. Legal Issues in Preserving Client Rights. In *Preservation of Client Rights: A Handbook for Practitioners Providing Therapeutic, Educational and Rehabilitation Services,* eds. G. T. Hannah, W. P. Christian, and H. B. Clark, pp. 3–13. New York: Free Press.

Martinson, R. 1974. What works? Questions and answers about prison reform. *The Public Interest* 35:22–54.

Marwell, G. and D. Schmitt. 1967. Dimensions of compliance-gaining behavior: An empirical analysis. *Sociometry* 30:350–364.

Mary, N. 2005. Transformational leadership in human service organizations. *Administration in Social Work* 29(2):103–118.

Maxwell, G. and A. Morris. 2004. What Is the Place of Shame in Restorative Justice? In *Critical Issues in Restorative Justice*, eds. H. Zehr and B. Toews, pp. 133–142. Monsey, NY: Criminal Justice Press.

Maxwell, G. M. and A. Morris. 1993. *Family, Victims and Culture: Youth Justice in New Zealand.* Wellington, New Zealand: Social Policy Agenda and Institute of Criminology, Victoria, University of Wellington.

Mayer, J. and N. Timms. 1969. Clash in perspective between worker and client. *Social Casework* 50:32–40.

McCambridge, J. and J. Strang. 2003. Development of a structured generic drug intervention model for public health purposes: A brief application of motivational interviewing with young people. *Drug and Alcohol Review* 22:391–399.

McCambridge, J. and J. Strang. 2004. The efficacy of single-session motivational interviewing in reducing drug consumption and perceptions of drug-related risk and harm among young people: Results from a multi-site cluster randomized trial. *Addiction* 99:39–52.

McCold, P. and B. Wachtel. 1998. *The Bethlehem Pennsylvania Police Family Group Conferencing Project.* Pipersville, PA: Community Service Foundation. Retrieved 07.07.-7 online at http://fp.enter.net/restorativepractices/BPD.pdf.

McDermott, F. 1975. *Self-determination in Social Work.* London: Routledge-Kegan Paul.

McDonnell, L. 2004. *Seven Years of Welfare Reform: Weighing the Results.* Minneapolis, MN: The University of Minnesota Centers for Urban and Regional Affairs and Advanced Studies in Child Welfare.

McFarland, B. 1995. *Brief Therapy and Eating Disorders: A Practical Guide to Solution-Focused Work with Clients.* San Francisco: Jossey-Bass.

McFarland, D. 2001. Student resistance: How the formal and informal organization of classrooms facilitate everyday forms of student defiance. *American Journal of Sociology* 107(3):612–678.

McGowan, B. G., and E. M. Walsh. 2000. Policy challenges for child welfare in the new century. *Child Welfare* 79(1):11–27.

McGrath, R. J., ed. 1995. *Vermont Clinical Practices Guide for the Assessment and Treatment of Adult Sex Offenders.* Vermont Center for Prevention and Treatment of Sex Offenders, Burlington, VT.

McGuire, D. 1980. *A New American Justice.* Garden City, NY: Doubleday.

McGuire, J., ed. 1995. *What Works: Reducing Re-offending—Guidelines from Research and Practice.* Chichester: John Wiley.

McIvor, G. 1990. *Sanctions for Serious or Persistent Offenders.* Social Work Research Centre, University of Stirling.

McMahon, A. 1998. *Damned if You Do, Damned if You Don't: Working in Child Welfare.* Ashgate: Aldershot.

McNeece, C. and B. Thyer. 2004. Evidence-based practice and social work. *Journal of Evidence-Based Social Work* 1(1):7–25.

McNeill, F. 2003. Resistance Focused Probation Practice. In *Moving Probation Forward Evidence Arguments and Practice*, eds. Wing Hong Chui and M. Nellis, pp. 146–162. Essex, England: Pearson Longman.

McPhee, D. M. and L. R. Bronstein. 2003. The journey from welfare to work: Learning from women living in poverty. *Affilia* 18(1):34–48.

Meichenbaum, D. and D. Turk. 1987. *Facilitating Treatment Adherence.* New York: Plenum Press.

Melendez, M. P. and M. C. La Sala. 2006. Who's oppressing whom? Homosexuality, Christianity and social work. *Social Work* 51(4):371–377.

Melnick, G., G. De Leon, J. Hawke, N. Jainchill, and D. Kressel. 1997. Motivation and readiness for therapeutic community treatment among adolescents and adult substance abusers. *American Journal of Drug and Alcohol Abuse* 23:485–506.

Melton, G., J. Petrala, N. Poythress, and C. Slobogin. 1987. *Psychological Evaluations for the Courts*. New York: Guilford.

Mendonca, P. and S. Brehm. 1983. Effects of choice on behavioral treatment of overweight children. *Journal of Social and Clinical Psychology* 1(4):343–358.

Merton, R. 1980. Social structure and anomie. In *Theories of Deviance* (2nd ed.), eds. S. Traub and and C. Little, pp. 105–138. Itasca, IL: F. E. Peacock.

Miles, S. 2006. *Oath Betrayed: Torture, Medical Complicity and the War on Terror*. New York: Random House.

Milgram, D. and J. Rubin. 1992. Resisting resistance: Involuntary substance abuse group therapy. *Social Work with Groups* 15(1):95–110.

Milgram, S. 1963. Behavioral studies of obedience. *Journal of Abnormal and Social Psychology* 67:371–378.

Miller, D. and B. S. Carlton. 1985. The etiology and treatment of anorexia nervosa. *Adolescent Psychiatry* 12:219–232.

Miller, E. T., A. P. Turner, and G. A. Marlatt. 2001. The Harm Reduction Approach to the Secondary Prevention of Alcohol Problems in Adolescents and Young Adults: Considerations Across a Developmental Spectrum. In *Adolescents, Alcohol, and Substance Abuse*, eds. P. M. Monti, S. M. Colby, and T. A. O'Leary, pp. 58–79. New York: Guilford.

Miller, G. 1991. *Enforcing the Work Ethic: Rhetoric and Everyday Life in a Work Incentive Program*. Albany: State University of New York Press.

Miller, O. A. and R. J. Gaston. 2003. A model for culture-centered child welfare practice. *Child Welfare* 82:235–250.

Miller, S. 1983. Practice in Cross-Cultural Settings. In *Handbook of Clinical Social Work*, eds. A. Rosenblatt and D. Waldfogel, pp. 490–517. San Francisco: Jossey-Bass.

Miller, T., M. Cohen, and B. Wiersema. 1996. Victim Costs and Consequences: A New Look. National Institute of Justice, U.S. Department of Justice.

Miller, W. 1962. The impact of a total community delinquency control project. *Social Problems* 9:168–191.

Miller, W. 1989. *Handbook of Alcoholism Treatment Approaches*, eds. R. Hester and W. Miller. New York: Pergamon.

Miller, W. R. 1983. Motivational interviewing with problem drinkers. *Behavioral Psychotherapy* 11:147–172.

Miller, W. R. 1985. Motivation for treatment: A review with special emphasis on alcoholism. *Psychological Bulletin* 98:84–107.

Miller, W. R. 2001. Foreword. In *Adolescents, Alcohol, and Substance Abuse*, eds. P. M. Monti, S. M. Colby, and T. A. O'Leary, pp. x–xiii. New York: Guilford.

Miller, W. R., R. Benefield, and J. Tonigan. 1993. Enhancing motivation for change in problem drinking: A controlled comparison of two therapist styles. *Journal of Consulting and Clinical Psychology* 61(3):455–461.

Miller, W. R. and S. Rollnick. 2002. *Motivational Interviewing: Preparing People for Change*. New York: Guilford.

Miller, W. R. and V. C. Sanchez. 1993. Motivating Young Adults for Treatment and Lifestyle Change. In *Issues in Alcohol Use and Misuse by Young Adults*, ed. G. Howard, pp. 52–71. New York: Guilford.

Miller, W. R., R. G. Sovereign, and B. Krege. 1988. Motivational interviewing with problem drinkers: II. The drinker's check-up as a preventive intervention. *Behavioural Psychotherapy* 16:251–268.

Mills, C. W. 1971. *The Sociological Imagination.* New York: Penguin.

Ministry of Community and Social Services. 2000. *Risk Assessment Model for Child Protection in Ontario* (Revised). Toronto: Queen's Printer for Ontario.

Minnesota Department of Human Services. 2007, February. Welfare Reform Outcomes of Racial/Ethnic and Immigrant Groups in Minnesota. St. Paul: Author.

Monti, P. M., S. M. Colby, and T. A. O'Leary. 2001. *Adolescents, Alcohol, and Substance Abuse.* New York: Guilford.

Moore-Kirkland, J. 1981. Mobilizing Motivation: From Theory to Practice. In *Promoting Competence in Clients: A New/Old Approach to Social Work Practice,* ed. A. Maluccio, pp. 27–54. New York: Macmillan.

Mor Barak, M., J. Nissly, and A. Levin. 2001. Antecedents to retention and turnover among child welfare, social work and other human service employees: What can we learn from past research? A review and metanalysis. *Social Service Review* 75(4):625–661.

Morisee, D., L. Batra, L. Hess, R. Silverman, and P. Corrigan. 1996. A demonstration of a token economy for the real world. *Applied and Preventive Psychology* 5:41–46.

Morris, P. A. and L. A. Gennetian. 2003. Identifying the effects of income on children's development using experimental data. *Journal of Marriage and Family* 56:716–729.

Morton, T. 1999. The increasing colorization of America's child welfare system: The overrepresentation of African America. *Policy and Practice* 57(4):23–36.

Mullaly, R. 1997. *Structural Social Work: Ideology, Theory and Practice,* 2nd ed. Oxford: Oxford University Press.

Mullen, E. 2004. Facilitating Practitioner Use of Evidence-Based Practice. In *Evidence-Based Practice Manual: Research and Outcome Measures in Health and Human Services,* eds. A. Roberts and K. Yeager, pp. 205–210. New York: Oxford.

Mulroy, E. A. and M. B. Tamburo. 2004. Nonprofit organizations and welfare-to-work: Environmental turbulence and organizational change. *Administration in Social Work* 28(3/4):111–135.

Munson, C. E. 1995. Loss of control in the delivery of mental health services. *The Clinical Supervisor* 13(1):1–6.

Munson, C. E. 2002. *Clinical Social Work Supervision,* 3rd ed. New York: Hayworth Press.

Murdach, A. 1980. Bargaining and persuasion with non-voluntary clients. *Social Work* 25(6):458.

Murdach, A. D. 1996. Beneficence re-examined: Protective intervention in mental health. *Social Work* 41(1):26–32.

Murphy, C. and V. Baxter. 1997. Motivating batterers to change in the treatment context. *Journal of Interpersonal Violence* 12(4):607–619.

Murphy, C. and C. Eckhardt. 2005. *Treating the Abusive Partner: An Individualized Cognitive-Behavioral Approach.* New York: Guilford.

Murphy, J. J. 1996. *Solution-Focused Counseling in Middle and High School.* Alexandria, VA: American Counseling Association.

Murphy, J. J. 1996. Solution-Focused Brief Therapy in the School. In *Handbook of Solution-Focused Brief Therapy,* eds. S. D. Miller, M. A. Hubble, and B. L. Duncan, pp. 184–204. San Francisco: Jossey-Bass.

Murphy, J. J. and B. L. Duncan. 1997. *Brief Intervention for School Problems.* New York: Guilford.

Nagda, B. A., M. L. Spearmon, L. C. Holley, S. Harding, M. L. Blassone, D. Moise-Swenson, and S. De Mello. 1999. Intergroup dialogues: An innovative approach to teaching about diversity and justice in social work programs. *Journal of Social Work Education* 35(3):433–449.

National Association of Social Workers (NASW) Code of Ethics. 1999. http://www.socialworkers.org/pubs/code/code.asp (accessed October 3, 2008).

National Association of Social Workers (NASW). 2001. *Standards for Cultural Competence in Social Work Practice.* Washington, DC: NASW.

National Center for Health Statistics (NCHS). 2002. *Vital Statistics of the United States.* Washington, DC: U.S. Government Printing Office.

Nelsen, J. 1975. Dealing with resistance in social work practice. *Social Casework* 56:(10):587–592.

Newbeck, K. and N. Cazenave. 2001. *Welfare Racism.* New York: Routledge.

Newsome, S. 2004. Solution-focused brief therapy (SFBT) groupwork with at-risk junior high school students: Enhancing the bottom-line. *Research on Social Work Practice* 14:336–343.

Nickerson, P. 1995. Solution-focused group therapy. *Social Work* 40:132–133.

Nooe, R. 1980. A model for integrating theoretical approaches to deviance. *Social Work* 25(5):366–370.

Norcross, J. C., L. E. Beutler, and J. F. Clarkin. 1998. Prescriptive Eclectic Psychotherapy. In *Paradigms of Clinical Social Work*, Vol. 2, ed. R. A. Dorfman. New York: Brunner/Mazel.

Norman, E., ed. 2000. *Resiliency Enhancement: Putting the Strengths Perspective into Social Work Practice.* New York: Columbia University Press.

O'Connor, G. 1988. Case management: System and practice. *Social Casework* 69(2):97–106.

Office of National Drug Control Policy. 2003. *National Drug Control Strategy, Update* 2003. Rockville, MD: Author.

Ogawa, B. K. 1999. *Color of Justice. Culturally Sensitive Treatment of Minority Crime Victims,* 2nd ed. Boston: Allyn and Bacon.

O'Hare, T. 1996a. Court-ordered versus voluntary clients: Problem differences and readiness for change. *Social Work* 41(4):417–422.

O'Hare, T. 1996b. Readiness for change: Variation by intensity and domain of client distress. *Social Work Research* 20(1):13–18.

Okamoto, S. and C. Le Croy. 2004. Evidence-based practice and manualized treatment with children. In *Evidence-Based Practice Manual: Research and Outcome Measures in Health and Human Services,* eds. A. Roberts and K. Yeager, pp. 246–252. New York: Oxford University Press.

Okun, B. F., J. Fried, and M. L. Okun. 1999. *Understanding Diversity: A Learning-as-Practice Primer.* Pacific Grove, CA: Brooks/Cole.

Omnibus Budget Reconciliation Act of 1987. P.L. 100-203. http://www.sa.gov/.

O'Neill, J. V. 2004. Tragedies spark worker-safety awareness. *NASW News* 49(4):9.

Orme, J. 2002. Social work: Gender, care and justice. *British Journal of Social Work* 32: 799–814.

Osborne, C. J. 1999. Solution-focused strategies with involuntary clients: Practical applications for the school and clinical setting. *Journal of Humanistic Education and Development* 37(3):169–172.

Osgood, C. and P. Tannenbaum. 1955. The principle of consistency in the prediction of attitude change. *Psychological Review* 62:42–55.

Palmer, S. 1983. Authority: An essential part of practice. *Social Work* 28(2):120–125.

Palmer, S. E., R. A. Brown, and M. E. Barrera. 1992. Group treatment program for abusive husbands: Long-term evaluation. *American Journal of Orthopsychiatry* 62(2):276–283.

Pandya, V. and W. J. Gingerich. 2002. Group therapy intervention for male batterers: A micro-ethnographic study. *Health and Social Work* 27(1):47–55.

Panepinto, W. C., J. A. Garrett, W. R. Williford, and J. A. Prieke. 1982. A short-term group treatment model for problem drinking drivers. *Social Work with Groups* 5:33–40.

Parton, N. and P. O'Byrne. 2000. *Constructive Social Work: Towards a New Practice*. London: Macmillan.

Pazaratz, D. 2000. Task-centered child and youth care practice in residential treatment. *Residential Treatment for Children and Youth* 17(4):1–16.

Pearson, F., D. Lipton, C. Cleland, and D. Yee. 2002. The effects of behavioural/cognitive behavioural programs on recidivism. *Crime and Delinquency* 48(3):476–496.

Pecora, P., J. Whittaker, A. Maluccio, R. P. Barth, and R. D. Plotnick. 2000. *The Child Welfare Challenge: Policy, Practice, and Research*. New York: Aldine de Gruyter.

Pecora, P. J., K. R. Reed-Ashcraft, and R. S. Kirk. 2001. Family-centered Services: A Typology, Brief History, and Overview of Current Program Implementation. In *Balancing Family Centered Services and Child Well-being*, eds. E. Walton, P. Sandau-Beckler, and M. Mannes, pp. 1–33. New York: Columbia University Press.

Pence, E. and M. Paymar. 1993. *Education Groups for Men Who Batter: The Duluth Model*. New York: Springer.

Pence, E. and M. Shepard, eds. 1999. *Coordinating Community Responses to Domestic Violence: Lessons Learned from Duluth and Beyond*. Thousand Oaks, CA: Sage.

Pennell, J. and G. Burford. 2000. Family group decision making: Protecting children and women. *Child Welfare* 79(2):131–158.

Perloff, R. 1993. *The Dynamics of Persuasion*. Hillsdale, NJ: Lawrence Erlbaum.

Peterocelli, J. V. 2002. Processes and stages of change: Counseling with the transtheoretical model of change. *Journal of Counseling and Development* 80(1):22.

Peters, R., A. Haas, and M. Hunt. 2001. Treatment Dosage Effects in Drug Court Programs. In *Drug Courts in Operation: Current Research*, ed. J. Hennessy, pp. 63–72. New York: Haworth Press.

Peters, R. and M. Murrin. 2000. Effectiveness of treatment-based drug courts in reducing criminal recidivism. *Criminal Justice and Behavior* 27(1):72–96.

Peters, T. J., ed. 2001. Clinical Pathology. In *International Handbook of Alcohol Dependence and Problems*, eds. N. Heather, T. Peters, and T. Stockwell, pp. 593–603. New York: John Wiley.

Petr, C. G. 1998. *Social Work with Children and Their Families: Pragmatic Foundations*. New York: Oxford University Press.

Petrosino, A., C. Turbin-Petrosino, and J. Buechler. 2004. Scared straight and other juvenile awareness programs for preventing juvenile delinquency (Cochrane Review). In *The Cochrane Library*, issue 2. Chichester, UK: John Wiley.

Peyrot, M. 1985. Coerced voluntarism: The micro politics of drug treatment. *Urban Life* 13(4):345.

Pharr, S. 1988. *Homophobia: A Weapon of Sexism*. Iverness, CA: Chardon.

Pinsof, W. 1983. Integrative problem-solving therapy: Toward the synthesis of family and individual psychotherapies. *Journal of Marital and Family Therapy* 9(1):19–35.

Pirog-Good, M. and J. Stets-Kealey. 1985. Male batterers and battering prevention programs: A national survey. *Response* 9:8–12.

Poertner, J. 2006. Social administration and outcomes for consumers: What do we know? *Administration in Social Work* 30(2):11–24.

Poland, S. 1994. The role of school crisis intervention teams to prevent and reduce school violence and trauma. *School Psychology Review* 23(2):175–190.

Pollack, S. 2004. Anti-oppressive social work practice with women in prison: Discursive recon-strctions and alternative practices. *British Journal of Social Work* 34:692–707.

Popple, P. and F. Vecchiolla. 2007. *Child Welfare Social Work: An Introduction.* Boston: Pearson.

Powers, E. and H. Witmer. 1951. *An Experiment in the Prevention of Delinquency: The Cambridge-Somerville Youth Study.* New York: Columbia University Press.

Preston, M. S. 2004. Mandatory management training for newly hired child welfare supervisors: A divergence between management research and training practice? *Administration in Social Work* 28(2):81–97.

Prochaska, J. O. and C. C. DiClemente. 1982. Transtheoretical therapy: Toward a more inte-grative model of change. *Psychotherapy: Theory, Research and Practice* 19:276–288.

Prochaska, J. O. and C. C. DiClemente. 1984. *The Transtheoretical Approach: Crossing the Tradi-tional Boundaries of Therapy.* Homewood, IL: Dow Jones/Irwin.

Prochaska, J. O. and C. C. DiClemente. 1988. Toward a comprehensive model of change. In *Treating Addictive Behaviors,* eds. W. R. Miller and N. Heather. New York: Plenum Press.

Prochaska, J. O., C. C. DiClemente, and J. C. Norcross. 1992. In search of how people change. *American Psychologist* 47:1102–1114.

Prochaska, J., J. Norcross, and C. C. DiClemente. 1994. *Changing for Good.* Avon Books: New York.

Prochaska, J. O., W. F. Velicer, J. S. Rossi, M. G. Goldstein, B. H. Marcus, W. Rakowski, C. Fiore, L. L. Harlow, C. A. Redding, D. Rosenbloom, and S. R. Rossi. 1994. Stages of change and decisional balance for twelve problem behaviors. *Health Psychology* 13:39–46.

Proctor, E. K. and L. E. Davis. 1994. The challenge of racial difference: Skills for clinical prac-tice. *Social Work* 39(3):314–323.

Purdy, F. and N. Nickle. 1981. Practice principles for working with groups of men who batter. *Social Work with Groups* 4(3/4):111–122.

Putnam, M. L. 1995. Crisis intervention with adolescents with learning disabilities. *Focus on Exceptional Children* 28(2):1–24.

Racially disproportionate incarceration of drug offenders. 2000. *Human Rights Watch* 12, No. 2 (May):G.

RAND Health Research Highlights: Mental Health Case for Youth. 2001. Retrieved from http://www.rand.org/publications/RB/RB4541/ (accessed January 31, 2004).

Ratnasuriya, R. H., I. Eisler, G. I. Szmukler, and G.F.M. Russell. 1991. Anorexia nervosa: Out-come and prognostic factors after 20 years. *British Journal of Psychiatry* 158:495–502.

Rawlinson, J. G. 1970. *Creative Thinking and Brainstorming.* London: British Institute of Management.

Raynor, P. 1978. Compulsory persuasion: A problem for correctional social work. *British Journal of Social Work* 8(4):411–424.

Raynor, P. 2003. Research in Probation: From Nothing Works to "What Works." In *Moving Probation Forward Evidence Arguments and Practice,* eds. W. H. Chui and M. Nellis, pp. 74–91. Essex, England: Pearson Longman.

Reamer, F. G. 1983. The concept of paternalism in social work. *Social Service Review* 57(2):254–271.

Reamer, F. G. 1987. Informed consent in social work. *Social Work* 32(5):425–429.

Reamer, F. G. 1994. *Social Work Malpractice and Liability: Strategies for Prevention.* New York: Columbia University Press.

Reamer, F. G. 1999. *Social Work Values and Ethics,* 2nd ed. New York: Columbia University Press.

Reamer, F. G. 2000. The social work ethics audit: A risk-management strategy. *Social Work* 45(4):355–366.

Reamer, F. G. 2001a. *The Social Work Ethics Audit*. Washington, DC: National Association of Social Workers.

Reamer, F. G. 2001b. *Ethics Education in Social Work*. Alexandria, VA: Council on Social Work Education.

Reamer, F. G. 2003a. Boundary issues in social work: Managing dual relationships. *Social Work* 48(1):121–134.

Reamer, F. G. 2003b. *Social Work Malpractice and Liability*, 2nd ed. New York: Columbia.

Reamer, F. G. 2005. Ethical and legal standards in social work: Consistency and conflict. *Families in Society* 86(2):163–169.

Reardon, K. 1991. *Persuasion in Practice*. Newbury Park, CA: Sage.

Regehr, C. and B. Antle. 1997. Coercive influences: Informed consent in court-mandated social work practice. *Social Work* 42(3):300–306.

Reichman, N. E., J. O. Teitler, and M. A. Curtis. 2005. TANF sanctioning and hardship. *Social Service Review* 79:216–235.

Reid, D. 1984. Child protective services: What happens when our values conflict with those of our clients? *Practice Digest* 6(4):15–16.

Reid, K. 1986. The use of confrontation in group treatment: Attack or challenge? *Clinical Social Work Journal* 14:224–237.

Reid, W. 1978. *The Task-Centered System*. New York: Columbia University Press.

Reid, W. 1982. Understanding resistance: Seven social workers debate. *Practice Digest* 5(1):10–11.

Reid, W. 1985. *Family Problem Solving*. New York: Columbia University Press.

Reid, W. 1992. *Task Strategies: An Empirical Approach to Clinical Social Work*. New York: Columbia University Press.

Reid, W. 2000. *The Task Planner: An Intervention Resource for Human Service Professionals*. New York: Columbia University Press.

Reid, W. and P. Hanrahan. 1982. Recent evaluations of social work: Grounds for optimism. *Social Work* 27:328–340.

Reid, W. J. 2002. Knowledge for direct social work practice: An analysis of trends. *Social Service Review* (March):6–33.

Rein, M. and S. White. 1981. Knowledge for Practice. In *Handbook of the Social Services*, eds. N. Gilbert and H. Specht, p. 624. Englewood Cliffs, NJ: Prentice-Hall.

Rempel, M. and C. Depies-Di Stefano. 2001. Predictors of Engagement in Court-Mandated Treatment: Findings at the Brooklyn Treatment Court, 1996–2000. In *Drug Courts in Operation: Current Research*, pp. 87–124. New York: Haworth Press.

Reynolds, P. 1982. *Ethics and Social Science Research*. Englewood Cliffs, NJ: Prentice-Hall.

Rhodes, M. 1986. *Ethical Dilemmas in Social Work Practice*. Boston: Routledge and Kegan Paul.

Richards, S., G. Ruch, and P. Trevithick. 2005. Communication skills training for practice: The ethical dilemma for social work education. *Social Work Education* 24(4):409–422.

Ritchie, M. 1986. Counseling the involuntary client. *Journal of Counseling and Development*. 64(April):516–518.

Roans, M. and K. Hoagwood. 2000. School-based mental health services: A research review. *Clinical Child and Family Psychology Review* 3(4):223–241.

Roberts, A. R. 1982. A National Survey of Batterers. In *The Abusive Partner*, ed. M. Roy, pp. 230–243. New York: Van Nostrand.

Roberts, A. R. 1998. *Battered Women and Their Families: Intervention Strategies and Treatment Approaches*, 2nd ed. New York: Springer.

Roberts, A. R., ed. 2000. An Overview of Crisis Theory and Crisis Intervention. In *Crisis Intervention Handbook: Assessment, Treatment, and Research*, 2nd ed., pp. 3–30. New York: Oxford University Press.

Roberts, D. 2002. Racial disproportionality in the U.S. child welfare system: Documentation, research on causes and promising practices. Working paper no. 4. Baltimore, MD: Annie E. Casey Foundation.

Robin, M. and R. Spires. 1983. Drawing the line: Deviance in a cross-cultural perspective. *International Journal of Group Tensions* 13:1–4, 106–131.

Robinson, G. 2003. Risk and Risk Assessment. In *Moving Probation Forward Evidence Arguments and Practice*, eds. W. H. Chui and M. Nellis, pp. 108–128. Essex, England: Pearson Longman.

Robinson, T. and P. Davis-Kennington. 2002. Holding up half the sky: Women and psychological resistance. *Journal of Humanistic Counseling, Education and Development* 41:164–177.

Rock, C. and S. Collins. 1987. Contract or con trick? *British Journal of Social Work* 17:199–211.

Rodenborg, N. A. 2004. Services to African American children in poverty: Institutional discrimination in child welfare? *Journal of Poverty: Innovations on Social, Political and Economic Inequalities* 8(3):109–130.

Rodgers, H. R., Jr., and L. Payne. 2007. Child poverty in the American states: The impact of welfare reform, economics, and demographics. *The Policy Studies Journal* 35(1):1–21.

Roffers, T. and M. Waldo. 1983. Empathy and confrontation related to group counseling outcomes. *Journal for Specialists in Group Work* 8(3):106–113.

Rohrbaugh, M. 1999, June. Demand-withdraw interaction and the ironic maintenance of alcoholism. Symposium conducted at the meeting of the American Psychological Society, Denver, CO.

Rohrbaugh, M. and V. Shoham. 2001. Brief therapy based on interrupting ironic processes: The Palo Alto model. *Clinical Psychology: Science and Practice* 8:6–81.

Rohrbaugh, M., H. Tennen, S. Press, and L. White. 1981. Compliance, defiance and therapeutic paradox: Guidelines for strategic use of paradoxical interventions. *American Journal of Orthopsychiatry* 51(3):454–467.

Roloff, M. and G. Miller. 1968. *Persuasion: New Directions in Theory and Research*. London: Sage.

Rooney, R. H. 1977. Adolescent Groups in Public Schools. In *Task-Centered Practice*, eds. W. J. Reid and L. Epstein, pp. 168–182. New York: Columbia University Press.

Rooney, R. H. 1981. A Task-Centered Reunification Model for Foster Care. In *The Challenge of Partnership: Working with the Parents of Children in Foster Care*, eds. A. Maluccio A. and P. Sinanoglu, pp. 101–116. New York: Child Welfare League of America.

Rooney, R. H. 1992. Strategies for Work with Involuntary Clients, 1st ed. New York: Columbia University Press.

Rooney, R. H. 2000. How can I use authority effectively and engage family members? In *Handbook of Child Protection Practice*, eds. H. Dubowitz and D. DePanfilis, pp. 44–46. Thousand Oaks, CA: Sage.

Rooney, R. H. 2002. Working with involuntary clients. In *Social Workers' Desk Reference*, eds. A. Roberts and G. Greene, pp. 710–713. Oxford: Oxford University Press.

Rooney, R. H. and A. A. Bibus. 1995. Multiple lenses: Ethnically sensitive practice with involuntary clients who are having difficulties with drugs or alcohol. *Journal of Multicultural Social Work* 4(2):59–73.

Rooney, R. H. and A. A. Bibus. 2000. Clinical Practice with Involuntary Clients in Community Settings. In *Social Work Practice: Treating Common Client Problems*, eds. H. E. Briggs and K. Corcoran, pp. 393–406. Chicago: Lyceum Books.

Rooney, R. H. and A. A. Bibus. 2001. Clinical practice with involuntary clients in community settings. In *Social Work Practice: Treating Common Client Problems*, eds. H. E. Briggs and K. Corcoran, pp. 391–406. Chicago: Lyceum Books.

Rooney, R. H. and M. Chovanec. 2004. Social Work with Involuntary Groups. In *Handbook of Social Work with Groups*, eds. C. D. Garvin, M. J. Galinsky, and L. M. Gutierrez, pp. 212–226. New York: Guilford.

Rose, S. 1998. *Group Therapy with Troubled Youth: A Cognitive-Behavioral Interactive Approach.* Thousand Oaks, CA: Sage.

Rose, S. and B. Black. 1985. *Advocacy and Empowerment: Mental Health Care in the Community.* Boston: Routledge and Kegan Paul.

Rose, S. R. and M. F. Fatout. 2003. *Social Work Practice with Children and Adolescents.* New York: Pearson.

Rosenberg, C. and J. Liftik. 1976. Use of coercion in the outpatient treatment of alcoholism. *Journal of Studies on Alcohol* 37:58–62.

Rosenfeld, B. 1992. Court-ordered treatment of spouse abuse. *Clinical Psychology Review* 12:205–226.

Rouse v. Cameron, 125 U.S. App. D.C. 366, 373 F.2d 451 (1966).

Rowan, T. and B. O'Hanlon. 1999. *Solution-Oriented Therapy for Chronic and Severe Mental Illness.* New York: John Wiley.

Roy, V., D. Turcotte, L. Montminny, and J. Lindsay. 2005. Therapeutic factors at the beginning of the intervention process in groups for men who batter. *Small Group Research* 36(1):106–133.

Rozovsky, F. 1987. *Consent to Treatment.* Boston: Little, Brown.

Rubin, A. 1975. Practice effectiveness: More grounds for optimism. *Social Work* 30(6):469–476.

Russell, M. 1995. *Confronting Abusive Beliefs: Group Treatment for Abusive Men.* Thousand Oaks, CA: Sage.

Ryder, R. and R. Tepley. 1993. No more Mr. Nice Guy: Informed consent and benevolence in marital family therapy. *Family Relations* 42:145–147.

Sackett, D., S. Straus, W. Richardson, W. Rosenberg, and R. Haynes. 2000. *Evidence-Based Medicine: How to Practice and How to Teach EBM*, 2nd ed. Edinburgh, UK: Churchill-Levigness.

Sackett, D. L., W. Rosenberg, J. Muir-Gray, R. Haynes, and W. Richardson. 1996. Evidence-based medicine: What it is and what it isn't. *British Medical Journal* 312:71–72.

Sadoff, R. 1982. *Legal Issues in the Care of Psychiatric Patients: A Guide for the Mental Health Professional.* New York: Springer.

Sagarin, E. 1975. *Deviants and Deviance.* New York: Praeger.

Saleeby, D., ed. 1996. The strength perspective in social work practice: Extensions and cautions. *Social Work* 41(3):296–305.

Saltmarsh, R. 1976. Client resistance in talk therapies. *Psychotherapy: Theory, Research and Practice* 13:34–39.

Saltzman, A. and K. Proch. 1990. *Law in Social Work Practice.* Chicago: Nelson-Hall.

Salus, M. 2004. *Supervising Child Protective Services Caseworkers.* Washington DC: U.S. Department of Health and Human Services.

Sanford, J. and B. Arrigo. 2005. Lifting the cover on drug courts: Evaluation findings and policy concerns. *International Journal of Offender Therapy and Comparative Criminology* 49(3):23–44.

Saunders, D. 1982. Counseling the Violent Husband. In *Innovations in Clinical Practice*, Vol. 1, eds. D. A. Keller and L. G. Ritt, p. 20. Sarasota, FL: Professional Resource Exchange.

Saunders, D. 1984. Husbands who batter. *Social Casework* 65(June):347–353.

Saunders, D. 1996. Feminist-cognitive-behavioral and process-psychodynamic treatments for men who batter: Interaction of abuser traits and treatment models. *Violence and Victims* 11:393–414.

Schein, E. H., I. Schneier, and C. H. Barker. 1961. *Coercive Persuasion: A Socio-Psychological Analysis of American Civilian Prisoners by the Chinese Communists.* New York: W. W. Norton.

Scheurman, J., T. L. Rzepnicki, and J. Littell. 1994. *Putting Families First: An Experiment in Family Preservation.* New York: Aldine de Gruyter.

Scheyett, A. 2006. Danger and opportunity: Challenges in teaching evidence-based practice in the social work curriculum. *Journal of Teaching in Social Work* 26(1/2):19–29.

Schlenker, B. and S. Wowra. 2003. Carryover effects of being socially transparent or impenetrable on strategic self-presentation. *Journal of Personality and Social Psychology* 85(5):871–880.

Schlosberg, S. and R. Kagan. 1988. Practice strategies for engaging chronic multi-problem families. *Social Casework* 69:3–9.

Schmitz, C. L., C. Stakeman, and J. Sisneros. 2001. Educating professionals for practice in a multicultural society: Understanding oppression and valuing diversity. *Families in Society, The Journal of Contemporary Human Services* 82(6):612–622.

Schopler, J. H. and M. Galinsky. 1981. When groups go wrong. *Social Work* 26:424–429.

Schneider, R. L. and L. Lester. 2001. *Social Work Advocacy.* Belmont, CA: Brooks/Cole.

Schroeder, L. 1995. *The Legal Environment of Social Work.* Revised edition. Washington, National Association of Social Workers.

Schultz, J., L. Brown, and R. Butler. 1996, November. *Promoting safer sex among HIV-positive youth.* Abstract presented at the International Conference on AIDS Education, Atlanta, GA.

Schwam, K. 1998. The phenomenon of compassion fatigue in perioperative nursing. *Association of Operating Home Nurses Journal* 68:642–648.

Schwartz, W. 1976. Between Client and System: The Mediating Function. In *Theories of Social Work with Group*, eds. R. R. Roberts and H. Northen, pp. 186–188. New York: Columbia University Press.

Scott, J. 2006. Job satisfaction among TANF leavers. *Journal of Sociology and Social Welfare* 33(3):127–149.

Seabury, B. 1976. The contract: Uses, abuses and limitations. *Social Work* 21:16–21.

Seabury, B. 1979. Negotiating sound contracts with clients. *Public Welfare* 38:33–38.

Seccombe, K. 1999. *"So You Think I Drive a Cadillac?" Welfare Recipients' Perspective on the System and Its Reform.* Boston: Allyn and Bacon.

Seibel, D. and E. Dowd. 1999. Reactance and therapeutic noncompliance. *Cognitive Therapy and Research* 23(4):373–379.

Selekman, M. 1999. The solution-oriented parenting group revisited. *Journal of Systemic Therapies* 18:5–23.

Sheafor, B. W. and C. R. Horejsi. 2003. *Techniques and Guidelines for Social Work Practice.* New York: Allyn and Bacon.

Sheppard, V. B. and R. Benjamin-Coleman. 2001. Determinants of service placements for youth with serious emotional and behavioral disturbances. *Community Mental Health Journal* 37(1):53–65.

Sherman, W. R. and S. Wenocur. 1983. Empowering public welfare workers through mutual support. *Social Work* 28:375–379.

Shields, S. A. 1986. Busted and branded: Group work with substance abusing adolescents in schools. *Social Work with Groups* 9:61–81.

Shireman, C. and F. Reamer. 1986. *Rehabilitating Juvenile Justice.* New York: Columbia University Press.

Shoham, V. and M. Rohrbaugh. 1997. Interrupting ironic processes. *Psychological Science* 8:151–153.

Shoham-Salomon, V. 1989. You're changed if you do, changed if you don't: Mechanisms underlying paradoxical interventions. *Journal of Consulting and Clinical Psychology* 57:590–598.

Shonfeld-Ringel, S. 2001. A reconceptualization of the working alliance in cross-cultural practice with non-Western clients: Integrating relational perspectives and multicultural theories. *Clinical Social Work Journal* 29(1):53–64.

Showalter, D. and C. Williams. 1980. Marital and family counseling in prisons. *Social Work* 2(5):224–228.

Shulman, L. 1999. *The Skills of Helping Individuals and Groups,* 4th ed. Itasca, IL: F. E. Peacock.

Shulman, L. 1993. *Interactional Supervision.* Washington, DC: National Association of Social Workers.

Shulman, L. 1995. Supervision and Consultation. In *Encyclopedia of Social Work* (19th ed.), editor-in-chief, R. L. Edwards, pp. 2373–2379. Washington, DC: National Association of Social Workers.

Shupe, A., W. A. Stacey, and L. R. Hazelwood. 1987. *Violent Men, Violent Couples.* Lexington, MA: Lexington Books.

Silvergleid, C. S. and E. S. Mankowski. 2006. How batterer intervention programs work: Participant and facilitator accounts of processes of change. *Journal of Interpersonal Violence* 21:139–159.

Simons, R. 1982. Strategies for exercising influence. *Social Work* 27(3):268–274.

Simons, R. and S. Aigner. 1985. *Practice Principles: A Problem-Solving Approach to Social Work.* New York: Macmillan.

Singer, M. T. and J. Lalich. 1996. *Cults in Our Midst: The Hidden Menace in Our Everyday Lives.* San Francisco: Jossey-Bass.

Sjostrom, S. 2006. Invocation of coercion context in compliance communication-power dynamics in psychiatric care. *International Journal of Law and Psychiatry* 29:36–47.

Skickel, S. A. and K. M. Satchwell. 1991. The school counselor and discipline: A three-state survey. *School Counselor* 39:111–115.

Sklare, G. 1997. *Brief Counseling That Works: A Solution-Focused Approach for School Counselors,* pp. 43–64. Thousand Oaks, CA: Corwin Press.

Slonim-Nevo, V. 1996. Clinical practice: Treating the non-voluntary client. *International Social Work* 39:117–129.

Smith, R. and R. Seitzer. 2002. *Race, Class and Culture.* Albany, NY: SUNY Press.

Smith, T. E. 1985. Group work with adolescent drug abusers. *Social Work with Groups* 8(1):55–63.

Snyder, L. 1989. Health care needs of the adolescent: Position paper. *Annals of Internal Medicine* 110(11):930–935.

Solomon, B. 1983. Value issues in working with minority clients. In *Handbook of Clinical Social Work,* eds. A. Rosenblatt and D. Waldfogel, pp. 866–887. San Francisco: Jossey-Bass.

Solomon, R. L. 1977. An opponent process theory of acquired motivation: The affective dynamics of addiction. In *Psychopathology. Experimental Methods,* eds. J. D. Maser and M. E. P. Seligman, pp. 66–103. San Francisco: Freeman.

Specht, H. and R. Specht. 1986. Social work assessment: Paths to clienthood: Part I. *Social Casework* 67:525–533.

Spencer, P. C. and S. Munch. 2003. Client violence toward social workers: The role of management in community mental health programs. *Social Work* 48(4):532–544.

Sprenkle D. H. and C. L. Storm. 1983. Divorce therapy outcome research: A substantive and methodological review. *Journal of Marital and Family Therapy* 9(12):39–59.

Springer, D. W., C. Lynch, and A. Rubin. 2000. Effects of a solution-focused mutual aid group for Hispanic children of incarcerated parents. *Child and Adolescent Social Work Journal* 17(6):431–442.

Stalans, L. 2004. Adult sex offenders on community supervision. *Criminal Justice and Behavior* 31(5):564–608.

Stalker, C. A., J. E. Levene, and N. F. Cody. 1999. Solution-focused brief therapy—One model fits all? *Families in Society: The Journal of Contemporary Human Services* 80(5):468–477.

Stanton, M. D. 1980. Family treatment approaches to drug abuse problems: A review. *Family Process* 18:251–280.

Stein, T. 1987. The vulnerability of child welfare agencies to class-action suits. *Social Service Review* 61(December):636–654.

Stein, T., E. Gambrill, and K. Wiltse. 1978. *Children in Foster Homes: Achieving Continuity of Care.* New York: Praeger.

Stein, T. and T. Rzepnicki. 1983. *Decision Making at Child Welfare Intake: A Handbook for Practitioners.* New York: Child Welfare League of America.

Stephens, R. S., R. A. Roffman, S. A. Fearer, C. Williams, J. F. Picciano, and R. S. Burke. 2004. The marijuana check-up: Reaching users who are ambivalent about change. *Addiction* 99(10):1323–1332.

Stephens, S. A. 2001. The effectiveness of motivational enhancement therapy in adolescent smoking cessation. Dissertation Abstracts International: Section B: *The Sciences and Engineering*, Vol. 62, 2–B: University Microfilms International.

Sterling, E. 2004. Drug policy: A challenge of values. *Journal of Religion and Spirituality* 24(1/2):51–81.

Stevens, A., D. Burto, W. Heckmann, V. Kerschl, K. Oeuvray, M. Van Ooyen, E. Steffan, and A. Uchtenhagen. 2005. Quasi-compulsory treatment of drug dependent offenders: An international literature review. *Substance Abuse and Misuse* 40:269–283.

Stewart, P. 2004. Afrocentric approaches to working with African American families. *Families in Society, The Journal of Contemporary Human Services* 85(2):221–228.

Stewart, S. and C. Anderson. 1984. Resistance revisited: Tales of my death have been greatly exaggerated (Mark Twain). *Family Process* 23(March):17–20.

Stolz, S., L. Wienckowski, and B. Brown. 1975. Behavior modification: A perspective on critical issues. *American Psychologist* 30(11):1027–1048.

Stosny, S. 1994. Shadows of the heart: A dramatic video for the treatment resistance of spouse abusers. *Social Work* 39(6):686–694.

Stosny, S. 1995. *Treating Attachment Abuse: A Compassion Approach.* New York: Springer.

Strand, V. C. and L. Badger. 2007. A clinical consultation model for child welfare supervisors. *Child Welfare* 86(1):79–98.

Streeter, C. L. and C. Franklin. 2002. Standards for school social work in the 21st century. In *Social Worker's Desk Reference*, eds. A. Roberts and G. Greene, pp. 612–618. New York: Oxford University Press.

Strom-Gottfried, K. 1998. Informed consent meets managed care. *Health and Social Work* 23(1):25–33.

Strom-Gottfried, K. and K. Corcoran. 1998. Confronting ethical dilemmas in managed care: Guidelines for students and faculty. *Journal of Social Work Education* 34(1):109–119.

Strom-Gottfried, K. and N. Mowbray. 2006. Who heals the helper? Facilitating the social worker's grief. *Families in Society* 87(1):9–15.

Sturkie, K. 1986. Frameworks for comparing approaches to family therapy. *Social Casework* 67:613–621.

Sullivan, D. and L. Tifft. 2004. What Are the Implications of Restorative Justice for Society and Our Lives? In *Critical Issues in Restorative Justice*, eds. H. Zehr and B. Toews, pp. 391–404. Monsey, NY: Criminal Justice Press.

Surgenor, L. 2003. Treatment coercion: Listening carefully to client and clinician experiences. *International Journal of Law and Psychiatry* 26:709–712.

Swanson, J., M. Swartz, E. Elbogen, R. Wagner, and B. Burns. 2003. Effects of involuntary outpatient commitment on subjective quality of life in persons with severe mental illness. *Behavioral Sciences and the Law* 21:473–491.

Syers-McNairy, M. 1990. *Women Who Leave Violent Relationships: Getting On with Life.* Doctoral dissertation. School of Social Work, University of Minnesota.

Taft, C. T., C. M. Murphy, J. D. Elliott, and T. M. Morrel. 2001. Attendance enhancing procedures in group counseling for domestic abusers. *Journal of Counseling Psychology* 48(1):51–60.

Taft, C. T., C. M. Murphy, P. H. Musser, and N. Remington. 2004. Personality, interpersonal and motivational predictors of the working alliance in group cognitive behavioral therapy for partner violent men. *Journal of Counseling and Clinical Psychology* 72(2):349–354.

Tam, T. and L. Mong. 2005. Job stress, perceived inequity and burnout among school social workers in Hong Kong. *International Social Work* 48(4):467–483.

Tarasoff v. the Regents of the University of California, 17 Cal. 3d 425, 131 Cal. Rptr. 14, 551 P. 2nd 334 1976.

Tatar, M. 2001. Counsellors' perceptions of adolescence. *British Journal of Guidance and Counseling* 29(2):213–231.

Tavantzis, T., M. Tavantzis, L. Brown, and M. Rohrbaugh. 1985. Home-Based Structural Family Therapy for Delinquents at Risk of Placement. In *Handbook of Adolescent and Family Treatment*, eds. M. P. Mirkin and S. L. Koman, pp. 69–88. New York: Gardner.

Taylor, M. F. and K. J. Bentley. 2005. Professional dissonance: Colliding values and job tasks in mental health practice. *Community Mental Health Journal* 41(4):469–480.

Taylor, M. J. and A. S. Barusch. 2004. Personal, family, and multiple barriers of long-term welfare recipients. *Social Work* 49(2):175–183.

Teen Parenting Service Network. 2005. Year in review: Fiscal year 2005. Chicago, IL: UCAN.

Tevyaw, T. O. and P. M. Monti. 2004. Motivational enhancement and other brief interventions for adolescent substance abuse: Foundations, applications, and evaluations. *Addiction* 99:63–75.

Theander, S. 1985. Outcome and prognosis in anorexia nervosa and bulimia: Some results of previous investigations, compared with those of a Swedish long-term study. *Journal of Psychiatric Research* 19:493–508.

Thibaut, J. and H. Kelley. 1959. *The Social Psychology of Groups.* New York: John Wiley.

Thio, A. 1978. *Deviant Behavior.* Boston: Houghton-Mifflin.

Thomas, E. and M. Yoshioka. 1989. Spouse interventive confrontation in unilateral family therapy for alcohol abuse. *Social Casework* 70:340–347.

Thomas, E. J., C. Santa, D. Bronson, and D. Oyserman. 1987. Unilateral brief therapy with the spouses of alcoholics. *Journal of Social Service Research* 10:145–162.

Thomas, H. and T. Caplan. 1999. Spinning the group process wheel: Effective facilitation techniques for motivating involuntary client groups. *Social Work with Groups* 2(4):3–21.

Thomlison, B. 2003. Characteristics of evidence-based child maltreatment interventions. *Child Welfare* 82:541–569.

Thyer, B. and L. Myers. 2000. Approaches to Behavioral Change. In *The Handbook of Social Work Direct Practice*, eds. P. Allen-Meares and C. Garvin, pp. 197–216. Thousand Oaks, CA: Sage.

Tober, G. 1991. Motivational Interviewing with Young People. In *Motivational Interviewing: Preparing People to Change Addictive Behavior*, eds. W. R. Miller and S. Rollnick, pp. 248–259. New York: Guilford.

Todd, T. 2000. An essay for practitioners—Solution focused strategic parenting of challenging teens: A class for parents. *Family Relations* 49(2):165–168.

Togo, P. 2006. *The Nexus of Parenting Practices and Acculturation Challenges among African Immigrants and Refugees in the United States.* Doctoral dissertation. School of Social Work, University of Minnesota, St. Paul, MN.

Tohn, S. L. and J. A. Oshlag. 1996. Solution-Focused Therapy with Mandated Clients: Cooperating with the Uncooperative. In *Handbook of Solution-Focused Brief Therapy*, eds. S. D. Miller, M. A. Hubble, and B. L. Duncan, pp. 152–183. San Francisco: Jossey-Bass.

Tolman, R. and L. Bennett. 1990. A review of quantitative research on men who batter. *Journal of Interpersonal Violence* 5:87–118.

Tolman, R. M. and G. Bhosley. 1987. A comparison of two types of pregroup preparation for men who batter. *Journal of Social Service Research* 13:33–44.

Tolson, E. R. 1981. Toward a Metamodel for Eclectic Family Practice. In *Models of Family Treatment*, eds. E. R. Tolson and W. J. Reid, pp. 332–354. New York: Columbia.

Townsend, B. 2000. The disproportionate discipline of African American learners and related school suspension and experience. *Exceptional Children* 66:381–391.

Trattner, W. I. 1999. *From Poor Law to Welfare State: A History of Social Welfare in America*, 6th ed. New York: Free Press.

Trotter, C. 1990. Probation can work: A research study using volunteers. *Australian Journal of Social Work* 43(2):13–18.

Trotter, C. 1993. *The Effective Supervision of Offenders.* Unpublished PhD thesis. La Trobe University, Melbourne.

Trotter, C. 1996a. The impact of different supervision practices in community corrections. *Australian and New Zealand Journal of Criminology* 29(1):29–46.

Trotter C. 1996b. Community corrections—Punishment or welfare. Book review essay. *International Criminal Justice Review* 6:121–130.

Trotter, C. 1999a. Don't throw the baby out with the bath water—In defence of problem solving. *Australian Social Work* 52(4):51–55.

Trotter, C. 1999b. *Working with Involuntary Clients.* London: Sage.

Trotter, C. 2000. Social work education, pro-social orientation and effective probation practice. *Probation Journal* 47(4):256–261.

Trotter, C. 2002. Worker skill and client outcome in child protection. *Child Abuse Review* 11:38–50.

Trotter, C. 2004. *Helping Abused Children and Their Families: Towards an Evidence-Based Practice Model.* Sydney: Allen Unwin.

Trotter, C. 2006. *Working with Involuntary Clients: A Guide to Practice*, 2nd ed. London: Sage.

Tsui, M.-S. 1997. Empirical research on social work supervision: The state of the art 1970–1995. *Journal of Social Services Research* 23(2):39–54.

Tsui, M.-S. 2005. *Social Work Supervision: Contexts and Concepts.* Thousand Oaks, CA: Sage.

Turkat, I. and V. Meyer. 1982. The Behavior Analytic Approach. In *Resistance: Psychodynamic and Behavioral Approaches,* ed. P. Wachtel, pp. 157–184. New York: Plenum Press.

Turnell, A. 2006. Constructive child protection practice: An oxymoron or news of difference? *Journal of Systemic Therapies* 25(2):3–12.

Turnell, A. and S. Edwards. 1999. *Signs of Safety: A Solution and Safety Oriented Approach to Child Protection.* New York: W. W. Norton.

Turner, L. and W. Shera. 2005. Empowerment of human service workers: Beyond intra-organizational strategies. Worker empowerment. *Administration in Social Work* 29(3):79–94.

Tuszynski, A. 1985. Group treatment that helps abusive or neglectful parents. *Social Casework* 66:55–56.

Tweedie, J. 2001. Sanctions and Exits: What States Know About Families that Leave Welfare Because of Sanctions and Time Limits. In *For Better and for Worse: Welfare Reform and the Well-being of Children and Families,* eds. G. J. Duncan and P. L. Chase-Landsdale, pp. 81–99. New York: Russell Sage Foundation.

Tyler, T. R. 1989. The psychology of procedural justice: A test of the group value model. *Journal of Personality and Social Psychology* 57(5):830–838.

Tyuse, S. and D. Linhorst. 2005. Drug courts and mental health courts: Implications for social work. *Health and Social Work* 30(3):233–240.

Understanding and addressing racial disproportionality in the front end of the child welfare system. 2005. *Evidence for Practice* 1 (July); available at http://cssr.berkeley.edu/bassc/public/dispro_summ.pdf (accessed 10/10/08).

Up and out: A jobs strategy that works. *Star Tribune.* March 26, 2005, A-12.

The Urban Institute. 2006, June. A decade of welfare reform: Facts and figures. Washington, DC: Author.

U.S. Census Bureau. 2003. http://www.census.gov/hhes/www/poverty/histpov/hstpov4.html.

U.S. Department of Health and Human Services, Substance Abuse and Mental Health Services. 1995. *National Household Survey on Drug Abuse: Population Estimates 1994.* Washington, DC: Author.

U.S. Department of Justice. 2007, April 27. Family group conferencing. Restorative Justice Fact Sheet: Office of Justice Programs, National Institute of Justice, Office for Victims of Crime, National Institute of Corrections, and Office of Juvenile Justice and Delinquency Prevention: U.S. Department of Justice. Retrieved from http://www.ojp.usdoj.gov/nij/publications/rest-just/CH5/5_grpcnf.htm (accessed July 6, 2007).

Usher, C. 2004. Measuring and Evaluating Effectiveness of Services to Families and Children. In Roberts, A. and Yeager, *Evidence-Based Practice Manual: Research and Outcome Measures in Health and Human Services,* pp. 423–430. New York: Oxford University Press.

Vance, J. and P. Elofson. 1999. *Family Group Conferences: Implementation with Native American Families.* Seattle, WA: Northwest Institute for Children and Families and Division of Children and Family Services.

Van Soest, D. and B. Garcia, eds. 2003. *Diversity Education for Social Justice.* Alexandria, VA: Council on Social Work Education.

Van Voorhis, R. M. 1998. Culturally relevant practice: A framework for teaching the psychosocial dynamics of oppression. *Journal of Social Work Education* 34(1):121–133.

van Wormer, K. 1987. Group work with alcoholics in recovery: A phase approach. *Social Work with Groups* 10(3):81–98.

van Wormer, K. 2004. Restorative justice: A model for personal and societal empowerment. *Journal of Religion and Spirituality in Social Work* 23(4):103–120.

van Wormer, K. and S. G. Bednar. 2002. Working with male batterers: A restorative-strengths perspective. *Families in Society* 83(5/6):557–565.

Vasilanki, E., S. G. Hosier, and W. Cox. 2006. The efficacy of motivational interviewing as brief intervention for excessive drinking: A meta-analysis review. *Alcohol and Alcoholism* 41:328–335.

Vera, E. M. and S. L. Speight. 2003. Multicultural competencies, social justice and counseling psychology: Expanding our roles. *The Counseling Psychologist* 31:253–272.

Videka-Sherman, L. 1985. Harriett M. *Bartlett Practice Effectiveness Project: Report to NASW Board of Directors*. Washington, DC: NASW.

Videka-Sherman, L. 1988. Meta-analysis of research on social work practice in mental health. *Social Work* 33(4):325–337.

Vodde, R., and J. P. Gallant. 2002. Bridging the gap between micro and macro practice: Large-scale change and a unified model of narrative-deconstructive practice. *Journal of Social Work Education* 38(3):439–458.

Vohs, K., R. Baumeister, and N. Ciarocco. 2005. Self-regulation and self- presentation: Regulatory resource depletion impairs impression management and effortful self-presentation depletes regulatory resources. *Journal of Personality and Social Psychology* 88(4):632–657.

Wahab, S. 2005. Motivational interviewing and social work practice. *Journal of Social Work* 5(1):45–60.

Waites, C., M. Macgowan, J. Pennell, I. Carlton-LeNay, and M. Weil. 2004. Increasing the cultural responsiveness of family group conferencing. *Social Work* 49(2):29.

Waldorf, D. 1971. Social control in therapeutic communities for the treatment of drug addicts. *International Journal of Addictions* 6:29–43.

Walker, D., R. Roffman, and R. Stephens. 2004. The Teen Marijuana Check-Up: A brief motivational enhancement intervention for adolescent marijuana smokers. *Minuet, A Publication of the Motivational Interviewing Network of Trainers* 11(1):11.

Wallace, K. 1967. An Ethical Basis of Communication. In *Ethics and Persuasion,* ed. R. Johannesen, pp. 41–56. New York: Random House.

Walsh, J. 2003. The Psychological Person. Cognitions, Emotions and Self. In *Dimensions of Human Behavior. Person and Environment* (2nd ed.), ed. Elizabeth D. Hutchinson. Thousand Oaks, CA: Sage.

Walton, E., J. Roby, A. Frandsen, and R. Davidson. 2004. Strengthening at-risk families by involving the extended family. *Journal of Family Social Work* 7(1):1–21.

Walton, E., P. Sandau-Beckler, and M. Mannes, eds. 2001. *Balancing Family-Centered Services and Child Well-Being*. New York: Columbia University Press.

Wambach, K. G. and D. Van Soest. 1997. Understanding Oppression: Linking Knowledge to Practice. What Social Work Students Must Know and Care About Oppression. In *Encyclopedia of Social Work*. Supplement to 19th ed. Washington, DC: National Association of Social Workers.

Warrick, J. and W. Pincus. 2008. Station chief made appeal to destroy CIA tapes. *Washington Post,* January 16, 2008, p. A01.

Wasow, M. 1984. Deinstitutionalization. *Practice Digest* 6(4):10–12.

Wathney, S. and D. Baldridge. 1980. Strategic interventions with involuntary patients. *Hospital and Community Psychiatry* 31(10):696–701.

Watzlawick, P., J. H. Weakland, and R. Fisch. 1974. *Change:Principles of Problem Formation and Resolution*. New York: W. W. Norton.

Weatherly, R. and M. Lipsky. 1977. Street level bureaucrats and institutionalized innovations; implementing special education reform. *Harvard Educational Review* 47(2):171–197.

Weaver, H. N. 2000. Activism and American Indian issues: Opportunities for social workers. *Journal of Progressive Human Services* 11(1):3–22.

Weaver, H. N. 2004. The elements of cultural competence: Application with Native American clients. *Journal of Ethnic and Cultural Diversity in Social Work* 13(1):19–35.

Wegner, D. 1997. When the antidote is the poison: Ironic mental control processes. *Psychological Science* 8(3):148–150.

Weidman, A. 1986. Family therapy with violent couples. *Social Casework* 676:211–218.

Weil, A. and K. Finegold, eds. 2002. *Welfare Reform: The Next Act.* Washington, DC: Urban Institute.

Weinberg, M. 2006. Pregnant with possibility: The paradoxes of "help" as anti-oppression and discipline with a young single mother. *Families in Society: The Contemporary Journal of Social Services* 67(2):161–169.

Weiner-Davis, M. 2001. *The Divorce Remedy: The Proven 7-Step Program for Saving Your Marriage.* New York: Simon and Schuster.

Weinger, S. 2001. *Security Risk: Preventing Client Violence Against Social Workers.* Washington, DC: National Association of Social Workers.

Weiss, R. 2003. Adherence to pharmacotherapy in patients with alcohol and opiod dependence. *Addiction* 99:1382–1392.

Weissman, A. 1976. Industrial social services: Linkage technology. *Social Casework* 57(1):50–54.

Weist, M. D., A. Goldstein, L. Morris, and T. Bryant. 2003. Integrating expanded school mental health programs and school-based health centers. *Psychology in the Schools* 40(3):297–308.

Weitzman, J. 1985. Engaging the severely dysfunctional family in treatment: Basic considerations. *Family Process* 24:473–485.

Welch, M. 1999. *Punishment in America: Social Control and the Ironies of Imprisonment.* Thousand Oaks, CA: Sage.

Wells, K. and S. Guo. 2004. Reunification of foster children before and after welfare reform. *Social Service Review* 78:75–95.

Wells, R. 1982. *Planned Short-Term Treatment.* New York: Free Press.

Werthamer-Larsson, L. 1994. Methodological issues in school-based services research. *Journal of Clinical Child Psychology* 23(2):121–133.

Westbrook, T. M., J. Ellis, and A. J. Ellett. 2006. Improving retention among public child welfare workers: What can we learn from the insights and experiences of committed survivors. *Administration in Social Work* 30(4):37–62.

Whatules, L. J. 2000. Communication as an aid to resocialization: A case study of a men's anger group. *Small Group Research* 31(4):424–446.

White, M. and D. C. Epston. 1990. *Narrative Means to Therapeutic Ends.* New York: W. W. Norton.

Whiting-Blome, W. and S. Stieb. 2004. Whatever the problem, the answer is "evidence based practice"—or is it? *Child Welfare* 83(6):611–615.

Whittaker, J., K. Greene, R. Blum, K. Blum, K. Scott, and R. Roy. 2006. Integrating evidence-based practice in the child mental health agency: A template for clinical and organizational change. *American Journal of Orthopsychiatry* 76(2):194–201.

Whyte, W. H. 1956. *The Organization Man.* New York: Simon and Schuster.

Wilder Research Center. 2003. *The Issues Behind the Outcomes for Somali, Hmong, American Indian, and African American Welfare Participants.* St. Paul, MN: Author.

Wile, D. 1981. *Couples Therapy: A Nontraditional Approach.* New York: John Wiley.

Wilk, R. 1988. Involuntary outpatient commitment of the mentally ill. *Social Work* 33:133–137.

Williams, C. W. 2005. Personal responsibility. *Poverty and Social Justice Section Connection*, Summer, NASW:8–9.

Williams, O. J. 1994. Group work with African American men who batter. Toward a more ethically sensitive approach. *Journal of Comparative Family Studies* 25:91–104.

Wilson, S. and C. Tiles. 2006. Mentoring the statutory child protection manager—A strategy for promoting proactive outcome focused management. *Social Work Education* 25(2):177–188.

Winett, R. and R. Winkler. 1972. Be still, be quiet, be docile. *Journal of Applied Behavioral Analysis* 5:499–504.

Wing Hong Chui. 2003. What Works in Reducing Re-offending: Programs and Principles. In *Moving Probation Forward Evidence Arguments and Practice*, eds. Wing Hong Chui and M. Nellis. Essex, England: Pearson Longman.

Wodarski, J. 1980. Legal requisites for social work practice. *Clinical Social Work Journal* 8(2):94–97.

Wood, K. 1978. Casework effectiveness: A new look at the research evidence. *Social Work* 23:437–458.

Woodruff, S. I., C. C. Edwards, T. L. Conway, and S. P. Elliott. 2001. Pilot test of an Internet virtual world chat room for rural teen smokers. *Journal of Adolescent Health* 29(4):239–243.

Wortman, B. and J. Brehm. 1975. Responses to uncontrollable outcomes: An integration of reactance theory and the learned helplessness model. In *Advances in Experimental Social Psychology*, Vol. 8, ed. L. Berkowitz, pp. 278–336. New York: Academic Press.

Wright, R. A., J. Greenberg, and S. S. Brehm. 2004. *Motivational Analysis of Social Behavior*. Hillsdale, NJ: Lawrence Erlbaum.

Yan, M. C. and Y. L. Wong. 2005. Rethinking self-awareness in cultural competence: Toward a dialogic self in cross-cultural social work. *Families in Society* 86:181–188.

Yatchmenoff, D. 2005. Measuring client engagement from the client's perspective. *Research on Social Work Practice* 15(2):84–96.

Yates, P. 2003. Treatment of adult sexual offenders: A therapeutic cognitive-behavioral model of intervention. *Journal of Child Sexual Abuse* 12(3/4):195–232.

Yochelson, S. and S. Samenow. 1985. *The Criminal Personality. The Change Process*, Vol. 2. New York: Jason Aronson.

Yoo, J., and D. Brooks. 2005. The role of organizational variables in predicting service effectiveness: An analysis of a multilevel model. *Research on Social Work Practice* 15(4):267–277.

Yu, M. M. and T. Watkins. 1996. Group counseling with DUI offenders: A model using client anger to enhance group cohesion and movement. *Alcoholism Treatment Quarterly* 14(3):47–57.

Zappay, A. 1995. The politics of empowerment. *Social Work* 40(2):263–267.

Zaslow, M., K. A. Moore, K. Trout, J. P. Scarpa, and S. Vandivere. 2002. How are children faring under welfare reform. In *Welfare Reform: The Next Act*, eds. A. Weil and K. Finegold, pp. 79–101. Washington, DC: The Urban Institute Press.

About the Editor

Ronald H. Rooney is a Professor at the School of Social Work, University of Minnesota. He is the author of *Direct Social Work Practice*, now in its seventh edition. Dr. Rooney has provided more than one hundred consultations and trainings related to involuntary clients and child welfare across the United States, Canada, Taiwan, Korea, and Holland. He was the first recipient of the Keith McFarland Teaching Award of the College of Human Ecology at the University of Minnesota. He is a consultant for the Teen/Parenting Service Network of Chicago, Illinois.

Contributors

Julie Altman is an Associate Professor at Adelphi University School of Social Work in Garden City, New York, where she also directs the child welfare training program. Dr. Altman holds a doctorate from the University of Chicago and a master's of social work from the University of Michigan. Her research interests are in the field of child welfare, specializing on issues of parenting, immigration, client service use, and welfare reform. Most recently, Dr. Altman was a Fulbright Scholar at the University of the West Indies, lecturing and doing research on child rearing and child welfare services in Trinidad and Tobago. These findings will inform the work she does with New York City's diverse immigrant child welfare community. Prior to her academic career, Dr. Altman worked as a child welfare practitioner.

James Barber commenced at RMIT University as the Deputy Vice Chancellor in January 2006. Prior to that he was dean of the Faculty of Social Work at the University of Toronto, where he won the Pro Humanitate Award for his book *Children in Foster Care* (co-written with Paul Delfabbro). Before moving to Canada, Dr. Barber held a range of senior academic positions at Flinders University of South Australia, including director of the research institute, head of the school, and associate dean of research. While at Flinders University, Dr. Barber received the Vice Chancellor's Award for Excellence in Teaching in 2000. His direct practice experience spans a variety of human service settings, including street youth work, palliative care, psychiatric social work, child protection work, and drug prevention in the heroin unit of Melbourne's notorious Pentridge Prison.

Tony Bibus is a Professor and Chair in the Social Work Department at Augsburg College in Minneapolis, Minnesota. A graduate of the doctoral program at the University of Minnesota School of Social Work (1992), he is a licensed social worker. He has worked since 1970 in juvenile corrections, child welfare, family-based services, and social work education. He has taught, trained, and published in such areas as supervision, cultural competence, welfare reform, social work regulation, and work with involuntary clients.

Michael Chovanec is an Associate Professor at the College of St. Catherine/ University of St. Thomas School of Social Work in St. Paul, Minnesota, where he has taught for eleven years. He received his doctorate from the University of Minnesota in 1995, and his dissertation examined the dropout problem in domestic abuse treatment. He has been a clinician for more than ten years and works part-time as coordinator and group facilitator for a county domestic abuse program, which he helped to develop in 1988. One of his first experiences with involuntary groups was facilitating a group of patients on a locked mental health hospital unit.

Glenda Dewberry Rooney is a Professor in the Social Work Department at Augsburg College, Minneapolis, Minnesota. She has extensive experience as a clinical and management consultant in child welfare and family service agencies, including culturally sensitive agencies. Her practice experience includes child welfare and adult mental health. Dr. Rooney is active with several organizations and coalitions that address the issue of the disparities that exist in child welfare for children of color. Her current professional and research interests are linking practice methods and ethics, involuntary clients, and the experience of families within the child welfare system. She is the author of *Direct Social Work Practice: Theory and Skills*.

Cynthia Franklin is a Professor at the University of Texas at Austin, School of Social Work, and holds the Stiernberg/Spencer Family Professorship in Mental Health. She is also coordinator of the clinical concentration for the masters in social work program. Dr. Franklin is an internationally known scholar and leader in school mental health practice. She has written on such topics as how to help at-risk youth not to dropout of high school; the effectiveness of solution-focused, brief therapy with at-risk youth in schools; and how to help pregnant and parenting youth stay in school and become self-sufficient. Dr. Franklin is the author of several books including *The*

School Services Sourcebook: A Guide for School-based Professionals; Taking Charge: A School-based Life Skills Program for Adolescent Mothers; and *Family Treatment: Evidence-based Practice with Populations At-Risk.* She has won numerous awards including a lifetime achievement award presented to her by the Solution-focused, Brief Therapy Association for her work with forgotten children. Dr. Franklin has also been active in the mental health practice. She is a clinical member of the American Association of Marriage and Family Therapy and holds practice licenses in clinical social work and marriage and family therapy. Before going into academia full time, Dr. Franklin served in the ministry and conducted a clinical practice for ten years.

Debra Gohagan is a Professor at the Department of Social Work, Minnesota State University, Mankato. She received her doctoral degree in social work at the University of South Carolina (2000). Dr. Gohagan has more than twenty years experience as clinical social worker with children, couples, and families in a wide variety of public and private settings, including residential treatment centers, psychiatric hospitals, mental health centers, and child welfare agencies, as well as private practice. Current professional interests include child welfare, technology and teaching, and solution-focused treatment approaches.

Melinda Hohman is a Professor at the School of Social Work, San Diego State University, San Diego, where she has worked since 1995. Dr. Hohman teaches courses in substance abuse treatment, research, and social work practice. She also coordinates the undergraduate social work program. Dr. Hohman's research interests include substance abuse assessment and treatment services and the overlap of substance abuse treatment and child welfare services. She has been a trainer in motivational interviewing since 1999, training community social workers, child welfare workers, probation officers, and addiction counselors across Southern California. Dr. Hohman is currently the project director of motivational interviewing training for more than 2,000 employees of the California Division of Juvenile Justice (Cal-METRO Project), which is conducted through the Center on Criminality, Addiction Research Training and Application, Department of Psychiatry, University of California at San Diego.

Laura Hopson is an Assistant Professor at the University at Albany School of Social Welfare. She is interested in interventions that reduce risk and build protective factors for youth, especially in school settings. Current research projects involve implementation and evaluation of evidence-based prevention programs in schools.

Carol Jud has worked in the field of child welfare for the past fifteen years. Currently, she works at Hennepin County as a Supervisor in the Aging and Disability Services area.

Chris Kleinpeter is a Professor at the Department of Social Work, California State University, Long Beach, where she has worked since 1994. Dr. Kleinpeter teaches graduate courses in mental health and addiction treatment, human behavior, and social work practice. Dr. Kleinpeter's research interests include mental health and addiction treatment services. She has been a trainer in motivational interviewing since 2001, training community social workers, child welfare workers, probation officers, and addiction counselors across Southern California. Dr. Kleinpeter has been the Co-PI on grants, including a process and outcomes evaluation of the co-occurring court in Orange County, California, and an evaluation of enhanced services provided to Orange County drug court participants, including vocational counseling, psychotherapy, and additional drug testing. She also conducted research in the areas of surrogate motherhood and distance learning. Her administrative roles have included coordinator of the distance education program and associate director and coordinator of academic programs. Dr. Kleinpeter is licensed as a clinical psychologist and clinical social worker in California. She has more than ten years of clinical experience in inpatient and outpatient mental health settings.

Chris Trotter is an Associate Professor in the Department of Social Work at Monash University in Australia. He has authored *Working with Involuntary Clients,* now in its second edition, which is also available in German, Japanese, and Chinese; and *Helping Abused Children and Their Families.* He worked for many years as a social worker and manager in child protection, juvenile justice, and adult probation and parole. Dr. Trotter has developed a worldwide reputation for his work on involuntary clients and has been a consultant in Australia, Canada, Europe, United Kingdom, and Asia to assist probation services and child protection agencies to implement effective practices.

Index